The Immobile Empire

"The Reception of the Diplomatique & his Suite, at the Court of Pekin"
James Gillray, September 14, 1792

The
IMMOBILE
EMPIRE

Alain Peyrefitte

TRANSLATED FROM THE FRENCH

BY JON ROTHSCHILD

Alfred A. Knopf
New York
1992

THIS IS A BORZOI BOOK
PUBLISHED BY ALFRED A. KNOPF, INC.

Library of Congress Cataloging-in-Publication Data
Peyrefitte, Alain.
[Empire immobile. English]
The immobile empire / Alain Peyrefitte ; translated from
the French by Jon Rothschild.
p.   cm.
Translation of: L'Empire immobile ou Le Choc des mondes.
Includes bibliographical references and index.
ISBN 0-394-58654-9
1. Great Britain—Foreign relations—China.
2. Macartney, George Macartney, Earl, 1737–1806.
3. British—Travel—China—History—18th century.
4. Great Britain—Foreign relations—1789–1820.
5. China—Foreign relations—Great Britain.
6. China—History—Ch'ien lung, 1736–1795.
I. Title.
DA47.9.C5P4913   1992
327.41051—dc20   92-329   CIP

Manufactured in the United States of America
First American Edition

Nothing could be more fallacious than to judge of China by any European standard.

LORD MACARTNEY, 1794[1]

The Chinese and Mongolian empire is the realm of theocratic despotism. The state is fundamentally patriarchal; it is ruled by a father who also presides over what we would regard as matters of conscience. . . . The head of state in China is a despot, and he leads a systematically constructed government with a numerous hierarchy of subordinate members. . . . the individual has no moral selfhood. . . . History is still predominantly unhistorical, for it is merely a repetition of the same majestic process of decline. . . . no progress results from all this restless change.

HEGEL, 1822[2]

Hegel's idea that China was mired in immobility is easily refuted. . . . Yet Hegel was right.

ETIENNE BALAZS, 1968[3]

Contents

III ▪ IN THE SHADOW OF THE EMPEROR

IV ▪ THE REAL MISSION BEGINS

V ▪ NEW DEVELOPMENTS, FRESH HOPES

VI ▪ AFTER MACARTNEY OR A SPIRAL OF MISFORTUNE

Illustrations follow page 282.

Acknowledgments

It is difficult to express my appreciation to all the many people who helped me in gathering the profuse documentation that went into this book.

Professor Hou Renzhi, archeologist at the University of Peking, accompanied me to the imperial city of Jehol, in Macartney's "Tartary." His assistance in reconstructing the embassy's itinerary and locating its residences was quite precious. Professor Zhang Zhilian of the University of Beida and Mr. Xu Yipu, general director of the Imperial Archives, guided me in sifting through the court letters and the Chinese bibliography. Father Yves Raguin did indispensable, though ultimately fruitless, research in the Qin archives transferred to Taipei. Zhu Yong shared with me his meticulous research in the archives of the Grand Council and the Grand Secretariat, both housed in the Forbidden City.

Three brilliant young Sinologists—Roger Darrobers, Pierre-Henri Durand, and Sylvie Pasquet—translated, from the difficult language of the Manchu court, the unpublished documents that I was able to bring back from Peking. Roger Darrobers also accompanied me on the last three of my eight trips to the People's Republic, Hong Kong, and Macao, tracking Macartney's steps. They were aided, in various labors of decoding and translation, by Fan Ke-li, Liu Huijie, Xiao-Ming Huang, Huo Datong, Guat-Kooi Peh, William Shen, Bérangère Lecoq, Belinda Palmer, P.-H. Genès, and Marie-Thérèse Chabord.

Mr. W. R. Erwin procured for me the Thomas Staunton manuscript held by Duke University. Dr. Min Chih-chu, conservator of the Wason Collection at Cornell, and Dr. B. Johnston, conservator of the manuscript department at the University of Nottingham, also supplied me with unpublished materials. Professor Kazuo Enoki, director of the Toyo Bunko of Tokyo, afforded me the manuscript journals of Macartney and Alexander preserved there. Mr. Jacques Dupont, French ambassador to South Africa, gave me access to Macartney's papers at the University of Witwatersrand in Johannesburg and at the South African Library in Capetown. Professor J. L. Cranmer-Byng, of Toronto, whose erudition stretches well beyond the bounds of his book reproducing most of Macartney's journal, and Professor Roebuck, of Colraine, who knows everything there is to know about Macartney's life, were generous in their assistance. Michael Galvin allowed me to examine Lord Amherst's journal and gave me permission to reproduce excerpts from it.

Fathers Dehergne and Duclos opened the archives of the Society of Jesus in Chantilly to me, Fathers Baldacchino and Bendinelli those of the Lazarists in Paris and Rome, Father Lenfant those of the foreign missions. In Macao Monsignor Teixeira, superior of Saint Joseph, and Mrs. Adelina Costa Braga, director of the archives, allowed me access to the civil and ecclesiastical records of the Portuguese colony.

Xavier Walter helped me search through the vast literature on relations between the West and the Far East during the seventeenth, eighteenth, and nineteenth centuries and compiled the indexes and the various annexes. Françoise Kearns helped me locate precious documents about Macartney, the two Stauntons, Amherst, and the missionaries—in Britain (especially the Public Record Office and the India Office), Ireland, and the United States. Michelle Levieil and Françoise Auger—assisted by Chantal Jacquelin and Nathalie Brochado—patiently and meticulously typed five successive drafts of the book.

The Sinological expertise of the following people was of great help to me: Professor Jacques Gernet, General Jacques Guillermaz, Father Claude Larre, S.J., Professors Marie-Claire Bergère, Lucien Bianco, Marianne Bruguière-Bastid, Michel Cartier, Charles Commeaux, Jean-Luc Domenach, Danielle and Vadim Elisseeff, François Joyaux, André Lévy, Kristofer Schipper, Léon Vandermeersch, Pierre-Etienne Will, Erik Zürcher. Father Armogathe, Professors Georges Balandier, François Crouzet, Jacques Lacant, Serge Lebovici, Jean Meyer, and René Pommeau, consulted in the fields of their expertise, gave me useful advice. Finally, my friends Jacques Bompaire, Jean-Jacques de Bresson, Vincent Labouret, Jacques Leprette, Alain de Lyrot, and Philippe Moret offered me their criticism with their customary frankness.

I express my friendly gratitude to them all.

It should go without saying, however, that the author alone is responsible for this book.

A Note on Spelling

Except for a few names with well-established English spellings (Peking, Nanking, Canton, Tientsin, Jehol), the Chinese names in this book are spelled according to the official, pinyin transcription system. While a meticulous effort was made to preserve the original punctuation and spelling (and, very often, misspellings) in all quotations from eighteenth- and nineteenth-century English sources, the idiosyncrasies in the spellings of Chinese personal and place names mentioned within these sources would, unfortunately, only confuse the reader. To prevent misunderstanding, these Chinese names have been put into pinyin.

Introduction*

History thrives on the testimony of kings and on that of their
valets.

VOLTAIRE[1]

THERE IS PERHAPS no more striking instance of the clash between advanced
and traditional societies than the proud encounter, at the end of the eighteenth century, between Britain and China—the first country to be gripped
by the industrial revolution and the most brilliant of all civilizations rooted
in custom. The confrontation between the industrialized countries and the
Third World—or between North and South, as it is gingerly put today
—was tainted at the outset by colonial conquest, which inflicted intolerable
damage on the soul of the colonized peoples and often aroused a sense of
guilt among the colonizers for their acts of plunder, once the intoxication
of domination had passed. The majority of these cultural collisions involved
"civilized man" on the one hand and the "noble savage" on the other. But
there was a uniqueness to the encounter between two societies that, having
undergone separate development for centuries, considered themselves the
world's most civilized—and not without good reason. This made their
confrontation especially exemplary, lending it the purity of a laboratory
experiment.

In the years after the Second World War, many noble families brought
to ruin by the new regime in Poland sought to raise funds by putting
antiquarian books up for sale. So it was that in 1954, in a Cracow bookstore,
I purchased a *Bibliothèque des voyages*[2] previously owned by the scion of
an aristocratic line. These accounts of exploration[3] bore the *ex libris* of one
Prince Adam Czartoryski,† who, in a paradoxical consequence of the
partition of Poland, became in 1802 the minister of foreign affairs in the
government of Tsar Alexander I. (The two Russian invasions, a century
and a half apart, caused the rise of the ancestor and the ruin of his
descendants.)

This collection was remarkable in two respects. First, in the second

---

* Notes important for understanding the text are asterisked and printed at the foot of the page;
references and more rarefied observations are numbered and printed at the end of the book,
pp. 565–96.
† This same prince will reappear in our story in chapter 83.

half of the eighteenth century, Europe was gripped by a frenzy of pere-grination. There had been a similar period in the late fifteenth and early sixteenth centuries, and it had taken some 250 years to digest the many finds of those journeys. But now a new leap forward had been taken, and the last remaining "unexplored" territories of the world were penetrated. Second, most of these works had been translated from English. The earlier great explorations had been monopolized by the Spanish and Portuguese, and later by the Dutch. But now it was the turn of the English, a people small in number but great in vigor, far outstripping the France of Bougainville and La Pérouse. Their presence was felt everywhere as they swept through most of the planet's archaic societies, dragging them into the modern world, often against their will and without really willing it themselves.

Of all these accounts, the ones I found most fascinating were two "Reports on the Journey to China and Tartary in the Company of the Embassy of Lord Macartney." One was written by Sir George Staunton, who had been second in command of the mission, the other by John Barrow, its comptroller, the same man who recounted the story of the mutiny on the *Bounty*. These twelve volumes[4] were a complete revelation to me. I knew nothing of eighteenth-century China save what had been said by Leibniz, Voltaire, and the Jesuits: that it was a wondrous empire, perfectly governed by an "enlightened despot" whom Europe might well envy.

But I had no idea that in the midst of the French Revolution, the British dispatched a large expedition to the Chinese Empire in an effort to open it to English penetration. Or that they, a nation of 8 million,[5] were so confident of their status as "the most powerful nation of the globe" that they intended to deal on an equal basis with a country whose population was 330 million, one-third of the human race. Or that the Middle Empire—"the only civilization under heaven"—flatly rejected their every request.

Nor did I know that they discovered a China quite different from the one idealized by the Enlightenment. They set about to destroy this myth irrevocably, denouncing the writings of the Catholic missionaries as pure fabrication. Instead they came to believe that the supposedly incomparable model was in fact fossilized by ritual and steeped in vanity.

Most remarkable of all was an apparently trivial incident that sym-bolized Macartney's failure: he refused to kowtow to the emperor, as stipulated by court protocol. The episode would have enchanted Montes-quieu, who believed that Caesar had been killed because the tyrant, contrary to custom, neglected to rise before the Senate. The republicans had suffered the most arbitrary acts in silence, but this insolence triggered their assault:

"Men are never so deeply offended as when their customs and traditions are violated, which is always a sign of contempt."[6]

The Celestial Court was outraged. The emperor cut the mission short, and the ensuing conflict ignited a tragic chain reaction: the clash of the two nations, the collapse of China, British domination of Southeast Asia in the nineteenth century, malevolent misunderstanding between the West and the Third World in the twentieth.

HAVING COME TO propose change and exchange, Macartney and his companions found in China a closed society with a system as self-contained as a billiard ball, one so comprehensive, exacting, and exigent that any refusal to bend before it entailed great risk. It could be circumvented only through evasion, misappropriation, or inertia. In other words, through nonaction, but rarely through initiative. Innovation was prohibited, reference to precedent the rule. The "canonical texts"—those that inspired Confucius or were inspired by him—contained the solution to every problem. They covered everything. To change anything in them would be presumptuous.

If change was to be prevented, then exchange was better avoided. The British, on the other hand, had raised business to new heights, and intended to raise it higher still. They understood that trade benefited both seller and buyer, who were like two lovers, each depending on the other for satisfactions neither could provide singly. Manchu China, however, was quintessentially scornful of the merchant, suspicious of business, and dismissive of foreign inventions. A vigorous domestic market had arisen, but foreign trade was throttled by a bureaucratically controlled monopoly. Macartney's mission to China was an encounter between those with the most developed civilization of free exchange and those most refractory to it.

The expedition thereby goes to the heart of the mystery of the "underdevelopment" of traditional societies and the "development" of advanced countries, whose encounter will likely dominate the centuries to come.

IT WAS IN AUGUST and September 1960, from my base in Hong Kong, that I first entered the Chinese universe. I was immediately struck by this society's resemblance to the one described by Macartney's companions. It has been said that every Chinese bears in his genes the entire heritage of Qianlong's empire, and China had a very Chinese way of rebelling against itself. Even while seeking to break with its past, it plumbed that past for precedents to grasp in asserting its own invariance.

The country was still overpopulated, and still threatened by poverty, anarchy, and decomposition. Its medicine remained faithful to acupuncture, herbs, and the twelve pulses the English physicians had found so hilarious. Most of all, in face of the uncertainties of existence, the Chinese continued to rely on the collective: the group, rather than the individual, determined what should or should not be thought or done.

The fact that in 1960 the Chinese still upheld Qianlong's assessment of the Macartney expedition underscored this continuity. Although they used Marxist terminology, the history texts, university courses, and intellectuals all maintained that the emperor had been right. Macartney had manifested an "imperialist," "capitalist," and "colonialist" attitude, and everyone endorsed Qianlong's stinging reply: "We have no need of anyone. Go home! Take back your gifts!" Exactly what Mao had just said, when he expelled Soviet technicians and "advisers" and proclaimed, "Let us rely on our own strength."

Despite the disaster of the Great Leap Forward, many Chinese officials were still convinced that China was superior to all other countries. At best the West might contribute a few minor formulas. If China had suffered so much hardship over the past 120 years, it was because the country had been plundered by rapacious nations. It was not China's fault. Within a few years, backwardness would be overcome and the country would recover the preeminence it had held for millennia.

IN JULY AND AUGUST of 1971, when I led the first official Western mission granted entry to the People's Republic since the outbreak of the Cultural Revolution five years before, I was struck by the strange similarities between the Maoist state and the one Macartney had confronted.

There was the same cult of the emperor, Mao merely replacing Qianlong. Everything hung on his will. In matters of everyday management, power was similarly delegated to a prime minister who interpreted the thought of the living god and maneuvered among intrigues and factions, lacking any support save approval from above. There was the same concern for the rituals of protocol, which expressed respect for tradition and hierarchy. And the same adherence to a common set of references that provided the answer to everything, Mao Zedong Thought standing in for Confucius Thought, the Little Red Book for Kangxi's Sacred Edict.*

The land was as predominant as ever. If Qianlong was contemptuous

---

* Except that the Confucianism of the elite coexisted with a syncretistic popular religion combining Buddhism and Taoism, whereas Maoism, sweeping aside everything in its path, sought to become the sole, universal credo.

of the products of the English industrial revolution and of merchants of any nationality, and if Mao relied on the peasants rather than the workers, it was because nearly all the population lived in the countryside and depended on agriculture. The same secret conflicts would burst suddenly to the surface, heralded by slender clues understood only after the fact. In September 1971, after returning to Europe, we (along with everyone else) learned that Marshal Lin Biao, Mao's beloved disciple and an enthusiastic promoter of the Little Red Book, had supposedly died in a plane crash while fleeing to Moscow. We then recalled that in mid-July the Chinese chief of protocol had recommended that I toast Mao and Zhou Enlai, but not Lin Biao, who was nevertheless Mao's designated successor at the time. Some years after their return, Macartney and his companions learned that the favored chief minister, Heshen, had been the victim of a similar drama. In China, in our day as in the past, the Tarpeian cliff lies within the Capitoline dome.

There was the same distrust of foreigners, who could only disturb the Chinese Order. Their curiosity was dangerous, and they had to be closely watched. The same collective reflexes: on stifling summer nights, the Chinese still sleep in the streets. The same frugality, the same bowl of rice and cooked vegetables, the same chopsticks. Clothes of the same blue-gray cotton fabric. The same taste for tobacco.

Even revolutionary violence testified to the hardiness of heritage. The "feudalist" and "reactionary" lurking within each Chinese had to be extirpated. If the upheavals of "liberation" were sealed in blood, it was because the weight of tradition was too great: liberated peasants still trembled before their dispossessed masters. It was not enough to eliminate examinations, grades, and the privileges of the mandarin bureaucracy that the party bureaucracy had quite naturally replaced. Social classes had to be crushed, intellectuals humiliated, the hierarchy shattered. So it was that China shifted back and forth between the murder of the past and its rediscovery. Red and gold banners trumpeted the slogan "May the old serve the new!" Mao's stunning achievement was to make the Chinese feel that they were remaining faithful to their heritage even while abolishing it.

MY BOOK ON modern China in turmoil appeared in 1973, and it contained many references to the Macartney mission. Quite a few readers asked me how they could obtain copies of accounts of it. I was tempted by the idea of republishing them, for the expedition was unknown in France. True, the reports of Staunton and Barrow had been translated at the time.[7]

Napoleon had read them, and they were said to have inspired his famous remark "When China awakens, the world will tremble." But in France the episode had been forgotten since then. Even erudite works made no mention of it. Sinologists, compelled to specialization by their small numbers, had devoted no study to it. I thus began a long effort to track down the sources.

In England the results of the mission had dispelled illusions. If China was determined to remain sealed, then the doors had to be battered down. Apart from the semi-official accounts by Staunton and Barrow, four other reports had been published at the time: one by Samuel Holmes, a soldier in the guard, which had a naive simplicity; one by Aeneas Anderson, the ambassador's valet, which was "compiled" by a tendentious journalist; one by William Alexander, one of the two painters who accompanied the expedition (as photographers would today), an account as vivid as his watercolors;[8] and finally, one by Hans Christian Hüttner, a German and a private tutor to the ambassador's page,[9] whose work was described by the Lazarist Father Lamiot, a missionary in Peking, as "nothing to write home about."[10]

Two additional reports came later: from James Dinwiddie, an "astronomer" who was appalled at "the infantile credulity of the Chinese,"[11] and from Lord Macartney himself,[12] parts of whose journal were belatedly published by Helen Robbins in 1908, after the unexpected discovery of the manuscript. A detailed, critical edition of that journal was issued in 1962 by Professor J. L. Cranmer-Byng.[13]

WOULD IT BE possible to take the lazy way out and republish one of these accounts? The trouble was that they complemented and corrected one another, and as I continued the hunt, I discovered other texts, some never published, some never even cited. Young Thomas Staunton, Macartney's page, who was eleven years old when the mission set out, kept a diary[14] that candidly notes what his father and the ambassador diplomatically concealed. His schoolboy efforts often outstrip those of the adults for accuracy. In 1817 he also wrote a report on the second British mission to China, led by Lord Amherst, and in 1856 he issued his memoirs. Other sources included the notebook of Sir Erasmus Gower, who commanded the squadron; the log of the *Hindostan*, kept by Captain William Mackintosh, a seasoned businessman and veteran of commercial voyages in the Far East; the journal of Edward Winder, the mission's secretary and Macartney's cousin; the scientific notes of Dr. Hugh Gillan, the expedition's physician; correspondence between the official representatives of the East

India Company in Canton and the "gentlemen" back in London; correspondence between Macartney and Henry Dundas, the home secretary and strong man   the Pitt government. In all, there are some fifteen eye-witnesses to the expedition from the British side.

Could the English view be balanced by that of other Westerners? There are writings by Charles de Constant, a Swiss citizen, and by four French-men: Jean-Antoine d'Entrecasteaux, Louis XVI's envoy in Canton in 1787; J. F. Charpentier-Cossigny, who responded to Staunton's report in 1799, after a long stay in Canton; Louis-Chrétien de Guignes, who headed the French mission in Canton from 1784 to 1799; and Jean-Baptiste Piron, a representative of the French East India Company, who was present when Macartney passed through Macao. Of these five witnesses, the last two wrote substantial reports (conserved in the Quai d'Orsay) on the vexed relations between the English and the Chinese. But the missionaries—French, Spanish, Italian, and Portuguese—then living in Peking and Macao took a special interest in the expedition. The well-known Jesuit Father Joseph-Marie Amiot devoted his last missives to it, and the Jesuit archives contain dozens of letters that would have been published, like the earlier *Lettres édifiantes et curieuses*, had not the Society of Jesus been dissolved in 1773. The archives of the Lazarists and of the foreign missions in China contain material as well.

In Macao I had the opportunity to visit Monsignor Manuel Teixeira, the most erudite of Portuguese historians. Having been brought to China as a child, he has spent his long life scouring the archives of the Portuguese governors and the Catholic missions. In 1966 the Seminary of Saint Joseph in the old Portuguese city, which he directed, was home to about a hundred European priests and Chinese seminarians, nearly of whom fled to Hong Kong at the first sign of trouble during the Cultural Revolution. "Like a flock of sparrows!" Father Teixeira sadly commented, adding that "the days when priests sought martyrdom are long gone." The father found himself alone with the most aged of his colleagues, and thereafter he devoted his time to the publication of the *Annales de Macao*.[15]

Father Teixeira believes that the object of the Macartney mission was to prepare a raid against Macao as much as to open China to trade. "The English were basically jealous," he told me. "Little Portugal had been settled in Macao for 250 years, and the English either had to get their hands on another Macao or else take ours. Macartney did detailed research on the Portuguese defenses. But the missionaries were not deceived by this ploy. We can always get along with the Chinese. With the English, never!"

What a paradox! During the French Revolution and the Napoleonic wars, Portugal was Britain's ally. But the Portuguese missionaries in China were fervent opponents of the English, whom they considered "arrogant miscreants." Monsignor Teixeira had simply taken up the cause of the Portuguese priests Macartney had dealt with. On the other hand, even when France and the United Kingdom were at war, the French priests in Peking did all they could to aid the English.

While affording me the benefits of his research, Father Teixeira mimicked Macartney's introduction to Qianlong: "He bent one knee, scornfully, like this. It was an insult to the emperor! The Portuguese missionaries kowtowed every day, without even being asked. In Macartney's place, I would have kowtowed not once, but ten times, a hundred times! And it would have worked. Closer and closer ties between China and the West would have been woven little by little, except that those two egotists—Macartney and the cardinal of Tournon, eighty years before him—wrecked everything. Instead of bowing to Chinese rites, as he easily could have done, the cardinal ruined two centuries of missionary efforts with his stupid intransigence." Monsignor Teixeira's long beard, as white as his robe and as wet with sweat, trembled with indignation as he parodied the pretentious posturing of the pope's envoy.

The published and unpublished texts I was able to assemble came to about twelve thousand pages. It would have been impossible to publish them all and a shame to be content with any one of them. I therefore undertook to synthesize all this testimony in the form of a continuous account.

BUT THE CHINESE view was still lacking. In 1928–29 *Zhongghu Congbian*, a limited-circulation bulletin issued by the Chinese Archives, published several imperial edicts on matters relating to the Macartney mission that had previously been known only from English sources. But it seemed impossible that the imperial bureaucracy had not also devoted some correspondence to this unprecedented expedition.

In 1980 I asked a professor of history at the University of Peking to aid me in this investigation. He had edited the translation of my book *Le Mal français* into Chinese,* and he promised that he would encourage one of his students to probe the Imperial Archives for court letters and mandarin memoranda dealing with the English expedition.

---

* A colloquium held at the University of Wuhan on this work (published in China under the title *The Bureaucratic Disease*) concluded that *le mal français* and *le mal chinois* were identical. I personally would not go that far, but it must be said that the idea was not new in China. In 1895 Yenfu wrote: "In France after the Revolution there were three republics in succession, but the authoritarian power of the administration emerged strengthened."[16]

In the meantime, in 1981, 1984, 1986, 1987, and 1988, I sought to retrace, in sections, the expedition's itinerary: Macao, the Zhoushan Islands and the port of Ningbo, the Gulf of Beizhili, Tientsin, Peking, the drive through the Tartar lands to Jehol (Chengde), the overland journey through the interior from Peking to Canton, via Suzhou and Hangzhou, and back to Macao. On the excursion to Jehol it was my good fortune to be accompanied by Professor Hou Renzhi, a University of Peking specialist in archeological research into the Manchu epoch. He knew all the buildings, surviving or long demolished, that Macartney and his companions might have stayed in or simply seen in Peking and its environs and on the road through the Tartar lands. In Jehol we spent two days charting the various edifices that had been standing during the mission's stay in that "mountain residence where the court took refuge from the scorching summer heat."

In 1987, during my seventh trip, I had the most agreeable surprise any researcher could hope for. A young student named Zhu Yong had spent more than a year sifting through papers stored in the deep cellars of the Forbidden City. He had assembled the equivalent of 420 pages, handwritten in the concise language of the imperial bureaucracy. I examined this treasure close up. Reams of rice paper, uniformly folded, accordion-style. They contained court documents written in India ink: edicts of the emperor, instructions signed in his name by the chief minister or by one of the other five Grand Councillors, memoranda sent to the emperor by the highest mandarins. There were even marginal vermilion notes: observations handwritten by the emperor himself, who spent several hours a day reading and annotating this correspondence.[17] The pages seemed perfectly fresh, as though they had been written the evening before and ironed to eliminate every crease.

I was handed microfilm copies of this correspondence with all the solemnity with which a priest might have given me the Holy Sacrament, and it was pointed out to me that no such complete corpus of court correspondence had ever before been assembled. I was told that the "privilege of being granted a copy demonstrates that the policy of opening adopted by the Third Plenum in December 1978 extends to the archives," that most sensitive of all domains, the collective memory of the Chinese people.

This unprecedented imperial correspondence will soon be available to public inspection. A number of significant extracts from it will be found in the present work. The reader, for example, may be surprised to discover a two-century-old incident not unlike the *Rainbow Warrior* affair, and to learn that the British offered the Chinese a military alliance against France. These letters have the ring of calls to vigilance in the face of danger. In them we see an enormous organism preparing to manufacture the antibodies with which to repel the foreign body that had dared to invade it.

In 1988, during my eighth visit, I had the double satisfaction of receiving the complete collection of imperial correspondence on the Amherst mission of 1816 and of learning that Zhu Yong's thesis, reexamining history in the light of the political choices of 1978, would include harsh criticism of Qianlong's policy of sealing China shut and rejecting modernization.

STENDHAL ONCE described the novel as "a mirror that walks along the route." This book was constructed through the play of thirty mirrors—or, rather, cameras—perched on the shoulders of the protagonists or planted along the mission's path. I have simply arranged and compared the testimony, most often letting the witnesses speak for themselves. The points of view are sufficiently varied that, with two centuries of hindsight, we may not only grasp the truth of events that were obscure for the witnesses, but also shed some light on the great questions raised by this failed rendezvous of history.

Until the sixteenth or seventeenth century, China was the most developed country in the world, surpassing Western Europe in the richness of its inventions and the refinement of its civilization. Why did it allow itself to be so far outdistanced that by the nineteenth century portions of its territory were colonized as though inhabited by Stone Age tribes, and by the twentieth it had become one of the world's poorest and most backward countries? How is it that some countries "awaken" while others remain dormant or return to slumber? Will we someday be threatened by the fate that befell China?

Three-quarters of a century before the emperor Qianlong's encounter with Macartney, Peter the Great sought to have Russia imitate the West, whatever the cost. Qianlong's grandfather Kangxi—a contemporary of both Peter and Louis XIV—had glimpsed that same necessity. Three-quarters of a century after Macartney's failure, the Meiji emperor felt it implacably for Japan. The Japanese, long hitched to China's wagon, struck out on their own at the very moment that Chinese civilization, once the principal hearth of their own, was dying in its own ashes. Why did Qianlong—at the geographical and chronological midpoint between Peter the Great and the Meiji emperor—disdainfully dismiss the foreign contributions that had been offered him?

Does exchange inevitably entail the obliteration of identity? Does it have to mean moving toward an ethnic and cultural cross-breeding producing coffee-colored mulattoes with slightly slanted eyes living in a civilization of Coca-Cola and chewing gum? Is uniformity the only alternative to fresh outbreaks of closed-minded, tempestuous nationalism or the convulsions of fundamentalism? Will our children succeed in devising a harmonious synthesis of tradition and modernity, striking a balance between fidelity to oneself and openness to others?

Clearly, the answers to these questions will increasingly weigh heavily in determining the fate of peoples. To see how the Macartney mission fits into the fabric of this planet's destiny, we have only to follow the itinerary of one of its chief witnesses, Thomas Staunton. The three major episodes of his adventure offer us the beginnings of some answers to our questions and open a portal on unknown horizons.

Prologue

The Witness to Three Stages
(1793, 1816, 1840)

> You who live—and above all you who are just beginning to
> live—in the XVIIIth century, rejoice!
>
> CHASTELLUX, *De la félicité publique*[1]

IT WAS STILL DARK in Manchuria at four in the morning on September 14,
1793. In the capital encampment in Jehol, where the Imperial Court was
spending the summer, paper lanterns lit the emperor's tent,[2] to which only
four members of the large British mission were to be granted entry: Lord
Macartney; his deputy, Sir George Staunton; his interpreter, Father Li, a
Tartar priest* and a graduate of a Naples seminary; and the twelve-year-
old page, Thomas Staunton, Sir George's son. The child had looked forward to this moment ever since his departure from England a year before:
he was to carry the train of the cloak of the Knights of Bath worn by the
ambassador. He alone among the seven hundred Englishmen of the mission
had taken the trouble to learn Chinese during the ocean crossing, and he
had done so effortlessly, with the facility of a gifted youth.

At seven o'clock they were brought before the emperor. All those
present—court attendants, Tartar princes, envoys from vassal nations—
performed the kowtow: three genuflections, each accompanied by three
acts of prostration, the forehead touching the ground nine times in all.
Except for the English, who merely went down on one knee; Lord Macartney insisted on shunning a ritual he considered humiliating for his
country. He was seeking to become the very first envoy from any country
to be accredited as a permanent representative to the Son of Heaven and

---

* The term *Tartar*, the only appellation in use in Europe at the time, referred to various peoples
of northern China other than the Han Chinese, primarily the Manchus and the Mongols. Until
the sixteenth century, these peoples had been called *Tatars*, from a Persian word probably of
Turkic origin.

to deal with China on an equal basis, in the name of his king, a man he called "the sovereign of the seas" and "the most powerful monarch of the globe."

Macartney climbed the steps of the imperial rostrum, his page bearing his train. He held aloft the gold filigreed box containing his written credentials from George III. The emperor handed Macartney a carved scepter of white stone, his gift to King George, and another of jade, for the ambassador himself. Macartney and his page descended the rostrum backwards. Then Sir George, accompanied by his son, climbed the stairs to pay his respects. The monarch gave Staunton a carved scepter as well. Informed that the page knew Chinese, he untied a yellow silk purse from his belt and—a rare privilege—handed it to the child, indicating his desire to hear the boy speak. Fluently, Thomas* told the sovereign how grateful he was to have received a gift from his august hands. Qianlong was visibly delighted, as though the child's gracious performance had eclipsed the unseemly behavior of his master.

TWENTY-THREE YEARS LATER, on August 28, 1816, Sir Thomas Staunton, having risen in age and rank, prepared for the second audience to be granted a British mission by the Son of Heaven. The great Qianlong had been succeeded by his son Jiaqing, and Thomas, too, had replaced his father as the second-ranking member of the mission. The new ambassador was Lord Amherst.

The British had arrived in Peking exhausted. Forewarned by the events of 1793, ever since their arrival in China they had steadfastly maintained that they would not kowtow.

Sir Thomas had spent the past twelve years in Macao and Canton as a commissioner and later the senior official of the British East India Company. Having been the first Englishman to learn the Chinese language, he had since become the first British Sinologist to reveal to the West the other face of China, the one masked by the idealized view presented by the missionaries. He was a more valuable adviser to Amherst than his father had been to Macartney, for he knew Chinese and the Chinese in depth.

Immediately upon their arrival in Peking in the middle of the night, Lord Amherst and Sir Thomas were rushed to a court in the Summer Palace. They were to be cast forthwith at Jiaqing's feet. They were grabbed

---

* Actually his name was also George: the father was George Leonard, the son George Thomas. In order to avoid confusion, I will always refer to the son as Thomas, just as his father did.

by the shoulders, they resisted, and a scuffle broke out. Were they actually refusing to see the emperor? They were immediately ejected.

TWENTY-FOUR YEARS LATER, on April 7, 1840, a debate raged in the House of Commons. Several English merchants in Canton were facing a death sentence, and a military expedition against China was being prepared. Sir Thomas Staunton, honorable member of Parliament for Portsmouth, the city from which he had embarked, forty-eight years before, with the first British mission to the Middle Empire, rose to speak.

"The question with regard to the opium was not a question of morality or policy, but a question whether there had been any breach of international law. For a time, certainly, when the laws against opium trade were in a state of obeyance: when the viceroy of Canton gave the use of his own vessel to bring up the opium to Canton, they could not feel surprised that foreigners did not feel themselves bound very strictly to obey the edicts of the government. . . .

"To attempt to punish those under the new law, who had arrived in China under the old law, must be condemned by all parties as a most atrocious injustice. . . . An American merchant has well described the conduct of the Chinese towards the English as resembling their treatment of a refractory village—put them to the sword!. . . . Let the House recollect that our empire in the East was founded on the force of opinion; and if we submitted to the degrading insults of China, the time would not be far distant when our political ascendancy in India would be at an end." The stakes of the impending war, Staunton said, were incalculable: the British had no right to engage in battle if they were to lose it, and no right to shirk combat if they were to win it.[3]

He was heard in religious silence, for everyone was aware that no member of Parliament, indeed no British subject, knew China as well as he did. A few minutes later, his concluding peroration was met with prolonged applause, as he announced that he believed, "though very reluctantly, that this war is absolutely just and necessary under existing conditions."[4]

AT ELEVEN he was the page of the first British ambassador to Peking, at thirty-five the deputy of a new ambassador, at fifty-nine a member of Parliament and a resolute supporter of the Opium War. Such was the career of this most favored witness to half a century of events of world importance.

Relations between the Far East and the West, of course, did not begin in 1793. Far from it. But 1793 was the astonishing point of departure of a protracted confrontation whose costs both China and the West are still paying.

It was a year that seemed so completely French to the French! Indeed, it might well be argued that the full energy of history, creative and destructive alike, was focused on the events in Paris. France went to war against Europe not to gain new provinces but to "bring down tyrants."

What a contrast to the tranquillity that reigned in the two most powerful countries of the world! Yet in that same year, in a kind of nonevent, these countries would shape the history of the two centuries to come. Not much seemed to be happening in the United Kingdom or in China. Fascinated though they were by what was happening in France, the British simply remained on the sidelines and observed the arrival of thousands of distraught immigrants. In China, the emperor Qianlong was completing the fifty-eighth year of his reign. He knew nothing of the Convention, nor of the French Republic, and when news of both finally arrived in Peking, it was regarded as the pointless story of a tempest raging across an unknown ocean.

Despite its small size and modest population, England was the Western country experiencing the most rapid ascent, at a time when the market economy, mechanization, and the industrial revolution were taking their first faltering steps on the European continent. China was at its apogee. During the long and glorious reign of the emperor Qianlong, the country's population had more than doubled,* and so had the area of the territories over which Pax Sinica held sway: Annam, Cochin China, Siam, Burma, Nepal, Tibet, Korea, Manchuria, Mongolia, Turkestan, and central Asia as far as the Aral Sea and even to the Caspian. Never in history had so many bowed to a single authority.

Until then, only tenuous trade links had been woven between these two summits of human accomplishment. But what if the two worlds had broadened their contacts, mutually enriching each other with what each did best? What if the country that, centuries before all others, had invented printing and paper, the compass and the rudder, gunpowder and firearms, had blended its discoveries with those of the country that had just tamed steam and was about to master electricity? Cultural exchanges between

---

* According to estimates made at the time and confirmed by more recent historical demographic studies, China's population stood at 140 million to 160 million in 1730, just before Qianlong acceded to the throne, and rose to 340 million in 1796, when he abdicated. See note 5 to the Introduction.

China and Europe would surely have spurred leaps of progress on both sides. Talk about a cultural revolution!

Such was the opportunity history offered the Far East and the West, an opportunity aborted by a dialogue of the world's most powerful deaf. Instead there was a clash of pride, each party imagining itself the center of the universe and consigning the other to a barbarous periphery.

China refused to open itself to the world at the very moment that the British were seeking, willy-nilly, to open the world to all forms of exchange. In just fifty years the two extremities of Eurasia would move from cultural collision to armed conflict.

Thomas Staunton was the "engaged observer" of this great missed opportunity.

I

THE JOURNEY
TO CHINA

(September 1792–June 1793)

A naval empire has always given the peoples who have possessed it a natural pride, because, feeling themselves able to insult others everywhere, they believe that their power is as boundless as the ocean.

CHARLES DE MONTESQUIEU, 1748[1]

England's plan is to create free and independent settlements on the coasts of China.

JEAN-ANTOINE D'ENTRECASTEAUX, 1787[2]

Whatever each man can separately do, without trespassing upon others, he has a right to do for himself.

EDMUND BURKE, 1790[3]

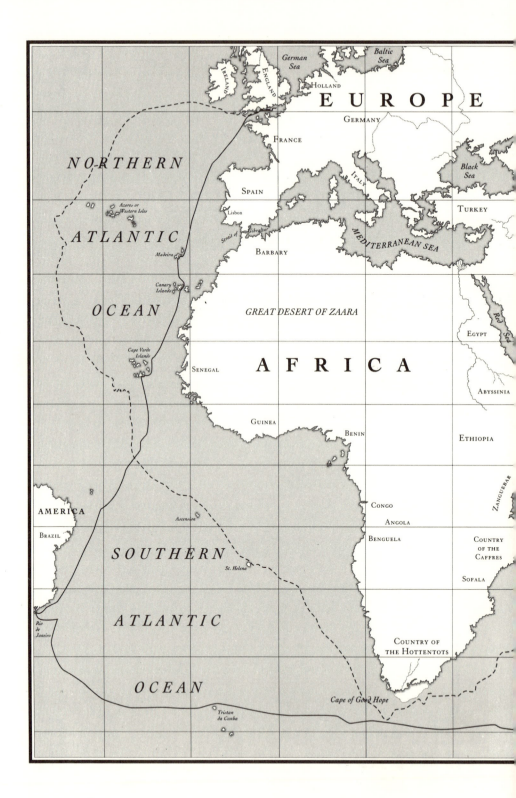

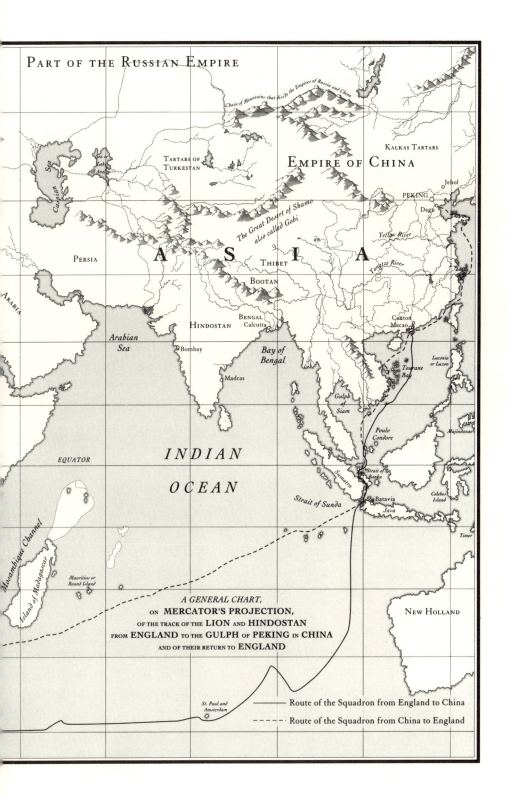

PART OF THE RUSSIAN EMPIRE

Chain of Mountains that divide the Empires of Russia and China

KALKAS TARTARS

TARTARS OF
TURKESTAN

EMPIRE OF CHINA

Jehol

PEKING

Dagú

*Sea of
Lake
of Aral*

*Caspian
Sea*

A S I A

*The Great Desert of Shamo
also called Gobi*

Yellow River

PERSIA

THIBET

Yangtze River

BOOTAN

Canton
Macao

ARABIA

HINDOSTAN

BENGAL
Calcutta

*Arabian
Sea*

Bombay

*Bay of
Bengal*

Luconia
or Lazon

Madras

*Tourane
Bay*

*Gulph
of
Siam*

*Poulo
Condore*

Majindanao

EQUATOR

INDIAN

Sumatra

*Strait of
Banka*

Celebes
Island

OCEAN

Strait of Sunda

Batavia
Java

Timor

Mozambique Channel

*Mauritius or
Round Island*

Island of Madagascar

NEW HOLLAND

A GENERAL CHART,
ON **MERCATOR'S PROJECTION**,
OF THE TRACK OF THE **LION** AND **HINDOSTAN**
FROM **ENGLAND** TO THE **GULPH** OF **PEKING** IN **CHINA**
AND OF THEIR RETURN TO **ENGLAND**

*St. Paul and
Amsterdam*

———— Route of the Squadron from England to China

- - - - Route of the Squadron from China to England

1

Departure

(September 26–October 8, 1792)

THEY CAST OFF with the morning tide, heading due west, quickly leaving Portsmouth harbor behind: the *Lion*, a sixty-four-gun warship; the *Hindostan*, a 1,200-ton three-masted vessel owned by the East India Company; and the *Jackall*, a brig. Lord Macartney, eager to take advantage of the favorable wind, "resisted his inclination" to accept the king's invitation to stop at Weymouth for a visit with the royal family.[1] As he stood on the rear deck of the *Lion* and breathed the sea air, he felt exhilarated at the prospect of this adventure. No British sovereign had ever assembled so impressive an embassy, and no European state had ever sent anything like it to China.

As a former ambassador to the Russian tsarina and a former governor of British colonies in the Caribbean and in India, Macartney was no newcomer to diplomacy. Nor was Sir George Staunton, his deputy, who had been an invaluable aide to Macartney in his last two postings and would be quite capable of taking command of this expedition should the need arise. King George III was sending two brilliant emissaries to China. In all, the mission had nearly a hundred members: diplomats, scions of the British aristocracy, scholars, physicians, painters, musicians, technicians, soldiers, and servants. Counting the sailors, almost seven hundred men were involved.[2] It had taken days to bring them all aboard.[3]

The newspapers and diplomatic dispatches were full of news of France: abolition of the monarchy, massacres in the prisons, proclamation of a republic, defeat of the Prussians at Valmy. Macartney was astute enough to realize that the United Kingdom would not remain aloof from all this turmoil for long. His friend Edmund Burke[4] had hazarded the prediction that the universal upheaval then occurring in Europe would entail the common ruin of religion, morality, tradition, and respect for authority. He feared a monstrous degeneration of the human race that would return it to a state of savagery.[5]

The mere fact that this mission was leaving on schedule despite the impending war was proof enough of its importance. Every ship would be needed, but these three could not possibly be recalled. A courier on horseback could overtake an army, but once a naval squadron sailed, it was in God's hands alone.

Macartney was also accredited to approach other sovereigns of the Far East: the emperors of Japan and Annam and the kings of Korea, Manila, and the Moluccas. He was authorized to visit any country that might help in his principal mission: to open China to British trade. England was already a global power, and London had no intention of putting all its eggs in a single Continental basket. The British state took the long view, and it was now investing in its future.

On that same day, on the other side of the world, representatives of the East India Company who had left London in April and arrived in Canton on September 20 asked the Chinese merchant guild of that city to arrange an interview with the viceroy. They had been instructed to hand the viceroy a message from Sir Francis Baring, the company president. That message said, in part, "His Majesty, desirous of improving the connection, intercourse and good correspondence between the Courts of London and Peking, and of increasing the commerce between their respective subjects, resolved to send his well-beloved Cousin and Counsellor the Right Honorable George Lord Macartney."[6] The objective of the expedition—exchange on an equal basis—was thus being presented to Chinese officials at the very moment that the ships were casting off.

THE FAVORABLE east wind did not last. The temperature dropped, and a swell arose. A whistling storm whipped the halyards, and the crews furled the mainsails and hugged the reefs. It was an inauspicious start to the crossing. How would the ships hold up under the typhoons of the China Sea?

Young Thomas Staunton, who had read Voltaire, wondered whether the ship might split in two like Candide's near Lisbon. Sir Erasmus Gower, commander of the squadron, decided to seek shelter at the inlet of Tor Bay.

The *Lion* and the *Hindostan* spent two days making repairs and awaiting the *Jackall*, which they had lost track of in the storm. On September 30 they decided to go on without the missing ship. On October 1 they sailed past Ushant, an island off the west coast of Brittany. A moderate wind soon carried the ships through the Bay of Biscay, which John Barrow described as "like the 'Wavering Nation' . . . whose shores it laves, . . . ever in a state of restlessness, even in the midst of a calm."[7]

They sailed quickly, perhaps too quickly: "On the 8th the *Lion* sprung her fore-top mast in crowding too much sail."[8] The damage was quickly repaired, and young Thomas admired the agility of the seamen as they crawled through the yards and rigging. His father had great hopes for the boy, his sole surviving son. The child's manners were impeccable: he seemed to sense instinctively exactly what was required of a scion of the gentry. Learning was a game to him—he could recite a page of a newspaper after reading it just once—and for the past several weeks his main occupation had been the Chinese language. He spent all his time with the two interpreters, communicating with them in Latin.[9]

The passengers relished the comforts of the *Lion*, a great vessel of the high seas. As he listened to the five German musicians playing Handel and Haydn, Macartney felt relieved that neither the indispensable interpreters nor the precious cargo of gifts for the emperor had been aboard the *Jackall*, possibly lost with all hands and goods.[10]

The interpreters were among the mission's most essential members, and it had not been easy to find them. No suitable candidates were available in the United Kingdom, Sweden, or Lisbon,[11] and the British had preferred to avoid the various French monks who had served in the Middle Kingdom and were well versed in Chinese, since they might have been tempted to serve their own country, Britain's eternal rival, rather than George III. Staunton had therefore traveled to Italy the previous winter, visiting the Collegium Sinicum in Naples and meeting with two Chinese priests who wanted to return to their homeland. They had been located by Sir William Hamilton, His Majesty's minister to Naples, the same man whose wife, a former prostitute, would later arouse Lord Nelson's uncontrollable passion.[12] Fathers Li and Zhou did not speak a word of English, but their Latin was serviceable. Sir George had also been kind enough to offer free passage to Macao to two other returning Chinese priests, Fathers An and Wang. The five of them had gathered in London in May.

As for the gifts to the emperor, they were the centerpiece of a dazzling display that was meant to prove that England was not only "the most powerful nation of the globe" but also its most advanced civilization. Staunton had made sure that these gifts, brilliant testimony to British genius, were securely stowed aboard the *Lion* and the *Hindostan*.

IN THE ERA OF the Enlightenment, as in the time of Columbus, what we now call the Far East, from Pakistan to Korea, was known as the "East Indies." And to an Englishman, the East Indies meant the East India

Company, which was now in serious trouble. "To say that the Company is doing badly," Edmund Burke had declared in 1783, "is to say that the country is doing badly."[13] What's good for the company is good for England.

In an effort to encourage the tea trade, over which the company held a monopoly, William Pitt, the British prime minister, had lowered tariffs from 10 percent to 1 percent.[14] Imports of Chinese tea had tripled in two years. But the trade remained one-sided, since the Chinese seemed to want nothing in return. "I cannot recollect any new article that is likely to answer," one of the company directors wrote, "almost everything has been tried."[15] The one article he didn't mention was opium. Trade in that commodity had begun decades ago and had expanded rapidly since 1780. No one spoke of it aloud, but it was on everyone's mind. With that single shameful exception, the Chinese market was closed to English exports, choked by the bottleneck of Canton. London had finally concluded that only agreements at the highest level could remove the obstacles.

Back in 1787 Pitt and his friend Henry Dundas, then president of the company's governing board, had decided to send an ambassador to China. Colonel Charles Cathcart, an officer who had served with distinction in Bengal, enthusiastically set sail. But when asked their view of this mission, company officials in Canton did not mince words: "The Chinese government looks with contempt on all foreign nations. Its ignorance of their force give it confidence in its own strength. It does not look on Embassies in any other light than acknowledgments of inferiority."[16]

The episode went badly. The expedition was buffeted by storms and racked by epidemics. After it rounded the Cape of Good Hope, Cathcart himself fell ill and died within sight of China. When his ship, the *Vestal*, returned to London at the end of 1788, Macartney suggested to Pitt that his friend Staunton be sent to try again. But three years passed before a decision was made. The diplomats hesitated, but industrialists stepped up the pressure.[17] Gradually the idea arose that an expanded mission might be entrusted to Macartney himself, who had scored repeated successes in Russia, the Caribbean, and India. Dundas, who was now home secretary but still followed Asian affairs closely, formally proposed the idea to Macartney in October 1791.[18]

Macartney accepted the challenge. The impending conflict in Europe would inevitably favor the careers of military officers rather than diplomats like himself, and he would be better off defending British interests far from the battlefields, at the head of a lavish embassy. Three days before Christmas, he informed Dundas of his terms for accepting the assignment:

a payment of fifteen thousand pounds for each year he was away from Britain and a promotion to the rank of earl.*

He also demanded the right to choose the members of the mission. They "should consist of persons either immediately useful in the negotiation," he told Dundas, "or who, by being versed in such sciences or arts as are admired in China, might then increase the respect for the country of which such men are natives."[19] Beginning with his right-hand man. There must be no repetition of the Cathcart experience: if anything happened to Macartney, the mission would have to continue under the command of a duly accredited deputy. Macartney's friend Staunton was therefore named plenipotentiary minister. Sir George, in turn, insisted that his son serve as the page who would be needed for the various ceremonies. Young Thomas already spoke elegant French and Latin, which he studied under the strict supervision of Hans Christian Hüttner, his German tutor, who would go along on the voyage as well.

The ambassador was also accompanied by a comptroller, John Barrow; two secretaries, Acheson Maxwell and Edward Winder; three attachés; two physicians, Drs. Hugh Gillan and William Scott; and a military escort with its officers. But even that was not enough. Macartney was convinced that if the British were to demonstrate sufficient culture to challenge the millennial Chinese claim to a monopoly of civilization, they would have to arouse admiration for their peacetime and wartime technology. "The most curious and striking experiments, especially such as from their novelty are not likely to have been exhibited by the missionaries in China: steam engines, cotton machines & etc.—could not fail to gratify a curious and ingenious people." And: "It has been thought necessary on various accounts to be provided in all Oriental Embassies with a military guard."[20]

Macartney hoped that the mission's men and material would both play a role in determining the image England would present to the Chinese emperor. Dundas somewhat sarcastically reminded Macartney "that he was not leading a delegation of the Royal Society," but Macartney stood his ground. Granted, uppermost in his mind were the abuses suffered by British merchants in Canton and his country's long-standing aims: to open new ports to trade, to gain a territorial concession for the establishment of a permanent warehouse, and to penetrate the Chinese market. But he believed that his embassy should be a delegation of the Royal Society as well.[21]

---

* This proposal was accepted: Macartney immediately became Viscount of Dervock (the name of his estate in County Antrim), and it was agreed that he would be named an earl upon his return from China. Half on signature, the balance on delivery.

The expedition would therefore have its artists—the painters William Alexander and Thomas Hickey—and its scientists, chief among them Dr. James Dinwiddie, an astronomer and physicist skilled in mechanics and optics. No one would be more adept at eliciting Chinese admiration for the hot-air balloons and the very latest hoists.

MACARTNEY AND STAUNTON met in the company headquarters in the heart of the City of London to prepare their embassy. The superb offices were in striking contrast to the company's precarious position in Canton. The negotiations that Cathcart had not had a chance to open six years earlier would now have to be conducted in an even gloomier atmosphere. In fact, the company had initially opposed this entire project, fearing that any initiative at all would only further irritate the Chinese. This mission was the brainchild of politicians, not merchants, who believed that excessive ambition might well compromise the positions that had already been won, however tentative they were. But once the politicians carried the day, the company backed down. If the mission was inevitable, the company directors would do whatever they could to ensure its success, giving Macartney and Staunton all the information they had.[22]

As a former governor of Madras, Macartney was well placed to appreciate the close link between Chinese and Indian affairs. He also knew how important the Canton trade was to the company. The Indian empire was itself somewhat shaky. It was ravaged by famine, and the rebellions among the rajahs fomented by the French during the last war had not been easily put down. After the peace of 1783, Parliament decided that a trading company could not rule over such a populous empire alone. The English settlements in India were therefore brought under tighter Crown control.

During his tenure as governor of Madras, Macartney had come to believe (as Dundas did) that events in China would determine India's future, an idea that had steadily gained ground in London. The conquest of the Chinese market would help defray the costs of British rule in India.

The rising importance of the Indian opium trade during the eighteenth century had aroused heated debates in the House of Commons. The Honorable Philip Francis, for instance, had condemned the "pernicious" cultivation of poppies—"the most noxious weed that grew"—in India.[23] It speaks well for British honor that a member of Parliament denounced the profits being made from an enterprise that looked more and more like slow genocide. But an unruffled Dundas replied that opium was a widespread consumer good in Asia and that the more of it was exported from

India to China, the less money would flow out of Britain to India. Macartney would have preferred that "we could substitute rice or any other better production in its [opium's] place,"[24] but he soon made his peace with reality.

Europe was running a larger and larger trade deficit with Asia,[25] selling next to nothing in China apart from a few clocks and other minor manufactured goods. Meanwhile, Chinese exports of tea, porcelain, silk, and curios were rising steadily. The only way out was to balance Europe's Chinese imports with the export of industrial goods. Once the Chinese market was opened, contraband Indian opium would no longer be necessary. For the moment, however, it was paying for the tea. Britain took a world view of its trade, if not a moral one.

DUNDAS HAD GIVEN Macartney his official instructions on September 8, 1792. They contained a solemn preamble: "A greater number of His Majesty's subjects than of any other Europeans have been trading for a considerable time past in China—The commercial intercourse between several Nations and that great Empire has been preceeded, accompanied, or followed by Special communications with its Sovereign—others had support of Missionaries who . . . were frequently admitted to the familiarity of a curious and polished Court, . . . while the English traders remained unaided, and . . . unavowed at a distance so remote as to admit of a misrepresentation of the national character and importance, and where too their occupation was not held in that esteem which ought to procure them safety and respect."[26]

The British cabinet wondered about the nature of the restrictions being imposed on European trade in Canton, and the ambassador was told to find out whether this treatment was the result of a deliberate policy, "jealousy of our national influence," corruption, or the abuses of a provincial administration operating outside the control of the capital. "The propriety of fixing this Embassy on a person thus dignified [as yourself] is enforced by the decided opinion of those who have been most experienced in the Company's concerns at Canton, and who have been Witnesses of the vexations under which they labour."[27]

". . . you will procure an audience as early as possible after your arrival," Dundas explained, "conforming to all ceremonials of that Court which may not commit the honour of your Sovereign or lessen your own dignity, so as to endanger the success of your negotiation. . . . While I make this reserve I am satisfied you will be too prudent and considerate to let any trifling punctilio stand in the way of the important benefits which may be obtained by engaging the favourable disposition of the Emperor and his ministers."[28] In other words: honor the rites without dishonoring us, but don't sacrifice the mission by standing on ceremony. There followed seven points summarizing suggestions Macartney himself had earlier made in writing to Dundas.[29]

1. Open new ports for British trade in China.
2. Obtain the cession of a piece of territory, or an island, as close as possible to the areas of tea and silk production, where British merchants can reside year round and in which British jurisdiction is exercised.
3. Abolish the abuses of the system now in effect in Canton.
4. Create new markets in China, especially in Peking.
5. Open the other lands of the Far East to British trade, through bilateral treaties.
6. Request the establishment of a permanent mission in Peking.
7. And last but not least, an intelligence mission: "You will naturally in the course of your residence in China extend your remarks as far as can be done without exciting jealousy, . . . to every circumstance likely to throw a light upon the present strength, policy, and government" of China, "now less understood in Europe than they were in the preceding century."[30]

It was a wide-ranging program, whose colonial aspirations were already discernable.

There had, of course, been precursors to this mission. Portugal tried five times between 1521 and 1754, but had done nothing for the past forty years. The Netherlands tried three times between 1656 and 1686. Russia, more persistent and geographically nearer to China, had dispatched seven caravans between 1656 and 1767. France had sent missionaries, but no official representatives.[31] In all, there had been fifteen missions, with quite unspectacular results.[32]

Twenty years later, Thomas Staunton summed up the feeble achievements of these fifteen "embassies": "This great Empire, too well assured of the competency of its own natural and artificial resources to be induced to seek, and if not too powerful, at least too distant and compactly united, to be liable to be compelled to enter into alliances and close connections with the Powers of Europe, has never yet, except in a precarious and limited degree, admitted of any species of intercourse with them."[33] Macartney was determined to break this skein. Though his embassy was only the sixteenth, it would be the first to be truly worthy of the name.

Actually, only the Russians had managed to hold genuine negotiations with the Chinese. As rivals for control of the vast Asian plains inhabited by Tartar nomads, these two countries were simply unable to ignore each other.[34] It was now Macartney's task to show the Chinese that a new power had been born in the West. The vessels of the United Kingdom, overturning geography, would bring England as close to China as the barbarian state beyond the steppes. Great Britain would now be China's maritime neighbor, and Macartney intended to make his country just as inescapable to China as its Russian land neighbor was.

2

"The Lords of Human Kind"

(October 9–27, 1792)

> . . . in a nation like ours, . . . commerce has kindled an universal emulation to wealth, and . . . money receives all the honours which are the proper right of knowledge and of virtue.
>
> SAMUEL JOHNSON, 1759[1]

ON OCTOBER 9 the British reached the waters of the Portuguese island of Madeira, where, on a previous voyage, William Mackintosh, the captain of the *Hindostan*, had lost his ship and its entire crew. He and his cook, both ashore at the time of the disaster, were the sole survivors.[2] The island's governor, alerted by Lisbon to expect the squadron, greeted the British ships with a ceremonial salvo.

The English were most welcome on this island, whose wine they bought and where they owned some twenty trading companies with enough capital to shield them from any threat of competition. The Portuguese had been effectively colonized in their own colony, and Macartney and Staunton savored this triumph of the mercantile civilization whose messengers they were. The poverty of the Portuguese was in sharp contrast to the unabashed prosperity of the British commercial establishments.[3]

Women walked along the roads carrying bundles of "broom," which they used for firewood. "The poorness of their food . . . added to the severity of their labour, and the warmth of the climate, give them the appearance of age at an early period of life."[4] Garbage was commonly thrown in the streets, to the delight of wandering pigs. Malnutrition caused epidemics and scurvy among the multitudes of poor, while the rich few were racked by gout. Rich and poor alike suffered from smallpox. The British, good Protestants all, were quick to draw a connection between the island's evident backwardness and its "Roman" religion.[5] Staunton was reminded of southern Italy, where he had recruited the interpreters, Macartney of his native Ireland and of the wretchedness of the archaic Catholic smallholdings of Connemara.

AS HE SAILED toward the world's oldest, largest, and most populous empire, Macartney repeatedly told himself that his real purpose was to affirm a new truth: that Great Britain was now "the most powerful nation of the globe" and George III the "sovereign of the seas." His letters, notes, and reports are riddled with these expressions. This revelation, undoubtedly disagreeable to his hosts, would be presented as politely as possible, Qianlong being described as holding primacy in the East, George III in the West. But the mission itself belied this purely formal concession to courtesy. The fact was that the East was going to have to open its doors to the West, whose masters now proclaimed, asserting their own power and interests, that the world was one and that they intended to travel it and trade in it freely.

"He who controls trade controls the world's wealth, and therefore the world itself," Sir Walter Raleigh had affirmed during the reign of Elizabeth I,[6] and every British citizen knew the words to the anthem of that ambition: "Rule, Britannia / Britannia rules the waves." As rulers of the waves, eight million Britons were confident that they could speak as masters to three hundred million Chinese.

English pride had been born—the pride of a nation of mounting power and irrepressible energy, the horizon of whose ambition lay in the borderless world of the seas. Just after the victories of the Seven Years' War, Oliver Goldsmith had written of his countrymen:

> Pride in their port, defiance in their eye,
> I see the lords of human kind pass by.[7]

In 1776, when Adam Smith's *The Wealth of Nations* was published, the exchange economy he analyzed was a living reality practiced by merchants, capitalists, and entrepreneurs. Where the French *philosophes*, his contemporaries, speculated about the theoretical organization of an ideal world, Smith described a system whose reality and power he could see around him.

Smith was a strong believer in the beneficent effects of nature's bounty: supply would always elicit demand. If there was poverty, private initiative would deal with it. Personal interest was the mother of ingenuity and innovation.[8] Technological cross-fertilization and the universality of trade—such was the revolutionary idea Macartney meant to sell Qianlong.

Smith's thought had become official doctrine. In 1787 Pitt held a great banquet to which Smith was invited. As they approached the table, the British prime minister turned to the Scottish economist and said, "After you, sir, for we are all your disciples."[9]

In 1753 the curmudgeonly but fascinated Samuel Johnson formulated a moralist's critique of this developing consumer society, whose products were unknown yesterday, indispensable today, and outmoded on the morrow.[10] The term *industrial revolution*, conjuring up images of workshops rattled by the deafening din of the earliest machines, is but a pale reflection of this soaring economic creativity. The truth is that the economic revolution that swept England during the eighteenth century was based most of all on ships like the ones carrying this expedition. Throughout his career, Macartney had been a deliberate agent of this roaring maritime and commercial revolution.

The complex interplay of supply and demand had quintupled the tonnage carried by the British merchant fleet in just one century. Roads and canals, banks and mines were opened throughout the kingdom. Production of iron and wool leaped from the handicraft to the industrial stage. The porcelain and cotton industries were born. Factories sprouted everywhere. The widespread development of machinery and the huge sums required for all these investments gave rise to two new species: the worker, who lived only by dint of his labor in the factory, and the industrialist.

The great entrepreneurs—like Robert Peel, Sr., or Richard Arkwright—were honored, courted, and often knighted. When Wedgwood had a leg amputated in 1768, the entire aristocracy of London gathered at his bedside.[11] British nobles, free of the fear of divestiture that haunted their counterparts on the Continent, took pride in their economic activities. The first canals were dug by a duke; crop rotation was introduced by a lord. A new world was being born, not all at once and not by deliberate design, but through the cumulative effects of countless interactions.

But the most important revolution of all was the one that gripped people's minds, and these were minds that thought of everything all at once.[12] Mercantile wealth, naval power, financial prosperity, agricultural productivity, and population growth all stimulated one another. But they would have soon reached their limits had it not been for an absolutely new phenomenon that James W. Watt and Matthew Boulton described to King George III in these terms in 1775: "Sir, we sell what the world desires: power."[13] Partly, this was a play on words: *power* in the dual sense of energy and political might. But the adage reflects the advent of the modern economy. The pastoral world of mills driven by donkeys was gone. The horse gave way to the steam engine, an innovation comparable to the mastery of fire, the birth of agriculture, or the various inventions that China had been unable to exploit: printing, gunpowder, the compass.[14] Without steam there would have been no machinery, but only (as in China) brilliant but isolated inventions devoid of development potential.

Macartney had closely followed this chain of inventions, each one triggering the next, and the holds of his ships contained many samples of them.

The economic explosion, born in trade, had spilled out of the British Isles and had now launched Macartney on this voyage. Though prosperity had come first to England, it had not neglected the colonies, beginning with those in North America, enriched in 1763 by the absorption of French Canada. The emancipation of the thirteen colonies in 1783 had been a challenge quickly surmounted: British exports to the new United States recovered rapidly.

In India the three trading centers the British had controlled since the seventeenth century—Bombay, Madras, and Calcutta—soaked up the products of the subcontinent and cast maritime routes ever eastward. The British were building an empire in the Phoenician style,[15] and they would have preferred to do so without direct colonies. Opening the doors of China was part of a more general plan.[16] Dundas had been trying to persuade the Dutch to cede the island of Rhio, opposite Singapore, to the British Crown.[17] And the first English settlers, mainly convicts, had arrived in Australia.

This network of trading posts was meant to sell the world all the products that were spun and woven, forged and fashioned, by the workers of the United Kingdom. Commerce and Industry were to join hands, like two heroic silhouettes on a commemorative medal.

Shortly after 1763 Lord Clive, flushed with his recent victories over the Mogul Empire and the French, proposed that he be sent to conquer China by armed force. The elder Pitt rejected the offer, arguing that it would be lunacy to try to subjugate such a great mass of humanity.[18] Now, thirty years later, the question was whether diplomacy would be any more effective.

Could "progress"—which was not yet called "development"—be imposed by force, guile, or even charm on a people who insisted that the "occasions on which the Master talked about profit . . . were rare"?[19] Confucius never read Adam Smith.

THE CROSSING from Madeira to the Canary Islands was a delight. Late on the fourth day, Tenerife seemed to rise up out of the sea. "On Sunday the

21st, we saw with pleasure the Peak of Teneriffe (supposed to be the highest single mountain in the world)," wrote Samuel Holmes, a soldier in the ambassador's guard.[20]

There had been no plans to lay over in Santa Cruz, where the winter moorage was execrable,[21] but Sir Erasmus Gower decided that a stopover would be useful after all. It would give the *Jackall* time to catch up, and the expedition could stock up on wines that traveled better than those of Madeira. The men of the escort were proud to find that the best vintage of all was labeled London Particular.[22]

In principle, Madeira, the Canaries, and the Cape Verde islands were Iberian colonies, but by the end of the eighteenth century their only real purpose seemed to be to foster British trade—or rather, Anglo-Saxon trade, since the Americans were already buying what wine the English couldn't use.[23]

Spanish reserve made contact with the islanders somewhat difficult, but fortunately there were many English residents only too happy to offer their hospitality. The local Spanish aristocracy seemed to spend most of its time in church. Holmes advised his readers to supply themselves "plentifully with dollars" if they wished "a welcome reception from the selfish Spaniards here."[24]

Some of the British "made an excursion to the Peak." A few, "more adventurous than the rest, got within half a mile of the top, by climbing over rocks and precipices upon their hands and feet."[25] In the middle of the following century the British invented mountain climbing in Switzerland and Savoy, and here they were already exercising their taste for self-created challenges, risk, the thrill of striving, and the spirit of enterprise.

In the harbor a strange flag fluttered from one vessel's mast: the tricolor of the new French Republic. Barrow reports that the French commander greeted the British squadron with a volley of cannon fire, more challenge than salute, several cannonballs splashing loudly into the sea. "Like a true Gascon he had boasted, as we afterwards heard, that, concluding from the sight of our squadron war must have broken out between England and France, he had prepared to receive us with one broadside at least, in order to do all the mischief he could, *pour l'honneur de la Grande Nation,* before he struck his colours. Yet these are the people who are loudest in complaining of the tyranny of the English in exercising the sovereignty of the seas."[26]

ON EACH ISLAND, the local Portuguese and Spanish governors honored "Lord Macartney, viscount of Dervock, ambassador of His Gracious Majesty," with cannon salvos and gala dinners. As scions of the Europe of the Ancien Régime, united by the snobbery of the nobility, they were naturally impressed by their guest. But any reader of *Gentleman's Magazine* could have put them at ease. Macartney was in fact a man of the new era, and his genealogy was a good deal less glorious than his career.

He had taken full advantage of more than one stroke of luck, most recently the death of Colonel Cathcart. This latest opportunity had come his way because he had been fortunate enough to acquire diplomatic experience in St. Petersburg, military expertise in the Caribbean, and knowledge of the Orient in Madras. At the age of twenty-seven he had been recommended for the posting to the court of Catherine II by Henry Fox, the first Lord Holland and hardheaded negotiator of the Treaty of Paris, who was then at the height of his power. Macartney owed this protective sponsorship to a fortuitous encounter in Geneva with Fox's son Stephen, who had been tearing a path through the gaming tables of the Continent at the time.[27]

But luck alone does not forge a destiny. Character counts too, and Macartney had plenty of that. Viewing a portrait of his friend painted by Joshua Reynolds in 1764, the elder Fox examined the burning gaze and self-assured brow and exclaimed, "It resembles him excessively!"[28] And Fox, who had just divested France of the greater part of its colonial empire and established British maritime supremacy, was himself no stranger to ardor and self-assurance.

It was that same combination of luck and character that accounted for Macartney's having had his portrait painted by such a famous artist at such an early age. He was, after all, only the great-grandson of a Scottish emigrant—George Macartney, also known as Black George[29]—who had joined a settlement in papist Ireland in 1649. Through hard work and shrewd marriages Black George, his son, and his grandson had augmented the family holdings until they included houses, farms, and mills. Their landholdings and their political activity (in the current that was beginning to be called Whig) brought them affluence and fame.

Black George's son, the future Lord Macartney's grandfather, held a seat in the Irish parliament for fifty-four years (1700–1754). By the end of his life, all his hopes were riding on his only grandson, our hero. The youngster had been carefully educated in the classics, Greek, Latin, and French. At the age of thirteen he enrolled in Trinity College, Dublin, a Protestant sentinel in a Catholic land. Most of his classmates were sixteen or seventeen, but Macartney's family lied about his age.[30]

In the autumn of 1757 the twenty-year-old Macartney left for London, where he was to receive legal training, though he had no intention of ever pleading cases in court.[31] His purpose was to begin weaving a fabric of friendly connections in a milieu that had no equivalent on the Continent. Napoleon later called it "the oligarchy." It was here that winners and losers were sorted out, the men who could make a name for themselves separated from those who just couldn't cut it. This was the source of power—if you knew how to grasp it.

But the real training ground for the British elite was the "grand tour" of the Continent. Macartney duly sailed for Calais at the end of 1759. No fewer than forty thousand Britons left for Europe annually, spending two, three, or even five years abroad, depending on their resources and their connections. It was a rite of passage, but a costly one.[32] The aim was to learn to observe, to judge, to admire—and to feel definitively superior, if only by appropriating the accumulated cultural capital of all of Europe.

Though he inherited the family patrimony at the age of twenty-two, it was in Geneva that Macartney truly made his fortune, for it was there that he ran into Stephen Fox, son of the victor of the Seven Years' War. Macartney ardently set about protecting his new friend from various con men and from his own passion for gambling. He remained constantly at Fox's side, bringing him back to London safe and sound in July. The grateful Fox family was utterly smitten with the young Irishman. At the end of the year, when Stephen returned to Geneva, Henry Fox asked Macartney to go along as his son's mentor.

That second trip was like a fairy tale. Fox's name earned Macartney introductions to people he never would have dreamed of approaching otherwise. He had an audience with the duke of Württemberg.[33] He visited Rousseau in Neuchâtel and Voltaire at Ferney. "Who in the world is this young man," exclaimed the latter, "who knows so much about so many things at such a tender age!"[34] Macartney so impressed the great man that Voltaire gave him written introductions to Choiseul and to the philosophers Helvétius and d'Alembert. "*Mon illustre philosophe*," Voltaire wrote to Helvétius, "this will introduce a very well educated English gentleman who thinks much as you do, finding our nation most amusing."[35] This was the century of Enlightenment, and Macartney was absorbing its photons at the very source.

But if he found wisdom, he also struck gold. The Foxes brought him into a milieu where pounds were counted in the thousands, at a time when a weaver in a factory made less than half a pound a week.[36] None of these people spent much time cooling their heels in waiting rooms. Despite his talent for writing, his peerless memory, his mastery of French, Latin, and Italian, his tireless energy, and his taste for mature ladies, Macartney never would have been able to rise so high had it not been for the Foxes. Lord Holland gave him a chance, and Macartney seized it.

He entered the world of the British elite, a world whose stage was the planet. Maritime trade was the hearth in which the oligarchy forged its power, tested its men, and renewed its energies. The British carried the freight of five continents. Total British merchant tonnage was double the French tonnage, quadruple the Dutch, Swedish, and Danish, and ten times the Spanish. The English sold in Batavia what they bought in Rio, bought in India what they would resell in Europe. But even that was not enough. It was never enough. Macartney had now set sail to convince Qianlong that this traffic must be allowed to grow.

3

When China Was the Rage in Europe

(October 27–November 30, 1792)

THE EXPEDITION reached the Cape Verde islands on November 1. Drought had reduced these islands to little more than a way station, but the strength of the British Empire was based on just such points of support in allied territories: "unofficial" colonies in the Iberian world.

In the port of Santiago was another French ship flying that annoying tricolor. But the shape of the vessel seemed vaguely familiar, and the British suddenly realized that it was none other than the *Resolution*, the ship on which Captain Cook had won his glory and lost his life. The French had somehow recovered it and renamed it *La Liberté*. Macartney shared his companions' anger at seeing this famous ship profaned by *sans-culottes*. "I am not ashamed to confess," wrote Barrow, "that my feelings were considerably hurt in witnessing this degradation of an object so intimately connected with that great man."[1]

They waited for five days, and when there was still no sign of the *Jackall*, they decided to go on without it.

Two days earlier, the French Republic, having defeated the Austrians at Jemappes, had begun its occupation of Belgium.

AS A PRODUCT of the British oligarchy, Macartney was now its willing servant, and his brilliant career had always revolved around trade. In France a man on the rise might be appointed intendant of a *généralité* or *maître des requêtes*. His path to the top might take him briefly to the provinces, but he would soon return to a posting in the capital. In England such men were sent abroad on trade missions. After being knighted in 1764, Sir George Macartney was dispatched to Russia to renegotiate the trade agreement the two countries had signed in 1743. Prime Minister Grenville advised him to take along a copy of the Navigation Act of 1651, but this proved unnecessary, since Macartney "memorized the entire corpus . . . to the point where he could recite any part with ease."[2] The ambassador was twenty-seven years old.

Catherine II and her minister Panin were so taken with Macartney that he won several unexpected concessions. British traders would be taxed at the same rate as the Russians themselves, and they would have the right to operate in all the territories under Russian rule. While the French ambassador, the marquis de Bausset, was graciously willing to remain in the background, Macartney made it a point of honor—and therefore an affair of state—when he was denied a position he considered worthy of the envoy of His Gracious Majesty during a diplomatic reception.[3] Questions of protocol assumed an inordinate importance in his mind. He became abrasive.

On his return from Russia in 1767, he was greeted as a great diplomat. It was then that he married the daughter of Lord Bute, a former prime minister. The marriage set tongues wagging. Lady Bute complained that her daughter was marrying beneath her station, and there were mutterings about the husband's careerism and the bride's ugliness.[4] Macartney might well have anticipated the words of a Parisian dandy who married a rich but ugly woman about a century later: "She's a great catch, as dowries go." Unfortunately, the same man referred to the bridal bedroom as an "expatiatory chapel." Nevertheless, throughout their many separations, Macartney always began his letters to his wife, "My dearest love."[5]

He sampled political life, holding a seat in Parliament for a few months, and later (1769–72) served in Dublin as "chief secretary" (de facto governor) of Ireland.[6]

In 1775 he was named captain general and governor of Grenada, the Grenadines, and Tobago. When his archipelago was thrown into turmoil by the war of American independence, he proved himself an energetic administrator and a courageous leader. In June 1779, during the war, the French admiral d'Estaing sailed into the waters off Grenada with twenty-five "ships of the line," twelve frigates, and 6,500 men. Macartney tried to hold his ground with twenty-four artillery pieces and 300 volunteers. The archives of the French navy contain a record of Macartney's response (in French) to Admiral d'Estaing's insistence that he lay down his arms: "Lord Macartney is ignorant of Count d'Estaing's force; he knows his own, and will defend the island to the utmost of his power."[7] Half of his troops were killed or wounded, and Macartney himself was taken prisoner.

He arrived in La Rochelle on September 4, 1779, and was sent on to

Limoges, where he soon became the darling of high society even though he was under house arrest. He still fumed, however, at having been forced to surrender without receiving the consideration he felt was due him. "I do not know," he wrote to his minister, "whether or not Admiral d'Estaing's behavior, so contrary to custom, or the pillaging which he authorized and his rejection of an honourable surrender were approved by his compatriots, but he has established a painful precedent, one from which the French will undoubtedly suffer in due course."[8] Macartney would never compromise his dignity.

On September 9 he wrote to Count de Sartine, Louis XVI's minister of the navy: "If Your Excellency has no objection, I would very much like to repair to Paris as soon as possible, along with Monsieur de Montrésor, my aide de camp, who is, like me, a prisoner. Having been robbed of all my personal effects during the taking of Grenada, I find myself in circumstances that lend this journey the greatest necessity."[9] Sartine did even better, exchanging Macartney for a French prisoner in British custody. In November 1779 he was sent back to London.[10]

But formally he was "still a prisoner of war, though allowed to visit London on his parole." His "release," which would enable him to leave for India, was the subject of negotiations with the Court of France, conducted on his behalf by George Staunton in 1780.[11]

IT WAS IN MADRAS that Macartney first encountered the East India Company, whose interests, bound inextricably to those of King George, he would later defend in China.

India was a major source of British wealth, and like the Caribbean, it was threatened by the French. Lord North, the prime minister, assigned Macartney to Madras, where he acted as governor of one of the company's three "territories." Macartney now found himself in one of the British government's major trouble spots, and he was soon engrossed in maintaining relations with the rajahs and nabobs whose continuing cooperation was critical to British interests.[12]

Macartney never regretted having accepted this trusted mission. The stipend he received as governor of Madras made him rich: he accumulated savings of thirty-five thousand pounds.[13] But he resolved to resist the temptations of "this dangerously voluptuous country that has led thousands to the worst excesses."[14]

He returned from Madras six years later with clean hands and a clear conscience, rare attributes at the time. Pitt offered to name him governor-general of India. Macartney, believing that he was now indispensable, replied that his price for accepting the post was admission to the English peerage. (At the time he was merely an Irish baron.) But here he set his sights too high, and Pitt withdrew the offer.[15]

Parliament, on the other hand, hailed his incorruptibility. He was praised in the Commons[16] for having rejected a gift of thirty thousand pounds offered him by the nabob of Karnataka, who had been seeking to reestablish his rule and had already worked his way around the company, leaving Macartney as the sole obstacle. He told his superiors that if the order to restore the nabob were confirmed, in violation of the principles that had guided his activities, "my resignation should immediately follow the receipt of their orders."[17]

On at least one occasion, Macartney's uncompromising virtue put his life at risk. He had ordered Staunton to arrest a Major General Stuart on charges of corruption. On their return to London, the general challenged Macartney to a duel. Though he had no illusions about his skill with firearms, especially in a contest with a seasoned officer, Macartney refused to back down. Here is the letter—miraculously preserved in a private collection—that he wrote to his wife on the eve of the duel, a letter she would never read.

London, June 8, 1786

My dearest love,

When you receive this letter, I shall be no more. To leave you is the only pain I feel at this moment, but I trust that we shall meet again in a happier world, for, if the step I am now obliged to take be forgiven, I know of no other crime to sit heavy upon me.

My will, which Sir George Staunton will deliver to you, will show you that I retain to the last the same affection and confidence which I have ever reposed in you. Let me recommend to your care and friendship my niece, Miss Balaquier, Sir George Staunton, Captain Benson, and Mr. Acheson Maxwell. Adieu.

Macartney[18]

All the man's qualities are on view here: pride in his own integrity; indomitable courage; faith in the hereafter (despite his skepticism toward organized churches); attentive affection for his wife; fidelity to his three friends and collaborators, whom he would lead to China seven years later; sober self-expression and self-control.

This letter was probably written a little before four in the morning. The two men faced off in the pale Hyde Park dawn, twelve paces apart. Macartney was nearsighted, and Stuart asked whether the distance was not perhaps too great for His Lordship. He also pointed out that Macartney's weapon was not cocked. Shots were exchanged, and Macartney was wounded. In principle that should have settled the affair, but Stuart protested that His Lordship had offended him so deeply that first blood was not enough. Macartney agreed to a duel to the death, but the witnesses managed to separate the adversaries.[19]

AFTER THE DUEL, Macartney temporarily withdrew to Ireland. At his estate in Lisanoure he rediscovered the charms of rural life and self-reliance, aided by the annuity for life of fifteen hundred pounds the company had granted him.[20] From time to time he attended sessions of the House of Lords in Dublin. But most of all, he read. The catalogue of his library, which I examined,[21] is revealing of his personality. There were English classics and French works, texts by *philosophes* and freethinkers. Many travel books. He had the complete collection of the twenty-five-volume *Lettres édifiantes et curieuses*, written by Jesuit missionaries in China and published by the Society of Jesus between 1735 and 1773, together with *Recherches philosophiques sur les Egyptiens et les Chinois*.[22] An *Armorial of France*, *Arms of Nobility and Peerage*, and an incomplete collection of *Gentleman's Magazine* round out the portrait of a man who had labored to make himself a great lord.

From Lisanoure, from London, where he had bought a house on Curzon Street, and later from his residence in Parkhurst (whose name he would bear when he finally achieved the coveted English peerage), he followed the now inextricably interlinked affairs of the kingdom and the empire. He was primarily interested in the Orient, on which he had become an expert.

Macartney was a man on the move in an England on the move. But this England was not simply one of wealth, lords, and entrepreneurs. The new factories were filled with a new working class, and the populace of London was prone to wild rioting. This other England, however, was still English: full of energy, steeped in life's struggles, and fiercely nationalist. The steerage compartments of the *Lion* and the *Hindostan* were packed with men who had come, willingly or otherwise, from that England. China would not impress them.

When France imploded in revolution, England was briefly tempted by the fever of the new. But in the end it resisted the temptation—most probably because it was already steeped in the new.

AFTER THE Cape Verde islands, the trade winds forced a wide detour. A powerful wind off the West African coast virtually compelled the squadron to sail across the Atlantic to Rio de Janeiro. This was exactly how the Portuguese explorer Pedro Alvares Cabral had discovered Brazil while trying to sail around Africa. The *Lion* and the *Hindostan* caromed like billiard balls toward the port of Rio.

On November 18 the squadron crossed the equator, and the tropical climate did not agree with his lordship. On November 22 Macartney was stricken by an attack of gout that lasted a month. But he bore his pain in silence,[23] and his companions never even noticed.[24]

Macartney spent many long days reading. He had stocked the *Lion*'s library with nearly every book on China published in Europe over the past century. The company had given him twenty-one volumes of files.[25] He also delved into his own notebooks, which contained meticulously transcribed accounts of conversations about China that he had copied down over the years, convinced that this country would one day be his destiny.

He may have imagined that he was already well acquainted with that land. He drank his Chinese tea in Chinese porcelain cups. His lacquered Chinese writing case had mother-of-pearl pictures of people in Chinese dress. The grounds of the estates of his wealthiest acquaintances shunned the French style of geometrical landscaping and imitated Chinese gardens instead: they were filled with a lovely disorder of varied species of plants, little white marble pagodas, and miniature gullies spanned by superfluous arched walkways. China was all the rage in Europe, whose palaces were hung with tapestries featuring Chinese motifs and filled with bric-a-brac from the Celestial Empire. And since the real thing cost a fortune, there was a thriving market for imitations. Chinese ornaments were manufactured in Bristol and Limoges. European tastes were shaped to the "Chinese model" by Sèvres and Meissen porcelain, Chippendale furniture, and Lyons silks.

Daniel Defoe had mocked this fashion trend as early as 1708, noting that the queen herself appeared in Chinese dress and that English homes were filled with Chinese trinkets.[26] And Louis-Sébastien Mercier: "What wretched luxuries these Chinese porcelains are! With a touch of its paw, a cat can do more damage than the plunder of twenty acres of land."[27]

Did Macartney realize that his contemporaries' infatuation with China actually masked a deep lack of understanding of this land across the world? The works of art they so admired were utterly different from what they were used to, but it was just this difference, and not the beauty of the works, that charmed them. They were often unable to tell real from fake. The Chinese themselves churned out thousands of vases complete with ancient-looking patinas for their distant, inexpert customers.[28] The European taste for exoticism proved no key to understanding the real

China, which, however omnipresent in the West, remained completely foreign to it. Communication was illusory. The messages the Europeans thought they read in all the Chinese products were figments of their own imagination.

THERE WAS ALSO an intellectual side to this fad for all things Chinese, but here Macartney suspected the error. Zealous Jesuit missionaries had introduced "enlightened" minds to the moral laws and beliefs shaped by the precepts of Confucius. La Mothe Le Vayer, private tutor to Louis XIV, rhapsodized: "*Sancte Confuci, ora pro nobis.*"[29] Leibniz urged the sovereigns of the West to apply themselves to the Chinese school, to exchange scholars with China so as to discover the universal truth from which divine harmony would spring. He even proposed to the Sun King that an ideographic writing system inspired by Chinese be devised and taught to all the world's peoples.[30] Oliver Goldsmith, who had already written *Persian Letters*, published his *Chinese Letters* in 1762, and the novel *L'Espion chinois* featured mandarins touring Europe in an effort to foster awareness of the unseemliness of European morals.

All this enthusiasm, some of it profound, some frivolous, stemmed from a single conviction: that China offered a model of government in which men ruled themselves and man was ruled by reason—with no church and no religion,[31] a green paradise of free thought.[32] All that was needed was to copy that model, whose flattering reputation had spread throughout Europe. In China, Voltaire affirmed, the prince was surrounded by men of letters whose advice and even reprimands he heeded, under the people's watchful and demanding eye. The passion had even been set to rhyme:

> *Vossius apportait un traité de la Chine*
> *Où cette nation paraît plus que divine.*[33]

Certain wits expressed their admiration ironically. Boulainvilliers, for instance, commented: "The Chinese are sadly lacking in Revelation and therefore blind. But over the past four thousand years their ignorance has failed to deprive them of the marvelous benefits of affluence, art, study, tranquillity, and security."[34]

The fad even found its way into economics, another field in which the Chinese were held to be models—not so much by the practical British (who needed no advice on how to cultivate their land, dig their mines, or run their looms), as by the French, ever enamored of theory. In his *Le Despotisme de la Chine* (1767), the physiocrat François Quesnay argued that his own system tallied perfectly with Chinese notions of cosmic harmony, the primacy of agriculture, and the role of the state as organizer of the economy.[35]

The scholars of the Enlightenment questioned every aspect of European society and no aspect of Chinese society. Their critical spirit, so trenchant in its westward slash, lost its edge when pointed east. In their urge to denounce the hellishness of a Europe vilely subjugated by the clergy, they hailed the supposedly rational paradise of atheist China. In the process they completely ignored the cruelty of the emperors, the seismic upheavals born of dynastic changes, the torture of oppositionists, and all the rebellions, ever renascent yet ever drowned in blood. Willful blindness was impervious to evidence.

The rare discordant views were confined to the dark recesses of libraries. Had Macartney read Captain Dampier's scathing account, written in the late seventeenth century? Or Berkeley, who considered the writings of Confucius a collection of simplistic precepts containing nothing comparable to the teachings of Christ? Or Defoe, who denounced the nation "which was self-sufficient, exclusive in policy, and looked upon bustling Wigh merchants as indesirable barbarians"?[36] In any event, there is no doubt that he was familiar with the one great thinker of his time who stubbornly resisted the wave of Sinomania: Montesquieu, who took most of his information from the Jesuit Foucquet (who, orally at least, was quite critical of his colleagues' writings).[37] Montesquieu accused the Society of Jesus of having been far too credulous: "I have always said that the Chinese are not the honest people that the *Lettres édifiantes* would have us believe."[38]

Macartney had read the severely critical passages of *The Spirit of the Laws*: "Therefore, China is a despotic state whose principle is fear." "The stick governs China."[39] And the life of the Chinese "is entirely directed by rites . . . Chinese legislators have had two objects: they have wanted the people to be both submissive and tranquil."[40] To alter a ritual would be to shake the edifice of obedience.

Were the Jesuits mere dupes? No, but they felt constrained not to publish anything about China that might offend the Chinese. To do otherwise might have brought their missionary venture to an abrupt end. Their letters were edifying in the literal sense: not only were they free of denigration, but they were deliberately meant to encourage admiration for China and to build support for their own enterprise. Not a few brilliant Sinologists acted similarly under Mao, consciously or otherwise, in an effort not to cut themselves off from their life's work.

The *philosophes* can be less easily excused, for they let themselves be brainwashed, although it should be noted that eventually Voltaire got over his China craze, accepting Montesquieu's critique and even going beyond it. This is apparent in various scattered phrases. As early as 1755, he wrote: "These Chinese to whose land we have traveled, risking so many perils, have not yet realized how superior to them we are."[41] Sixteen years later he denounced the defects of the Chinese writing system: "It took years to print a poem that could have been printed in two days had the Chinese condescended to adopt the alphabet of other nations."[42] Finally, he argued that Chinese science was mired in empiricism: "It is hardly surprising that the Chinese invented gunpowder fifteen hundred years before we did, for their land is full of saltpeter."[43]

In other words, Voltaire could have disabused his contemporaries of their illusions as early as the 1750s. He chose not to do so, despite having expended so much effort trying to convince them. Why? Perhaps the answer is provided by another enthusiast of the era, the author of *L'Espion chinois*: "Voltaire never wrote about *things*; he produced books only to fill them with *words*."[44] Voltaire held varying convictions in succession, and he lacked the scruple to disavow them as they changed. He was not honest enough to publicly retract an argument he had made too often: that the Chinese had proved that society could dispense with theology, the church, and perhaps even God. In the end he came to agree with the few lucid observers, but he never made amends for his earlier views.

The dialogue of the deaf therefore dragged on, Europe doing all the talking, asking the questions and giving the answers, while China played the mute.

4

Protected by the British Fleet

(November 30, 1792–January 21, 1793)

ON NOVEMBER 30 the two vessels sailed into the "magnificent harbour of Rio de Janeiro."[1] "The shores of the harbour," Staunton wrote, "were diversified and embellished with villages, farms, and plantations."[2] The English found the town lovely. The stone houses, the straight paved streets, and the "refreshing fountains" fed by a huge aqueduct combined to make for a "pleasant stay."[3]

Our Protestants were struck by the contrast between the Brazilians' pronounced taste for pleasure and their strict observance of a religion whose exoticism made it seem all the more "Roman." Services were announced by bells and fireworks; chanting processions lasted into the night; holy images were posted at intersections. The Puritan irritation of Samuel Holmes, the soldier, was piqued: "The inhabitants are a people sunk in effeminate luxury, of a temper hypocritical and dissembling; . . . superstitious, ignorant, rich, lazy, proud, and cruel, and, like the inhabitants of most southern climates, prefer show and state to the pleasures of society or a good table."[4]

There were many convents, and Holmes had dark suspicions about what might be going on inside.[5] Macartney complained of a "general depravation": "the most scandalous libertinism in the women" and "unnatural propensities" among the men. A few Brazilian officers invited "some of the midshipmen of the *Lion* into their apartments," but the "little youngsters . . . instantly drew their hangers and stood upon their defense with true English dignity."[6]

For a Catholic country, however, Brazil seemed surprisingly prosperous, though our visitors noted with pride that the Brazilians were narrowly dependent on British ships, without which they would have had no whales, precious "for their oil" and even more "for their sperm [*sic*], ambergris." A British whaler was anchored in the harbor, with its haul of "sixty-nine whales, each worth, upon an average, two hundred pounds sterling."[7]

England had established a veritable whaling empire in the South Atlantic.

British naval protection was also indispensable to the slave trade. "The average price was about twenty-eight pounds sterling each."[8] In other words, one whale equals seven slaves. And without the slaves, no sugar plantations.

The British visited the depots where the slaves, "imported, chiefly, from Angola and Benguela on the coast of Africa," were locked up. "This spot was appropriated to the purpose of cleansing, annointing, fattening, rendering sleek and saleable, and concealing the defects of, this class of beings."[9] Twenty thousand slaves were brought to Brazil each year, about five thousand of whom were sold in Rio.[10]

The majority of Brazil's foreign trade was controlled by British firms based in Lisbon. "All the gold of Brazil passed through the United Kingdom, which held Portugal under its yoke," one contemporary observed.[11] Indeed, these indirect colonies were even more lucrative than the direct ones, whose costs of government the British had to bear. It was an arrangement that might be profitably extended to Macao and—why not?—to all of China.

They raised anchor on December 17, 1792. In Paris the trial of Louis XVI had begun.

YOUNG THOMAS STAUNTON's eye was as sharp as his voice, which he raised to his teachers without fear or insolence. Undaunted by his future assignment as his father's page, he spent most of his time studying Chinese with Father Li, whom the boy took to calling "Mr. Plumb," *li* being the Chinese word for "plum tree." The three other priests—Zhou, An, and Wang—began teaching him to write Chinese characters. He had a good ear for the tones of the language, and his eye easily retained the shape of the characters.

At first George Staunton attended the lessons too, but once he found that his fifty-six-year-old mind was too rusty to keep pace with his son's agility, he gave up the lessons in favor of the shipboard library. There he discovered that although caravans of camels had plied the central Asian silk route at least as early as the third century B.C., the Mediterranean peoples saw few Chinese, of whom Pliny the Elder wrote: "Like savages, the *Seres* [men of silk] shun the company of others and wait for traders to seek them out."[12]

Which was exactly the purpose of this mission, since in some respects trade with China under the emperor Qianlong had changed little since ancient times: though the West knew nothing of China, it could not do without Chinese products like silk, furs, and spices. Seneca chided his countrymen for "bankrupting themselves that their wives might wear silk veils whose transparency offends modesty."[13] Bankrupting themselves: even then, China wanted nothing from the West. It exported without importing, and Rome ran out of money. The barbarian invasions put an end to this one-way trade, and the silk route remained severed for a long time. But in that first confrontation of cultures, the West had been dominated.

A second confrontation occurred in the Middle Ages, when new silk routes were opened on land and sea, but with similar results. The Chinese had invented the rudder and the compass, while the Normans plied their coasts in rowboats. Chinese holy books were printed, while Carolingian scribes copied theirs by hand.[14] Great Britain was no more than a barbarous Western backwater, while China had achieved the perfection of an immutable civilization. Sir George was now preparing for the third confrontation.

TWO WEEKS LATER, the squadron sighted whales again, near Tristan da Cunha, a barren rocky island midway between Rio and the Cape of Good Hope: "Whales of every kind were seen sporting here-abouts, . . . their enormous snouts rising sometimes above the waves."[15] On January 7, 1793, the squadron rounded the cape, about a hundred miles off the coast. Despite the southern summer, the fog seemed tinged with snow.[16]

ON JANUARY 15, 1793, as the *Lion* creaked softly in the gentle swell of the Indian Ocean, Lord Macartney bent over the trunk where he kept the journal he had begun back in 1764, the year he left for St. Petersburg.[17] He flipped through a section of one notebook that brought him back to an evening spent in that city at the home of Prince Galitzin, where he had been introduced to a man named Bratishchev, a high state official who had served in Irkutsk and had traveled to Peking to discuss border problems with the Chinese. Bratishchev, one of the few Russians who spoke Chinese, told Macartney that dealing with China was like "sailing in fog."

The Russians were the only real rivals of the British in China. The Portuguese were in decline despite their enclave of Macao, as were the Dutch (despite Indonesia) and the Spanish (despite the Philippines). The French, who might otherwise have tried to harvest the seeds sown by their missionaries, were hampered both by their commercial weakness and by their domestic upheavals, which were to keep them off world trade routes for quite some time. The Americans, whose first ship had docked in Canton in 1784, were still dwarfs. The Russians, however, had begun expanding in central Asia even before the reign of Peter the Great, though since the 1720s their ambitions had been thwarted by the Manchu emperors.

The British now sought to step into the breach. Their presence in India gave them a common border with the Chinese Empire, or at least with its vassal states of Burma and Tibet. Four-fifths of the Western ships moored in Canton were British,[18] and the time seemed ripe to take advantage of the Russian retreat and the convulsive impotence of France.

Bratishchev told Macartney that the Chinese were incredibly ignorant of anything but China itself, which they thought of as the vast middle section of the earth, in turn pictured as a square along whose outer edges were scattered all other countries, worthy only of paying tribute or of being haughtily ignored. In the late sixteenth century, when the Italian Jesuit Matteo Ricci showed the Chinese a globe, they were incredulous. "China is too small," they declared.[19] Ricci's sphere was too far removed from their conception of the universe, whose center China occupied, under the vault of a gigantic tortoise shell.

Macartney remembered that Bratishchev had told him that Chinese superiority had been regarded as axiomatic for as long as China had existed. Peoples were either "civilized" or "barbarian" depending on whether or not they had submitted to Chinese culture. In the Mandarin language a barbarian who had pledged fealty to China was referred to as "baked"; before that he was "raw." Human beings therefore fell into three categories: the "men with black hair" (their term for themselves), who alone were civilized; the baked barbarians, who had declared their obeisance to the Celestial Order; and the raw barbarians, who were either unable or unwilling to partake of the benefits of civilization. (The former was pardonable; the latter was not.)

We now know from Imperial Archives that each foreign mission to China, from the Latin merchants of ancient Rome to the monks sent by the popes of the Gothic age, was registered as a "vassal delegation." Even France was listed as a "tributary country" as of 1689, the date of the arrival of the first French Jesuits, whom Louis XIV had deliberately refrained from formally accrediting.

No one was immune to the solicitations of civilization. Whether he knew it or not, whether he wanted it or not, the raw barbarian began to be baked the moment he approached the Chinese hearth, where all was molded, from kaolin to human clay.

That evening in St. Petersburg weighed heavily on Macartney's mind as he now approached the hearth. He would not perform the gesture of allegiance. Alleged Chinese superiority would now have to confront the reality of British superiority.

On January 21 the French Convention sealed the foundations of the republic with the blood of the king: Louis XVI was guillotined. The Court of St. James was in mourning.

5

A Whiff of China

(End of January–June 16, 1793)

ON FEBRUARY 1, after another two weeks of solitary sailing, the squadron arrived at New Amsterdam Island, whose beaches were strewn with seals.[1] Five men were spotted on shore, thought to be victims of a shipwreck.[2] But they turned out to be three Frenchmen* and two Englishmen who had been dropped off on this deserted island to prepare "a cargo of twenty-five thousand seal skins for the Canton market."[4] "The Chinese, it seems, have a particular art in dressing seal skins, depriving them of the long and coarser hair, leaving only the soft fur, or underdown, and at the same time rendering the skin or leather thin and pliant."[5]

The men were "remarkable for the squalor and filth of their persons, clothes, and dwelling. Yet none of them seemed anxious to catch an opportunity of abandoning the place."[6] That same day, February 1, the Convention in Paris declared war on the king of England. But while their countries fought, these five men would toil together, killing twenty-five thousand seals and skinning the carcasses as they lay rotting on the shore. Such was the barbarism aroused even then by the passion for fur, which had so powerfully gripped the mandarins that pelts were pretty much the only item that could be sold to China, apart from opium.†

They cast off the following day,[8] and on February 25 the squadron drew within sight of Java, without having encountered any other ship. Despite the lemons recommended by Cook, there were several cases of scurvy among the crew.[9] The *Lion* was relieved to find the *Hindostan* waiting at Java's western tip.[10] The two vessels had been separated for many long days.

---

* Louis XVI took a special interest in the fur trade. His instructions to La Pérouse included an order to stop in Canton to investigate the tanning procedure.[3]

† This episode fascinated Fernand Braudel, who devoted a long passage to it in *Civilisation matérielle, économie et capitalisme*.[7]

It had taken two months to get from Brazil to Java. Two months without sighting another sail, the only stopover being those two rocky outcroppings in the sea's immensity, final resting places of thousands of seals. Yet even there the presence of Britain, China, and world trade had been felt.

Long days at sea meant long bouts of reading and thinking, as well as long conversations. At first Macartney hadn't much cared for the four priests, who were, after all, not only Chinese but papists and Neapolitans to boot—quite a cross for an Irish Protestant to bear. Father Li's teeth were ruined by smoking; the man never seemed to be without his long-stemmed pipe. Father Zhou had a penchant for munching dried water-melon seeds, a habit not easily tolerated by a gentleman. But they knew their country's history well, and Macartney bombarded them with questions in Latin, as the fluency of his days at Trinity College came back to him.

As he listened to the priests and devoured the books in the ship's library, Macartney began to form a clear impression of the history of relations between China and the West. There were times when the Chinese dragon tranquilly uncoiled its rings, and others when it curled nervously in upon itself. But this society, which seemed periodically to collapse and then pull itself together again, never really changed. The unending cycle of order and disorder formed an immobile history quite different from England's headlong rush to constant progress and the conquest of an ever-expanding world.

Where did the emperor Qianlong stand in this millennial ebb and flow? Was he more favorable to opening or to closure? He had welcomed Western missionaries, who boasted that he held them in the highest esteem. But he had also persecuted Chinese converts and priests, quelled revolts savagely, expelled all Europeans except for the handful who were useful to him, and restricted their merchants to the ghettos of Macao and Canton. He had also censored anything critical of his Manchu dynasty, banning ten thousand books, burning two thousand others, and executing hundreds of writers. Though he had widened China's borders, he had not opened them.

Macartney knew that the emperor was old and somewhat hard of hearing. The missionaries had reported that Qianlong wanted two ear trumpets. But would he be deaf to the advances of "the most powerful nation of the West"?

In the thirteenth century the Tartar-Mongol dynasty of Genghis and Kublai Khan had opened China up. But their Ming successors had closed the gates again. Chongzhen, the last Ming emperor, was brought down by a peasant revolt and felt so thoroughly abandoned by Heaven that he hanged himself. Observing the empire's decomposition, the Manchus had seized the helm. Once again China was governed by foreigners. The Tartar-Manchus could have followed the example of the Tartar-Mongols and opened China's doors, but instead they emulated the Mings. The teeming, multifaceted country celebrated by Marco Polo was long gone.

With the single exception of the great Kangxi, Qianlong's grandfather and a contemporary of Louis XIV's, the Tartar-Manchus wanted only to savor their prey in peace. The land these foreigners occupied had already been sealed to the outside world for the nearly three centuries of Ming rule. The better to possess it, they double-bolted the gates.

Europeans had paced back and forth outside those gates for some four centuries, but Macartney now believed that he could find the way in.

ON MARCH 6, 1793, they reached the port of Batavia (Djakarta), in the Dutch East Indies. Civilization at last. China seemed very near.

The Dutch, traditional rivals of the British, were uneasy about this expedition. "The secret apprehensions that had been entertained by them were frankly acknowledged; as well as the intentions of their agents at Canton to join in counteracting his Excellency there as much as lay in their power."[11] Macartney felt he had to placate his hosts, and in the end they agreed that both nations could prosper jointly in the vast Chinese market. The governor of Batavia assured Macartney that in due course conciliatory instructions would be sent on to Canton.

The harbor, with its countless junks flying sails ribbed like dragonfly wings, made it seem as if they were already in China. "It is impossible to express the pleasure that appeared to agitate the two Chinese on board our ship, when they discovered one of their own country's vessels."[12]

The English had their first cultural shock: it was easy to tell the Dutch houses from the Chinese. The inhabitants of the latter—low, narrow, and dirty, made of wooden planks or, more rarely, dingy bricks—lived one atop another. The Dutch houses, spacious and clean, were of red brick, often decorated with marble and freshened by flowing fountains.

But the British were surprised to find that the "greatest number of the Dutch settlers in Batavia . . . appeared wan, weak, and languid."[13] The vessels of the Dutch East India Company wallowed in the harbor. Malay and Chinese pirates attacked them within sight of the city itself, for there were no warships to defend them. The Dutch lived in fear of an attack from Mauritius, colonized by France in 1712. The city would have been quite incapable of repelling any such aggression, since its "fortifications were by no means, such as would be deemed formidable in Europe."[14]

MASSES OF CHINESE immigrants had come to seek their fortune in Batavia long ago. Those who remained in the city were merchants, brokers, and retailers. In the countryside they were farmers, agricultural laborers, and servants. They were so energetic that they were undaunted even by work in the cane fields, for which black slaves had been imported. International trade had made many of them rich: the Chinese scattered along the rim of the China Sea adapted very well to the mercantile economy, showing a talent they had been discouraged from exploiting in China itself.

The Dutch feared both their numbers and their success, and in 1740 the Dutch East India Company seized upon rumors of rebellion to organize an anti-Chinese massacre. Some twenty thousand to thirty thousand people were killed, the equivalent of ten St. Bartholomew's Day massacres in a matter of hours.* "The dreadful deed was not approved by the directors of the Company in Holland; and much apprehension being entertained that the fact would excite the indignation of the emperor of China." Would he take revenge against the company's dealings—and perhaps against its personnel—in Canton? An emissary was dispatched to explain and excuse the radical measure, and the Dutch were pleasantly surprised. The emperor "calmly answered, that 'he was little solicitous for the fate of unworthy subjects, who, in the pursuit of lucre, had quitted their country and abandoned the tombs of their ancestors.' "[15]

The emperor who made that comment was the young Qianlong, expressing qualities that would mark his entire reign: contempt for trade, profit, and international exchange; condemnation of any Chinese tempted by things foreign; devotion to immobility.

Compared with the bustling Chinese, the Dutch cut a sorry figure indeed. Java was full of pestilential swamps and racked by "cyclical fevers" whose second or third outbreak was often fatal.[16] The British met one "lady" who had arrived ten months earlier with eleven members of her family and had already lost her father, six sisters, and a brother-in-law.[17] Though they could get rich here very quickly, few Europeans stayed.

Their life-style was unlikely to infuse them with vigor. Mornings they spent smoking and drinking—wine, gin, and beer. "It is not very uncommon for one man to drink a bottle of wine in this manner before dinner," which was served at one in the afternoon.[18] After dinner they napped.

---

* Two centuries later, under Sukarno, five hundred thousand supposed Communists, many of them Chinese, were massacred in Indonesia.

Bachelors and passing travelers were attended to by female slaves who fanned them as they slept.[19]

But not every country's history was immobile. Three or four French merchant ships put into port, "carrying into the Eastern world, in addition to the natural products of their country, the monstrous doctrines of the Rights of Man." The crew of one of these ships, imbued with these new ideas, raised a demand for culinary equality: "The crew, it seems, had one day taken it into their heads that, by virtue of the sacred and inalienable principle of all men being equal, they had a right to enjoy as good a dinner as their officers, no matter who should pay for it; and accordingly, having followed the dishes into the cabin, they seated themselves at table, inviting, in the most obliging manner, the captain and other officers to partake of their own dinner with them. These gentlemen, however, finding their authority and their property at stake, thought it prudent to make application to the government of Batavia for a few German troops to instruct their crew in the rights of discipline, and in the duties of obedience and subordination."[20]

The powerful swiftly united against the "rabble," notwithstanding the fact that in this case the powerful were citizens of belligerent countries: the French Republic had been at war with Great Britain and the Netherlands for five weeks. True, no one in Batavia knew that yet, since it would take six months for the news to arrive. But everyone could see the conflict coming. It would last more than twenty-two years.

THE EXPEDITION spent only about ten days in Batavia, lifting anchor on March 17 in order to enter the Strait of Banka while the monsoon winds were still favorable. This last leg of the journey began auspiciously. Captains Gower and Mackintosh bought a French two-masted brig to carry some of the squadron's cargo. They renamed it the *Clarence*, in honor of the king's brother, the admiral-duke.

But just then the *Jackall* reappeared, complete with all hands. Severely damaged by the storm off the coast of Portsmouth, the ship had turned back for repairs. It just missed the rest of the squadron in Madeira, and again at the Cape Verde islands. It had then sailed around Africa without dropping anchor even once. The crew, reduced to minimal rations, seemed exhausted, but Lieutenant Saunders was hailed for having successfully brought his vessel halfway around the world alone.[21]

The euphoria, however, was brief. The wind came up, and the crews were ravaged by "fevers and dysentery" caused by "the lack of proper conveniences on board."[22] They had to wait nearly two months for the monsoon winds to change direction. The Malay pirates, on the other hand, did not change theirs. The scourge of this region, they scoured the seas for prey, seemingly able to come out of nowhere at any moment. But "they were careful to observe a proper distance from us, as we had too formidable an appearance for them."[23]

There were deaths among the crew. The decks and steerage were washed with vinegar, the ships fumigated. "It is inconceivable," Macartney wrote, "how soon habit reconciles people to almost every accident and misfortune. The death of the nearest friend makes very little impression on the survivors, who from the frequency of losses and the resignation of seamen to the accidents of their profession go on as if nothing unusual happened, and seem perfectly resigned to the miseries of their profession."[24] The able-bodied traded with the Malays, bringing monkeys and multi-colored birds aboard.

"On Sunday the 28th [of April] we arrived in the Straits of Banca . . . the entrance into the China Sea."[25] This time they made it. On May 10, 1793, they crossed the equator again, south to north. Despite the squalls, the temperature passed ninety degrees Fahrenheit. The crews of the *Clarence* and the *Jackall* had to probe the shallow seas constantly. "Several of the seamen were afflicted with a dysentery, which . . . left little hope of its being subdued, until the diseased were removed from the ships to some convenient shore, which might afford good air and fresh provisions."[26] The "bodies of some amongst us was one entire sore from head to foot. . . . To cheer our present sufferings, we were encouraged with the assurances that these things would wear away . . . as we advanced to the northward, otherwise despair would nearly have driven us all mad."[27]

THE SQUADRON SOON reached the coast of Cochin China, the European name for Vietnam at that time. Navigation was now easier, the winds more clement. Cultivated hillsides could be seen on shore. Junks, sampans, and fishing boats plied the waters. On May 25, within sight of the Bay of Tourane (Da Nang), the British reached "the southern extremity of that great continent which may, properly, be called Chinese."[28]

Indeed, Cochin China had been an integral part of the Chinese Empire, and though it had won independence, the bonds of vassalage had not been severed. Annamite princes performed the kowtow and paid tribute to their suzerain, the Son of Heaven. Macartney believed that its close relations with China made this country worthy of the embassy's attention.

Approaching the shore was no mean feat, since the maritime maps were inaccurate. They tried hailing several of the nearby fishing boats, but all fled. The *Hindostan* sent a launch after one of them, and a terrified old man was brought aboard. After being soothed with a few Spanish dollars,* which he recognized, the old man steered them through the channel and took to his heels the moment they docked.[29] The Cochin Chinese might well have taken this for an invasion, for the country was gripped by an interminable revolutionary struggle. One of the two contending parties had been expecting some friendly assistance from France, which, mired in its own convulsions, was hardly in a position to intervene.

The embassy protested that its intentions were peaceful. The local commander cautiously replied that he would await instructions from the capital. He allowed them to take a few, meager supplies aboard. But forty-eight hours later, the governor of Tourane approached on a galley, followed by nine skiffs loaded with supplies. Macartney was invited to come ashore. He understood the reasons for this sudden amiability when his hosts asked whether he would be interested in selling them some weapons. Disinclined to get involved in a civil war, he explained that he was anxious to meet the Great Emperor as soon as possible. This was language that the governor, a respectful tributary, understood very well.

But the British did accept the governor's invitation to a banquet.[30]

They enjoyed this visit to a graveyard of French ambition. In a treaty signed in Versailles in 1787 the Annamite prince Anh had ceded the Bay of Tourane and the island of Poulo Condore to France in exchange for French protection that enabled the prince to triumph over his enemies. The French opened settlements on the island of Callao. Staunton speculated that "the French might have had in contemplation to be able, by means of a settlement on the coast of Cochinchina, to procure Chinese articles at a cheaper rate than could be obtained by any foreigners trading immediately to China."†[31]

But the French settlement was a thing of the past. As Macartney saw it, the future lay in China itself. His crews rested, his holds reprovisioned, he now set sail for his final stopover: Macao.

---

* See the appendix on Money and Currency.

† It was true that the Chinese government charged no export duties on commodities transported by its own subjects on their own ships. But Staunton may well have overestimated the commercial expertise of the French, who were not known for their brilliance in this domain.

II

ANOTHER PLANET

(June–September 1793)

Should any foreigner enter China secretly, he will be forbidden to return to his country, lest he perchance conspire among his own to effect the Empire's ruin. This is why Chinese who treat or converse with foreigners, without the permission of the sovereign, are punished severely.

NICOLAS TRIGAULT, S.J., 1617[1]

When a citizen is not permitted to leave the land in which he has, by chance, been born, the meaning of this law, manifestly, is: "this country is so ill governed that we forbid any individual to leave it, lest everyone else follow suit."

VOLTAIRE, 1764[2]

The sole object of the policy of the Tartar-Chinese Court is to maintain the people in tranquillity. Scant heed is paid to commerce with foreign nations. Embassies are received only inasmuch as they can be regarded as marks of submission. When such embassies are admitted, those composing them are assigned conductors, interpreters, and servants dependent on a minister to whom they are obliged to account. The ambassadors cannot speak a single unreported word; cannot take a step beyond the residence that is assigned to them; can neither receive visitors nor undertake visits, save those of etiquette; there are no banquets and no spectacles, save those granted by the sovereign.

JOSEPH-MARIE AMIOT, S.J., 1789[3]

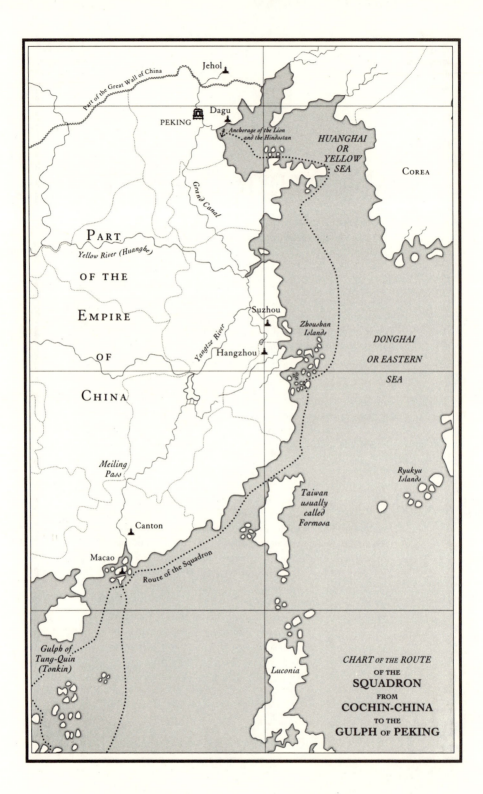

Part of the Great Wall of China

Jehol

Dagu

PEKING

Grand Canal

*Anchorage of the Lion
and the Hindostan*

HUANGHAI
OR
YELLOW
SEA

COREA

P ART

OF THE

EMPIRE

OF

CHINA

Yellow River (Huanghe)

Yangtze River

Suzhou

Hangzhou

*Zhousban
Islands*

DONGHAI

OR EASTERN

SEA

*Meiling
Pass*

*Ryukyu
Islands*

Canton

*Taiwan
usually
called
Formosa*

Macao

Route of the Squadron

*Gulph of
Tung-Quin
(Tonkin)*

Luconia

CHART OF THE ROUTE
OF THE
SQUADRON
FROM
COCHIN-CHINA
TO THE
GULPH OF PEKING

6

Macao

(June 19–23, 1793)

The Portuguese gain nothing by Macao; if it could be purchased by our company, it would be a most consequential
acquisition.

DAVID SCOTT, 1787[1]

ON JUNE 19, 1793, after nine months at sea, the British finally came within
sight of the Chinese mainland. The following morning they dropped anchor
off Macao. But Macartney did not go ashore. Having reached China, he
now feared being snared by it, and he had no intention of entering the
country through the traditionally obligatory gate. Nor would he linger in
Macao, which, though it was China, was not quite the Chinese Empire.
Instead the ambassador sent Staunton ashore to meet with the company
commissioners.

Sir George skirted several small and barren islands and disembarked
in an old colonial city. Greenish mold hung from the houses. Twisting
alleyways led to a fortress crowned with cannon. Staunton spent four long
days in this extraordinary condominium jointly administered by a Portuguese governor who had jurisdiction over the Europeans and Chinese
mandarins who ruled over their own compatriots. The Portuguese were
virtually quarantined, unable to leave their peninsula, access to which was
barred by a wall with a single gate, through which Chinese alone could
pass. The mandarins came and went at will.[2]

The Sino-Portuguese enclave was a marriage of two cultures, Far
Eastern and Far Western. For nearly two and a half centuries it had been
the "base camp" of all the European mercantile companies and missionary
enterprises, playing a role that would later be usurped by Hong Kong: a
sort of airlock between two worlds.

Company officials filled Staunton in on the latest information about
Peking's intentions. A courier sent to meet them in Batavia had told the
British that things were going reasonably well, but they were eager for

details about how the news of their impending arrival had been received in China. It will be recalled that company representatives had sought an audience with the Canton authorities on the day the squadron left Portsmouth.

The requested interviews had been granted. On October 11 company officials met with the superintendent of customs (the hoppo), and on October 18 with Governor Guo Shixun, successor to the former viceroy, General Fukang'an, who was now in command of a military expedition in Tibet.

These Chinese officials were already well aware that the British of Canton were not your run-of-the-mill barbarians. Where the Portuguese, the Dutch, and all the other agents and missionaries routinely kowtowed, the British had always refused, and this refusal had itself been ritualized. As the Chinese and British representatives gathered in the superintendent's office, a cannon shot rang out, announcing the arrival of a letter from the court. The British immediately excused themselves, not out of discretion, but in order to avoid kowtowing to the yellow silk packet containing the imperial message. Once the mandarin had read the august correspondence, the British returned. This was a modus vivendi that the British and Cantonese had worked out among themselves; Peking may have been unaware of it.[3]

The governor's report to the emperor on the October 18 meeting was filed in the archives of the Grand Council. "Upon their arrival in Canton," he wrote, "the English barbarians asked to be taken to the governor's palace and to the customs office to present a request. We immediately granted them an audience. Their report states that the king of England, having been unable to convey his congratulations to Your Majesty on the occasion of your eightieth birthday two years ago, has now dispatched his envoy, *Ma-ga-er-ni*,* to offer tribute. Custom requires that barbarians, once granted permission to enter a port, present the viceroy of the province with a copy of their sovereign's request, along with a list of the articles of tribute. The king of England, however, has supplied us with neither of these two documents. We have only the letter submitted by the English merchants. Your humble slaves dare not transmit such a document to Your Majesty."[4]

The British apparently considered it seemly to allow a royal embassy to be announced by such contemptible wretches as merchants. Well, such drivel was unworthy of the emperor. The mandarins knew how dangerous it could be to submit a document that failed to conform to the immutable etiquette. "The English merchants have no knowledge of the composition

---

* The literal retranscription of the Chinese version of Macartney's name.

of the tribute, which was still being prepared when they left their country. But the articles in question are numerous and heavy. Should they be obliged to take the land or river route from Canton to Peking, it is to be feared that some pieces of the tribute might be damaged. Moreover, their ships are already at sea, sailing for Tientsin. It would doubtless be improper for the foreigners to moor in a port of their own choosing; nevertheless, we cannot ask the king of the English to send his ships back to Canton, for too much time would be lost in transit. . . . We suggest that Your Majesty order all viceroys and governors of the provinces of Zhejiang, Fujian, and Zhili to instruct their subordinates to inspect these ships and to allow them to pass."

Upon receipt of this report, Qianlong wrote in the margin, in his vermilion brushstrokes, "I will transmit my instructions to you."[5]

And so he did. Twice. He noted with satisfaction the arrival of an embassy that could "contribute to the Emperor's glory."

IMPERIAL CONSENT was issued on December 3, 1792, and relayed to Canton by Viceroy Fukang'an himself, now returning to his capital after victories in Tibet against the Gurkha warriors of Nepal. It reached the company on January 5, 1793, through the intermediary of the guild.* There was no hitch on that front:[6] merchants had no difficulty talking to other merchants.

Orders went out to all the ports of the China Sea: the British were to be honorably greeted but closely watched. The viceroys and governors of the coastal provinces immediately acknowledged receipt of the emperor's instructions. Here, for example, is the response of Liang Kentang, viceroy of Zhili: "Your servant observes that Your Majesty's virtue and immense prestige have spread so far and wide that the foreign Barbarians spare no effort in undertaking long voyages to manifest their loyalty and to bring tribute. And at the very moment that the Barbarians are sailing to bear witness to their reverence, our victorious elite troops are returning in triumph from Tibet. What a glorious dynasty, registering stunning successes the like of which no one has ever seen! Your servant cannot contain his joy, and it seems to him that in the circumstances it would be appropriate to reward the British for the sincerity they are demonstrating in their desire to contemplate Civilization."[7]

---

* The merchant guild, or hong, was granted a monopoly on foreign trade in 1720. The term *guild*, however, should not be misinterpreted. The hong was not an association of free merchants similar to a Western medieval guild, but an official organization closely controlled by the bureaucratic state. Its power, like all power in China, emanated from the emperor.

Here is the reaction of Jiqing, viceroy of Shandong: "Your slave* has had the port zones of Shandong inspected. If the tribute-bearing ships drop anchor here, local officers will have to be doubly vigilant, taking the British in hand and conducting them to the capital as swiftly as possible. The Barbarians, who will have sailed more than ten thousand *li*,† will then be able respectfully to contemplate Your Majesty. Upon receipt of this instruction, Your slave issued orders to all the prefectures, asking that they retransmit them to all the coastal cities. Your slave will send qualified officials to unload the tribute and transport it to Peking."[8]

Proud jubilation at the humble pilgrimage from the ends of the earth. A watchful eye on the barbarians, who could never be trusted. The reception system was in place.

In the meantime, Staunton was busily setting up a system of his own, one designed to account for any possible future difficulties. As the official narrator reconstructing the story after the fact, he complained of the jealousy of Britain's European competitors and the hostility of corrupt local mandarins.

It was true that some of the Europeans in Macao and Canton were worried. The letters the British brought with them from Batavia allayed the concerns of the Dutch. The Portuguese, however, were expected to do everything in their power to place obstacles in the embassy's path.[9] Once the letters from the court arrived, the mandarins became more cooperative, though at bottom they remained "as ill-disposed as ever." The superintendent of customs,[10] "whose consciousness of having merited reprehension for well known acts of his office, always connected in his mind the subject of complaint with the views of the Embassy."[11] He feared that an official examination of his conduct was in the offing, and therefore began scheming to paralyze the early initiatives.

Macartney, who was keeping a journal not meant for publication, tried to focus on the positive aspects of all this news, and Staunton's report of his four-day stay in Macao fully reassured him. Imperial instructions to the mandarins had opened all of China's ports to his ships. For the moment at least, what more could he ask? Staunton explained that in the meeting with the British merchants the governor had initially insisted that the embassy disembark in Canton and take the land route to Peking, as foreign

---

* In general, when Manchu mandarins addressed the emperor, they referred to themselves as *nucai*, "Your slave." Han Chinese mandarins tended to say *chen*, "Your servant." The Chinese mandarins did not regard themselves as slaves of the sovereign of the steppes.

† A *li* was equivalent to about a third of a mile. The expression "ten thousand *li*" was an idiom, not to be taken literally.

visitors always did. He had backed down only when they argued that there were "several presents, which from their size, nice mechanism and value could not be conveyed through the interior of the country without risk of much damage and injury."[12]

Macartney was amused when Staunton told him that the British commissioners had found it impossible to avoid revealing some details about the gifts the embassy was carrying. The mandarins had claimed that they could not announce the embassy's arrival to the court without appending an exact list of the gifts, for it was by judging their quality that the monarch would assess "the degree of consideration and respect in which he was held by the prince who sent them."[13] An initial and largely imaginary list had been duly drawn up. It would not be the last.

If the squadron moored in Canton, the mandarins would surely again step up the pressure. But they could not prevent the British from sailing up the coast. How could they forbid what the emperor had already authorized? All was in order.

This was the very heart of the system. Throughout the empire, the mandarins represented the emperor, who was at once the executive, the legislature, and the judiciary. In fact, the mandarins virtually embodied the emperor, "father and mother of the people." As faithful interpreters of his will, they were far more likely to exceed instructions than to fall short: zeal was not punished, but disobedience was—mercilessly. In addition to representing the emperor, they also (and somewhat arbitrarily) collected taxes. The margin between what they levied and what they passed on to higher echelons varied in proportion to the greed of the local mandarins. That margin was both the true measure of their power and the source of intimidation and corruption.[14]

In Canton the guild held a monopoly on trade with the Europeans, a privilege the viceroy and the hoppo were prepared to sell off to certain merchants for a high premium, payable to their own private accounts. They also forced the guild to kick back a slice of the profits,[15] an extra expense that the foreign companies were ultimately compelled to bear. Barrow noted that the government's principal officers "invariably . . . arrive poor and, in the course of three years, return [to Peking] with immense riches."[16] The foreign merchants, who had no right to appeal to Peking, had only one recourse: to grease the wheels by offering the authorities "gifts," using the guild as a go-between.

Such was the Celestial bureaucracy so envied by the Enlightenment. It was this system that the embassy meant to attack. The British of Britain wanted an open China, but the British of Macao and Canton preferred to work things out under the status quo, even if it meant having to charge their European customers a little more.

THE FOUR CHINESE priests who had been traveling with the embassy scattered during the stopover in Macao. Fathers An and Wang, who had been granted free passage from Portsmouth, decided to disembark. Father Zhou, one of the two interpreters, asked to do likewise, even though he had been drawing a salary of 150 pounds a year since coming aboard.[17]

The British saw this as breach of contract, but the fact was that these intermediaries were in an awkward situation. There had been a touch of terror in their excitement upon seeing those Chinese junks in Batavia. It was illegal for any Chinese to leave China or to work for barbarians, except on the emperor's orders. Zhou and Li were doubly guilty: they had left the empire without authorization, and they had served a foreign power— actually two foreign powers: first the Holy See and now England.

Sometimes curiosity got the better of fear. "Some Canton Chinese travel to England, but fear of discovery induces them to return to Canton as soon as possible, and they never speak of their journey."[18]

Zhou jumped ship despite Staunton's exhortations, while Li agreed to stay on, showing a "greater firmness of mind . . . though exactly in the same predicament."[19] Li was a Manchu, a member of the ruling nation, but it is not clear that this lessened the risk. His main hope was to pass as a Westerner: "He was a native of a part of Tartary annexed to China, and had not those features which denote a perfect Chinese origin. . . . He put on an English military uniform, and wore a sword and a cockade."[20] Staunton seems not to have understood all the pressures bearing down on the Chinese churchmen: as priests, they had been unable to let their hair grow, and for Chinese men the penalty for not wearing the pigtail decreed by the Manchus was death. By passing as a European, Li hoped to escape that terrible fate.

Macartney was philosophical about the loss of Father Zhou: "His companion, who remains with us, though not so complete a scholar, is a man of much better temper, has a very good understanding, and is sincerely attached to us."[21] But here Macartney underestimated the difficulties he would later face. Li's excellent attitude could not compensate for the inadequacy of his knowledge of court language. In a country where official ranks were determined by literary competitions, a high-school graduate's style would not suffice where a doctorate's expertise was wanted.

Though three of the priests left the squadron, two others came aboard: Fathers Robert Hanna and Louis-François-Marie Lamiot, French Lazarists who had been waiting in Macao for a way to get to Peking, where they intended to offer the emperor their services as mathematicians and as-tronomers. They embarked on the *Hindostan*, since Macartney was reluctant to let Frenchmen get too close to the embassy's leadership on the *Lion*.

The *Lion*, the *Hindostan*, the *Clarence*, and the *Jackall* cast off on Sunday, June 23, as the tolling bells of Macao's many churches summoned the faithful to Mass. Macartney and Staunton watched the peninsula recede onto the horizon. The harbor was well protected by small neighboring islands. It would have suited the Crown and the Royal Navy very nicely indeed.

7

Skirting Canton

(June 23–24, 1793)

THE SQUADRON sailed along the coast, about a dozen miles offshore. Macartney enjoyed the view of the mouth of the Pearl River, which his ships, unlike those of all previous Western arrivals, would not have to navigate. His interest was Peking, not Canton, and he meant to get there by sea, the shortest and freest path. Taking this route would reduce the travel time by at least a month and would also enable him to avoid the scheming maneuvers of venal functionaries on land.

In Macao Staunton had learned of the imperial edict instructing pilots to stand by in every port, ready to escort the British squadron to Tientsin or any other city they might choose. The mission was already beginning to change things in Canton: some obstacles to trade had been lifted; requests from company agents were better received; there had even been talk of abolishing the exorbitant duties that had been imposed on trade in Macao.[1]

These developments seemed to confirm what Macartney had already sensed: if the situation in Canton was to be alleviated, the city itself would have to be bypassed. That would be a relief in any case. Just about everything he had heard about Canton worried him.

The former company commissioners whom Macartney and Staunton had grilled in London had given a bleak account of life in Canton's ghetto for Europeans. The "factories" of the various trading companies—which served simultaneously as stores, warehouses, offices, and residences, each flying its country's flag—were infested with rats. The living conditions of the subjects of His Gracious Majesty serving the China trade were "unworthy of the age or of British subjects."[2] Westerners were denied all contact with the Chinese, who were forbidden, on penalty of death, to teach their language to barbarians. Every new crisis threatened the entire European colony.

The Admiral Anson case was an example. In 1741, his holds crowded with sick sailors, Anson sailed into the Pearl River in search of supplies in Canton. The authorities informed him that his sixty-gun warship, the *Centurion*, could not sail upriver to the city. He got permission to arrive in a launch and decided to request an audience with the viceroy. But company representatives persuaded him to reconsider, managing instead to work something out with the guild.

Finally reprovisioned, the *Centurion* set sail. It captured a Spanish ship and then returned again, followed by its captive, now also in need of supplies. This time the Cantonese authorities demanded the taxes due for two merchant vessels. The argument was just beginning to get bitter when a fire suddenly broke out in a neighborhood of the city where the houses were built of wood. The fire was brought under control thanks only to the efforts of Anson's seamen, and that turned the situation around.

The viceroy suddenly agreed to receive Anson to express his appreciation. The admiral took the opportunity to protest the exorbitant taxes, the bureaucratic mean-mindedness, and all the other harassment.[3] Back aboard his ship, Anson boasted that his strong words had taught the Chinese some respect, and Macartney would have liked to take inspiration from this example, except that he knew that the moment Anson cast off, harassment of the British merchants actually got worse. The lesson of the Anson incident seemed to be that once the moment of confrontation had passed, the agreement the British thought they had won from the Chinese turned out to be illusory. Canton was surely not the place to negotiate. Peking was.

Macartney also learned of another misadventure that had occurred twenty-eight years after Anson's. In 1769 the *Granby* docked at the Canton customs office carrying a "treasure" in company cash. Inspectors tried to board the ship, there was an altercation, and the customs officials wound up in the muddy water. The ship was impounded, but the company continued to insist that a vessel carrying a treasure in cash ought not to be searched. With the *Granby* immobilized, the crew went ashore to visit the local dives.

One night a commissioner noticed that some of the men seemed to have decided to sleep Chinese-style, stretched out along the dock in the open air. The next morning, three of them were found dead. Five others died the next day. The British charged that their men had been poisoned. There were calls for revenge. Autopsies showed no trace of poison, but the Chinese authorities must have felt guilty about something, because they suddenly canceled the investigation of the *Granby*, which was now free to go.[4]

The Anson affair had concluded with a fire; in the *Granby* incident, never fully explained, there were eight suspicious deaths. Clearly, something was amiss in Chinese-European relations in Canton. The Chinese merchants, on the other hand, treated their European customers like royalty. How pleasant the Chinese would be if only they were not subject to their own government's terror![5]

Anything could provoke an incident. A certain Captain Elphinstone[6] had been forbidden to continue loading his ship because he had had the temerity to bring into the English factory a pretty young Indian girl whom he had met in Madras and intended to take back to England for various dubious purposes. The Chinese claimed that he had violated the law barring foreigners from bringing women into China. Elphinstone objected that the charge was ludicrous. In fact, he claimed, they were simply trying to "fleece" him. He was right about that: the incident cost him five hundred dollars. But he was also wrong. No "liaisons" were allowed, whether familial or extramarital. Bachelors only! The Chinese were quite intractable on this point, possibly out of concern to protect the purity of the Chinese race against barbarian women, who were considered even more dangerous than the men. In any event, they insisted that the foreign settlement, apart from being strictly temporary, must also be wholly free of women.

Macartney was well informed about the kind of life the British led in Canton: held to ransom by a menacing bureaucracy, they enjoyed no liberty or dignity whatever.

His task was to find a way to circumvent this obligatory transit point through which China conducted its trade with the rest of the world. Previous attempts to do this had failed. The man who had come closest to success was one Captain Flint, forty years earlier.

In 1753 the company asked Flint to try to open a trading post in Ningbo, on the coast of central China well north of Canton. Flint and his men arrived there two years later and were very well received. He filled his holds with merchandise and made a second trip the following year. But when he arrived for the third time in 1757, he was stopped in the harbor. Half his cargo was seized, and the cannon were removed from his ship, without explanation.[7]

Qianlong then issued an edict reiterating that all foreign trade had to be conducted exclusively in Canton.[8] China reverted to type. The gate was bolted, and the emperor sent the British back to square one: Canton.

The viceroy of Zhejiang province immediately ordered Flint to leave. He set sail, but instead of returning to Canton, he headed north to Tientsin, becoming the first Englishman to enter that city. His intention was to go all the way to Peking and see the emperor, but the best he could do was to convince a local mandarin to convey his request for an audience to the court. Flint then returned to Canton without waiting for a reply.

But it was waiting for him when he got there, in the form of a convocation to the viceroy. Suspicious company commissioners insisted on going with him. The moment they entered the palace court, they were divested of their swords and hauled in front of the viceroy, to whom they were ordered to kowtow. They refused. For having traveled to Tientsin in violation of the imperial will, Flint was condemned to three years' relegation to Macao, followed by banishment from all Chinese territory.[9] The Tientsin mandarin who had been so foolish as to convey Flint's request to the Peking court was decapitated.

Macartney took a dim view of Flint's conduct: "On the footing that Mr. Flint was sent, what else could have been expected? A private individual commissioned by a few other individuals trading at Canton, whom the Chinese had not yet learned to respect as they ought, was dispatched without a passport in a small vessel . . . to accuse the regency of Canton. . . ."[10] Macartney, in contrast, was duly accredited by the "sovereign of the seas," the "most powerful monarch of the globe." Moreover, he would arrive in a great warship.

The ultimate result of Flint's initiative came in 1760, when an imperial edict stiffened the restrictions on foreign trade.[11] Foreigners were ordered to leave Canton on the Chinese New Year, withdrawing to Macao until autumn. Chinese were ordered not to trade with or work for foreigners, under penalty of deportation. Foreigners were denied the right to learn Chinese and were permitted to have contact only with interpreters accredited by the Canton guild. Chinese officials had to be present aboard any foreign merchant ship during its stay in Chinese waters. Foreigners were forbidden to bear arms or to send couriers abroad without permission from the Chinese authorities. Finally, any foreigner involved in an incident with a Chinese would be subject to Chinese jurisdiction.

It was when he learned of this edict that Lord Clive, the newly appointed governor of India, proposed to His Majesty's cabinet that Britain seize China by force.[12] The edict had been issued thirty-three years before Macartney's mission, but that was a mere instant in a country that, over "four millennia," had always found ways to restabilize the status quo, despite repeated upheavals, explosions, and dislocations. The restrictive, dishonorable situation in Canton had not changed since Flint's abortive initiative. Macartney had now been instructed to put it right.

He believed in his own good fortune. Just as he had once learned the Navigation Act by heart, so he now memorized a comment made by Father

Amiot (the celebrated dean of the Jesuits in China, whom Macartney hoped to meet in Peking) about the "Tartar-Chinese Court": "Embassies are received only inasmuch as they can be regarded as marks of submission."[13]

Macartney had eluded the Canton trap, and he was confident that he would also find a way to elude the pitfalls of the absurd customs of the Peking court. The squadron sailed past the mouth of the Pearl River and headed for the high seas.

8

Strange Beings

(June 26–July 5, 1793)

THE NEXT STOPOVER was to be the Zhoushan Islands, in Zhejiang province. The winds were favorable, and the squadron covered seven hundred miles in six days. They had maritime maps drawn by British traders earlier in the century, when the trading post in Ningbo was still active. But beyond that city lay unknown seas.[1]

ON JUNE 26,* as the British were leaving Canton, Guo Shixun, military governor of Guangdong province, of which Canton was the capital, wrote to the emperor: "Sea winds being irregular, it was not impossible that the tributary ships might moor in one of the ports of Guangdong after all. Your slave Guo Shixun therefore ordered the prefects of Macao and Xiang-shan to remain at the ready, and upon their entry into port, to escort them, with soldiers formed up into ordered ranks so as to display rigor. But reports from the subprefect of Xiangshan and the customs chief of Macao indicate that the tributary ships left Macao with the wind in their sails. It appears that they mean to travel along the Zhejiang coast."[3]

As Macartney proudly pressed on to the Zhoushan Islands, Chinese couriers galloped for Peking. The English fly was approaching the Celestial web.

The *Lion* was the first to arrive in the waters of the archipelago. The captain selected a moorage where they could wait for the other ships, which took three days to catch up. Thousands of junks came out to admire the unprecedented spectacle, and the exoticism cut both ways: "A Chinese pilot came on board with some of his people, who . . . examined everything with great curiosity, and observing the Emperor of China's picture in the

---

* It took the authorities in Canton six days to react to Staunton's stopover in Macao. But the journey from Macao to Canton was not easy: a three-day trip in the best of circumstances.[2]

ambassador's cabin, immediately fell flat on their faces, and kissed the ground several times with great devotion."[4]

Kowtowing to a mere image! Macartney noted the gesture with amusement, never dreaming of taking it as a warning. This very first encounter presented him with the chief difficulty his mission would face, but he refused to see it. In February 1792 he had received a very clear memorandum from the man who had served as physician to the Cathcart mission: the ambassador would have to perform the ninefold prostration without taking it as a mark of submission. Lord Macartney had merely shrugged.[5] He knew of the problem, but would not acknowledge it.

In Zhoushan, as in Macao, the ambassador left local contacts to his deputy. He remained aboard the *Lion* in a secure mooring some fifty miles from the main island, while Sir George set out on the *Clarence*, threading his way through the archipelago, stopping first at the island of Luowang. These were Staunton's first real contacts with Chinese soil, and he felt as though he had landed on another planet.

They disembarked on a "small level plain recovered from the sea, which was kept out by an embankment of earth, at least thirty feet thick. . . . The plain was, indeed, cultivated with the utmost care, and laid out, chiefly, in rice-plats, supplied with water collected from the adjacent hills into little channels."[6] Staunton admired the neatness of the work but also noted that "instead of the dung of animals" it was fertilized with "matters more offensive to the human senses," namely human excrement.[7] He went on to point out that "previously to its being sown," the rice was steeped in "liquids of an analogous nature," which "is supposed to hasten the growth of the future plant, as well as to prevent injury from insects in its tender state."[8]

A peasant approached these Martians. He wore clothes of blue cotton, small boots, and a conical straw hat held in place by a cord tied under his chin. Stupefied, he led the travelers to his village and showed them into a house, where another dumbfounded farmer gaped at them. "The house was built of wood, the uprights of the natural form of the timber. No ceiling concealed the inside of the roof, which was put together strongly, and covered with the straw of rice. The floor was of earth beaten hard, and the partitions between the rooms consisted of mats hanging from the beams." Even today, most Chinese families live in single rooms partitioned by mats. "Two spinning wheels for cotton were seen in the outer room; but the seats were empty. They had probably been filled by females, who retired on the approach of strangers."[9] In our own day too, the women of the countryside are often equally shy.

The next day the *Clarence* entered the harbor of Dinghai, capital of the Zhoushan Islands. "In consequence of the regulations of the vigilant government of China, a report of her approach had already reached Zhoushan; a Chinese vessel anchored near her, from which an officer came on board."[10] The military governor of the city greeted the British with great courtesy. Provisions were brought aboard, and a banquet was held in the governor's palace. The spacious reception hall was ringed by galleries supported by columns of varnished wood painted red. It was lit by lanterns hanging from silken cords studded with acorns. Some of these lanterns were of "thin silk gauze," others of animal horn so "thin and transparent" that at first the travelers took them for glass. Staunton observed: "The usual method of managing them . . . is to bend them by immersion in boiling water, after which they are cut open and flattened; then they easily scale, or are separated into two or three thin laminae, or plates. . . . It is a contrivance little known elsewhere, however simple the process appears to be."[11] A delegation was sent to invite the ambassador to come ashore, and only the expressed desire of the British to proceed to the emperor without delay brought the festivities to a close.

In accordance with court instructions, the governor had pilots ready to guide the British along the coast to the next province, where other pilots would take over, and so on until they reached Tientsin. But Staunton wanted no part of the coastal waterway. He explained that he meant to go on to Tientsin by the quickest possible route, the high seas. The mandarin was nonplussed. "The idea of a direct navigation to the gulf of Peking, without any intermediary stop, was altogether new" to him. "He thought proper to consider of it till the next day."[12]

Chinese documents give us the name of this perplexed officer—Ma Yu—and the British had no idea of the problems they had created for the hapless brigadier general. A few days before, another British ship had passed through the islands. It had been sent by the company just in case Macartney decided to bypass Macao. Ma Yu never mentioned this other ship to Staunton, a bit of discretion for which the Celestial hierarchy would never have reproached him. But he also failed to report it to the hierarchy, and that dereliction earned him condemnation in an edict issued by the emperor himself, who insisted that Ma Yu "must be punished."[13] The British were not the only ones under surveillance.

They took advantage of the overnight delay to visit the town of Dinghai. Staunton felt that its many canals, spanned by humpbacked bridges, and its narrow streets, paved with flat stones, made it seem like "Venice, but on a smaller scale." Modern visitors would likely find the comparison somewhat exaggerated.

Everything about Dinghai seemed surprising to the Europeans, who could hardly decide what to look at next. "The houses . . . were low, and mostly of one story. The attention, as to ornament, in these buildings was confined chiefly to the roofs, which, besides having the tiles that covered the rafters luted and plastered over, . . . were contrived in such a form as to imitate the inward bend of the ridges and sides of canvas tents, or of the coverings of skins of animals. . . . On the ridges of the roofs were uncouth figures of animals."[14] The British rationalists never imagined that the rooftop figurines were supposed to ward off evil spirits.

The shops displayed clothing, food, furniture, and even gaily painted coffins. Live fowl were on sale, along with live fish and eels (kept in jars filled with water), and even dogs bred for the frying pan. Sticks of incense used in the temples were available everywhere.

"Loose garments and trowsers were worn by both sexes; but the men had hats of straw or cane which covered the head; their hair, except one long lock, being cut short or shaved."[15] The Manchu conquerors had imposed the "pigtail" on Chinese men back in the seventeenth century. Anyone who rejected this token of allegiance was subject to the death penalty, which was applied as late as the 1720s. By the end of the eighteenth century, however, no one dreamed of shirking the humiliating obligation.

"Throughout the place there was an appearance of quick and active industry, beyond the natural effect of a climate not quite thirty degrees from the equator; a circumstance which implied the stimulus of necessity compelling, or of reward exciting, to labour. None seemed to shun it."[16] A cliché was born: "No one in China is idle. There are no public promenades, for there is no time for promenading."[17] Then as now, visitors were struck by the unending, anthill-like turbulence.

In the streets, Staunton wrote, "none asked alms."[18] French observers were more acute: "There are some beggars, especially lepers."[19] Father Lamiot noted that "if the English saw no beggars, it was because they were hidden from them."[20] Hüttner made a comment that would be apposite even today: "Thousands of the poor were prepared to carry on their shoulders whatever could not be loaded into carts."[21] A Chinese was ever ready for any effort, in exchange for a sapek or a bowl of rice. Familial solidarity was striking too. Sharing was a rite. "No question of gratitude among relatives," an uncle said to his nephew.[22]

Activity reigned, and beggars were scarce. Eighteenth-century China enjoyed a prosperity that would ultimately stimulate unbridled population growth and thus bring the country to ruin.

THE BRITISH SAW Chinese women—"even in the middle and inferior classes"—with mutilated feet. "They appeared as if the forepart of the foot had been accidentally cut off, leaving the remainder of the usual size, and bandaged like the stump of an amputated limb. They undergo, indeed, much torment, and cripple themselves in great measure, in imitation of ladies of higher rank, among whom it is there the custom to stop, by pressure, the growth of the ankle as well as foot from the earliest infancy; and leaving the great toe in its natural position, forcibly to bend the others, and retain them under the foot, till at length they adhere to, as if buried in, the sole, and can no more be separated."[23] Mothers kept constant watch over their daughters "to deter them from relieving themselves from the firm and tight compresses, which bind their feet and ankles. . . . The young creatures are indeed obliged, for a considerable time, to be supported when they attempt to walk; ever afterwards they totter; and always walk upon their heels."[24]

Prejudices were inviolate. "Some of the very lowest classes of the Chinese, of a race confined chiefly to the mountains and remote places, have not adopted this unnatural custom. But the females of this class are held by the rest in the utmost degree of contempt, and are employed only in the most menial domestic offices."[25]

The Chinese women who willingly submitted to this suffering inspired Staunton to an observation in comparative sociology of which Montesquieu would have approved: "In forming conjectures upon the origin of so singular a fashion among Chinese ladies, it is not very easy to conceive why this mode should have been suddenly or forcibly introduced amongst them by the other sex. Had men been really bent upon confining constantly to their homes the females of their families, they might have effected it without cruelly depriving them of the physical power of motion. No such custom is known in Turkey or Hindostan, where women are kept in greater habits of retirement than in China. Opinion, indeed, more than power, governs the general actions of the human race; and so preposterous a practice could be maintained only by the example and persuasion of those who, in their own persons, had submitted to it. Men may have silently approved, and indirectly encouraged it, as those of India are supposed to do that much more barbarous custom of widows burning themselves after the death of their husbands. But it is not violence, or the apprehension of corporal suffering, but the horror and disgrace in consequence of omitting, and the idea of glory arising from doing, what is considered to be an act of duty, at the expense of life, which leads to such a sacrifice. In that instance, ages must have past to ripen prejudices of a consequence so dreadful."[26]

Macartney took a more relativistic view: "We have not yet indeed pushed it to the extreme point the Chinese have done, yet we are such admirers of it, that what with tight shoes, high heels, and ponderous buckles, if our ladies' feet are not crippled they are certainly very much contracted."[27] Then he lifted a corner of the veil: a missionary "assured me that in love affairs the glimpse of a fairy foot was to a Chinese a most powerful provocative."[28] Today we know that these dwarf feet were a major sexual fetish. Born of such terrible suffering, they later became the focus of the most intense pleasures. Fondling them was an obligatory part of foreplay.[29] A woman who wanted to call attention to herself would allow her silk-wrapped foot—her "golden lotus"—to slip out from under the hem of her dress. A go-between once said to a suitor: "You must boldly touch her foot. If she lets you, the game is won."[30] Erotic Chinese paintings depict scenes in which the only clothing worn by the woman is the silk shoe that covers her fetish foot.[31]

Staunton noticed another oddity in the governor's palace in Dinghai. "On several tables were placed in frames, filled with earth, dwarf pines, oaks, and orange trees, bearing fruit. None of them exceeded, in height, two feet. Some of those dwarfs bore all the marks of decay from age: and upon the surface of the soil were interspersed small heaps of stones, which, in proportion to the adjoining dwarfs, might be termed rocks."[32]

Records of these potted landscapes date back to the fourth century. A thousand years later the Japanese imitated them, calling them bonsai. They were the botanical equivalent of bound female feet, produced with equal dedication and by the same method: compression through binding, which stunts growth. A strange yen for the miniature.

But the "people of black hair" were also discovering the "people of red hair," and the surprise was mutual. "They collected now in multitudes round the strangers. . . . They were familiar, but without insult, scoff, or uproar."[33] ". . . they could not refrain from bursting into fits of laughter on examining the grease and powder with which our hair was disfigured."[34] The travelers seemed uncomfortable in their European clothes, quite ill suited to the subtropical summer heat. The people in the crowds around them were lightly dressed.[35]

First impressions are crucial, and the accounts of the British are redolent with the enthusiasm of discovery. Though Dinghai was really no more than a modest port, for them it had the incomparable allure of the wholly new. But it was here, too, that they heard the first of the loud guffaws that would track them across China. They considered themselves the lords of the earth, but here they were objects of derision.

9

Rounding Up Pilots

(July 6–18, 1793)

THE NEXT MORNING, July 6, the British had their second meeting with the military governor of Dinghai. The general, dressed in a superb robe with a lion (representing his military function) embroidered on the chest, was accompanied by two mandarins and several lower-ranking officers. They sat on chairs covered in "English scarlet cloth" and went through the ritual Chinese tea drinking. The magistrate gave a spirited speech, the gist of which was translated by Mr. Plumb: "that the mode of navigation from province to province along the coast had been, at all times, the practice amongst the Chinese, and must, consequently, be best to follow in the present instance."[1] There was always a ritual.

Staunton replied "that the greater size, and different construction of the English ships, required a different method to be followed in this respect than what usually was practiced; that as Ningbo might furnish such pilots as could not be found at Zhoushan, they would immediately proceed thither in search of them."[2]

The military governor could not possibly admit the naval superiority of a tributary vassal, but Staunton's cold resolution alarmed him. Naively, he confessed that if the British went looking for pilots that he had failed to provide, he might be accused of not having received the embassy with the proper respect. The governor said that this "might occasion the loss of his office and his dignity." He pointed to his cap with its red mandarin's button, representing the second grade. To "avoid the possibility of disgrace," the governor "immediately undertook to find out persons qualified to conduct the squadron in the desired route."[3] The British thought it a strange spectacle: a high-ranking officer displaying such reverential fear of the emperor.

Troops soon returned with "a set of the most miserable looking wretches I ever beheld; who were thrust into the hall, and dropping on their knees, were examined in that attitude, as to their qualifications. Some, it appeared, had been at the port of Tientsin, but were no seamen; others followed the profession, but had never been at that port."[4] The soldiers set out anew. They returned with two men who seemed to qualify, though they had long retired from sea duty. In vain, they fell to their knees to beg that they be left alone. Barrow, the comptroller, could not help feeling sorry for them: "The governor was inexorable; and they were ordered to be ready to embark in the course of an hour."[5]

Barrow concluded from this incident that "long voyages are never undertaken where they can be avoided; but that the commerce of the Yellow Sea is carried on from port to port; and that the articles of merchandize so transported must necessarily have many profits upon them, before they come to the distant consumer; which may, in some degree, account for the high prices many of the products of the country, as we afterwards found, bore in the capital. In like manner was the inland commerce of Asia conducted by caravans, proceeding from station to station, at each of which were merchants to buy or exchange commodities with each other, those at the limits of the journey having no connection nor communication whatsoever with one another."[6]

This was one reason why the superb British vessels aroused such astonishment: "At the sight of our large ships, . . . a vast number of boats, issuing from every creek and cove, presently crowded together, in such a manner, and with so little management, as to render it difficult to pass through without danger of oversetting or sinking some of them; a danger, however, to which they seemed quite insensible."

Barrow was surprised at how vulnerable the junks were. They stood so high above the waterline that they were unable to withstand typhoons, and they were loaded with wood piled so high "upon their decks, that no extraordinary force of wind would seem to be required to overturn them."[7] Examining paintings dating back two hundred years, Anderson observed that "the junks of the last century, and those of the present day, are invariably the same."[8] He might have said as much in the 1990s as well, except that by then more and more of these boats had motors instead of sails.

Navigation was archaic: "they have no means of ascertaining the latitude or longitude of any place."[9] Nevertheless, they claimed that several of their ancient navigators had made long voyages, on which they were guided "by charts of the route, sometimes drawn on paper, and sometimes on the convex surface of large gourds or pumpkins." Though they knew it was true, the British found it hard to believe that the Chinese had not only invented the compass, but used it "when the greatest part of Europe was in a state of barbarism."[10]

It was a strange situation. Europeans borrowed the compass from the Chinese only several centuries after its invention, but they used it to cross oceans and discover continents, while the Chinese, who had reached the African coast well before the Europeans, now declined to venture beyond local seas, at the very moment that Europeans were sailing to the Far East—thanks to China's inventive genius. What accounted for the decrepitude of the Manchu fleet, given the splendor of the navy under the Songs, the Mongols, and the earliest Mings?

In the meantime, the Chinese had an idiosyncratic interpretation of the compass. The emperor Kangxi, Qianlong's grandfather, once said: "I have heard Europeans say that the needle obeys the north. In our oldest records it is said that it turns to the south. . . . The farther I proceed, the more convinced I am of their [the ancients'] knowledge."[11]

Thus did the emperor take sides in the eternal quarrel between old and new: the present is no more than the past debased. Himself a northerner, the Manchu added this somewhat surprising argument: "Moreover, as all action grows languid, and nearly is suspended towards the north, it is less likely that the virtue, which gives motion to the magnetic needle, should proceed from that quarter." Indeed, Chinese palaces, temples, and the Forbidden City itself all faced south, because "the south alone is considered as containing all the attractive power."[12]

Compass or not, the British were quite surprised that such poorly designed structures as the Chinese ships "were able to make so long and dangerous a voyage as that to Batavia."[13] But shipwrecks were frequent: "ten or twelve thousand subjects from the port of Canton alone are reckoned to perish annually by shipwreck."[14] When a Chinese vessel prepares for a voyage abroad, "it is considered as an equal chance that she will never return."[15]

As usual, Macartney raised a good question, wondering at the "extraordinary ignorance of the Chinese in the art of navigation, for although above two hundred and fifty years are elapsed since they have been acquainted with Europeans, and although they see and admire our ships and our seamanship yet they have never in the slightest point imitated our build or manœuvres but obstinately and invariably adhere to the ancient customs and clumsy practice of their ignorant ancestors; and this negligence is the more extraordinary as there is no country where naval skill is more requisite."[16]

ONE OF THE PASSENGERS on the *Clarence* got sick from eating too much "acid fruit he had found on shore." In those days, illness and death were constant threats on ships, and the slightest twinge was taken very seriously. Since the *Clarence* had no physician or pharmacy aboard, the British had no choice but to ask a Chinese doctor for help. He, "without asking any questions about the symptoms or origin of the complaint, with great solemnity felt the pulse of the left arm of his patient, by applying gently his four fingers to it; then raising up one of them, he continued to press with the other three, afterwards with two, and, at last, with only one, moving his hand for several minutes backwards and forwards along the wrist, as if upon the keys of a harpsichord, as far towards the elbow as the pulse could be distinguished. He remained the whole time silent, with eyes fixed, but not upon the patient, and acting as if he considered every distinct disease to be attended with a pulsation of the artery peculiar to itself, and distinguishable by an attentive practitioner. He pronounced the present complaint to come from the stomach, as indeed was obvious from the symptoms, of which it is very probable he had information before he came; and which soon yielded to appropriate medicines, supplied, at the patient's request, by him."[17]

Staunton's skeptical tone prefigures the attitude taken by Western physicians over the next two centuries: no salvation outside Western (scientific and rational) medicine; the twelve pulses of the Chinese, like their medicinal herbs and their acupuncture, were "charlatanism."

THE GOVERNOR PAID a visit to the ship. He was surprised at the height of the mast and the "dexterity of the sailors running up the shrouds. . . . the Chinese sailors . . . generally carry on the manœuvres of navigation upon deck."[18] The *Clarence*, having taken its pilots on board, now set out to catch up to the *Lion*.[19]

On July 7 it rejoined the rest of the squadron. One of the pilots was assigned to the *Lion*, the other to the *Hindostan*. Staunton proudly announced that "the squadron was arrived at the utmost boundary of recorded European navigation. The sea from thence, for about ten degrees of latitude and six of longitude, was utterly unknown, except to those who dwelt in the neighbourhood of its shores." This was the Yellow Sea, "bounded by China, Tartary, and the peninsula of Corea."[20]

They cast off on July 8, and the pilots were useless the moment the ships were out of sight of the familiar coast. "When . . . a European pilot arrives upon the deck of a vessel, on board of which his assistance is required, he takes at once the helm, and exercises his functions like a dictator among the Romans. . . . But the Chinese, in the present instance, were too much awed by the novelty of their situation."[21] Did they believe that since China lay at the center of the world, oceans were the antechambers of the void? In any event, the sounders were more useful than the pilots.

A comparison of British and Chinese testimony reveals a twofold gap between their civilizations. The court was stunned by the rapid pace set by the English ships, particularly since they were sailing in seas unknown to them. One mandarin wrote a memorandum pondering the reasons for this performance.[22] But as the squadron headed for Tientsin, the imperial postal system worked wonders in keeping Peking informed of British progress. Chinese couriers on horseback, wearing little bells on their clothes, galloped along the overland route. The moment a courier heard the bells of his predecessor, he hurried to take the relay. The Chinese postal system outclassed the British just as decisively as the British fleet outclassed the Chinese. Where the sea was concerned, China was entering its fourth century of slumber. As early as the 1500s, Britain had opted for the sea, China for the land, and their exploits in their chosen domains were unequaled.

In defense of China's primitive naval expertise, Staunton charitably noted that necessity was "the great inventress of social arts." Even the Greeks, so admirable in their science and "the acuteness of their minds," were never able to determine "the position of a ship at sea; satisfied that they could, by the observation, in the day time, of some part of the coast of the Mediterranean, in which they generally sailed, or of the many islands scattered through it, and, in the night time, of the stars, obtain such information as they wanted in that respect. The Chinese, indeed, enjoy a similar advantage, as their seas resemble the Mediterranean, by the narrowness of their limits, and the numerous islands with which every part of them is studded. It is to be observed, likewise, that the art of navigation, improved among Europeans, dates its origin nearly from the same period when their passions, or their wants, impelled them to take long voyages over the boundless ocean."[23]

A penetrating observation. But why had the Chinese never felt these "passions" or these "wants"? Were they wholly lacking in the thirst for knowledge, which spurs discovery, and the thirst for profit, which seeks out new applications for the fruits of discovery?

On July 12 the fog was so thick the ships "lost sight of each other, notwithstanding we kept firing guns every half hour, and were answered until about 12 o'clock at night."[24] These waters were unknown to the Westerners, and it is the explorer's habit to name newly discovered lands. Sir Erasmus Gower was no exception, covering his maps with new labels: Cape Macartney, Cape Gower, Staunton's Island.[25] Fortunately the Chinese knew nothing of this. One wonders what they would have thought of "tributaries" taking symbolic possession of the empire's shores. In our own day, nationalism and ideology have reversed the process. During the Cultural Revolution the main street in the Peking neighborhood where foreign embassies are concentrated was renamed Anti-Imperialist Avenue. The street the Soviet embassy was on became Anti-Revisionist Street. Victoria Avenue in Tientsin was renamed Liberation Avenue, and taxi drivers had already begun calling Victoria Peak Hong Kong. To put new names on things is to remake them.

While the British happily busied themselves with Chinese geography, the Chinese were preparing to take their visitors in hand. An imperial letter sent by chief minister Heshen to Liang Kentang, the viceroy of Zhili, warned: "The English tributary ships left Macao on June 20 and reached Dinghai on July 4; their progress north, at full sail, has been very swift. But when they arrive in Tientsin, their massive hulls will prevent them from entering the shallow waters, and the men and articles of tribute will have to be loaded onto boats that can anchor in the inner ocean. To pass from the inner ocean to the canal, the men and articles of tribute will again have to be reloaded onto smaller boats. The successive loading and unloading will take time. May Liang Kentang and Zhengrui deal with the tributary envoy with all the requisite care."[26]

Liang Kentang replied: "Your servant has already enjoined all Your officials to hire all the required boats, since the articles of tribute are quite numerous."[27]

IN PARIS ON JULY 17, four days after stabbing Marat to death, Charlotte Corday donned the red dress of a parricide and mounted the scaffold of the guillotine.

10

"The Renown of the English Name"

(July 19–31, 1793)

ON JULY 19 the *Lion* dropped anchor in the Bay of Zhitao. The pilots, justifying the low esteem in which they were held by the British, mistook the place for the Miao Islands, which lie much farther north.

The embassy would soon disembark, and Macartney had a solemn proclamation read to the crew of all four ships telling them how to behave: "It is impossible that the various important objects of the Embassy can be obtained, but through the goodwill of the Chinese; that goodwill may much depend on the ideas which they shall be induced to entertain of the disposition and conduct of the English nation, and they can judge only from the behaviour of the majority of those who come amongst them. The impression hitherto made upon their minds, in consequence of the irregularities committed by Englishmen at Canton, are unfavourable even to the degree of considering them as the worst among Europeans. . . . Though the people of China have not the smallest share in the government, yet it is a maxim invariably pursued by their superiors, to support the meanest Chinese in any difference with a stranger, and if the occasion should happen, to avenge his blood,* of which there was a fatal instance, not long since, at Canton, where the gunner of an English vessel, who had been very innocently the cause of the death of a native peasant,† was executed for it. . . . Peculiar caution and mildness must consequently be observed

---

* Nowadays, any Western diplomat posted to China who kills a Chinese in an automobile accident is automatically expelled from the country, regardless of who was at fault. It is the result, not the intention, that counts.

† According to other sources, it was a cannoneer of the *Lady Hughes* who, in 1784, accidentally killed two Chinese boatmen. He was firing an honorary salvo and did not realize that the guns were loaded.[1]

in every sort of intercourse or accidental meeting with any of the poorest individuals of the country."[2]

The ambassador asked the members of the crew and the mission to maintain order, temperance, and discipline, "so as to enhance the renown of the English name." In the event of misconduct, he would consider it his "duty to punish any offender." Moreover, he "would let Chinese justice take its course"—a terrible threat. Macartney must have regretted having to accept such a possibility, since one of his objectives was precisely to win the exemption of his compatriots from Chinese judicial authority. But the members of his retinue did not know that.

No one was allowed to go ashore without his permission, and once on shore, no one could leave the camp, nor engage in trade of any kind. "His Excellency will gladly relax these strictures once the negotiations are sufficiently advanced to assure the mission's success."

This expedition was intended to foster commerce, yet it now prohibited trade until it had attained its goal. Here there was no hypocrisy, but simply sound knowledge of Chinese attitudes, at least on this issue. Staunton and Barrow spared no effort in explaining to their readers just how contemptuous the Chinese (or rather the mandarins) were of commerce. The Chinese absorb their prejudices against foreigners "from their earliest youth," Barrow wrote.[3] And Staunton noted: "There are, properly, but three classes of men in China. Men of letters, from whom the mandarins are taken; cultivators of the ground; and mechanics, including merchants."[4]

A secret committee of company directors had authorized Macartney to demote the commander or any other officer of the *Hindostan* found "guilty of disobedience of orders from His Excellency during the continuation of the Embassy to China."[5] Macartney was painfully aware that the British had a reputation as wicked merchants—the worst possible combination.

If he was to have any chance of broadening commercial relations, he would have to begin by presenting himself in a new light. Yet the ban on trade was not without its inconvenient aspects. Provincial mandarins who dealt with the British expedition would be disappointed to learn that the gifts it carried were meant for the emperor alone. No presents for the Chinese intermediaries? Not even the watches and music boxes they were so fond of, which they bought cheap and resold dear, or passed on to powerful protectors? After all, friendship unmaintained tends to wither.

While the king of England's ambassador was making his wishes known to his retinue, the emperor was busily reminding his own officials of the immutable rules: "In dealing with Barbarians, one must find the mean between prodigality and parsimony. When the English tributary envoy arrives, you must not receive him with greater ceremony than the ancestral regulations prescribe. Nevertheless, this being his first visit to our illustrious country, and coming as it does after a long voyage, he ought not to be treated identically to the envoys of Burma, Annam, and others who bring tribute often."[6]

Special treatment for the English envoy. But not too special: "It appears that the tributary envoy is to arrive in Jehol, there to gaze upon Us in an audience, sometime after August 26. He can then be invited to a banquet and receive gifts, along with the Mongol princes and dukes and the Burmese and other tributary envoys. That would be quite appropriate."[7]

"Let us not offend envoys who come from so far," the emperor wrote. The barbarian who aspires to Civilization must not be hurriedly panfried; better to bake him at a low heat.

A "SMALL SQUARE RIGGED European vessel" suddenly came into view.[8] It was the *Endeavour*, under the command of Captain Proctor, "the vessel which was fitted out by the East India Company to cruize for us off the island of Zhoushan, and to pilot us to the nearest port to Peking." Not finding the squadron, the ship "had been cruizing at the mouth of the Yellow Sea, where we could not well enter without discovering each other."[9] The company had taken precautions, making sure that Macartney would get the latest news from Peking even if he decided to bypass Macao. The *Endeavour* joined the squadron, which now consisted of five ships.

On July 20 the British reached Dengzhou Fu, where they found that Miao was not the mainland port they had imagined, but an island, and that they were moored in a dangerous harbor.

The prefect of Dengzhou Fu, a high-ranking mandarin whom Macartney found "courteous, intelligent, and inquisitive,"[10] came aboard the *Lion*. He offered the ambassador the means of transport required for a land journey to Peking. "The Court had issued orders to this effect." The Chinese had a real horror of sea voyages, but Macartney wanted to sail on. A new pilot informed him that the Gulf of Beizhili presented no danger this time of year, and junks that could carry the expedition's baggage upriver to Tien-tsin were waiting. "They are large and so constructed that there is no danger of our packages being wetted or damaged."[11]

The five ships set sail on July 22. At dawn on the twenty-fifth they arrived at the mouth of the Baihe River, but the alluvium-choked gulf was impassable, and the squadron therefore had to moor five miles offshore, in a mere seven fathoms of water. Campbell and Hüttner went on ahead to Dagu in the *Jackall*.

That evening they returned to the squadron to report to Macartney that they had been very well received.

True, they had been bombarded with questions about the expedition —the number, ages, and qualifications of its members, the strength of the *Lion* and its escort, the gifts, and much else—and a secretary noted down their answers. But they had also been told that two great mandarins were to come aboard the *Lion* to pay their respects to the ambassador and to discuss arrangements for the journey to Peking.[12]

This was to be Macartney's first personal contact with the Celestial bureaucracy, in whose formidable cogwheels the expedition would now be enmeshed.

11

Delivery of the Tribute

(July 31–August 5, 1793)

THE TWO MANDARINS duly arrived at noon on July 31. "They had never seen a ship of the *Lion*'s construction, bulk, or loftiness. They were at a loss how to ascend her sides; but their chairs were quickly fastened to tackles, by which they were lifted up."[1]

According to Macartney, a third mandarin, higher in rank, was "afraid of the sea" and preferred to remain on dry land.

Imperial archives tell us that the British misunderstood. It was in fact for reasons of protocol that the third mandarin, the legate Zhengrui, did not come aboard.[2] Great mandarins did not condescend to *climb* aboard foreign ships. Instead their soldiers went aboard and secured a bamboo walkway that was lowered from a higher point of the imperial junk. The grand personage then used the walkway to *descend* to the barbarian vessel. But the impressive dimensions of the *Lion* made this ritual impossible, and it would not have befitted the dignity of an imperial legate to dangle like a spider from the end of a rope. A loss of face for him would have been tantamount to a loss of face for the emperor he represented.

Seven large junks drew near, loaded with provisions that included "20 bullocks, 130 sheep, 120 hogs, 100 fowls, 100 ducks, 160 bags of flour, 160 bags of rice," and numerous other supplies that Macartney described as "so great and so much above our wants that we were obliged to decline accepting the larger part of them."[3] Chinese hospitality was ever "respectful of forms, even toward enemies."[4]

The two mandarins were named Wang and Qiao.[5] Wang, a military officer, wore a cap with a red coral button (the insignia of the second grade) and a peacock feather given to him by the emperor in appreciation of his services. Qiao, who sported a blue button (one grade below the red), was a man of letters. "After a number of compliments and civilities in the Chinese manner, we proceeded to business."[6] They first arranged details of the transfer of the presents, of which the British were of course asked to provide a new list. The operation would take four to five days.

There followed a lavish and friendly meal aboard the *Lion*. The Chinese quickly learned to manipulate their knives and forks with great skill. They much enjoyed the English alcohol—gin, rum, and cherry brandy—and Macartney noted that "upon taking their leave, they shook hands with us warmly."* The chairs were even more necessary for their departure than they had been for their arrival.

Delighted to have done the honors aboard the *Lion*, Macartney did not suspect that he had just enjoyed his very last opportunity to play lord of the manor. Once on land, under the tutelage of their two amiable mentors, the British would be closely supervised: ushered in, out, and around, never again masters of their own movements.

STAUNTON SKETCHED quick portraits of Wang and Qiao, who were to accompany the embassy for many long months: Qiao, "the civilian mandarine, was a man of grave, but no austere, manners. His demeanour indicated a plain and solid understanding. He was not formal in discourse; neither appearing to aim at any thing brilliant in himself, nor to be dazzled by it in others. A faithful and benevolent discharge of his duty seemed to be the sole and simple object of his pursuit. He had been preceptor to some of the imperial family; and was considered as a man of learning and judgment."[7] The typical Confucian man of letters, as seen by his British counterpart: thoughtful, modest, authoritative without the slightest ostentation.

Wang, "the military mandarine," was "in the true character of his profession, 'open, bold, and brave.' . . . He was above the middle size, erect, and uncommonly muscular. In the Chinese armies, where the bow and arrow are still in use, and generally preferred to fire arms, his activity and strength, as well as his other martial qualities, were highly prized. And, though he was no boaster, in his deportment was sometimes perceptible an honest consciousness of his prowess and achievements. But instead of any arrogance or roughness in his disposition, good nature was conspicuous in his countenance, and his manner testified to his willingness to oblige. He was cheerful and pleasant in his conversation, banishing all reserve, and treating his new friends with the familiarity of old acquaintance."[8]

---

* This seems surprising. Chinese under the Manchu dynasty generally did not shake hands, but bowed several times.

A diptych of the Celestial bureaucracy, with its civilian and military facets. A balance has always been sought between the two. Though civilians (the Chinese call them "men of letters") hold ascendancy, military influence is strong. Mao and Deng, for instance, though glorious survivors of the Long March and absolute masters of the Red army, held supreme power as civilians. In China, as in the Roman Republic (and in democracies as well), the toga outranks the uniform.

There have, however, been some exceptions to this rule. For a time, the military held precedence under the Manchu conquerors. The same was true under the warlords of the 1920s, and the army was used to halt the excesses of the Cultural Revolution. The military has always been the last resort against the turmoil to which China is prone. But Wang never lastingly imposed his will on Qiao.

AS COOLIES TRANSFERRED the crates from the British ships to the junks, Macartney drew up another list of their contents. He decided that a description of the gifts "somewhat in the Oriental style" would enhance their glamour.[9]

By "Oriental" he seems to have meant bombastic, and in this he overlooked the first principle of Chinese courtesy: the donor is supposed to understate the value of his gifts, in order not to humiliate the recipient. But since Macartney could not bring himself to characterize his presents as a collection of "little nothings," mere "trinkets from our poor country," he wound up sounding arrogant.

It would not, he began, "be becoming to offer trifles of momentary curiosity, but little use. His Britannic Majesty had been, therefore, careful to select only such articles as might denote the progress of science, and of the arts in Europe, and which might convey some kind of information to the exalted mind of His Imperial Majesty."

This was followed by a presentation of the chief articles. "The first and principal [the planetarium]* . . . represents the universe, of which the earth is but a small portion. This work is the utmost effort of astronomical science and mechanic art combined together, that was ever made in Europe. It shews and imitates, with great clearness and with mathematical exactness, the several motions of the earth, according to the system of European astronomers; likewise the eccentric or irregular motions of the moon around it; and of the sun, with the planets which surround it, as well as the

---

* Other descriptions make it clear that the planetarium was a working model of the solar system as known at the time, driven by complicated, clocklike gear mechanisms.

particular system of the planet, called by Europeans Jupiter, which has four moons constantly moving about it, as well as belts upon its surface; and also of the planet Saturn, with its rings and moons; together with the eclipses, conjunctions, and opposition of the heavenly bodies. Another part indicates the month, the week, the day, the hour, and minute, at the time of inspection. This machine is as simple in its construction, as it is complicated and wonderful in its effects; nor does any so perfect remain behind in Europe. It is calculated for above a thousand years. . . .

"Another article consists of a globe, representing the heavenly firmament. . . . Corresponding to this celestial globe, is one representing the different continents of the earth, with its seas and islands; distinguishing the possessions of the different sovereigns, capital cities, and great chains of mountains. It is executed with particular care, and comprehends all the discoveries in different parts of the world, made in the voyages undertaken for that purpose by order of His Britannic Majesty, together with the routes of the different ships sent on those expeditions."

Macartney cleverly slipped some politics, and even a touch of intimidation, into his description: "His Britannic Majesty, who is acknowledged by the rest of Europe to be the first maritime power, and is truly sovereign of the seas, wished as a particular mark of his attention to His Imperial Majesty, to send some of his largest ships with the present Embassy. He was however obliged to fix on vessels of less considerable size, on account of the shallows and sands of the Yellow Sea, little known to European navigators; but he has sent a complete model of the largest British ship of war [the *Sovereign*], mounting one hundred and ten cannon of considerable calibre. This model shews every minutest part of such a stupendous structure." A discreet way of pointing out that neither the *Lion*, with its sixty-four guns, nor the four ships that accompanied it gave an accurate picture of the powerful fleet London could dispatch to Canton should the need arise.

There was special mention of the "howitzer mortars" and the various portable arms: carbines, rifles, and pistols. Another allusion to the overwhelming superiority of British weaponry, but also an implied offer of unlimited sales of the world's most outstanding artillery. Macartney also cited the "sword blades for cutting through iron without losing their edge"—a hint that Britain also enjoyed superiority in special steels.

There was an equally detailed and pompous description of the Herschelian telescope, the chronometers, the Wedgwood porcelain, the Parker lenses, and the fabrics.

Finally there were paintings: portraits of "the royal family" and of "eminent persons"; "representations of . . . cities, towns, churches, seats, gardens, castles, bridges, lakes, volcanoes, and antiquities; likewise of battles by sea and land, dockyards, . . . horse races, bull fighting, and of most other objects curious or remarkable in the dominions of His Britannic Majesty."

Wang and Qiao declared themselves very impressed, and the British found that they liked these two escorts more and more. In fact, they were totally smitten. We know nothing of how Wang and Qiao felt, since they did not have the right to communicate directly with the emperor. The report of this first meeting between Macartney and the Celestial bureaucracy was therefore written by the third man, the legate Zhengrui, who had not actually attended. "The tributary ships," he told the emperor, "came as far as the port of Tientsin. When Your slave proposed to go aboard the ships to instruct the Barbarians in etiquette, the envoy, *Ma-ga-er-ni*, believing himself a man of high rank, judged himself worthy of an interview on an equal footing. Had Your slave repaired forthwith to meet him, propriety would have been violated."

(A note in the margin at this point in the report, written in the bright red ink reserved for the emperor, reads: "Excessive. I cannot agree with you." This particular imperial legate was more imperial than the emperor.)

"Your slave therefore instructed Intendent Qiao and Colonel Wang, with whom he had left the port, to board the ship and issue the following proclamation: 'The imperial legate Zhengrui has come to examine the tributary memorandum [in other words, the letter from George III] and the list of articles of the tribute. He has sent us aboard to seek them.' The tributary envoy then came forward and, turning in the direction in which Your slave stood in the distance, expressed himself as follows: 'We have been showered with Celestial kindness.' The envoy also received Intendant Qiao and Colonel Wang with great respect. Your Majesty's portrait was hanging in the middle of a cabin of one of the great ships; the frame was of gold, studded with pearls and gems. The tributary envoy dared not seat himself before it.

"Among the articles of tribute is a very large one, disassembled and packed in crates. According to the Barbarians, all the articles can be transported to Jehol save this one, to which their King is much devoted and which would surely suffer irreparable damage were it to be assembled in Jehol and then disassembled. Your slave requests imperial instructions. . . . England lies far away, across several oceans. Its envoy has traveled tens of thousands of *li* in an eleven-month journey in order to present this tribute. This is unprecedented in history. It is a very great exploit carried out under Your glorious dynasty."[10]

The purpose of the legate's memorandum seems to have been less to inform His Majesty of what was happening than to tell him what he wanted to hear.

Fathers Zhou, An, and Wang, as well as Fathers Hanna and Lamiot and even young Thomas, had worked very hard to translate the original list of presents and the letter of accreditation. The Chinese version, conserved to this day in the Imperial Archives, was drafted on the basis of a Latin translation provided by Hüttner. It is riddled with gibberish. The object the British called a "planetarium," for example, was simply phonetically transcribed.

The missionary priests attached to the emperor edited this Chinese translation, since "the style of writing in that language for the court" is "familiar only to those who are employed about the palace."[11] They retranslated "planetarium" with this charming image: "geographical and astronomical musical clock."[12]

The vicissitudes of this recopied double translation may well be imagined. The Chinese and the British each had their own learned language. Classical Chinese as used by the empire's officials was incomprehensible to the illiterate, even when spoken aloud. Latin, though declining with the rise of "the universality of the French language," was still the lingua franca of the European intelligentsia, enabling the British to communicate with Chinese priests schooled in Italy.

In twentieth-century China, classical Chinese is rarely taught except in universities, and even there few students learn it. In Europe Latin is hardly used even in churches. On the other hand, businessmen from France or Germany who visit China speak to the Chinese in Macartney's language. In this particular cultural collision, the English expedition eventually carried the day—against two "celestial" bureaucracies and against all other competitors as well.

But these initial encounters severely taxed the embassy's linguistic resources. One of the two interpreters had been lost in Macao, and the one who remained, a Tartar, had his work cut out for him. Sir George and young Thomas did the best they could, with very different results, as Staunton was only too glad to admit, paternal pride softening his personal disappointment. A "trial was now made of the skill of the two persons belonging to the Embassy, to whom the Chinese missionaries had endeavoured to communicate some knowledge of their language. . . . One of these persons applied to this study with the uninterrupted diligence of mature age, but had the mortification of finding that as yet he could scarcely understand a word of what was said to him by these new comers, to whom his pronunciation was equally unintelligible: while the other, a youth, who certainly took less pains, but whose senses were more acute, and whose organs were more flexible, proved already a tolerably good interpreter."[13]

It was a surrealistic situation: the embassy's hopes for success rested on a Manchu priest and an English child. The former, who had left for Europe as an adolescent, knew little of China beyond his memories, the latter nothing beyond his books. And both were wholly ignorant of politics.

Did they at least succeed in their first task? They did not. "There are many incorrect characters," a report by Zhengrui reveals. The objects Macartney had described in such loving detail were never referred to by the mandarins other than by their number in the list. No one ever wondered what they might be for; the important thing was to make sure that the set was complete.

The Chinese began loading the crates onto large junks on August 2. It was no small task. A report from Viceroy Liang Kentang, dated August 3, explains: "In all, there are 590 pieces to be transferred from the Barbarian ships to the port. The handling operations are proceeding without interruption but are not yet complete. The passengers of the ships will enter the port only after the tribute has been entirely unloaded."[14] In other words, the members of the embassy would not be authorized to disembark until the Chinese had taken delivery of all the gifts. The "tribute" was their passport.

The job was finished on August 4.[15] It had to be repeated in Dagu, where the inventory was loaded onto smaller junks that would carry it upriver to Tongzhou (about a dozen miles from Peking). There the expedition would finally go ashore. "The Chinese sailors are all very strong and work well, singing and roaring all the while, but very orderly and well regulated, intelligent and ingenious in contrivance and resource. . . . Mandarins . . . received the articles and gave accountable notes for them, so that no loss or mistake is likely to happen."[16]

"Thinking the Chinese were little skilled in the use of the mechanic powers, we had provided . . . double pulleys to tranship the heavy packages," wrote Winder. The precaution was "very needless, for they managed by their own method the heaviest things with incredible ease and dispatch."[17] Hüttner was no less surprised: "We feared that the large pieces would not survive transfer from the ships to the junks undamaged. These fears proved groundless, because of the numbers of men employed and because of their extreme attentiveness. The strength of the Chinese is greater than might be expected of a people nearly all of whose diet consists of rice and water, whereas our seamen receive meat and strong beverages daily."[18]

These observations would remain true today. Chinese handling skills are undeniable, and their diet still consists essentially of rice and boiled vegetables. The beef and mutton the British enjoyed in 1793 remain rarities.

Reassured by all this diligence, Lord Macartney decided to let the *Lion* and the *Hindostan* sail off. The sea bottom was uncertain, the crews prey to illness. He therefore sent the ships back to the Zhoushan Islands, where supplies could be taken on in deeper water. But Captain Mackintosh, the commander of the *Hindostan*, would go with him to Peking. He could then return to England with the first reports of the initial negotiations.

When the ambassador disembarked from the *Lion* on August 5, the crew treated him to three cheers and a nineteen-gun salute.[19] But the seamen were "much disappointed and not a little mortified" to have come so far without "being able to see the so famed capital of China."[20]

Two men were particularly annoyed at being left behind: Fathers Hanna and Lamiot, the French priests who had joined the expedition in Macao but were now denied permission to disembark. One does not enter the emperor's service in the company of a barbarian envoy. The priests were told to return to Macao and apply to the viceroy of Canton, as the immutable procedure stipulated. It would not be changed, not even as a favor to a great embassy.

12

" 'Tis New to Thee"

(August 5–7, 1793)

THE PREREQUISITE of the gifts having been dealt with, the baggage, soldiers, and servants were all packed into junks with a low enough draft to sail upriver to Dagu. Macartney and his retinue, however, had the satisfaction of entering Chinese territory on the three lightest British ships, the *Jackall*, the *Clarence*, and the *Endeavour*.

The flotilla sailed into the mouth of the Baihe River on August 5. Once again the British were taken aback by the large number of boats around them and by the crowds that gathered on the riverbanks. "Great numbers of houses on each side, built of mud and thatched, a good deal resembling the cottages near Christchurch, Hampshire."[1] "The young children were mostly naked. The men in general were well-looking, well-limbed, robust, and muscular," though they ate "very little meat."[2] It never occurred to Macartney—described by one of his companions as subject to "a violent fit of the gout"[3] because of "his gastronomic indulgence"—that this compulsory frugality actually fostered good health.

His lordship was even more charmed by the women: "Among those who crowded the banks we saw several women, who tripped along with such agility, as induced us to imagine that their feet had not been crippled in the usual manner of the Chinese. It is said, indeed, that this practice, especially among the lower sort, is now less frequent in the Northern Provinces than in the others. These women are much weather-beaten, but not ill-featured, and they wear their hair, which is universally black and coarse, neatly braided, and fastened on the top of their heads with a bodkin."[4] The dazzled ambassador fell into an uncharacteristic lyricism: "I could scarcely refrain from crying out with Shakespeare's Miranda in *The Tempest*: 'Oh wonder! How many goodly creatures are there here! How beauteous mankind is! Oh brave new world that has such people in it!' "

He had apparently forgotten Prospero's disenchanted warning to the princess: " 'Tis new to thee." Macartney was as happy as a Christopher Columbus whose triumphal voyage had finally brought him to Cathay. "The troops were drawn up on the southern bank," he wrote, "and made a tolerably good appearance. The mandarins, Wang and Qiao, who had dined with us aboard the *Lion*, now came to visit us, and pressed us much to accept their invitation to a banquet on shore which had been prepared for us; but being a good deal fatigued, I declined it, and proceeded up the river about a mile further to the yacht provided to convey me to the city of Tongzhou, within twelve miles of Peking. This yacht was clean, comfortable, and convenient." Macartney naturally assumed that the other members of the mission had been equally pampered: "Similar care and attention seemed to have been paid to all the other gentlemen."[5]

Not so. Dinwiddie, the astronomer, had less pleasant memories. Compelled to stretch out on a bench for the night, he was so uncomfortable that he took refuge on the outside deck, where he tried to sleep leaning against a coil of cable.[6]

In the People's Republic, as under the empire, the heads of delegations, considered "distinguished guests," are treated with a refined solicitude in sharp contrast to the rustic simplicity of the welcome reserved for everyone else. Hierarchy in Chinese society was strict, and so it remains.

THE EMBASSY spent three days in Dagu. Gifts, baggage, and men all had to be transferred from the large junks to smaller boats that could sail farther upriver, to Tongzhou. Thirty-seven were required. A veritable fleet.

The members of the embassy, accompanied by about a hundred mandarins, were well pleased with these boats in which they would spend the long days of the journey to Peking. They now entered the immense network of rivers that furrowed China. "In China and Indostan," Adam Smith had written admiringly, "the extent and variety of inland navigations save the greater part of this labour [of land transport], and consequently of this money, and thereby reduce still lower both the real and the nominal price of the greater part of their manufactures."[7] One reason the economist so admired this particular aspect of the "Chinese model" was that it was precisely during the 1770s that the British began to build canals linking their various industrial basins, thus closing a millennial gap with China.[8]

These "yachts" were much better suited to British ideas of comfort than the crude junks they had sailed on until then. Each had six cabins for gentlemen, two that served as galleys, and one dining hall. "In the windows, transparent silk fluttered in the breeze."[9] The wood was coated with a yellow varnish that far surpassed the varnishes of Europe in brilliance and delicacy.[10] Hüttner expressed one discreet regret: "These boats had all the necessary conveniences, save the one we Europeans regard as the most essential."[11] A privation that would follow them everywhere.

Several high-ranking mandarins informed Macartney that the viceroy of Beizhili, sent by the emperor to meet him, had just arrived from Baoding, a hundred miles distant. At eight o'clock that morning, August 6, the ambassador, Sir George, young Thomas, and Mr. Plumb climbed onto palanquins "of bamboo, covered with satin, and carried by four stout fellows, two of them before and two of them behind."[12]

Escorted by a contingent of cavalry, they made their way to the Hai-shenmiao, "or Temple of the Sea God, where the viceroy had taken up his quarters."[13]

Tents decorated with streamers had been set up in the temple grounds. Several companies of soldiers armed with sabres were on hand, and there were horsemen with bows and arrows. But not a firearm in sight. The viceroy cordially greeted the four visitors at the temple gates, then invited them into a large hall, which was soon filled with members of his entourage.

After the ceremonial tea, "inquiries about our health," and expressions of "the Emperor's satisfaction at our arrival," they came to the point: "We now entered upon the business."[14] Macartney's impatience is palpable. It was impossible to get anything done without the pointless but obligatory exchange of compliments, a practice that remains a source of exasperation to visiting Western businessmen who have planes to catch and sometimes manage to get signatures on contracts only moments before departure.

Macartney "informed the viceroy that the train of the embassy consisted of so many persons, and that the presents for the Emperor and our own baggage were so numerous, and took up so much room, that we should require very spacious quarters at Peking." The viceroy then told the ambassador that the emperor wished to see him in Jehol, in "Tartary," the "mountain capital where he sought to escape the summer heat."

Macartney was disconcerted. This was a major complication. If they had to go as far as Jehol, many of the gifts would have to be left behind in Peking, for they would certainly be damaged in such a long land journey. He could only reiterate his hope that the embassy "would be attended with all the good effects expected from it."

Exactly who told Macartney that he would have to go on to Jehol? According to Zhengrui's report, it was Wang and Qiao, speaking to the ambassador on board the *Lion* on July 31. According to Macartney's journal, it was Liang Kentang, during their meeting in the Temple of the Sea God on August 6. Which of them distorted the record? Was Zhengrui trying to conceal the fact that Wang and Qiao had failed to perform a task that was actually his responsibility? Or was Macartney trying to suggest that really important news was conveyed to him only by the highest-ranking officials? In any event, the Imperial Archives make it clear that the Chinese had long assumed that the barbarians would contemplate the Son of Heaven in the Tartar lands.

More immediately, the ambassador asked the viceroy to arrange for medical treatment for his "sickly" seamen and to grant Sir Erasmus Gower permission to have the ships repaired, either at Miao Island or in Zhoushan, "for the advancing season required his speedy departure from the Gulf of Beizhili."[15]

"It is impossible," Macartney wrote enthusiastically, "to describe the ease, politeness, and dignity of the Viceroy during the whole conference, and the attention with which he listened to our requests and the unaffected manner in which he expressed his compliance with them. With regard to the ships, . . . he offered to supply them with twelve months' provisions immediately." His lordship noted in passing: "I hope this does not forebode his wishes for our speedy departure."[16] Macartney did not suspect that the Chinese never even imagined that he wished to remain permanently.

But how could anyone be suspicious of this venerable and pleasant old viceroy with his long silver beard, small sparkling eyes, and benign aspect?[17] Liang Kentang's career had been exemplary.[18] Born in 1715, he won his doctorate in the examinations of 1756 and went on to serve as district magistrate, prefect, provincial judicial commissioner, and deputy governor of Hunan. In 1791 he became viceroy of Beizhili, winning his peacock feather and yellow jacket. His path now crossed Macartney's, but his career continued after their encounter. At more than eighty years of age he took part in the banquet held to honor the "thousand grand old men." At eighty-five, being too old to serve actively in the administration, he was granted the honorary title of governor-general of the grand canal. He was the very model of the enlightened official whose "ease, politeness, and dignified carriage . . . could not be exceeded by the most practised courtier in modern Europe."[19]

WHEN THEY RETURNED to their junks, the British were treated to the most lavish meal they had yet been offered. As he ate, Macartney had plenty of time to ponder the two new issues that had arisen in his conversation with Liang.

The emperor's stay in Jehol had upset his plans. His aim was to open a permanent legation, one that could be located only in the capital, a capital as fixed as those of Europe. He also wanted spacious premises, and not only because of the gifts. He would not entertain the remarkable proposal Zhengrui had made to Campbell and Hüttner during their scouting trip on July 26:[20] that any merchandise the British had brought along for sale be stored in the Catholic missions. The British had nothing to do with the missionaries, and in any case they had nothing to sell. What they wanted were premises of their own.

Another of Macartney's objectives was to open the Zhoushan Islands to British trade, and he had cleverly used his squadron's difficulties as an excuse to ask permission to moor his ships there temporarily.

On the question of the Peking residence, Macartney had the feeling that he had made his point, and he was to be given satisfaction on the issue of the squadron's moorage. He therefore felt reasonably content. The Chinese were less happy. The viceroy noticed immediately that the ambassador was ignorant of the rites. The imperial edict stipulating the terms of his audience with the emperor had been read to him; in his account of the meeting, however, Macartney does not even mention this formality, which seemed trivial to him.[21]

But it was precisely on this point that the court would judge him, and he had already been found wanting, as is shown by the correspondence sent to the court in Jehol by the mandarins.[22] Instead of prostrating himself nine times before the emperor's edict, as all the Chinese had done, the envoy of the king of the Western Ocean merely doffed his cap. The viceroy had been told not to be too exigent about etiquette, but simply to observe and report.[23] He therefore said nothing to Macartney, but he described the scene for the emperor:

"On August 6 *Ma-ga-er-ni* and others disembarked to request an interview. Your slaves made it known that the Great Emperor had an Instruction to communicate to them. The envoy, having removed his hat, stood deferentially. Your slaves proclaimed to him as follows: 'Our Great Emperor has specifically instructed us to see to you. While en route to Jehol, you shall have the right to food in the residences, and after touching the ground with your forehead before the Great Emperor, you will be invited to a banquet and will receive gifts. Upon your return to your country, you will be granted a year's worth of grain. As to meat and other perishable foodstuffs, local officials will provide you with these.' The envoy and others, having listened respectfully, were filled with gratitude. The interpreter spoke in these terms on the envoy's behalf: 'We have come from afar to celebrate the Ten Thousand Year anniversary by touching our forehead to the ground.' Your slaves, having proclaimed the welcoming edict, invited the tributary envoy and the others to enter the great hall of the East and to proceed with the customary salutations.* *Ma-ga-er-ni* and the others again removed their hats and saluted by joining hands; they were most deferential." The report absolves the offender's intentions, which were highly respectful. But he had no manners.

Having made his report, the viceroy began to take some distance from the mission. At dawn the next day he sent Wang to tell Macartney of his intention to pay a visit. But because of his advanced age, he would not be able to cross the walkway to the junk. Macartney replied that he would be "sorry to be the occasion of the Viceroy's risking either his person or his health for the sake of a visit of ceremony."[24] Wang explained that the viceroy would come as far as the walkway on his palanquin and would then present his "visiting ticket." He hoped that the ambassador would regard this gesture as an actual visit.

And so it was. The viceroy arrived with great pomp, preceded by a military parade and accompanied by an impressive retinue of mandarins. They all knelt as the palanquin was placed on the ground. Liang then handed his calling card to an officer, who passed it on to the interpreter. Then, without further ado, the viceroy returned to his quarters.

Macartney could hardly believe his eyes, but he was determined not to take offense. The night before, the viceroy seemed like a man who would be undaunted by a journey of a hundred miles, yet this morning he claimed to be unable to cross a walkway to a junk. In other words, he was more than willing to receive visitors, but not to go visiting. Yet he had been subtle enough to demonstrate his superiority only with his opposite number's prior approval. A subtle lesson in the diplomatic arts.

As for the calling card, that was common practice in China at the time (and is all the rage again today, inspired by the businessmen of Hong Kong, Japan, and South Korea, who are virtually obsessed with it).

Barrow tried to save face for the embassy by noting that the dimensions of the calling card were commensurate with the honor being paid to Macartney: "The old viceroy of Beizhili's ticket to the Embassador contained as much crimson-coloured paper as would be sufficient to cover the walls of a moderate-sized room."[25]

But Macartney would have had every reason for outrage had he been aware of the contents of a letter from the court being conveyed to Liang and Zhengrui at the very moment the three men were talking. "The post of viceroy is august," it said. "Were Liang Kentang to accompany the tributary envoy, the latter might well find in this a source of conceit." The

---

* In other words, to kowtow before a table of perfumes, on which inscriptions represented the "real presence" of the emperor.

venerable old man was therefore advised to leave town, on the pretext of having to inspect some construction work on the banks of the Yongding River. "In this way we must keep these visitors from afar in check."[26] Spoken like the good Tartar horseman the emperor was: handle the reins with firmness and flexibility.

In this same message, however, Qianlong took a conciliatory line on the kowtow, acknowledging differences in culture: "If the English do not submit to the ceremonies, let them simply observe the customs of their own land. There is no point in forcing them to kowtow."

It sounds like a stunning concession, but in fact the emperor was not backing down at all. He knew the difference between the essential and the secondary, and his leniency applied only to gestures of submission to his emanations: the kowtow to an edict, an imperial banquet, a table of perfumes, or a legate. Qianlong was prepared to forgo such symbolic homage, whose ritual significance was in any case well beyond the meager ken of these Western barbarians.

Qianlong then chided Zhengrui with this acid barb: "Were this envoy to prostrate himself before you, it would do honor neither to him nor to you."[27] With such a kowtow, the barbarian would be honoring not the physical person of the legate, but the spiritual presence of the emperor, represented by his legate. And if he kowtowed without knowing what he was actually doing—namely, submitting to the perfection of the Celestial Order so as to prepare himself to receive civilization—then the gesture would do no honor to him either. After all, is there anything honorable in the greeting of a dog that has been taught to sit up and beg?

In a new letter to the same mandarins, however, Qianlong shifted the emphasis.[28] He now compared Macartney to the Annamite sovereign Nguyen, who, though himself a king, gracefully submitted to ceremony, even kowtowing to a mere dish of food. Macartney was not a king, but an envoy pledging his allegiance. He therefore owed the imperial legate respect.

Qianlong's recommendations continued to waver between exigence and leniency. On the one hand, "treated too favorably, a Barbarian becomes arrogant." On the other, foreigners had to be allowed to practice their own "customs" (he used the word *su*, connoting "vulgar practices"), which were quite distinct from "ceremonies" (*li*). The latter, representing the supreme expression of ritualized courtesy, were incomprehensible to barbarians who had not yet been baked in the Celestial hearth.

In a letter to the chevalier de Guignes, who still believed himself the representative of the king of France in Canton (though, actually, Louis XVI had been beheaded seven and a half months earlier), Father Raux wrote: "The vessels of Ambassador Macartney are in Tientsin, and six

missionaries have been convoked to Jehol."[29] Indeed, on August 7 Heshen*
had selected several of the most competent members of the Western missions, skilled clockmakers well acquainted with astronomy and geography,
and ordered them to Jehol.[30] They had been summoned in their capacity
as experts in Western affairs and languages. The emperor, too, was getting
ready.

* Heshen, Qianlong's all-powerful favorite, was the chief minister, who presided over the Grand
Council, the Grand Secretariat, and other state organs. The British referred to him as "prime
minister" or "Grand Colao."

13

Gifts or Tribute?

(August 8–10, 1793)

THE PREPARATIONS for departure went smoothly. The "machinery and authority of the Chinese Government," Macartney marveled, "are so organized and so powerful, as almost immediately to surmount every difficulty, and to produce every effect that human strength can accomplish."[1] The envoy of the world's most antibureaucratic society could not help admiring its most bureaucratic.

On the evening of August 8 Macartney called out the regimental band to celebrate the success of the operations. The astronomer remarked that the martial airs made very little impression on the Chinese seamen.[2]

The following morning the Chinese responded with deafening copper gongs and drums, which gave the signal to cast off. All the boats had "the noisy instrument of the gong," Winder remarked, "on which they incessantly beat, and deprive the traveller of rest. In fleets they serve for signals to the vessels to stop or proceed, and to the trackers."[3]

In less than an hour the entire fleet had begun its journey upriver, moving at a pace of about five miles an hour.[4] It would take two days to cover the eighty winding miles to Tientsin, the next stopover. The astronomer wrote that the meanders made for an enchanting landscape. In just a few hours, the compass needle made an entire revolution of the dial.[5] "At every instant," writes Hüttner, "we passed boatmen who were quick to gape at us, amazement on their faces; many burst into laughter, pointing at one or another singularity in our persons or our dress. A countless crowd of curious onlookers instantly assembled on the riverbanks."[6]

Inveterate sailors, the British carefully examined the many cargo boats. "Several of them are of great size: from 100 to 160 feet long though seldom more than 25 feet broad. They are built very strong, of the shape of a long flat-bottomed trough curved upwards at each end, but the poop considerably higher than the prow and projecting a vast way behind the sternpost which thus appears almost in the middle of the vessel. The sails are of mats or of cotton, made like a fan to fold up with bamboo sticks, and when wanted to be set are drawn up from the deck with great labour (for they are ignorant of the use of the double pulley). . . ."[7]

Anderson counted six hundred boats over a twenty-four-mile stretch of river and at least twice as many anchored along the banks; "nor shall I hesitate to add, that, on the most modest computation, we beheld at least half a million of people." There were "elegant villas and delightful gardens; while the more distant country offers the prospect of splendid cultivation and landscape beauty."[8]

Among the banners that gave the flotilla its festive air were several that seemed somewhat disturbing. "The Chinese," Hüttner noted, "must have been quite flattered by the arrival, from so distant a land, of an embassy so large as to occupy so many boats, for they had written on the banners, in large characters in the language of their country: envoy paying tribute to the Great Emperor."[9] On these banners, as on the list they had been given, the mandarins had replaced the word *li* ("present") with *gong* ("tribute"). The ambassador expressed displeasure at the substitution, but the mandarins explained that gifts for the emperor were always called *gong*.[10]

The explanation sounded plausible, but it would not do. Macartney meant to become the first permanently accredited ambassador to the emperor. He was not simply one more temporary envoy declaring his country's submission. As such, he was carrying *presents*, not tribute. But the relevant documents show that the Chinese refused to recognize this distinction. From the outset they were determined to treat this mission with the same protocol, and the same vocabulary, as any other.

The emperor saw to this personally. When the list of presents reached Jehol, Qianlong was keenly irritated by the "whimsical title" Macartney had appropriated for himself in the Chinese translation: *qin chai*, or "legate of the sovereign," which was exactly Zhengrui's title. The emperor reacted immediately, issuing an edict on August 6: "In an effort to honor the envoy, the English interpreter has imitated the titles of Our Court. To act in this way is to be ignorant of the weight of words. In conformity with the rites, *Ma-ga-er-ni* is entitled only to the appellation *gong shi* [conveyor of tribute]."[11]

In conformity with the rites. In other words, with what had always been and must forever remain: "in all future translations the title should be replaced by 'tributary envoy' or 'vassal envoy.'"

There was only one emperor, and that was China's. To accept the term *legate of the sovereign* would be to concede equal status to the king of

England. Furthermore, Macartney had to be defined not in terms of his relation to the man who had sent him, but in terms of what he was coming to do: declare allegiance.

As the pillar of universal order and humanity's sole intercessor before Heaven, the emperor could admit to no equal. He was the first of all men of letters and the guardian of custom. "The gentleman widely versed in culture but brought back to essentials by the rites," said Confucius, "can . . . be relied upon not to turn against what he stood for."[12] No barbarian would ever be permitted to approach the Celestial Order without conforming to China's words and rites.

Zhengrui was then asked to slip this phrase into his conversation: "The Celestial Court already possesses the objects that your country is bringing in tribute."[13] That would stop the tributary envoy from taking pride in the allegedly extraordinary character of these objects.

This was in fact a deliberate attempt to deflate the British, and the Korean tributaries, impartial witnesses, reveal the emperor's bad faith: "These English offerings, original and ingenious, were unequaled among the Westerners."[14] Which was just what the British themselves thought.

Like Macartney, the emperor intended to leave nothing to chance. The impending clash over ceremony was not rooted in mere superficial touchiness. Deep convictions were at issue—respect for cosmic order on one side, sense of honor on the other. The disagreement was not due, as the British imagined, to misguided interference by junior officials; nor, as the Chinese believed, was it a matter of barbarian ignorance. For the British, it was the refusal of a people who felt borne by the wings of history to humble themselves; for the Chinese, it was the defense of the rituals, long ago established once and for all, that lay at the very foundation of civilization itself. The impasse of protocol masked a confrontation of two different worlds.

As though dreading the collision, Macartney managed to avoid any incident for the time being, pretending that the use of the word *gong* on the banners was a mere lexical inaccuracy. But he was no fool. An entry in his (unpublished) account of the mission, dated November 9, 1793, indicates that he feared that any protest on this subject would not only fail to achieve a rectification, but might even bring his mission to an early end.[15]

EVEN A MARITIME people finds it tedious to stay on the water when land is but a gangplank away. A few of the British had been granted the privilege of going ashore in Macao, Zhoushan, or Dagu, but most had left their vessels only to transfer onto the junks. The astronomer, determined to bring back a wealth of information that would dazzle the learned societies of Europe, therefore marked August 10 as a red-letter day.

To begin with, he performed the first measurement of latitude "ever conducted on this river." Result: 39° 10 min. N. The same as Toledo, Spain. Next Dinwiddie went looking for plants. He noticed a specimen that was used to make dye and plucked a sprig of it. Linnaeus had never catalogued it. Another first, of which the scholar was quite proud. A Chinese onlooker came over and handed Dinwiddie a worthless vegetable, provoking general hilarity. He complained that the Chinese of the lower classes indulged in such silly jokes at every opportunity.[16] His curiosity about the plants was soon overwhelmed by Chinese curiosity about him, and the astronomer had to beat a retreat to avoid being smothered by the crowd.

On dry land, even more than on the yachts, the British were at the mercy of the natives, whether gawking onlookers or military officers supposedly protecting the visitors from gawking onlookers. "Whenever a European went ashore . . . the presence of a soldier with him announced the immediate protection of the government; and might have been intended also, as a check upon his conduct."[17]

From August 5 on, the food was Chinese, and the British reacted with a mixture of fascination and revulsion. "A separate table for the gentlemen in each yacht was served up in the manner . . . of the country; . . . The Chinese method of dressing victuals, consisted chiefly in stewing animal substances, divided into small square morsels, mixed with vegetables, and seasoning them with a variety of savoury sauces, and a combination of tastes. . . . Among the most expensive articles, and accounted the greatest delicacies, were the nests of a particular species of swallow . . . and the fins of sharks. . . ."[18]

Anderson, the valet, was frankly disgusted: "We received our usual supply of provisions, which we were obliged to dress ourselves, as the Chinese are so very dirty in their mode of cookery, that it was impossible for the inhabitants of a country where cleanliness is so prevailing a circumstance of the kitchen, unless impelled by severe hunger, to submit to it."[19] Nevertheless, even he had to admit that the Chinese were experts in rice, the only touch of cleanliness in their cuisine: "They . . . wash it well in cold water; after which it is drained off through a sieve: they then put the rice into boiling water, and when it is quite soft, they take it out with a ladle, and drain it again through a sieve: they then put it into a clean vessel, and cover it up; there it remains till it is blanched as white as snow, and as dry as a crust, when the rice becomes a most excellent substitute for bread."[20] And still does. "The yellow people," Claudel remarked, "never touch bread. Instead they eagerly devour a semiliquid food."[21]

Anderson was not impressed by Chinese table manners: "The table on which they eat their meals is no more than a foot from the ground, and they sit around it on the floor: the vessel of rice is then placed near it, with which each person fills a small basin; he then with a couple of chopsticks picks up his fried vegetables, which he eats with his rice; and this food they glut down in a most voracious manner."[22]

Food was of paramount social importance to the Chinese, and meals were scheduled with ritual regularity. The sailors took their meals at sunrise, at eleven in the morning, and at seven in the evening.[23] "If there is one thing we take very seriously, it is neither study nor prayer, but food," a Chinese of our century once commented. "For us, eating is one of the rare joys of human destiny."[24]

The only Chinese the British had any real contact with were those who served them, and since the interpreter was monopolized by the ambassador, they had to communicate in sign language. But that did not stop the visitors from spinning theories. To read their accounts is to witness the birth of the classic stereotype of the sly and deceitful Chinese, quick to steal and equally quick to confess his misdeeds unashamed. "Some of the Chinese on board the junks practised the art of dissimulation in keeping back part of the provisions, which, however, were always given up with a good grace. A very barefaced trick was attempted by the cook serving two fawls, each without a leg. When signified that fawl had two legs, he laughingly pointed to the dish into which they had been put."[25]

Montesquieu accused Chinese merchants of using three scales, two of them false: "a heavy one for buying, a light one for selling, and an accurate one for those who are on their guard."[26] Barrow was even more sweeping: "A Chinese merchant will cheat . . . ; a Chinese peasant will steal . . . ; and a Chinese prince, or a prime minister, will extort the property of the subject."[27] The comptroller considered theft a Chinese national sport, but since neither he nor any of his companions had any dealings with merchants or peasants, it seems clear that they were merely repeating gossip picked up from the British in Canton.[28]

These Puritan individualists were repulsed by Chinese individuals, whom they found swinish, deceitful, and immoral, but they were struck by China's collective discipline and power. Yet another cliché was born, one resented by the Chinese to this day: the image of the country as a turbulent "anthill" of demented "ants." Seen close up, the Chinese elicited faintly contemptuous smiles from the British, but the panoramic view was one of supreme order.

As the junks continued up the Baihe, the British were treated to a never-ending, constantly shifting spectacle, even at night: "As soon as night came on, the banks were illuminated with variegated lights, from lanterns whose transparent sides were made of different coloured paper, some white, some stained with blue, and others red. The different numbers of lanterns hoisted on the masts' heads of the various vessels in the river denoted the ranks of the passengers they held; all which, together with the lights from the cabins of the junks, reflecting the water, produced a moving and party-coloured illumination."[29]

Another witness comments on the acoustical aspect of this strange sound-and-light show: "The sentinels of shore have, each of them, a piece of hollow bamboo, which they strike at regular intervals, with a mallet, to announce that they are awake and vigilant in their respective stations. This custom, as I was informed by the peyings, or soldiers themselves, is universal throughout the Chinese army."[30]

As along the Nile, there were pyramids. But these were of salt. You can still see them in the environs of Tientsin today, a region riddled with saltern marshes. Barrow estimated the total quantity of salt at six hundred million pounds, and Staunton commented: "When in the former govern-ment of France, several of its provinces were subjected to the gabelle or duty upon salt, a calculation was carefully made of the average consumption of that article. It was then deemed to be considerably under twenty pounds weight in the course of the year, for each individual. . . . But upon the supposition of the entire quantity of twenty pounds being annually con-sumed by every Chinese, the present collection of that commodity was sufficient for thirty millions of people for a year."[31] While the Chinese sought to impress their visitors with lights, the pragmatic, trade-minded British counted consumers and calculated potential profits. If the population of this province could consume six hundred million pounds of salt, how many yards of Manchester cotton could they absorb?

AUGUST 10, 1793, was the first anniversary of the overthrow of the French monarchy. Paris solemnly celebrated the rule of Reason. La Vendée was in flames.

14

The Journey Upriver

(August 11–14, 1793)

SALT PYRAMIDS were about the only new wrinkle in the landscape, and the journey up the Baihe grew monotonous. The British were relieved to reach Tientsin on August 11. This was their first big Chinese city, and they had never seen such a vast concentration of humanity, not even in London or Paris. Located at the confluence of three rivers, Tientsin was "the general emporium for the northern provinces of China."[1] Yet it seemed like an enormous suburb, resembling the Thames at Limehouse rather than Westminster, or the Seine at Javel rather than Notre-Dame. "But neither the buildings nor the river would bear any comparison, even with those parts of Redriffe and Wapping. Everything, in fact, that we had thitherto seen wore an air of poverty and meanness."[2] Tientsin gives much the same impression today. It is a gloomy city in which even the inhabitants seem bored.

"If anything excited admiration, it was the vast multitude of people that, from our first arrival, had daily flocked down to the banks of the river, of both sexes and of all ages." In those days, such a human multitude could be assembled nowhere but in China. The "populace stood in the water, the front rank up to the middle, to get a peep at the strangers."

The British thought all the Chinese looked alike. "It was an uncommon spectacle to see so many bronze-like heads stuck as close together . . . as Hogarth's group, . . . but it lacked the variety of countenance which this artist has, in an inimitable manner, displayed in his picture."[3]

Barrow enjoyed the boisterous, colorful display of official splendor: the ringing of the gongs, cymbals, and trumpets; the stage that had been set up near the river, from which actors sang, accompanied by shrill instruments; the pavilions and pagodas elegantly decorated with silk ribbons and hangings. He loved "the buzz and merriment of the crowd." But he had no illusions: "The arrival of Elfy Bey in London drew not half the crowd;

and yet the Chinese account us much greater barbarians than we pretend to consider the Mamlukes."[4] People laughed and pointed, the typical mob reaction to the unusual. Few people better fit Freud's definition of gregariousness: "The individual feels incomplete when alone, but the herd rejects all that is new or unusual."[5]

In fact, the display of pomp was a show staged by the Chinese for their own enjoyment. If the "people of the Western Ocean" were its star attraction, they were also its hostages. Macartney's journal strikes a single note of anxiety: in the midst of the many smiling faces, he suddenly spied a scowling mask. Standing on the dock with the other officials, alongside the aged viceroy, was the legate Zhengrui, the man who had refused to board the *Lion*.

The astronomer describes the scene: The gentlemen, "in full dress," were "conducted, with much parade, to a pavilion erected on purpose. To keep the crowd at a distance, the officers whipped them most unmercifully." His lordship, Sir George, and the interpreter took their places on a raised platform, to the left, facing the viceroy and the legate on the right. Seated below were the gentlemen on one side and the mandarins on the other. The pavilion "was covered and lined with mats painted on the inside, and supported by pillars, apparently of bamboo, wrapt round with red silk. A matting, and over that a kind of thin silk gauze, covered the floor."[6]

Another banquet was held. The legate's overt hostility was in sharp contrast to the viceroy's benevolent urbanity, but agreement was finally reached on the mission's itinerary.* It would sail upriver to Tongzhou, a journey of seven days, and from there make the day-long, overland crossing to Peking, twelve miles distant. The embassy would probably remain in the capital for several days to unload the gifts and baggage and to arrange for porters and teams of oxen to carry them to Jehol.[7]

Macartney reiterated his intention to leave the bulk of the presents in Peking. The legate objected. He had just been instructed "to convey *all* the objects of tribute to His Majesty."[8] Macartney replied that some of the gifts might be fatally damaged by such a journey and that on no account would he offer the emperor imperfect or damaged goods, which would be "unworthy of His Britannic Majesty to give and of His Chinese Majesty to receive." Fortunately for Macartney, the viceroy seemed amenable to his suggestion. They therefore stuck to the original arrangement, though

---

* Imperial Archives cast some doubt on Macartney's version of events. He suggests that the itinerary was the subject of delicate negotiations, but in fact it had been set down in Chinese documents weeks before.

Macartney felt "great disquiet and apprehension from this untoward disposition so early manifested by the legate."[9]

Actually, Zhengrui was merely following Chinese procedure. Tributary missions were supposed to place *all* their tribute at the emperor's feet. By insisting on leaving the most precious objects behind in Peking the British were lowering their own prestige. The legate yielded, but he must have thought these barbarians mad.

MACARTNEY WAS surprised by the flighty curiosity of the Tientsin mandarins, quite unlike the reserve of the other escorts. They shamelessly examined everything the British had, including their clothes, books, and furniture. "In seeking out the nearest resemblance between these persons and Europeans," Staunton wrote, "the character of gentlemen of rank in France, while the monarchy subsisted there, occurred readily to the mind. An engaging urbanity of manners, instantaneous familiarity, ready communicativeness, together with a sense of self-approbation, and the vanity of national superiority, piercing through every disguise, seemed to constitute their character."*[10] It was almost as though Staunton had seen the viceroy's memorandum to the emperor: "We plan to hold a banquet for the envoy on Your Majesty's behalf. Having set foot on China's soil, he may now admire the brilliance of a superior country."[11]

The archives reveal that the seemingly light-hearted courtiers were in fact quite shocked by the behavior of the British. This succulent meal was an offering not from the viceroy but from the emperor. Apparently unaware of this, the British simply ate heartily, failing to kowtow (as the Chinese did) when the food was brought to the table.

In their reports to Jehol the legate and the viceroy mention that the tributary envoy "removed his hat and touched his forehead." This latter expression was the standard euphemism for the kowtow. But how could he have "touched his forehead" without prostrating himself? In effect, these expert men of letters had invented a pious metaphor—an ambiguous formulation combining the Western idea of the doffed hat and the Chinese idea of the kowtow. Their intent was apparently to suggest that *Ma-ga-er-ni* had been as respectful as he knew how to be.

It was during this banquet that the worthy old viceroy snatched his own chestnuts from the fire, announcing that, "in accordance with a previous instruction," he now had to take his leave to oversee construction projects on the Yongding riverbank.[12]

---

* In 1804 the French translator of Staunton's book omitted this passage.[10]

Zhengrui was more long-winded in his own report, discussing the various contortions of the tributary envoy, the imperial portrait aboard the *Lion* (which he had not seen), the gifts the British preferred to leave in Peking, and their uneasy surprise when they learned that the audience would be held in Jehol. Finally, he noted that the improper appellation usurped by the tributary envoy had been stricken from the list of presents and no longer appeared in any of the documents.[13]

FOR STAUNTON the most notable occurrence was the clandestine arrival of a young Chinese who had been seen lurking around the yacht. "A youth was introduced," he wrote, "clean and composed in his dress, of a modest countenance, and humble in his deportment. He proved to be a young neophyte, a sincere convert to the doctrines of Christ, and a fervent disciple of the missionary who had regenerated him from the paganism of his ancestors. He was devoted to the commands of his ghostly father, and performed now a service of no little danger, in bringing letters to the Embassador, without permission either from the magistrates of the place from whence he came, or those where he now arrived."[14]

Staunton discovered that this young convert had taken such fearful precautions because Chinese did not have the right to communicate even among themselves, let alone with foreigners. China had no public postal system. "Expresses are continually sent on horseback . . . to the Emperor alone. . . . Slower messengers are employed for the ordinary purposes of government, and the use of the mandarines. These are charged sometimes, through particular favour, with the packets of individuals. But the provident attention of the Chinese government preserves carefully the advantage of giving information to, or withholding it, as it may deem expedient, from the body of the people."[15]

The letters, in French, were from the French missionary Joseph de Grammont, a fifty-seven-year-old Jesuit who had lived in China for a quarter of a century.[16] The first of them, dated three months earlier, was both a warning and an offer of services, and its content was as enigmatic as the manner of its delivery. Father de Grammont asked Macartney to employ him in helping to prepare the details of the embassy's reception in Peking, but he also implored him not to tell anyone that he had received the letter, which had been written in May, when inaccurate reports suggested that the embassy had already arrived in Tientsin. "I have set everything in motion, Milord, to encourage the Chinese to the most favorable possible disposition. I hasten to warn Your Excellency that it is essential not to let anyone know of the secret and principal reason for His* mission before His arrival in Peking. I hope to be of some small use to Your Excellency if, having received my letter, He deigns to honor me with His orders."[17]

Had this initiative come from the ambassador, no one would have taken it amiss. It would have been considered natural for a European arriving in China to seek the aid of another European well versed in Chinese life. An initiative in the opposite direction, however, was out of the question. As a servant of the emperor, the priest had no right to offer his services to anyone else.

The second message, dated just a few days before, warned the ambassador against a Portuguese missionary by the name of Bernardo d'Almeida, who, according to de Grammont, had been designated to serve as Macartney's interpreter in Jehol, despite—or because of—his well-known hostility to the English. "Were the affairs of the embassy to be dealt with in Peking, as I had hoped, my mind would be at rest, because it would then have been easy for me to counter the evil impressions that may be made by the foolhardy words of this Portuguese. But since the Emperor and his entire Court are now in Jehol, to which city I would be unable to follow Your Excellency without being summoned by the government, I am deathly concerned about the behavior of this Portuguese." Father de Grammont then proposed himself as a replacement for d'Almeida.

Was the Jesuit naively pursuing his own personal goals?[18] For the moment, Macartney declined to answer him. But once in Peking, he found that the priest's information was accurate: though he spoke neither English nor French, Father d'Almeida had indeed been designated by the court as the embassy's official interpreter.

Macartney requested authorization to select an assistant, someone whose language he spoke, from among the European missionaries in the emperor's service. Wang and Qiao assured him that a favorable response was likely.[19] The ambassador had not yet discovered that "as a direct refusal to any request would betray a want of good breeding, every proposal finds their immediate acquiescence; they promise without hesitation, but generally disappoint by the invention of some sly pretence or plausible objection."[20] He would later find this out (to his cost), but he never really managed to accept it: "They have indeed so little idea of its [the truth's] moral obli-

---

* The missionary, addressing Macartney in the third person, suggests that he knows the goals of the embassy just as well as the ambassador does.

gation, that they promise you everything you desire, without the slightest intention of performance."[21]

HIS RETINUE, less preoccupied than Macartney, paid more attention to the theatrical production mounted by the Chinese. Amid multicolored silk ribbons and pennants, actors twirled swords, spears, and lances in daring leaps greeted by cries of admiration from the audience. The female roles were played by men, "as the Chinese never suffer their women to appear in such a state of public exhibition as the stage." The Europeans were assured that these actors were eunuchs.[22]

The orchestra was made up of wind instruments resembling trumpets, French horns, and Scottish bagpipes, but the music was far too dissonant for British ears. Still, "we had every reason to be satisfied with the entertainment, the circumstances of which were replete with novelty and curious amusement."[23] Western impressions of the Peking Opera today would probably be similar.

Macartney's journal seems to suggest that this show was a special production for the British. But another witness lets the cat out of the bag. The astronomer writes that this "insipid" presentation actually began before the embassy's arrival and continued after it set sail, the Europeans' departure going unnoticed by the audience.[24] The Chinese never let themselves be distracted at their theater.

The flotilla prepared to cast off. The astronomer was quite critical of the equipment of the Chinese soldiers posted on the banks. Their heavy steel helmets and leather chinstraps seemed ideally suited to self-strangulation; their bows and arrows looked like London museum pieces depicting the wars of Antiquity; the rare muskets were in a sorry state.[25]

Holmes was frankly amused. The soldiers had pipes in their mouths and fans in their hands. Some of them stood, while others sat. They wore jackets "beset with thin pieces of iron or brass, which imitates an English brass nailed trunk."[26]

Staunton learned that these unsoldierly soldiers were in fact not professionals, and as a ranking official of a country that had never been comfortable with conscription, he was curious about the terms of their enlistment. "After the salutes were over," he wrote, "the gaudy dresses or uniform of the soldiers, worn upon extraordinary occasions, together with their arms, were said to be deposited in the storehouse of the station until they should again be wanted. In the intervals the men . . . are occupied in manufactures; or in the cultivation of the land."[27] You would think you were in Switzerland.

The members of the embassy reboarded their boats as the opera continued. They were saluted by cannon fire, though "guns they cannot properly be called, being nothing more than a piece of hollowed wood; one end of which is stuck in the ground, and filled with powder, is fired right into the air."[28] "The fleet set sail," Anderson observed, "amidst the greatest concourse of boats and people I ever beheld:—indeed, so great was the crowd of both, that I considered it to be impossible for us to pass without being the witness of considerable mischief."[29]

He was right to worry. One old junk carried so many onlookers that the "uppermost part of the deck" collapsed, and some forty people fell into the water, "and several of them were unfortunately drowned. Some were, indeed, saved by clinging to the ropes which were thrown out to them; though it was very evident to those who witnessed the accident, that curiosity rather than humanity prevailed on the occasion; and that the people were more anxious to get a sight of the foreigners, than to save the lives of their countrymen."[30]

A present-day Chinese has judged such behavior this way: "There are some rather bizarre heroes who would cast themselves into the water to save a child. No married man would do so. The mob is indifferent, for it must protect itself."[31] Hardened to grief, amused by novelty, insensitive to the death of others—characteristics retained by the Chinese masses today.

THE FLOTILLA NOW moved up the Baihe River by day and by night, towed by men onshore. Our travelers found the procedure astonishing. "On all the rivers of the Empire, there are Chinese whose sole occupation is to tow junks. Every hauler wears a piece of wood, the ends of which are tied to ropes set into the mast and the prow of the junk."[32] Anderson: "These pieces of wood being thrown over their heads, rest upon their breasts, . . . and when they are all ready, the leader of them gives the signal."[33]

Thus harnessed like beasts of burden, the haulers worked to a pace set by a rhythmic chant of *hoy-alla-boy*, the Chinese "heave-ho." The use of this refrain is "universal . . . among the class of labouring Chinese."[34] This type of haulage was still practiced in the 1970s.

Anderson felt sorry for these unfortunates: "I have sometimes seen them wading up to their very shoulders, and dragging one another, as well as the vessel, after them."[35] The astronomer admired their ability to pull against the current, to lift themselves out of waist-deep mud, and even to swim across tributaries of the Baihe—and all this so happily, with a kind of natural goodwill at doing their duty.[36] In fact these were forced-labor brigades, and on the return trip some of the conscripted haulers fled. But those unable to escape did seem more or less content with their lot.

The British never left their junks during the five-day trip upriver from Tientsin to Tongzhou, August 11 to 16. They were deafened by cicadas, the shrill voice of the Chinese summer, north and south, then as now. Mosquitos attacked in swarms. Even today these humid plains are not really rid of them. Macartney's agronomist's eye took in the various crops: corn, sorghum, millet, rice, cucumbers, fruit trees. He learned that droughts and locusts often caused famines. "On these occasions, robberies are frequent, and not to be repressed by all the power of government, but as they are only committed through absolute hunger and necessity, so they usually cease at the return of plenty."[37]

To make up for the shortage of housing, there were many boats "having a range of ten or twelve distinct apartments built upon the deck, and each apartment contained a whole family."[38]

As they observed cargo heading for the capital, the British noted one "article of commerce" whose use "puzzled us not a little to find out." It "consisted of dry brown cakes, not much larger but thicker than those we call crumpets. A close examination, however, soon discovered the nature of their composition, which, it seemed, was a mixture of every kind of filth and excrementious substances, moulded into their present shape, and dried in the sun. In this form they are carried to the capital as articles of merchandize, where they meet with a ready market from the gardeners in the vicinity; who, after dissolving them in urine, use them for manure."[39]

Anderson also noted, without further comment: "This evening, two of the Chinese belonging to our junk stripped themselves naked, and, picking off the vermine, which were found in great plenty on their clothes, proceeded to eat them with as much eagerness and apparent satisfaction, as if they were gratifying and delicate food."[40]

The Chinese escorts did what they could to enliven these rather dreary days. Qiao, a charming traveling companion, was unexpectedly animated during the tea ceremony, dancing and singing, humming along to songs played on the flute by Thomas Hickey, one of the painters, while tapping out a rhythm on the teacups with his fan.[41] "There is something quite exquisite about the courtesy of well-educated Chinese," Father Huc would confirm fifty years later.[42]

Qiao even offered the British some amusement at his own expense by trying to speak their language. The astronomer noted that he had little trouble with "very well" and "How do you do?" but no luck at all with "broth." What foreigner hasn't struggled with the English *r* and *th*?[43]

The monotony of the landscape was finally broken by the sight of one of the palaces used by the emperor on his travels. The sumptuous building, its yellow tile roof gleaming in the sun like polished gold, made quite a contrast to the miserable hovels with walls of mud-packed wicker, covered with thatch, or sometimes with grass. Only the state dared flaunt its opulence. In this, as in much else, the empire was not very different from Communist China: individual wealth was always suspect, at least during the regime's first three decades.

Staunton was struck by how different the Chinese landscape was from the European countryside, riddled with chateaus: "Every large building was said to be destined for some public use; or for the habitation of a man in office. Such, if there were, to whom fortunes had descended from their ancestors, but who held no department under government, were certainly not ostentatious in their possessions; and enjoyed their riches in obscurity."*[44]

To build, after all, is to assert permanence, and in China no particular situation is guaranteed to last. The state bestows honors and functions and withdraws them with equal ease, just as Heaven may bring a dynasty down by withdrawing its mandate. "The great creations of the Chinese," Teilhard de Chardin later noted, "are made of dust, their solid substances (jade, bronze, porcelain) serving only as trinkets."[45] "To go forward when employed and to stay out of sight when set aside," as Confucius put it.[46] A minor incident now showed the British how true this was.

Some of the provisions spoiled in the heat, and Macartney was stunned by the swift punishment meted out to those responsible. On Wang and Qiao's orders the mandarins in charge of supplies were "deprived of their buttons" (in other words, demoted), while the servants were whipped with bamboo sticks.

Macartney tried to intercede on their behalf: "Though we were heard with great attention, and received very flattering answers, we easily perceived that no indulgence was to be expected on such occasions."[47] He was beginning to understand that while the Chinese were always accommodating in words, in practice they never deviated from custom.

---

* Undoubtedly a slight exaggeration, as proved by the villas of Suzhou and Hangzhou. The artistry of Chinese gardens, so widely imitated in the West, was originally developed by wealthy men of letters (albeit behind high walls) and later copied by merchants.

15

A Lesson in the Kowtow

(August 15, 1793)

THE VICEROY and the legate had sent the court cautious reports on the tributary envoy's behavior at the Tientsin banquet. But these reports caused confusion in the Grand Council in Jehol, where the clever metaphor was taken literally. Macartney had "touched his forehead"? How was it that he had behaved so badly upon receipt of the imperial edict in Dagu and so well upon being served the banquet in Tientsin? Had he really made such rapid progress?

Heshen wrote back to the viceroy on August 14, requesting clarification.[1] "We know that the Western peoples are ignorant of the ceremony in which the forehead touches the ground. Perhaps the viceroy's letter, failing to distinguish this nuance, was erroneous in indicating that the envoy touched his forehead to the ground."

Had he really done so, then the matter was settled. On the other hand, had he merely bowed his head, he must be advised that in the emperor's presence he would have to conform to the ritual to which all tributaries, even kings, submitted. A man-to-man warning, delivered in confidence, was required. Macartney must be told: "If you do not learn to perform this ceremony, you will be the laughingstock of all the envoys of the vassal countries, who will regard you as boors." Moreover, he would fail in the mission with which the king of England had entrusted him. "There is no point in concealing the truth."

The tone taken in this letter is quite different from the earlier affability. Just a month ago, the emperor seemed prepared to grant the envoys from across the seas some leeway. A mere eight days before, there had been talk of allowing each side to honor its own national customs. What had changed? An intriguing comment in the Lazarist archives suggests one possible explanation: "At first the kowtow ceremony seemed not to be a great problem; the mandarins did not insist on it. But the government's attitude suddenly changed when word of the embassy's aim was received: what it was asking was not something that could be purchased with jewels and fine words. The rejection of the kowtow was a pretext."[2]

When word of the embassy's aim was received? The letter from George III had not yet been delivered. Only the British were supposed to know what Macartney intended to discuss with Qianlong.

Perhaps there had been a leak. Or perhaps the emperor had given further thought to the improprieties of the letter listing the gifts, concluding that they could not be written off to mere ignorance after all. One thing is certain: though the exact reason for the shift was not yet clear, a decisive turn in the fortunes of the mission occurred during those first two weeks of August.

Heshen's letter, dated August 14, arrived the next day. Zhengrui, the legate, immediately realized that he stood to lose his mandarin's button over this business. Something had to be done. Macartney was suddenly torn from his contemplation of the landscape by a visit from his guides.[3]

Zhengrui was accompanied by Wang and Qiao, who seemed more solemn than during their usual courtesy visits. The emperor, they explained, was well pleased. He had placed two fine residences at the embassy's disposal, one in the city of Peking, the other six miles into the countryside but more pleasant and very close to the Summer Palace, the Yuanming Yuan. And the schedule had been finalized: ceremonies marking the emperor's birthday would be held in Jehol in mid-September, after which the embassy would immediately return to Peking. The emperor would soon follow, so it would not be necessary to bring all the gifts to Jehol after all. Macartney expressed relief.

"They then introduced the subject of the court ceremonies with a degree of art, address, and insinuation that I could not avoid admiring."[4] The Chinese began by talking about dress. Chinese clothes, they said, were better than Western ones, for they impeded neither genuflection nor prostration. "They therefore apprehended much inconvenience to us from our knee-buckles and garters, and hinted to us that it would be better to disencumber ourselves of them before we should go to court."[5]

Macartney reassured them. He pretended to believe that the emperor would prefer the British envoy to pay him the same homage he would have paid to his own king.

The three mandarins then described the kowtow, as though Macartney were ignorant of it. Macartney replied that he intended to send a letter to Peking on this matter. The mandarins changed the subject, explaining that "the Emperor did not mean to hunt this autumn as usual, but to remove with his court very early to Peking on purpose that we might not be delayed. I told them His Imperial Majesty would judge from the King's letter, and from my representations, what was expected of me at my return to England, and what time would be sufficient to enable me to transact the business I was charged with."[6]

Macartney may have cloaked his rejection of the kowtow in excessively accommodating circumlocutions. Or the interpreter may have garbled the message. Or perhaps Zhengrui was simply too optimistic, convinced that he had brought the foreigners to their senses. Whatever the reason, the legate reported to the court that the British were "deeply ashamed of their ignorance of ceremony" and that, under his direction, "they were regularly practicing prostrating themselves, touching their foreheads to the ground."[7] Zhengrui must have known he was lying, and that his deceit could cost him dearly. He therefore left himself an out: "Nevertheless, the Barbarians are rather strongly inclined to forget the prostration."

The Chinese also raised another subject of dissatisfaction: Tibet. Here again, clothing was involved. Macartney was told that British troops in Bengal had given aid to Tibetan insurgents. Europeans fighting against Chinese armies on "the Roof of the World"? They had allegedly been recognized by their hats. An astonished Macartney denied it: "I was very much startled at this intelligence, but instantly told them that the thing was impossible."[8]

A few days later the Chinese asked him whether the British would be willing to aid them in suppressing the Tibetan rebels. His lordship smelled a rat. He replied that British possessions in India were much too far from the combat zones to allow any kind of intervention. "Because if our troops could come thither to the assistance of the Emperor's troops, they could equally have come to the assistance of his enemies."[9]

The slowness of the means of communication had put Macartney in a delicate situation. He had left England in September 1792, before hearing any news of the fighting that had occurred in the Himalayas six months earlier. The Gurkhas, a warrior people of Nepal, had launched an expedition against Tibet in the autumn of 1791, fomenting rebellion among the local population. The authorities of this Chinese protectorate appealed to Peking for aid, and Qianlong quickly intervened. In the spring of 1792 a Chinese army commanded by Fukang'an, the viceroy of Canton, crushed the Gurkhas. Nepal was forced to declare itself a tributary of the empire, and the Tibetans paid a high price for the Chinese intervention. London had been completely unaware of these developments when Macartney's embassy left Portsmouth, and the British in Macao knew nothing of them in June 1793, when the expedition passed through. The news arrived only on September 8. Not until his return to Canton did Macartney find out, to his relief, that his denials of British complicity with the Gurkhas were accurate.[10]

Difficulties of communication caused tragic misunderstandings several times during this planetary epic, but this was primarily a case of negligence on the part of Lord Cornwallis, the governor-general of India, who had not thought to send Macartney a message in Batavia.

But if the British had not intervened, who was wearing those "hats" the Chinese had spotted among the Gurkha turbans? Had there been some mistake? An optical illusion due to the great altitude? Perhaps a few sepoy deserters from the British army?

Macartney tried to extract himself from the awkward impasse as best he could. But his enthusiasm, so keen in Dagu, was now blunted. He seemed anxious and upset, shaken by his uncertainty about the situation in Tibet. In fact the incident was over and done with, but only the Chinese knew that. Why did they raise it now? Perhaps the embassy's objective had been discovered, and someone was trying to sabotage it. The man who was spreading these rumors was General Fukang'an himself, the viceroy of Canton, who had led the punitive campaign. And he had every reason to distrust the British.

MACARTNEY WAS ASKED whether he had a personal gift for the emperor. Though he had not thought of this, he had the presence of mind to reply that he hoped that the emperor would be so kind as to accept a coach (his own). He took the opportunity to add that he had also arranged for some presents for the Chinese New Year, which fell on January 31, 1794.

This was a way of making it clear that he would be happy to remain in Peking at least until then. "I have entertained a suspicion, from a variety of hints and circumstances, that the customs and policy of the Chinese would not allow us a very long residence among them."[11] He remembered that it had been mentioned that the emperor planned to return to Peking quickly, giving up his hunting season. In order to open more serious negotiations with the embassy, or to avoid delaying its departure? What if the Chinese refused to allow the mission to stay beyond the forty days ordinarily granted to tributary delegations by the Tribunal of Rites?[12]

Macartney saw that the legate was having trouble concealing his hostility. On the other hand, he believed he had won over Wang and Qiao. Whenever the legate's back was turned, they made no secret of their dislike of their Tartar colleague, who had "the exclusive privilege of corresponding with the Court upon our affairs, and whom they consider a sort of crazy and morose man."[13]

On disembarking in Tongzhou, Macartney took careful note of how the embassy was treated. The greeting was attentive: more food than they could eat, repeated military honors, banners, music, and fireworks at night.[14] They were given everything and never permitted to pay.[15] But Macartney was beginning to see all this largess as a by-product of rituals that were slowly but surely hemming him in.

British freedom of movement, for instance, was narrowly restricted. When "we desired to make little excursions from our boats into the towns, or into the country, to visit any object that struck us as we went along, our wishes were seldom gratified. The refusal or evasion was, however, attended with so much expression, artifice, and compliment that we soon grew reconciled and even amused with it. We have indeed been narrowly watched, and all our habits, customs, and proceedings, even of the most trivial nature, observed with an inquisitiveness and jealousy which surpassed all that we had read of in the history of China."[16]

Macartney was learning fast. Though he had ignored the banners inscribed Envoy Paying Tribute to the Great Emperor, he realized that they heralded a basic misunderstanding that would not be easily dispelled. "There is no point in people taking counsel together who follow different ways," said Confucius.[17] Macartney had set out for China with very definite principles, which he believed were universal. But he was now beginning to realize that they would open no doors in China. He felt as if he were being stuffed into a funnel by a hand gloved in silk.

16

Residing in a Temple

(August 16–21, 1793)

TONGZHOU WAS as far as they could go by boat. Peking was only twelve miles away, but the embassy now had to wait several days while the flotilla was turned into a caravan. Macartney wanted to go on ahead, leaving Staunton behind to see to the unloading of the baggage. Permission denied. In Chinese eyes, he was a bearer of tribute, and as such could not be separated from it.

They waited. So near and yet so far. "At six o'clock this morning [August 17] two palanquins were sent for Lord Macartney and Sir George Staunton, who, . . . were carried to the temple . . . escorted by a party of Chinese soldiers and an immense concourse of spectators."[1] The others, confined to their junks, witnessed yet another masterpiece of baggage handling.[2] The expedition's cargo was taken from twenty-seven junks and stored in two vast bamboo warehouses, called pandals, that had been built in just a few hours. "Such rapidity in the movement of such a great number of packages, most of them of enormous weight, could have been seen nowhere else but in China, where everything is at all times under State command."

Once again the great capitalists had cause to admire the efficiency of the state economy: "Even the most laborious tasks are undertaken and executed with a readiness and even a cheerfulness which one would scarcely expect to meet with in so despotic a government. The Chinese seem able to lift and remove almost any weight by multiplying the power: thus they fasten to the sides of the load two strong bamboos; if two are not sufficient, they cross them with two others."[3] There was no shortage of manpower, nor of bamboo.

Anderson marveled at the meticulous vigilance of the Chinese: "At the gate of this inclosure there were two Chinese officers, who inspected all cases and packages which were brought from the junks: the first took their dimensions . . . and then pasted . . . a counterpart of their minute on every separate article; nor was a single box, package, or parcel, suffered to pass, until it had undergone this previous ceremony."[4]

The retinue joined Macartney in the temple in which the embassy was lodged—or rather, to which it had been assigned. One of the twelve bonzes remained, to keep the flame of the altar burning in the sanctuary. The rest were withdrawn, turning the temple into a caravansary for the honored visitors.

Inns did exist, but they were little more than wretched huts in which ordinary travelers could have a cup of tea and stretch out on the floor, for a small price. Guests had to supply their own bedding, and customers who couldn't pay had to leave their blankets behind.[5] In Peking traveling merchants were housed in the headquarters of their guilds, and candidates for the imperial examinations had special hostelries of their own. The Chinese hotel system was so rudimentary (and remained so into the 1980s) that when the state wanted to honor respected guests, temples had to be requisitioned.

These places of worship also served as gathering places for community life. It was here that romantic assignations took place, and here too that troops were sometimes quartered. The temple was the most beautiful setting in any town.[6] Lavishly decorated, even today it is often the only structure worth visiting in many cities, but it is almost always empty. Many temples were laid waste by soldiers earlier this century, long before the tempest of the Cultural Revolution.

The British were served lunch: 12 times 12 dishes, the 144 plates of honor still customary in our own day. No longer shielded by their junks, they now had to suffer these awkward banquets in public. A crowd gathered to laugh at their ineptitude with chopsticks.[7]

Was there any way at all to make an impression on the Chinese? In a harbinger of things to come, Macartney resorted to his military apparatus. He had his personal guard posted at the outer gate, "that they might attract the notice of the Chinese, and elevate the consequence of the diplomatic mission, in the general opinion of the people of the country; a circumstance on which the success of it was supposed, in great measure, to depend."[8]

The British gawked at the Buddhist temple. They were surprised that in China, unlike in the West, religion had not spawned an original architecture. The temples were no different from the imperial palaces or princely residences. Geomancy dictated a north-south orientation, and there were horned roofs surmounted by protective figurines or menacing gargoyles, paved courtyards, and pavilions supported by columns varnished in red.[9]

Even the many sacred inscriptions were not peculiar to the temples. China was devoted to the written word, and the country was like an enormous library. "Adages and maxims are everywhere: on pagodas, monuments, merchants' signs, and the doors of private houses."[10] The authors have changed, but the taste for quotations offered for public contemplation persists.

"One notices various statues, in wood or porcelain, of male and female divinities"[11] arranged into a Celestial hierarchy mirroring mandarin society. The British were offended by these sculptures, whose "anatomical proportions" are "outrageous."[12]

The monks who had been displaced by the embassy returned at the hours of prayer. "Opposite to the servants quarter was a small square building" that contained "an altar, with three porcelain figures as large as life placed upon it; there were also candlesticks on each side of it, which are lighted regularly every morning and evening, and at such other times as persons come there to pay their devotions. Before these images there is a small pot of dust, in which are inserted a number of long matches, that are also lighted during the times of worship."[13]

The rooms the monks had left to the British were clean and pleasant. The beds consisted of platforms "of boards, raised upwards of a foot above the surface of the floor. . . . A thick woolen cloth . . . was spread upon the platform, and with the addition of a cushion, formed the whole of the bedding. . . ." In China "at least the common people, continue to wear at night a considerable part of the dress which covers them in the day."[14] Except in summer, when they slept nude. Both practices are still common.

China and its clergy were hierarchically structured, and the barbarians were treated hierarchically as well: "The separate apartments, belonging to the superiors of the monastery, were now allotted to the principal persons of the Embassy. In some of the other rooms the priests had suffered scorpions and scolopendras to harbour thro' neglect."[15] The astronomer had to share a room with seven companions. "But such was the heat that two gentlemen were to have prefered the portico, and in consequence of the appearance of a scorpion another gentleman followed."[16]

Despite the presence of the British, throngs of worshipers continued to visit the temple. Staunton was amused at the resemblance between Buddhist and "Roman" worship. The statue of Shengmu, or Sacred Mother, was "a representation which might answer for that of the Virgin Mary." She was depicted "sitting in an alcove with a child in her arms, and rays proceeding from a circle, which are called a glory, round her head, with tapers burning constantly before her."[17] And the monks—with their long, coarse woolen robes, "bound with cords round the waist," living an ascetic, cloistered life of fasting and penance—inevitably recalled the Franciscans.[18]

In principle the government "does not interfere with mere opinions," prohibiting "no belief which is not supposed to affect the tranquillity of society"—such as Christianity. But the British found this particular proscription a good deal less outrageous than the ban on Western trade, and it had not tarnished China's reputation for tolerance among the European intelligentsia: "There is in China no state religion. . . . The Emperor is of one faith; many of the mandarins of another; and the majority of the common people, of a third, which is that of Fo [Buddha]."[19]

A somewhat oversimplified assessment. The most widespread religion was syncretistic: part Buddhist, part Taoist. This or that parish, brotherhood, or individual might recognize one or another holy figure. It was a matter of local piety and personal preference more than deliberate theological choice. The mandarins took a dim view of the popular Taoist religion, whose diversity ill suited the official order and whose initiation rituals escaped the regime's control. As far as the British were concerned, there was "no more superstitious nation." Macartney noted that "sheep and oxen"[20] were sacrificed to Confucius.

On the eve of a marriage, a journey, or any "undertaking of importance" the Chinese would visit the temple to address the divinity. "This is performed by various methods. Some place a parcel of consecrated sticks, differently marked and numbered, which the consultant, kneeling before the altar, shakes in a hollow bamboo, until one of them falls on the ground; its mark is examined, and referred to a correspondent mark in a book which the priest holds open."[21] Others used "polygonal pieces of wood" that "were thrown into the air. Each side has its particular mark." The side that appeared when the die fell sent the priest to the corresponding page of the book of destiny. "If the first throw be favourable, the person who made it prostrates himself in gratitude, and undertakes afterwards, with confidence, the business in agitation. But if the throw should be adverse, he tries a second time, and the third throw determines, at any rate, the question."[22] The same procedures may be seen in Communist China today, where temples closed since the Cultural Revolution are now being reopened to worship.

"Few Chinese," Staunton wrote, "are seldom said to carry the objects, to be obtained by their devotion, beyond the benefits of this life."[23] Here he spoke too soon. Countless examples attest to belief in a future life. Father Le Comte, for example, tells of being asked to baptize an old man seeking to escape the fate the bonzes had predicted for him: reincarnation as a horse.[24]

AN ECLIPSE of the moon was supposed to be visible in the Chinese sky on the night of August 21. The astronomer checked the calculations. At first he had trouble understanding the chronology Wang presented to him, but once he worked his way around the interpreter's mistakes, he saw that it was accurate. The British knew that one of the tasks of the European missionaries attached to the court was to predict astronomical events, but what really impressed them was the government's political manipulation of the phenomenon. "As the party passed along the streets, they observed, in several places on the sides of houses, the projection of a lunar eclipse, which was to happen soon afterwards."[25]

Taking advantage of the reverential fear eclipses aroused among the populace, the emperor arrogated to himself the exclusive right to eliminate the element of surprise. Among the Chinese, imperial predictions of eclipses inspired "veneration for that superintending power from whence such knowledge was immediately derived to them."[26]

Having penetrated the secrets of the heavens, the court was more than merely metaphorically Celestial. And the emperor was careful to maintain exclusive access to this knowledge. His science thus offered proof of his own holiness and thereby kept science itself beyond the reach of the masses. The emperor's Christian astronomers made him a great wise man:

> Nothing in all this universe is secret to him,
> And for him our fate is an open book.[27]

The emperor's power rested on the knowledge of the few and the ignorance of the many, a state of affairs that perpetuated that ignorance and transformed it into respect, thus keeping the people in their place.

But the most exact science of all was the science of government. The emperor "never ventures on any undertaking of importance at the approach of such an eclipse, but affects to withdraw himself from the presence of his courtiers, to examine strictly into his late administration of the empire, in order to correct any error, for the commission of which the eclipse may have been an admonition, and invites his subjects to offer him freely their advice."[28] The absolute despot summons his subjects to free examination of his conduct. Let a hundred flowers bloom.

"When the eclipse began, we heard a frightful commotion. Bells, gongs, clappers, and drums made a noise so dreadful that the dragon, who held the moon in his claws, might be frightened and thus abandon his prey."[29] The dragon was the most honored animal in China. A being of the other world, he would sometimes (though rarely) appear in the clouds. More often he remained coiled at the bottoms of lakes. If awakened, he would shake the world. He was neither good nor evil, but simply a part of the order of the universe. The clamor intended to make him release his lunar prey, like the noise made to bring the soul of a dying relative back into his body, was considered a thoroughly practical initiative.[30]

The embassy had no love for the missionaries, who had not "been disposed to confer a real service on the Chinese" by instructing "a few of their youth in the principles of arithmetic and the mathematics." Why had they kept the Chinese in such obscurantist darkness? Barrow pointed an accusing finger: "It would be too great an instance of self-denial, to relinquish the advantages and the credit which their superior skill had gained them over a vast empire, by making the individuals of that empire participate in their knowledge."[31]

As our travelers saw it, the system endured because the Celestial bureaucracy and its Western supernumeraries had a common interest in it. Immobility was guaranteed by the advantages drawn from it by those who perpetuated it. The missionaries had become accomplices in superstitions they might have been expected to oppose. They were the emperor's partners in maintaining a system of popular ignorance and hidden knowledge.

Thus did the British Protestants, advocates of the universality of Western knowledge, denounce the Catholic clergy's dedication to obscurantism. But their view was unfair. The real history of missionary efforts to spread Western science in China from the sixteenth century onward suggests that it was rather the British who were guilty of ignorance. It was not the priests' fault that they had done no more than dig a tiny niche in the walls of Chinese indifference and hostility. The ambassador himself would soon find out just how thick those walls really were.

17

A City of Wood

(August 19–20, 1793)

ANDERSON WAS the boldest tourist: "This morning [August 19] I took the opportunity to visit the city of Tongzhou, with its suburbs; and with no small fatigue, and some trouble, I traversed the greatest part of it." Like most Chinese cities, this one was square. It was "defended by a very strong lofty wall, with a deep ditch on the outside of it in the most accessible parts . . . three gates . . . are . . . defended by ramparts mounted with cannon: there is also a strong guard within them towards the city, in a state of regular duty. These gates are always shut at ten at night, and opened at four in the morning."[1]

The single-story houses were of wood, except for the mandarins', which were of stone or brick. "Glass is not any where used in China for windows, and the common substitute for it is a thin glazed paper, which is pasted on the inside of a wooden lattice."[2] There was little or no furniture. The façades, often color-washed, revealed the residents' status: only mandarins could have red walls. The decor of the shops was pleasingly elegant. Streamers indicated the nature of the merchandise. The "most wretched habitation is equally furnished in regard to its idols, . . . every kind of vessel that navigates the sea, or the river, being provided with its deity and its altar."[3]

The sidewalks (still a rarity in Europe at the time) and the mats stretched from house to house above the narrow streets to block out the sun would have made it very pleasant to walk around—except for the press of the crowd. The curiosity cut both ways. "I was sometimes surrounded by twenty or thirty [people], who pressed so much upon me, that I was frequently under the necessity of taking shelter in shops, till the crowd that persecuted me was dispersed; and, in return for the protection afforded me, I made some purchases of fans and tobacco-pipes."[4]

Anyone who traveled in China had these little misadventures, at least until the early 1980s, when the presence of foreigners in the big cities (though not in remote villages) became commonplace.

The court dress and powdered wigs of the British were shocking enough to the Chinese, but surprise became outright stupor at the sight of the black servant one of the Englishmen had taken aboard in Batavia. "The jet hue of his complexion, his woolly head, and features, peculiar to the negroes, nothing like which had been remembered to have been seen before, in this inland part of China, led some of the spectators almost to doubt, whether he belonged to the human species; and the boys exclaimed that it must be a black demon, *fan-quee.* . . ."[5] African students arouse similar (and not always benevolent) curiosity in Chinese universities today.

Anderson claimed that the Chinese were shocked by the black man not because of the color of his skin, but because he was a slave. That seems hard to believe. Though rare, slavery did exist in China. "A tolerable horse and a man slave are usually about the same price," Barrow noted.[6] And Staunton reported that "a man may sell himself . . . in certain cases, such as . . . to assist a father in distress, or if dead, to bury him in due form."[7]

We get some sense of just how incredulous Anderson was when we read in his journal that the Great Wall was built "in the short space of a few years."[8] His eye was sharp, but he was so naive about this "best of all worlds" that those of his reflections not based on direct observation may be safely disregarded. For instance, when he turns his pen to the "negro," Coombes.

THE BRITISH SAW no one who looked like a beggar. "No small portion of the people seemed, it is true, to be in a state approaching indigence; but none was driven to the necessity, or inured to the habit, of craving assistance from a stranger."[9] When famine threatened, the emperor came to the rescue: "He orders the granaries to be opened; he remits the taxes to those who are visited by misfortune; he affords assistance to enable them to retrieve their affairs; he appears to his subjects, as standing almost in the place of Providence, in their favour: he is perfectly aware by how much a stronger chain he thus maintains his absolute dominion, than the dread of punishments would afford. He has shewn himself so jealous of retaining the exclusive privilege of benevolence to his subjects, that he not only rejected, but was offended at, the proposal once made to him, by some considerable merchants, to contribute towards the relief of a suffering province."[10] In fact, however, famine was a lethal threat in China, despite the emperor's granaries.

In fat and lean years alike, the state system prevailed. No private fortune was allowed to elicit the people's gratitude.[11] The British were definitely far from home, while yesterday's China is close to today's.

THEY WERE INTRIGUED by a strange, eleven-story building "perfectly solid in the first and second story. There is not even the appearance of a door or window in either. There are no remains of steps, or other means of ascent to the third story."[12] Though covered with grass and moss, the monument was well maintained.* Its foundation was said to antedate the Great Wall. Now supremely useless, long ago, according to Staunton, it may have been "a watch-tower, to guard against the sudden approach of the Tartar enemy."[13]

Some of the British were "supplied with horses, to ride about in the neighbourhood." They admired the fertility of the countryside, where it would soon be time for the autumn harvest. The main crops were millet and corn, introduced from America during the sixteenth century (a rare instance of an imported innovation). The grain was flailed with sticks or crushed under horses' hooves. A large roller was also used for this purpose. The winnowing machines were so similar to those used by the peasants of Europe that Staunton took it as confirmation that this was indeed a Chinese invention. Chinese agricultural techniques, communicated to Europe by missionaries, had contributed to the eighteenth-century agrarian revolution in the West. Lightweight plows equipped with seeders were another Chinese invention.[14]

The animals were kept out of sight and were given their feed of beans and mashed straw in cowsheds. China was short on pastureland. Nor were there any villages, just scattered huts "without fences, gates, or other apparent precaution against wild beasts or thieves."[15] The British admired this degree of security. Their own society was far more violent, not only in the cities, but also on the highways and in the countryside.[16]

The peasant women "carry on most of the tasks which can be exercised within doors. Not only they rear silk-worms, and spin the cotton, . . . but the women are almost the sole weavers throughout the empire. Yet few of them fail to injure their health, or at least their active powers, by sacrificing, in imitation of females of superior rank, to the prejudice in favour of little feet. . . . Notwithstanding all the merit of these helpmates to their husbands, the latter arrogate an extraordinary dominion over them, and hold them at such a distance, as not always to allow them to sit at table, behind which, in such case, they attend as handmaids."[17]

---

* In August 1986 the same eleven-story pagoda in Tongzhou was being restored.

This custom, always a feature of Confucian households,[18] is still prevalent among the popular classes, particularly in the south and in Taiwan. It seemed more outrageous to the British than it would have to a peasant of the Rouergue or of Corsica.

Staunton waxed ethereal. The dominion of men over women, he wrote, "is tempered, indeed, by the maxims of mild conduct in the different relations of life inculcated from early childhood amongst the lowest as well as highest classes of society. . . . Plain sentences of morals are written up in the common hall, where the male members of the family assemble. Some one, at least, is capable of reading them to the rest."[19] These observations would be equally valid today. It makes one wonder how the many bloody upheavals that mark China's history were possible, up to and including the savage outbursts of the Red Guard youth.

Old people lived with the younger members of their families, serving "to moderate any occasional impetuosity."[20] Old age was always considered a virtue to be honored. Father Amiot tells us that in 1785 Qianlong brought to Peking 192 families whose patriarchs had six generations of living descendants. Four of these men were more than a hundred years old. "The Emperor sent them magnificent gifts and personally composed verses in their honor."[21] In Maoist China these ancient traditions were adopted by the party. Family members—or neighborhood work teams—would gather to read the writings of Mao Zedong Thought. According to a principle set forth by Zhou Enlai, all the various types of committees were to be based on the "triple union of ages"—youth, adults, and the elderly—which would ensure the presence of their respective qualities: impetuousness, strength, and moderation, blended as judiciously as in primitive societies.

The culmination of this respect for age was ancestor worship. Every household had a family tree, and forefathers were constantly recalled as examples. The clan would gather at their tombs at least once a year, and family members never lost track of one another.

British admiration for these close family ties was typical of Westerners among whom the more restricted nuclear family was fast becoming the rule. Every member of the Chinese extended family had a duty to aid all the others. Staunton concluded, rather too hastily, that "institutions of public benevolence" were "rendered little necessary, where the link which unites all the branches of a family, brings aid to the suffering part of it without delay, and without humiliation."[22] In effect, social security was provided by the family, while the state intervened only when major catastrophes outstripped the resources of clan solidarity. But Sir George's formula could well be turned on its head: it was the state's inadequacy that forced the family to play this role. This remains true today: the state's inability to pay pensions to peasants is one reason for the fierce popular resistance to the government's policy of one-child families. Without sons, who will take care of us in our old age?

Social cohesion, respect for hierarchies, duty of filial piety, ancestor worship: these Confucian virtues have defied the passage of centuries, down to our own day.

18

Gathering Clouds

(August 16–21, 1793)

IN THE MEANTIME, Macartney was concentrating on his mission, and there were more and more signs of trouble. First came a new letter from Father de Grammont, dated August 16, alluding to but not explaining various rumors then current in Peking: "I implore Your Excellency not to scorn my offer of service. Matters here are handled quite otherwise than elsewhere, and that which would be seen as just and reasonable among us is here often regarded as mere ill will and unreason."[1]

What were the motives of this tenacious priest? Gratitude for the protection Britain had accorded the Society of Jesus? Hope that the success of the mission might ameliorate the lot of foreigners in China? Belief that the embassy was seeking to help propagate the faith? If so, he could not have been more wrong. This expedition of nearly seven hundred members with not a clergyman among them was imbued with the spirit of the Enlightenment: indifference to the religion of their own state, overt contempt for the "Roman" confession. Since the good father was surely not so naive, it seems more likely that his repeated initiatives were motivated in no small part by internal rivalries within the narrow circle of missionaries. And fear of imperial reprisal is a more than adequate explanation for his apparently fanciful mania for secrecy. The letter Macartney received on August 17 was no more explicit than its two predecessors had been, but its insinuations must have alarmed him.

The next morning Wang informed Macartney that the caravan would be ready to leave on August 21. It would pass through Peking and proceed directly to the Summer Palace, where the ambassador would find a European missionary at his disposal. Wang made no mention of this missionary's nationality, but the information seemed to confirm de Grammont's warnings. The court meant to assign Macartney an interpreter, most probably this d'Almeida against whom the priest had warned. In imperial as in People's China, in Tsarist Russia as in the Soviet Union, the interpreter's task is not to translate local realities in the manner most practical for the visitor, but to present them in the manner most flattering to the regime. Every intermediary, collaborator, or servant must therefore be selected by the authorities themselves.

That night Wang and Qiao came to see Macartney alone, explaining that a temporary indisposition prevented "the Tartar" from accompanying them. Macartney suspected a diplomatic illness.[2]

In fact, Zhengrui was anxiously awaiting the court's reaction to the highly optimistic report he had sent from Tientsin, and in view of the uncertainty, he preferred to avoid direct contact for the moment. The chief minister's directives, sent from Jehol on August 18, arrived the next day: "Your report has been read. When the tributary envoy arrives in Jehol, he will have to respect the etiquette. You are to instruct him in all the details. He will be shown into the audience only after being versed in the salutations of the kowtow."[3]

The orders were clear, but it remained to apply them. Zhengrui knew very well that his head was on the block.

The time had come to dot the *i*'s, or perhaps the *yi*'s, which in Chinese means "customs." The British were beginning to realize that China was probably the world's most ritualized society. "A man . . . has no way of taking his stand unless he understands the rites," the master said.[4] Ritual was the foundation of Confucianism, and Confucianism was (and remains) the essence of Chinese cultural identity. Of the Thirteen Classics in the syllabus of the imperial competitions for the mandarin examination, three were devoted to rituals. Of the six Court Tribunals, which roughly corresponded to ministries, the Tribunal of Rites was expressly charged with ensuring their permanence, primarily by overseeing the movements of envoys and the receipt of tribute, but also by controlling the "system of examinations," itself one of the chief instruments in the perpetual reproduction of this system.

Having counted his chickens before they hatched, Zhengrui now feared that his entire career was at stake. He therefore subcontracted the mission to Wang and Qiao, who might be better able to sugarcoat the pill. Macartney anxiously took note of their attempt.

The two colleagues broached the subject while accompanying the ambassador back from a visit to the pandals. "They told us that the Emperor's answer was come to our request of having a European missionary to attend us, and that we might choose any of the Europeans in the Emperor's service then at Peking."[5] That was good news, though it later proved to be false. Macartney was also told that the emperor held the British in "the highest esteem." That seemed worrisome. The Chinese, even today, insist on the most pleasant possible language when they know that disagreements are inevitable.

Finally they came to the point. Wang and Qiao explained that the kowtow was simultaneously an insignificant detail and a major obstacle. To bolster their argument they knelt on the ground and "begged me whether I could not perform it. On my declining it, they applied to my interpreter to do it, who, although a Chinese, said that he could only act as I directed him; they seemed a little disappointed in finding me not so pliant in this point as they could wish."[6]

For his part, Macartney was disappointed that they had not been more consistent: "They are wonderfully supple, . . . though . . . not very sumptuous in regard to veracity, saying and unsaying, without hesitation, what seems to answer the purpose of the moment. . . . when we hinted to them any contradictions that occurred, . . . [they] seemed to think them of trifling consequence." But they were polished enough not to show displeasure at their failure: "We then entertained them with a concert of music, which they appeared to be much pleased with."[7]

On the morning of August 19, near the pandals, Macartney met with Wang, Qiao, and the "Tartar legate," who had apparently recovered from his indisposition. The ambassador presented them with eight small brass cannon, ready to be shipped with the rest of the gifts and baggage. The astronomer affirms that these were "capable of firing seven shots a minute."[8] The legate treated the artillery pieces offhandedly, claiming they were nothing new for China. Macartney did not believe that for a moment, but he was beginning to realize that the Chinese would never acknowledge inferiority in any domain whatsoever. Since it was out of the question for the mandarins to admire the gifts, they preferred to ignore them in a kind of incantatory disdain: British superiority would contravene Celestial Order; therefore it could not exist.

An incident during the artillery demonstration annoyed the mandarins. Seeing some people across the river, more than five hundred yards away, they tried to wave them off with loud cries and frightened gestures. ("The Chinese are naturally such timid cowardly fellows," Holmes reported, that "the very sight of these pieces strike them with terror, and the report will immediately drive them to a considerable distance, like so many frightened sheep.")[9] But the British were shooting blanks, and Lieutenant Parish stood just a few yards in front of the mouths of the cannon as they fired. The mandarins were keenly irritated by this. The astronomer drew a philosophical conclusion: the more ignorant men are, the more offended they become at the revelation of their ignorance.[10]

"That night," reads an entry in Macartney's journal dated August 19, "died of dysentery after a long illness Henry Eades, a cunning artist in brass and iron."[11] Eades was the first member of the expedition to die on Chinese soil. Dysentery felled many others later on, especially during the return trip, by which time the funerals were hasty affairs. Eades, however, was buried with quite a fanfare, "in order," Anderson says, "to inspire in the Chinese a high idea of our funeral ceremonies"—and probably of their military execution as well.

"As no clergyman accompanied the embassy," Anderson notes, "I was appointed to read the funeral service of the Church of England on this melancholy occasion."[12] Had Louis XV or Louis XVI sent an embassy to China, it surely would have included priests, and much would have been made of the encounter between Christianity and Confucianism. But the British, while perhaps not mere envoys of the East India Company, were Protestant advocates of "universal priesthood." Everyone was his own minister.

"At nine o'clock the procession began in the following order: detachment of the royal artillery, with arms reversed; the coffin supported on men's shoulders; two fifes playing a funeral dirge; the person appointed to officiate at the grave; the mechanics, servants, & c. two and two; the troops then followed, and closed the whole. . . . Thus we proceeded, with all due solemnity, to the burying ground."[13] The authorization given the British to bury one of their own in a Chinese cemetery showed "a liberality that would not have been practiced in some of the countries of enlightened Europe." Meaning: enlightened but Catholic. The Chinese, however, may have regarded burial in Chinese earth as symbolic of a particularly definitive and radical assimilation to Celestial Civilization. A kind of eternal kowtow.

As expected, the ceremony was a resounding success, drawing a crowd "that the most splendid spectacles would not assemble in the cities of Europe." The soldiers formed a circle around the grave. Prayers were read, and the casket was buried. The detachment fired three volleys. Anderson cast a curious glance at the surroundings. "In the burying ground was a great number of marble and stone monuments with inscriptions on them. Some of these memorials were gilt, and enriched with various devices of no ordinary sculpture; this funeral spot is very extensive, but without any enclosure. There are, indeed, no public places of burial, but near large towns and cities; as, in the country, every one is buried on the premises where he had lived."[14]

The British discovered that the location of graves was a delicate matter determined by geomancy. Coffins were hermetically sealed with various layers of lacquer and sometimes remained in private houses for months while awaiting the selection of a favorable site for burial, such as a tomb in the middle of a cultivated field. In those parts of China that are not flat, cemeteries are often located on high ground or in stony, uncultivated earth. "What was considered of importance: the common people, food, mourning, and sacrifice," Confucius said.[15] A compromise had to be found between the dual obligations of cultivating the soil and guarding the cult of the ancestors.

19

Passing Through Peking

(August 21, 1793)

THE EMBASSY reached Peking on August 21 and continued directly through the city to their quarters near the Yuanming Yuan, or Garden of Perfect Brightness, some six miles to the west.

The travelers had spent the night on benches, their camp beds having been sent ahead the evening before. They were thus scarcely refreshed.[1] Drums (which often sounded during the night watch in Chinese cities) had awakened them at two in the morning. Four palanquins were reserved for the ambassador, Sir George, his son, and Mr. Plumb. As for the others, their two-wheeled carts had neither springs nor seats, and there was nothing for it but to sit cross-legged on the floor, Chinese-style.[2]

British composure may have been ruffled by the discomfort: "We were then summoned to prepare for our departure, when a scene of confusion and disturbance took place among ourselves, which, whatever its real effects might have been, was not calculated at least to give any very favourable impression of the manners and disposition of the English nation. . . . it was a matter of no inconsiderable difficulty for the mandarins to assign the people to their respective vehicles."[3] Chinese settling a dispute among the British! The procession set out at four in the morning.

It was led by three thousand porters carrying six hundred packages, some of them so enormous that it took thirty-two men to lift them. A similar number of officials kept order and directed the bearers. Then came eighty-five wagons and thirty-nine handcarts filled with wine, beer, and other European produce, plus munitions and various unbreakable objects. The eight artillery pieces followed.[4]

Behind the baggage came the Tartar legate, the court mandarins, and their large retinue, traveling in chairs, on horseback, or on foot. Then the ambassador, and finally his escort, whose vehicles were "not unlike in appearance to our funeral hearses."[5] Wang and Qiao brought up the rear.

The carriages were jolted by every bump in the road, and the British pondered the superiority of their coaches, while calculating the profits to be made by exporting them to China.

As the procession passed through the city of Tongzhou, vast crowds gathered along the way. The heat became unbearable as the morning wore on.[6]

Macartney sat in his palanquin and contemplated the enormous paving stones, each one twenty feet long by four feet wide. He wondered how such gigantic slabs of granite had been transported. A white marble bridge with five arches* drew his admiration.[7] "The road to Peking," Winder wrote, "is a hundred and fifty feet wide, shaded with statch trees. The middle part is flagged with standards twenty feet long and broad in proportion."[8] At nine in the morning the travelers finally entered the capital, the "tender object of our aspirations."

Guards of honor fired salvos from atop the city walls. "The outside of the city wall, though not perfectly perpendicular, was smooth, but the inside was upon a considerable bevel; the rows of bricks which form it, being placed, like steps, one above and behind the other, such as are described to be the faces of the Egyptian pyramids."[9] But the British did not view these walls with a tourist's eye. How effective was the enclosure? Its height and thickness were certainly impressive,[10] yet there were no cannon, only loopholes for archers. "Over the gate was a watch tower several stories high. In each story were port-holes for cannon, painted, as sometimes on the sides of merchant vessels which have none," Staunton noted, not without irony.[11]

Once in the capital, the British discovered a human sea whose tide never seemed to ebb. "Different trains" led young brides to their husbands, to the sound of "squalling music." Families in mourning accompanied, "with lamentable cries, corpses to their graves." Mandarins walked in processions "bearing umbrellas and flags, [and] painted lanterns." "Troops of dromedaries" brought coal from the Tartar lands. Carts and wheelbarrows groaned under the weight of vegetables. "All was in motion."[12]

The convoy had trouble clearing itself a path. "The sides of the street were filled with an immense concourse of people, buying and selling and bartering their different commodities. . . . Pedlars with their packs, and jugglers, and conjurers, and fortune-tellers, mountebanks, and quack-doctor commedians and musicians, left no space unoccupied."[13]

The muddle of sounds included the "loud bawling" of merchants

---

* Similar to the famous Palikao bridge in Tongzhou, where Cousin-Montauban, commanding Anglo-French forces, clashed with imperial troops in 1860. In fact, it might well have been the very same bridge, for I found no other along the indicated line of march.

hawking their wares, barbers snapping their scissors, and street quarrels.[14] "A file of soldiers now moved along with the procession on each side of the road, armed with whips, which they continually exercised in order to keep off the crowd. . . . We observed, however, that though the soldiers were very active and noisy in brandishing their whips, they only struck them against the ground, and never let them fall upon the people."[15]

The "crowds of people that surrounded us," Anderson wrote, seemed motivated by curiosity more than respect. "I cannot but feel some degree of regret, that no alteration was made in the ordinary travelling, and shabby appearance, of the embassy, on such an important occasion. . . . the appearance of the Ambassador's attendants, both with respect to the shabbiness of their dress, and the vehicles which conveyed them, bore a greater resemblance to the removal of paupers to their parishes in England, than the expected dignity of the representative of a great and powerful monarch."[16] The valet's pride was hurt.

IN TIENTSIN the British had seen no women, but here in Peking they were plentiful. Anderson remarked on their "great delicacy of feature, and fair skins by nature, with which, however, they are not content, and therefore whiten them with cosmetics; they likewise employ vermilion, but in a manner wholly different from the application of rouge among our European ladies, for they mark the middle of their lips with it by a stripe of its deepest colour, which, without pretending to reason upon it, certainly heightened the effect of their features. Their eyes are very small, but powerfully brilliant, and their arms extremely long and slender." They wore "a sharp peak of black velvet or silk, which is ornamented with stones, and descends from the forehead almost between their eyes." (This sort of small hat is still worn by elderly women in Peking.) And most of all: "their feet, free from the bandages . . . were suffered to attain their natural growth."[17] Anderson did not realize that these women were not Chinese but Manchu. Peking was the capital of the Tartar conquerors. Staunton commented on the beautiful horsewomen: "A few Tartar ladies were on horseback, and rode astride like men."[18] Amazons of the steppes.

Anderson took advantage of the slowness of the march to approach several of these superb creatures. He knew no Chinese, but had learned the word *chou-au*, "beautiful." The women "seemed to be extremely diverted, and gathering round me, but with an air of great modesty and politeness, they examined the make and form of my clothes, as well as the texture of the material of which they were composed." Upon taking his leave, he shook hands, not without some anxiety about possible reactions from the women's husbands, but they did not "appear to be at all dissatisfied with my conduct."[19] He concluded, rather too hastily, that women in China were more free and their husbands less jealous than he had been led to believe. Not for a moment did he suspect that he himself was but a fleeting object of derision.

He was torn from his gallantry by quite another attraction, a "funeral procession, which proved to be a very striking and solemn spectacle." At least "fifty or sixty men," marching eight abreast, carried "on their shoulders with long bamboos crossing each other" a "large bier or platform" on which lay the coffin, "covered by a canopy decorated with curtains of satin, enriched with gold and flowers, and hung with escutcheons." Musicians played a "kind of dirge." The friends and relatives of the deceased brought up the rear of the procession.[20] They were dressed in white (which remains the color of mourning in China today). But Staunton noted that white mourning clothes should be somewhat soiled, because the etiquette "excludes every appearance of personal care or ornament from those who are supposed to be overwhelmed with grief."[21] "The most splendid of our coffin furniture," Barrow added, "would make but a poor figure if placed beside that intended for a wealthy Chinese."[22]

Luxury was the privilege of the dead, for they alone were beyond giving offense to the emperor and could therefore flaunt their wealth. Barrow wrote that coffin making was "a trade of no small rate in China."[23] Fifty years later, Father Huc would write: "The well-to-do invariably select a casket of their choice well in advance" and keep it in their homes.[24] The coffin stays at home not only before death, but after it as well. "At Canton," Winder commented, "we visited a rich merchant, and in an appartment of his house lay the embalmed body of his father, in a coffin of dark mahogany colour,* where it had lain above a year—and cost 4,000 taels."[25] It was waiting for a geomancer to indicate a favorable burial site to the deceased's descendants.[26]

STAUNTON OBSERVED that Peking's broad boulevards and low houses were in sharp contrast to the narrow streets and tall buildings of the great cities of Europe. The roads, he said, were "airy, gay, and lightsome."[27]

The avenue they were traveling on had been watered to hold down the dust. It was spanned by what looked like wooden *Arcs de Triomphe*. Large gilded characters named the people commemorated by these arches:

---

* The internal coffin was enclosed in an external one, a true luxury in a country where wood is scarce.

worthy state officials, victorious generals, and even a chaste widow. Monuments like these are still typical in Chinese cities.*

Sir George admired the shops, over some of which "were broad terraces, covered with shrubs and flowers. Before the doors several lanterns were hung, of horn, muslin, silk, and paper."[28] Barrow missed the domes and bell towers of Europe. The regularity of the streets, "laid out in straight lines,"[29] the absence of windows on the façades, and the small size of the houses gave the city "the appearance and regularity of a large encampment." A century and a half later another visitor commented that the thousands of "low, curved houses are reminiscent of rows of tents."[30] The geometrical layout of the streets would have pleased Baron Haussmann or American city planners, but it was disappointing to a man whose internal landscape had been shaped by his own, Gothic and baroque, city.

Our travelers got one fleeting glimpse of the Forbidden City as they walked along the "eastern wall of the Imperial palace, called the yellow wall, from the colour of the small roof of varnished tiles with which the top of it is covered."[31] The observation was accurate, the interpretation incomplete. The yellow that limned the wall, "gleaming like gold" on the roof of the Winter Palace, was a sacred color whose use was reserved for the emperor alone.

THE BRITISH LEFT Peking at noon, and their taxing long march finally ended near the village of Haidian, a couple of leagues into the countryside. When they reached their residence, they were left to wait while Macartney went off to negotiate their living arrangements. Time dragged on, and they grew impatient. When they went looking for the ambassador, they found him embroiled in a quarrel with the mandarins over the cramped conditions of the rooms.

But no one had the energy to argue, and in the end they gave in. The exhausted astronomer went to bed, noting in his journal that the embassy had "arrived at the journey's end."[32] Eleven months after leaving Portsmouth.

---

* There is an impressive triumphal arch on the street of the Confucian temple, in front of the building in which the mandarin examinations were held.

20

The Garden of Perfect Brightness

(August 22, 1793)

THE BRITISH WERE escorted to their new residence, a "country cottage" on the outskirts of the Yuanming Yuan, or Garden of Perfect Brightness, which Europeans would later call the Summer Palace. The huge park "contained a vast variety of elegant little buildings; in the front of most of them was a large canal for bathing, and other useful purposes."[1]

The apartments were decorated with paintings. Staunton admired the miniature landscapes, in which the rules of perspective were faithfully observed. He was far less critical than the astronomer, who felt that these paintings "exhibit a most complete ignorance of knowledge of the art of painting. People at a distance figure taller than a house at hand, and do not touch the ground."[2] But both agreed that the Chinese knew nothing of shadow and light. "A lake was represented, with trees and houses near it, almost on every side," Sir George wrote, "but a Chinese would consider it as a blemish, to render the shadow of any of those objects perceptible on the water."[3] How proud they were that Western art had mastered the techniques of relief!

In Staunton's view, European discoveries like shade and light or chiaroscuro demonstrated the absolute superiority of the West, which had not only established the "laws of science" but also penetrated the "laws of art." The British were as dismissive of Chinese painting as they were of the twelve pulses of Chinese medicine. For them, Europe's art and science were fully mature, while those of other civilizations were still in their infancy. Father Attiret, on the other hand, acknowledged that to understand Chinese art, one had to be completely immersed in it: "I had to forget everything I had learned."[4] The Enlightenment British could not imagine a taste different from their own, and they consequently assumed that the

Chinese were technically incompetent, which was simply not the case. The fact was that they were quite skillful, able to copy meticulously the European paintings, reproductions of which they had been given, according to Alexander, the expedition's best painter.[5]

In this domain the clash of cultures bred utter intolerance.

STAUNTON WAS concerned about maintenance. These buildings "had been inhabited by Embassadors from foreign courts,* . . . but had now been empty for some time, and wanted repairs."[6] Anderson put it more crudely: "This habitation . . . was inhabited by . . . centipes, scorpions, and musquetos, which infested it in every part."[7]

The British were reduced to sleeping in the hammocks and cots they had used during their voyage. "The natives have no such comfortable article of furniture [as a bed] in their houses, but sleep on a kind of mattress."[8] In fact, each culture had its own kind of bed. Most Chinese today still make do with a frame of wooden planks, or in the winter with a platform of bricks that can be heated from below.

The residence was cut off from the outside world by a high and carefully guarded wall: "nor was any person belonging to the embassy permitted, on any pretence whatever, to pass its boundaries, mandarins and soldiers being stationed at every avenue to keep us within the precincts of this miserable abode; so that we were in reality in a state of honorable imprisonment."[9]

Lieutenant Colonel Benson, a brisk and distinguished officer, "was so hurt and mortified at being denied the liberty of passing the walls of the palace, that he made an attempt to gratify his inclinations, which produced a very unpleasant affray, when he was not only forced back from his design, but threatened with very illiberal treatment from the Chinese who were on duty at the gates."[10] It was "very humiliating" for the British to be "made prisoners" while on a mission that "by the laws of European nations possesses almost universal privileges."[11] All the British, from noble lord to simple soldier, considered themselves a conquering people, and they were unaccustomed to such insidious contempt.

Neither Holmes nor Anderson nor any other Briton of comparable rank had any idea of what was going on at the top, between Macartney and the chief Chinese dignitaries. But missions abroad always entailed encounters at all levels, and relations between lower-ranking British and

---

* Today this area is part of the campus of Beida University of Peking, and its buildings are used to house foreign students.

Celestial personnel soured fast. The former, certain that they were not being treated as the emperor would have wished, accused the latter of displaying an excess of spite. This embassy had come to Peking partly to redress wrongs being committed in Canton, and now that they had arrived, they already had to consider asking the sovereign to redress further wrongs committed by his servants in the capital itself.

While Holmes approved of Benson's attempt to leave the grounds, Anderson wondered whether it might not "have been more discreet to have . . . submitted with patience to those regulations, which, however unpleasant, were such as were adopted by, and might be the usage of, that government, whose partial favour and friendship it was the interest, and therefore, the duty of the British embassy, by insinuating address and political manœuvre, to obtain and establish."[12]

As for Macartney, he flatly declared the residence "unacceptable." True, the country house and its park were "charming and delightful."[13] But he was not interested in a remote retreat. He wanted to be in Peking itself.[14] If he was not to be allowed to remain in China as long as he had hoped, then he would at least insist that he be quartered in the heart of the Chinese capital. He never imagined that he could be quarantined in Peking just as effectively as he was in these woods, and he misjudged the topography of power: moving to Peking would actually take him farther from the imperial seat.

Macartney raised the issue during Zhengrui's courtesy call on August 22. "The Tartar legate . . . said that there was a Grand Secretary* on the road from Jehol particularly appointed to attend to our affairs, and that he would send one or two of the European missionaries to me to-morrow. As the Legate seemed to be in a better humour than usual I took the opportunity of mentioning the subject of my quarters." To Macartney's great surprise, the legate replied that "he thought there could be no objection" to a change.[15]

In fact, a Peking residence had already been set aside for the embassy upon its return from Jehol, one intended to display the beauties of the capital. "It is the task of the officials of the Imperial House," chief minister Heshen explained, "to assess the extent of cleaning and decoration that may be necessary."[16] This had not yet been done, but since Macartney insisted on it, the residence could be prepared for occupation in four days.

The same instruction had outlined a detailed program of tourism. The ambassador was to be shown what he needed to see and no more. "He

---

* By "Grand Secretary," Macartney apparently meant one of the six members of the Grand Council.

shall be permitted to take walks through the Yuanming Yuan,* and to visit Lake Wanshou,[17] where he will have the opportunity to observe the nautical games. When he arrives in the capital to receive the imperial edict, he will be authorized respectfully to admire the magnificence of the pavilions. These sites will have to be prepared for the holding of the nautical games. Finally, the Emperor grants the tributary envoy permission to visit Lake Kunming† and to sail on a dragon-ship. The waters must be deep enough. You shall see to the dragging of the lake, that all may be perfect."[18]

The Potemkin villages toured by Catherine II were no more carefully stage-managed. Macartney was to be taken on a trompe l'oeil visit, but the illusion itself was as revealing as a plunge into China's depths.

---

* The Garden of Perfect Brightness contained a replica of the Versailles palace, designed by Jesuits.
† This is the lake at which the empress Cixi (or Tseu-hi) had a famous marble boat constructed, around 1890, using credits meant for the navy.

21

Meeting the Missionaries

(August 23–24, 1793)

ON AUGUST 23 Zhengrui came to see Macartney again, accompanied by six bearded missionaries dressed as mandarins—which was indeed the rank they held. Emotions ran high on both sides. For the British, this was the first encounter with some of the men whose curious and edifying "Letters," read by all educated Europeans, had created the fascination with China that was partly responsible for Macartney's visit. In fact, it might be argued that they were China's missionaries to Christendom as much as Christendom's to China. For their part, the priests may have seen the British as missionaries of a new type and rivals for the emperor's favor. If so, their concern was misplaced. The Son of Heaven was no more interested in the god of trade than he was in the God of Abraham.

The two Europes met under a watchful Chinese eye.

Four of the visiting priests were Jesuits and top-ranking Catholic mandarins: Father Bernardo d'Almeida, the Portuguese president of the Tribunal of Mathematics (the man Father de Grammont had warned Macartney about); Andres Rodrigues, another Portuguese, vice-president of the same tribunal;[1] Louis de Poirot, a Frenchman, the emperor's official portraitist;[2] Father Giuseppe Panzi, an Italian, who was also a painter. The other two were clockmaker-mechanics: Father Joseph Paris, a French Lazarist, and Father Piero Adeodato, an Italian Augustine who later served as interpreter for Barrow and Dinwiddie as they saw to the assembling of the gifts.[3]

These foreigners, granted entry to China on the strength of their scientific expertise, had only bolstered Qianlong's conviction that his country had no further need of outside support. The Jesuits had begun by casting cannon for the Mings to help them repel the Manchus; later they did the same for the Manchus to help them quell the last supporters of the Mings. Since foreign scholars were prepared to offer their services for no other recompense than the greater glory of the Celestial Empire, it was hard to see why the emperor should yield even an inch to the pretensions of this embassy.[4] When the British arrived in Tientsin, for instance, two more Lazarists were traveling with them, seeking the honor of joining the court.

Macartney was told that the missionaries who had been summoned to Jehol had been promoted in the mandarin ranks, a move meant to honor the embassy. A court letter dated August 19 reveals that d'Almeida and Rodrigues had been issued the pale blue button of the third grade, while Poirot, Panzi, and Adeodato received the white glass button of the sixth.

Macartney was uneasy about d'Almeida's promotion. A mere glance at the president of the Tribunal of Mathematics was enough to convince him that Father de Grammont's description had been accurate. This was clearly a man "of malignant disposition jealous of all Europeans, except those of his own nation, and particularly unfriendly to the English."[5] But Macartney hit upon the right response. He spoke to d'Almeida, who was supposed to be his interpreter, first in English and then in French. The Chinese were taken aback when the Portuguese stood mute, and d'Almeida was enraged by this public demonstration of his incompetence. "His mortification upon this occasion he had not sufficient temper to conceal, and almost instantly expressed very unfavourable sentiments of the Embassy to an Italian missionary who stood near him. As they conversed in Latin, he probably imagined that I should not understand or overhear him, but his looks and gestures would have been alone sufficient to discover the state of his mind if his tongue had been silent. At this visit I reminded the legate of my wishes to move to Peking, on which occasion Bernado [*sic*] very impertinently interfered. . . . All the other missionaries seemed shocked at and ashamed of his behaviour."[6]

Macartney then loosed his Parthian shot, asking one of the Frenchmen to express to d'Almeida his regret at being obliged to decline his services, since he himself did not understand Portuguese.

It was a strange argument. Macartney and his companions spoke to their own interpreter, Mr. Plumb, neither in English nor French but in Latin.[7] For Macartney to reject d'Almeida on the grounds that he did not know Portuguese seemed a flimsy pretext in an age when every educated European was taught the language of Cicero.[8]

In claiming proficiency in no foreign language but French, Macartney was effectively extending a privilege to the French missionaries. True, French was the diplomatic language of the era: it was in French that the European allies discussed their war plans against France. But there was another factor as well: Macartney had no fear of the French. The British were jealous of Portugal's base in Macao, but France had been swept from the Far Eastern map. As Van Braam, commissioner of the Dutch East

India Company in Canton, had observed: "The French nation is zero to China."[9]

Moreover, the revolution would now cut any link these priests might have had with their homeland, since there could be no doubt of their hostility to the anticlerical republic. Their position was so precarious that Macartney could consider them allies.

The British refrained from speaking Latin until d'Almeida left for Jehol. Neither Macartney nor Staunton mentions this decision in his journal, but an amused Dinwiddie does. He wondered how anyone could have believed that a true scholar might not know Latin, the language in which the majority of scientific works were written. "The gentlemen were much at a loss to know the reason for this prohibition." *Tu loqueris latinum, Domine, num?* one of the priests asked Dr. Gillan. "Learned doctors not speak Latin," the doctor replied, in broken English. "To try to impress the Portuguese fathers with the idea that the gentlemen of the Embassy could not speak Latin, was not only lowering their dignity, but asserting what evidently was not true," Dinwiddie complained. At one point Sir George sent a letter to the Yuanming Yuan reminding Dinwiddie of the prohibition on the use of Latin in the presence of the Portuguese or of the Italian priest Adeodato. Unfortunately, the letter fell into the hands of the very same Adeodato, who duly passed it on to the astronomer, glancing ironically at the Latin inscription on the outside of the envelope: *Fiat responsio*, awaiting your response.[10]

In the end they had little choice but to call a halt to the charade. Adeodato was accepted as interpreter, but only to help the British experts make themselves understood to the Chinese workers, and that by way of Latin, "a language which, a few days before, the gentlemen could not understand."[11] But Macartney's ploy worked: he managed to keep his own interpreters, Mr. Plumb and young Staunton.

Their rough translations may explain why Macartney also believed that he had finally disposed of his bête noire, Zhengrui. That was his impression when Wang and Qiao announced the arrival of the "Grand Secretary" Jin Jian, a "cousin of the Emperor" who was now to take charge of the embassy.

Actually Jin Jian was not a replacement for the cantankerous legate. Nor was he a Grand Councillor or Grand Secretary, but merely a minister of public works, and he was "cousin" to the emperor only in that his sister had been one of Qianlong's countless concubines. He was not even Manchu, but Korean.[12] Although he had indeed been assigned to see to the embassy's reception in Peking, he was to share that responsibility with his vice minister, Yiling'a, and with Zhengrui. The three of them were now formally placed in charge of the escort, but the archives make it clear that the two ministers were anything but eager to contest Zhengrui for the perilous honor of guiding this mission.

From Jehol the emperor bombarded the three men with questions. He saw no reason why the astronomical instruments could not be brought to him safely, and he refused to believe that they could not be dismantled and taken back to Peking once having been set up for him. On August 16 he ordered "skilled craftsmen" to be sent to the Yuanming Yuan to "aid the Barbarian craftsmen in setting up the objects and to conscientiously learn to do it as well as they do."[13] Zhengrui replied to the emperor individually, and Qianlong complained that he did not understand why his report had not been countersigned by the two ministers. All these contraventions of custom were beginning to irritate the Son of Heaven. When the two offending mandarins replied, the impatient emperor wrote a vermilion marginal notation about the Chinese craftsmen who had been assigned to observe and imitate their European counterparts: "There is absolutely no reason they cannot learn."[14]

ON THAT SAME DAY, August 23, Macartney was taken to what Westerners have called the Summer Palace ever since European troops destroyed it in 1860. A more accurate name would have been the Year-Round-Except-Summer Palace, since it was only in summer that Qianlong withdrew to Jehol. The Chinese expression *yuanming yuan*, the only one Macartney used, properly reflects what this palace was to the emperor: the garden of perfect brightness, or, in other words, the Chinese garden of gardens. It was Qianlong's masterwork, as much as Versailles was Louis XIV's.

Macartney was struck by the magnificence of the landscape, dotted with flowers, herbs, and fountains. He saw only a part of the immense park, which contained several hundred pavilions linked "by passages apparently cut through stupendous rocks, or by fairyland galeries."[15]

Macartney was the first Briton to view this palace, which had been designed by Frenchmen and became legendary when Britons and other Frenchmen destroyed it. The palace itself, very much in the Louis XIV style, was ringed by Chinese pavilions that seemed lost in the park's immensity. Qianlong was clearly convinced that with this grandiose replica of Versailles and Schönbrunn, he had mined all the ideas of the Europeans, who now had nothing more to offer him. After all, what Western sovereign could boast of living in a Chinese palace?

But our travelers would have considered it a blow to their own self-esteem to admit how charmed they were. "The outer façade of the palace is richly ornamented with dragons and gilded flowers," wrote Hüttner.

"From afar, it is stunning. As one approaches, however, one notices the inferiority of the gilding and the crudeness of the execution, and all its charm soon vanishes."[16]

Macartney was supposed to be granted the honors of this palace only on his return from Jehol, and to alter a program decreed by the emperor was out of the question. The purpose of this visit was therefore only to show him where those of the presents that he did not take to Tartary would be stored. Since these gifts were tribute to the emperor, their proper place was the throne room.

Macartney was led into a hall built on a granite platform and ringed by a double colonnade supporting a roof lavishly decorated with five-clawed dragons, another of the emperor's prerogatives. (High-ranking dignitaries were entitled only to dragons with four claws.)[17] The room was more than fifty yards long by twenty yards wide. Its tiled floor was of gray and white marble covered with rugs, and it was illuminated on only one side. Opposite the windows, on a platform raised several steps above the floor, stood the carved mahogany throne, whose British workmanship Macartney immediately recognized. Above the throne was an inscription: *Zheng Da Guang Ming Fu*. Macartney offered a Latin translation: *Verus, Magnus, Gloriosus, Splendidus, Felix* ("Upright, Great, Glorious, Famous, Fortunate").[18] On either side of the throne were enormous pheasant feathers* deployed in a fan. In front was an altar where offerings of tea and fruit had been placed, since the emperor was always considered to be present here, in spirit if not in body. "Through the astonishing power of absence do I reign," Segalen had the emperor say. "My two hundred and seventy palaces, joined by impenetrable galeries, are filled with my traces alone."[19]

In a memorandum dated August 25, the three mandarins escorting Macartney reported (jointly, as the master willed): "The tributary envoy and his subordinates went to the hall of Uprightness and Clarity. They looked solemnly at one another. Having learned that the throne was located there, they immediately removed their hats and saluted, hands raised, their gaze turned upward. Your slaves observed that their attitude was highly deferential. As he admired the splendid room, the envoy felt in his heart a great respect for so much magnificence."[20] Zhengrui must have found it most awkward to put his name to this document, which contained no mention of a kowtow.

The "men of black hair" did not report what happened next, because they did not get it. Macartney was stunned by the sudden tinkling of a

---

* In Chinese mythology the pheasant plays a part similar to that of the phoenix in the West. Its tail feathers, which can be more than six feet long, are considered good-luck charms.

familiar tune. It turned out that the noise was coming from a clock in one corner. Imported from London, it marked each hour by chiming a different melody from John Gay's *The Beggar's Opera*.[21] An English clock relentlessly chiming the equivalent of Tin Pan Alley tunes in the throne room of the Son of Heaven, every hour on the hour. The surrealism of the scene eluded both Qianlong and the Jesuit clockmakers who periodically serviced the device. It was a private joke that only the British could appreciate.

That first visit to the Yuanming Yuan was also to be Macartney's last. It was from this same palace that Lord Amherst was physically ejected twenty-three years later. Yet a third British noble, Lord Elgin, entered it in 1860, commanding the troops that would loot and burn it. Today ruins are all that remain of that eighth wonder of the world, testimony to a threefold encounter between East and West: Jesuits drew up its plans and supervised its construction; diplomats passed through it without understanding it; soldiers destroyed it.

22

The Palace of Discovery

(August 23–24, 1793)

NOT EVERYTHING about this guided tour was so pleasing. Macartney found to his "great surprise" that the legate was back. This was "an unpleasant circumstance, because, as he is a Tartar and has powerful connections at the Court, our friends Wang and Qiao are obliged to pay him great deference, and dare not exert themselves in our favour as much as they are inclined to do."[1]

Here Macartney was the victim of a classic phenomenon of diplomacy: he imagined that his companions were more highly placed than they really were. Actually, the prime minister knew nothing of Wang and Qiao.[2] The Chinese made a comparable error. "According to the list of tribute," says a court letter of August 6, "the envoy was specially selected for this mission among very high ranking nobles. If he is not a prince, he is nevertheless a member of the royal family." The rhetoric of the courts of Europe—"our well beloved cousin, the honorable Lord Macartney"—had been taken literally by the Celestial bureaucracy.[3]

On both sides information was constantly distorted by illusion, suspicion, dissimulation, and silence, and the result was mutual lack of understanding. "When what is said does not sound reasonable, affairs will not culminate in success," said Confucius.[4] If the master was right, then Anglo-Chinese relations in 1793 were doomed.

Montaigne, too, held that the true causes of misunderstandings were "grammatical." Further evidence of this came the next day, August 24, when Staunton returned to the Yuanming Yuan with Barrow, Dinwiddie, Thibaut, Petitpierre,[5] and other "artisans and technicians" to organize the unloading of the gifts that would not be taken to Jehol.

Chinese palace personnel had already begun unpacking what they considered articles of tribute that properly belonged to the emperor, since without handing them over, the embassy would not have been given permission to disembark. Mr. Plumb gallantly opposed this interpretation of the Tartar legate, thus launching a lexical controversy. The objects in question, he said, were not *gongsi* (articles of tribute of which the recipient takes delivery immediately upon their arrival), but *songli*—gifts*—whose donor was free to present them at a time of his own choosing.

Ultimately, this change in terminology was enough to alter the whole character of the mission, but for the moment the stakes were more modest: who was to be responsible for all this delicate equipment? Minister Jin Jian "put an end to the conversation by saying that the expression of *songli* was proper enough."[6] After all, there might well be problems with these machines; better not to take possession of them until they were fully assembled.[7]

The rest of the embassy was preparing to settle into their new quarters in Peking before going on to Jehol. But let us remain with Barrow and the astronomer in the Yuanming Yuan, an ideal vantage point from which to observe the deterioration of the atmosphere.

They began opening the crates. The packing had been so carefully attended to that even after such a long journey, very few objects were damaged.[8]

The terrestrial globe was to be placed on one side of the throne, the celestial globe on the other. The "lustres," as might be expected, were to be hung from the ceiling. The planetarium was to be placed at one end of the hall,[9] the Vulliamy clocks, the barometer, the Wedgwood porcelain, and Fraser's orrery at the other.[10] In all, it was "an assemblage of such ingenuity, utility, and beauty as is not to be seen collected together in any other apartment, I believe, of the whole world besides."[11]

It looked like a preview of the British pavilion at an international exhibition.† A "stunning display of Western genius" in what was then called "the arts": applied science and technology. The British had highlighted two fields they knew to be of special interest to the Chinese: porcelain and astronomy.

As far as the porcelain was concerned, this was a bit of a gamble, but Wedgwood's style had changed enough to make him more than a mere

---

* Here the British faced a quintessentially Chinese difficulty. The entire social and political order was closely linked to the preservation of correct appellations, which were in turn intimately related to the corresponding written characters, alleged to represent the very essence of things. The closer one came to the living mystery of the Son of Heaven, the more crucial terminological accuracy became. The moral struggle of each individual consists precisely in the effort to achieve an ever-closer approximation of the correct appellation of the Confucian virtues. It was a kind of Chinese version of scholastic nominalism.

† The first French exposition of "the products of art and industry" was held in Paris in 1799. The British exhibit in China showed that the idea was already in the air.

imitator, and the ploy paid off. Macartney noted that most of the officials who came to the Yuanming Yuan to see the gifts "affected to view them with careless indifference." But he added: "They could not however conceal their sense of the beauty and elegance of our Derby porcelain, when they saw the ornamental vases belonging to the Vulliamy clocks."[12] Wedgwood in particular exhibited a copy of the Barberini, a famous antique vase whose prominent white figures against a field of blue inspired the style of porcelain that still bears his name.

The Wedgwood firm had seized the promotional opportunity offered by Macartney's visit. It was a new sales technique that would flourish in the coming century.[13]

The astronomical part of the exhibit was more complicated. It took no fewer than eighteen days to assemble the planetarium. The British were aided by the Chinese workers who had been ordered by the emperor to learn the procedure, which they proved quite capable of doing.* The astronomer even mentions one point on which the European technicians had to defer to their colleagues: with a red-hot iron, the Chinese succeeded in cutting a convex glass panel where the British had failed with a diamond.

On the other hand, Dinwiddie would have happily done without the intrusive rubbernecking of the palace servants and the nervous snickering of the eunuchs every time something went wrong.[14] The slow pace at which the British worked kindled Chinese suspicions that they lacked competence. One mocking Chinese noted that the British moved around a lot, but did not seem to get much done.[15]

Dinwiddie would have preferred that no one be authorized to witness these laborious preparations. The ignorant must always be taken unawares, and the effect would have been far more spectacular had the planetarium been revealed in its full splendor all at once.[16] Like any good producer, the astronomer knew that rehearsals should never be open to the public.

Moreover, Dinwiddie and Barrow inevitably felt belittled by being left out of the trip to Jehol and reduced to the lowly status of workers. In the Grand Council archives they appear at the end of a list of recipients of minor gifts. Artisans and merchants occupied the lowest rung of the Celestial hierarchy, even lower than peasants.

The slowness of the assembly process sharpened the emperor's irritation at the British insistence that their machinery be permanently exhibited in the throne room. It had already been assembled and dismantled in England, so why not in China too?

---

* Since Ricci brought his magnificent pendulum clock to Peking, various court craftsmen had become experts in precision mechanics and clockmaking.

The emperor believed—quite rightly—that the British were trying to make themselves indispensable. "By seeking to demonstrate the prodigious perfection of these instruments and the skill of his technicians, the tributary is trying to make himself important." But neither Zhengrui nor Jin Jian dared to intervene in a matter that clearly lay beyond their competence. Qianlong accused Zhengrui of letting himself be manipulated, noting that the legate, "who has held posts only in Zhejiang and Tientsin," was "naive," never having "seen the clocks and other mechanical devices of the Westerners in Canton and Macao."[17]

Precision mechanics were an ancient Chinese passion. In the thirteenth century Kublai Khan, the first Mongol emperor, showered favors upon Guillaume Boucher, a French goldsmith taken prisoner by Mongol cavalry in eastern Europe, after Boucher built him a monumental automaton: a great tree with leaves and fruit of silver, at the base of which stood four lions, also of silver, whose mouths spewed mare's milk. The tree was topped by an angel sounding a trumpet.[18]

Qianlong was a seasoned but jaded aficionado of this passion, while the rustic Zhengrui was only just discovering the world. A great number of European watches and pendulum clocks were brought into China through Canton during Qianlong's reign. The court was especially keen on music boxes with figurines inside, and the emperor had quite a few of these, which he distributed among his palaces and residences.[19] Court astronomers serviced them for him. Qianlong saw no real difference between a planetarium and a watch. He felt that anyone who could take a clock apart ought to be able to put a planetarium back together.

23

A Distraught Scholar

(August 24, 1793)

ONE DAY Father Rodrigues and three other Portuguese missionaries, the bishop of Peking among them, arrived with great ceremony at the Yuan-ming Yuan to attend a demonstration of the British astronomical equipment and to report back to the emperor.[1] These men, officials of the Tribunal of Mathematics, were following the path of Matteo Ricci, who in 1593, exactly two hundred years earlier, had used his maps of the world, dials, spheres, and clocks to propel himself ever higher in Celestial society, eventually becoming, effectively, a naturalized Chinese.[2]

The tribunal was actually more concerned with astronomy and astrology than with mathematics. One of its tasks had been to establish a national calendar, since governing the world of men required matching the harmony of the universe.[3] This calendar, published in the *Peking Gazette*, designated lucky and unlucky days and seasons for government ceremonies and undertakings—everything from major public works to military campaigns. But the calendar had its influence on daily life as well: trips, marriages, the laying of the first stone of a new house, and so on.

Lucky and unlucky days are still listed in the popular almanacs that have always been available in Hong Kong, Taiwan, and among overseas Chinese and are now sold freely again in the People's Republic as well.

"Whether," Barrow declared, "the men of letters, as they call themselves, really believe in the absurdities of judicial astrology, or whether they may think it necessary to encourage the observance of popular superstitions, on political considerations, I will not take it upon me to decide. If, however, they should happen to possess any such superior knowledge, great credit is due them for acting the farce with such apparent earnestness, and with so much solemnity. The duration of the same system has certainly been long enough for them to have discovered, that the multitude are more effectively governed by opinion than by power."[4] Father Huc put it this way: "The Chinese prefer the authority of the pen to that of the sabre."[5]

The missionaries had been integrated into this system, reinforcing the Middle Empire's astrological convictions by lending them the support of astronomical science. But lately the prop had grown frail.

The members of the Tribunal of Mathematics apparently expected to be shown music boxes, "those curious pieces of musical mechanism which, in the Canton jargon, are called *Sing-songs*, and that nothing more was necessary than to wind it up like a jack." Instead they found themselves staring at a complicated astronomical device, and they turned out to be so ignorant of astronomy that the British could not even manage to explain the workings of the planetarium to them.[6]

Dinwiddie and Barrow were stunned, for astronomer-missionaries had a great and time-honored reputation in the West. When Shunzhi, the first Manchu emperor, acceded to the throne in 1644, the country's system of dates was in total disarray. Not a single almanac was accurate. Barrow was amused to find that a Chinese astronomer had been strangled in 1670 for having assigned that year thirteen months.*[7] The Jesuits immediately seized the opportunity,[8] convincing the Manchu court of the ignorance of its councilors "in a matter of the last importance to the government."[9]

Barrow noted that these first Jesuits were highly knowledgeable Germans. But: "After these the Portuguese succeeded to the appointments of regulating the calendar. . . . Fortunately for these gentlemen, the Chinese have no means of detecting any little inaccuracies that may happen in their calculations."[10]

Exit the tribunal. The next day Father Gouvea, the Portuguese bishop of Peking, secretly appealed to the British for help.

These "experts" had been allowed into China specifically on the strength of their scientific competence. But their cover had been wearing thin, and yesterday their emperor had stood naked in his new clothes. The bishop confessed that in fact he and his colleagues had no idea how to forecast an eclipse, predict the phases of the moon, or calculate the times of sunrise and sunset, tasks they were reputed to perform at the court.

Up to now they had managed to squeak by with the help of a manual published in Paris, *Connaissance des temps*. Since they knew the difference in longitude between the two capitals, they were able to make the necessary adjustments. But the French Revolution had cut them off from their source: the precious almanac no longer arrived. Their trickery was about to be exposed.[11] Disaster loomed.

---

* In this case Barrow's irony was quite misplaced. He clearly did not realize that the lunar calendar requires the addition of an extra month every six years. Most probably the unfortunate Chinese astronomer simply picked the wrong year.

This man so enamored of China was in great danger of being deported, perhaps even beheaded, a fate not a few of his colleagues had suffered for lesser crimes than this deceit. The letters of the Jesuits after 1773, when their society was dissolved, generally reflect great disarray, but this prelate was in a particularly perilous position. Dinwiddie took pity on the distraught "scholar," giving him a collection of "nautical almanacks" calculated for the Greenwich meridian up to the year 1800.[12] Seven years of peace of mind for the astronomer-bishop who knew no astronomy.

Connaissance des temps was a sign of the times. France, divided against itself, was preparing for war against the entire continent of Europe. Meanwhile, Britain stepped into the breach in China. The Greenwich meridian displaced the Parisian.

The British accused the Jesuits of concealing European science from the Chinese in a deliberate attempt to maintain their own monopoly. This view was a comfortable conjunction of anti-Chinese rancor and hatred of the Catholic church. Barrow in particular never considered the recalcitrance of the Chinese educated classes. For him science was a quintessentially Western product, and to refuse to share it was a crime against the life of the mind. But he took no account of the much-vaunted knowledge of the Chinese themselves—or of their rejection of foreign learning.

The fact that the Jesuits enjoyed imperial protection ought not to foster any illusions on this score. Most Chinese men of letters considered Christianity and the Western sciences (presented by the missionaries as a single package) as no more than a collection of heresies. Beginning in the late sixteenth century, a "fundamentalist" backlash produced a trenchant defense of traditional Chinese science against the assault of the "barbarian devils."

"Now," the great mathematician Mei Wending wrote, "with the introduction of the new [Western] method, we abolish all the traditional way of following [astronomy]." And he asked, rhetorically: "Is it that all the experiences of the past are not fit to be used?"[13] Why should China have to copy the West, when it was actually the West that had copied China? "As a result of the burning of books in the Qin dynasty [221–206 B.C.], most of the classics in China were lost. But the branches abroad still preserved the originals. It is from this that Western learning has its origin."[14]

The imported clocks, telescopes, harpsichords, and weapons were admittedly fascinating. But they were also resented as a threat. A deep movement against Western technology developed.[15] Not mere wounded pride, but also a will to defend a threatened identity is apparent in this typical, amusing yet pathetic, dismissal of Western gadgetry: "Even though [the barbarian machines] are skillful, what good will they do to one's mind? Now take the case of the self-alarm clock; it is nothing more than a clepsydra which requires more than ten gold pieces to manufacture it; . . . with regard to machines such as cannon, they will set on fire the gunners before annihilating the enemy. . . ."[16] Ricci's map of the world? Unacceptable! "China should be in the centre of the world, which we can prove by the single fact that we can see the North Star resting at the zenith of the heaven at midnight."[17]

From the end of the sixteenth century to the end of the twentieth, there has been an unbroken current of Chinese scholars who refuse to consult non-Chinese works, striving to keep their heritage intact by guarding it against Western intrusion.[18] Fundamentalism hunkered down behind the ramparts of fidelity to Chinese values. Where it dared not deny "scientific" superiority, it sought instead to change the subject, putting things in their proper perspective: "It is better to have no good astronomy than to have Westerners in China. If there is no good astronomy, this is no worse than the Han situation when astronomers did not know the principle of opposition between the sun and the moon, . . . still the Han dynasty enjoyed dignity and prosperity for four hundred years"[19] "Better a Chinese train that runs late than a capitalist train that runs on time," was a slogan during the Cultural Revolution. This passion for self-reliance runs like a red thread through Chinese history right up to the death of Mao. The Gang of Four—who were in fact slightly more numerous than that— dogged the tracks of the West for ten years, extirpating such accomplices of the "bourgeois order" as Beethoven and Antonioni.

Throughout all these centuries, of course, some men of letters have sought to produce a synthesis of Chinese traditions and Western inventions. But they have always been a minority, and the evidence suggests that Qianlong was not one of them. Here, for instance, are some verses he composed about the gifts the British gave him:

> Though their tribute is commonplace, my heart approves sincerely,
> Curios and the boasted ingenuity of their devices I prize not.
> Though what they bring is meagre, yet,
> In my kindness to men from afar I make generous return,
> Wanting to preserve my good health and power.[20]

Why, then, did Qianlong pay two visits to the exhibition of presents? Why, during the months of August and September, did he attach a more than ritual importance to them? What accounts for the inordinate space occupied in imperial correspondence by the Macartney mission, which seems to have eclipsed Qianlong's every other concern that year? The truth is that there were two sides to the emperor's attitude: public scorn and private attraction.

The British sneered at "papist obscurantists" who prospered amidst Chinese gullibility. But here again the truth was more complex. The British were true representatives of their century, and as such were enamored of an Enlightenment they supposed was universal. They knew nothing of relativism, and they underestimated the unshakable power of a deeply rooted culture.

But be that as it may, Westerners did not tattle on their own kind: no member of the embassy ever said a word to the Chinese about their disdain for the missionaries or the extent of their ignorance. The emperor continued to believe that the world's best astronomers were in his employ. "The tributary envoy," he commented with pride, "can see that the Celestial Court also has people capable of understanding astronomy and geography, of assembling clocks and of helping to put these instruments together. No longer will he dare to claim that he alone possesses the secret of these things, and his intolerable boasting will cease."[21]

24

The Science of Government

(August 23–28, 1793)

ALL MANNER of Chinese, "from princes of the blood to plain citizens,"[1] soon began streaming in to view the exhibit of presents. "All the men of letters and rank, who held employments in the state, and whose attendance had been dispensed with at Jehol, flocked to the Yuanming Yuan."[2] Much like the Chinese whom Ricci had encountered two centuries earlier, they were surprised that China took up such little space on the globe, and they suspected that the "men of red hair" had deliberately reduced their country's size. Outraged, they turned rapidly from the globe.

The astronomer considered their reaction puerile: "They act like children; easily satisfied, they are just as easily bored." It is true that the "childish" behavior of the Chinese has since been noted by many travelers, Chinese included. As Lu Xun pointed out, "the government treats adults like infants."[3] If they resembled children, perhaps it was because the command structure of their society prevented them from growing out of childhood, just as a bonsai gardener prevents trees from growing and ligatures dwarf young girls' feet.

Freud would probably have joined Dinwiddie in arguing that the Chinese were *unable* to become adults. If one believes that children attain adulthood only by "murdering" the father, it is hard to see how the father can be "killed" in a country in which ancestor and emperor worship—two cults embodying and sanctifying an unassailable paternal perfection—are imposed and ritualized by the collective mentality. Mao left the first of these forms of worship virtually untouched and even strengthened the second. This twofold cult remains the shared religion of most Chinese to this day, and it has mired them in a psychic infantilism that meshes perfectly with their xenophobia and their rejection of innovation. As Father Teilhard de Chardin wrote, "The mass of Chinese—a mass enormous, unimaginative, and inert—are instinctively hostile to foreigners who propose changes for which they feel no need."[4] To prohibit whatever might displease one's ancestors is to reject all novelty.

Three of the emperor's grandchildren disrupted the demonstrations every day. One of them had a gem-studded British pocket watch (by Cumin of London) that had stopped years ago. It began working again after one of the embassy's craftsmen cleaned it thoroughly. A second prince was unimpressed. The British must be very proud of their scientific knowledge to make such a display of this machinery, he commented.[5] The British and the Chinese, each equally convinced of their own superiority, treated one another with condescending irony. There was little mutual admiration between these two nations, each of which considered itself the world's most powerful.

BARROW WAS witness to yet another cultural chasm: the one separating the British aristocracy from the Celestial bureaucracy.

Among the gifts were three volumes of engravings, portraits of the flower of British nobility. The emperor requested that the name of the subject be inscribed under each portrait, in Chinese and Manchu. This raised the classic difficulty of phonetic transcription, and the Chinese calligraphers had a hard time of it. The duke of Marlborough, for instance, became *Too-ke Ma-ul-po-loo*. The British found it all quite amusing.

But it was the turn of the Chinese to laugh when Barrow, indicating the rank held by each person, came to the portrait (by Joshua Reynolds) of the duke of Bedford, painted when he was a child. He proposed *Ta-gin*, "great man of the second order." The Chinese, who failed to see how anyone so small could be great, thought Barrow was referring to the father. Barrow then explained that to enter the House of Lords, the son of a lord had to meet just two requirements: to be born and to have a dead father. "They laughed heartily at the idea of a man being born a legislator, when it required so many years of close application to enable one of their countrymen to pass his examination for the very lowest order of state-officers."[6]

The laughter of the Chinese made the British realize just how absurd hereditary positions were, and they had no real answer to their hosts' hilarity. They did not see that rights of lineage might act as a barrier to state omnipotence, nor did they perceive the ideology of the bureaucratic state that lay behind the Chinese meritocracy. They felt inadequate. Their own intelligence told them that their own society was in the wrong.

Although China has been Westernized in many respects during the past two centuries, the West has come closer to China in terms of bureaucratization. The privileges of the nobility have been breached throughout Europe, even in traditionalist England, and a system of state examinations now holds sway. This is more than mere convergence. The Chinese example, held up as a model, contributed powerfully to the rise of meritocracy in Europe.*

The Chinese seemed intrigued by the mixture of power and family ties in Britain. The seven young members of the aristocracy whom Macartney had brought along with him had been introduced as relatives of his, and the emperor ordered Zhengrui to find out exactly what the kinship ties were. He asked whether Staunton junior had an official title. Respectful as he was of barbarian customs, the emperor decided to offer special presents to these seven young gentlemen, who in British protocol ranked just above the musicians.[7]

WITH MORE justification than Louis XIV, Qianlong could well have proclaimed, *L'Etat, c'est moi.* But the ideology embodied by this sovereign was about to be stymied by the coach Macartney intended to offer the emperor as a personal gift. After his tiresome experience with Chinese vehicles, the ambassador was eager to demonstrate the excellence of British spring suspension, and Staunton was still dreaming of massive exports to this immense market.

Chinese interest, however, was focused not on the suspension system but on the driver's seat. A horde of mandarins climbed aboard, testing the softness of the cushions and fingering the upholstery. The raised position of the seat and its "smart edging, . . . ornamented with festoons of roses," lent it such an imperial air that the Chinese had no doubt that it was meant for the emperor himself. Meanwhile, an attentive examination of the "windows, blinds, and skreens" of the coach's interior convinced them that it was suitable for none but the "Emperor's ladies."

When Barrow disabused one aged eunuch of this illusion, "he asked me, with a sneer, whether I supposed the . . . [Great Emperor] would

---

* On this issue (unlike most others) the experience of the Macartney mission confirmed the accounts of the missionaries. But both idealized the situation to some extent, ignoring various factors: the hereditary status of the imperial family and the Manchu nobility, the instances of exemption from the mandarin examinations and of special permission to compete for higher positions, the inherited positions granted to some families whose ancestors had rendered significant service to the state. And of course, there was also corruption.

suffer any man to sit higher than himself, and to turn his back towards him."[8] So much for the golden goose of exports.

DINWIDDIE AND BARROW felt the Chinese pressure more than Macartney did, for they bore the brunt of it in the Yuanming Yuan. In the midst of their careful preparation of a demonstration meant to dazzle the court and the city alike, they suddenly received an order to "deliver all gifts immediately, even those not yet assembled or unpacked." The perceptive Dinwiddie realized that their stay in China would be brief.

As he gloomily contemplated his useless planetarium, he realized that the scientific aspect of this mission was doomed. And he had a foreboding of its diplomatic failure as well. He wrote in his journal that when he asked the Chinese whether the inventors of such an extraordinary machine must not be superior men, he was told that these objects, curious as they were, seemed of little importance. "Do you possess the science of government?" he was asked.

In China there was an art, and even a science, of government, one that permeated society itself. Simply by taking possession of the unchanging structure of the Celestial bureaucracy, three hundred thousand Manchus were able to govern a thousand times as many Chinese.

In their eyes this bureaucracy was a wondrous machine, far more subtly conceived and assembled than Dinwiddie's planetarium. Every actor had an assigned role. The emperor ruled, his Grand Council governed, his mandarins administered, his peasants cultivated the land, his craftsmen manufactured what was needed, his merchants traded. The cogs meshed perfectly, and everyone was content. Those few who dissented faced "bambooing," the iron collar, or beheading. Glorious indeed was the art of governing!

Their prejudices seemed so deeply rooted, the astronomer commented, that force alone could vanquish them.[9] He was the first of our witnesses to come to the conclusion that fifty years later would appear inescapable to the West: only war could overcome such profound condescension.

25

A Gilded Prison

(August 24–26, 1793)

ON AUGUST 24 Zhengrui handed the ambassador a letter from Sir Erasmus Gower bringing news of the squadron, which had arrived safely in Zhoushan, and requesting instructions. Macartney prepared a response, to be carried by the imperial post, and gave it to Zhengrui the next day. In it he told Gower to take the ships back to Canton.

The legate demanded to know the contents of both Gower's letter and Macartney's response. As the emperor's designated supervisor of British activities, he felt he had to know everything about his "charges." Macartney, eager to avoid an incident, agreed to keep his inquisitive interlocutor informed. Apparently pleased to find the ambassador so accommodating, Zhengrui then proposed a training session in the kowtow. But here the ambassador called a halt, dismissing Zhengrui with a promise that he would present him with a document on this matter in a day or two.[1]

The poor salt inspector now found himself in a real quandary. How could he admit to the emperor and the Grand Council not only that the tributary envoy was not practicing the kowtow, but also that he was actually preparing a written proposal on the subject, as if it had not already been settled by two thousand years of ceremony? The problem was getting ugly. Hoping to save his mandarin's button, he decided to play for time. Once he had the envoy's note, he would at least know where he stood.

In the meantime, he would go out of his way to show the emperor that he was granting the British no indulgence whatever. Without telling Macartney, Zhengrui sent the ambassador's reply to Gower to Jehol instead of Zhoushan, with a recommendation that the British be denied permission to return their ships to Canton.

On August 26, however, Macartney's other wish was granted: the embassy was transferred to Peking, to the heart of the Tartar city, all except Barrow, Dinwiddie, and the two mechanics, who stayed behind in the Yuanming Yuan in the service of science. Macartney found the new residence "magnificent."[2] It consisted of eleven pavilions of gray brick "so well joined one to the other that the cement that bonds them is almost imperceptible, and they appear as smooth as marble." In front of the pavilions was a courtyard paved with broad flat stones and embellished by an "open terrace supported by beautiful columns of wood and adorned with elegant balustrades."

The apartments, painted or wallpapered, were "spacious and airy." The residence assigned to the ambassador even had a theater. Some private individuals maintained troupes of performers, as French lords did during the seventeenth century; others merely purchased their services on holidays.[3]

Anderson admired "the superiority of the Chinese in the art of house painting, to which they give a gloss equal to japan, that not only preserves the colours from fading, but never suffers any injury itself from the exposition of air, or sun, or rain."[4] But his enthusiasm was misplaced. The Grand Council archives reveal that the court had expressly ordered the residence repainted for the British.[5] The paint gleamed because it was barely dry.

Beneath the floor of each apartment was "a stove, or furnace of brickwork."[6] The furniture was spare and low. In those days the Chinese lived on their haunches, as the Japanese still do. Armchairs had become fashionable under the Tang dynasty, but the Manchus, a people of the steppes used to sitting on the ground in their tents, revived the ancient custom. The apartments were partitioned by folding screens, which also constituted the only decoration apart from the lanterns of gauze, paper, or transparent animal horn. The walls were bare. There were no rugs or mirrors.

By way of beds, Barrow says, there were "mats or stuffed mattresses, hard pillows or cushions" placed on "a bench of wood or a platform of brick-work."[7] But the beds Barrow saw were meant only for sleeping. He would have been less critical of the ones in the women's apartments, which were designed for other purposes. Very wide, replete with soft cushions, and draped with net curtains, they protected marital intimacy from the assaults of mosquitos and the comings and goings of domestic life.[8]

The residence the British were staying in had recently been confiscated from one Muteng'e, a former Canton hoppo demoted for going somewhat too far in lining his own pockets by fleecing Europeans. The mandarins could not resist sharing an imperial witticism with the British. It seems that when it was suggested to the emperor that the embassy be lodged in these quarters, he replied: "Most certainly, you cannot refuse the temporary occupation of a house to the Embassador of that nation which contributed so very amply towards the expense of building it."[9] Barrow was not amused by this cynical retort, for he felt that it proved that the emperor "was well aware of the extortions committed against foreigners at Canton." He might punish excess, but he never contemplated putting an end to the practice.

Macartney had hoped that the move to Peking would break the embassy's isolation, but he now found that he was not even allowed to look out over the walls of the residence. "Some few, prompted by curiosity, ventured [to peep over the walls]; but being observed by the soldiers on the outside, a terrible clamour was instantly raised about our ears: 'The Place,' as it was named, in which we were, was in a few minutes filled with mandarins, and threatenings thundered out against any future transgressors."[10]

The British reacted like prisoners: every detail of daily life acquired inordinate importance. They could not get used to Chinese food.[11] All the dishes, they complained, were ground or boiled: "They have not the least notion of any other method of preparing them."[12] Only the soups pleased British palates. Hüttner regretted that the Chinese did not drink milk, and he went to extraordinary lengths to acquire some.[13]

The mandarins kept watch on the servants, who were "the most thievish set of villains on the face of the earth." Holmes reports that it was "common practice" for them "to keep back one half of our bread, sugar, tea, and sometimes whole pieces of meat. . . . They were not induced to rob us through want; had that been the case, we might have overlooked their impudence, but the meanest of them had a superfluity of the best provisions: it was disposed of, for a third of its value, to those people who originally sent it to us, and perhaps served in a different manner the next day, at our own table."[14]

The Chinese were "unaccountably suspicious and fearful" of any foreigners.[15] Service and surveillance were blended like sweet and sour tastes in Chinese cuisine. "Whether out of attention or distrust, they had sent us at least a dozen mandarins. What a remarkable spectacle it was to see them scurrying through the palace all day!" Though they seemed very busy—one furnishing milk, another bread, another opening doors—the British were convinced that they spent most of their time observing their prisoner-guests and reporting back to the emperor.* The members of the embassy were even followed into their rooms, and "each mandarin was accompanied by a servant carrying his pipe." Though isolated from the outside world, the British were denied the right to isolate themselves.[16] "Nine shepherds for every sheep," a Chinese adage says.

---

* Here the British simply flattered themselves. Only Zhengrui and the two ministers were authorized to correspond with the emperor.

Upon their return to Europe, our travelers received many offers from publishers, and they could not resist painting portraits of this city that they had lived in but never seen. Their descriptions owe more to conversations with missionaries than to direct observation. But the best sources of information about a country are often resident compatriots whose view may be more balanced, and therefore sharper. The missionaries played this role for the embassy, with more sincerity to what they spoke in private than what they wrote for public consumption.

In their own houses, the Chinese lived "as close as the teeth of a comb."[17] In a single dwelling "a whole family of three generations, with all their respective wives and children, will frequently be found. One small room is made to serve for the individuals of each branch of the family, sleeping in different beds, divided only by mats hanging from the ceiling. One common room is used for eating."[18] Several generations under the same roof: a recommendation of Confucianism and a product of necessity to boot. Today more than ever.

In view of this overcrowding it was not surprising that the "Chinese live, indeed, much in the open air."[19] They loved fresh air so much that on hot summer nights entire families would sleep in the street, a custom that can still be observed today, especially in the most torrid cities, such as the "three ovens": Chongqing, Wuhan, and Nanking.

"The streets are broad," Hüttner notes, "and though they are watered in summer, one is nevertheless choked by the dust."[20] Dust still invades everything in Peking today, from lungs to apartments. Torn out of the steppes by the wind, it falls back upon the city in rains of sand that cover the capital in yellow, the imperial color.

The swarming tumult concealed a level of organization that led Staunton to observe, "The city partakes of the regularity and interior safety of a camp; but is subject also to its constraints."[21] He further noted: "Great order is preserved among such multitudes; and the commission of crimes is rare. Every tenth house-keeper, somewhat in the manner of the ancient tithing-men in England, is answerable for the conduct of the nine neighbouring families."[22] Families and guilds stood in for the mandarins (with their consent) in settling disputes. As for prostitution: "In the suburbs only, public women are registered and licensed. They are not indeed very numerous, being proportioned to the small number of single men, and of husbands absent from their families to be found in the metropolis."[23]

Staunton's idealized account foreshadows the portraits of a pure and austere China painted by enthusiastic visitors between 1950 and 1980. Take his comment about the "tithing-men," for example. According to Lazarist Father Lamiot, the system Staunton described was actually ancient history.

"Even Confucius spoke nostalgically of this police, which had been abolished long before his time."[24] The mission's mandarin escort must have subjected the British to a most edifying discourse—no crime, no vice—while making sure that whatever they were not supposed to see, like beggars and prostitutes, was kept well out of sight. But the antiseptic atmosphere did not prevent one of the mandarins from "frolicking among the flowers and willows,"[25] returning with a dose of "the kick of Venus" for his trouble. Mercurial ointment imported from the West through Canton cured the malady,[26] which was known as the "Canton ulcer,"* since it was through that city that syphilis entered China from America in 1511, less than twenty years after the European discovery of the New World. Corn and sweet potatoes had the same origin, but took much longer to arrive.[27]

The Europeans of Canton, who were expressly forbidden to bring any women into China, affirmed that "with enough money and sufficient disdain for one's health, one can procure as many as one wants."[28]

The money went not only to the prostitutes, but also to the Celestial bureaucrats. One witness who had spent more than ten years in Canton, where he later met Macartney, reported: "If mandarins or soldiers catch you in the boats [of the prostitutes], they make many threats but release you after extorting a large sum, the amount depending on the rank you hold in society."[29] One wonders whether Anderson, who boasted of having "taken the measure of a lady's foot"[30] on a boat in Canton, was aware of the risk he had taken.

Dinwiddie scorned the accounts of China that had been so popular in Europe, complaining that they unfairly presented the Chinese as the most polite and pacific people on earth. The members of the embassy, he countered, had seen no evidence of such gentility, but had witnessed angry clashes even in the corridors of the palace itself. He concluded that the Chinese had been depicted in a thoroughly Confucian manner: as they should be, not as they are.[31] The truth is that when the Chinese are polite, they are very polite, while their outbursts of brutality are brutal indeed. Even the highly sheltered and closely chaperoned embassy heard tales of the "bare club" bandits who ravaged the countryside and played their part in peasant revolts.[32]

The various witnesses saw things from very different points of view. Macartney and Staunton were constantly involved in court rituals, doing all they could to ease the tribulations of the embassy and to secure the future of Anglo-Chinese relations—not to mention their own futures. They

---

* Canton today is full of advertisements for antisyphilis treatments; the disease seems to be flaring anew in the region.

were therefore subject to constraints comparable to those felt by the missionaries, who, as we have seen, described China in such laudatory terms that one might well wonder why China had not sent missionaries to Europe instead of the other way around. But Dinwiddie and Barrow were under no such pressures, and as they traveled back and forth between the Yuanming Yuan and Peking, they had more opportunities to observe the man in the street. Like Anderson and Holmes, but with a lucidity these men lacked, they retained the detachment typical of supporting players.

China is an empire of word and deed. To speak of it in dithyrambic terms is to enter the Chinese Order itself, in a kind of intellectual kowtow. Staunton, compelled to play along with the games of ritual in order to save face, did so fairly often. His companions declined to follow suit, and thereby found themselves suspended between the real China and an imaginary one. They sometimes forgot that for the Chinese, the imaginary China was also real.

26

Europeans Turned Chinese

(August 27–29, 1793)

SEVERAL OF THE missionaries began to visit the embassy in its Peking residence. These men "all wear the Chinese dress, acquire the language of the country, and in outward appearance are scarcely to be distinguished from the other inhabitants."[1]

Strangely, there was no sign of Father de Grammont. But another French priest, Father Nicolas-Joseph Raux, soon became a regular caller. He introduced himself the day after the embassy moved in and informed Macartney "that he had permission to attend us, and that he would wait upon me every day to receive our commands and execute our commissions."[2]

That was a relief. The worrying shadow of Father d'Almeida, already on his way to Jehol, had been lifted. Father Raux was the leader of the Lazarists, who had been sent to China to take over from the Jesuits after Pope Clement XIV, yielding to pressure from the entire European intelligentsia, dissolved the Society of Jesus in 1773. Father Raux, accredited as a "mathematician," had arrived in April 1785, accompanied by two colleagues, a "painter" and a "clockmaker." Macartney soon took a liking to this florid, loquacious, and corpulent priest who had immersed himself in Chinese reality.

Father Raux described his hectic schedule in a letter to his sister: "I am responsible for a mission of seventy-three people. Every day I am obliged to speak four languages: French, Latin, Chinese, and Tartar. I must reply to an infinity of letters, as well as attending to catechism, sermons, confessions, and the other sacraments, in addition to visiting important personages from time to time."[3] "He was a picture of health," commented the Dutch ambassador, Isaak Titsing, who met Father Raux in 1795. His Chinese "clothes suited him admirably, and he spoke Chinese with a melodious fluency which made it sound pleasant."[4]

A bit of a bon vivant, the priest arrived each day with little presents from his convent: "some excellent French bread, sweetmeats, and confections, very fine large figs, and a quantity of grapes, both red and white, the latter of a most delicious flavour, and without stones. He told me they were originally brought to the Jesuits' garden from Chamo,* on the borders of the great desert of Gobi."[5] "Once we discovered the secret of producing excellent wines in Peking by adding a certain quantity of sugar to the must of the grape," Father Raux explained, "we ceased to long for European wine, which fetches a very high price here."[6] (The missionaries of Shala, on the outskirts of Peking, manufactured their own red wine until 1949.) Father Raux's bread and wine suggest that however Chinese these missionaries may have appeared, their assimilation was not quite complete.

Macartney also received a "charming letter" from Father Joseph-Marie Amiot, accompanied by his portrait. Amiot was an almost mythical figure, a patriarch who had been in China for forty-two years and had witnessed the entire Jesuit venture, in all its glory and persecution. He was one of the principal authors of the *Mémoires concernant l'histoire de la Chine* and the *Lettres édifiantes et curieuses*. Now very sick, he was unable to travel,[7] and he died in Peking in October 1793, just a few days after Macartney's mission left the capital.

Father Raux treated Macartney to a gripping account of the state of Christianity in China. There were some 5,000 Christians in the capital and perhaps 150,000 in the entire empire. Barely one baptized citizen per 2,000 Chinese was a fairly meager balance sheet for such a dedicated apostolate.[8] Why were there so few adherents, 241 years after the death near Canton of Saint Francis Xavier, 211 years after Father Ricci's arrival in Macao? "In the arts and in politics," Father de Grammont explained, "the Chinese are perhaps more enlightened than any other people. But they are imbeciles when it comes to religion. Any of our seven-year-olds could perceive how absurd their superstitions are. They are so stubborn in their prejudices, and so full of self-esteem, that scarcely anyone will convert."[9]

A single source of recruitment of neophytes remained, Father Raux told Macartney, and that was newborn babies abandoned on the streets: "The police send a cart round the city at an early hour every morning, which takes them up and conveys them to a fosse or cemetery appointed for their burial. The missionaries often attend and preserve a few of these children which appear to them to be healthy and likely to recover. The rest are thrown indiscriminately, dead or alive, into the pit. But Father

---

* Chamo (Shamo) means "desert." The Muslims of central Asia, ignoring the Islamic ban on alcohol, cultivate grapes and manufacture wine.

Raux assured me very seriously that his brethren always first christened those that appeared to have any life remaining in them, *pour sauver leur âme*."[10] To save their souls. The Protestant strikes an ironic tone when discussing such "superstitions." And the priest speaks of these practices as though oblivious to their horror.

Travelers of the past three centuries have been stunned by infanticide in China. But the Middle Empire held no monopoly on the abandonment of unwanted newborns, particularly in the eighteenth century. In Paris in 1771, an average year, the Enfants-Trouvés hospital took in 7,600 babies, a good number of whom soon died of lack of milk and care. In a register of grievances dated 1788, we read: "The depositing of newborns in the street delivers them to the voracity of animals."[11] And in England, *Oliver Twist* postdates the Macartney mission by forty-five years. In China, however, there were few if any hospitals to take abandoned newborns in, and nearly all of them went straight to mass graves or to Catholic missions.

Our witnesses were puzzled. Barrow, for instance, commented: "How very weak then, in reality, must be the boasted filial affection of the Chinese for their parents, when they scruple not to become the murderers of their own children."[12] And from Staunton: "Habit seems to have familiarized a notion that life, only, becomes truly precious, and inattention to it criminal, after it has continued long enough to be endowed with a mind and sentiment; but that mere dawning existence may be suffered to be lost without scruple, though it cannot be without reluctance."[13] Hüttner: "We saw some instances of it: during famines some poor people eat their children."[14] Huc wrote, chillingly: "Newborns are mercilessly killed. The birth of a male baby is a blessing, the birth of a girl a calamity."[15] And that was—and still is—the heart of the matter: a girl, destined to become her mother-in-law's servant immediately upon her marriage, is no more than an extra mouth to feed for twenty years, whereas a boy not only remains with his parents to care for them in their old age (and ensures that they will be worshiped after their death) but also enriches the household with a new servant: his future wife.

Infanticide was not illegal. Chinese census figures for some areas in Macartney's time show as many as 150 boys for every 100 girls.[16] Nor has infanticide been eradicated even in our own day, despite energetic condemnation of it since 1949. In certain rural counties of the People's Republic there are as many as five boys per girl, and however ardently Chinese women may pray to the Heavenly Weaver to bless them with handsome baby sons, five-to-one seems a suspiciously high success rate. Draconian measures against overpopulation have aggravated the scourge. Couples are now forbidden to have more than one child, and if fate decrees that the first born be a girl, some families find it hard to resist the temptation of eliminating her to clear the way for a possible boy.*[17]

The missionaries were the only people in China to pluck survivors from this massacre, and most Chinese Christians were not converts but adopted children. As such, they attracted less suspicion from the Celestial authorities, and the church became their natural, as well as their spiritual, family. This may well account for the intensity of their devotion.

By 1793, however, Qianlong's persecution of Christianity had had its effects. "The Chinese," Father Raux told Macartney, "seem to be less jealous of religious conversions than formerly, owing to the discretion of the present missionaries."[18] There was no cause for levity here, for the persecution was by no means solely rhetorical. The most recent repression dated from 1785, and the next wave would not be long in coming. Driven out of the provinces, Christianity was now tolerated only in Peking, where the court needed the knowledge of the missionaries and therefore learned to live with them.

The good fathers, now teaching catechism only to children abandoned by their parents, had themselves been abandoned by the West. From one monsoon to the next, the penniless Father Raux waited vainly for Paris to send help. In an August 1793 letter to Louis-Chrétien de Guignes, a Canton resident, formerly an agent of the king but now also forgotten by France, Father Raux wrote: "Last April I had the honor of asking that you take charge of our affairs in Canton pending the arrival of a French missionary assigned to our apostolate."[19] Which missionary never came.[20]

In such precarious conditions, the missionaries were hardly a problem to the Celestial authorities. But they continued to act for God's greater glory: "With God's help everything is possible," Father Raux told his sister. "I am content with my fate, for I have reason to believe that the Lord knows that I am here. Alive or dead, we are with Him."[21] The British seemed taken aback by this holy faith: "It must have appeared a singular spectacle . . . to see men actuated by motives different from those of most human actions, quitting for ever their country and their connections, to devote themselves for life to the purpose of changing the tenets of a people they had never seen; and in pursuing that object, to run every risk, suffer every persecution, and sacrifice every comfort; . . . by talent, by humility, by application to studies foreign to their original education; . . . overcoming the prejudice of being strangers in a country where most strangers were

---

* In 1984 the authorities responded to the widespread resistance of couples by relaxing the rules somewhat.

prohibited, and where it was a crime to have abandoned the tombs of their ancestors."[22]

Monsignor Gouvea, a man of "no great measure of learning," paid another visit, accompanied by priests of various nationalities, all of whom surreptitiously warned Macartney to have no confidence in their bishop: The "Portuguese have formed a sort of system to disgust and keep out of China all other nations. . . . In a conversation with an Italian a few days ago, he told me that all the missionaries except the Portuguese were our warm friends, but that the Portuguese were friends of nobody but themselves."[23]

Far from regarding these clique rivalries with sarcasm, Macartney, in accordance with the recommendations of Henry Dundas and Father de Grammont, decided to avail himself of the services of the missionaries to press his case. At least his visitors could tell him something of the atmosphere of the court.

A Sovereign Under the Influence

(August 28–29, 1793)

FATHER RAUX described the situation for Macartney. Only four of the emperor's twenty sons[1] were still alive. "He is of so jealous a nature that no person as yet knows with certainty which of them he intends for his successor."[2] Succession in the empire was not by birthright, but by "designation of the heir," as in Roman law. Qianlong's grandfather, Kangxi, who reigned for sixty years, had had an unhappy experience with this system, finding himself compelled to depose his designated successor, who ultimately died in prison. Kangxi's son and eventual successor, Yongzhen, took a lesson from this precedent and kept the name of his heir secret, recording it in a sealed box and in a document he carried with him at all times. The name in that box was Qianlong's, and he in turn decided to follow his father's example.[3] But in the end the precaution was pointless: Qianlong abdicated in 1796 at the age of eighty-five, publicly designating his son Jiaqing as his successor.[4]

Qianlong did not allow his sons "to interfere in his government." He ruled alone, "reading all the dispatches himself, and often entering into the minutest detail of affairs."[5] In reporting this assertion by Father Raux, Macartney had no doubt that it was fully confirmed by the experience of his own embassy. But sometimes the emperor did heed the advice of the six major personalities of the state, the members of the Grand Council. In principle they were all equal, but in fact one was more equal than the others.

The man who enjoyed the emperor's full confidence was Heshen, "a Tartar of obscure origin but considerable talent, whom he has raised by degrees from an inferior post in his guard to his present elevation, having been struck by his comeliness at a review twenty years ago, and confirmed ·

in the prepossession by finding his character correspond to his figure. He is in such high favour that the Emperor not long since gave one of his daughters in marriage to this minister's eldest son, and conferred on him many other marks of distinction."[6] We may suppose that the priest actually told Macartney a lot more about the storybook tale of Heshen's role in the life of the normally dutiful Qianlong. But an ambassador's report requires a touch of reserve, and Macartney was therefore content merely to drop hints. Contemporary documents reveal, however, that Heshen was not only the emperor's favorite minister but also his lover.

The imperial harem provided the setting for many a love story, but this may be the strangest such tale in the whole history of the Chinese court. As a very young man, Qianlong fell hopelessly in love with one of his father's concubines. When the empress found out, she decided to deliver her son from the woman's spell by summoning the malefactor and forcing her to strangle herself with a silken cord. Forty years later, as the emperor Qianlong was reviewing his guard, a handsome young man in the very front rank caught his eye. The youth so resembled the woman Qianlong had loved and lost that he could scarcely tell them apart. Many Chinese believe that the souls of those who die violent deaths wander aimlessly until being reincarnated, and as a Lamaist Buddhist, Qianlong believed in metempsychosis. He was convinced that this young man was the reincarnation of his beloved, and it was said that with him Qianlong found the happiness that had been denied him so long ago.[7]

The emperor was completely entranced. Heshen, thirty-five years his junior, was a strong and handsome man who loved life. He had a keen intelligence, and though not a genuine man of letters, he was noted for his winning conversation and clever turn of phrase. In short order he became viceroy, grand councillor, chief minister, and tutor to the prince who would one day become the emperor Jiaqing.

One of the Jesuits epitomized Heshen's position in a single image: "The Emperor is old, and every country has its Pombals and Pompadours."[8] Pombal was the favored prime minister of King José of Portugal, Madame Pompadour the mistress and inspiration of Louis XV. Heshen was all of these things to Qianlong.

As supreme mandarin, the chief minister would ordinarily serve as the Celestial bureaucracy's spokesman before the emperor. But the personal relationship between Qianlong and Heshen had thrown the system out of kilter. Instead of helping the hierarchy of scholar-bureaucrats to exercise their right of counsel (and of censure), Heshen had become an impassable screen shielding the emperor and thereby aggravating the absolutism of this system.

The "second minister," Fuchang'an, was another Tartar. Father Raux had little to say about him except that he had arranged for his older brother to marry one of the emperor's nieces. But the brother in question, General Fukang'an, had pursued a brilliant career of his own, waging victorious punitive campaigns in Taiwan and Tibet and expertly governing the province of Canton, the territory most exposed to foreign influence.[9] Fuchang'an, still a young man, had been named to the Grand Council "even though he seemed more a favorite than a man of competence." He owed his position mainly to his friendship with Heshen.[10]

Eventually both fell victim to palace intrigue, and Jiaqing had them arrested immediately after Qianlong's death.[11] Heshen was condemned to end his own life with the silken cord, just like the concubine whose reincarnation he was presumed to be. The death sentence against Fuchang'an was commuted, but he was ordered to assist Heshen in his suicide.[12]

The third Manchu member of the Grand Council, Agui, was too old to play any active role in state affairs. But the emperor still consulted him, as is clear from several of his marginal notes to state documents, such as: "What is the opinion of the normally so clear-sighted Agui on this matter?"[13] The three other members of the highest organ of the state—two Chinese and a Mongol—carried less weight. As we shall see, one of them, the Mongol Songyun, served as Macartney's escort on the return trip to Canton. But whatever their competence, they did not have the sovereign's ear as the others did.[14]

The success of this mission clearly depended on the aging emperor and his favorite, Heshen. Macartney realized that he would have to speak personally to one or the other of these men, explaining, convincing, cajoling—in short, negotiating. But the picture painted by Father Raux left him puzzled. He wondered whether these powerful court personalities would ever be more than ghostly presences concealed by the invisible curtain of ritual etiquette.

IN THE MEANTIME, the Chinese were as concerned about the envoy's ships as they were about the envoy himself. The British had asked the authorities in Zhejiang for "a piece of vacant land where the squadron could establish a camp and care for its sick."[15] The emperor replied immediately: "Let the sick be confined to this enclosure and let the inhabitants not approach them."[16] The quarantine was justified. Between August 6 and August 29 five men died aboard the *Lion*: a soldier, a cooper, two seamen, and an officer. The crew swabbed the deck with vinegar and fumigated and aerated the ship.[17]

On August 25 a memorandum from Changlin, viceroy of Zhejiang, explained: "The sea bottom around Zhoushan island is dangerous, all sand and mud. It is therefore not possible to establish a camp there. At the port of Cengang, northeast of the island, the ships would have a secure mooring and the men could camp nearby." Assembling the men and the ships in one place was far more practical for the authorities assigned to keep watch over the foreigners. "Good," the emperor wrote in the margin of Changlin's report.[18]

No aspect of the movement of the ships or the behavior of the barbarians escaped him. But he was under the influence, and the whole court knew it. Everyone but him.

28

The Emperor's Vermilion Brush

(August 28–31, 1793)

ZHENGRUI THOUGHT it had been a clever idea to send Macartney's August 25 letter to Gower to the court instead of to Zhoushan. The emperor disagreed, considering it a major blunder. Why delay the departure of six hundred barbarians who had actually asked to cast off? When he found that the salt commissioner had once again acted without consulting with his colleagues, he lost his temper. On August 28 Heshen issued a reprimand, which the three mandarins received on August 30. They must have been chilled indeed by the emperor's rage.[1]

The letter bore his mark, for the text drafted in his name by the chief minister was annotated with his own vermilion marginal notes. The three mandarins kowtowed to this red ink: it was as though His Holy Majesty had rebuked them in person.

Heshen dealt first with the crux of Zhengrui's latest memorandum: "Since the horde of men on board the ships are unaccustomed to the climate, the envoy wants to send them home forthwith. We ought to let them do as they please." But Zhengrui had not actually told the court what his reply to the tributary envoy had been, nor indeed if he had replied at all. The emperor condemned this lacuna with his red brush: "Not a word in the report."

Are we to conclude from this silence, Heshen asked, that Zhengrui does not consider it advisable for the ships now anchored in Zhoushan to depart immediately? Does he believe that it would be better to wait for all the barbarians to leave together? Here the terrifying red brush added: "Absurd!" The chief minister then instructed Zhengrui to convey the tributary envoy's request to Viceroy Changlin as soon as possible, so that the vessels moored in Zhoushan could cast off.

"Remember that there are no less than six or seven hundred officers and crew members aboard these ships. Their prolonged stay in Zhoushan would entail enormous expenses. Since they themselves now wish to return, why should we forgo such a savings?" The emperor was counting pennies. Having noted that the British ate mainly meat, he had already urged that their provisions of rice and flour be reduced.

Jin Jian, Yiling'a, and Zhengrui were then sharply called to order: reports that arrive without all three signatures suggest unacceptable dissension among them. They had been jointly assigned to accompany the tributary mission, and they were duty bound to collaborate. "Jin Jian and Yiling'a, Zhengrui's hierarchical superiors, should never have let him sign a report alone.* Does Zhengrui imagine that as an imperial legate posted to the tributary envoy, he now commands an authority exceeding that of the ministers? Or have these ministers unilaterally divested themselves of their responsibilities? One of these two explanations must necessarily be the true one."

Words failed the court in condemning "these unspeakable petty quarrels," which were "unfortunately typical of the imperial house."† The entire house was now pilloried in the persons of these three unworthy mandarins.

Even after receiving this reprimand, the three colleagues were not fully aware of just how angry the emperor was. The tracks of his rage appear in the margins of the letter drafted in his name by the chief minister, and these vermilion brushstrokes give us a behind-the-scenes glimpse of a household exchange between Qianlong and his favorite.

The Son of Heaven was manifestly exasperated, and every underling was to feel his ire. Heshen, who drafted the letter, received his own share of imperial wrath. He had preceded the ritual injunction "Obey these instructions" with Jin Jian's name alone, and Qianlong chided him: "This time you forgot Yiling'a and Zhengrui. How can you be so stupid?"

It seems unlikely that the mandarins escorting the British embassy would have been allowed to read such a severe reproach of the chief minister, for that would have violated the rules of the Celestial hierarchy. The usual procedure was that the original of a court letter, annotated by His Majesty, would be sent to its addressee, who would make a copy of it and return the original to the emperor for further annotation. This is

---

* The reference is to the memorandum sent to Jehol on August 26 along with Macartney's intercepted letter to Gower.
† The imperial house was in charge of internal government organization and functioned as an autonomous administration within the Forbidden City.

probably what happened here, and the Son of Heaven therefore had two opportunities to explode.

Ensconced in his summer residence in the Tartar lands, the eighty-three-year-old monarch was beginning to grumble about this embassy, a birthday bouquet that was fast turning into a fistful of thorns. Zhengrui's errors of judgment had hobbled the bureaucratic machine; clearly his promotion from the administration of salt taxes and customs controls had raised him to his level of incompetence, as Heshen cruelly pointed out in an ironic barb on August 16.[2] His inadequacy had disrupted a command system as delicate as the mechanism of a clock.

We now know, however, that it was the emperor himself, with his very Confucian sense of proportion, who had decided that Macartney should be escorted from Dagu to Jehol by a lowly functionary of the salt-tax department. Macartney must not be permitted to boast that he had been accompanied by anyone as important as the viceroy of Beizhili: "That would make the tributary envoy presumptuous."[3] The emperor meant to puncture British pride by consigning care of the embassy to a salt-tax collector. But the tactic had backfired: Zhengrui was simply not up to the task.

The tone gets sharper from letter to letter, attaining a crudity barely credible in such a normally subtle bureaucracy: "The salt administration is clearly unlucky to have such an idiotic functionary."[4] His report was "complete nonsense." How could he have taken it upon himself "to prevent the ships from leaving"?[5] The foam generated by this fresh lather spilled onto Jin Jian and Yiling'a as well: "Why has Zhengrui alone signed a report that should have been issued jointly by the three of you? His ideas are a muddle; he is contemptible and ridiculous."[6]

Heshen hurried to put his own two cents in, telling the malefactors just where they had gone wrong. The style was typical. In China the state reads men's souls. Indeed, this is its hallmark, and subordinates must be made to feel their own guilt. For mandarins, deliberate wrongdoing was more reprehensible than "objective" errors, and Heshen, speaking for the emperor, spared no one. Jin Jian and Yiling'a were "unworthy," "ludicrous," and "odious."

The quarrel between the court and the three mandarins threatened to go on endlessly, scornful admonishment pouring down from the court, expressions of confusion rising up from the underlings. But a vermilion marginal note, probably appended on September 2 to a report dispatched by the three guilty parties the day before, brought a temporary end to the exchange: "Such verbosity is futile." The comment may have been aimed at the Grand Councillors as much as at the mandarins in the field.[7]

It is not unusual for bureaucracy to produce such absurd results. Initiative at the lower echelons is paralyzed by the higher-ups, who then rebuke their underlings for immobility, with all the vehemence typical of refined gentlemen who have temporarily lost their composure. Qianlong was well aware of the negligence of those who served him. It was as if the first of all Chinese had brief flashes of wakefulness from the narcissistic slumber in which the entire nation was held by its two-thousand-year-old system.

Tension was far greater among the Chinese than among the British. The rigidity of their system infected the former with the endless factionalism of mandarins warring over their buttons, while the latter closed ranks in a world wholly foreign to them. My country right or wrong. The British saw the Chinese as a threat that had to be confronted with unanimity. Despite their disillusionment, weariness, and occasional edginess, no real internal dissension is apparent among our witnesses.

THE IMPERIAL STORM passed. But more trouble was brewing for poor Zhengrui. These barbarians definitely had no idea how to live.

On August 29 the ambassador handed him the promised note about court ceremony. It was a bad business.

Zhengrui was not the only one to be terrified by this note. Try as he might, Macartney could find no one willing to translate it. Neither the mandarins, nor the missionaries, nor even his own Manchu interpreter wanted to get involved in such a grave affair of state. After all, many an imprudent official had been "bambooed," imprisoned, or even beheaded for merely transmitting a barbarian message to the court in violation of the prescribed ritual. The Flint experience was an example. In the end, Father Raux agreed to translate the note but not to copy it out. He would not even let his secretary do that. The risk was simply too great.[8]

Luckily for Macartney, young Staunton was now able to write passable characters. The remarkable tale of the translation and recopying of this note is recounted by Staunton and Anderson. It had to go from English (which Father Raux did not understand) to Latin, to standard Chinese, to official Chinese. After which it was transcribed by the boy from London.

Fear of any initiative not in strict accordance with the accepted code was so pervasive that it is hard to see how any significant change could occur in China except as the consequence of crisis. "A religious adherence to ancient customs, without much investigation of their origins, was a principal feature in the Chinese character," Macartney wrote.[9]

"Adherence to ancient customs" hardly covered the ground. He might well have said "holy terror of their violation." This episode—comic, cruel, and crucial—epitomized the entire mission.

What was it that Macartney proposed in this terrifying note? Simply that a Chinese official of rank equivalent to his own stand before a portrait of George III and perform whatever ceremony Macartney himself performed before Qianlong. Reciprocal and simultaneous prostrations before the greatest sovereign of the East and the greatest sovereign of the West.

Zhengrui's face darkened as he read the note. Such an equivalence was out of the question. There was only one emperor, and that was the Son of Heaven. Other monarchs were mere kinglets. Wang and Qiao enthusiastically proposed to proceed "on the spot" to this ceremony, which at least offered a way to get the tributary envoy to bow down. But Macartney cooled their ardor. He knew that their kowtow to a portrait of George III would be meaningless without imperial endorsement.

He must also have known that Zhengrui's unconcealed opposition was the correct stance from the Chinese point of view and that the emperor would never acknowledge the king of England as his equal, even through the intermediary of a mandarin. But despite the difficulties he knew lay ahead, he pressed on.[10]

"We must impose our will on these Englishmen," the emperor repeated, "demonstrating to them the effectiveness of our system and the superiority of our civilization."[11] This would be another constant factor in relations between China and the West over the two centuries to come. Not even debacle would undercut Chinese confidence in Celestial superiority. In 1867, seven years after the sacking of the Summer Palace, a high-ranking mandarin wrote: "I have heard that in their dispatches and treaties the puny hobgoblins or petty monsters whom they [the barbarians] have the audacity to call 'Emperors' are placed on a level of equality with His Sacred Majesty."[12]

Such coded language was so foreign to Macartney that he failed to grasp its meaning. He did not realize that Zhengrui had been chosen as his escort precisely because of his mediocre rank. In fact, he assumed that Zhengrui must have been a top official if he had been granted the honor of accompanying the ambassador of His Gracious Majesty. Two centuries later, we know more about the motives of the two sides than they did themselves, for we are confidants of both, and of history itself.

29

Jehol Is Not the Place
to Do Business

(August 30–September 1, 1793)

Lord Macartney would have done better to come to Canton,
and once there, to propose, with firmness, moderation, and
perseverance, a treaty of commerce.

CHARLES DE CONSTANT, February 1793[1]

MACARTNEY CONCLUDED his preparations on Friday, August 30, and planned
to set out for Jehol on Monday, September 2. When he announced that
he would spend the two intervening days "viewing the buildings, triumphal
arches, and other things most worthy of observation in the city of Peking,"
he was told that this would have to wait until he returned from Tartary,
since "it was improper that an Ambassador should appear in public till
after he had been presented to the Emperor."[2] Macartney pointed out that
he had already appeared in the capital—before a public numbering in the
millions.

Diplomatic custom in Europe forbade ambassadors to conduct any
official activity before presenting their letters of accreditation. But at least
they were free to wander about. Celestial tradition prohibited conveyors
of tribute from so much as appearing outdoors until their missions had
been accomplished.[3] The interdiction on tourism may also have been a
subtle way of suggesting to the tributary envoy that if he showed no
flexibility, neither would his hosts.

Macartney assumed that the Chinese would surely understand the
obvious fact that official missions could not set out on Saturday or Sunday.
By Chinese reckoning, however, it was not Friday, August 30, 1793, but
the twenty-fourth day of the seventh lunar month of the fifty-eighth year
of the Qianlong era. "The Chinese have no set days of rest," one observer
noted with astonishment.[4]

Today these differences have largely disappeared, though the Chinese continue to observe the lunar calendar for their holidays. But for centuries the Chinese did not count centuries. An emperor assuming the throne was considered a god whose accession marked the opening of an era, just as the birth of Christ opened the Christian era. In France the year 1793 marked the birth of the revolutionary calendar, the first in the West to attempt to break with Christian chronology. Maoist China lacked that audacity, but even today the Chinese do not think of their history in terms of centuries or millennia before or after Christ. Few Chinese could answer the question, What were the centuries of Yuan rule? But every schoolchild knows that the Yuan dynasty came after the Song and before the Ming.

CUSTOM DICTATED that Macartney offer Qianlong a personal gift, "something portable to be delivered into the Emperor's hands by my own at the time of my introduction." The coach would not do, since it could not be *handed* to the emperor. Moreover, the "principal great men in the Ministry," as well as the emperor's sons, favorite ministers, and several others "expected to be gratified in the same manner."[5]

All the presents Macartney had brought with him were listed in the document given to the court, and he was therefore "a good deal at a loss what to fix upon." He found himself compelled to turn to members of the embassy, from whom he purchased objects they had brought along to sell despite his own strict prohibition of such sales. Captain Mackintosh agreed to part with a collection of "watches of very fine workmanship" for the profit they would have fetched in Canton. The captain did pretty well for himself in this exchange, but business is business.

And that "would be the last of the presents." Once again the information came from Father de Grammont, who wrote to Macartney again on August 30. This time his letter must have raised the ambassador's hopes for his mission's success. The priest had produced yet another masterpiece of self-promotion and sly denigration:

> The mandarins seem quite content with Your Excellency's most dignified manners and with the magnificent gifts. The more obstacles that are placed in the path of my desire to pay Him my respects, the more widely do I sing the praises of His illustrious nation: its power, its riches, its credit, and its love for the sciences. . . .
>
> I base myself upon the advantages that would accrue to the Empire from trade with England. I point out that every year there arrive in Canton some fifty or sixty English vessels which spend immense sums in that city; that the vessels of all other kingdoms, taken together,

represent scarcely a fourth of that total; that English trade, already so lucrative for the Empire, would be even more profitable were it freed from the impediments now weighing upon it in Canton, and that it could well be extended to any other port in which vessels were not compelled to wait four or five months before unloading their cargo, often being obliged to return during the monsoons, at the risk of being lost at sea.

It is well that Your Excellency know who His friends are. The Portuguese d'Almeida has now been named to the Tribunal of Astronomy, a subject of whose most basic principles he is ignorant. He once had the opportunity to treat Heshen for a slight indisposition, and this was the origin of his good fortune, which in turn emboldened him to seek the honor of being named Your Excellency's interpreter. He will, however, soon enough be divested of this good fortune and this honor, if Your Excellency can prevent him from acting as interpreter in Jehol. . . . For the rest, my sole complaint against this missionary is his pretensions against the English nation. . . .

Upon his return from Jehol, Your Excellency will have many a present to bestow in Peking. [There follows a list, which Macartney later put to good use.] It is essential that d'Almeida have nothing whatever to do with the distribution of these gifts. I would only alert Him that MM. Poirot and Raux are unschooled in the ways of the world.[6]

In addressing Lord Macartney, this priest, the scion of an illustrious family and the son of a marquis, was inhibited neither by ecclesiastical solidarity nor by Christian charity. In those days "rank" and "the ways of the world" outweighed all other considerations in all the world's courts.

"According to the letter with which Your Excellency has honored me, I find that it may be impossible for me to see Him before His departure for Jehol, and in the light of certain pronouncements which I have heard, I foresee that neither will it be easy for me to see Him after His return."[7] These lines must have given Macartney pause. Did de Grammont have information that the embassy's days would be numbered after Jehol?

But the very next day, August 31, Macartney finally met this prolific letter writer. De Grammont apologized for not having come sooner, attributing the delay to the "jealousy" of the legate, who did not appreciate de Grammont's "having talked so much of the Embassy, of the power and grandeur of the English nation, of the magnitude of its commerce with, and its importance to, the Chinese Empire."[8] Macartney immediately realized that the priest was quite well informed. But de Grammont may have been too polite to be completely honest. He concluded with this pirouette: "I shall remain here in tranquillity, convinced that it is not in Jehol that Your Excellency must do business."⁹ If Jehol is not the place to do business, Macartney must have wondered, what am I going there for?

THE WORN "English poste-chaise" in which Macartney meant to make the trip to Jehol "greatly attracted the notice of the Chinese," who "were so anxious to understand all its parts, that they made various drawings of it. But so familiar are the eyes of these people to the glare and glitter of colours and gilding, that, however they might admire the mechanism and contrivance of the carriage, they did not hesitate to express their disapprobation of its exterior appearance."¹⁰ Anderson himself, however, had to admit that it "did not possess any very uncommon degree of attraction."¹¹

When the time came to distribute ceremonial clothing for the entry into Jehol, a large crate of green clothes trimmed in gold was opened. But "their appearance awakened a suspicion that they had already been frequently worn, and on tickets, sewed to the linings, were written the names of their former wearers; and as many of these tickets appeared, on examination, to be the visiting cards of Monsieur de la Luzerne, the late French ambassador, it is more than probable, that they had been made up for some gala, or fête, given by that minister. But they were never intended for actual service." The British took it all in good humor: "The Chinese may not be supposed to be capable of distinguishing on the propriety of our figure, . . . but we certainly appeared in a very strong point of ridicule to each other."¹²

In the meantime Alexander, the embassy's painter, went to the Yuanming Yuan "with a blue-button mandarin" to make a drawing of the planetarium. "On our return, we were met on the road by a young mandarin of the royal family, with a retinue of about twenty attendants on horseback. Agreeably to Chinese etiquette we were obliged in compliment to him to drive off the road and to alight till he had passed. My conductor endeavoured to persuade me to kneel before this august personnage, who seemed much amused by my declining this mode of respect."¹³ The innocent Alexander, smug in his British good conscience, never suspected that the mandarin's smile may have been tinged with disapproval of his "barbarity."

DUNDAS AND MACARTNEY had insisted on including rapid-fire cannon among the gifts for the emperor despite the company's warning: "We cannot resist the apprehension . . . having offered them a specimen of what they can neither imitate nor resist. . . . It is well known what difficulties the Company had to encounter formerly in regard to guns and fire-power."[14] But the government and its ambassador ignored this prudent advice. Were they hoping to sell the Chinese artillery as well as Wedgwood porcelain and Lancashire linen? Or were they simply trying to demonstrate British military power and technological expertise?

The legate was disturbed by the embassy's firepower: "He who had expressed himself, before, so anxious that all the presents should accompany the Ambassador to Jehol, was of opinion now that the field pieces should be left behind, as the Emperor was to return soon to Peking. The gunpowder also, . . . was become an object of suspicion with him. He desired it to be delivered up."[15] An edict issued in 1757 strictly forbade foreigners to possess firearms in China. The rules were the rules.

On September 1 Zhengrui wrote to his master: "Tomorrow morning Your slave will leave the capital, escorting the tributary envoy. After his arrival in Jehol six days hence, he will be able to contemplate Your Celestial countenance in an audience."[16]

Jin Jian came to wish Macartney well, telling him that the emperor much appreciated the measures that had been taken "to place the sick men of the *Lion* in a camp separate from Zhoushan and to prevent the seamen from dispersing." Orders had been issued that Gower was free to go: he "should do as he wished."[17]

Macartney seems not to have noticed that the prime concern of the Chinese was to establish a cordon sanitaire around his compatriots in Zhoushan. The emperor wished them "bon voyage." In other words, good riddance. Six hundred fewer meat eaters to feed. Six hundred fewer spies to spy on.

III

IN THE SHADOW
OF THE EMPEROR

(September 2–October 6, 1793)

Between Chinese and Europeans it is always the conventional and the approximate that prevail, giving one the sense of living in fluid and elusive surroundings.

TEILHARD DE CHARDIN[1]

. . . it will give us the utmost satisfaction to learn that Our wishes in that respect have been amply complied with and that as We are Brethren in Sovereignty, so may a Brotherly affection ever subsist between us.

GEORGE III to QIANLONG[2]

There is no truth in the word of strangers.

CHILAM BALAM, Mayan poem[3]

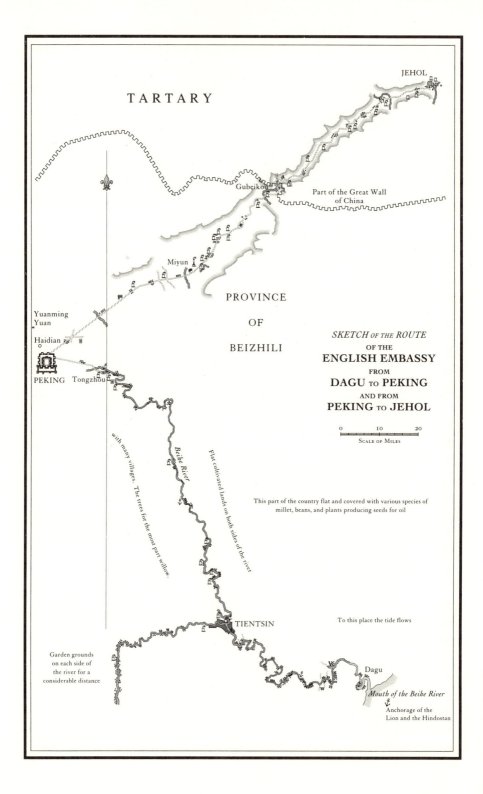

TARTARY

JEHOL

Part of the Great Wall
of China

Gubeikou

Miyun

PROVINCE

OF

BEIZHILI

Yuanming
Yuan

Haidian

PEKING   Tongzhou

SKETCH *OF THE* *ROUTE*
OF THE
ENGLISH EMBASSY
FROM
DAGU TO **PEKING**
AND FROM
PEKING TO **JEHOL**

0   10   20

SCALE OF MILES

This part of the country flat and covered with various species of
millet, beans, and plants producing seeds for oil

Beihe River

with many villages. The trees for the most part willow.

Flat cultivated lands on both sides of the river

TIENTSIN   To this place the tide flows

Garden grounds
on each side of
the river for a
considerable distance

Dagu

Mouth of the Beihe River

Anchorage of the
Lion and the Hindostan

30

Toward the Great Wall

(September 2–5, 1793)

THE DRUMS SOUNDED at one in the morning on Monday, September 2. "The bedding was then sent on in carts; and the Ambassador, with his attendants, . . . quitted the palace at half an hour past three o'clock, under a strong escort of Chinese cavalry." Despite the early hour, the crowds were so thick that it took nearly four hours to cross the city. "At seven o'clock we passed through the city gate, and in about half an hour had exchanged the suburbs for a rich and finely cultivated country."[1]

Macartney shared his post chaise with young Staunton, whose father, hobbled by an attack of gout, was carried on a palanquin. The seventy members of the retinue (forty of them soldiers) traveled on horseback or in wagons. Two hundred Chinese porters carried the gifts and baggage. Twenty-one of Macartney's companions remained behind in Peking, and Alexander, the painter, was miffed to be among them: "To have been within fifty miles of the famous Great Wall, that stupendous monument of human labour, and not to have seen it, I have to regret for ever. . . . That artists should be doomed to remain immured at Peking . . . is not entirely to be accounted for!"[2]

At two in the afternoon the caravan halted in Nanshishee, twenty-five miles into the countryside, where the travelers settled into one of the emperor's residences, on the outskirts of a huge park. But they could admire the palace only from afar, being granted entry to just one pavilion. The mandarins seemed increasingly numerous, and Wang and Qiao led them in climbing aboard the ambassador's coach, admiring "the ingenuity of the springs, and the various contrivances for raising and lowering the glasses, curtains, and jalousies."[3] The British were served refreshments, which were stored in "hermetic containers" and carried the entire way by porters. "To our dinner each day was added a regale of Jooaw and samtshoo: the former is a bitter wine of the country; and the latter, a very strong spirit distilled from rice and millet, whose appearance resembles that of British gin."[4]

The British moved from residence to residence during the six days it took to cover "the one hundred and sixty miles" from Peking to Jehol. They were told that these were imperial lodgings, and that their use was a "privilege . . . considered to be a most flattering mark of distinction, as it is never granted to the first mandarins of the empire."[5] They imagined that the Chinese had decided to pamper their cherished guests by lodging them "at the Emperor's."

In fact they had no idea of the fate they had barely escaped. Originally, Zhengrui had suggested storing the "tribute" in the imperial residences and billeting Macartney and his retinue in private homes. Private homes! When all contact with the local population was to be prevented! Qianlong's angry vermilion brush declared: "Your report is completely devoid of intelligence. If the tribute is to be stored in the outbuildings of the imperial residences, why billet the mission in local homes? Let them be lodged either in pavilions belonging to my retinue—and of this you may tell them—or in the residences of princes—though that must not be revealed. Things will be much simpler if the envoy and the tribute are kept in one place."[6]

In other words, the pavilions of courtiers and eunuchs were appropriate to the mission's rank, but not the pavilions of the emperor himself. The residences of his sons might possibly be made available, but knowledge of this privilege must be kept from the envoy, lest he become presumptuous. In the end, however, these precautions were pointless: the British informed their readers that they stayed "at the Emperor's."

Qianlong also issued orders about the pace of the journey, instructing his mandarins not to hurry. "Arrive during the first ten days of the eighth [lunar] month."* The embassy must be "tactfully managed" so as to progress "with slow steps." The emperor did not want these irritating guests on his hands in Jehol for too long. He even offered Zhengrui an excuse for the slow pace: "The British are not used to hard work. It would be uncomfortable for them to travel on horseback."[7] The members of the embassy, however, were quite satisfied with their "no very tardy progress."[8] The Chinese were deliberately going slowly, but the British thought they were moving fast. It is almost as if they were describing two different journeys.

---

* In other words, between September 5 and September 14; the embassy in fact arrived on the eighth.

Though Macartney's people believed they had been granted the honor of the emperor's hospitality, they were well aware that they were forbidden to travel on the special road maintained for his use. This imperial pathway occupied the center strip of the great Peking to Jehol highway. Ten feet wide and raised a foot above the roadway, it was built of moistened sand and clay packed so hard that it had the "firmness of polished marble." This part of the road, Hüttner explained, was "as clean as the parquet floor of a salon."[9] Winder commented: "The road is as smooth as a billiard table; the middle part being solely reserved for His Majesty's convenience. On either side is an excellent road for the use of travellers; it is shaded with handsome trees, and, at stated distance, are cisterns constantly supplied with water to lay the dust."[10] Hüttner speculated that "when the Emperor passes, there is probably no finer road in all the world than this. As we traveled out and back, we saw groups of men busily maintaining its entire length."[11] Macartney estimated that some twenty-three thousand men were working on the road, divided into teams of ten posted every hundred yards or so.

The route was guarded day and night by sentries. On the eve of the emperor's passage, no one was allowed to set foot on it. Once he passed, however, it was abandoned to one and all and quickly deteriorated. It therefore had to be rebuilt twice a year: on the eve of the emperor's departure for Jehol and just before his return to Peking. Hüttner speculated that if the Chinese could "manipulate air and light as well as earth, they would bestow upon their Emperor the exclusive right to air more pure and light more soft."[12]

The second day of the journey took the embassy through mountainous terrain, from Nanshishee to Miyun. Outlined against a ridge ten miles to the west they glimpsed the Great Wall, which the caravan would cross much farther to the north.

In Miyun they spent the evening with a Tartar officer to whom Wang showed great deference, though formally they held the same rank. Macartney felt that this man was well informed "of the pre-eminence of Great Britain in Europe as a civilized, ingenious, and powerful nation,"[13] and he therefore considered him "sensible" and "gentlemanlike." How was it that a Tartar knew anything about Europe? According to Father Raux, one of the many tasks of the head of the French mission was "to visit leading personages and answer the thousand questions they ask about Europe, the sea, and science."[14] This officer may well have participated in such discussions.

There was a dramatic change in the landscape. The fields were now devoted to pasturage, supporting vast herds of small cattle and bulky sheep with "a short thick tail, which is a lump of fat, and weighs several pounds"[15]—still a typical feature of Mongolian sheep today.

On the third day the embassy reached You-chin-sa. Near the pavilion where they would spend the night, Macartney and the officers of his guard inspected a small walled town that the ambassador describes in such detail that it almost sounds as though he were planning to storm it.[16]

When the British asked why there were no cannon on the walls, Qiao replied that they were "not necessary," since China had "no enemies with artillery." The ramparts were meant only to protect the emperor's treasures and granaries from looters. Macartney noted the explanation without comment. This country seemed to have virtually no artillery, but his had plenty. The Chinese claimed to have been familiar with the use of cannon since the time of Ghengis Khan, in the thirteenth century. By 1621, however, when the Portuguese in Macao gave the Ming emperor a gift of three mortars, the city senate had to send "three men to instruct the Chinese how to use them."[17] How could they have fallen so far behind after having been so far ahead? The continuity of progress was an article of British faith, yet here there had been regression, the Chinese illustrating one of their own proverbs: "He who does not advance retreats."

THE ROAD ROSE steadily higher, and the caravan skirted dangerous cliffs. They passed a weeping willow on the bank of a small river, and were told of the Chinese poet who once called the willow "the tree in whose arms swans and birds huddle, to which we owe the music that fills the air and keeps loneliness at bay on summer days."[18] Even Anderson was touched. In this China far from the human swarm, where there was solitude and open space, the British felt at home.

The route Macartney took six days to cover can now be driven in six hours. The riverbanks and ravines, the thick-tailed sheep, the Great Wall, and the small villages are little changed, and you can still see weeping willows and pyramid-shaped rocks resting on their apexes. But the emperor's palaces are gone without a trace.* We know all the details of the sack of the Summer Palace, whose ruination lies heavy on the conscience of the West. But no one knows who sacked the palaces of the Imperial Way, and no one has ever repented of their destruction.

---

* Hou Renzhi, the scholar of archeology with whom I made this trip, assured me that these palaces disappeared "during recent decades." But no one could supply a more exact date: during the rule of the warlords, the anti-Japanese war, the civil war, the Cultural Revolution?

During a lull in conversation the legate, who was about to leave the caravan to go on ahead to Jehol to prepare for its arrival, incidentally told Macartney that his letter to Sir Erasmus Gower had never been delivered. The ambassador was astonished, but declined to make an issue of it. One wonders what accounts for his surprising composure. Diplomacy, resignation, or simply the heedless unconcern of a man on vacation?[19]

DESPITE HIS ATTACK of gout, Staunton observed that tobacco was being grown "in the low grounds of this part of the country." The Chinese smoked it "through bamboo tubes." Smoking was a "prevalent" habit among "persons of both sexes."[20] "Every female from the age of eight or nine years," Barrow wrote, "wears . . . a small silken purse or pocket to hold tobacco and a pipe, with the use of which many of them are not unacquainted at this tender age."[21] Anderson confirms that children, "as soon as they have sufficient strength or dexterity to hold a pipe in their hands, are taught by their parents to smoke. . . ."[22] "Girls of not more than ten years old, or younger," Staunton reports, "coming from the houses near the road out of curiosity to see the strangers pass, were observed to have long pipes constantly in their mouths."[23] Well-bred Chinese, says Macartney, "consider it as a compliment to offer each other a whiff of their pipes,"[24] and Anderson explains that smoking was considered "not only as an habitual amusement, but . . . as a preservative against all contagious diseases."[25] Smoking was so common in China that when someone was deathly ill they said, "He can't even smoke anymore,"[26] where we would say, "He's on his last legs."

Later, on their way to Canton, the British saw a great many tobacco plantations. Staunton wrote that it was "now the season for curing tobacco" and that this was "performed mostly in the open air." He assumed, incorrectly, that tobacco was native to China, since "foreign usages" are rarely adopted.[27] Our travelers constantly invented hypotheses they had no way of verifying. In Europe, however, their reports were taken as gospel truth.

Today we know that it was Spanish and Portuguese explorers who first brought tobacco to China, from South America. Its popularity spread during the decline of the Ming dynasty, when cultivation of other cash crops (mainly tea, cotton, indigo, and sugarcane) also expanded at the expense of grain, fostering the rise of a merchant class and a concomitant spurt of urbanization. This economic and commercial growth paralleled a weakening of the central government. Another constant feature of Chinese history: the slackening of the regime's mechanisms of control leading to a spread of innovation.

China is still far and away the world's leading producer and consumer of tobacco. In a small hotel in the Chinese interior, not far from Ningbo, I once met an American engineer working on a three-year project to build factories on behalf of Philip Morris. Graphs in hand, he explained to me that China would provide an unparalleled cigarette market for many years to come.

In a country where nearly everyone smokes and the state holds a monopoly on supply, smuggling is highly profitable. "Cigarette kings" commanding far-flung networks of accomplices are regularly denounced in the official press. Trains, postal vehicles, and army trucks all play their part in the black-market tobacco trade, which sustains a veritable mafia readily capable of paying off state officials and laundering money.[28]

In 1793 the British embassy also observed that the Chinese, while not disdaining ginseng and cinnabar, had a real passion for opium.[29] Macartney had been instructed not to raise this issue,[30] and it never came up during his mission. But he was well aware of the profitable and thinly veiled traffic in this commodity being run by the East India Company. "The use of this narcotic," wrote the Dutchman André-Everard Van Braam, "has spread so far and wide in the Empire in the course of the past twenty-five years that two thousand four hundred crates are now consumed annually."[31] He also pointed out that the Chinese authorities in Canton were accomplices in this traffic.

The opium trade and the cultivation of poppies have not been entirely eradicated in Communist China. Poppies are grown in an area straddling Yunnan province, Vietnam, Laos, Thailand, and Burma. But today the poison flows from East to West.

The British passed a caravan of "at least two hundred dromedaries and camels carrying heavy loads of wood and charcoal. . . . This large drove was under the direction of one man, who seemed to manage them all without the least difficulty. These animals are among the most docile of brute creation; besides, the length of time they can fast, and the burthens they can bear, render them invaluable in the commerce of the east."[32]* The camel, Father Huc later wrote, seemed "born for servitude."[33]

ON THE MORNING of September 5 the British crossed a steep hill known as Nantianmen, or Heaven's Gate. It was here that they got their first close

---

* Until the 1950s, they came to Peking by the hundreds, but today they can be seen only beyond the Great Wall, in Manchuria, Inner Mongolia, and Turkestan.

view of what Neil Armstrong later called the only human construction visible from the moon: the Great Wall.*

They passed through a valley hemmed in on both sides by sheer slopes. The road wound through a narrow pass with a stream at the bottom. The wall, which sealed the pass and climbed the mountainsides, was in a state of disrepair. It still is.

The British entered a populous city, Gubeikou, and were greeted by three volleys of artillery: "At the end of the town . . . there was a temporary triumphal arch erected in honour of the embassy, finely decorated with streamers and silks of various colours."[34] A double file of soldiers stretched from the arch to the Great Wall. It was the first time the British were impressed by a Chinese military exercise. "I never saw a finer display of military parade. . . . They were all arrayed in a kind of armour, which consisted of a loose coat or robe, in imitation of a coat of mail, with steel helmets that covered their heads and shoulders."[35] Seventy companies of eighty men each stood in close columns, each company wearing a different uniform and carrying its own standard.

These were not placid Chinese, but elite troops of the Manchu "banners," the eight military detachments identified by the colors of their flags: yellow, white, blue, or red, with or without borders. They carried no umbrellas, fans, or pipes. Their bows, Lieutenant Parish observed, were made of an "elastic wood," and the strings were of "silk threads . . . firmly woven." Chinese and Tartars both "value themselves on their skill in the use of this weapon."[36] "We had the army form up in ranks," the legate reported to the emperor. "They displayed their arms and banners, such that all was brilliant and impeccable."[37] A double-edged honor for the British.

Half an hour later, Macartney and his companions reached the foot of the wall. Macartney ordered Lieutenant Parish and his men to measure the ramparts, parapets, walkways, and towers. He considered the wall "the most stupendous work of human hands" and speculated that at "the remote period of its building China must have been not only a very powerful empire, but a very wise and virtuous nation . . . to have had such foresight and such regard for posterity as to establish at once what was then thought a perpetual security for them against future invasion. . . ."[38]

---

* Etiemble contests this assertion, arguing that a wall no more than a few yards wide could not be seen from so far away, even if it is almost four thousand miles long. A human hair becomes invisible at a very short distance, no matter how long it is. *Geographical Magazine* has shown that Armstrong's "Great Wall" was actually just a cloud formation, but the Chinese are much enamored of the more flattering claim.

In fact, that was an oversimplification. Qin Shihuangdi, who unified China in the years 220 to 210 B.C., actually linked various existing walls together. He did not build *the* wall, which at the time was no more than a modest levee of hardpacked earth. The brick and stone were added a thousand years later and were reinforced by the Mings later still. More than one invader breached it, but it did effectively prevent ordinary travel in the countryside, in both directions.[39] Its effect was less to impede invasions than to block escapes, and it is still harder to get out of China than to get in. The Great Wall is a state of mind more than an instrument of military defense.

The Chinese were irritated by the meticulous observations of the British, who swarmed over the wall measuring everything, notebooks in hand. These old walls were considered part of the landscape—something to look at but not to visit—and their hosts almost suspected the English of harboring some dark design. In this they were not far wrong, for Lieutenant Colonel Benson and Lieutenant Parish were hard at work on a secret aspect of their mission: to prepare for a less pacific expedition, just in case the present amicable approaches came to nothing.

But most of the British simply wanted to take home souvenirs. They picked up chunks of brick and guarded them as jealously as if they were "wedges of the most precious metal."[40]

IN FRANCE, on that same day, other Englishmen disembarked in Toulon, responding to the appeals of the inhabitants. In Paris throngs of *sansculottes* converged on the Convention, which placed "the Terror on the agenda."

31

In the Tartar Lands

(September 6–8, 1793)

BEYOND THE GREAT WALL lay the country the British called Tartary, a fallow, barren, savage land of mountains and valleys. "Instead of a level range of various and unceasing cultivation, of the habitations of wealth, the crowd of population, and the exertion of industry; we beheld a wide and barren waste, sinking into valleys and rising into mountains." They came to the foot of a very tall peak, where a road had been cut into the rock, "another proof of the genius and indefatigable spirit of the Chinese people in all works that relate to public utility."[1] It was so steep that the wagons needed extra horses to climb it.

That night there was an incident involving the two Chinese mandarins and a Tartar servant accused of theft. The Tartar acted impertinently, and Wang and Qiao immediately ordered him beaten with bamboo sticks. The servant was indignant at being beaten by Chinese *in Tartar lands*, and even a second bambooing failed to calm him. "On this occasion," writes Macartney, "Wang could not help saying to our interpreter: 'A Tartar will always be a Tartar.'" (Wang apparently did not realize that the interpreter, Mr. Plumb, was himself a Tartar.)

The servant seemed convinced that he was within his rights, and Macartney tried to intervene on his behalf. They were, after all, in Tartar territory, not in China itself. But the mandarins merely laughed, confident in the numerical superiority of their people and the power of the Celestial hierarchy.

That evening Macartney was pleasantly surprised to hear from Qiao that his proposal concerning the court ceremony had every chance of being approved by the emperor.[2]

THE DIFFICULT TERRAIN slowed their march. On the fifth day, September 6, they covered only thirteen miles. As they climbed higher into the mountains, it got colder. Macartney noticed many people "with very large goitres or wens growing on the outside of their throats as in the Valais and the Tyrol."[3]

Hüttner reports that one mandarin approached them and asked to see "the admirable rarities which we were bringing for the Emperor,"[4] adding that he had heard that the British were carrying "a fowl that eats coal, a dwarf a foot and a half tall, an elephant the size of a cat, and a magic pillow that transports he who lays his head upon it to the place of his wish." All this, the mandarin said, was "surely true," because "he had read it in the newspapers."[5]

These fantasies were the stuff of Chinese imagination. A dwarf elephant was a bonsai elephant. China's fairy tales are rife with such extraordinary creatures. And why shouldn't the barbarians be capable of traveling from place to place on magic carpets? The embassy, after all, was carrying one of the hot-air balloons that were all the rage in Europe at the time.

Macartney confirms Hüttner's story, in his usual understated way. The interpreter, he says, "amused us" with a newspaper report of similar idiocies (including one new wrinkle: "a horse the size of a mouse"). He casually mentions that this particular newspaper came from Tientsin.[6] Had Mr. Plumb picked it up when they passed through that city a month earlier, not daring to show it to his employers until now?

It is hard to say whether these stories were spontaneous rumors of the sort that can spread so easily among a population with a blunted critical spirit and a pronounced taste for chimeras, or the product of a deliberate campaign of disinformation designed to present the Westerners as freaks of nature, amusing but insignificant oddities. Perhaps it was a subtle way of erecting a psychological barrier between civilization and barbarism, an obstacle as impassable as a Great Wall of stones cemented in blood.

FOR QUITE SOME time the British had seen no cultivated fields. But now they glimpsed several cleared strips on the flank of a sheer mountainside. Such feats of relentless agriculture can still be seen along the very same road today: tiny terraced gardens cut into steep slopes.

Far above a man worked one parcel, on a rise so nearly vertical that it was hard to see how he could even stand without tumbling into the void. When the British peered at him through their telescopes, they saw that he was hanging from a rope tied around his body. "In this manner he had decorated the mountain with those little cultivated spots that hung about it. Near the bottom, on an hillock, this industrious peasant had erected a wooden hut, . . . where he supported, by this hazardous industry, a wife and family."[7] It looked like a Chinese engraving: a vast, dizzying landscape, a lone, minuscule individual moving within it—one small man integrated into the Great Whole.

The peasant-acrobat's cabin was ringed by a small vegetable garden that probably produced barely enough to feed his own family, at the risk of his life. "The whole of these cultivated spots," Anderson wrote in obvious admiration for the man's courage and ingenuity, "do not amount to more than half an acre; and situated as they are, at considerable distances from each other; and, abstracted from the continual danger he encounters, the daily fatigue of this poor man's life, they offer a very curious example of the natural industry of the Chinese people."[8]

A remarkable encounter between nascent industrial civilization and the rural tradition, between tomorrow's England and eternal China.

ON SEPTEMBER 7 they came within sight of Jehol. The mandarins explained that the entire countryside around the city was reserved for the emperor's use. But as Confucius said, food is even more important than funerals,[9] and Qianlong would have been derelict in his duty as a sovereign had he failed to cause the nourishing earth to bear fruit. He therefore decreed: "The land shall lie idle when we pass it, but it may be ploughed afterwards. In this way the land will not lie fallow, and, in addition, will be a great blessing to the soldiers."[10]

This journey was in many ways a first. True, the glassy smooth imperial roadway was off-limits to the British, and their horses limped, stumbled, and balked on the rocky path. Many of the saddles were missing one or both stirrups, and the "servants of the mandarins left early with the good mounts, leaving the emaciated nags to us."[11] But none of that mattered. The travelers were thrilled at the prospect of succeeding in this historic mission, and the smallest tidbit of information amused them, as when they discovered that it was considered a friendly gesture to whip another man's horse, an act they had first taken as a mark of discourtesy. What was polite here was uncouth elsewhere. Everyone is a someone's barbarian.

These six days were like a vacation for the embassy. "The country here indeed has a very Alpine appearance much resembling Savoy and Switzerland."[12] Perhaps it was the rarefied mountain air, but the British climbed toward Jehol in a careless mood of delectable insouciance.

At eight in the morning on the seventh day, September 8, they reached a village barely two miles from the imperial residence. Here, Macartney reports, they paused to "dress and marshal the procession for my public entry."[13]

The caravan was reminiscent of a royal entrance into a Western city, a street parade in a Flemish carnival, or a Corpus Christi procession of the sort evoked so effectively by Jean Brodin in *La République*: an entire society displayed itself with a pomp meant to tell its story. The order of march, Macartney writes, "made a very splendid show":

A hundred mandarins on horseback;*
Lieutenant-Colonel Benson;
Twelve light dragoons, in three ranks of four;
Lieutenant Parish;
Fife and drum;
Eight artillery men in two rows of four;
A corporal of artillery;
Lieutenant Crewe;
Sixteen infantrymen in four rows of four;
A sergeant of infantry;
Eight servants in four rows of two [wearing the "rich green and gold livery" of the French embassy];
Two couriers [similarly dressed];
Four musicians [ditto];
Six gentlemen of the embassy, two by two, in gold-embroidered scarlet uniforms;
Lord Macartney, Sir George Staunton, and his son, in a chariot;
A servant in livery behind [Anderson adds that it was "the black-boy, dressed in a turban"].[15]

It took the procession nearly two hours to cover the last couple of miles to the palace in Jehol, where the gifts had already been delivered. They advanced through a "prodigious concourse of people, whom curiosity had led to see such a spectacle as they had never seen before, and will never, I believe, behold again."[16]

Anderson, however, struck a note of sarcasm: "There was somewhat of a parade in all this business, but it was by no means calculated to impress a favourable idea of the greatness of the British nation, on the minds of those who beheld it." While the soldiers and the gentlemen of the embassy cut a "respectable figure," the "rest of the company exhibited a very awkward appearance: some wore round hats, some cocked hats, and others straw hats: some were in whole boots, some in half boots, and others in shoes with coloured stockings. In short, unless it was in second-hand coats

---

* An exaggeration? Thomas Staunton speaks only of "several."[14]

and waistcoats, which did not fit them, the inferior part of the suite did not enjoy even the appearance of shabby uniformity."[17]

As the "carnival" slowly advanced to the strains of *God Save the King*,[18] the diplomats, too, may have wondered whether this display was "calculated to impress a favourable idea of the greatness of the English nation." The spectators, who expected to see an unusual people, must not have been disappointed.

32

The Crisis of Ritual

(September 8–9, 1793)

IT IS NO EXAGGERATION to call Jehol the empire's second capital.* The emperor spent three months in the city every summer, and power in China was so highly centralized that the capital was located wherever the emperor happened to be.

"The choice of this district," wrote Kangxi, Qianlong's grandfather, "cannot encroach upon my duties. In harmony with the natural contours of the country, I have built pavilions in the pine groves, thereby enhancing the natural beauties of the hills. I have made water flow past the summer-houses as if leading the mountain mists out of the valleys. . . . When I find pleasure in orchids, I love uprightness; when I see the pines and bamboos, I think of virtue; when I stand beside limpid brooks, I value honesty; when I see weeds I despise dishonesty."[1]

But Jehol was also a wretched city of twisting, dirty streets and sorry wooden huts,[2] and travelers had to cross that part of it in order to enter the imperial domain. Had Qianlong not continued his grandfather's works, building his dream palace and parks, had his presence not brought pomp and luxury to this place each summer, Jehol would not have been worth the "tedious and troublesome journey" required to reach it.[3]

But his presence also made it a vast military camp: "The garrison during the Emperor's residence is about a hundred thousand men."[4] Qianlong took no chances. Even outside Peking, a Manchu army stood at his side, shielding him from any rebellion.

Capital, slum, and military base, Jehol was also a center of Lamaist Buddhism, and the British arrived during a great gathering of pilgrims and lamas dressed in homespun yellow robes. "They did not seem . . . to

---

* Etymologically, Jehol (or Rehe in the pinyin transcription) means "hot stream," and there are in fact hot springs in the city, which is now called Chengde. The name Jehol was used both for the site of the imperial summer residence and for the entire Tartar province.

be much respected by the surrounding multitude; nor did their own demeanor imply any consciousness of dignity, or any attention to exterior decorum, which persons of rank in China are generally solicitous to maintain."[5]

Our Protestants, of course, were firm anticlericalists, and antimonasticism had been virulent in England since Henry VIII's Anglican reform. But their disdain for the Buddhists would not have offended Qianlong's subjects, whose view of the bonzes was shaped by their portrayal in popular plays as thieves, swine, drunkards, and libertines, an image not unlike that of monks in the satirical farces of medieval Europe.[6] Nor does classical Chinese literature spare the female bonzes, presenting them as licentious messengers of eroticism.[7]

IT WAS A GLOOMY Sunday. Once again a palace-prison had been prepared for the British. Three tiled courtyards ringed by galleries formed terraces in the mountainside. The kitchens and common areas opened onto the first level, the apartments of Macartney and Staunton onto the second, and the rooms of the gentlemen of the embassy and their servants onto the third.[8]

There were no high-ranking dignitaries anywhere in sight. Only idlers "of the lower classes" watched the procession, and Anderson makes no secret of his resentful humiliation: "Not a mandarin appeared to congratulate the Ambassador on his arrival, or to usher him, with that form which his dignity demanded, to the apartments provided for him. In short, we came to this place with more than usual ceremony; but we entered into it with as little, as any of those where we had been accommodated during our journey."[9] This was particularly strange, since Macartney had expected that Heshen himself would greet him "on his entry at Jehol."[10]

Lieutenant Colonel Benson kept his soldiers at the ready, waiting for the chief minister. "In this state of suspense we remained from our arrival till past four o'clock; in the course of which time we had paraded at least a dozen times, as several mandarins came to take a curious view of us, and every one of them was supposed, in his turn, to be the Grand Colao."[11] The day dragged on, and dinnertime drew near. Heshen was obviously not coming.

News of two important events was received in Canton on that same day: war between France and England had been declared on February 1, and a British expedition had been sent to Tibet under the command of Captain Kirkpatrick. With no extra ship available, the company thought it too risky to entrust a letter containing such dramatic news to the imperial post. Only on October 5 was a small ship dispatched to Tientsin, and the message never reached the ambassador.[12]

Though Macartney was as uneasy as his companions, he tried to put the best possible face on the situation: "Soon after we arrived at this place, the Legate came and gave me back my paper about the ceremonial, and said that if I delivered it myself to the Minister I should receive the answer. Our interpreter also came and told me from Wang and Qiao that the Emperor had seen my entry and procession from one of the heights of this park, and was much pleased with them, and that he had immediately ordered the first Minister and another Grand Secretary to wait upon me."[13]

That order was soon countermanded. The chief minister's retinue was said to be too numerous for this palace. Macartney was therefore told to make his own way to Heshen, who in any case was having difficulty walking as the result of a knee injury.*

Macartney responded to Heshen in kind. Who did they think he was? This was no way to treat the ambassador of the world's most powerful nation! He therefore declined the invitation, claiming that the long journey had tired him. A knee for a knee. Staunton, he said, would present his credentials to the chief minister that evening.

As long as he had received no news of his note, Macartney could still hope that there would be no objection to his proposal. Qiao, after all, had suggested as much. But now the note had been returned to him—"sealed," Staunton explains. Zhengrui even claimed that he had "kept the memorial the whole time in his possession."[14] The British did not believe that for a moment. Clearly, Zhengrui had been told what to say. But what did it all mean?

The ambassador was now in a tight spot. His diplomatic indisposition had only exasperated the emperor. Wang and Qiao feared that the court might suspect them of having somehow inspired the dreaded note, and they implored Staunton to ask his son to sign it with his Chinese name, "to certify it to be his writing."[15] Imperial wrath would spare the head of a child, but not of a mandarin.

Sir George duly went to see the chief minister, accompanied only by young Thomas and Mr. Plumb.

Staunton junior admits that they were received quite casually. "That evening," he writes, "we went to see the prime minister. . . . He was sitting with four other ministers. He greeted us cooly, speaking to us in a proud and imperious tone. He gave us some hot milk and provided a seat for

---

* From young Staunton's indiscretions we learn that high-ranking Celestial dignitaries *never* made the first visit.

my father, but not for Mr. Plumb or me. After conversing with him for about an hour, we returned."[16] A single touch of kindness in the glacial welcome: the British taste for milk had been noted.

The father says even less about the meeting than the son. Staunton, like the ambassador, always avoids "dramatizing." But he does not contradict the boy's account. "At the audience of the Colao, he was seated on a platform covered with silk, between two Tartar and two Chinese mandarins of the state."[17]

He speaks of these "mandarins" as though they were mere members of Heshen's retinue, but in fact Staunton had before him very nearly the entirety of the empire's government: five-sixths of the Grand Council (the aged Agui was probably the missing member).[18] In this initial confrontation, Heshen had no wish to act alone.

He curtly "went through the formality" of requesting that the minister plenipotentiary explain the objective of the embassy, and Staunton promptly presented him with a Chinese translation of the king of England's letter to the emperor. This message said:

> His Most Sacred Majesty George III, by the Grace of God King of Great Britain, France [sic] and Ireland, Sovereign of the Seas, Defender of the Faith, and so forth, To the Supreme Emperor of China Qianlong, worthy to live tens of thousands and tens of thousands thousand Years, sendeth Greeting.
>
> We have taken various opportunities of fitting out Ships and sending in them some of the most wise and learned of Our Own People, for the discovery of distant regions, not for the purpose of conquest, or of enlarging our Dominions, which are already sufficiently extensive for all Our wishes, not for the purpose of acquiring wealth, or even of favouring the commerce of Our subjects, but for the sake of increasing Our knowledge of the habitable Globe, of finding out the various productions of the Earth, and for communicating the arts and comforts of life to those parts where they were hitherto little known; . . .
>
> We have been still more anxious to enquire into the arts and manners of Countries where civilization has been perfected by the wise ordinances and virtuous examples of their Sovereigns thro a long series of ages; and, above all, Our ardent wish had been to become acquainted with those celebrated institutions of Your Majesty's populous and extensive Empire which have carried its prosperity to such a height as to be the admiration of all surrounding Nations. . . .
>
> We have the happiness of being at peace with all the World. . . . Many of Our subjects have also frequented for a long time past a

remote part of Your Majesty's dominions for the purpose of Trade. No doubt the interchange of commodities between Nations distantly situated tends to their mutual convenience, industry, and wealth. . . .

We are indeed equally desirous to restrain Our Subjects from doing evil or even of showing ill will in any foreign Country, as We are that [they] should receive no injury in it. There is no method of effecting so good a purpose, but by the residence of a proper Person authorized by Us to regulate their conduct and to receive complaints against them, as well as any they might consider as having just cause to make of ill treatment towards them.

By such means every misunderstanding may be prevented, every inconvenience removed, a firm and lasting friendship cemented and a return of mutual good offices secured between our respective Empires.

All these considerations have determined Us to depute an Embassador Extraordinary and Plenipotentiary to Your Court. . . . Our right trusty well beloved Cousin and Counsellor, the Right Honourable George Lord Viscount Macartney. . . . [There follow some twenty lines on his career and talents.]

And in order to avoid every possibility of interruption in this available communication which we wish to establish and maintain with your sublime Person and Court, and which might happen after the departure of Our said Embassador Extraordinary whose presence may be necessary to Our affairs elsewhere or in case of his death or occasional absence from Your Capital, We have appointed our trusty and well beloved Sir George Staunton [about fifteen lines on his virtues] to be Minister Plenipotentiary to Your August Person, with Credentials likewise under Our great Seal. . . .

We rely on Your Imperial Majesty's wisdom and Justice and general benevolence to Mankind so conspicuous in Your long and happy reign that You will please to allow Our Ambassador and Representative to Your Court to have the opportunity of contemplating the example of Your virtues and to obtain such information of Your celebrated institutions as will enable him to enlighten Our people on his return; He, on Our part being directed to give, as far as Your Majesty will please to desire it, a full and free communication of any art, science, or observation, either of use or curiosity, which the industry, ingenuity and experience of Europeans may have enabled them to acquire: And also that You will be pleased to allow to any of Our Subjects frequenting the coasts of Your dominions and conducting themselves with propriety a secure residence there, and a fair access to Your markets. . . .

. . . it will give us the utmost satisfaction to learn that Our wishes in that respect have been amply complied with and that as We are Brethren in Sovereignty, so may a Brotherly affection ever subsist between us. . . .

Imperator Augustissime
Vester bonus frater et Amicus
[Most August Emperor, Your Good Brother and Friend]
Georgius R[19]

Staunton then delivered the ambassador's memorandum on the question of ceremony, which Zhengrui had returned that afternoon. He requested a written response that the ambassador could study.[20] Heshen "affected to be a stranger" to Macartney's memorandum, but he nonetheless seemed "prepared to make objections to the proposal it contained." Neither side would budge. "The discussion terminated by the Colao's desiring his reasons to be reported to the Embassador for his consideration."[21]

But Heshen said nothing about a written response. Did that mean that the subject was still open to discussion?

This meeting was by no means private. "Throughout the interview, the hall was filled with people employed in the palace, who were allowed to hear what was being said. It seemed as though in dealing with foreigners who had come from so far, there was no point in hiding anything from the Chinese." The regime's rule of secrecy did not apply to relations with foreigners, and for good reason: the intent here was not to negotiate, but to manifest the immutable order. The presence of a large number of witnesses probably encouraged the chief minister to strike "an air of dignified reserve; and in his manners and conversation, he seemed willing to convey the idea, that whatever civilities he shewed to the English minister, were the condescensions of national as well as personal superiority."[22] But that did not prevent the Chinese from resenting British "pride."

Each camp had stated its position, and the crisis of ritual was now inescapable. Imperial archives show that Qianlong had come to view this embassy in an increasingly unfavorable light. He was annoyed by the ambassador's claim of weariness and by his dispatch of his deputy to see Heshen in his place. And toward what end? To present a "paper of ignorance." The reference may have been to the letter from King George, the memorandum on ceremony, or both, and it is likely that the comment was meant to condemn their content as well as their form.[23]

On September 8, the very day of the embassy's arrival in Jehol, the emperor issued an edict stipulating a ceremony that offered what he must have considered the absolute limit of tolerable concessions. Here he waived the kowtow in favor of a single prostration: "The [Chinese] officers shall lead the British envoy and his adjunct to the foot of the steps. The British, prostrating themselves, shall wait as the Emperor gives them a gift for their king. The officers shall present themselves before the Emperor and perform the three genuflections and the nine prostrations, heads touching the ground. These marks of reverence effected, they shall usher forward the English, who shall perform one prostration, heads touching the ground, before returning to their place."[24]

But now the British had upset these plans by resubmitting their note, and the emperor was angry: "The more magnanimous we are toward them, the more conceited they become."[25]

The idea of reciprocity suggested by Staunton was quite inconceivable to Qianlong, who considered himself the summit and guarantor of universal order. No one could be likened to him. To propose a ceremony based on reciprocity was therefore absurd.

Equally absurd were King George's extravagant suggestions: that China should avail itself of British progress (as if China were not sufficient unto itself!); that British subjects in Canton should not be obliged to endure injustice (as if the emperor could have committed injustice!); that an English representative should take up permanent residence in Peking (as if it had not always been the duty of barbarians to leave the empire once they had delivered their tribute!); that Qianlong should consider George III his "friend and brother" (as if the one and only Son of Heaven could have friends and brothers!). So much unpardonable nonsense in so few words!

On September 9 Qianlong declared: "I am extremely displeased!"

His fury abated the next day, but before "coming to his senses" he actually contemplated canceling the audience and sending Macartney back to Zhili, where he had first come ashore.[26]

Macartney's attempt at a clever compromise was rejected. It was once again solemnly explained to him that if he wanted to see the emperor, he would have to prostrate himself. Nothing less would do. The ball was now in his court.

He spent two days pondering his next move. In the meantime, the Chinese sought to break his will by keeping him isolated while harrying him with fresh initiatives.

Macartney seems not to have realized the full extent of the danger. When Wang, Qiao, and the legate paid another visit to prevail upon him to withdraw his ceremonial innovation, the ambassador insisted that an independent sovereign had to be treated differently from a tributary prince. He was still convinced that the emperor was unaware of his proposal, and he remained confident that once it was actually submitted to him, he would surely accept reciprocal and simultaneous homage to the world's two most powerful nations.[27]

Was Macartney really as confident as his journal suggests?* If so, it may have been because he interpreted Chinese irritation as a sign of weakness. He pointed to the contradiction in their arguments. The mandarins pleaded with him to submit to the ritual prostration as a trivial formality, but the kowtow suddenly assumed the highest importance when it was a matter of a Chinese bowing to a portrait of the king of England.[28]

He never realized that from their own point of view, the logic of the Chinese was flawless. Nothing was more natural than kowtowing to the emperor, a daily habit with centuries of history behind it. But no one had ever seen a Chinese bow to another monarch. There was, after all, only one Son of Heaven.

When his interlocutors went so far as to warn him to think of his own security, Macartney proudly replied that his attachment to his king took precedence over any consideration of personal safety, which was his way of calling their bluff. British honor was at stake, and he had not forgotten his protest to Catherine II's chief of protocol, nor his proud response to Admiral d'Estaing, nor his acceptance of a duel to the death.

Staunton, however, sensed the gathering threat. The atmosphere was getting hostile: ". . . the conversation which passed at the palace with the Colao, spread rapidly through Jehol. Several persons, who saw in the Embassy, only a few solitary foreigners, entirely at the mercy of the court which they came to visit, were at a loss to conceive how they could presume to propose conditions to it, or hesitate to obey its pleasure."[29] Had some of the Chinese leaders considered subjecting Macartney to the fate that befell Peres, the first Portuguese ambassador, who died in prison in the 1520s after evincing too much "disrespect for customs"? Two and a half centuries do not amount to much in an empire several millennia old.

Staunton mentions, not without pride, that the Chinese were surprised by the obstinacy of the British. But he did not realize that most of all they were outraged by their impropriety and stunned by their lack of awareness. Rumor had it that the embassy might not even be granted an audience with the emperor.[30] That might well have been the case had Heshen and Wang not soothed the emperor's fury.[31]

---

* Many of the entries in this journal may have been altered later. Macartney took notes daily but edited them at his leisure during the return voyage.

33

Victory

(September 10, 1793)

ON SEPTEMBER 10 the trio of Zhengrui, Wang, and Qiao paid another visit. Young Staunton, laconic as usual, noticed a change: "The first [Zhengrui] was degraded two degrees of his Mandarinate. Cool weather."[1]

Especially for Zhengrui. But why? The two Chinese, delighted that their Tartar superior had been sanctioned, offered an explanation the moment his back was turned. In one of his reports, they said, he had told Qianlong about the portrait of the emperor hanging in one of the cabins of the *Lion*. When he next saw his legate, Qianlong asked whether the painting was a good likeness. The evasive Zhengrui was then forced to admit that he had not actually seen it with his own eyes, his fear of the water having prevented him from boarding the ship. But he had earlier informed the emperor in writing that he had carried out the explicit instruction to greet the tributary envoy on his vessel.[2] He had therefore been caught lying to the emperor, a serious crime.

The archives of the Grand Council, however, show that it was Wang and Qiao who were lying this time, most probably under orders. The legate's disgrace actually had nothing to do with the portrait. True, Qianlong was surprised to find that his image was displayed aboard the *Lion*. He wondered how the British had acquired such a painting and why it did not figure on the list of presents. But he had already scolded Zhengrui (at the beginning of August)[3] for not having gone aboard the *Lion*. That particular incident had been closed long ago.

The real reason for the Tartar legate's disgrace was far more serious, recent, and simple. After the August 11 banquet in Tientsin, Zhengrui had reported that the barbarian had "touched his forehead" when the food was brought to him. It was that formulation that now ensnared the legate,[4] since Macartney's memorandum proved that Zhengrui had lied. When questioned in Jehol and presented with the evidence of the envoy's proposal on ceremony, Zhengrui had acknowledged that in fact Macartney had not "touched his forehead" during the banquet. Nor had he ever practiced the kowtow. Wang and Qiao, of course, could not have given Macartney the true explanation, since to do so would have breached the rules of ritual. On the other hand, to claim that Zhengrui had suffered a serious sanction for the venial sin of not telling the truth about the emperor's portrait might enhance British understanding of His Imperial Majesty's fearsome authority.

The legate's optimistic dissimulation had set the stage for the crisis that was now in full bloom, and his demotion was punishment not only for his outright lies, but also for what he had concealed, namely his inability to manipulate this barbarian. Chinese documents indicate that he was demoted by one grade.[5] He had been specially promoted for this mission, and having failed, he was now busted back to his original rank. The emperor also took away his peacock feather, issuing him a crow's feather instead.[6] (Two centuries later, during the Cultural Revolution, the dunce cap would replace the crow's feather.)

This style of punishment is still common today. In the West, punitive sanctions target the malefactor's function: you can get suspended, silenced, or even promoted ("kicked upstairs"). But in China the sanction targets your dignity. You keep your post, but do not escape disgrace. The color of the button is there for all to see. Demoted mandarins had to note in their correspondence: "Mandarin, formerly of the————class, but now degraded to the————class."[7]

Zhengrui might well have suffered a worse fate, such as bambooing or exile. The "last stage of public degradation," Barrow says, "is an order to superintend the preparation of the Emperor's tomb, which implies that the person so sentenced is more fit to be employed among the dead than the living."[8]

In China today ministers and party leaders are suddenly and publicly denounced, even while remaining in their posts (provided they engage in self-criticism). Press and poster campaigns have replaced the withdrawal of the peacock feather.

Zhengrui continued his mission, and even tried to regain the prince's favor by manifesting renewed zeal. But the Briton was unmoved.

The mandarins were feverishly seeking a solution, and suddenly someone had an idea. Suppose a portrait of King George III were hung on the wall behind the emperor's throne. Macartney would then be prostrating himself before his own king, though from the Chinese point of view he would be kowtowing to the emperor. It was a circuitous, elegant, and therefore thoroughly Chinese way of saving face for the ambassador while not violating the Celestial Order.

The trouble was that Macartney would not prostrate himself before his own sovereign even once, let alone nine times. The most he would do was go down on one knee; he touched both knees to the ground only before God.

He repeated that he could not pay greater homage to another sovereign than he would pay to his own. The puzzled mandarins then asked how British subjects greeted their king. Macartney dropped to one knee and mimicked kissing the king's hand. He explained that he would be willing to do the same for the emperor. The three mandarins then "retired seemingly well satisfied."[9]

As this glimmer of hope appeared at the summit, uneasiness was mounting among the rank and file. The leaders negotiated, and the personnel eyed one another. Tartar mandarins carefully examined the French livery worn by the British servants, fingering the braid and finding that it was not gold but yellow cloth.[10] Anderson thought the Manchus were laughing at him, but that was just another misunderstanding. Yellow was the imperial color, and no one had the right to wear it without explicit permission.

Those members of the mission not directly involved in the negotiations grew increasingly tense. The condescension of these Manchus grated. Macartney advised Winder to inform the servants that if there were any complaints about the quantity or quality of the food, they should leave their plates "untouched" and "intimate the grievance" to the ambassador himself. What was the meaning of that? Their meals had always been lavish. The next lunch, however, clarified the warning: barely enough was served to satisfy half the embassy. Reduced rations.[11]

The men did Macartney proud. Prisoners they might be, and hungry to boot, but they would never bow down! They took this ill treatment as an "insult . . . to the crown and dignity of the first nation in the world." Let the opprobrium fall upon the offenders! Leaving their pittance on their plates, they alerted the ambassador, who immediately sent Mr. Plumb to "insist on more hospitable usage." Five minutes later, their tables were covered with steaming dishes, which had obviously been ready in the kitchens but had been held back to test the British. Anderson wondered whether this had been a mere prank (which speculation he dismissed) or an attempt to save money, which "could be no object to the treasury of the Chinese Emperor." It was "considered, therefore, as an enigma," which the men decided to ignore once the new meal had been served.[12]

Punish the barbarians. Show them that if they fail to respect customs, generosity might cease at any moment. A little harassment, a little extra pressure.

Immediately after this lunch, Qiao informed Macartney that he had just had a long conference with the chief minister and that they were now leaning toward one of two formulas that might suit the British: either reciprocal, Chinese-style prostrations or the simple English genuflection.

Shortly afterwards, the legate arrived to announce that they had opted for the genuflection. Just one last point. It was not customary to kiss the emperor's hand. To compensate for the elimination of hand kissing, Macartney would have to go down on both knees. He replied that he had already given his answer to that suggestion: on all occasions when the Chinese custom was to kowtow, he would genuflect on one knee. The legate insisted that even so, hand kissing was out. Macartney agreed, adding: "As you please, but remember it is your doing, and according to your proposal, is but half the ceremony, and you see I am willing to perform the whole one."[13] In the end, not only Zhengrui but the entire court, including Heshen, had given in.

Macartney had won, and in the process saved the expedition. He was amused at being told to dispense with the hand kissing. As it turned out, he would not even pay Qianlong the homage he would have paid to his own king. A gesture Westerners considered a mark of humility was seen by the Chinese as sacrilegious contact with the imperial person. So much the better!

Macartney attributed his victory to the proximity of the emperor, who he thought had overruled the rigid lower echelons, always "more royalist than the king." He believed that he had pierced the wall of silence erected around the sovereign by his entourage, and he was equally convinced that things would go much better in Canton once His Majesty learned what was really happening there. All he had to do was to supply this ill-informed sovereign with the proper information. The embassy had already proved its worth, and the future seemed bright. Everything was well in hand.

Macartney won the battle of form, but his own journal contains evidence of his underlying defeat, though he seems unaware of it. On September 11 he mentions the preparations for the emperor's birthday celebration, which were taking up all the chief minister's time. On the thirteenth Macartney notes: "To-morrow being the grand festival at Court *and* [emphasis added] the day appointed for our first presentation, we are busily employed in getting ready for the occasion."[14]

The British were to be presented to the emperor during festivities held in his honor and not in theirs, and they would be but one attraction in the day's events. What would they be able to get out of the spectacle for which they were so feverishly preparing? Far from being cleared up, the misunderstanding had only deepened.

Teilhard de Chardin once called China a "plastic and recalcitrant bloc."[15] Macartney was about to find out how true this is.

34

To Each His Own Truth

(September 10, 1793)

WHAT ACCOUNTS FOR the Chinese volte-face that filled the British with such euphoria? The court, though offended and determined to offend, could not bring itself to cancel the ceremony. To send the British home without granting them an audience would have been an irreparable affront, and there was no telling how these "red-haired devils" might react. Of course, no one imagined that they could do much harm to the empire so far from their bases. The real risk entailed in expelling the British lay on the home front. It would ruin the emperor's party instead of enhancing its brilliance, for an expulsion would have amounted to an admission that the emperor had been insulted, and that his councillors had allowed an insolent barbarian delegation to get so close to the throne without revealing their true intentions. Any publicity given to the assault on the rites might even make it seem as though Heaven had allowed the dynasty's mandate to be violated.

The security of the leading mandarins, the emperor's dignity, and the future of the Manchu dynasty itself made it urgent to find some way to save appearances. But only appearances. There would be plenty of time to deal with reality later. In a country with a five-thousand-year-old history, revenge is a dish best served cold. Macartney's original proposal, implying the equality of king and emperor, was clearly inappropriate. Had the Chinese agreed to let a minister bow down to a portrait of George III, the British victory would have been unalloyed.

For the moment, then, the agreed-upon solution suited everyone: certainly Macartney, who would greet the emperor as though he were the king of Prussia (without even kissing his hand); but also the Chinese, who could claim that in the benighted minds of these decidedly raw barbarians a genuflection was equivalent to a kowtow.

Macartney won this test of wills because he was the sole judge of his own tactics. His instructions gave him carte blanche, and he therefore had the luxury of waiting until he had entered the throne room itself before deciding whether to kowtow or genuflect. The court, however, could not wait. In a system that codified everything, improvisation was tantamount to attack. The emperor, his ministers, and the mandarins of the Tribunal of Rites had to be sure of everything in advance. They were the ones who needed some solution, no matter how unsatisfying. The unprecedented ceremony, universally considered inconceivable just a day earlier, was accepted at the last minute because now, a mere four days before the audience, the court was unable to extract itself from the awkward position it had been placed in by the combination of Zhengrui's negligence and Macartney's obstinacy.

Macartney, however, seems not to have understood that this outcome contained an ambiguity that would cost him dearly. In British eyes, a genuflection was a worthy expression of respect for a great emperor on the part of the ambassador of a great king. In Chinese eyes, it was the crude yet incontrovertible expression of the vassal status of a boor.

Macartney was free to translate his genuflection into English, but the court would read it in Chinese. However clear Macartney's words had been, they left no trace in the written historical record. Once his note disappeared into the archives, only the gesture would remain. The British offered their version of it to their own public: they had asserted their independence. The Chinese would present theirs to the Chinese: the English had performed a gesture of submission.

Official Chinese documents are utterly silent on this breach of order, the substitution of crude barbarian "customs" (*su*) for the "rites" (*li*) of civilized man. Many years later, the Chinese authors of the "Essay on the History of the Qing Dynasty," who had access to the archives of the Tribunal of Rites, would write that "the officials discussed with Macartney what form the ceremony would take. He argued in favor of an audience analogous to that of the English Court; an imperial edict consequently permitted the use of the Western ceremony."[1]

But the edict itself disappeared.

Under the reign of Qianlong's successor, Jiaqing, the official line was that "when the Ambassador entered His Majesty's presence, he was so overcome with awe and nervousness, that his legs gave way under him, so that he grovelled abjectly on the ground, thus to all intents and purposes performing an involuntary kowtow."[2] On the word of a mandarin! The initial lie, soon given credibility by repetition, ultimately evolved into acknowledged fact. In the end the Chinese came to believe their own words. In 1816 the emperor Jiaqing affirmed in an edict that he had seen Macartney prostrate himself before his august father.[3]

MACARTNEY SAVORED his victory: British protocol had prevailed over immemorial Chinese practice. But retaliatory measures were already being prepared.

Qianlong's wrath was commensurate with the scope of the offense he had suffered, and he was determined to chastise the impertinent foreigners. The alien invader would be mercilessly cast out. On the very day he was pretending leniency, the emperor issued angry instructions to "His Excellency Wang Wenxiong," none other than our old friend Wang, the escort's highest-ranking mandarin after Zhengrui:

> For the tributary envoy's visit to the capital, my initial intention, following the example of the eighteenth year of Qianlong,* was to permit him to visit various famous sites and to attend theatrical performances. Moreover, in view of the long distance he has traveled across the seas, it was also my intention to grant him still higher favors.†
>
> But now the envoy has decided to feign illness. He is causing many lapses in the rites. Yesterday I ordered the chief minister of the Grand Council to meet him. Taking indisposition as a pretext, he failed to respond to this invitation, instead sending his deputy, who presented a note full of absurdities. In conformity with his role as minister, Heshen was obliged to criticize it harshly. He enjoined the English to conform to the rites of protocol, but they persist in using illness as an excuse to gain time. This is proof of their presumption and their arrogance.
>
> I am extremely displeased. I have already ordered their supplies reduced. In these conditions, there is no point in giving them the planned gifts. As for the sites of the capital, it is not worth taking the trouble to prepare them. Once they have attended the birthday banquet, let us immediately order the envoy to return to Peking.
>
> During your interviews with the envoy, follow the same protocol as the chief of the Grand Council. Precedence dictates that you occupy the place of honor. When the envoy visits you, you must not rise. It will suffice to prepare a bench and to order him to sit.
>
> All those items of this country's tribute that have already been

---

* The last European embassy, led by Pacheco, had come from Portugal in 1753, the eighteenth year of Qianlong's reign. When there was no obvious rite, the most recent precedent had to be followed.

† It may be objected that the Portuguese had come just as far, but the Chinese knew next to nothing of geography.

assembled can remain where they are. There is no point in moving them. When they leave, the gifts planned for the king shall be set outside Wumen Gate.* Wang shall be charged with conveying them to the residence.

Accepting presents is forbidden.† We shall give the envoy one or two days in his residence to prepare his affairs and depart. There is no point in allowing him to wait for my return to the capital. Zhengrui remains in charge of escorting him back to the borders of Shandong.

When Barbarians manifest sincerity and respect, I shall unfailingly treat them with kindness. When they are full of themselves, they do not merit the enjoyment of my favors. The ceremonial must therefore be curtailed, so as to make it clear to them what our system is. Such is the road to follow with the Barbarians.

Let this edict be followed and respected![4]

There is a notation in the margin in the emperor's hand: "What is the opinion of the normally so clear-sighted Agui on this matter? Let these instructions be communicated to him."

The modern reader is likely to be as surprised by this imperial anger as Macartney would have been had he been aware of it. But this was an issue not of diplomacy, but of religion, and the edict has all the conviction of the Psalm: "Be wise now therefore, O ye kings: be instructed, ye judges of the earth. Serve the Lord with fear, and rejoice with trembling. Kiss the Son, lest he be angry, and ye perish from the way, when his wrath is kindled but a little. Blessed are all they that put their trust in him."[5]

Let the barbarians manifest their submission, and they will be well treated. Let them act with presumption, and they will suffer the consequences. The meager lunch was deliberate harassment ordered by the emperor himself. Other punishments would follow. Macartney was to be dismissed without delay, deprived of the promenades and spectacles of Peking.

But this edict had other purposes as well: to reassure the court, the Celestial bureaucracy, and enlightened public opinion in Peking; to restabilize the shaken order; to ensure that history would forget an infringement of the rules that now had to be tolerated so as to avoid an explosion whose consequences would have been incalculable. "Rites prevent disorder, as dykes prevent floods."[6] The breach in the dike had to be promptly sealed. Public opinion would be told that the barbarians had

---

* The large interior gate in the Forbidden City.

† The reference is to the personal gifts Macartney had been advised to distribute, which he had purchased in extremis from Mackintosh.

yielded to the court ceremony, but they would be punished for their failure to respect that same ceremony. Reprisals would compensate for the violation of the rite, but the violation itself would never be acknowledged.

Macartney had no notion that he had barely escaped being sent home without an audience, nor did he suspect that he would now be given his walking papers immediately after the emperor's birthday party. The punishment anticipated the crime, which had not yet been committed. But to forestall any ill effects, it was announced to Chinese officials before the ceremony, at a time when Macartney, still fondly hoping to remain in Peking at least until spring, believed that he could now let his ships go south without him.

35

The Aftershock

(September 11–14, 1793)

THE EMPEROR and his ministers did their best to put a good face on a bad business, but echoes of the scandal reached Peking, where Barrow and Dinwiddie were still at work assembling all their machinery. The September 10 directive hit like an earthquake.

When they went to the throne room at the usual hour, they found it locked. In the courtyard the mandarins and the aged eunuch who held the keys gathered as though facing disaster. No one said a word to Barrow or Dinwiddie. Finally Father Adeodato told them the stunning news: his lordship had refused to submit to prostrations, and the court had accepted the British position.[1]

The great mandarins of the Tribunal of Rites were shocked. "It was impossible to say what might be the consequence of an event unprecedented in the annals of the empire. . . . the Emperor, when he began to think more seriously on the subject, might possibly impeach those before the criminal tribunal who had advised him to accede to such a proposal, on reflecting how much his dignity had suffered by the compliance; and . . . the records of the country might hand it down to posterity, as an event that had tarnished the lustre of his reign, being nothing short of breaking through an ancient custom, and adopting one of a barbarous nation in its place."[2]

In Peking, as in Jehol, the British felt the effects on their menu: portions were less ample than usual. The adjustment of the astronomical machinery, which had fascinated the mandarins and princes, ceased to draw their attention. And the old eunuch grumbled about these Englishmen who were "so full of themselves"—the very term used in the imperial edict.

Two centuries later, the effects of the aftershock could still be felt. Despite all the evidence to the contrary, most of the Chinese historians and archivists with whom I was able to discuss this subject refused to admit that Macartney had dispensed with the kowtow. Such a breach of their country's immemorial customs seemed quite implausible to them.

In Jehol the diplomatic minuet continued. The ambassador paid a visit to the chief minister. But by now the show of smiles masked a game of grimaces, as in the Peking Opera.

ON SEPTEMBER 11 Wang, Qiao, and Zhengrui came to escort Macartney and Staunton to see Heshen, who received them in a modest apartment. This time his courtesy was in marked contrast to the chilly reception to which Staunton had been treated three days earlier. Heshen was a handsome man of about forty, straightforward, lively, and well spoken. On his right sat Fuchang'an, "a handsome, fair man also, of about thirty years old." On his left were two older mandarins, the presidents of the tribunals of Rites and of Revenue.

As if nothing at all were amiss, Macartney told Heshen how happy he was "to have an early opportunity of waiting upon him." He said he hoped to deliver his king's message to the emperor as soon as possible. He made no attempt to press the advantage of his success.

He said he was glad to learn that the emperor was in good health, and reported that "it would give sincere pleasure to the greatest sovereign of the West to hear such good news . . . of the greatest sovereign of the East."[3] The implicit principle of equality had now become explicit, no rhetorical flourish softening its presumptuousness.

Though this formulation was quite unacceptable to Heshen, he let it pass without comment and replied amicably to Macartney. The rituals, he said, would be relaxed "on account of the very great distance from which the Embassy had been sent, and of the value of the presents." Macartney would see the emperor on the following Saturday, the great court holiday.

Heshen asked about the situation in Europe. Macartney informed him that England was "at present at peace with all the world." There was just one small difference of opinion with Russia over Turkey. The situation in India? It had been brought about contrary to British desires, under the pressure of incessant revolts by the nabobs, who conspired with other European powers which dreamed of gaining control not only of the Indian princes but also of the imperial government of China.[4]

Here the ambassador's target was the French revolutionaries, who might seek to export their "hatred of tyrants" all the way to China. Macartney gave his little speech. Britain was not a colonial power. Evil men in France and Portugal (which he did not name) had forced Britain, despite itself, to expand its modest bases to imperial dimensions. This profession of pacifist faith—"the King of England . . . is a lover of peace"—would be a constant theme, and for good reason. The Chinese regarded the British as especially aggressive, and they would ultimately decide that in this they had not been mistaken.

As his visitors took their leave, Heshen mentioned that he hoped he would have "frequent opportunities" of seeing Macartney again, though not in Jehol, where "the bustle and hurry of business and the festivals of the Emperor's anniversary must necessarily engage the greater part of his time." Macartney, too clever by half, took this assertion at face value.

Young Staunton, who accompanied his father and the ambassador to this meeting, was less naive. "Today we went again to the Colao, who received us more nicely than before and in a more interior part of the palace. He gave us warm milk twice." But despite the two bowls of milk, the boy considered the audience a nonevent. The adults, in their innocence, took it for a happy success. The child's view was the correct one.[5]

That afternoon a clearly relieved Wang and Qiao added to the euphoria by obligingly repeating flattering comments the chief minister had supposedly made about his guests. Later Zhengrui brought the British "a present of fruit and sweetmeats," compliments of Heshen.[6]

The Chinese version of this nonevent was put to astonishing use, in the form of a new edict.

Qianlong and Heshen had now had time to think things over, and they apparently decided that wrath had been a poor counselor. To order a punishment was to acknowledge that a crime had been committed. Though none had been named in the circular, word would certainly get around, especially among the mandarins. Would they consider the punishment sufficient? The members of the Celestial government may have known nothing of the logic of Europeans, but they knew their own people well enough, and as Macartney correctly observed, the "Chinese are now . . . awakening from the political stupor they had been thrown into by Tartar impression [oppression], and begin to feel their native energies revive. A slight collision might elicit fire from the flint, and spread flames of revolt from one extremity of China to the other."[7] The violated rite might strike the spark, if not tomorrow then in fifteen years' time. The entire detestable episode therefore had to be reshaped for public opinion. Everyone in China had to believe that the customary rites had been scrupulously observed.

The earlier edict could not be retracted, but it could be used to establish a pious lie. Heshen would deal with the Macartney problem through successive corrections.

A new imperial letter, dated September 11, now suggested that the barbarians had in fact yielded:

Yesterday we decided that the envoy, unversed in the requirements of etiquette, would be quickly sent away after Our birthday celebrations. . . . The first and second envoys, admonished by the ministers of the Grand Council, have now come to an understanding; they are repentant and respectful of the rites. They have come from afar; upon their arrival at our Court, they were ignorant; we were therefore compelled to take some restraining measures.* Now that they are entirely obeying the rules, we must regard them with renewed benevolence.[8]

In fact nothing had changed between the issuing of these two edicts. The British had not suddenly agreed to bend a second knee, and the Chinese had already decided to swallow the affront. But the ire of the September 10 edict had been too revealing of the damage done to the Chinese Order. Qianlong and Heshen therefore decided to pretend that the British had backed down. The emperor had to save face, and defeat was therefore turned into victory.

Heshen took the opportunity to take credit for the barbarians' supposed change of heart, portraying himself as the man who had succeeded in getting them to understand an etiquette that had been beyond their ken. To justify his own nonconformist rise in this country of conformism, Heshen always sought ways to assert his authority. The Celestial hierarchy was partly to blame for this complicated affair, and the supreme chief of all the mandarins could not resist the pleasure of humiliating them (though they would later exact their revenge).

As always in China, there was a moral lesson to be drawn from the incident. Heshen explained that it had been necessary to "reeducate" the barbarians. This word, so popular in Mao's China, has a long history. Anyone who deviates from the line set down from above must be straightened out. Throughout Chinese history, trials have been held to punish breaches of orthodoxy. Noncomformist men of letters have often found it convenient to live in isolation and to cease writing. But if the malefactor properly repents, the regime may show leniency.

There was every sign, however, that this new circular was pure fiction. The unseasoned reader might conclude that the tributary envoy, having finally come to his senses, had decided to abide by the eternal rules of Celestial etiquette. Yet the text, carefully examined, does not say that. The lie is effected by omission. The emperor never says exactly which rules were infringed, nor does he offer any details about the sudden obedience

---

* This was obviously meant to justify the reduction of the embassy's rations in both Jehol and Peking.

of the barbarians. Moreover, despite his alleged renewed benevolence, none of the punishments were lifted. The timing of the embassy's expulsion stood unaltered. The circular concluded by instructing princes and ministers residing in Peking not to invite the ambassador to their homes but to confine him to his own residence. The program of tourism was held in abeyance. As we shall see, it was never reinstated.

In all the eighteen months of detailed imperial correspondence—including the many instructions on how to treat the British and the copious reports to the emperor about their behavior—there is not a single specific account of the incredible breach of ritual.[9] The September 11 edict was immediately published in the Official Chronicles of the empire, which contain barely a mention of the imperial audience itself. That, of course, could not be described without revealing the truth, or at least without lying more energetically than by mere omission.

The essential point—that Macartney did not kowtow—was officially concealed, until eventually the facts were forgotten. This subtle falsification had consequences many years later. In 1816 Lord Amherst was confronted with the official truth: that his predecessor "had kowtowed to Qianlong." When he refused to do likewise, he was expelled. The measures taken by Heshen, tantamount to the erasure and reconstruction of memory in a kind of collective brainwashing, were successful well beyond the author's relatively short life. A compilation of Qing poetry from the 1860s (after the sacking of the Summer Palace) contains these lines, attributed to one Chen Wenchu:

> Englishman, in the fifty-eighth spring of the Qianlong era,
> Your country brought its tribute of rare and precious objects.
> The Son of Heaven allowed you to become his vassal.
> Englishman, if you sincerely open your heart to the August Emperor,
> Your request must conform to the rules.
> Your envoy must learn the rites.[10]

THE TWO NEXT DAYS were spent unloading the gifts and bringing them to the palace, a process that, in view of the uncertainty, had earlier been postponed. They consisted of two hundred bolts of cloth; two large telescopes; two compressed-air rifles; two handsome hunting rifles (one inlaid with gold, the other with silver); two pair of saddle pistols (ornamented "in the same manner"); two boxes each containing seven bolts of Irish cloth; two elegant saddles; two large boxes containing the finest carpets of English manufacture.[11]

The British were confident that the gifts would impress, even though the most important ones had been left behind in Peking. But they had no notion of how jaded Qianlong actually was. Father Amiot tells us that he had been spoiled long ago by the clever Jesuits, who had presented him with such gifts as a "magnificent" watch, complicated fountains with clock-like movements, a mechanical lion that could take a hundred steps, and an automaton in human form. The good fathers were actually afraid that someday the emperor might tell them, "You have made a man that walks; now make one that talks."[12]

The following day was devoted to preparations for the audience with the emperor.[13] Staunton assembled the embassy personnel to transmit the ambassador's final instructions.

Everyone was to be at his post at three in the morning, the servants dressed in their green and gold livery, wearing shoes and silk stockings. No one was to wear boots. The soldiers and servants were not to wait for the ambassador to come out of the audience, but were instead to return to the residence immediately. His "Excellency had every reason to suspect that, in a few days, the present restrictions, . . . would be removed, and every indulgence granted them which they could reasonably desire: and . . . any deviation from this order would tend to risque the loss of that mediated favour. His Excellency seriously expected [his orders] to meet with a general and willing obedience."[14]

36

The Morning of the Big Day

(September 14, 1793)

SATURDAY, SEPTEMBER 14. The moment had come. Macartney would finally speak personally to the emperor. But he sensed that little business would be transacted in this first interview, which would not be a private meeting. More like a ritual audience at St. Peter's Basilica in Rome.

We have no Chinese account of this historic encounter—just the brief mention in the court records. That silence is eloquent. Of our six witnesses—Macartney, the two Stauntons, Winder, Hüttner, and Anderson—the last three saw only its beginning. They were not admitted to the most holy of inner sanctums.

"AT THREE IN THE MORNING the ambassador and his retinue, in ceremonial dress, set out for the Emperor's Court."

Anderson describes the procession. It formed in the courtyard of the residence, whose gallery was lit with "Venetian" lanterns, so named because the prototype had been brought back to Europe by Marco Polo. But once the contingent moved away from the lanterns, "the morning was so dark that we could not distinguish each other."[1]

Yet the Chinese were masters of artificial illumination. As he stumbled through the darkness, Anderson must have thought of the "profusion of lamps and other lights" in the mandarins' palaces, which "in my unexaggerated opinion, would serve the palace of an European sovereign for a month."[2] Chinese literature abounds in processions "ringed with lanterns that made them as bright as day."[3] And once they got close to the emperor's tent, there were streaming lights.

Why did the Chinese make the British walk more than a league in thick darkness, stumbling against one another like blind men? A handful of torchbearers could have easily lit the way. It is hard to resist the conclusion that this was more of the harassment through which the court meant to exact payment, with interest, for the concession that had been made on the kowtow.

Despite the darkness, Lieutenant Colonel Benson tried to organize an escort to lead the ambassador's palanquin. The maneuver was unsuccessful.[4] The clusters of Chinese porters scurried along with their usual rapidity,[5] and Anderson and his companions had to run after the palanquin as it disappeared into the night.

Chaos peaked when "we found ourselves intermingled with a cohort of pigs, asses, and dogs, which broke our ranks, such as they were, and put us into irrecoverable confusion."[6] Animals rule the night in China. "In the public streets of Peking," says Barrow, who remained in that city while Macartney went on to Jehol, "after five or six o'clock in the evening, scarcely a human creature is seen to move, but they abound with dogs and swine."[7]

The ever-dignified Macartney makes no mention of these complications. The walk to the emperor's tent, he says, a distance of "about three miles," lasted "little more than an hour."[8] Like the Chinese historians, he shapes reality by omission. His servants and soldiers are more forthcoming: "The pedestrian part of the suite [was] . . . a little out of breath with running; and the gentlemen on horseback, not altogether insensible to the risk of accidents from the dark hour of the morning." They arrived at the palace at about four o'clock, in the most complete disorder: "It appeared . . . to be rather ridiculous to attempt to make a parade that no one could see."[9]

His lordship descended from his palanquin, Thomas holding the hem of his cloak. They were followed by the other gentlemen, "amidst an immense concourse of people. . . . The servants &c, returned accordingly to order, and the soldiers marched back with fife and drum."[10] Like the servants, they must have wondered why they had come.

Exit Anderson, the footman. A pity, for he was a sharp observer.

HÜTTNER, who remained on the scene until the emperor's arrival, picks up the account: "Chinese etiquette required that we wait at least several hours for the Emperor. Most of the courtiers were therefore obliged to spend the night outside the palace, in tents."[11]

The Tartar tents, round and vaulted, were not held up by posts but were "made of bamboo interwoven with considerable skill and covered with thick felt. One of them was much taller and larger than the others. Hung in yellow, decorated with a rug, and bedecked with painted lanterns and garlands, it contained a throne for the Emperor."[12]

The entire ceremony, the most solemn of the year, would take place in the tent. There were tents in which to await the emperor's arrival, and another where he would be worshiped. Here in Jehol, Qianlong was the khan of the Manchu Tartars, and he received his visitors not in a palace, but in a camp.

The ambassador and his retinue cooled their heels in one of the small neighboring tents. A horde of Tartar courtiers "pointed and prodded at us, with their customary coarseness. The Chinese are relatively more polite."[13] A curious remark. These masters of China, whom Hüttner depicted as so different from the Chinese, are now quite indistinguishable from them, drowned in the mass.

But at least the British got a glimpse of the court, the entirety of which had gathered for the emperor's birthday. All the Tartar princes were there, plus several viceroys, governors of districts and cities, and perhaps five or six hundred mandarins of all types and all ranks, along with their servants. There were also soldiers, itinerant balladeers, and musicians. Several thousand people, all awaiting the simultaneous appearance of the emperor and the sun.

The British were not the only foreigners. "They pointed out to us other ambassadors of darkened complexions, who were also to be presented to the Emperor on that same morning. They wore turbans, were barefoot, and chewed areca nuts. The Chinese not being very astute geographers, they hesitated and were ultimately unable to tell us any more than the Chinese name of the land from which this delegation had come. We supposed that they were from Pegu [Burma]."[14]

And there you have it. The people sharing the honor of this collective audience were not "ambassadors," as Hüttner claims, but bearers of tribute invited to celebrate the emperor's birthday. The Chinese barely even knew where they came from.

Half an hour after sunrise, a horseman approached. Everyone formed up into ranks, and a deep silence fell over the crowd. Music was heard in the distance, and "we remarked in the expressions of all those present that sensation which is always produced by the expectation of extraordinary happenings."[15]

Striking a suddenly phlegmatic air, Hüttner comments: "The luxurious indulgence of an Asiatic prince is always certain to make a powerful impression on the senses, and hence on the hearts, of the superstitious peoples of the Orient."[16] But Hüttner himself sounded pretty oriental in the presence of this particular prince.

Several ministers, dressed in yellow and riding horses "as white as snow," were the first to arrive. They dismounted and formed into a row near the great tent. Immediately after them came the musicians and the guard. Then finally the emperor himself, carried on an open chair by sixteen men dressed in gold. He was followed by other ministers and the chief mandarins.

As he passed through the lines of courtiers, people dropped to their knees and repeatedly touched their foreheads to the ground. The British went down on one knee.

The emperor entered his tent, followed by the princes, the high mandarins, and finally the vassals—Macartney, the two Stauntons, and Mr. Plumb walking among them. Hüttner was asked to remain at the threshold, and he did so. "The sun had just come up, illuminating the vast park. It was a beautiful morning, the profound silence of nature interrupted only by the melodious chanting of a solemn hymn, to a most sweet instrumental accompaniment and an equally sonorous cymbal."[17]

Anderson had returned to the residence with the embassy's guard, while Winder, Hüttner, and the rest of the retinue were halted at the gates of the sanctuary. None of them witnessed the encounter with the emperor. But let us linger over a few of the frames of the film they offer us.

Anderson describes Macartney's and Staunton's attire. They wore robes and cloaks, which made them look more Chinese, but their intent was neither to appear picturesque nor to dazzle. The British had come to understand that in China the robe was a symbol of dignity, concealing shape, distinguishing its wearer from the savage and the lowly worker, and highlighting differences of rank and function.

All the court dignitaries wore robes. Those of the mandarins had circular, embroidered crests on the chest, those of the princes and ministers square crests on the backs. Yellow jackets signaled imperial blood or a very special indulgence. The British had also remarked upon the peacock feathers—one, two, or three in number. Carried in an agate tube, they symbolized the emperor's personal esteem: "He, to whom three feathers had been presented by Imperial favour, thought himself thrice great and happy."[18] The language of dress has largely died out in the West, but in the eighteenth century it was still current, and traces of it remain even now: in the army, the universities, the courts, and the church.

Macartney, ever alert, had selected his wardrobe "to show the attention I always paid, where a proper opportunity afforded, to oriental customs and ideas." Staunton did likewise. "Over a rich embroidered velvet," Macartney writes, "I wore the mantle of the Order of the Bath,* with the

---

* This was England's second-ranking order of knighthood, after the Garter.

collar, a diamond badge, and a diamond star." Sir George was also dressed "in a rich embroidered velvet . . . and, being a Doctor of Laws in the University of Oxford, wore the habit of his degree, which is of scarlet silk, full and flowing."*[19]

This time the British were determined to avoid the laughter aroused by their trousers, stockings, and tailored jackets, which had earned them the nickname "devils," since in the Chinese theater only devils wore tight clothes.[20] Staunton thought that Chinese modesty accounted for their reaction to European dress: "The Chinese idea of decency goes so far that they hide, for the most part in their loose and flowing robes, the bulk and form of their limbs. . . . Even in the imitation by art, the human figure, either naked or covered only with such vestments as follow and display the contour of the body, is offensive to Chinese delicacy; a delicacy which has retarded the progress of painting and sculpture."[21]

Nudity was allowed only in off-color engravings, and even the most erotic statuettes concealed the women's bound feet, or "golden lotus."[22] The only completely nude Chinese figurines were the ones doctors used to examine female patients without touching or seeing their bodies.

MACARTNEY CLAIMS that they waited "an hour" for the audience. In fact it was a good two hours more than that. The accounts of various witnesses agree that the embassy left its residence at three in the morning and arrived at the palace at four; the emperor did not show up until seven. This was the interval required by the protocol of yet another Chinese custom: the longer the wait, the greater the honor. Low-ranking mandarins used the same technique with their supplicants. But it would have hurt Macartney's and Sir George's pride to admit that they spent three long hours waiting, and it is likely that they did not want to offend the national honor of their readers too much either.

Everyone—princes, ministers, and top mandarins—had to wait the same as everyone else. But the ambassador and his deputy do not mention that they shared their tent with tributary vassals.

Macartney had had an inkling of this unpleasant amalgam back in Macao. A March 24 edict had stipulated that "the English and the Burmese and Mongol tributaries shall be dealt with all together."[23] When this news reached Canton in May, the merchants of the Chinese guild were dismayed, and the gentlemen of the company could neither ignore it nor conceal it

---

* Staunton also held a doctorate in medicine from the University of Montpellier and was therefore entitled to wear the French toga. But national dress was essential on this occasion.

from the ambassador.[24] In their accounts, Macartney and Staunton make it sound as if they were the sole heroes of these festivities, but Staunton junior, who rather enjoyed the proceedings, is more forthcoming, reporting that the embassy was mixed in with the princes who had come from all the vassal territories of China for the emperor's birthday.[25] The kid just couldn't keep his mouth shut.

His father, on the other hand, had an eye for any detail that might flatter British patriotism, and he mentions one that he took as a good commercial omen: "Several of the courtiers were partly dressed in English cloth, instead of silks or furs, in which only it had hitherto been allowed to appear before his Imperial Majesty. As there had not been lately any particular scarcity of those materials, the regulation which permits the use of English cloths at court, was understood to be intended as a compliment to the British Embassy; and it was so presented to the Embassador."[26] Father Lamiot, however, dismisses this proud allegation: "European clothing was permitted at the Court well before this expedition."[27]

THE SIZE OF THE THRONG was itself part of the homage to the emperor. All these illustrious figures, normally surrounded by courts of their own, "were, in this place, confounded in the crowd, and their grandeur lost in the contemplation of that of his Imperial Majesty," cooed Staunton.[28]

No one was surprised by the waste of time. They simply waited patiently for daybreak, like seasoned hunters not yet softened by luxury. This was a millennial tradition: ministers scheduled for an audience with the emperor in Peking would arrive at the palace gates in the middle of the night, there to await a sovereign who never appeared before dawn.

Several people who honored Macartney with their curiosity were pointed out to him: "a brother of the Emperor . . . ; two of the Emperor's sons, and as many grandsons."[29] One of the two sons was the man who would succeed Qianlong, the future emperor Jiaqing, whose false eyewitness testimony figured in the controversy over the kowtow during the Amherst mission some twenty years later.

Halting conversations were struck up here and there, and one tributary prince from the shores of the Caspian seemed to know "somewhat more of Europe than the rest." Not that he understood any European languages. In fact he "spoke the Arabic language," of which the British knew not a word. Nevertheless, he "seemed to take a greater interest in what related to the Embassy." Barbarians easily find points of common interest among their own kind.

One of the guests was an old acquaintance: Liang Kentang, the viceroy who had greeted the British in Tientsin before going off to inspect construction work on the riverbank. He endeavored to share with his colleagues the "esteem" in which he held the English ambassador.[30]

Or at least so the English believed.

37

At the Emperor's Feet

(September 14, 1793)

EVEN THE NORMALLY reserved Staunton waxed lyrical when describing the emperor's appearance. "Heaven is high, the Emperor distant," says a Chinese adage. But now he was suddenly close, and Staunton seems in seventh heaven. "He soon appeared from behind a high and perpendicular mountain, skirted with trees, as if from a sacred grove, preceded by a number of persons busied in proclaiming aloud his virtues and power. He was seated in a sort of open chair, or triumphal car, borne by sixteen men."[1]

He was dressed in brown silk and wore a velvet cap that reminded Staunton of the hats of the Scottish Highlanders. A single large pearl was affixed to the crown.

In 1790 Father Amiot had described the eighty-year-old emperor this way: "He walks with a firm step, and is loud and sonorous of voice; though his vision is good enough to read and write, he is slightly hard of hearing."[2] In 1795 the Dutchman Van Braam wrote: "He bears all the features of his old age. His eyes . . . are watery; his eyelids barely open. His drooping cheeks are flaccid."[3] Five years separate these contradictory assessments; 1793 was the midpoint between them, and according to the members of the embassy, the sovereign had not yet begun to show his age. Hüttner thought he looked like "an alert man of fifty years" who carried himself with considerable "grace."[4] Winder says that his face bore no trace of old age, that his appearance was pleasing, and that "he appears to be about . . . sixty."[5] Macartney says the same,[6] and both of them attributed Qianlong's excellent health to the regularity with which he rose before dawn and retired with the sunset.

Here is the young page's account of the historic moment when Qianlong passed before the group of Britons: "We left the tent, as we were told that the Emperor was coming. We then stood by the side of the road which the Emperor was to pass. He came in a gilt chair supported by 16 men. As he passed we went upon one knee and bowed our heads down to the ground."[7]

To the ground? In the manuscript, these three words are neatly crossed out. Because they were inaccurate, or because they suggested an acrobatic contortion easily performed by a child but difficult for most adults and downright impossible for gout-ridden men like young Thomas's father and the ambassador? The boy was well aware of the kowtow controversy. Had he described the gesture expected of the embassy and then crossed out the key words in an effort to emphasize that they had in fact refused to perform it? Or was the deletion made at the behest of his father, lest what the boy had written be taken as a victory for Celestial protocol?

Does the existence of these crossed-out words cast doubt on Macartney's real response to the exigencies of Chinese ceremony? Is it possible that the British were hiding something, with the complicity of a child clever enough to understand the import of his silence?

Let us admit that there seems to be room for doubt. The unpublished account of another witness, Winder, complicates matters even further, for he is alone in reporting: "As he passed, we were led from our tent and drawn up in a line, opposite to a row of mandarins and Tartar princes. We paid our respect in the usual form of the country, by kneeling *nine times to the ground*."[8]

Nine times? In "the usual form of the country"? But isn't this precisely a kowtow? Were Macartney and the elder Staunton, the official narrators, simply lying? Had they actually capitulated without admitting it? Winder, who jotted his observations down day by day, editing them as he went along, seems an unimpeachable witness.

The truth is that everyone viewed the same scene but saw it very differently. Let us try to reconstruct what happened.

To get a clearer idea of the problem faced by the British, try practicing a kowtow in front of a mirror. Start in a standing position. Then kneel down. Bend forward until your forehead touches the floor; raise your torso and bow again until your forehead touches the floor a second time, then a third. Then stand up straight and begin again. Kneel three distinct times, rising to a standing position between each genuflection, touching your forehead to the floor three times during each stage of kneeling.

The entire procedure will have taken at least a minute, even if you hurried. If you tried to maintain a little dignity, as the people gathered in Jehol would have done, two minutes is a more likely estimate. A thousand or so mandarins performed these movements in unison, and during these two minutes, the imperial palanquin passed majestically through the crowd.

Now imagine the British. As the crowd kneels for the first time, they do likewise, going down on one knee. As the others touch their foreheads to the ground, they bow their heads. Picture it as a Catholic Mass in which some worshipers remain standing, merely lowering their eyes as others kneel. The mandarins, still on their knees, then raise their torsos. It seems unlikely that the British would keep their heads bowed, so let us assume that they raise them. The crowd then prostrates itself again, and the British bow their heads. When the crowd rises, the British do likewise, not wishing to remain on one knee while everyone else is standing. And so on. Unable to avoid the collective movements, the British follow along, simply abbreviating them. It is difficult to imagine them remaining on one knee for two full minutes while the Chinese stand up three times. Is it any more likely that they would have remained standing while the Chinese continued to kowtow? At first I thought so, but Winder's manuscript seems to resolve the ambiguity.

Macartney's problem had to do with the form of the gesture and not its repetition. He insisted on touching only one knee to the ground and on not bowing his head too low. Absorbed in contesting the form, he forgot that the strange, threefold repetition was also an essential part of the kowtow, and since the first kowtow faced by the British was a collective one, it seems almost inevitable that they would follow each of its phases, paying their respects, as Winder says, "in the usual form of the country." But the Chinese did not see it that way. Since British foreheads never touched Chinese soil, their gesture was not "in the usual form of the country."

In their accounts, Macartney and Staunton emphasize the difference in the gesture and conceal the repetition. But they do not overtly lie. None of their accounts says that they knelt but a single time. Had they done so, while repeated reverence was being displayed all around them, it seems likely that they would have boasted of the difference. Winder must therefore be right. The British were carried along by the crowd, and they probably felt that they had made concessions better passed over in silence. But they had not been carried along far enough to satisfy the Chinese.

ONCE THE EMPEROR disappeared into the tent where the audience would be held, the High Mass of vassalage could begin. Winder, who remained at the entrance to the tent, reports: "When he was seated on his throne, the most profound and rather awfull tranquillity prevailed. Sweet music at intervals agreeably broke the general stillness, while the tinkling of little bells, whose sound was ravishing to the ear, added to the solemnity of this great event."[9] He was the only one to comment on this bell. According to

Franciscan reports, it was a custom begun by the Mongols back in the thirteenth century.

Macartney entered the vast yurt of the Tartar emperor, which resembled a theater. Three small flights of stairs led to a platform. The center stairs were for the emperor alone. The ones on the left were for guests being granted the honor of an audience, the ones on the right for the ministers, who would attend the audience on their knees, the same position in which they attended meetings of the Grand Council. The rest of the court sat on the ground.

Let us follow the scene as young Thomas describes it. When he entered the tent, the emperor was already seated on the throne. "The gentlemen [of the embassy] then stood at the entrance of the tent, and Lord Macartney, my father, Mr. Plumb, and I went up to the edge of the platform and made the same ceremony as before. Then Lord Macartney climbed up on the platform, presented the letter from the King and gave some small presents, watches. The Emperor gave him a piece of carved serpentine for himself and another stone in the same shape as the other but white for the King of England. The ambassador then came down, and my papa and I went up and made the proper ceremony. The Emperor gave my papa a stone . . . and took off a little yellow purse hanging by his side and gave it to me. He wanted me to say a few words in Chinese, which I did, to thank him for the present."[10]

So much for the view of the Western child, who makes it sound as though both sides were improvising in an atmosphere of sweetness and light. Yet the ceremony had been strictly scripted.

The same scene looked quite different from the immutable Chinese point of view. For them, it was the child who brought the real "tribute." He spoke Chinese. He had been "Sinified." He had taken a step toward the emperor and had thus been transformed into a civilized being, a Chinese. He therefore richly deserved an exceptional favor, for he had made up for the rudeness of the barbarian grown-ups. They were raw, whereas he was now baked.

We have no direct Chinese testimony of this encounter, but we do have the records of the Tribunal of Rites. The ceremony described by Staunton junior conformed to the stipulations of the court letter of September 8, minus the kowtow. The established sequence of the official ceremony had been followed: entrance, gesture of homage at the foot of the staircase, kneeling on the second step, conversation with the emperor. The sole infringement of the time-honored rules was the elimination of the nine prostrations. Everything else was strictly observed. Imperial guards were stationed on either side of the platform, and when the tributary envoy reached that platform, the task of escorting him shifted to one of the two presidents of the Tribunal of Rites,* who wore the court dress in the appropriate colors, with embroidered dragons. "The Emperor deigned to question the tributary envoy in benevolent and gracious terms. The president of the Tribunal of Rites received the questions and transmitted them; the interpreter translated them; the envoy replied to them; the interpreter translated his words; the president of the Tribunal of Rites then transmitted them to the Emperor."[11] In other words, the tributary envoy did not address the emperor directly, nor did the emperor reply to him. The ambassador handed his letter of accreditation not to the emperor, but to a mandarin, who kowtowed and then passed it on to the emperor. The British witnesses, however, mention nothing that might even smack of submission. Now it was their turn to lie by omission.

Earlier the British had been drawn by the crowd into repeated genuflections, but when they stood alone at the platform, they reverted to the appropriate gesture: one knee upon the ground a single time.

But Macartney and Staunton senior leave out the more humiliating gesture of homage at the base of the staircase, which is reported only by the more truthful Staunton junior. The ambassador's account merely states: "Holding in both my hands a large gold box enriched with diamonds in which was enclosed the King's letter, I walked deliberately up, and ascending the side-steps of the throne, delivered it into the Emperor's own hands, who, having received it, passed it to the Minister, by whom it was placed on the cushion."[12]

It seems highly unlikely that he actually delivered the box "into the Emperor's own hands." The Rites called for Macartney to hand the box not to the emperor but to a mandarin, who would kowtow and then place it on the cushion. It is doubtful that the court would have accepted the innovation suggested by Macartney's account. That was not part of the agreement.

For the British, delivery of the letter from the king was merely the pretext for this journey; for the emperor, it marked its end. But Macartney did not know that yet. Qianlong, he writes, "then gave me as the first present from him to His Majesty the *ju-eu-jou* or *giou-giou*,† as the symbol of peace and prosperity, and expressed his hopes that my Sovereign and he should always live in good correspondence and amity. It is a whitish,

---

* Under the Manchu dynasty, each tribunal had two presidents, one Chinese, the other Tartar.
† Cranmer-Byng (p. 368) explains: "By this Macartney meant a *ju-i*, which was usually a piece of jade carved in the form of a sceptre. It was considered to be a symbol of good luck, the phrase *ju-i* meaning 'what you will.' As such it was often given by Chinese emperors to their great officials as a special mark of favour."

agate-looking stone about a foot and a half long, curiously carved, and highly prized by the Chinese, but to me it does not appear in itself to be of any great value.

"The Emperor then presented me with a *ju-eu-jou* of a greenish-coloured stone of the same emblematic character; at the same time he very graciously received from me a pair of beautiful enamelled watches set with diamonds, . . . and which, having looked at, he passed to the Minister."[13]

Then it was the Stauntons' turn. "Sir George Staunton . . . now came forward, and after kneeling upon one knee in the same manner which I had done, presented to him two elegant air-guns, and received from him a *ju-eu-jou* of greenish stone nearly similar to mine."[14]

Macartney does not condescend to report the episode of the conversation between the emperor and the child, but Staunton could not resist a bit of boasting about his offspring. Here again, his tone becomes lyrical: "During the ceremonies, his Imperial Majesty appeared perfectly unreserved, cheerful, and unaffected. Far from being of a dark and gloomy aspect, as he has sometimes been represented, his eyes were full and clear, and his countenance open." But the necessity of communicating through interpreters made the interview tiring. "His Imperial Majesty, adverting to the inconvenience arising from such a circumstance, inquired from Heshen whether any person of the Embassy understood the Chinese language; and being informed that the Embassador's page, a boy then in his thirteenth year, had alone made some proficiency in it, the Emperor had the curiosity to have the youth brought up to the throne,* and desired him to speak Chinese. Either what he said, or his modest countenance or manner, was so pleasing to his Imperial Majesty, that he took from his girdle a purse, hanging from it for holding areca nut, and presented it to him."[15]

We know that Qianlong had a weakness for young boys, but he was not alone in this penchant. "The commission of this detestable and unnatural act," Barrow notes in a tone of reprobation, "is attended to with so little sense of shame, or feelings of delicacy, that many of the first officers of state seemed to make no hesitation in publicly avowing it. Each of these officers is constantly attended by his pipe-bearer, who is generally a handsome boy from fourteen to eighteen years of age, and is always well dressed. In pointing out to our notice the boys of each other, they made use of

---

* In accordance with the rite, Macartney stopped one step below the level of the emperor's throne, but the boy was invited to mount the platform. Qianlong was hard of hearing, and he wanted the boy close to him. The ambassador, however, communicated through two intermediaries, the interpreter and the minister.

signs and motions, the meaning of which was too obvious to be mis-interpreted."[16]

Charmed by the young boy's grace, Qianlong gave him the purse,[17] which was still warm from his body and was therefore considered to have magical powers. "Purses are the ribands of the Chinese monarch, which he distributes as rewards of merit among his subjects; but his own purse was deemed a mark of personal favour, according to the ideas of Eastern nations, among whom any thing worn by the person of the sovereign, is prized beyond all other gifts."[18] (Mao once offered a basket of mangos to a visiting delegation; having been touched by the Great Helmsman, the ordinary fruit became holy, and party members schemed to get their hands on it. The mangos were eventually bottled in alcohol, "that this admirable testimony of Mao Thought might be preserved forever.") The emperor's gift "procured for the young favourite the notice and caress of many of the mandarines, while others perhaps envied his good fortune. This Imperial purse is not at all magnificent, being of plain yellow silk, with the figure of the five-clawed dragon, and some Tartar characters worked into it."[19]

Lord Macartney descended the stairs, and other tributary envoys immediately approached the throne. The two leaders of the British mission say nothing about these other supplicants. So far they had not even reported the presence of other envoys, and Macartney now did so only in the most offhanded manner.

"I forgot to mention," he writes, "that there were present on this occasion three ambassadors from Tatze or Pegu and six Mohammedan ambassadors from the Kalmucks of the south-west, but their appearance was not very splendid."[20] The Muslim emissaries were chiefs of the Torguts, a tribe of the Kalmuks who had fled eastward in late 1770 after being driven from the Volga plains by Russian expansion. Qianlong brought them under his protection and resettled them in the region of Urümqi, present-day Chinese Turkestan.[21]

After the ritual presentations came the ritual banquet. The three Britons and their interpreter were seated "upon cushions at one of the tables on the Emperor's left hand."[22] Macartney was right to take note of this: the left was the place of honor. The Tartar princes and court mandarins were seated at other tables, each according to his rank, in accordance with the note of September 8. "When the Great Khan holds court and has a banquet," Marco Polo wrote, "he sits . . . at a table raised above the others. His first wife sits beside him on his left; on his right, lower down, so that their heads are level with his feet, sit the Khan's sons in order of age, beginning with the eldest, followed by his grandsons and other members of the imperial family. The barons sit on a lower level still."[23] Imperial archives show that this terraced arrangement was still in effect five centuries later, under the Manchus. The British did not breathe a word of it.

The meal was lavish, and Macartney mentions that the emperor honored him with favors, sending "several dishes from his own table, together with some liquors, which the Chinese call wine, not, however, expressed from the grape, but distilled or extracted from rice, herbs, and honey."[24]

Qianlong even summoned Macartney and Staunton to approach him once more during the meal, giving them "a cup of warm wine with his own hands." They "immediately" drank it "in his presence." He politely asked the age of the king of England, "and, being informed of it, said he hoped he might live as many years as himself, which are eighty-three."[25] George III was only fifty-six.*

The emperor's manner was "dignified but affable, . . . and his reception of us has been very gracious and satisfactory." The "order and regularity in serving and removing the dinner was wonderfully exact, and every function of the ceremony performed with such silence and solemnity as in some measure to resemble the celebration of a religious mystery."[26] The British are suspiciously discreet about exactly how they thanked the emperor for all these favors. They must at least have bent a knee and bowed their heads. How many times and how far we do not know.

In the meantime, festivities were being held outside for those not honored to share the emperor's tent. Wrestlers, acrobats, tightrope walkers, and mimes performed for the full five hours of the ceremony.[27] This ritual, too, is as old as China itself. From the time of the Han dynasty (and probably even earlier) shows were staged in honor of foreign delegations and on other state occasions. Court life was festive.

We have but a single Chinese report of this entire ceremony, and it is, as always, laconic: "The Emperor, enthroned in the Great Tent in the Park of Ten Thousand Trees, granted an audience to the envoy of England, *Ma-ga-er-ni*, the vice-envoy *Si-tan-ton*, and the others, along with the Mongol princes and nobles and the envoys of Burma and others; a banquet was offered them, as well as various rewards."[28] This was no more than a repetition of the court letter of March 24, repeated on May 12 and on other occasions as well. Sticking to litany was the surest means of avoiding error. The note was followed by a poem composed by Qianlong to com-

---

* The emperor very nearly got his wish. George III died in 1820, at the age of eighty-three, after reigning sixty years, just as Qianlong had. But the British king went insane years before his death, and his son, the future George IV, assumed the regency in 1811.

memorate the "submission" of the British. It begins: "Formerly Portugal presented tribute; Now England is paying homage." This "homage," of course, was pleasing, and the approximate kowtow, crude as it was, earned England its place on the official list of "kingdoms of the western ocean" that had pledged their allegiance to China.

When the meal ended, the audience was over. The ambassador rejoined the rest of his retinue outside the tent. The procession then formed and, in accordance with protocol, he was escorted back to his residence.

Macartney had finally seen the famous emperor. Even spoken to him. But without saying a thing.

38

The Paradise of Ten
Thousand Trees

(September 15–16, 1793)

AFTER THE AUDIENCE with the emperor, the British were treated to four
days of equestrian tourism in the vast imperial parks. They began in the
Garden of the East. "The Emperor, having been informed that in the
course of our travels in China we had shown a strong desire of seeing
everything curious and interesting, was pleased to give directions to the
first Minister to show us his park or garden at Jehol. It is called in Chinese
Wanshu yuan, which signifies the paradise of innumerable trees."*[1] To
enjoy this "uncommon favour," Macartney and his companions "rose this
morning at three o'clock, and went to the Palace, where we waited, mixed
with all the great officers of state, for three hours (such is the etiquette of
the place) till the Emperor's appearance."†[2]

He arrived just as he had the day before, with guards, musicians,
standard bearers, and men to carry his parasols. "Observing us as we stood
in the front line [he] graciously beckoned us to approach, having ordered
his people to stop." Imperial archives show that this apparently unexpected
encounter had in fact been planned to the smallest detail on September
13. "He entered into conversation with us, and with great affability of
manner, told us that he was on his way to the pagoda, where he usually
paid his morning devotions; that as we professed a different religion from
his, he would not ask us to accompany him."[3] Qianlong, like the other
leaders of his dynasty, was a devotee of Lamaism, a variety of Buddhism

---

* The word *paradise* is a strictly English "oriental" exaggeration. Wanshu Yuan means Garden
(or Park) of Ten Thousand Trees.
† This time Macartney admits to the three-hour wait, declining to reduce it to the single hour
claimed in his embellished description of the imperial audience.

to which Shunzhi, the first Manchu emperor, had converted despite the efforts of his tutor, Father Schall.[4]

Qianlong informed Macartney that he had ordered the chief minister and Grand Councillors to "conduct us through his garden, and to show us whatever we were desirous of seeing there." Macartney expressed to His Majesty his "increasing admiration of everything I had yet observed at Jehol."[5] Finally, the emperor took the opportunity to speak to Thomas for a moment, asking him to make a drawing of the purse he had given him the day before. The child relates the conversation proudly.[6]

The foreigners had been granted a great favor, for tourism was not generally permitted in these gardens, which were the emperor's personal property.

"My imperial grandfather," Qianlong wrote, "built the Summer Palace as a means of ruling and pacifying the frontier peoples."[7] In other words, far from being a mere caprice, Jehol was the product of a military campaign, the continuation of war by other means. But the grandson confessed his pure pleasure in the site: "As for the high mountains, the steep cliffs, the water and the forests, the wandering storks and deer, the soaring eagles and the playing fish, the buildings in the shadow of the precipices, the pavilions beside the brooks, the luxuriant grass and the ancient trees, they have a natural beauty that makes one forget worldly cares."[8]

While the emperor said his prayers in the pagoda, Macartney and the ministers retired to one of the pavilions for a light snack. They then rode three miles through gently undulating grounds whose contrasts were carefully designed to offer pleasing views. This park, "kept in the highest order," reminded Macartney of "the approach to Luton in Bedfordshire," a reference to an estate owned by his father-in-law, Lord Bute, and designed by the famous Lancelot Brown. Had Brown visited China, Macartney added, one "should have sworn" that he had drawn "his happiest ideas from the rich sources which I have tasted this day."[9]

The honored guests arrived at the banks of "an extensive lake" and boarded a "large, magnificent yacht." Boats had been prepared for the retinue, all decorated with "numberless vanes, pennants, and streamers." The "shores of the lake have all the varieties of shape which the fancy of a painter can delineate, and are so indented with bays or broken with projections, that almost every stroke of the oar brought a new and unexpected object to our view." Islands had been situated "only where they should be, each in its proper place and having its proper character." These islands were all different: some had pagodas, others were "quite destitute of ornament"; some were "smooth and level," others "steep and uneven";

others still were "frowning with wood, or smiling with culture." The visitors admired "forty or fifty palaces or pavilions," all "furnished in the richest manner, with pictures of the Emperor's huntings and progresses; with stupendous vases of jasper and agate; with the finest porcelain and japan."[10]

It would be, Macartney commented, "an endless task" to "attempt a detail of all the wonders of this charming place . . . in the course of a few hours I have enjoyed such vicissitudes of rural delight, as I did not conceive could be felt out of England. . . ."[11] Stunned that so many marvels could exist elsewhere, Macartney rivaled the Chinese in narcissism.

None of the ministers told Macartney of a tragic accident in this idyllic setting that nearly brought the Qianlong era to a premature end. "On October 14, 1788," wrote Father Raux in an unpublished letter, "the Emperor, engaged in a hunt near Jehol, was caught in a horrifying downpour. The floodwaters reached to his neck. The chief minister, Heshen, and several other large men held their master's chair as high as they could, yet they were very nearly swept away by the river, and owe their lives to the intrepid courage of a number of Mongols who possessed excellent mounts and knew how to swim. Sixty-three persons of the imperial retinue were drowned, and the number of common people who perished is unknown."[12] Another enduring feature of life in China: tragic floods.

MACARTNEY WAS SO impressed by this visit that he devoted a long passage in his "Observations on China" to horticultural comparisons between East and West. "There is certainly a great analogy between our gardening and the Chinese," he wrote. But "our excellence seems to be rather in improving nature, theirs to conquer her and yet produce the same effect. . . . His [the Chinese gardener's] point is to change everything from what he found it, to explode the old fashion of the creation and introduce novelty in every corner. If there be a waste, he adorns it with trees; if a dry desert, he waters it with a river or floats it with a lake. If there be a smooth flat, he varies it with all possible conversions. He undulates the surface, he raises it in hills, scoops it into valleys and roughens it with rocks."[13]

Macartney took a relaxed view of the controversy over which nation had invented the art of landscaping: "Whether our style of gardening was really copied from the Chinese, or originated with ourselves, I leave for vanity to assert, and idleness to discuss. A discovery which is the result of good sense and reflection may equally occur to the most distant nations without either borrowing from the other."[14]

England and China both excelled in the horticultural arts, and Macartney found little to criticize in the Garden of the East. He did not "much admire" the water lilies with which the lakes were "overspread." And: "Artificial rocks and ponds, with gold and silver fish are perhaps too often introduced, and the monstrous porcelain figures of lions and tigers usually placed before the pavilions, are displeasing to an European eye. But these are trifles of no great moment, and I am astonished that now, after a six hours critical survey of these gardens I can scarcely recollect anything besides to find fault with."[15]

As the visit came to a close, Heshen informed Macartney that there was bigger and better yet to come. This was only the Garden of the East; the marvels of the Garden of the West still awaited him.

Though Macartney discoursed at length on the differences and similarities of English and Chinese gardens, he strangely failed to understand what Jehol really was. The emperor had created a Celestial microcosm, a reconstruction of the Middle Empire containing replicas of some of its most famous landmarks and monuments: the Potala of Lhasa, the Tashilhunpo of Xigaze, the pagoda of the Hill of Gold in Zhenjiang, a Xinjiang mosque, the Yangtze, the Grand Canal, Lake Kunming. Here in the middle of Manchuria, the unsuspecting Macartney viewed reconstructions of sites in southern China, Tibet, and Turkestan. It was a kind of Disneyland, a theme park of the wonders of the Chinese world, an architectural bonsai. In Jehol, a mere six days from the capital by palanquin, Qianlong could enjoy a miniature empire boasting all the natural charms that China had to offer.

MACARTNEY'S SPIRITS rose. The taste of tourism had given him his first opportunity to speak to people who mattered, and he felt that his real diplomatic mission had finally begun.

He was accompanied by the most important state leaders, all of them Tartars, wearing short, gilded jackets over their robes. Macartney called them the "Knights of the Yellow Vest."[16] There was Heshen, the chief minister; Fuchang'an, the "second minister"; his brother, General Fukang'an, breaker of rebellions; and Songyun, a forty-one-year-old Tartar-Mongol with a reputation for incorruptibility,[17] who had recently been named a Grand Councillor. Songyun had just returned from the Siberian border town of Kiakhta, where he had conducted complex negotiations leading to a trade treaty with Russia.[18] When he learned that

Macartney had been ambassador to St. Petersburg, Songyun asked intelligent questions about Russia.*

Heshen, on the other hand, seemed to lack warmth despite his outward courtesy, and Macartney expressed astonishment when a well-meant compliment was taken amiss. The ambassador remarked that the creation of this paradise was "worthy of the genius of the great Kangxi." Heshen, clearly surprised, asked how it was that an Englishman knew that the park had been built by Kangxi. Macartney replied that "as the English were a wise and learned nation, and acquainted with the history of all countries, it was not to be wondered at that they should be particularly well informed of the history of the Chinese, whose fame extended to the most distant parts of the world." But Heshen gave Macartney no credit for his interest in the Middle Empire, apparently finding his curiosity "impertinent." To know China was to offend it.

Where Fuchang'an, the "second minister," was "very gracious" toward the British, his brother, the general, was equally open in his aversion to the "men of red hair." As a former viceroy of Canton, he "knew them too well not to fear them." That morning, when Macartney approached the emperor, the general had pulled the ambassador "by the sleeve" and "touched my hat with his hand to indicate his wishes that I should take it off on the occasion, a thing that could scarcely have occurred to any of his brother courtiers, as the salutation of the hat is entirely a European custom, . . . the Asiatics never uncovering their heads, even in the presence of their most elevated superiors."[19] Since Macartney had insisted on European rites, Fukang'an would at least make sure that he did not evade the appropriate gestures of humility.

Macartney tried to win the great soldier over by inviting him to review "the exercise of my guard and their military evolutions, with the latest European improvements." But Fukang'an declined the proposal with what Macartney regarded as great coldness tinged with unreasonable vanity, "saying that nothing of that kind could be a novelty to him." Macartney, however, had "doubts whether he ever saw a firelock in his life; at least, I am sure I have never seen anything above a matchlock among all the troops in China."[20] That would still be true half a century later, during the Opium War.

The British were somewhat mortified to find that the pavilions of the

---

* Songyun's published "memoirs" do not even mention Macartney, with whom he later spent five weeks. A Chinese professor suggested to me that Songyun may have feared being chided for their friendly relations.

Garden of the East contained "every kind of European toys and sing-songs; with spheres, orreries, clocks, and musical automatons of such exquisite workmanship, and in such profusion, that our presents must shrink from the comparison and 'hide their diminished heads.' "[21] There was even a planetarium. Macartney's guides told him that these treasures were "far exceeded by others of the same kind in the apartments of the ladies and in the European repository at Yuanming Yuan." In other words, China teemed with objects equally as precious as the gifts the British were so proud of.

Macartney recognized some of the British-made music boxes as having once belonged to the superb collection known as "Cox's museum." Fukang'an mistakenly concluded from Macartney's enthusiasm that the envoy had never seen such things before. He "exultingly demanded, whether such performances were to be found in England," and it was his turn to be "not a little mortified," when it was explained to him that "it was precisely from thence they came to China."[22]

AMID THESE mutual expressions of superficial national pride, Macartney raised a specific issue. Captain Mackintosh, he explained, was still in Peking, and Macartney wished to send him back to Zhoushan. Mackintosh could then set sail for Canton and then for London, carrying the envoy's report of the imperial audience. Fukang'an replied that it was "not proper" for foreigners to "be allowed to traverse the Chinese empire."[23]

Hence arose the "Mackintosh affair." Imperial archives tell us that the rejection of Macartney's request, far from being the whim of a general jealous of British superiority, had been decreed by the emperor himself. Qianlong saw no reason why Mackintosh was needed on the *Hindostan*; the ship, after all, had returned from Dagu to Zhoushan without him. Besides, such a superfluous and extravagant journey would have required the cooperation of the entire Celestial machinery, and the emperor was growing increasingly annoyed with these Englishmen, who seemed determined to make themselves at home. (Even in today's China, groups of visitors are expected to remain together. The Chinese detest having tourists wander off on their own.)

Deciding not to press the issue, the ambassador instead requested an interview with Heshen, who claimed to be too busy with preparations for the emperor's birthday celebrations. The chief minister repeated that "he hoped to have frequent opportunities of seeing" Macartney at the Yuanming Yuan and of "cultivating my friendship there."[24]

As Father de Grammont had predicted, no affairs of state would be dealt with in Jehol. But Macartney did manage to get Heshen to agree to read a note on the issue.

On September 16 the restrictions on the ambassador's retinue were lifted, and Staunton and several others decided to go horseback riding. Mandarins and soldiers followed at their heels, the chaperons "in dread that some inconvenience might result from indiscretion or imprudence on the part of the strangers." The mandarins, Staunton observed, "have little idea of the use or pleasure of walking abroad, merely for the sake of exercise, or for seeing prospects, . . . unless with the military, and, consequently, suspicious views."[25] Holmes made a similar point more directly: "The unaccountable jealousy, and strange conduct of the Chinese, surprised us very much."[26]

Little has changed in this respect, and perhaps the Chinese have a point. Once deprived of its mystery, a state becomes more vulnerable. There is an old Chinese fable that tells of the sudden appearance of a donkey in the province of Guizhou, where no such animal had ever been seen. The tiger was frightened by the donkey's braying and hid in his den. But after observing the newcomer carefully for a time, he leaped upon the poor donkey, broke his spine, and devoured him. Suppose the British lion took it into its head to break the spine of the Chinese dragon? The dragon might be wiser to remain coiled and concealed.

In the meantime, the British observed, assessed, took notes. Reconnaissance. Visceral Chinese paranoia about spies was in fact based on acute awareness of the risk,[27] but since there was nothing to fear here in Jehol, the Chinese resigned themselves to supplying these Englishmen with horses and guides. The British scaled the high ground and enjoyed a grand panoramic view of the fertile Jehol Valley, watered by the great Luan River. Traces of one of its recent floods were still visible, and the surrounding mountains had lost their tree cover. Deforestation and flood, the one bringing the other in its wake. Both plague China to this day.

The British saw several Lamaist monasteries and admired a mountain peak topped by an enormous mushroom-shaped rock.* They were allowed to examine it close up, but were forbidden to climb onto it, which would have been "an impropriety." They gazed down into the imperial gardens "consecrated to the use of the ladies of the palace." From their vantage point, they could see some of them "walking through the grounds; though at the distance of three or four miles."[28]

---

* This oddity of nature, resembling an enormous mallet with its handle stuck into the ground, is equally impressive today.

ON THAT SAME DAY, September 16, the chief minister summoned the ambassador's physician. After the previous day's ride through the Park of Ten Thousand Trees, Heshen's every move brought pain. Dr. Gillan found the court doctors gathered at his bedside, and Heshen described the symptoms: pain in his joints and a swelling in the lower abdomen that seemed to come and go. The Chinese doctors were unfamiliar with these details, because: "They pretend that the pulse, like a general interpreter of animal life, explains every state and condition of the body and that by means of it alone they can immediately discover the seat, nature and cause of disease without asking any question of the patient, or those around him. . . ." Heshen's physicians "had early decided that the whole of his complaints and all their change of place and symptoms were owing to a malignant vapour or spirit which had infused itself into, or was generated in his flesh. . . . In consequence of this opinion . . . the method of cure was to expel the vapour or spirit immediately, and this was to be effected by opening passages for its escape directly through the part affected. This operation had been frequently performed and many deep punctures made with gold and silver needles . . . with exquisite pain and suffering to the patient." Heshen, "apprehensive of injury to some part of the genitalia," had refused to undergo similar operations to the lower abdomen, though he had accepted them in the arms and legs.[29]

To avoid offending his colleagues, the British physician gravely took the patient's pulse, in both wrists. He did, however, explain that it was pointless to take it anywhere else, "because we know that all the pulses corresponded together and communicated with the heart and each other by means of the circulation of the blood, so that from knowing the state of one artery, or pulse, we knew the state of all the rest." The chief minister and his physicians were dumbfounded by that assertion. At Gillan's invitation Heshen touched his right index finger to the left temporal artery and his left index finger to his right ankle. To "his great surprise he found the beats of his pulses simultaneous."

Gillan diagnosed "two distinct complaints": rheumatism and "a complete formed hernia." He strongly advised against any puncturing of the abdomen, as "the worst consequences would have followed." Heshen asked Dr. Gillan for written explanations and instructions.

Was the chief minister really "promptly cured of his most urgent illness," as the British proudly claimed? If so, the embassy made no gains from the incident. "Thus I see," Macartney wrote, "that the same strange jealousy prevails towards us which the Chinese Government has always shown to other foreigners, although we have taken such pains to disarm it, and to conciliate their friendship and confidence."[30] Unable to obtain an interview with Heshen, Macartney decided to write to him. Young Staunton was assigned to copy out Mr. Plumb's translation and to check it for accuracy.[31]

In the meantime, Heshen offered a rare kind word and gesture. Thoroughly satisfied with Dr. Gillan, he gave him a gift of a piece of silk and told him that his ideas were "so brilliant and reasonable, and so different from the notions credited in Asia, that they seemed to come from an inhabitant of another planet."[32]

An apt phrase. Though these two civilizations had undergone quite separate development, they would now be forced to live together, for better or worse. European awareness of China had been based on utopian imagination rather than reality, and now that Britain was taking the measure of reality, utopia would be dispelled and intervention would become inevitable. China would be compelled to suffer the spread of Western technique.

The encounter of 1793 was truly a clash of two planets. This was not a case of explorers arriving in a land of head-hunting savages, but of the mutual discovery of two refined yet incompatible cultures, one celestial and lunary, the other quite down-to-earth: mercantile, scientific, and industrial. Heshen knew that the moment was historic, and that China could no longer remain its own immutable self. But he did not realize that however the country reacted, whether it accepted or resisted this new situation, everything was going to be turned upside down.

39

The Emperor of the Tartars

(September 17, 1793)

IN JEHOL the Manchu emperors returned to their origins. This dynasty controlled the empire through two interwoven networks: the Tartar hereditary nobility,* with its military vocation, and the Chinese mandarinate, the civilian elite, recruited essentially through competitive examinations. Their stay in the Tartar heartland gave the British more insight than most other visitors into the strange phenomenon of Manchu rule, which ultimately lasted nearly three centuries.

Macartney was visited by a young Tartar dignitary, Poo-ta-vang, who wore a red button and a peacock feather and proudly offered the ambassador his version of the origins of the ruling dynasty. The emperor, he said, was a direct descendant of Genghis and Kublai Khan, whose dynasty conquered and governed China for more than a century before being dethroned by the Mings.† The Tartar princes with whom Macartney had dined were the heads of the clans. It was they who were entitled to raise the armies known as "banners."

The Manchu nobility was enamored of the bow and arrow. "They seemed a good deal surprised," Macartney wrote, "when I once told them . . . that we had left off the use of the bow in Europe, and fought chiefly with firearms in its place. The bow is the Emperor's favourite instrument of war, and I observe that he is always represented in the pictures as shooting at stags, wolves, and tigers with arrows, and never with a musket."[2] It was much more exciting to shoot an arrow from a galloping horse than to stand on the ground and aim a rifle. Noble arms for noble prey, an equal chance for the hunter and the game.

---

* The hereditary system was degressive: rank diminished with each successive generation, disappearing at the seventh.[1]

† This supposed genealogy was wholly imaginary. The Manchu dynasty was actually descended from the Jürchen, the so-called Golden Horde. The nomads of Jehol were neither Mongols nor even, strictly speaking, autochthonous Manchus, but conquerors of Manchuria.

Macartney devoted considerable space to the Tartars in his "Observations on China," written during the return trip. "Most of our books," he pointed out, "confound them [Tartars and Chinese] together, and talk of them as if they made only one nation under the general name of China; but whatever might be concluded from any outward appearances, the real distinction is never forgotten by the sovereign, who, though he pretends to be perfectly impartial, conducts himself at bottom by a systematic nationality, and never for a moment loses sight of the cradle of his power."[3]

"The science of government in the Eastern world," Macartney continued, "is understood by those who govern very differently from what it is in the Western. . . . It matters little whether a Bourbon or an Austrian fills the throne of Naples or of Spain, because the sovereign, whoever he be, then becomes to all intents and purposes a Spaniard or Neapolitan, and his descendants continue so with accelerated velocity. George the First and George the Second ceased to be foreigners from the moment our sceptre was fixed in their hands. . . . The policy of Asia is totally opposite. There the prince regards the place of his nativity as an accident of mere indifference. If the parent-root be good, he thinks it will flourish in every soil and perhaps acquire fresh vigour from transplantation. . . . A series of two hundred years in the succession of eight or ten monarchs did not change the Mogul into a Hindu, nor has a century and a half made Qianlong a Chinese. He remains at this hour, in all his maxims of policy, as true a Tartar as any of his ancestors."[4]

The irreducible differences Macartney detected between Manchus and Chinese could also be seen between Chinese of different provinces, each of which had its own recalcitrant identity. Father Huc later noted that there were "as many differences between the eighteen provinces as there are between the various states of Europe."[5] Until recently the Taiwanese state officially considered young citizens born on the island as natives of the mainland provinces from which their parents or grandparents had come. In France Chinese of Peking origin rarely associate with Cantonese, whom they have difficulty understanding. It is the fate of great empires to suffer such particularities. Nevertheless, all Han Chinese had a sense of belonging to a single civilization and a single homeland, and they considered the rule of the Manchus a foreign tyranny.

What Macartney failed to grasp was the extent to which the Manchus, while governing China with an iron hand, had nevertheless been gradually assimilated, adopting the Chinese writing system and Confucian culture and finally even abandoning their own language. To paraphrase Horace's remark about Greece after the Roman conquest, vanquished China conquered its fierce conquerors. After the 1911 revolution, the Manchus prudently melted into the mass, renouncing their collective identity in the interests of personal survival. Not until 1979 did people begin to dare to identify themselves as Manchu again.

The Sinification of the Manchus, while neglected by Macartney, was exaggerated by Barrow and Hüttner. But that did not prevent them from gathering considerable evidence of underlying hatred, which had already sparked local revolts and, some sixty years later, contributed to unleashing the deadly Taiping Rebellion.

Barrow considered Manchu conduct "a master-piece of policy little to be expected in a tribe of people that had been considered but as half civilized."[6] The Manchus were cleverly pragmatic in ensuring their grip on the country. Having been summoned to China to help put down a rebellion,* they placed their chief on the vacant throne and cast themselves in the mold of the Middle Empire and the Celestial bureaucracy. Curiously, they insisted on imposing the humiliating shaved head and pigtail, which Chinese men wore rolled up in their hats and cut off at the first impulse of revolt.

Barrow and Hüttner believed that the Manchus had concluded from the unhappy experience of the Mongols that violence and sectarianism had to be repudiated: "In all the civil departments of the state they appointed the ablest Chinese, and all vacancies were filled with Chinese in preference to Tartars. They learned the Chinese language; married into Chinese families; encouraged Chinese superstitions; and, in short, omitted no step that could tend to incorporate them as one nation."[7]

Nevertheless: "In proportion as the Tartar power has increased, they have become less solicitous to conciliate the Chinese. All the heads of departments are now Tartars; and most of the offices of high trust and power are filled by Tartars. And although the ancient language of the country is still preserved as the court language, yet it is more than probable that Tartar pride, encreasing with its growing power, will ere long be induced to adopt its own."[8]

We now know that most of this was erroneous. In fact it was mainly in the early years that the Manchus acted with ferocity, whole populations being massacred in the years immediately following the establishment of the Qing dynasty. Resistance to the obligatory pigtail provoked riots that

---

* China had been in turmoil for twenty years, and the Manchu emperor of Mukden, whose young empire was organized on the Chinese model, was exerting growing pressure on the northern border. In 1644 the rebel Li Zicheng took Peking. Chongzhen, the Ming emperor, committed suicide. When the loyalist general Wu Sangui appealed to the Manchus for aid in ousting the usurper, the Manchus drove Li Zicheng out of Peking and took power themselves, holding it for 267 years.

were repressed in blood, after which the master race settled down to rule over a people enslaved. Segregation was complete, mixed marriages strictly forbidden. The northern half of Peking was emptied of its inhabitants and reserved for the Manchus. All the women in the palace, without exception, were Manchus, even the servants.[9] Just to be on the safe side. All the eunuchs, equally without exception, were Chinese. The palace environment therefore provided absolute assurance against impure offspring: the only available women were Manchu, and all the Chinese men on the scene were castrated.

Barrow's remarks about the distribution of posts in the state apparatus were also exaggerated. Generally a kind of parity was observed: one Tartar, one Han Chinese. But this, of course, masked an enormous disparity, since the population of the country included some three hundred thousand Manchus and three hundred million Chinese. It was like Marius's pâté: one horse, one rabbit.

When the British sought to generalize or to make predictions, they often erred. In this case they had it backwards: the savagery occurred at the beginning; in the long run, Sinification prevailed.

Their diagnosis was accurate. Barrow observed that "the Chinese are greatly disaffected, and not without reason, at the imperious tone now openly assumed by the Tartars; and although they are obliged to cringe and submit, in order to rise to any distinction in the state, yet they unanimously load them with 'Curses, not loud, but deep.' "[10]

But their prognosis was way off. The British believed that the Tartars would ultimately prevail over the Chinese. In reality, however convinced they were that they would remain masters forever, the Tartars were virtually swallowed up. No one saw the turnabout coming, since no one accurately gauged the indestructible force of a culture protected by a massive ethnic group. Secret societies aimed at ousting the Manchus and restoring a truly Chinese empire were increasingly active, but when the Tartars were finally dethroned, the empire itself did not survive them. With the revolution of 1911, the Manchus vanished into thin air, and many peasants longed for a restoration of the Mings,[11] a dynasty that had collapsed centuries earlier precisely under the blows of peasant revolt. Revolutions rarely achieve what is expected of them.

On the other hand, the British were right to surmise that this country, which considered itself the center of the world, was in truth the center of what would someday be called the Third World.

The testimony of the British, if not their prophecy, is quite credible. Here is Barrow giving us the inside dope: "I could observe that the young men of the royal family at the Yuanming Yuan spoke with great contempt of the Chinese. One of them, perceiving that I was desirous of acquiring some knowledge of the Chinese written character, took great pains to convince me that the Tartar language was much superior to it; and he not only offered to furnish me with the alphabet and some books, but with his instructions also, if I would give up the Chinese, which, he observed, was not to be acquired in the course of a man's whole life."[12]

Staunton devoted long passages to the Mandarin language and its deficiencies,[13] and an impressed Hegel drew two far-reaching conclusions from them. The first, in *The Philosophy of History*: "The nature of their written language is at the outset a great hindrance to the development of the sciences."[14] The second, in *The Phenomenology of Spirit*: that it had been the mercantile opening to the outside world that had generated the need for alphabetic writing.[15] Whose inventors, after all, were the Phoenicians, the first great traders. Once thought takes to the seas and seeks to communicate, a supple tool is needed, and this flexibility in turn contributes to the advance of science. However barbarous Barrow may have considered his Tartar prince, the man sensed how paralyzing the Chinese writing system was. And the British commented on how different it was from the wondrous simplicity of the Latin alphabet and the fertile abstraction of algebraic language.

The butt of Tartar jokes was often a Chinese. "I could not forbear remarking, how very much these young princes enjoyed a jest levelled against the Chinese. An ill-natured remark, for instance, on the cramped feet and hobbling gait of a Chinese woman met with their hearty approbation; but they were equally displeased on hearing the clumsy shoes worn by the Tartar ladies compared to the broad flat-bottomed junks of the Chinese."[16] Hüttner remarked that "only with the greatest regret would even the lowliest of Tartars obey a Chinese mandarin."[17]

Tartar contempt for the Chinese was fully reciprocated. In Chinese, Hüttner observed, *Tartar* and *barbarian* were virtual synonyms: "In China the word 'Tartar' means 'brute.' At one point, when an Englishman complained of a toothache, one of our mandarins asked him, 'Why not ask the surgeon to give you something to kill the pain?' 'So I did,' the Englishman replied, 'but he recommended extraction of the tooth.' 'Oh,' exclaimed the mandarin, 'the Tartar!' "[18]

MARCO POLO HAD given a lavish description of the festivities organized by the Great Kublai Khan for his birthday, "the most important feast day apart from the first day of the year."[19] But Macartney must not have paid sufficient attention, for only now was he beginning to realize that he had been signed on to enhance the prestige of a birthday party that Tartars and Chinese alike considered the real reason for his mission.

On September 17 the British were taken to witness part of the strange celebration, a sacred ceremony with a hidden god.

At three in the morning the ambassador and his retinue, accompanied by Wang and Qiao, were brought to the palace, where they waited for the usual three hours or so. They were served fruit, tea, and hot milk. The festival finally began in the park, as all the state officials, in ceremonial dress, lined up in front of the imperial pavilion.

But this time the emperor never appeared. Instead he remained "concealed behind a screen, from whence, I presume, he could see and enjoy the ceremonies without inconvenience or interruption. All eyes were turned towards the place where His Majesty was imagined to be enthroned."[20] Muffled drums and deep-toned bells were heard in the distance. Then silence. Then the music began again, followed by another silence. The music was jarring to ears accustomed to the Handel and Purcell played by the embassy's German musicians during the ocean crossing: "Their instruments, it is true, are sufficiently varied, both as to shape and materials, but I know of none that is even tolerable to a European ear. . . . They have not the least notion of counterpoint, or of playing in parts."[21]

Some of the mandarins bustled about, "as if engaged in preparing some grand coup de théâtre." Music continued to alternate with silence. Finally the orchestra and voices reached full pitch, and "instantly the whole Court fell flat upon their faces before this invisible Nebuchadnezzar."[22]

Nebuchadnezzar? Macartney had certainly come a long way in a mere three days. On September 14, just after his audience with the emperor, he had written: "Thus, then, have I seen 'King Solomon in all his glory.' I use this expression, as the scene recalled perfectly to my memory a puppet show of that name which I recollect to have seen in my childhood, and which made so strong an impression on my mind that I then thought it a true representation of the highest pitch of human greatness and felicity."[23] But now his tone was sarcastic, his vexation bitter. It was as though he sensed how the official court register would record his presence at this ceremony: "The princes and high dignitaries of the imperial retinue, the Mongol princes and nobles, the envoys of Burma and England, paid their homage."[24] On the fourteenth Macartney believed that the audience was being held in his honor; on the seventeenth he is cited after the Manchus, Mongols, and Burmese.

THE ASTONISHED VISITORS also witnessed another strange rite. An immense red cloth was spread out on the ground. At each of its four corners stood a man with a whip. At the moment that the emperor was supposed to have mounted his throne, the cloth was whipped nine times, at intervals: after three strokes, the men put down their whips, picking them up again several minutes later. No one was able to explain to Hüttner the meaning of this ceremony.[25]

No present-day Sinologist has been able to explain it to me either. But ancient history affords us some clues. When Qin Shihuangdi, who unified the empire, went on his pilgrimage to holy Mount Xiang, a violent wind nearly prevented him from crossing the Yangtze. Furious, he ordered all the trees of Xiang felled and the mountain painted red, the color in which a parricide is dressed before his execution.[26] And the whip? After the fleet of Xerxes, another Asian potentate, was dispersed by a storm, he ordered the waves whipped as punishment. Perhaps the red cloth symbolized the punishment of hostile forces tamed by flagellation. Or perhaps the cracks of the whip were no more than an urgent appeal for silence.

The refrain of the ode composed for the monarch's birthday was translated for Macartney: "Bow down your heads, all ye dwellers upon earth, bow down your heads before the great Qianlong, the great Qianlong!" And the ambassador added: "And then all the dwellers upon China earth there present, except ourselves, bowed down their heads, and prostrated themselves upon the ground at every renewal of the chorus."[27] These few men touching but one knee to the ground as several hundred others brought their faces to the earth must have made an astonishing spectacle. Miscreants! A gesture of contempt sufficient to outrage the entire population of this empire on a day when, in the meanest temple and in nearly every private home, offerings were made "before placards wishing the Emperor ten thousand years of life."[28]

The longer Macartney observed such devotion, the lower his opinion of this devout people sank. And he was not alone. His cousin Winder reports: "The whole ceremony resembled more the adoration of deity, than that of subjects at the foot of their emperor's throne."[29] When the reverential homage was complete, everyone retired. At no time did the despot appear in public: "We saw nothing of him [the emperor] the whole day, nor did any of his Ministers, I imagine, approach him, for they all seemed to retire at the same moment as we did."[30] Mao, who nearly always acted the role of inaccessible hero of his people, invented nothing.

No one was allowed to disturb Qianlong's communion with Heaven, except for his direct descendants, who were granted brief access to him. Two years earlier he had written: "This year we reached the age of eighty-one years. The harvest is good and the rain fell at the right time. . . . On the eleventh day we invited our sons, grandsons, great grandsons, and our great great grandson to take part in an archery tournament at the Hill Palace. Our great great grandson . . . was only eight years old, but he was able to hit the bull's eye three times out of five. We were very pleased, and bestowed on him a yellow jacket. . . . We think of the blessings of Heaven, the fruits of our ancestors' good deeds, and the other blessings which have fallen to our lot."[31]

ON THAT SAME DAY, in Zhoushan, the squadron of His Gracious Majesty was likewise invited to participate in the adoration. The prefect Keshina reported that "the British officers led all the Barbarians to the prow of the ship, where they reverentially placed incense on a table, made salutations in the direction of the Palace, and hailed the imperial birthday. Upon which the controller Alinbao gave them, in Your name, provisions of beef, sheep, fruit, and flour. They made fresh salutations and thanked You for Your beneficence with much sincerity and respect."[32]

The shipboard log of the *Lion* strikes a somewhat more sober tone: "Fired twenty-one volleys of the lower batteries to celebrate the Emperor of China's birthday."[33]

40

The Party Continues

(September 17–18, 1793)

AFTER THE CEREMONIES, Heshen and the other high dignitaries who had earlier accompanied Macartney to the Garden of the East now took him to visit the Garden of the West.

Where the first trip had offered "the attractions of softness and amenity," the second presented "a strong contrast," exhibiting "all the sublimer beauties of nature." The park was "one of the finest forest scenes in the world, wild, woody, mountainous and rocky, abounding with stags and deer of different species, and most of the other beasts of chase not dangerous to man." A hunter's paradise. Oaks, pines, and chestnuts rose along "perpendicular steeps" and plunged down deep valleys. Palaces, temples, and monasteries ("but without bonzes") were scattered "at proper distances." There were rivulets and waterfalls.

They traveled on horseback, following terraced trails cut into the rock. After riding for several hours, they arrived at a pavilion built on a "summit so elevated as perfectly to command the whole surrounding country to a vast extent. The radius of the horizon, I should suppose, to be at least twenty miles from the central spot where we stood, and certainly so rich, so various, so beautiful, so sublime a prospect my eyes had never beheld."[1] In an illusion of perspective, the pagodas, palaces, villages, plains, valleys, and herds of cattle seemed almost close enough to touch. Macartney felt as though these sights lay at his feet and "that a step would convey me within reach of them."

Heshen pointed to a "vast enclosure below" that no one could enter except Qianlong, his women, and his eunuchs. But if no uncastrated man was allowed to look upon the emperor's wives, how had Father Castiglione managed to paint a portrait of the sovereign seated beside Xiangfei, the notorious "perfumed Muslim"? The Jesuit in fact painted in a studio, perhaps on the basis of sketches done by a eunuch who had been taught the principles of Western drawing.

Various travelers[2] had hazarded fanciful descriptions of the pleasures the emperor was said to enjoy in this enclosure. But Macartney, ever the skeptic, suspected exaggeration: "That within these private retreats various entertainments of the most novel and expensive nature are prepared and exhibited by the eunuchs, who are very numerous (perhaps some thousands) to amuse the Emperor and his ladies, I have no doubt; but that they are carried to all the lengths of extravagance and improbability those gentlemen [Attiret and Chambers] have mentioned I very much question. . . ."[3]

IN YET ANOTHER demonstration of the emperor's munificence, the British were served sweets in one of the pavilions. "The Chinese possess the art of confectionary in a very superior degree, both as to its taste, and the variety of its forms and colours."[4] Few today would agree. A lost art?

They were also given gifts: boxes containing silk and porcelain. These were from the emperor, and Macartney accepted them on one knee (a repetition of his original dereliction in Chinese eyes, but they made no protest).

The promenade concluded with a puppet show, which differed "but little from an English one." Macartney enjoyed the adventures of "Punch and his wife, Bandimeer and Scaramouch."[5] The characters were universal, the taste for spectacle eternal.

Macartney was well aware that he was making no progress in his mission. He had earlier mentioned a note to Heshen, and he now raised the issue again. His hosts listened politely but did not reply. The chief minister then took his leave, instructing Grand Councillor Songyun to accompany the ambassador to the replica of the Tibetan Potala.

The monastery was ringed by dozens of pagodas built at different levels, each within a separate enclosure, and the entire area was surrounded by a high wall. This copy of the Lhasa monastery was meant to celebrate the solidarity of the Manchu, Mongol, and Tibetan populations, all united in the Lamaist faith. Qianlong himself had written: "This year [1770] our sixtieth birthday fell, and in the next [1771] the eightieth birthday of Our August Mother, the Dowager Empress. The loyal princes from Mongolia and Xinjiang, etc., and the Chiefs of the Dzungar tribes, who had recently sworn allegiance to Us, gathered together to bring us good wishes. As a sign of our encouragement and friendliness toward them we had already [in 1767] begun to build this temple."[6]

Today the massive building is empty, but eight hundred lamas were in residence when Macartney visited it. He measured the dimensions of the impressive eleven-story quadrilateral whose square courtyard enclosed a "Golden Chapel." Monks were chanting their prayers. "The paraphernalia of religion displayed here—the altars, images, tabernacles, censers, lamps, candles, and candlesticks—with the sanctimonious deportment of the priests and the solemnity used in the celebration of their mysteries, have no small resemblance to the holy mummeries of the Romish Church as practised in those countries where it is rich and powerful."[7] Macartney's frequent antipapist flourishes were typical of the time. It was the age of Voltaire.

In the center of the chapel were three altars with "three colossal statues . . . all of solid gold." Macartney believed that these represented Buddha, his wife, and "some great Tartar divinity, whose name I forget." Actually, they were three manifestations of the Buddha. Today they are no longer (if they ever were) of solid gold, but of gilded wood.

The sanctuary was dedicated to Potala, or *Buddha-la*, "Mountain of Buddha." He was depicted "as riding upon dragons, rhinoceroses, elephants, mules, and asses, dogs, rats, cats, crocodiles, and other amiable creatures, whose figures he fancied and assumed, according to the lama mythology, for the edification and instruction of Tartars." Macartney described these "monstrous statues" as "all most horribly ugly, and so ill-represented, and so unlike anything in heaven or earth, or in the waters under the earth, that one would think they might be safely worshipped even by the Jews without incurring the guilt of idolatry." There were also "saints and bonzes without number, fully sufficient to match the longest catalogue of the Romish calendar."[8]

"The Emperor," Macartney reports, ". . . thinks that he is not only descended in a right line from Fo-hi [Buddha] himself, but, considering the great length and unparalleled prosperity of his reign, entertains of late a strong notion that the soul of Fo-hi is actually transmigrated into his Imperial body, *Nihil est quod credere de se possit* [There is nothing he is incapable of imagining of himself] . . . so that the unbounded munificence he has displayed in the erection of these pagodas may be looked on as not quite so disinterested for, according to this hypothesis, there has been nothing spent out of the family."[9]

These rather grumpy remarks may have been motivated in part by fatigue. Macartney, after all, was not a Tartar horseman accustomed to spending entire days in the saddle: "Our expedition of this day, from the time of our leaving home in the morning till our return in the afternoon lasted upwards of fourteen hours."[10]

The ambassador's irony (or admiration) might better have been directed to the aspect of this site that continued to elude him. The Potala of Lhasa was not the only famous Chinese monument to be replicated in Jehol.

Many others had been copied too, in spirit if not necessarily in their actual dimensions. It was as if Louis XIV had had models of the cathedrals of Reims or of Mont-St. Michel erected in Versailles, or perhaps a replica of the cathedral of Strasbourg, as a symbol of the fidelity of his new Alsatian subjects. Hadrian's Villa in Tivoli was similarly inspired. But Kangxi and Qianlong had no need of Western precedents. Theirs was a preestablished harmony of human universality.

Jehol had conquered China, and therewith the universe, and the Tartar emperor now held them prisoner here. But he was himself a prisoner as well. There was perhaps no more powerful man in all the world—and none less free.

In Paris on that same day, September 17, the *loi de suspects* ordered the arrest of relatives of emigrés and of all those whose relations, words, or writings might qualify them as supporters of "tyranny" . . . or of the Gironde.

THE NEXT DAY Macartney and Staunton were invited to the court. The emperor was putting on a show, or more precisely, an early matinee: from eight in the morning to noon, with no intermission. He sat in his throne facing the stage. The audience stood in boxes ranged alongside him. Up above, in compartments shielded by lattices, the women watched without being seen.

This was another exceptional moment for young Thomas, who strangely makes no note of it, though his father does: "They [the women] had not probably any view into the boxes; for the Emperor, being disposed to indulge their desire of seeing some person of the Embassy, one of the eunuchs conducted the youth already mentioned, out of the Embassador's box, upon a platform within the ladies' view."[11] Thomas Staunton was the first and last Englishman to be symbolically admitted to the Son of Heaven's harem.

Qianlong greeted Macartney obligingly, as though excusing himself. He explained that "considering the extent of his dominions and the number of his subjects, he could spare but little time for such amusements" as the theater.[12] Once, at a mature age, on the occasion of his mother's birthday, the emperor himself took to the stage, portraying the role of Lao Laizi, a legendary octogenarian. "Laizi, at the age of 80, had both parents still alive and, in order to make them forget their great age, he behaved towards them as if he were still a little child. Now the Emperor was seen to imitate him, and come creeping up, on all fours, to the front of the stage. . . . He made comic faces, dancing, and leaping about. The Dowager Empress was delighted."[13] Where lies the border between fiction and reality?

Even the Father of the People is childish before his own parents. This may, in fact, carry us to the very heart of Chinese immobility. In this empire, wrote Hegel, who had studied Staunton's account, "a *patriarchal relationship*" holds sway, and the "head of the family" is "the will of the whole. He acts in the interests of the common purpose, cares for the individuals, directs their activity towards the common end, educates them, and ensures that they remain in harmony with the universal end. . . . Ethical life has an immediate and lawless character, for this is the childhood of history."[14] Freud once commented: "Men cannot remain children for ever; they must in the end go out into 'hostile life.' "[15] They cannot be healthy if the "hate" that results "from the rivalry [with the father] for the mother" is constantly "inhibited."[16] Without the symbolic murder of the father, man is threatened by neurosis and remains inhibited. If his parents are the object of constant adoration, the parricidal wish is indefinitely deferred. Any innovation will then be seen as an insult to customs ritualized by the ancestors whom one is duty bound to worship.

Macartney tried to draw Qianlong into matters of diplomacy, but the emperor parried the attempt with a fresh round of gift giving: "I endeavoured in the turn of my answer to lead him towards the subject of my Embassy, but he seemed not disposed to enter into it farther than by delivering me a little box of old japan, in the bottom of which were some pieces of agate and other stones much valued by the Chinese and Tartars, and at the top a small book, written and painted by his own hand, which he desired me to present to my King, my master, as a token of his friendship, saying that the old box had been eight hundred years in his family."[17] Macartney himself was also given a book written and painted in the emperor's hand, as well as "several purses for areca nuts." Staunton got a purse too, and "other gentlemen of the Embassy" were treated to "some small presents." The "Tartar princes and chief courtiers" were handed "several pieces of silk and porcelain, . . . seemingly of no great value, . . . [but] appeared to receive them with every possible demonstration of humility and gratitude."[18] Then the show began.

Several plays were put on: tragedies, comedies, historical dramas, and mythological fantasies. Dialogue and musical passages alternated with battle scenes and murders. The actors wore "masks both before and behind so that their backs should never be turned to the Emperor."[19]

The performance ended with a "grand pantomime" that "seemed . . . to represent the marriage of the Ocean and the Earth. The latter exhibited her various riches and productions, dragons and elephants and tigers and eagles and ostriches; oaks and pines, and other trees of different kinds. The Ocean was not behindhand, but poured forth on the stage the wealth of his dominions under the figures of whales and dolphins, porpoises and leviathans, and other sea-monsters, besides ships, rocks, sponges, and corals, all performed by concealed actors who were quite perfect in their parts, and performed their characters to admiration." At the climax, a whale, "who seemed to be the commanding officer" of the festivities, "spouted out of his mouth into the pit several tons of water, which quickly disappeared through the perforations of the floor."[20] This *coup de théâtre* was "received with the highest applause, and two or three of the great men at my elbow desired me to take particular notice of it, repeating at the same time . . . 'Charming, delightful!' . . ."[21]

By now the spectators must have been dying to stretch their legs. Macartney was visited by two mandarins, "more confident and disengaged than the rest," who asked him whether he spoke Persian or Arabic. They were Kalmuks, persecuted in Russia and now living under China's protection.[22]

The morning plays were followed by an afternoon circus. At four o'clock Macartney returned to the great tent, where the emperor was already seated. "There were wrestling and dancing, and tumbling, and posture-making." Macartney, familiar with acrobatics from his days in India, seems unimpressed,[23] yet the jugglers he describes sound much like those performing in the circuses of Peking and Shanghai two centuries later, and they are incomparable indeed. "A fellow lay down on his back and then raised his feet, legs, and thighs from his middle perpendicularly so as to form a right angle with his body. On the soles of his feet was placed a round empty jar, about four feet long, and from two and a half feet to three feet in diameter. This he balanced for some time, turning it round and round horizontally, till one of the spectators put a little boy into it, who after throwing himself into various postures at the mouth of it, came out and sat on the top. He then stood up, then fell flat upon his back, then shifted to his belly, and after showing a hundred tricks of that sort, jumped down upon the ground."[24]

Next came another juggler who, also on his back, spun nine plates balanced on sticks attached to his boots and held in his hands. After "twirling and spinning" them all together for "a few minutes," he took them off "one by one, and placed them regularly on the ground without the slightest interruption or miscarriage."[25] Any Western visitor who had not been fortunate enough to serve as a governor of Madras in the eighteenth century would have marveled at such virtuosity.

But the weary Macartney was an increasingly unappreciative audience. He was disappointed at the apparent elimination of one part of the program. Where were the "feats of equitation"? He "had been always told that the Tartars were remarkably skilful in the instruction and discipline of their horses," and he had hoped to see a demonstration.[26] Had Wang and Qiao talked out of turn? Court correspondence confirms that the horsemen had been on the program.[27] But they did not appear.

Finally there were fireworks. In "novelty, neatness, and ingenuity of contrivance," Macartney admits, they "exceeded anything of the kind I had ever seen," including the Chinese fireworks in Batavia. There was "an immense network of fire," featuring "various forms and dimensions, round and square, hexagons, octagons, and lozenges, which shone like the brightest burnished copper, and flashed like prismatic lightning with every impulse of the wind." The display concluded "with a volcano or general explosion and discharge of suns and stars, squibs, bouncers, crackers, rockets, and grenadoes, which involved the gardens for above an hour after in a cloud of intolerable smoke."[28]

While continuing to ignore the purpose of this embassy, the emperor did not neglect the ambassador: Qianlong "sent to us a variety of refreshments, all of which, as coming from him, the etiquette of the court required us to partake of, although we had dined but a short time before." During all this entertainment, "dead silence was rigidly observed, not a syllable articulated nor even a laugh exploded during the whole performance."[29]

Silence at the festival's heart. Not the least astonishing aspect of these sacred ceremonies, which no other Western traveler had ever seen or recounted.

41

Court Secrets

THREE MONTHS LATER, as Macartney was preparing to leave China, Wang and Qiao shared some remarkable secrets with him. Perhaps he had finally won their confidence, or perhaps it was merely a moment of abandon on their part, now that there was nothing left to gain or lose, since Macartney would never be coming back. In any event, their revelations help us to decipher the somewhat disembodied personality of the man all Jehol held in terror.

Qiao and Wang began by explaining the emperor's daily routine. The ceremonies that ruled his life differed little from those of the Tang or Song dynasties, for the life of a Celestial sovereign was itself an immutable rite.[1]

He rose at three in the morning and said his prayers to Fo (Buddha) in his private pagoda. After the prayers, he read and annotated dispatches from the high mandarins who were authorized to write to him. At seven he had breakfast, then joined his wives in their gardens or in the palace.

Next he summoned the chief minister to discuss current business. The other Grand Councillors and Grand Secretaries then joined them for an enlarged council meeting. These ministers came to the court on foot, since it was forbidden to ride anywhere near the emperor. They would kowtow before the throne, even if the sovereign was momentarily absent, and remain on their knees throughout the meeting, never raising their eyes.

At three in the afternoon the emperor had a fifteen-minute lunch, in the presence of a single eunuch. Many dishes were served, but he merely sampled them. The kitchens were far from the court, and the plates had double bottoms so that embers could be added to keep the food hot. In the afternoon he attended to various diversions. Finally, he withdrew to read until bedtime, which was never later than seven in the evening.

"A principal eunuch is always in waiting during the night in order to conduct to him any of the ladies whom he chooses to call for."[2] Wang and Qiao said little else on this subject, but there was far more to report, since even the emperor's amorous recreation was ruled by ceremony.[3]

The ritual had been devised to guard against the formation of any emotional attachment. The Great Eunuch would offer the emperor a choice of plaques, each one bearing a name. When the sovereign picked one of them, the designated beauty was brought to him, wrapped in a sheet but otherwise naked, by another eunuch, who deposited her at the foot of the bed. The chosen woman then kowtowed and climbed onto the bed.

The Great Eunuch and his assistant remained outside a palace window. If the tryst exceeded the customary time allotted to it, the harem dignitary would shout, "It's time!" If there was no reply, he would shout again. When the emperor finally answered, both eunuchs entered, took the concubine from the bed, rewrapped her in her sheet, and escorted her out. No concubine could ever spend the night with the emperor.

Before leaving, the Great Eunuch would ask the emperor: "Might Your slave give birth?" If the reply was affirmative, a great registry was opened, and the date, hour, and circumstances of the encounter were recorded, along with other relevant information. If the reply was negative, the Great Eunuch would make sure that the embrace had no sequel.[4]

The ritual of imperial lovemaking was less strictly observed in the Yuanming Yuan and in Jehol than in the Forbidden City. And Qianlong undoubtedly found ways of circumventing the rigors of the ceremony.[5] It seems highly unlikely that he would have resorted to the eunuchs when he brought Heshen to his bed.

The oriental harem has always inspired fantasies among Europeans condemned to monogamy, especially male visitors traveling without women. Not all their revelations should be taken at face value, but they need not be summarily dismissed either. "In the Tartar lands," Hüttner writes, "all nubile young women are invariably presented to certain eunuchs who, being familiar with the Emperor's tastes, examine them and select some of them in his name. Young girls obtain permission to marry only once the eunuchs have declared them unsuited to serving the khan."[6] And Staunton: "At the death of an emperor, all his women are said to be removed to a particular building within the walls of the palace, where they continue for the rest of their days, secluded from the world. This building is termed the Palace of Chastity."[7]

Since the death of the first empress,[8] with whom he had had four sons, Qianlong had only eight wives: two queens of the first rank and six of the second, plus about a hundred concubines. It is a total that pales in comparison to the figures registered by the "emperors of perdition" during the late years of the dynasty, who were often unaware of the exact number of their thousands of concubines. Or at least such is the reputation ascribed to them by those who overthrew them and thereby became the arbiters of historical truth.

Wang and Qiao's final revelation: Qianlong's daughters were married to Tartar princes or nobles, never to Chinese.*

The two mandarins depicted the emperor as an erudite, devout, and affable man, affectionate to his subjects, merciless to his enemies. But they made no secret of his faults: pride, impatience when faced with obstacles, jealousy in protecting his power, distrust of his own ministers, outbursts of anger. The emperor did not even trust his own sons, and deliberately encouraged uncertainty about which of them would succeed him. One of his grandsons, Miencul, seemed to enjoy his special favor, being allotted some small part in state affairs.[9]

A few years earlier, Qianlong had begun setting dates for his retirement, but whenever a deadline approached, he found fresh excuses to postpone it. At the time of the Macartney mission it was set for 1796, but the emperor had a robust constitution and seemed unaffected by the infirmities of old age. Wang and Qiao doubted that he would ever abdicate.†

The emperor was interested in history and gifted with an artistic sensitivity; he had written many poems.[10] He had a horror of extravagance. Where his favorite, Heshen, decked himself in fine cloth and crimson, Qianlong's attire was always simple.

Not that he was a killjoy. Far from it. A tireless hunter, he loved pretty women and fine meals, seeing both as gifts of Heaven. He was not averse to the odd sentimental adventure, an occasional escapade in one of his many residences, or a romantic ride through Jehol's lovely hills.[11] But he was always attentive to his household. This polygamous, patriarchal husband was jealous of the dignity of his wives, whom he treated with courtesy and generosity. And he closely supervised the education of his sons.

Macartney took faithful note of the words of Qiao and Wang, whom he considered well informed (though Qianlong's advanced age inclined Macartney to suspect that their reports of their master's amorous exploits were exaggerated). Relations between the mandarins and the emperor had seemed so ritualized that he was astonished that his companions were even capable of forming personal opinions about their sovereign. But here were two human beings calmly discussing another. Character, incident, and anecdote had pierced the carapace of the sacred monarchy.[12]

---

* Mixed marriages were forbidden until the beginning of the twentieth century, a prohibition that (like the ban on foot binding) applied to all Manchus, and not just the imperial family.
† They were wrong. Qianlong kept his word, ensuring that his reign would be limited to the sacred figure of sixty years, not exceeding the reign of Kangxi, his illustrious grandfather, by even a single day.

THERE HAD BEEN three great passions in Qianlong's life, beginning with his youthful love for the beautiful Machia, the concubine of his father, Yongzheng. Establishing an intimate relation with one of the emperor's women was a crime so unforgivable that the only possible atonement was death. The fact that the perpetrator was the emperor's own son (who had already been named crown prince) compounded the crime with another offense: incest. Hence the drastic action taken by the young man's mother, who was then the ruling empress.

Qianlong never succeeded in winning the heart of his second great love, Xiangfei, the "perfumed Muslim," from whom an exquisite natural fragrance was said to emanate. After being taken prisoner, she remained obstinately faithful to the memory of her husband, who had been killed at her side, near Kashgar, by Qianlong's soldiers. In fact, she warned him that "if he tried to take her by force, she would kill him," and once she even drew a dagger from her sleeve in his presence, violating the rule that an unsheathed weapon could never be displayed before the Son of Heaven. When guards wrenched the knife from her grasp, she shouted haughtily, "I have many others." Qianlong did everything to overcome her cold rejection of him, even encouraging the Islamic faith in China and asking his Jesuit architects to build a replica of the mosque of her native city of Aksu—in the Forbidden City itself. Jesuits designing a mosque for a Lamaist sovereign! What could be more ecumenical?

As the emperor pined, the dowager empress stepped in to quash this second amorous scandal just as she had the first: the cause of the disorder was compelled to end her own life. Qianlong wept at the demise of the woman he called "the most beautiful breeze in Heaven and Earth," and he composed the words that appear on her tombstone:

> O deep sorrow, O lamentation without end.
> The short song has died away,
> And the moon's light has paled.[13]

A few miles from the oasis of Kashgar, on the edges of the Gobi desert near the Kazakh border, you can still read this inscription on the cenotaph adorning a mosque dedicated to the "perfumed Muslim."

FINALLY, in his seventh decade, Qianlong fell in love with Heshen, the supposed reincarnation of Machia. In violation of the rules of the Celestial

Empire, the emperor promoted a lover who had not distinguished himself through any public service. But this time his mother, who would live for two more years, did nothing: the lover was not female, and dalliances among men were none of her concern. Yet this situation was far more serious.

Heshen, unlike Machia and Xiangfei, ruled the heart of his master and lover. Power-hungry and inclined to embezzlement, he set about organizing a far-flung network of devoted supporters in the capital and the provinces. The public service system was corrupted, discontent aroused among the populace.[14]

In an effort to neutralize high officials uneasy at his ascension, Heshen sought backing among the only category of people (apart from the great dignitaries) who were allowed to approach the emperor: the palace eunuchs.

Venality, lust, and nepotism, resurgent under the nefarious influence of the all-powerful chief minister, combined to give the eunuchs an ability to influence events that they had lacked since the fall of the Mings. Macartney and Staunton believed that the decline of Manchu power under Qianlong was linked to a parallel decline of public and private morals accelerated by the eunuchs' newfound influence in the state apparatus. Staunton in particular offers an incisive description of these disquieting people: "Beginning as abject servants, the eunuchs are eager servitors of the secret pleasures of their master. Through groveling they achieve familiarity and favor. Then they acquire credit and authority. Ten thousand of them were once sent away [after the fall of the Ming dynasty], but since then their number has grown; at present they occupy all the lower posts, at least in the palaces of Peking and the Yuanming Yuan."

Relying on information from the mandarins and missionaries, Staunton explained the *cursus* of these men of power: "The qualification for such offices, consists in that operation, which in a few parts of Europe, is performed for meliorating the voice, and disqualifies for being a parent. But to be entrusted with the care of the ladies of the court, or to be allowed to approach their apartments, it is necessary to be what, without reference to colour, the Turks are said to have termed a black eunuch, which means, that all traces of sex should completely be erased. It may appear surprising to the English reader, that the operations for this purpose, however delicate in themselves, are performed, even upon Chinese of an adult age, with little accident or peril in respect of life. Such a fact is the more extraordinary, as the art of surgery is so little known in China, that not even letting blood by opening a vein is attempted there, and anatomy is not only unknown, but held in horror. . . . It is supposed that ligatures anointed with a caustic liquid, are mostly used upon this occasion in preference to the knife. The patient has been often found to walk abroad in the course of not many days, apparently as well in health as if nothing had happened to him. . . . If a man wishes to emerge out of the plebeian rank, and submits to become a eunuch, he is received in one of the palaces immediately, and promoted to some employment in it, which gives him the advantages and importance of a gentleman."[15]

The missionaries nicknamed these "black eunuchs" *rasibus*.[16] They carefully preserved their severed parts in alcohol, that they might be reattached to their corpses on the day of their death.

42

The Atmosphere Darkens

(September 19–25, 1793)

THE EMPEROR'S BIRTHDAY celebrations ended on September 18, and Wang proposed to Macartney that he leave for Peking on the twenty-first, three days before the emperor.

Macartney was still trying to get a note delivered to Heshen, and the message had now grown to include various requests: that Mackintosh be allowed to join the *Hindostan* in Zhoushan, that the ship be permitted to take on a cargo of tea or some other product, that its officers be authorized to engage in some personal trading, that Fathers Hanna and Lamiot be authorized to come to Peking, that Macartney himself be allowed to communicate freely with Canton.[1] This last request was something of a sore point. "The embassy was . . . shut out from the most necessary intercourse, with little prospect of redress," Staunton complains.[2] For an eighteenth-century European, the cardinal diplomatic privilege was the freedom and inviolability of the mail, but the Chinese were unyielding.[3] Since no one else wanted to recopy this note, Thomas was assigned to do it.

How would it be delivered? Macartney had no confidence in Zhengrui, and Wang and Qiao refused to get involved in matters that were properly in the Tartar's department. *"Il faut y penser,"* Macartney wrote in his journal.[4]

In the end he entrusted the mission to Father Li. "Thursday the 19th," Thomas notes. "Today Mr. Plumb went to the Colao with a note from the Embassador copied by me in Chinese."[5] The interpreter, dressed in European style, managed to elude the surveillance of the guards and got close to Heshen's palace, where he was finally intercepted by the populace and subjected to some "insult." But he broke free and made his way to one of Heshen's secretaries, who promised to deliver the message and "obtain a speedy answer."[6]

That evening Zhengrui, Wang, and Qiao brought Heshen's reply. All of Macartney's requests were granted save one: Mackintosh, having arrived with the embassy, would not be permitted to wander off on his own. In other words, Heshen effectively conceded nothing at all, since permission to trade had actually been granted months ago, unbeknownst to the British.

Mackintosh, the captain of the *Hindostan*, jewel of the company's fleet, was not just a long-serving officer, but one of the merchant-adventurers who had played such a great role in British expansion. He had extensive personal interests in the India trade, and had insisted on coming to Peking so as to acquire commercial information that might be worth its weight in gold. Failing that, he was anxious to get back to Zhoushan and at least transact some business. Otherwise he would have come all this way for nothing.[7] But the Chinese did not see it that way. To begin with, Mackintosh was nothing but a "contemptible merchant" anyway. In addition, he was part of a group, from which he had no right to separate. And if that wasn't enough, delaying the fleet's departure by having the ships wait for him to return to Zhoushan was a bad idea in any event. Finally, they did not want him carrying any messages. Four good reasons to make him stay with the group, the last of which alone would have sufficed. Curiously, Zhengrui read Heshen's note to Macartney aloud but testily refused to leave him a copy.[8]

Macartney wondered whether he had pressed his demands too far. He had heard that Heshen had called a special meeting about the embassy. General Fukang'an, former viceroy of Canton, had attended, and the former hoppo* had been summoned from his prison cell for the occasion. Macartney was unable to find out what had been said at that meeting, but he could not "avoid auguring the worst from the convention of such a divan."[10]

The atmosphere darkened on September 17 with the discovery of an infraction committed by a British soldier, one James Cootie. A Chinese soldier had given him some samtshoo, an alcoholic drink which he had apparently sampled, defying Macartney's prohibition. The ambassador decided to enforce the promised sanctions. Perhaps Cootie's punishment would give the "men of black hair" a higher idea of British discipline.

After being found guilty by a court martial, Cootie was sentenced to be caned. Troops lined up in the outer courtyard of the residence, and the victim was tied to one of the columns of the main gate. There he was given sixty strokes of the stick, in the presence of a large crowd of Chinese.

According to Anderson, the Chinese "expressed their abhorrence at

---

* None other than Muteng'e, whose confiscated palace served as the embassy's residence in Peking.[9]

this proceeding." Some of them commented that "they could not reconcile this conduct in a people, who professed a religion, which they represented to be superior to all others, in enforcing sentiments of benevolence, and blending the duties of justice and mercy." One mandarin is said to have cried out, "Englishman too much cruel, too much bad."[11]

I rather suspect that here Anderson ascribed his own opposition to corporal punishment to the Chinese. Or if not Anderson, then Coombes, his "editor," an advocate of progressive ideas who lost few opportunities to introduce them into the text. The Chinese were hardly repulsed by flagellation. Barrow, for instance, refers to the "common practice of flogging with the bamboo, . . . to which all are liable from the prime minister to the peasant."[12]

And it is not simply Barrow's word against Anderson's. Countless witnesses agree on this subject. Montesquieu was not exaggerating when he remarked that China was "ruled by the stick," and Chinese literature abounds with passages of this type: "The mandarin condemned the disloyal servant to a hundred strokes of bamboo. With the hundredth blow, the condemned man perished."[13] The transition from the Yuans to the Mings to the Qings brought no rise in clemency.[14]

In Anderson's view, there were good whippings and bad ones. Later, when two Chinese servants were beaten on the orders of a mandarin, he expressed no indignation whatever: "They were accordingly stretched on the ground, and being held down by two soldiers, were struck, in a very violent manner, across the hips, till the judge gave a signal for the punishment to cease."[15] Here no tear is shed, no commentary offered. Anderson (or Coombes) was an early specimen of the sort who exhibits indulgent indifference to the behavior of the "natives" and horror at the conduct of his Western compatriots.

ON SEPTEMBER 20, the eve of his departure for Peking, Macartney made a list of the presents the emperor had given the king. As a group of mandarins watched, lanterns, pieces of silk and porcelain, packages of tea, drawings, and Chinese boxes were packed into crates labeled George III. Rex. This packing was accompanied by repeated kowtows by the mandarins, awed by these objects that had been given by their emperor. The market value of the gifts, which the British considered very close to zero, was irrelevant.

Wang and Qiao informed Macartney that since the load was now lighter, the return trip would take six days instead of seven. The ambassador refrained from agreeing that the emperor had indeed failed to overburden them with gifts. He learned, without enthusiasm, that Zhengrui would accompany him back to Peking and intended "to visit us at the different stages where we meant to stop at."[16]

The procession departed on September 21, five days short of the first anniversary of the *Lion*'s embarkation from Portsmouth. Macartney faced an uncertain future as the embassy set out, leaving behind in Jehol not only its disappointed hopes but also another of its men, Jeremy Reid of the Royal Regiment of Artillery, who died after "having eaten no less than forty apples at a breakfast."[17] China definitely seemed not to agree with the British.

Hüttner attributed this death not to a silly bet but to an outbreak of dysentery. "The two mandarins escorting us were horrified at the thought that the disclosure of this man's death might cause their disgrace."[18] The problem was that no one was allowed "to die in one of the palaces of the emperor, lest he be reminded of his own mortality."[19] This is a frequent theme in traditional societies: the regime is life, and death must never sully it. Dying was also forbidden in Versailles.[20] Whenever the prohibition was violated, it was necessary "to pretend that the deceased still lived," until the corpse could be carried outside the grounds and buried by the roadside. Thomas confirms: "Sunday the 22nd. A fine day. We went . . . 9 miles before breakfast. . . . Here the soldier Reid was declared to be dead and was buried according to ceremony."[21]

Down below was a river "abounding in fine trout."[22] As he watched his companions' awkward attempts to fish, Macartney must have thought that the trout were slipping through their fingers much like the Chinese themselves.

In fact they were slipping much more quickly than he imagined.

On September 21, the day of the embassy's departure, an imperial instruction was sent to Changlin (hitherto viceroy of the province of Zhejiang, which included Zhoushan, but now promoted to viceroy of Canton), urging him to hasten the departure of the British fleet. The emperor told Changlin that if there was no mention of Mackintosh in the letter Macartney had sent to Sir Erasmus Gower several days before, then Changlin should instruct the fleet to raise anchor immediately. If Macartney's letter told the ships to wait for Mackintosh, then Changlin was to explain to the British officers that this was impossible. "If the officers refuse to cast off without Mackintosh, we will order the delegation to proceed directly to Zhejiang instead of going overland to Canton."[23]

The court's problem was clear enough: in reality the Chinese lacked the power to force the fleet to cast off. If Gower insisted on staying, he would—in which case the itinerary of the entire mission would be changed. One way or another, Mackintosh would not rejoin the squadron alone; if he went to Zhoushan, everyone else would go with him.

As the embassy made its slow, sad way out of Jehol, couriers set out for Zhoushan at a speed of six hundred *li* per day. Other messengers were dispatched to Jiqing, the viceroy of Shandong, and Guo Shixun, military governor and interim viceroy of Canton. A new edict was issued. After reading and rereading the letter from the British king, Qianlong and Heshen had finally grasped the embassy's true goals, especially its central objective: the establishment of a permanent residence in Peking, a totally inconceivable request that they were astonished to find embedded in the letter's dithyrambic banalities. This business of the kowtow was one thing. Irritating as it was, that problem had been settled quietly and without incensing the ambassador. But compromise on the request for a permanent legation was utterly unimaginable.

Until now the Chinese had done their best to delay an official rejection, but that moment would come, and China's two masters were concerned about how the British might react. For the moment, they decided to stall for time, and the governors dealing with these barbarians would have to take precautions. That was the gist of the September 21 edict: "The King of England has asked me for a right of permanent residence in the capital. Clearly an inadmissible request. Because I have treated them kindly, these Barbarians continue to put forward inappropriate requests. Ignorant as they are, it is possible that they may react spitefully to my refusal. They will not dare to undertake any action here, but it is not excluded that they may try to start trouble in Macao. Changlin will have to be vigilant when he arrives in his new post. To thwart any British schemes, he must ensure that the other Barbarians of Macao keep their distance from the British. Do not arouse their suspicions."[24]

The emperor chided his great mandarins for not dealing properly with the foreigners. "When I give orders to treat them well, they are shown too much consideration, to the point of making them arrogant. When I order a reduction in the favor shown them, they are treated badly. Let us act with discernment!"[25] The eternal problem with bureaucracies: they always go too far.

On September 22 Changlin sent a report to the emperor in Jehol: "Having been delayed by the consolidation of the dikes, I assigned the salt inspector Alinbao to instruct the British ships to cast off on their return trip. On September 12 he went to Dinghai with General Ma Yu. The commander was incapacitated by malaria. By the fifteenth he had improved and was able to take note of Your Majesty's edict and the envoy's letter. The Barbarians thank the Emperor for the signal favor he has done them in authorizing them to return to their homeland without further ado."

Thanks to the "comfortable circumstances of their quarters" and to "Chinese medicine," they have "recovered their strength." A few more days of rest and they would be "completely cured; they will then take to the sea."[26]

The entire imperial communications network was mobilized in an intensive circulation of official messages. This procedure, like most others, was immutable. The Son of Heaven would send an edict to a provincial dignitary. When the text arrived—carried by couriers covering nearly two hundred miles a day (six hundred *li*)—the dignitary, normally a viceroy or military governor, would kowtow to the edict, read it, and make a copy. He would then send the edict back, by similar courier, accompanied by his own report. When the edict and the report arrived at the court, the emperor would add his vermilion marginal notes, which were known as "rescripts." Fresh copies were then made, and the couriers would head back to the province at the same speed. The local dignitary would kowtow, read, and make another copy, which he would keep. The triple document—edict, report, and rescript—would then be taken back to Peking by a normal courier, covering some two to three hundred *li* per day. There it would be ceremonially archived. The characters written in the emperor's own hand made the document a holy object, and rescripts bearing the sacred marginal notations therefore had to be stored only in the Imperial Archives of the Forbidden City,[27] where we found them intact.

It was common for the emperor to address the same basic edict to all the provincial viceroys and governors, and we can therefore imagine the merry-go-round of couriers galloping off in all directions, returning to the court with reports, waiting for the rescripts, and then setting out again, regardless of the hour or the weather, transmitting His Celestial Majesty's will to all the nerve centers of China.

The true purpose of this admirable machinery was to guarantee an absolute identity between what the emperor wanted and what his "slaves" reported. Mandarins eagerly asserted what they did not know, failed to mention dangers of which they were well aware, and gave Qianlong the impression that the barbarians were thoroughly reverential. Sycophancy prevented them from doing otherwise.

Meanwhile, the emperor exhorted, gave orders, and issued reprimands, communicating only with the thirty or so men who were his eyes, ears, and arms in the provinces. It was as though he were talking to himself, goading himself, lecturing himself. And everyone was careful to make sure that the song of order, at least in this exchange of correspondence, was sung without a single false note.

THE RETURN TRIP from Jehol to Peking was the mirror image of the earlier journey from Peking to Jehol, and the journals of our witnesses contain little more than scattered gloomy remarks. When the procession arrived at the Great Wall, some of the British paid a second visit. The breach through which they had scaled the wall on the trip out had been plugged,[28] making the parapet impenetrable again. Apparently the barbarians had to be shown not only that China could protect itself with ramparts, but also that those ramparts were immediately repaired if damaged.

But the sealing of the fissure did not prevent the British from mounting the structure. In an entry dated September 23 Thomas writes: "In the evening I took a walk with Dr. Gillan to a part of the wall upon the top of [a] high mountain from which we had a fine view of the country, the wall, and two or three large villages in the valleys. We picked up several pieces of the wall and small shells which seemed to have fell from the bricks or mortar. We saw the Wall extend itself upon the tops of the highest mountain just upon the ridges. After having satisfied our curiosity we returned fatigued to the Inn where we had tolerable accommodations tho not so good as in the Emperor's Inns."[29]

The six days passed uneventfully, and our adult witnesses assure us that their accommodations in the common grounds of the imperial palaces were "irreproachable." But once again the child gives the game away: they had "tolerable accommodations" in an "inn." Wang and Qiao were as cordial as ever, "but the Legate still preserves the same vinegar aspect without relaxation."[30]

Macartney arrived back in the capital on September 26, nearly a month after his departure. Nothing had changed. He may well have wondered whether the entire trip to Jehol had not been a waste of time.

43

Back in Peking

(September 26–30, 1793)

THE AMBASSADOR and his retinue moved back into their residence in the capital at around noon on September 26. "Several Mandarines," Thomas reports, "came to pay their respects on our arrival. We found all the gentlemen except Mr. Barrow and Dr. Dinwiddie, who were at the Yuanming Yuan but came here in the evening. Mr. Maxwell told us some [news] from Europe which he learned from the Missionary. We also got letters from Mr. An* and heard that a brother of Mr. Plumb (who is a Blue Buttoned Mandarine) is just arrived from the southward of China and that Mr. Zhou came with him and is now at Peking. It is much warmer here than at Jehol."[1]

Mr. Zhou, of course, was the second interpreter recruited in Naples, the terrified man who had stayed in Macao. But now he had taken the risk of bringing Macartney a letter from the East India Company. It had been written on July 3, shortly after the squadron's passage through Macao on June 20. During those two weeks it had become clear that war between France and England was imminent. Taking account of the time it took for news to arrive, it had probably already been declared.[2] This would change the circumstances of the return trip: the *Lion* would no longer sail peaceful seas on the ambassador's behalf alone. Its sixty-four guns would make it the flagship of a company convoy that would brave the spring monsoons of 1794.

Since Macartney would have to wait for this convoy to be outfitted, he thought he ought to make the most of the delay. If failure loomed in China, why not try to compensate with success in Japan? London had instructed him to undertake an exploratory mission in that country as well. But if he was to sail for Japan, he would have to rejoin the *Lion* in

---

* One of the Chinese priests who had sailed from Europe with the squadron and had disembarked in Macao.

Zhoushan,[3] and he had already asked permission for the squadron to leave without him. Could he now turn around and ask that it wait?

For the time being, he did nothing, for he was not quite ready to abandon all hope of remaining in China somewhat longer. "We were all this morning employed in arranging the remainder of the presents to be sent to Yuanming Yuan," he wrote on September 27. "Our conductors seem pressing for us to finish this business, which, added to our own observations and intelligence from others, induces us to imagine that it is not intended we should pass the winter here."[4]

Information did not circulate freely in the little world of the embassy. Macartney considered secrecy a principle of command, and he refused to disseminate bad news. Anderson and his comrades were therefore naively preparing to winter in Peking. "Captain Mackintosh proposed to set off on the Monday to join his ship, the *Hindostan*, now lying at Zhoushan, and to proceed to Canton, there to take in his cargo for England, having seen, as he conceived, a favourable commencement of this important embassy, in which his masters, the East India Company, had such a predominant interest."[5]

On September 28 Anderson was bubbling with optimism: "The occupations of this day . . . were entirely confined to writing letters for England, . . . it then being considered by Lord Macartney as a settled arrangement with the court of Peking, that the English embassy should remain in that city during the winter, to carry on the important negotiations with which it was entrusted."[6]

Macartney was trying to bolster his collaborators' morale. But he was unaware of how thoroughly his pessimistic intuition was confirmed in the edicts that couriers were now carrying throughout the empire. The embassy's visits to the two imperial palaces of the capital had been canceled, as had the banquet with Qianlong and the various other festivities and receptions. Macartney would be granted the privilege of greeting the imperial palanquin at the Great Gate of the East when the emperor returned to Peking, but no more. Several days after that, he would be given the last of the presents and handed the imperial edict in reply to the letter from his king.[7]

Macartney had no idea what he was missing. Perhaps out of caution, the Chinese had never told him of the pleasant program that had been planned for him. The Englishman would now have to perform a few last indispensable rites, and then he would be sent on his way: "The tributary envoy will then have no further business here. It will remain only for him to pack up his gifts. He will set out for home before the fifth day of the ninth month [October 9]."[8]

The emperor ordered Zhengrui to make sure that all the articles of tribute were delivered to the Yuanming Yuan on the same day; if any were held in reserve, the ambassador might use them as an excuse to stick around.[9] Macartney notes that the impatient mandarins insisted that "our gentlemen might have an hundred, two hundred, or any number of hands that they chose to call for, to assist them."[10] Macartney was now less inclined to admire the efficiency of Chinese labor. The fairy tale had taken a nasty turn.

Once again the embassy was taken unawares, suddenly ordered to prepare their exhibit of presents for an imperial inspection. They had to hurry, but they managed to finish on time. Young Thomas, as usual the most precise, notes: "Friday the 27th. This morning we began to open the rest of the presents for the Emperor; some of which are very handsome. We heard that the Planetarium is quite finished and is now going at [the] Yuanming Yuan."[11]

By this time the British were less concerned about demonstrating their technical superiority than about encouraging the court to request their cooperation and instruction. Despite two centuries of effort, the Jesuits were still regarded as mere clockmakers and calculators of eclipses, and Macartney's ambition was to exploit Chinese curiosity so as to improve upon the mediocre results of this missionary infiltration. But it was wasted effort, as the amiable Father Raux could have told him. Five years earlier, commenting on "all the latest discoveries," the priest had written: "The phlegmatic Orientals were little impressed by the theory of aerostatic balloons, Mesmerism, and the planet Herschel."*[12]

Dinwiddie notes that at first the missionaries in the Yuanming Yuan fulfilled their task as interpreters most obligingly. But later they seemed to tire of the effort[13] and disappeared. The priests' absence was in fact far more significant than the astronomer realized: Lazarist archives indicate that the missionaries were actually being prevented from seeing the British.[14]

On September 28 the legate announced that the emperor would arrive on the thirtieth. Macartney was hobbled by rheumatism, but he could not afford to miss a meeting that might offer a chance for a real conversation. The compassionate Zhengrui advised him to take his time traveling to the site where the meeting would take place, "on the road at a place about twelve miles off." Zhengrui suggested that Macartney stop overnight at his former quarters near the Yuanming Yuan. On Sunday afternoon,

---

*Herschel was the name originally given to the planet Uranus, discovered by the English astronomer in 1781.

September 29, the ambassador finally summoned up the strength to move. He fell into bed exhausted the moment he arrived in Haidian.[15]

Macartney was not the only Briton to get sick. Dysentery now ravaged the embassy, and a section of the Peking residence was turned into a hospital to isolate the afflicted soldiers. Of the fifty men of the guard, eighteen were patients of Drs. Gillan and Scott.[16] Illness temporarily deprives us of one of our best witnesses, Hüttner.[17]

Young Thomas had gone on ahead of the ambassador, and he was enthusiastic about the Palace of Discovery: "Sunday the 29th. This morning I went with Mr. Barrow to the Yuanming Yuan. I saw all the presents laid out in order all in one end of the room. Indeed they made very beautiful appearance and were much admired by the Chinese."[18]

But according to the Dutchman Van Braam, who visited Peking in early 1795, even the superb planetarium undermined the British cause. "The missionaries remarked that several of the cogs were well worn and that the inscriptions on the parts were in German. They communicated these details to the chief minister, who, already offended by the British Embassy in many respects, passed the information on to the Emperor, adding that the British were deceitful imposters."[19] The Dutchman then reports: "The indignant Emperor ordered the embassy to leave Peking within twenty-four hours."

In fact there was no relation of cause and effect here. The Grand Council archives show no trace of this alleged report from Heshen, and Qianlong had set the date for the British expulsion long before. But the fact that such a rumor still circulated eighteen months later, at least among the missionaries, does reflect the failure of the British effort to dazzle the Chinese with scientific expertise.

THE FINAL ENCOUNTER with the emperor once again found the British playing bit parts in a pageant of imperial power. Awakened at the usual hour—three in the morning—on September 30, Macartney was taken to Miyun, north of the Yuanming Yuan, where a crowd of several thousand courtiers, mandarins, and soldiers waited.

Here is how the scene looked to the child: "We . . . posted ourselves at the side of the road where the Emperor was to pass. The road was lined for a considerable way with handsome painted flags supported by men. At last the Emperor passed in a pretty long train in which the Colao also was."[20]

The emperor came forward on a palanquin, followed by a two-wheeled carriage lacking any suspension system. As he waited at the roadside,

Macartney dreamed of how happy Qianlong would be to exchange this crude wagon for the comfortable coach he had given him. Sir George daydreamed too: "When such a carriage is compared with the easy, light, and elegant chariots imported there as presents, it is not likely that any national prejudice will long resist a sense of such a superiority in comfort and convenience; and it may therefore happen, that English carriages will become in China an article of merchandise, as well as watches or broad cloth."[21] The British were willing to take the best of both worlds, but the Chinese sensed that adopting British vehicles would mean exchanging their world for another.[22]

Macartney saluted the emperor as the procession passed. "We made the usual ceremony of bending one knee," says young Staunton.[23] He does not say how many times.

The procession moved on without stopping, and the crowd dispersed, leaving Macartney no choice but to return to Peking, where he arrived in the afternoon, "extremely tired and very much out of order."[24] All that trouble, just to genuflect! In the meantime, the emperor was once again forced to suffer the intolerable spectacle of this insolent little group looming above a crowd whose foreheads were pressed to the ground.

THE AX FELL SUDDENLY, when Qianlong issued a new edict to the viceroys and governors of Shandong, Zhejiang, and Jingnan. In effect, this was an expulsion order, though the interested parties were informed of it only a few days later:

> The British delegation will set out on October 7 and will travel by river to Zhejiang, where they will reembark. The governors of the provinces they cross must not meet them. They shall see to it that they are adequately provisioned, but with no more than is necessary. If the delegation seeks to delay, it will be necessary to compel them to advance.[25]

The court set down a definitive schedule, protocol, and itinerary. Since the departure had been moved up, Qianlong decided that the embassy should be conveyed to Zhoushan after all. Poor Zhengrui had earlier been accused of "hopeless stupidity" for making that very suggestion, but it is unlikely that he was given a chance to say I told you so.

When they returned from the ceremony, Barrow and several of his companions went riding with a detachment of Tartar cavalry. The speed of the gallop must have intensified their sense of confinement, for they turned back within sight of the city, entered it through a different gate and crossed neighborhoods they had not seen before. "But one of our conductors, who had thought it his duty not to lose sight of us, . . . hallowed out with all his might. We pushed forward, however, and got through the gate, but we were pursued with such a hue and cry, that we were glad to escape through one of the cross-streets leading to our hotel, where we arrived with at least a hundred soldiers at our heels."[26]

Close and constant surveillance made the travelers feel like rowdy college students on spring break. At one time or another nearly every European visitor to the People's Republic tries to play hooky just like Barrow.

In Paris on that day the Convention passed the *loi du maximum*, a decree that failed to halt soaring inflation but did provide for the copious use of the guillotine.

44

Shipwreck

(September 30–October 2, 1793)

DINWIDDIE, who witnessed the scene, tells us that the emperor came to view the gifts as soon as he arrived in Peking. Qianlong was probably doubly content to indulge his natural curiosity, since he knew that Macartney would not be present to do the honors of the "tribute." The ambassador, in fact, was informed of this imperial visit only the day after it happened, and he must have been mortified to have missed it. He makes no mention of the incident, but once again young Staunton gives the game away: "Today [September 30] the Emperor gave 4 ounces of silver to the gentlemen who arranged the presents."[1] These were "cast in the form of a Tartar shoe."[2]

The astronomer was not quite ready. The air pump, the Herschel telescope, and the Parker lenses[3] were still in their crates, and the court was quite annoyed by this delay. The Chinese believed that "putting together so complicated a machine as a system of the universe was an operation almost as easy and simple as the winding up a jack." Why wasn't it enough to mobilize "as many hands as are needed" to get the job done with dispatch? They made no distinction between advanced technology and manual labor, "imagining that labour, not skill, was the only thing necessary."[4]

On October 3 the lenses were finally mounted, and the emperor returned for a demonstration. The astronomer is our only witness to this visit. He writes that he had an excellent view of the emperor as he stood before the lenses. His face remained impassive,[5] and he spent no more than two minutes looking at them. He glanced at the air pump, and as he turned away, he commented that objects such as these were useful only for the amusement of children.[6] If Dinwiddie reported this cruel remark to Macartney, the ambassador did not see fit to mention it.

The astronomer gallantly pressed on. Of his vast scientific bric-a-brac he selected a few items that he thought might impress, but he failed to pique the interest of the chief minister and several top mandarins. It was most discouraging. The Chinese, he wrote, have ideas offensive to a European scientist.[7] He showed them that the Parker lenses could melt Chinese coins. Heshen used them to light his pipe, as though the apparatus were no more than a "cumbersome lighter." Then he asked a few questions: Could you set fire to an enemy city with these lenses? Would they work under a cloudy sky?[8] But he paid no attention to the answers. A foolhardy eunuch stuck out his finger, got burned, and pulled it back, provoking general hilarity. And that was that.

The British had no better luck with their military technology: "a mandarin came from the Emperor to request that the ordnance presents might be immediately sent to the palace of Yuanming Yuan, where they were to be proved and examined: but the Chinese thought themselves equal to the task of proof and examination; for the British artillery soldiers were never employed."[9] Did they really believe that they would be able to fire these cannon by themselves, or was it simply that they refused to acknowledge their inferiority in such a sensitive field? In any event, the British artillery men were dismissed as soon as they had delivered the pieces.[10] In 1860, after the sack of the Summer Palace, the cannon and mortars were discovered intact. They had never been fired, and they were shipped back to London.[11]

Once again Anderson (or perhaps Coombes) indulged in a bit of false reportage: "It was also reported, that when the brass mortars were tried in the presence of the Emperor, His Majesty admired the skill and ingenuity of these engines of destruction, but deprecated the spirit of a people who employed them; nor could he reconcile the improvements in the systems of destruction to the benign spirit which they represented as the soul and operating principle of their religion."[12] This was in fact the view of Anglo-Saxon "left liberals" of the Thomas Paine variety during the time of the French Revolution. Qianlong surely would not have shared it.

The scale model of the *Royal Sovereign*, the 110-gun pride of the British fleet, did briefly attract Qianlong's attention. He asked a few questions, but translation difficulties immediately arose. Father Adeodato, the expert clockmaker who was serving as interpreter, had no naval expertise, and it must not have been easy to translate deficient nautical Latin into Chinese, especially for someone who knew nothing about ships. Imperial interest soon flagged.[13]

A few curiosity seekers gathered. A "new channel of communication and intelligence has been opened," Macartney writes.[14] He was easily satisfied. These onlookers could not possibly have compensated for his loss of contact with the missionaries he had met with regularly before the trip to Jehol.

Bitterness mounted. Father Adeodato took Staunton and Barrow aside and told them of the secret distress of the missionaries. Behind the brilliant façade, they led miserable lives. Confined to Peking, they could leave the city only with the emperor's permission. If they made the mistake of letting a mandarin glimpse a watch in their cassock or a small clock on their work table, it was as good as lost. No rich man could enjoy his property in peace, since the mandarins resented his wealth. Any man who denounced another to the authorities would receive in recompense the post of the man he turned in. There were so many spies that nothing escaped them. And the missionaries were always the prime suspects in any crime.[15]

One day Dr. Dinwiddie felt a mandarin's hand in the pocket of his jacket. The astronomer's penknife was nimbly spirited away, disappearing into the wide sleeve of the mandarin's robe. Apparently encouraged, the man went for another pocket, but the astronomer pushed him away, loudly protesting that in England only pickpockets behaved in this manner.[16]

The emperor deigned to give the British who had put these machines together a gift: "This present was brought, after his departure from the hall, by the old eunuch, who took care to tell us that before we received it we must make nine prostrations according to Chinese custom." Barrow replied that he and his colleagues were not authorized to perform an act the ambassador had judged inappropriate. A Tartar prince observing the quarrel elegantly acknowledged defeat: it was a misunderstanding; all they wanted was for Barrow and his companions to do what the ambassador had done in Jehol. They therefore "placed one knee on the lowest step leading to the throne."[17]

We learn from a court letter that many of the gifts given to the embassy had originally been acquired as tribute from vassals. Each of the 650 British soldiers and sailors received a piece of Korean cloth, some white fabric from the Muslim territories, and some jute canvas from Burma.[18] These items were recycled like unopened boxes of chocolate passed from hand to hand at Christmas.

MACARTNEY'S ENTRY in his journal for October 1 contains this comment: "It seems that before our arrival . . . , some of the Emperor's Ministers had given it as their solemn opinion that we should be desired to depart at the end of our forty days, which period is pretended by the Chinese to be the term fixed by the laws of the empire for the stay of a foreign embassy."[19] *Before our arrival.* Macartney was trying to make it clear that his impending dismissal was unrelated to anything he had done. In one sense, he was right. He had begun to understand that from the very outset his embassy was fated to being regarded as no more than a somewhat grating variation on the theme of tribute.

The moment he got wind of the expulsion rumor, Macartney wrote to Heshen again, repeating his request that Mackintosh be authorized to rejoin the *Hindostan* in Zhoushan. For his part, he wished to set out for Canton after the new year, just as soon as weather permitted.* By that time the king's vessels would be in Macao, waiting to carry him back to England.[20] In other words, the ambassador intended to take his leave—but not until spring. Heshen asked him to come to the Yuanming Yuan on the following day, October 2, to discuss the matter.

Actually, Macartney received his marching orders not on the second, but on the first, as is clear from young Staunton's journal: "Tuesday the 1st of October. This morning Lord Macartney and my papa went to the Yuanming Yuan to receive some letters from Canton. They saw and spoke to the Colao there, who told them that it would be proper and convenient that we should go before the frost should set in."[21] This date is confirmed by Dinwiddie, who shared the carriage with Macartney and Staunton.[22] Was this a lapse of memory on Macartney's part, or did he deliberately alter the schedule in an effort to suggest that he had taken the initiative and to attenuate the humiliation of the hastily ordered dismissal?

Macartney says that Heshen cited four factors in urging the British to depart: the weather, his concern for the physical well-being of the embassy's personnel, their evident weariness, and their undoubted desire to return to their beloved native land. Sensing that this might be his first and last opportunity for serious discussion, the ambassador said his piece, effectively tossing a message in a bottle into the sea of this diplomatic shipwreck.

Here is Macartney's report of the conversation: "This morning, though much indisposed, I went to Yuanming Yuan, and found the Minister sitting with Fuchang'an and his brother Fukang'an, but no other Grand Secretaries attending. He began by delivering to me some letters which he said were just arrived by the post from Zhoushan. One of them was for Captain Mackintosh from his First Mate, and there were two from Sir Erasmus Gower to myself."[23]

Dinwiddie, an eyewitness, reports that these letters had been opened by the Chinese, but Father Adeodato had been unable to translate them.

---

* In 1794 the Chinese New Year fell on February 1, at which time the canals were normally frozen. Macartney intended to remain in Peking at least until spring.

As he handed them unsealed to Macartney, the unabashed Heshen asked what was in them. The guarantor of Total Order must know everything. No information could circulate without the authorities being aware of it before the addressee.[24] This was common practice until very recently; the Chinese would decide on a case-by-case basis whether or not to deliver a visitor's mail.

Macartney then told Heshen what he had just learned from the letters: that the *Hindostan* could not cast off without its captain, but that the *Lion* was preparing to leave Zhoushan. Heshen "said he hoped the *Lion* was not gone, for he imagined that, after so long an absence from home, I must be very desirous of soon returning to it; and that the Emperor, upon first hearing that I was ill and that I had lost some of my people by death since my arrival in China, remarked how much foreigners were likely to suffer from the cold winters of Peking, and had expressed his apprehensions that we should run great risk of injuring our health if we did not set out from it before the first frost set in."[25]

Macartney gallantly replied that he stood up to cold climates quite well. And since in Jehol the chief minister had spoken of his hope "to have frequent opportunities of seeing me at the Yuanming Yuan," Macartney wished to take "the earliest" of these to "explain to him fully my Sovereign's instructions to me, and to enter into negotiation upon the points contained in them."[26]

Barely pausing to take a breath, Macartney finally explained the objective of his embassy to Heshen: "It was the King's wish that I might be allowed to reside at his [the king's] expense constantly at the Emperor's Court, according to the custom in Europe, for the purpose of cultivating and cementing a firm friendship between two such powerful monarchs. I said that, with this view, I had been directed to propose that the Emperor would please to send a reciprocal Embassy to England, the care of which I would undertake to have managed in such a manner as I was sure would be highly satisfactory, as I should have proper ships with every accommodation prepared for the purpose of conveying it to England and bringing it back to China in safety, with every possible mark of honour and respect."[27]

Once under way, Macartney quickly went on to list all the commercial favors he had been asked to request, favors from which China would only stand to benefit.

Once again the trout slipped through British fingers. With his usual skill, Heshen "avoided entering into any discussion of these points." Instead he "turned the discourse upon the state of my health, assuring me that the Emperor's proposal for my departure arose chiefly from his anxiety

about it, for that otherwise my stay could not but be agreeable to him."
Heshen and his "two assessors" became even more friendly when Macartney finally rose to leave. Mr. Plumb "congratulated me on the fair prospect of my negotiation, and said that he expected the happiest issue from it."[28]

When he got back to his residence, Macartney learned that the missionaries were hard at work translating a letter from the emperor to the king of England from Chinese into Latin. A little later Wang and Qiao reported that the chief minister would see Macartney again the next day, most probably to deliver this imperial edict. In that event, "they advise me to ask permission to depart without delay." Macartney notes that he assumed that "they have been directed to hold this discourse to me."[29]

In other words, the Chinese wanted the ambassador himself to ask that his mission be brought to a close: "To go forward when employed and to stay out of sight when set aside," said Confucius.[30] Yet another ritual. So it had been with the two women Qianlong had loved so passionately: they too had been persuaded to implore the empress to grant them the favor of being permitted to end their own lives, and the empress had graciously agreed to their request.

But Macartney was not yet resigned to accepting this humiliating step, supposedly meant to spare him humiliation. Now rather despondent, he continued to temporize, though Sir Erasmus Gower's letter announcing the imminent departure of the *Lion* should have impelled him to act quickly.

The British had no idea how precarious their situation actually was. But the Chinese were not in a triumphant mood. Heshen's behavior was dictated by a mixture of impatience and caution. The British were barbarians, but of an especially dangerous variety, with numerous and powerful ships. Any possible temptation to retaliate had to be disarmed. Heshen, too, therefore temporized.

The court's chief fear was that Macartney would insist on remaining in Peking himself or on leaving one of his trusted deputies behind, possibly Sir George Staunton. It is curious that this idea, so feared by the Chinese, never actually occurred to Macartney. But the Chinese did not know that, and Zhengrui was ordered to take a wait-and-see attitude.

Heshen, meanwhile, was quite concerned about unpredictable British reactions. "If we tell the envoy categorically that no one of his retinue must remain in the capital after his departure, there is a danger that he might delay this departure, on the pretext of illness, for example, thus overstaying the customary deadline. Or he might try to withdraw the tribute. Or he might seek a pretext to decline to accept the imperial edict."[31]

The court had not forgotten Macartney's success in circumventing the kowtow. This infernal barbarian was capable of anything. There were other, well-codified ceremonies that now had to be fulfilled, and it was essential not to provoke any incident that might further disturb the natural order.

Qianlong was also bothered by less formal apprehensions. Another of his letters shows that behind this Englishman he saw England itself. These barbarians want "to spy on us" by demanding a permanent legation, and "there can be no question of that." But "the king of this country has sent a state message presenting a clear request. The envoy is not speaking in his own name."[32]

Another document makes these fears more precise: Macao is vulnerable to the British fleet. "We now understand that England holds supremacy among the nations of the Western Ocean." Worse: it is "the fiercest of the countries of the oceans."[33] The British even engage in "acts of piracy against the ships of the other Barbarians." Although the tributary envoy had "seen with his own eyes that the system of the Celestial Empire is strict and severe and that Barbarians from all lands have submitted to us," this did not change the fact that in Macao and Canton "the British vessels are the most numerous." "All precautions must be taken" in case this country "conspires" with the barbarian merchants to "stir up trouble." What a plum it would be for the British if they established a firm base in Peking from which to "acquire a monopoly" and "extract maximum profits" as the "obligatory intermediaries" for the merchants of other nationalities![34]

The ritual deadline had expired. The Briton must therefore request permission to leave. On October 2 the cavalry was informed of the situation and told to prepare for any possible consequences. The emperor reiterated his apprehensions, sending the requisite orders to the viceroys and military governors of the coastal provinces: "Take all necessary measures to forestall any possible British reaction."

It was a case of the carrot and the stick. First, when "Changlin arrives in Canton," he must "make it clear to the other Barbarians that the British delegation obtained no special privileges." He must "reassure the other foreigners and invite them to attend to their affairs so that they do not form a coalition with the British." "It appears that there are in Macao Western monks in whom the Barbarian merchants have complete confidence. Is that true of the British as well? If it is, then let us inform these monks of our plans, and let them act with appropriate discretion."[35] "It appears." Had d'Almeida or one of the other Portuguese "monks" in Peking told Heshen that he could count on other "monks" in Macao?

So much for the carrot. The stick was intimidation: the officers were told to display their banners and their arms. Dissuasion. A show of force in order not to have to resort to force.

"The maritime borders are the essential thing. Surveillance has been lax," and this must be urgently remedied so as to "make an impression on the Barbarians." "Prevent the seeds of trouble from sprouting." The barbarians must be dissuaded from "disembarking by surprise," especially "in the Zhoushan Islands and the smaller islands near Macao." The "ports and coasts" must be patrolled. "Assure their defense" while maintaining "the greatest secrecy." It is possible that "internal traitors" may link up with the barbarians to "garner some advantage." These potential traitors are "most detestable." It is essential "not to allow them any contact with the Barbarians." Traitors among the population must be exposed and punished with "the greatest severity."[36]

The imperial machine rumbled into action to expel the alien parasites and expose their potential accomplices. The incantatory rhetoric blended a touch of magic with a practical concern for effectiveness.

The *Lion*, a sixty-four-gun warship, moored near the Zhoushan Islands

A mandarin junk for provincial travels

The embassy's arrival in Tientsin

Macartney's residence in Peking (detail): stone pavilion shaped like a boat

The two mandarins
of the embassy's escort,
in court dress. *Above*,
Wang; *below*, Qiao

The emperor Qianlong being carried in his palanquin to the ceremonial tent
in Jehol

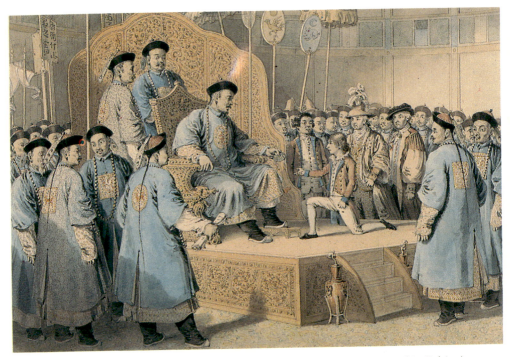

The imperial audience in Jehol, as imagined by Alexander (who remained in Peking).
Young Thomas kneels to accept the emperor's gift.

Lake and park in the imperial grounds, Jehol (painting by Alexander from a sketch by Lieutenant Parish)

On the Grand Canal, November 2, 1793. The embassy junks saluted by a Chinese military detachment.

Passing a lock on the Grand Canal, November 16, 1793

Haulers at work

Haulers eating rice
during a break

A dice game

Chinese preparing to
release fighting cocks

A mandarin's residence along the Grand Canal

Military post along the Grand Canal

Light infantryman in tiger combat gear

Infantryman in dress uniform

Rifleman with matchlock

Crime and punishment:
top, mandarin sentenc-
ing prostitute; *center*,
mandarin observing
beating with bamboo;
bottom, the yoke

Family of peasants

Chinese lady with her son,
accompanied by servant
with parasol

Wheelbarrow with sail

Cormorant fishing

View of Hangzhou

View of Suzhou

Funeral procession

Incense, sacrifice, and kowtow in a temple

November 7, 1793, Suzhou: "We spent three hours in the suburbs," reported Barrow, "before arriving in the city, where a large number of vessels had dropped anchor. The numerous inhabitants who were to be seen indoors and out in this immense city were better dressed and seemed more joyous than all the Chinese that we had seen up to that point."

Detail of a memorandum from a high-ranking mandarin, with vermilion note handwritten by the emperor Qianlong

45

A Scroll of Paper Enthroned

(October 3, 1793)

THE CHINESE were now satisfied with their psychological preparations. The time had come to act. In the early morning of October 3 Zhengrui summoned Macartney from his bed of pain, inviting him to attend, in ceremonial dress, a meeting with "the first Minister and several other Grand Secretaries . . . at the palace of the city." Macartney could not recall "ever having received an unpleasanter message in my life." Though "scarcely able to rise," he "got up immediately," dressed, and hurried to the Forbidden City.[1]

As it turned out, there was no need for haste, for he was treated to the usual three-hour wait. Macartney could scarcely contain his exasperation.

The strange ceremony was to take place in the hall of the Gate of Supreme Harmony. This was Macartney's only visit to the Forbidden City, but neither he nor Staunton had a word to say about this palace to which so few foreigners had ever been admitted. They were in no mood for sightseeing as they anxiously waited to find out what the imperial edict would say.

At the foot of a great staircase was a "fine yellow silk arm-chair," a throne not for the emperor, but for his letter, which was considered identical to his person. As their hosts kowtowed to the roll of paper, Macartney and his companions performed their "usual reverences," one knee to the floor, head bowed. Probably they genuflected nine times, since this was another collective kowtow. They then marched in a procession behind the armchair, which was "carried up in great state before us."[2]

Heshen explained to Macartney that the edict "would be sent to my house in the same pomp, but he did not tell me what was in it." It was as though the form were more important than the substance. The chief minister then pointed to several tables with a number of packages in yellow wrappers: the final gifts for the embassy.

Heshen did not display his usual courtesy, and Macartney gauged his hostility "by his decisive refusal of some magnificent presents which I had made him, and which I had every reason from himself to imagine he had accepted."[3] The ambassador and his deputy were sufficiently upset by Heshen's rejection of the presents to speak of it in front of Thomas. "I did not go," the child writes, "as I was not well. The Emperor then sent some presents to the King of England and to the gentlemen, servants and soldiers. We offered some presents to the Colao, which he would not accept of, nor would the Emperor take a carriage offered him by Lord Macartney."[4] So much for the export of coaches.

Macartney "was now almost fainting with fatigue and therefore requested the Minister's leave to retire." But he did have enough strength to mention the requests he had made the day before, and he asked that Sir George be allowed to stay to discuss these matters. Heshen "said I might send him a note of my requests, but he said it in such a tone as gives me no great hopes of success from it, especially as he chose to be quite silent on the subject of my former note."[5]

To the very end Macartney kept trying to read the chief minister's expression: yesterday he was lively, today sullen. The latter mood was probably a more sincere sentiment than the former, which had been designed to elicit a voluntary British departure but had succeeded only in drawing an impertinent plea for a longer stay.

Macartney was beside himself as he witnessed the final act of his failure. What an absurd ritual! A throne not for the emperor but for his letter. Reverential kowtowing to a piece of paper. His own presents rejected, though he had had every reason to believe they would be well appreciated. (The imperial letter of September 10 had forbidden anyone to accept them.)[6] Macartney suffered the affront in silence, but there is no doubt that he considered it as such.

The splendid spring-suspension carriage that Macartney had earmarked for Heshen had already been delivered, but as Anderson explains, since the Chinese "refused to accept it," the British now asked that it be returned to be "unslung and packed up; but no answer whatever was returned." They had so much to attend to that "there was no time to make further inquiries concerning the fate of this chariot, or the reasons of such an ungracious behaviour on the part of the minister by whom it was refused."[7] Perhaps the chief minister, having rejected it as a gift, now intended to confiscate it as booty.

Macartney left and Staunton remained. Heshen honored him with a bit of tourism. A walk around the grounds would ward off any conversation on matters of substance. The minister led Staunton and a few others into several pavilions, but they were shown the emperor's apartments only "at a distance."[8] The Forbidden City had to be worthy of the name.

Staunton, who paints vivid pictures of insignificant sites, mentions this most holy of holies only in passing. If China is the Middle Empire, the Forbidden City is the Middle of the Middle. But the normally sensitive Staunton was no longer paying any attention. In this context of failure, he lacked the heart for sightseeing.

In the meantime, the imperial edict pursued Macartney. Barely had he returned to his residence when it was brought to him by sixteen mandarins and their attendants, all of whom touched the floor with their foreheads nine times, while Macartney knelt and bowed his head before this document, carried on a luxurious litter. Then the presents were delivered, and the same ceremony was repeated.

The haste left no remaining shred of doubt. Macartney ceased to pretend to ignore the "hints already given," for he now feared that "they may possibly be imparted to us in a broader and coarser manner, which would be equally unpleasant to the dignity of the Embassy and the success of its objects."[9] He decided to request authorization to leave.

ON THAT SAME DAY, October 3, Changlin, still viceroy of Zhejiang, wrote as follows to the emperor:

> I went to Dinghai, where the Barbarian ships are moored. They told me: "The great Emperor has authorized us to leave. We would like to do so as soon as possible, but not all our sick men are cured. We ask for a few more days." Some twenty men are still sick and require care. I would have provoked panic among the Barbarians had I obliged them to leave. I therefore told them: "The climate does not agree with you. You have asked the Holy Indulgence of the Emperor, that you may care for yourselves in Zhejiang. The Emperor, granting an extreme favor, authorizes you to do so." I also told them: "Captain Mackintosh wishes to buy tea in Zhejiang and transport it back to England; he has been authorized to do so, and the taxes will be waived." The announcement of these instructions was unanimously acclaimed by the Barbarians, whose joy could be read on their faces.[10]

In other words, the British in Zhoushan were granted the favors Macartney had requested for them. But he was not told of this in Peking.

Changlin's report was addressed to all the members of the Grand Council. But it was accompanied by a postscript for the emperor's eyes only. That postscript is annotated with vermilion marginal notes in the

august hand, and the report, read in combination with the notes, amounts
to a long-distance conversation:

> Your slave reports to you in secret as follows: It is true that some
> Barbarians are ill, but their real intention is to gain time in order to
> permit Mackintosh to rejoin the ships and buy merchandise.
>
> EXACTLY.
>
> I think that if we grant them privileges in Zhejiang this time, they
> will become insatiable in the future, putting forward new indecent
> requests. They would use this as a precedent.
>
> ONE MAY WELL IMAGINE THAT IT WOULD BE SO.
>
> I checked and discovered that on several occasions in the past these
> men of red hair have come to Zhejiang to conduct trade. At the time,
> a certain Guo, who speaks their language, offered them his services
> to facilitate their transactions. This man is now deceased, but there is
> a Guo son, who presumably more or less speaks this Barbarian
> language.
>
> WE MUST BE ESPECIALLY WARY OF HIM. LET US REMOVE THIS MAN
> FROM THE SCENE BY HAVING HIM TAKE ANOTHER ROUTE. LIKEWISE FOR
> ALL THOSE WHO KNOW THE FOREIGNERS.
>
> I therefore alerted local officials to keep a close watch on him and
> to prevent him from establishing any contact with the Barbarians. But
> there is more. In 1756, when the Barbarians were forbidden to trade
> in Zhejiang, they left unpaid bills of fifteen thousand taels upon their
> departure. I have therefore had the merchants told that if they have
> any dealings with the foreigners, the latter will inevitably leave debts
> in their wake. The foreigners will therefore fail to find merchants
> willing to deal with them. In this way we can discourage the English
> from coming to trade in Zhejiang while avoiding any brutalization of
> them.
>
> THIS POINT OF VIEW IS QUITE CORRECT. YOU WILL RECEIVE INSTRUC-
> TIONS IN THIS REGARD.[11]

There were, then, several circles within the Forbidden City. Changlin's
report was meant to reassure the dozen or so members of the Grand
Council and Grand Secretariat. But the postscript, which the emperor
would show only to Heshen, alerted him to various matters that might
arouse his distrust. Any Chinese who knew the barbarians, any descendant
of anyone who once knew them, anyone who might be inclined to deal
with them, was a potential public enemy. The Chinese now had to maintain
surveillance not only over the barbarians, but also over Chinese who might
converse with these barbarians. Another invariant trait. At the beginning
of the seventeenth century, a Jesuit wrote: "So great and ubiquitous was

fear of foreigners that those of the mandarins who were acquainted with Father Ricci did not wish to speak to the fathers in their own homes."[12] Until the early 1980s, few Chinese dared to invite Westerners to their homes.

Meanwhile, back at the Yuanming Yuan the exhibition of presents was getting ridiculous. The old eunuch came forward and informed Dinwiddie, after repeated bowing, that the great crystal lusters had to be withdrawn, by order of the emperor, who wanted to rehang them in his own apartments.[13] Dinwiddie refused and returned to Peking disgusted. The moment his back was turned, seven men arrived to take the lamps away. Outright plunder. The emperor was icily disdainful of the scientific instruments, which he considered devoid of any interest, but he had been unable to resist the Chinese passion for lanterns.

When Barrow and Gillan arrived the following morning, they found considerable damage. The lamps were gone, their casings were shattered, the Parker lenses lay on the floor. It was a kind of premature "sacking of the Summer Palace." Dinwiddie cursed. These wonderful lenses—unparalleled in the entire world—were doomed to be forgotten forever. It was enough to convince him that nothing save its conquest by a more civilized power would be enough to make a great nation of China.[14] The Europeans who dismembered the empire during the following century were motivated by just that conviction.

46

A Suzerain's Letter
to His Vassal

(October 3, 1793)

IT WAS ON the afternoon of October 3 that Macartney received Qianlong's reply to George III. But the text had been ready since September 22, and court correspondence reveals that the first draft was actually composed on July 30 and submitted to the emperor on August 3, more than six weeks before the audience at which Macartney delivered the letter from King George to which this was supposedly a reply. Six weeks before the crisis over court ritual! The embassy's failure was therefore not merely the result of the refusal to kowtow, but was inevitable from the outset. We now know that the language of the edict was toughened in response to barbarian impertinence, but the essence of the reply would have been no different.

Qianlong's letter was primarily an acknowledgment of his acceptance of British vassalage. There was no reason not to prepare this largely ritualistic response well in advance, since it was essentially invariable, like a form letter requiring minor changes depending on the particular characteristics of this or that tributary people or their envoy.

But the three successive versions of this text in the three relevant languages were anything but invariable.

The original, written in classical Mandarin, strikes a tone of haughty condescension bordering on insult.

The missionaries who translated this text into Latin carefully altered the most insolent formulations, openly proclaiming their desire to remove "any offensive turn of phrase."[1]

The leaders of the embassy, however, did not want even that sanitized version to be made public in their lifetimes. (An abridgement was released only long after they all had died.) Instead they drafted an English summary of the Latin, and that summary subsequently came to be regarded as the official text, though effectively it is a forgery. From the already prettified version prepared by the missionaries, Macartney and Staunton deleted anything that might wound British pride. The British public was offered a bowdlerization of a bowdlerization.

Here is a complete English rendering of the original Chinese text.[2]

We, by the Grace of Heaven, Emperor, instruct the King of England to take note of our charge.*

Although your country, O King, lies in the far oceans, yet inclining your heart to towards civilization, you have specially sent an envoy respectfully to present a state message, and sailing the seas, he has come to our Court to kowtow and to present congratulations for the imperial birthday, and also to present local products, thereby showing your sincerity.†

We have perused the text of your state message and the wording expresses your earnestness. From it your sincere humility and obedience can clearly be seen. It is admirable and we fully approve.

As regards the chief and assistant envoys who have brought the state message and the tribute articles, we are mindful that they have been sent from afar across the sea, and we have extended our favor and courtesy to them, and have ordered our ministers to bring them to an imperial audience. We have given them a banquet and have repeatedly bestowed gifts on them in order to show our kindness. Although the officers, servants, and others, in charge of the ships, more than six hundred in number, returned to Zhoushan and did not come to the capital, yet we have also bestowed gifts on them generally so that all should receive favors equally.

As to what you have requested in your message, O King, namely to be allowed to send one of your subjects to reside in the Celestial Empire to look after your country's trade, this does not conform to the Celestial Empire's ceremonial system, and definitely cannot be done. Hitherto, whenever men from the various Western Ocean countries have desired to come to the Celestial Empire and to enter the Imperial service, we have allowed them to come to the capital. But once having come, they were obliged to adopt the costume of the Celestial Empire, they were confined within the Halls [their assigned residences], and were never allowed to return home.[3]

These are the fixed regulations of the Celestial Empire, and presumably you also know them, O King. Now, however, you want to

---

* This exordium was tactfully omitted from the Latin.

† Thus, in the eyes of History, based as it is on written documents, the English did kowtow, for so the emperor wrote.

send one of your subjects to reside at the capital. But he could neither behave like a Western Ocean man who comes to the capital to enter our service, remaining at the capital and not returning to his native country, nor could he be allowed to go in and out, and to have regular correspondence. So it would really serve no purpose.

Moreover, the territories ruled by the Celestial Empire are vast, and for all the envoys of vassal states coming to the capital there are definite regulations regarding the provision of quarters and supplies to them and regarding their movements. There has never been any precedent for allowing them to suit their own convenience. Now, if your country retains someone at the capital his speech will not be understood and his dress will be different in style, and we have nowhere to house him. If he is to resemble those Western Ocean men who come to the capital to enter the Imperial service, we must order him, without exception, to change his dress to that of the Celestial Empire. However, we have never wished to force on others what is difficult to do. Besides, if the Celestial Empire desired to send someone permanently to reside in your country, surely you would not be able to agree to it.* Furthermore, there are a great many Western Ocean countries altogether, and not merely your one country. If, like you, O King, they all beg to send someone to reside at the capital, how could we grant their request in every case? It would be absolutely impossible for us to do so. How can we go so far as to change the regulations of the Celestial Empire, which are over a hundred years old [a figurative expression], because of the request of one man—of you, O King?

If it is said that your object, O King, is to take care of trade, men from your country have been trading at Macao for some time, and have always been treated favorably. For instance, in the past Portugal and Italy† and other countries have several times sent envoys to the Celestial Empire with requests to look after their trade, and the Celestial Empire, bearing in mind their loyalty, treated them with great kindness. Whenever any matter concerning trade has arisen which affected those countries, it has always been fully taken care of. When the Canton merchant Wu Qiaoping owed money to foreign ships, we ordered the governor-general to advance the money out of the Treasury

---

* Heshen must have been quite disagreeably surprised when Macartney offered to escort a permanent Chinese ambassador to London. Here Qianlong not only avoids responding to this humiliating overture, but pretends to believe that the British would flatly reject any such request were the Chinese to make it. This was the most elegant method of ruling out the possibility.
† "Italy," which at the time did not exist, had never sent an envoy. Qianlong is probably referring to the pope, who sent legates on three occasions—in 1705, 1720, and 1725—in unsuccessful attempts to discuss not trade, but the question of rites.

and to pay his debts for him at the public expense, and to have the debtor-merchant severely punished. Presumably your country has also heard about this. Why, then, do foreign countries need to send someone to remain at the capital? This is a request for which there is no precedent and it definitely cannot be granted. Moreover, the distance between Macao, the place where the trade is conducted, and the capital is nearly ten thousand *li*,* and if he were to remain at the capital how could he look after it?

If it is said that because you look up with admiration to the Celestial Empire you desire him to study our culture, yet the Celestial Empire has its own codes of ritual which are different from your country's in each case. Even if the person from your country who remained here was able to learn them, it would be of no use, since your country has its own customs and regulations, and you would certainly not copy Chinese ones.†

The Celestial Empire, ruling all within the four seas, simply concentrates on carrying out the affairs of government properly, and does not value rare and precious things. Now you, O King, have presented various objects to the throne, and mindful of your loyalty in presenting offerings from afar, we have specifically ordered the Department of Foreign Tribute‡ to receive them. In fact, the virtue and power of the Celestial Dynasty has penetrated afar to the myriad kingdoms, which have come to render homage, and so all kinds of precious things from over mountain and sea have been collected here, things which your chief envoy and others have seen for themselves. Nevertheless we have never valued ingenious articles, nor do we have the slightest need of your country's manufacturers. Therefore, O King, as regards your request to send someone to remain at the capital, while it is not in harmony with the regulations of the Celestial Empire, we also feel very much that it is of no advantage to your country. Hence we have issued these detailed instructions and have commanded your tribute envoys to return safely home. You, O King, should simply act in conformity with our wishes by strengthening your loyalty and swearing perpetual obedience so as to ensure that your country may share the blessings of peace.

---

* A figurative expression. The actual distance was about half that.

† The wording is admirably precise: China, a civilized country, has *rites*, while barbarous England has only *customs*.

‡ The Celestial Empire had no ministry of foreign affairs, but only a department of tribute. The missionary translators prudently omitted any mention of this humiliating institution. It was only after the shock of the sacking of the Summer Palace in 1860 that China finally created a foreign ministry and sent its first envoys abroad.

Besides giving both the customary and extra gifts, as listed separately, to the chief and assistant envoys, and to the various officials under them as well as to the interpreters, soldiers, and servants, now, because your envoy is returning home we have issued this special edict, and confer presents on you, O King—elaborate and valuable things all, in accordance with the usual etiquette. In addition, we have bestowed brocades, gauzes, and elaborate curios; all precious things. These are listed separately.

Let the King reverently receive them and know our kind regard for him.

This is a special edict.

That is the complete text of the letter, free of the cosmetic surgery performed by the missionaries. Macartney himself never saw it in this pristine form, and even after his death, its true content was coyly masked.

Every one of George III's requests—that advanced British technology be exchanged for Chinese techniques, that the Macao-Canton trade be normalized and extended to other ports, that the living conditions of Europeans resident in China be improved, that new markets be opened, that a permanent embassy be established in Peking—was rejected on the grounds of sacrosanct, centuries-old rituals. That which had been codified could not possibly be changed. That which was bolted shut could not possibly be opened. There has probably never been a society more immobile or more resolutely sealed.

Its original flavor restored, this edict is not only the single most remarkable and important document in Chinese-Western relations from Marco Polo to Deng Xiaoping, but is also a most striking example of an aberration, traces of which may be found in the behavior of many peoples, though no nation has ever carried it quite so far as Manchu China. That aberration consists in a people's—or a culture's—belief, not only that it is superior to all others, but also that it can act as though it were alone in the world. It might almost be called collective autism.

47

A Message in a Bottle

(October 3–4, 1793)

THE PAINTER William Alexander, despite being deprived of any real news about the diplomacy going on at the top, had this to say on that sad October 3: "Little hope is now entertained that the chief objects of the Honourable East India Company will be obtained."[1]

Macartney's only option now was to draft the promised note to Heshen, and he marshaled what remained of his strength to do just that. Mr. Plumb and Staunton junior spent the next day working on the note, the former translating it, the latter copying it out.[2]

3 October 1793.

The King of Great Britain requests that His Imperial Majesty of China consider with favour the initiatives of his Ambassador.

He has instructed his Ambassador to ask His Imperial Majesty to be so kind as:

1. To allow the English merchants to conduct trade in the ports of Zhoushan and Ningbo, as well as Tientsin, in addition to Canton, provided that they obey Chinese laws and customs and conduct themselves peacefully;

2. To allow the English merchants to have a warehouse at Peking for the sale of their goods, in the same manner and in the same conditions as the Russians had formerly;[3]

3. To allow the English merchants some small, detached, unfortified island in the neighbourhood of Zhoushan as a magazine for their unsold goods, and as a residence for their people to take care of them, separated from the Chinese in order to avoid any quarrel or turmoil;

4. To allow them a similar privilege near Canton, or at least to

allow them to remain in Canton the year round should the need arise;* and that in addition, during their stay in Canton and Macao, they be allowed to ride on horseback, to practice their favorite sports, and to take exercise for their health—permission which they will take care to avail themselves of only in ways that do not disturb the Chinese;

5. To abolish the transit duties between Macao and Canton, or at least to reduce them to the standard of 1782;

6. To prohibit the exaction of any duties from the English merchants, over and above those settled by the Emperor's diploma, a copy of which is required to be given to them (as they have never yet been able to see it) for their unequivocal direction.†

The Ambassador would like to obtain from Prime Minister Heshen the favour of a written reply to these requests for the satisfaction of the King of Great Britain.[5]

That was exactly what Dundas had told Macartney: "Whatever may be the decision of the Imperial Government, unless, indeed, it should be a rejection of all your requests, it will be desirable to obtain it in writing."[6] It is somewhat surprising that Macartney seems not to have grasped the full import of the edict he had just received. The Son of Heaven understood the prose of the rationalist perfectly, but the rationalist failed to penetrate the veil of Chinese rhetoric. Was it mere fatigue or presumptuous credulity?

In any event, these requests were not nearly so "extravagant" as the proposal for a permanent embassy in Peking, and Macartney was astute enough to cite precedents. The British had indeed traded in Ningbo and Zhoushan in the past, as had the Russians in Peking. On the other hand, the Russians had long since been forced to retreat to Kiakhta, as the Westerners had been confined to Macao and Canton.[7]

The time had come to make some decisions. Macartney wondered whether there was any real point in staying around when the Chinese were doing all they could to encourage him to leave. Yet he was so cruelly disappointed. Though he believed he had done nothing wrong, that was small consolation for the failure of an enterprise that had begun with such high hopes. But what could be expected of ministers who trembled at the

---

* Immediately after the Chinese New Year, foreigners were required to leave Canton for Macao. They were authorized to return only in the autumn, with the first ship of the following monsoon. This twice-yearly migration was becoming increasingly costly.[4]

† The imperial tax was paid by the Chinese merchants of the guild, who recovered it in full from the foreign traders, usually adding a supplementary kickback, which they claimed was legally stipulated. The mandarins often levied their own charges as well. The European merchants therefore never knew how much they were really required to pay, and any official protest they might have made had to be channeled through the very same guild.

very thought of any novelty and who devoted most of their time to intrigues designed to assure their own futures in the closing years of this emperor's reign? Macartney commented that "most of the principal people, whom I have had opportunities of knowing, I have found sociable, conversable, good-humoured, and not at all indisposed to foreigners. As to the lower orders, they are all of a trafficking turn, and it seemed at the seaports where we stopped that nothing would be more agreeable to them than to see our ships often in their harbours."[8]

For the rest, he was dubious whether these supposedly immutable laws were really all they seemed. His impression was that they served mainly "as a general shield against reason and argument," and that they could be infringed when it was convenient to do so. The immutable law of the kowtow, for instance, had been relaxed on his account. Macartney had little choice but to acknowledge the temporary immobility of Qianlong's court, but he refused to recognize a more general Chinese immobility. A letter from the bedridden Father Amiot, delivered on the evening of October 3, comforted Macartney in this supposition. "However adverse" the Chinese government might be "in the beginning to any new propositions," the priest wrote, the same proposals might be brought "into a more serious and dispassionate consideration" once the initial novelty had passed.[9] In the meantime, he advised Macartney to depart.

Seeing no alternative, Macartney decided to do so. His note to Heshen therefore stated that as soon as he received the written reply to his requests, he would rejoin the *Lion* in Zhoushan, assuming that the vessel had not yet cast off. He also gave Heshen a letter to Sir Erasmus Gower asking him to wait. Otherwise they would have to return to Canton over land, since the *Hindostan* alone was not large enough to carry the entire embassy.

This was the signal Heshen had been waiting for. Late that evening the legate told Macartney that he was authorized to take his leave and that his letter to Sir Erasmus had been sent to Zhoushan at express speed. The emperor, enormously solicitous as ever, wished to spare the embassy the rigors of a journey during the cold season. He had therefore set the date of departure for October 7, three days hence.

On the morning of October 4, before Macartney actually knew when and if he was leaving, couriers set out carrying an edict to the viceroys and governors of Zhili, Shandong, Jingnan, and Canton: "The tributary envoy will depart on the seventh to return to Macao by the river route."[10]

The court had not yet received Changlin's October 3 report explaining that the British ships were still in Dinghai and would remain there for a few more days. The latest information in Peking—received on October 1 and communicated to Macartney by Heshen—was that the *Lion* was about to cast off. The emperor therefore assumed that Macartney would travel to Canton inside China and not by sea. It mattered little what route the barbarians took, so long as they returned to Macao as soon as possible, without creating any further difficulties. Viceroy Changlin, now being transferred from Zhejiang to Guangdong, would see to that. By any means necessary.

48

"We Quitted . . . Like Vagrants"

(October 5–7, 1793)

MOST OF MACARTNEY's retinue had been kept in the dark about all the negotiations, and on October 5 they suddenly found that it was time to go. "Today we were told that we should go the day after tomorrow," Thomas writes in his sole entry for that day.[1] Dinwiddie laments: "The 5th of October, at ten in the morning, suspense was put at an end, and the El Dorado dreams blasted for sure, by the intelligence that they had only two days to prolong their stay in the capital. But few experiments, comparatively speaking, had been wrought, and these were entirely lost on the most prejudiced of people. The want of an opportunity of performing some on aerostation was much regretted by the Ambassador; though his Lordship mentioned the balloon, the diving bell and the fire works, yet the principal mandarin heard the account without the least emotion or surprise."[2] As for Macartney himself, he merely noted: "So this matter is now settled."[3]

Since only Macartney and Staunton had had any real contact with the Chinese, most of the other members of the embassy were taken completely by surprise. Anger and confusion are apparent in the accounts of Anderson, Dinwiddie, and Thomas, and in other unpublished journals as well.

Wang and Qiao somewhat smugly informed the ambassador that the emperor had assigned an important personality, Songyun, to accompany the mission. Macartney remembered him from the visit to the gardens in Jehol, where they had exchanged memories of Russia.[4] Zhengrui would accompany the embassy only as far as Tientsin. Wang and Qiao did not yet know whether they would be going too.

The choice of Songyun—one of the six ministers of state who served on the Grand Council—showed that this was considered an important escort. A sudden surfeit of good manners now seemed to compensate for the earlier bitter snub.

Zhengrui, Wang, and Qiao arrived early in the morning on October 6 "to assist us in our preparations for departure to-morrow." Or rather, to hurry them along. Macartney was told that "there is a considerable number of great people at the Court who have expressed their being much pleased with us, and who wished that we had continued here longer."[5]

Thomas Staunton takes note of a single event on October 6: "Today one of the soldiers died." Another casualty. How many futile deaths for such a disaster! The pomp of Eades's funeral in Tongzhou seemed like ancient history.

Anderson (or Coombes) coolly notes: "In short, we entered Peking like paupers; we remained in it like prisoners; and we quitted it like vagrants."[6]

The preparations were especially hurried since an additional two-day delay initially approved by the chief minister in response to Macartney's entreaties had been annulled, Heshen having been overruled by the emperor: "You are wrong to hold the mission up. We must let them leave as soon as possible, because of the approach of winter, which threatens to disrupt their return."[7]

All the baggage had to be packed up in a single day, and many of the crates had disappeared. A few hastily nailed planks were all that protected the portraits of the king and queen. For lack of time, the canopy was wrenched off instead of dismantled; for lack of packing, it was given to Macartney's servants. Other objects fell prey to the Chinese. "They also contrived to purloin a very large quantity of wine; nor was it possible, in such a scene of hurry and confusion, to prevent those opportunities which they were on the watch to seize."[8]

They worked through the night and into the early hours of the morning. No one slept. Finally, on the brink of exhaustion, the British managed to load into the wagons what remained of their belongings after all the thievery. "An indescribable mess," Dinwiddie called it.[9]

October 7 was the day of departure, but before leaving Peking, the embassy had to have its final audience with the court.

Once again the ceremony was an affront—or rather, the affront took the form of a ceremony. The "audience" was no more than a brief stopover on the long day's journey. The embassy left its residence at noon, crossing the city and stopping at the pavilion of the chief minister, who greeted Macartney and Staunton in the company of the "second minister," Fuchang'an; his brother, Fukang'an; and several Grand Secretaries, all in ceremonial dress.[10] The final two rites of the tributary ceremony were now performed: the "delivery of the imperial gifts" and the "exit of the mission."[11]

The emperor had decided against a personal appearance.[12] But though he was physically absent, his holy spiritual presence had to be honored yet again. Heshen pointed to "two large rolls" lying on a table covered with yellow silk. One was the list of all the emperor's presents, the other his reply to Macartney's six requests.

"I said I hoped the answer was favourable to my wishes, as it might contribute in some degree to soften the regret which it was natural to feel on leaving the place of His Imperial Majesty's residence. He seemed as if surprised with the courtliness of such an address considering the circumstances of the moment."[13] Or perhaps Heshen was surprised that the Briton, ascribing greater importance to the second scroll than to the first, had once again demonstrated his failure to understand the very meaning of an embassy in Chinese eyes.

Heshen changed the subject, expressing the hope that "our tables had been properly served during our stay." He then "mentioned to me the Emperor's nomination of Songyun to conduct me to Zhoushan," apparently feeling that Macartney would be pleased by this nomination. "The Minister had a smile of affected affability on his countenance during the greater part of the time, but I thought Fuchang'an and his brother looked confoundedly sour at us. I have reason to suspect that there is some mystery in this appearance, and that a Court intrigue, which may be still on foot, relative to the affairs of the Embassy, has occasioned a disunion or difference of opinion among these great personages."[14]

Macartney emerged from this last audience convinced that he had been the victim of a cabal. Certainly he had seen plenty of those in the Court of St. James. "Raised in the seraglio, I know its twists and turns." And he sensed that such intrigues would be woven more skillfully in the world's most absolutist government than they were in a constitutional monarchy like the one he represented.

In all probability he was right about that. Intrigue alone cannot account for his failure, but it may well have had something to do with the haste of his dismissal. A letter from Father de Grammont suggests as much: "These gentlemen, like all foreigners who know China only from books, are unaware of the practices of this Court. They brought with them an interpreter even less informed than themselves. . . . Add to this the Emperor's advanced age and the fact that men of artifice and narrow spirit are everywhere, while all the great and favored personages are avid for presents and riches."[15]

Once ushered out, the ambassador had no choice but to set off on his return trip. The legate, Wang and Qiao, the hundred or so British gentlemen, and the soldiers, servants, and retinues of the Chinese escorts all formed into a procession that now left Peking and embarked on the long journey across China.

Before they left, a mandarin of the fifth class, with a white transparent button on his cap, was summoned. As he knelt, the two imperial scrolls were tied to his back with broad yellow ribbons. One of them, containing the list of presents, seemed derisory to Macartney, but the other, the reply to his six requests, would determine—or had already determined— whether this embassy might register some few concrete achievements or whether its failure would be complete.

The mandarin mounted his horse and took his place at the head of the procession, the ribbons of the fatal scroll fluttering in the breeze. Macartney left Peking in pursuit of a response that continued to elude him.

IV

THE REAL
MISSION BEGINS

(October 7–November 11, 1793)

Tseng Tzu said, "Conduct the funeral of your parents with
meticulous care and let not sacrifices to your remote ancestors
be forgotten, and the virtue of the common people will incline
towards fullness."

CONFUCIUS[1]

. . . a nation cannot long remain strong when every man
belonging to it is individually weak; . . . no form or combination of social polity has yet been devised to make an
energetic people out of a community of pusillanimous and
enfeebled citizens.

ALEXIS DE TOCQUEVILLE[2]

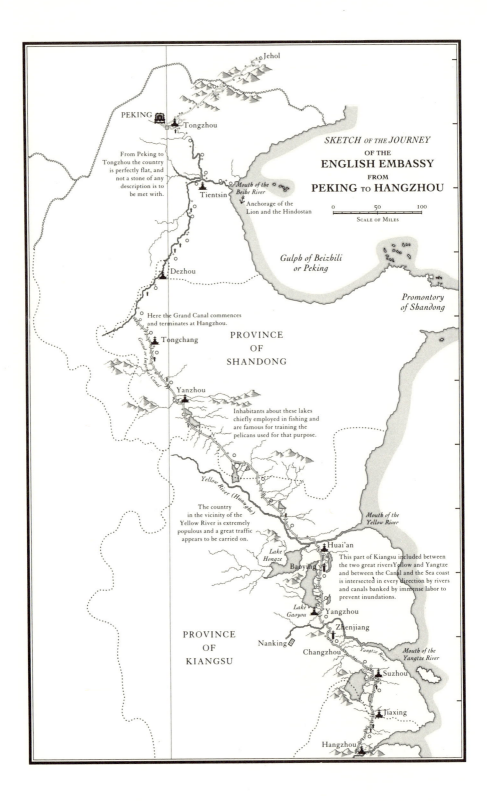

Jehol

PEKING

Tongzhou

From Peking to
Tongzhou the country
is perfectly flat, and
not a stone of any
description is to
be met with.

Tientsin

Mouth of the
Beibe River

Anchorage of the
Lion and the Hindostan

SKETCH OF THE JOURNEY
OF THE
ENGLISH EMBASSY
FROM
PEKING TO **HANGZHOU**

0   50   100

SCALE OF MILES

Gulph of Beizhili
or Peking

Promontory
of Shandong

Dezhou

Here the Grand Canal commences
and terminates at Hangzhou.

Tongchang

PROVINCE
OF
SHANDONG

Yanzhou

Inhabitants about these lakes
chiefly employed in fishing and
are famous for training the
pelicans used for that purpose.

Yellow River (Huanghe)

The country
in the vicinity of the
Yellow River is extremely
populous and a great traffic
appears to be carried on.

Mouth of the
Yellow River

Lake
Hongze

Huai'an

Baoying

This part of Kiangsu included between
the two great rivers Yellow and Yangtze
and between the Canal and the Sea coast
is intersected in every direction by rivers
and canals banked by immense labor to
prevent inundations.

Lake
Gaoyou

Yangzhou

Zhenjiang

Nanking

Changzhou

Yangtze River

Mouth of the
Yangtze River

PROVINCE
OF
KIANGSU

Suzhou

Jiaxing

Hangzhou

49

Responding to a Delay

(October 7–8, 1793)

Orthodoxy has an answer to everything.

ERNEST RENAN[1]

AFTER SAYING GOODBYE to Heshen, Macartney had to travel for three hours before he was allowed to take possession of the imperial letter.[2] That was in Tongzhou, the first stopover in a "yellow cruise" that was to last seventy-four days.

The procession halted at the same temple-hostelry in which the embassy had been lodged on its way to Peking. The mandarin carrying the scrolls dismounted and knelt before Macartney to be relieved of his imperial burden. The procedure had been quite deliberate: by the time the ambassador found out what was in the letter, he would be too far away to react.

The mandarins' angelic smiles and the ceremony surrounding the bearer of these scrolls cast a glow of unreality over what amounted to yet another sweeping rejection of British requests. Once again the Chinese original exhibits a sharpness of tone that the priest-translator excised from the Latin version and that was further softened in the English summary. This was not the reply of a prime minister to an ambassador's note, but another edict from the sovereign of China to the sovereign of Great Britain, the emperor's way of bringing the entire discussion to an end.[3]

"O King," the emperor wrote, "your envoy has gone beyond what has been set down by custom. He has presented many requests, which are absolutely counter to the generous manner in which the Celestial Empire treats foreigners and pacifies the four barbarian tribes.* The Celestial Empire rules over a multitude of lands, which it treats with equal kindness.

"Your country is not the only one to transact business in Canton. If all of them were to follow your example, formulating requests impossible

---

* A classical expression designating the countries beyond the empire's borders.

to satisfy and ceaselessly harrying us, how could we grant them what they wish?[4] . . .

"Your envoy has had the temerity to request that the merchant ships of your country henceforth be permitted to come to Ningbo and Zhoushan, as well as to Tientsin, there to conduct trade. Until now, when the countries of the Western Ocean came to buy and sell their products, they always did so in Macao,* where there is a merchant guild responsible for foreign trade. In the other ports there are neither guilds nor interpreters; no one would understand your language; it would be very awkward for everyone. With the exception of Macao, where trade has been authorized in accordance with long-standing custom, all the requests presented by your envoy for the practice of trade in Ningbo and Zhoushan, as well as Tientsin, can only be rejected."[5]

Likewise for "a warehouse in Peking" and "a small island, which would be quite useless in the absence of the guild and interpreters."[6] The other requests were ignored, and thereby rejected as well.

Strangely, this edict dismisses not only the six requests of Macartney's memorandum but also a seventh that he had not even made: Qianlong refused to permit the preaching of "the British religion," which in any case "is not the same as what the Christian religion had earlier been."[7]

The notion of asking for permission to proselytize had never even occurred to the British cabinet. Were the Chinese trying to protect themselves (just in case) by including this interdiction in a text that would now have the force of law? Was it their way of bolting the gate to a field that these barbarians, like the French, Italians, and Portuguese before them, might someday be tempted to explore?

In a letter to Lord Macartney written a year later, Father Poirot gave a somewhat peculiar account of this matter.[8] He explained that he had been dining in Peking with Father Raux when a mandarin suddenly ordered them to accompany him to his Haidian residence, near the Summer Palace. They had to hurry, for the city gates were about to close. When they arrived, the mandarin asked them to translate the rough draft of Heshen's reply to Macartney's requests. Since the text was so illegible that only the mandarin could decipher it, he had to dictate it to them phrase by phrase.

When he came to the passage about the "British religion," the two "highly surprised" priests tried to convince the mandarin that this must

---

* Whenever the emperor speaks of Macao, he means to include Canton. All foreign trade was funneled through these two cities, Canton playing this role only because of its proximity to the Portuguese enclave.

be a mistake, "that the English gentlemen were not seeking to propagate their faith but simply wanted branch offices for their merchants. But he was adamant." The missionaries were "deeply shocked" to discover that the text they were now translating into Latin stated that they themselves were in China "solely on behalf of the Emperor's civil service" and that they were "not permitted to preach the Gospel."[9]

As was their habit, the two translators softened the form of expression, but without altering the substance, since they feared that the Chinese might summon a third missionary to check their work. "As for the charge of having changed religion," Father Poirot added, "this has been known in China for more than a century. British traders have brought to Canton watches with very indecent miniatures."[10] (Once it was "indecent miniatures" brought to Canton through Macao; now it's pornographic videos smuggled into Canton from Hong Kong and hunted down by the virtuous People's Republic.)

Were the two priests trying to assure Macartney that they had had nothing to do with this business of prohibiting "the British religion"? Had they perhaps slipped a seventh request into the translation of the British memorandum requested of them by the court? If so, they had presented a proposal so brazen as to be utterly unacceptable, thereby eliciting a rejection that would long eliminate any possible Anglican competition. But this Machiavellian hypothesis seems implausible.[11] When Macartney raised the issue, Songyun did not deny that the emperor's reply had gone beyond the king's requests. The testimony of the ambassador and of the Grand Councillor agree on this point.

On the other hand, it is quite conceivable that the Portuguese missionaries (especially d'Almeida) may have suggested this superfluous refusal to Heshen, thus arousing Chinese suspicion. D'Almeida was treating Heshen for his chronic aches and pains at the time, and as Father Amiot once pointed out, "by the services he renders, a surgeon can procure more protectors for our Holy Religion than all the other missionaries with all their combined talents."[12]

FOR MACARTNEY this new edict was a crushing blow, one that broke the heady spirit of optimism he had expressed before his departure: "To bring human knowledge to perfection and to make society as happy as the imperfection of our nature will admit, perhaps nothing is wanted but a free and unrestrained intercourse with China."[13]

In Chinese eyes, this man of the Enlightenment was no more than a common merchant, a music-box peddler. But the honor of the embassy, now returning with its head hanging, required the concealment of this sweeping rebuff. In fact, Dundas's instructions to Macartney sound very much like an injunction to silence: it would be better if this *totally negative imperial response* did not exist. It ought to be kept secret.

The British therefore offered their compatriots an expurgated version of this second edict, just as they had of the first. In a long letter to Henry Dundas written from Hangzhou on November 9, 1793, this was all Macartney said of the two imperial edicts: "Except one subject in His Britannic Majesty's letter, that of a minister to reside in Peking after my departure, which is denied, not the least notice was taken of any others . . . , His Imperial Majesty thinking it sufficient generally to promise that he would treat our merchants kindly."[14]

The collapse of Macartney's dream was poignant: ". . . having been selected for this commission to China, the first of its kind from Great Britain, of which considerable expectations of success had been formed by many, and by none more than by myself, I cannot help feeling the disappointment most severely. I cannot lose sight of my first prospects without infinite regret."[15]

But Macartney had little time to indulge these depressing reflections. The local prefect* pointed out that the waters were low and getting lower every day. He "took occasion to observe how attentive and considerate it was in the Emperor to fix an early day in the season for our departure A few days later the river would have become too shallow to float our yachts." Macartney may not have understood everything about China, but this time he was not taken in. "This is certainly true," he wrote, "and shows how quickly the Court lesson reached this gentleman, and how aptly he had already learned it."[16] The ambassador had had about all the imperial solicitude he could take.

---

* "A Manchu Tartar," notes Macartney, adding, "Wang, the military commander, is a Chinese" (Cranmer-Byng, p. 158). This was an unusual situation. Manchu-Chinese parity in state posts (often relaxed in the provinces) was normally fulfilled in the opposite way, Tartar officers being flanked by Chinese civilians.

50

A Learned Grand Councillor

(October 8–10, 1793)

DEJECTION WAS NOW compounded by boredom. Tongzhou. The same town, the same boats. Yet Macartney wrote on October 8, "This morning I walked down to the waterside and found it would be some hours before the final arrangements could be made for our setting out. I . . . observed with pleasure the same care and attention for our accommodation down the river that we had experienced in ascending it."[1] He sounds determined to reassure himself, like a general on a tour of mess halls. Anderson was less enthusiastic: "There was, in the first place, no small difficulty in assorting the junks, with the persons who belonged to them. Nor were there a sufficient number of coolies to transport the different effects on board the vessels. In short, those attentions which were shewn to the Ambassador on his former abode in this city, seemed to have been forgotten."[2] Thomas adds that the boats "were not quite so good as those in which we were before."[3] Dinwiddie, too, speaks of haste and scramble.[4]

On the dock was a surprise: the carriage Heshen had refused to accept. It was standing "opposite the house appointed for the reception of the embassy, surrounded by crowds of Chinese." The fine coach, now in a sorry state, "many of its ornaments defaced," was tossed into the hold and carried through China from port to port, finally being unloaded in Madras.[5] One more humiliation.

The flotilla cast off on October 8, beginning a long river journey. Autumn is a dry season in northern China, and the water level in the canals and rivers was very low. The next day boats ran aground on several occasions.[6] So there had been good reasons, as well as ritual ones, for hurrying the departure.

Macartney reports that it was only on the afternoon of October 10 that "Wang came to tell me that Songyun had just received a letter from the Emperor, the contents of which he wished to communicate to me, and soon after I saw his yacht approaching mine very fast."[7]

After boarding the Grand Councillor's junk, Macartney thanked him for the courtesy he had shown him in the gardens in Jehol. Songyun replied that he had been assigned by imperial edict to make sure that all went well during the embassy's return to Zhoushan and to attend to its embarcation. If it turned out that the British ships had already left, then he was to accompany Macartney to Canton. The court had just (finally) instructed its officials to tell the ships to wait, if they had not already left.[8]

Macartney was thoroughly charmed. He was flattered that one of the six members of the Grand Council was to spend so many days with him. And Songyun's urbanity was a welcome relief after the loutishness of Zhengrui.[9] Staunton, too, showered praises on this "naturally affable" and "generous" man whose mind had been shaped by a "culture of letters" that had "extirpated his national prejudices." He was the only mandarin the British encountered who "travelled with a library."[10] Yet he was a Tartar-Mongol.[11] Over his robe he wore the short yellow vest, which bestowed "a sacred character" upon him. Once, when the interpreter ventured to "sit down before him," Mr. Plumb "was quickly called by him to his duty."[12]

Macartney had finally found an interlocutor of his own level, one who was especially well disposed to him since his fine words would have no further consequence. Half an hour later, Songyun paid Macartney a return visit. Once again they discussed their common experience in Russia. Songyun was surprised to hear that Macartney had spent three years there, and Macartney had some difficulty convincing him that relations between European nations were based on permanent ambassadors.[13]

The Mongol treated Macartney to another lesson in Chinese etiquette, explaining that foreign envoys were received only on great occasions—funerals, the coronation or birthday of an emperor—and that their stay was limited to forty days, a deadline extended to eighty days in certain exceptional situations. Only the emperor's extreme kindness would have enabled the embassy to stay much beyond the ritual deadline.*[14]

"He . . . entered a good deal into the manners and customs of China, which, he said, he knew were different from ours; but they could not be broken through without inconvenience and perhaps mischief to the State, and that therefore foreigners should not be surprised or dissatisfied at them."[15]

Macartney took the opportunity to sound Songyun out about the

_____

* Counting its travels, the embassy spent a total of more than six months on Chinese soil (nine months if you count Macao). But the time between its arrival in Peking and its departure from the capital was just forty days.

impression he had made at the court. He expressed his "concern on account of the ignorance" he "had been kept in with regard to many things." He feared that he had failed to be as agreeable to the emperor and his ministers as he would have liked. Macartney was clearly fishing for compliments, and Songyun obliged him, answering like "a complete courtier, assuring me that our behaviour had been such as showed we [were] . . . entitled . . . to every favour and regard that the laws of the Empire could authorize, that he did perfect justice to my sentiments and declaration, and would not fail to transmit them faithfully to the Court." But here is what Songyun reported to his master about this interview: "I had the envoy and his second brought aboard my junk to communicate Your instructions to them. They prostrated themselves upon the ground to thank You for permitting them to leave before the rigors of winter set in. Their thanks were manifestly sincere."[16]

The Grand Councillor left, and good old Wang and Qiao took over. They, too, sang of their sovereign's generosity, explaining that "forty vessels" were "employed in our present expedition," as well as "upwards of a thousand persons." Total expenses ran to 5,000 taels per day.

Macartney noted that 5,000 taels was the equivalent of more than 1,500 pounds sterling, and he doubted that so much had really been spent. In any case, he noted, there was a difference between "money charged and money actually expended." He recalled that Qiao had once told him of the compensation paid to some villagers in Shandong province who had lost everything in a terrible flood. The emperor ordered 100,000 taels for their relief, out of which the highest official concerned kept "twenty thousand, the second ten thousand, the third five thousand, and so on till at last there remained no more than twenty thousand for the poor sufferers." Macartney found that "the boasted moral institutes of China are not much better observed than those of some other countries, and that the disciples of Confucius are composed of the same fragile materials as the children of Mammon in the western world."[17]

ON OCTOBER 11 the waters were so low that the haulers had to drag the junks along the river bottom.[18] The nights and early mornings were increasingly frigid, though it was still very hot in the midafternoon.[19]

As they crossed China from north to south, the British encountered varied climates and correspondingly different types of agriculture. Here the main crop was sorghum, the grain from which the Chinese derive most of their alcohol, including *maotai*. The observant Staunton junior noted: "Friday the 11th. A cold morning. The wind right against us. . . . All the high millet [actually sorghum] which we saw coming up the river we now find cut down and in its stead the beginnings of a new crop."[20] The child was amazed: the intensive agriculture of this region was related to over-population; he had never seen anything like it in England.

Sorghum had been imported from Ethiopia, via Burma, in the sixteenth century and played an important role in Chinese population growth. At about the same time, the Portuguese in Macao introduced corn and potatoes from the Americas. Rice had been imported from Annam to Fujian. These new crops enabled the Chinese to bring additional land under cultivation, to introduce twice-yearly harvests, and to increase the yield. It is often forgotten that the Western discovery of America and the other great explorations may have benefited China as much as they did Europe. In the sixteenth and seventeenth centuries the Chinese population seems to have grown from something like 80 million to about 160 million, and it doubled again during Qianlong's reign. "The ground being in a constant state of tillage, ploughs of the most simple construction are found adequate to every purpose required from such an instrument. Where the ground is particularly light, men and women yoked to the plough, are able to draw it through the soil."[21]

The chief concern was irrigation. Ordinarily, opening the sluice gates was enough, since the rivers and canals were above ground level.[22] But when the water level dropped, inexhaustible Chinese patience closed the gap: two men "stood opposite to each other on two projecting banks, holding ropes fixed to a basket which swinging to and fro for a considerable time, they gave it a velocity that assisted in throwing the water into a reservoir dug near the river's bank; from whence it was communicated where wanted, by small channels."[23]

ON OCTOBER 12 Macartney had another meeting with Songyun. "We went over to the boat of a very great Mandarine who accompanies us all the way," young Thomas writes. There they received "an edict from the Emperor containing something as to our being well treated on the journey."[24] They were also told that Sir Erasmus Gower was still in Zhoushan with his ships.*[25] That was good news for Macartney, since it meant that his October 4 letter to Gower might arrive in time. It was also good news for the Chinese. The sooner the mission set sail, the happier they would be.

---

* This is an echo from Peking of Changlin's October 3 report from Zhoushan.

There was other good news too: the travelers would now be permitted to stroll along the riverbank. (The junks were moving more slowly than a man could walk.) Qianlong's orders had been strict—"No descent to the ground, no contact with the population"—but Songyun took it upon himself to relax them, though only out of sight of inhabited areas. Several days later he reported the liberty he had taken: "The envoy requested permission to walk along the riverbank from time to time in order to escape the deleterious effects of too narrow a confinement on board. His request seemed reasonable to me. I have therefore ordered that he and his retinue be allowed to leave their junks once away from any habitation. The envoy has been docile in his obedience and seems sincere in acknowledging Your benevolence."[26] Qianlong approved Songyun's initiative.

But Thomas indicated its limits: "Beyond Tientsin we stopt for about half an hour. In the meantime we walked a little in a small garden belonging to a miou [temple]."[27] Once the travelers sailed into Tientsin, however, they were prisoners in their junks again.[28]

In one of his private discussions with Songyun, Macartney returned to the "purposes" of his mission, which included "to recommend the King my master's subjects in China to protection and favour."[29]

Songyun quickly replied that the emperor had "lately given fresh orders to treat the English and other Europeans at Canton with indulgence and liberality." Macartney answered that he had no doubt of "the Emperor's good disposition towards us," but he was curious to know more about these fresh orders. Would British traders be informed of the favors the emperor was granting them? For instance, would the merchants cease being charged with "duties and taxes" that rose every year without explanation? If these were "not soon regulated," he said, "the English commerce, which is now carried on in sixty large ships annually, must be relinquished and given up, as unable to bear such heavy burdens."[30]

Songyun replied that "proper steps" to remedy this matter would "certainly" be taken, "but that the duties and taxes could not be fixed absolutely, because they must necessarily vary from time to time, according to the exigencies of the state, or of the particular provinces where they were levied." He admitted that the wars in Tonkin and Tibet had required an increase in duties. But these wars were now over, and peace should bring an easing of the tax burden.[31]

In his journal, Macartney does not say that he broached two other British aims as well: the opening of new trading ports and the establishment of a second Macao. Macartney believed that a British trading post was absolutely essential. Songyun held that there could be no access to China other than through the Portuguese post. No one would be permitted to trade in Ningbo, Zhoushan, Tientsin, or anywhere else. The ambassador should have no illusion on this score.*

Yet for the first time since his arrival in China, Macartney had the sense that he was engaging in a real dialogue. He was finally able to spend hours discussing his country's affairs with a leading state personality, just as an ambassador would do in a European capital.

What a godsend it was to be spending several weeks in the company of one of the six major ministers, a man who spoke daily to Qianlong and Heshen! At last Macartney was in a position to discuss the concrete objectives of his mission.

The counterfeit, ritualistic, Chinese-style "embassy" was ended. Substantive negotiations were on the agenda. The genuine, realistic, Western-style embassy could now begin.

---

* We know of this part of the conversation from Songyun's report to the emperor.[32]

51

Celestial Correspondence

(October 11–15, 1793)

> Moreover, any one who delays or postpones the execution of
> an Imperial edict for one day, shall be punished with 50 blows,
> and one degree more severely as far as 100 blows for each
> additional day of delay.
>
> TA T'SING LEU LEE (Chinese Penal Code)[1]

SONGYUN THOROUGHLY charmed Macartney, who regretted that this man
had not been his intermediary in Jehol and Peking. He briefly wondered
whether Songyun was trying to gull him, but answered his own doubts:
"Through all his discourse there is such an air of candour, frankness and
amity that if I am deceived in him, he must be the most consummate cheat
of the world."[2] He must have had winning ways indeed, for eighteen years
later, as viceroy of Canton, he also captivated the company's senior representative, the grown-up Sir Thomas Staunton, who would call Songyun
his "great friend."[3]

But imperial correspondence reveals that Macartney's distinction between the righteous Songyun and the odious Zhengrui was wholly imaginary. The British were quite naive to believe that the Celestial bureaucracy
was divided into good guys intent on fostering London's designs (such as
Songyun or Liang Kentang, the viceroy of Zhili) and bad guys bent on
defeating those designs (like Zhengrui or General Fukang'an). The reports
of the mandarins demonstrate that none of them was anything more or
less than a servant of His Holy Majesty. They were simply gifted with
endlessly variable tact.

This sort of illusion persists among twentieth-century Westerners
whenever they deal with totalitarian nations. They tirelessly distinguish
between "hawks" and "doves," mythological beasts whose supposed existence is carefully cultivated by these regimes themselves.

Songyun was indeed a "consummate cheat," if by *cheat* is meant an
official who refuses to reveal the confidential orders of his sovereign. He

refrained from letting Macartney know that he was empowered to call out the army against the British if need be.[4] But he had also been told "not to divulge anything and not to appear agitated, which could only arouse the suspicion of the Barbarians."[5] Discretion was the rule: let the barbarians show their hand, but reveal nothing of our own.

The archives, however, reveal everything. Jehol and Peking had been a subtle, gentleman's duel, with tipped foils. But the instructions issued to Songyun and all the relevant provincial governors on October 11 brought out the bare sabres.

> Because of the health problems of their crews, the Barbarian ships are still moored in Dinghai. Everything must be done to prevent them from establishing contact with felonious merchants* who might be tempted to trade with them. Let the envoy and his retinue cast off from Dinghai as soon as possible; that would be far more expedient than having to escort him all the way to Canton. Songyun and Changlin shall see to it that these Barbarians do not employ any pretext whatever for delay.
>
> The British have expressed a wish to make several purchases in Ningbo; they shall be permitted to buy tea and silk. But it would be advisable to dissuade the Chinese from dealing with them ever again, and the British from ever returning to trade in Zhejiang. We shall therefore remind the Chinese that in 1756 the British left 15,000 taels in unpaid bills when they departed Ningbo. I had been unaware of this fact, and I congratulate Changlin for having discovered it.
>
> Be sure to prevent any contact between the Barbarians and the population. If they ask permission to buy goods en route, let Songyun reply: To buy goods on the route would be contrary to the regulations of the Celestial Empire.
>
> There remains the case of the man Guo, whose deceased father once did business with the English. He has been arrested. Let him be brought to Peking, taking care that his path does not cross the embassy's. But there is no point in making him bear the yoke.†[6]

Songyun replied to this instruction on October 13, reporting the conversation he had had with Macartney the day before (the discussion the ambassador had considered so promising). Songyun's memorandum is graced with vermilion marginal notes dated October 15.

---

* A felonious merchant was any trader who sought relations with foreigners in the absence of a mandarin-controlled merchant guild.

† The yoke was a heavy wooden plank fastened around a prisoner's neck. One is pictured in the plates.

The envoy and his deputy removed their hats and respectfully listened to Your instructions on bended knee. The British acknowledged that they had procrastinated as to the modalities of their embarcation. . . . They now know that their ships have not yet left. They expressed gratitude for this.

When the envoy was already on the deck, he returned to my cabin to tell me: "We would like to be able to buy some goods as we travel, in the cities through which we pass." This Barbarian is greedy by nature.

RIDICULOUS PETTY GREED.

Your slave then repeated that Celestial regulations forbid the merchants of the cities through which the envoy will pass from trading with foreigners.

THESE RESTRICTIONS ARE WHOLLY WELCOME.

At these words, the envoy lowered his head in token of his fear and submission. I have forbidden him and his retinue to walk along the embankments when we pass through populated areas, and I have ordered the population not to approach.

EXCELLENT.

I will soon join Changlin in Zhejiang. There I will instruct the Barbarians to return to their country. Most of all the English must not establish any relations with felonious merchants.

THAT MUST BE AVOIDED AT ALL COSTS.[7]

This was not so much a report as a mirror held up to the emperor's face, and Qianlong clearly enjoyed looking at himself in it.

Two other memoranda were sent to the emperor at the same time. One came from Guo Shixun, military governor of Canton, and reached Peking at the end of October: "As soon as the delegation arrives in Guangdong, I will order the high civilian and military officials to come out to meet it, at the head of numerous suitably equipped and drilled soldiers, to make an impression on the delegation. The Barbarian is treacherous by nature, and it is difficult to trust him. If he renews his ill-considered requests in Guangdong, I will firmly reject them."[8]

The second came from Shulin, viceroy of Jiangxi and Jiangsu, and reached Peking on October 18: "All the military units are ready. I have secretly ordered the authorities to strike an impassively severe demeanor, the better to dissuade the Barbarians from lingering. I will not receive the envoy."[9]

Everything was in place for the expulsion of these irksome intruders. In Paris things moved even more expeditiously. Marie Antoinette's trial began on October 10. On the sixteenth she mounted the scaffold of the guillotine.

52

Works and Days

(October 17–18, 1793)

> The peasant is exposed to the periodic cataclysms of flood, drought, frost, hail, lizards, and insects. If, by chance, the harvest succeeds, the tax department and usurers contest him for it. Even before the grain leaves the field and the silk is taken from the loom, they no longer belong to him.
>
> SIMA GUANG, eleventh century[1]

WHEN THEY RETURNED to Tientsin on October 13, the British drew an even larger crowd than they had on their arrival. Holmes estimated that more than two million people gathered on the embankments, and he marveled that a single soldier with a whip, or even the mere sight of a mandarin, was enough to clear a path for the embassy: "They gave way in a moment, without the smallest appearance of ill nature; in fact, they durst not offer any resistance, so strictly are they kept in subjection, and the slightest disobedience punished on the spot with such severity."[2]

Lavish supplies for the embassy had been laid out on silk and brocade cloth, and everything was quickly brought aboard. Less than three hours after its arrival, the flotilla departed.[3]

Some unexpected traveling companions were added to one of the junks: two cows. Except in the Tartar lands, milk in the empire was used more or less only to raise veal. But since the British enjoyed adding a dash of milk to their tea, the cows would keep them supplied.

Macartney was pensive at this display of solicitude, coming so soon after his blunt dismissal. He wondered how to account for the "contradictions" in the Chinese government's attitude to the embassy. Why were they treated so royally yet sent home empty-handed? He could not resist spinning dreams again: "Perhaps they begin to find their mistake, and wish to make some amends for it."[4] Songyun was doing his job very well indeed.

Beyond Tientsin the flotilla turned right, leaving the river on which they had traveled to Peking and heading south along a powerful tributary, the River of Transports, generally used to convey the emperor's share of the harvests to his granaries. It was also called the Imperial Waterway, and it formed the first section of the magnificent north-south artery that unified China: the Grand Canal.

On October 16 young Staunton noted that "the country [is] much adorned with trees and interspersed with villages. . . . We continued our way through this river which winds considerably and is well banked to prevent innundations, which nothwithstanding frequently happens, as the country for the most part is as low or even lower than the surface of the water in the river."[5] The astronomer adds that the meanders sometimes formed complete circles, and since the river was crowded, it sometimes looked as though the boats were sailing above the earth in all directions.[6]

The twenty or so haulers assigned to each junk struggled against the strong current. Gently sloped embankments were shaded by superb trees. The fields were "neatly divided and admirably well cultivated, the farm houses picturesque, and every three or four miles are canals of different breadths either falling into the river or branching from it into the country."[7]

The British saw many military control points. "At every interval of a few miles, are military posts, at each of which soldiers are stationed to protect the internal commerce of the provinces, as well as travellers, from pirates and robbers."[8] These were the first in a long series of posts, for banditry was as old as China itself. "Theft is very frequent, but murder in the course of a robbery is rare," says one of the missionaries.[9] Barrow speaks of "bands of robbers that infest the weak and unprotected parts of the country" and "plunder the peasantry."[10] Traditionally winter was considered a bad time to travel, since the routes were infested with starving bandits.[11] But the mere presence of the soldiers inspired them to caution.

From the decks of their craft the British glimpsed images that gradually came to compose their view of China. Their leisurely observations mirror the slow pace of the haulers. In the meantime, the bureaucratic apparatus was in full swing, couriers galloping, messages flying back and forth, the emperor exhorting his mandarins to vigilance.

Here was the situation as of October 15. The embassy, guided by Songyun, had passed Tientsin and was sailing up the Imperial Waterway. The five British ships were still moored in Dinghai, in the Zhoushan archipelago. But Sir Erasmus Gower, having had no news of Macartney (whose October 4 letter had not yet arrived), planned to cast off the next day. Neither the emperor and Heshen in Peking nor Songyun and the embassy aboard their junks were aware of Gower's plans.

Jiqing, the new viceroy of the prefecture that included Zhoushan, had taken up his post in Ningbo. His predecessor, Changlin, en route to his new posting in Canton, was now ordered to turn back. Qianlong wanted him to return to Zhejiang to assist Songyun and Jiqing in overseeing the embassy's embarcation in Zhoushan.

On that same day the emperor sent new instructions to his mandarins. Qianlong, like Napoleon, was apparently convinced that "the most effective rhetorical device is repetition," and he reiterated his instructions relentlessly:

> The Barbarians are quite ridiculous to fish for small profits as they do. Try to entice them with the prospect of the purchases they can make in Ningbo, but on no account allow them to trade alone. They would enter into relations with felonious merchants or would be cheated by others. In addition, let no official give the appearance of dealing with them. Our officials should introduce them to merchants above all suspicion.
>
> Watch over them closely. Let them view our prosperity, but only from the junks. Do not let them walk along the ground. Be firm but tactful in all circumstances. They must fear us, yet they must also be overcome with gratitude.[12]

Neither aspect of this ambitious program succeeded: the British felt neither fear nor gratitude.

The same letter settled the outstanding question of personnel: "The mandarins Wang and Qiao may continue to accompany the envoy as they have since his arrival. There is no point in Zhengrui's going along. He shall do as Songyun commands him."[13]

As it turned out, Zhengrui left the procession at the border of Shandong province, unlamented by the British.

Two days later, on October 17, a report by Jiqing dated October 13, arrived from Zhejiang and was annotated by Qianlong. Here is the dialogue between the emperor and his manifestly energetic mandarin:

> JIQING: The five ships are still here.
> QIANLONG: Good.
> JIQING: All the coastal military units are in readiness and have received Your illustrious instructions. All measures have been taken to intimidate the Barbarian delegation during its passage through Zhejiang. I have arranged for training maneuvers by the navy. Any vessel seeking an unauthorized berth at any island or islet will be turned away or boarded. All internal treason must be prevented.
> QIANLONG: Very good. Act in conjunction with Songyun.

JIQING: To neutralize the felonious merchants whose only motivation is the lure of profit, I have reinforced the interdictions previously announced by Changlin. Every trader and courtier must be suspected as a matter of principle.

QIANLONG: In view of Changlin's meticulousness, I have asked him to return to Zhejiang. Consult with Songyun and with him, and all will go suitably.

JIQING: In all this, of course, I have acted without negligence, but equally without agitation, such that the population is in no wise uneasy.

QIANLONG: Even more correct.[14]

THE BRITISH WERE just beginning their river journey when, on October 16, the *Lion* left Zhoushan, contrary to the now common desire of the emperor and the ambassador. The messages Macartney had sent from Peking—held up by the censorship of the imperial post—had not arrived, and the court reacted so slowly (taking action only on October 8) that the emperor's instructions did not reach the moorage in time.

THE BRITISH IN the eighteenth century were devotees of progress, especially agricultural progress. They were ever on the alert for new techniques, and in this domain China enjoyed a limitless prestige: the entire country was considered a garden and granary.

Arthur Young had given Macartney a lengthy questionnaire about China's agriculture and property structure.[15] This famous observer of the French countryside before the revolution wanted to know about leases, areas under cultivation, and yields. If per-acre production was higher than in Europe, why did the poor eat rats, dogs, and carrion? Could a despotic regime effectively promote agriculture? Was excessive taxation a cause of scarcity? How did they raise water for irrigation? How were plows drawn? What kind of mulberries were fed to silkworms? How was the soil fertilized? How were grains harvested? Even more fascinating to this Enlightenment scholar were the questions about the sheep of Shanxi, which were fleeced twice a year; about the elephants that were reported to roam freely in heavily populated areas; and about the cadavers of the poor, which were said to be used to enrich the soil.

Sir George was as astonished by China's advanced methods of wheat production as Arthur Young had been, four years earlier, by the backwardness of French techniques. "Though the land was arid," Staunton wrote, "wheat was perceived growing. . . . It was about two inches above the ground; and though on a dry and sandy soil, where no rain had fallen for the three preceding months, it looked remarkably well. It was very neatly sown in drills, or dibbled, according to the methods used of late in some parts of England." The Chinese did not scatter seed, a technique that was far too wasteful: the grain "is apt to grow in some spots in clusters, while in others the ground is scarcely covered."

"A gentleman of the Embassy calculated, that the saving of the seed alone, in China, in this drill husbandry, which would be lost in broadcast, would be sufficient to maintain all the European subjects of Great Britain."[16] We may ignore the estimate itself. The important point was the enormous demographic disparity between the United Kingdom and the Celestial Empire.

So much wheat, yet no bread. Or at least no Western bread. Instead there was *mantou*, shaped like round fritters and steamed. Five hundred years after Marco Polo brought the recipe back from his travels here, the British were astonished to find that the Chinese, especially in the north, ate noodles, macaroni, and vermicelli.

STAUNTON NOTICED that the Chinese laughed when they were vexed, and he had an economic explanation for the phenomenon: it reflected the "gaiety of small holders." He took the opportunity to rebuke large British property, which had been formed by evictions: "At this season of harvest, an active cheerfulness seemed to pervade both sexes. They appeared to be sensible of labouring for their own profit. Many of the peasants are owners of the land they cultivate. There are no great and speculative farmers, aiming at monopoly or combination in the disposal of their produce, and overwhelming with their wealth the poorer husbandmen, till they reduce them at length to mere daily labourers."[17]

It sounds almost like a speech in an election campaign. The grass is always greener. The truth of the matter was that many of these Chinese peasants cultivated tiny scraps of land,[18] but such are the risks of jumping to conclusions. Staunton reviled the British society that he knew so intimately, but he idealized the Chinese countryside, through which he was merely passing. To paraphrase a Chinese adage, he was inspecting flowers from a galloping horse, and his mandarin escort unfailingly encouraged his flattering assumptions.[19]

Neither Macartney nor Staunton perceived the impoverishment China was suffering in the eighteenth century. The population nearly doubled during Qianlong's reign, rising from something like 150 million or 180 million to 340 million in the space of sixty years.[20]

Neither the expansion of land under cultivation nor the rise in productivity kept pace. In 1685 per capita land cultivation stood at about a third of a hectare, the vital minimum at the time. By 1793 it had fallen to a seventh of a hectare. The Chinese tried to meet the challenge with increasingly intensive agriculture: hand planting, irrigation, clearing of stubble. But poverty among the peasantry worsened, and revolts were more frequent. All this was carefully concealed from Macartney, who noticed neither the overpopulation nor (even then) the underdevelopment. The Chinese diet was worse than frugal: this was a malnourished population. In China, unlike in Great Britain, population growth had not been accompanied by economic change. True, the beginnings of the industrial revolution in the West aggravated poverty—but also reabsorbed it later. In China, however, a gap had opened between an expanding population and a stagnant production system centered exclusively on agriculture, a reflection of the immobility of Chinese society itself. Malthus, who read Staunton carefully, posed the problem well. In 1793 China had not yet experienced great turmoil, but prosperity was already on the wane. Though still at its apogee, the country was poised on the brink of decline.

The badly misled Staunton spoke of the "gaiety of small holders," but he ignored the ravages of usury, which, while much exaggerated by Maoist historiography, were certainly real. Land-hungry mandarin-usurers created the masses of landless peasants who later fought with the Taipings, the Boxers, and Mao.

The British swallowed the official story: that the providential state guaranteed the happiness of all. When the missionaries read Staunton's account, they commented ironically on several of his hasty conclusions.[21] He had failed to notice the growing injustice suffered by the people, which resulted in a regime that looked more and more like a police state. The threat of social unrest was one of the major reasons for the Manchu refusal to open the country to foreign influences. Mired in cliquish egotism, Qianlong and his mandarins feared losing their absolute power.[22]

Even the mandarins were imprisoned in a rigid honeycomb structure, and since they lacked autonomy themselves, they resolutely denied it to anyone else. No merchant or farmer could do anything contrary to the wishes of a bureaucratic pyramid that was itself immobilized by precedent and inhibition. The empire's ruling caste—the military Manchu minority that had reshaped the mandarin administration to suit themselves—was already on the defensive when Macartney's arrival signaled the coming Western invasion. And China had no strategy for dealing with Europe—except to enrich itself by taxing European merchants beyond all reason.

We can be more confident in Staunton when he describes what he saw without trying to elaborate a theory: "The walls of the village houses consisted mostly of indurated mud; or of masses of earth baked imperfectly in the sun, or moulded between planks into the shape of walls, and bound together with them, until it had acquired sufficient hardness to support a roof; or of wicker-work, defended by a coating of adhesive clay. The roofs were covered generally with straw, rarely with green turf. The apartments are divided by lattice-work hung with broad paper, containing either the figures of deities, or columns of moral sentences."[23]

Each cottage had a vegetable garden and a farmyard in which "they raised pigs, poultry, and especially ducks. The ducks are salted and dried and then sent to market in the big cities. The Chinese have long been masters of the art of causing duck eggs to hatch with artificial heat."

The little girl tending the ducks is a figure as popular in China as the little shepherd girl in European traditions. Farther south, Barrow saw the remarkable sight come to life: "The younger [women] of the family are sometimes employed in breeding ducks. . . . In a single vessel are sometimes many hundreds which, on the signal of a whistle leap into the water, or upon the banks to feed; and another whistle brings them back."[24]

In today's China, as under the Manchus, the people of the countryside live in brick hovels or cabins of wood or adobe with thatched or tiled roofs, or sometimes even in cavelike dwellings hewn from loess.[25] British descriptions of the vegetable gardens and agricultural techniques would suit the citizens of the People's Republic equally well. Two centuries of turmoil have left this multimillenary tableau largely unmodified.

The village women, spinning cotton at their wheels, sitting in front of their huts, or tending to the harvests, seemed coarse, indistinguishable from the men. "Their heads were large and round, and stature low. . . . Their shape was wholly concealed from the neck downwards by loose dresses; they wore wide trowsers from the waist to the small of the leg."

The travelers had an explanation for the ugliness of the women: "A custom which is said to subsist in China, must render beauty rare in the lower classes of life. It is assured, that the young maidens distinguished by their faces or their figure, are taken or purchased from their parents at the age of fourteen, for the use of the powerful and opulent. Accident had thrown a few of these within view of the gentlemen of the Embassy, who also considered them, from the fairness and delicacy of their complexions, and the beauty and regularity of their features, as entitled to admiration."[26] The most recent research confirms that this practice, too, continues.[27] The women who toil in the countryside are the countless castoffs of this selection process.

Sabotage the
Barbarian Vessels

(October 18–20, 1793)

THE FLAT COUNTRYSIDE dotted with walled towns and cities was reminiscent of Holland. Winter was approaching. "Few trees and the grain just springing up," writes Thomas. "Fine cold weather."[1] Macartney notes that the weather was "cold and pinching" whenever the wind shifted "to the northward."

Wang and Qiao told him that "a great many poor people die in these provinces for want of sufficient clothing." And: "It is chiefly their clothing that the Chinese trust to for a defence against the cold weather. They have no fireplaces nor fixed stoves in their houses; they . . . sometimes have braziers brought into their chambers, but these give only a short temporary heat and require too much trouble and attention to be regularly kept up."[2] Still true. In winter the Chinese wear multiple layers of wool clothing to keep warm.

The towns and villages were built well away from the river in order to avoid floods. After about a week of monotonous sailing, the astronomer was bored: in comparison with the Rhone or the Thames, there was no variety in the scenery visible from the boats.[3] Thomas Staunton, on the other hand, was more easily amused: "The river winds more than any other river I ever saw."[4]

The only incidents worth reporting involved the haulers. "A sufficient number of men were impressed by the mandarins to track the boats; but the pay allowed by government was not adequate to the labour, and many of them withdrew from the task whenever they found an opportunity of escaping unperceived. It often happened that a set of trackers were exchanged in the night, that fresh might be surprised and forced into the service. A superintendant, like a negro-driver in the West Indies, marches generally behind them with a whip, to quicken their pace, and prevent their desertion."[5]

On October 18 the travelers were greeted with military honors in Dezhou. A band played, and there was a lavish display of banners, torches, and lanterns.

On that same day Thomas wrote: "This morning we entered the province of Shandong, at which time the Tartar and some lower Man-darines left us but others came to take their place."[6] Shandong today is still one of China's richest provinces, but also one of the most overpopulated. Many of the inhabitants emigrate, seeking less crowded lands in Manchuria.

There was a full moon. "The observance of the usual ceremonies, which consist of firing their small petards, beating at intervals the noisy gong, harsh squalling music and fire-works, required that our vessels should remain stationary, and these nocturnal orgies ceased only with the ap-pearance of the sun."[7] Barrow reiterated his distaste for Chinese music.[8] Hüttner decided that "the Chinese have no ear."[9] Which was exactly what the Chinese thought of the British when they heard the embassy's mu-sicians.

Fields of wheat, sorghum, and tobacco stretched into the distance on both sides of the river. But the most common crop, Thomas noted,[10] was cotton, which the British found growing over immense stretches. But since most Chinese wore only cotton, even this enormous crop was insufficient to meet the country's needs, and cotton was imported from Bombay. In fact, it was the single most important item in the company's official trade, being exchanged for tea, silk, and porcelain.[11]

Staunton explains: "Adjoining to the fields of cotton, are others cul-tivated with indigo, with whose blue dye, the cottons used for the common people are generally coloured throughout the empire."[12] Blue cotton was the uniform of the toiling masses under Qianlong as under the Mings.[13] After the revolution the same uniform, even more strictly ob-served, was extended to everyone. Not until Deng Xiaoping's ascendancy in the late 1970s did the use of this monochromatic fabric begin to wane, especially in summer, as Chinese women led the men to multicolored dress.

MACARTNEY NOTED that as they approached large cities, the river was bor-dered by "large burying-grounds."[14] Staunton, too, was struck by the peo-ple's great respect for the dead. "The Chinese burying-places are no otherwise consecrated than by the veneration of the people, the remains of whose ancestors are deposited in them. The people preserve those sacred repositories, with all the care they can afford to bestow upon them. They . . . repair any breaches that accidents may have made, and remove any weeds that may have grown or dirt that may have been thrown around them."[15]

Indeed, to disturb a grave was to risk provoking the wrath of ghosts. The Chinese are terrified of unburied corpses, and literature abounds in abandoned dead who return to haunt their descendants. But the living also have ways of getting revenge. In China today, as in the past, there are thousands of stories about people playing dirty tricks on evil spirits. For instance, you can prevent them from returning to their coffins by stealing the lids, or you can torment the male children of their families, fooling the spirits by dressing boys as girls.

What, then, accounts for the indignation of Holmes, who proclaims: "The custom of burying their dead, or rather of disposing of them, disgusted us most of all. . . ."? Strangely, Chinese cemeteries were not always as well maintained as Chinese gardens: "You might sometimes see thousands of coffins wholly exposed, and the corpse in a state of putrefaction; others were half buried, or half covered with straw."[16] These abandoned dead were poor people, whose descendants (if any) lacked the wherewithal to afford decent tombs.[17] A terrible measure of their impoverishment.

MACARTNEY OBSERVES that the "mass of the people in China are gross idolators. . . . The vulgar, as elsewhere, are in general excessively superstitious. They are strict observers of lucky and unlucky days, and many of them, like their betters, are dabblers in chiromancy, divination, and astrology."[18]

According to Barrow, itinerant fortune-tellers made good livings going from house to house in the provinces predicting the future. "They are known by a wretched squalling flute on which they play, and are beckoned to call where their art is required. By being acquainted with the day and hour of a person's birth, they pretend to cast his nativity [draw his horoscope]."[19] The British had expected Confucian wisdom. Instead they found rampant superstition. Another myth collapses.

Chinese daily life is riddled with gestures meant to ward off ill fortune. Two furtive lovers, for instance, will scale a roof carrying burning sticks of incense to "scare away evil spirits."[20] The dead in their coffins receive warnings before the eternal nails of the lid are driven in, so that they will not panic at the sound of the hammer.[21] Bridges are built in zigzag patterns so that evil spirits will stumble over the railings and plunge into the water.

The ancient Greeks placed obols in the mouths of their dead relatives so that they could pay their toll across the river Styx. The Chinese slipped balls of agate or jade into the mouths of their dead to facilitate their entry into the land of shadows.[22] Another tradition that continues.

MACARTNEY NOTICED that the "prodigious" population "increases the farther we go southward. To-day we observed a great many women mixed with the men, but few of them handsome. They labour in the fields at harvest and other country business just like their husbands."[23] There was equality in toil, and toil was relentless. There are "no fixed days or stated periods set apart to rest from labour."[24] No Sundays, no paid holidays.

Macartney's observation was not meant to be critical. This was a time when the most modern of Europeans wished people to work without any break. "We have often groaned under the burden of an excessive number of holidays," reads a register of grievances drafted by an industrious French bourgeois in 1789. Labor schedules were also a point of contention between the Reformation and the Counter-Reformation. "It would be far better were it permitted to work on those days, for otherwise men become intoxicated and the animals go hungry. Our families would be more at ease if idleness were allowed only on Sundays and on four holidays a year."[25]

Barrow admired China for having so few holidays, and for celebrating those few so soberly: "The first of the new year in China, and a few succeeding days, are the only holidays, properly speaking, that are observed by the working part of the community. On these days the poorest peasant makes a point of procuring new clothing for himself and his family; they pay visits to friends and relations."[26]

Once again the British view was slightly too idyllic. New Year's Day, devoted by order of the emperor to agricultural rites, was a time of eating and drinking. Toasts were made to everyone's health, using cups made of rhinoceros horn. "Wishes more lasting than the mountains are exchanged—ten thousand years of life!" And: "Words forge friendships as strong as lacquer and glue."[27]

But Staunton, well aware of his own people's penchant for gin and beer, was right to consider the Chinese comparatively "sober and moral": "The Chinese are, perhaps, upon an average, better able to support moderate labour with little intermission than many of the lower classes in Europe. They are bred in better and sounder habits, and continue longer under the direction of their parents. They are, for the most part, sober; they marry early; they are less exposed to the temptations of debauchery; they are less liable to contract diseases which corrupt the springs of life."[28] But here again he went a little too far. The Chinese do drink.

To observe others is often to gaze into a mirror. Staunton's puritanism, while resistant to Confucianism, sought confirmation of its own preachings. And a French Catholic, observing the Chinese of Canton during the same period, drew conclusions not dissimilar to those of the British Protestant: "Constant toil maintains the strength of the Chinese and shields them from passion. Love is unknown here, ambition scarcely detectable. Though cupidity is widespread, it arouses emulation, industry, and effort."[29]

In any event, Confucianism has left ineradicable traces. Though the monastic rigor of the Mao era has been much relaxed, the Chinese authorities recently announced with pride that AIDS was unknown in China, except among foreigners.

But the Chinese did have one vice: gambling. According to Barrow, "They seldom part without trying their luck at some game of chance for which a Chinese is never unprepared."[30] "Gambling," Father Huc pointed out, "is forbidden by the laws of the Empire, but this legislation is so widely circumvented that the country resembles an enormous gambling den."[31]

The Chinese themselves were not above acknowledging this collective trait: "How many gamblers, ruining their families and squandering their property, have been degraded by gaming and have thus sowed the seeds of misfortune?"[32]

ON OCTOBER 20 the emperor summarized the state of his correspondence with Songyun:

"The edict of the fifteenth, in which we advised him to allow the Barbarians to view the countryside from their junks, was sent at the speed of 600 *li* per day and should have reached him on the seventeenth. If he replies immediately, we should have his report shortly. Songyun should arrive in Zhejiang to begin working with Changlin around November 15. If we notify him within a week, by the last days of November we will be informed of what he and Changlin have decided."[33]

As he surveyed his enormous empire, calculating the speed of the junks and the couriers, the emperor kept careful track of the flow of his orders and counterorders, including the replies to and execution of each instruction. There was good reason for Europe's fascination with China. Had any country ever been better—or at least more closely—governed?

On that same day Qianlong received a report, dated October 16, from Changlin, who was then still on his way to Guangdong, not yet having received the order to return to Zhoushan. In response to the edict of October 5, he had alerted all the coastal provinces. Here is the dialogue between the emperor and his mandarin, as recorded in Changlin's report and Qianlong's vermilion rescripts:

> With their own Barbarian eyes the English have beheld the rigor and strength of the Celestial institutions. It is therefore probable that they will attempt no violence. But since His Holy Majesty has exposed their deceit, it is better to prepare for any eventuality. Our maritime defenses are based primarily on bows and arrows, muskets, and a few cannon. The Barbarians have a profusion of weaponry on their ships. We must find a way to ensure our absolute superiority. Now, this summer I learned that there are, in the Ningbo prefecture, fisherman, called the Dan, who are able to dive to depths of several brasses.* If we could recruit such men to the army, we could have them swim underwater and destroy the rudders of the brigand ships, which would then be incapable of maneuvering and would be at our mercy.
>
> YOU CAN PREPARE FOR THIS EVENTUALITY WITHOUT NECESSARILY HAVING TO IMPLEMENT IT. I DOUBT THAT THINGS WILL COME TO THAT. AWAIT MY INSTRUCTIONS.
>
> This could be a decisive means of guaranteeing the supremacy of our fleet. Nevertheless, Prefect Keshina has pointed out to me that these fishermen would be disinclined to join the army, since the profits they make from their fishing are greater than the pay in grain allocated to recruits.
>
> NATURALLY.
>
> In my humble view, if the coastal defenses could avail themselves of such men, a single one of them would match many soldiers in effectiveness. The allocation could therefore be doubled. . . .
>
> I FEAR THAT THIS ADVANTAGE WOULD NOT SUFFICE TO PERSUADE THEM.
>
> Every man sent to another province could also be granted an indemnity of twenty taels in cash. This population of fishermen must be sufficiently attracted by the profit to agree to abandon the earnings of their fishing. Their enrollment would not only permit us to disable the Barbarian ships, but could also put an end to ordinary piracy.
>
> I respectfully await the instructions of Your Perspicacious Holiness.[34]

---

* A brasse was a measure of depth equal to about 5.25 feet.

THE PROVINCIAL GOVERNOR was well aware that he could not contemplate sabotaging foreign ships on his own account. But the sovereign, while not dissuading his viceroy from enticing the fishermen into this sabotage, had a sharper sense of his own responsibilities, and thus made sure that the governor would await specific instructions before taking any action. A good lesson in the workings of the state.

54

An Emperor
"Upon His Guard Against the Slightest Appearance of Innovation"

(October 21–23, 1793)

WINTER ARRIVED on October 21. It was "as if there had been frost during the night," wrote Thomas.[1] In the meantime, Macartney had had time to think about the emperor's two letters to his king, and he wondered why the second one had rejected an imaginary request for permission to preach Anglicanism. Songyun seemed willing to answer questions, so Macartney decided to ask him about this troublesome text.

He broached the subject by asking why the emperor's letter treated the requests as though they had come from Macartney himself, thereby suggesting that he had exceeded his instructions, a most disagreeable thing for an ambassador to do. It happened that the secretary who had copied out the emperor's letter was now "in the train of Songyun," and it was he who answered Macartney, explaining that this was "a Court artifice to elude an ungrantable demand." Chinese "urbanity," it seems, "does not admit a supposition that one sovereign can desire of another what is possible to be refused. It is, therefore, concluded that the request has never been made, or if made that the Ambassador has been guilty of an error in the delivery of his message, and to have asked from his own head what had never entered into that of his master."[2] Macartney decided to "let it pass," noting that "private and personal considerations must merge in the pursuit of public objects" and that there was a "wide difference between negotiating with an European and an oriental prince. . . . Even Louis XIV on occasion of one of his ships being fired at in the archipelago said there was no point of honour with such people as the Turks."[3] It is not surprising that Macartney would compare himself to Louis XIV, but it is interesting that he drew a parallel between the Chinese and the Turks.

On the matter of the phantom seventh request, Songyun replied that the court "had taken it for granted" that the British, "like the other Europeans," were energetic propagators of their faith. Macartney protested that the conversion of the Chinese was a matter of no interest whatever to the British. This was shown by the fact that neither the English merchants in Canton nor the embassy itself had any "priests or chaplains belonging to them."

Returning to the first edict, Macartney expressed surprise that it had "chiefly dwelt" on rejecting the request for a permanent embassy. Why had it avoided the questions of trade? And why had the second edict suggested that the British were seeking "exclusive privileges"? Macartney acknowledged that "we had only asked for ourselves," but insisted that "however grateful we should be for any favours granted to us, we by no means presumed to desire that his [the emperor's] bounty should not be extended to others."[4]

He then "renewed the subject of the grievances complained of at Canton," reiterating that if this situation were not speedily rectified, trade "would fall to decay, than which nothing could be more prejudicial to China." Here Macartney was merely repeating himself; the Chinese were not the only ones to parrot the words of their master.

Songyun tried to placate Macartney, assuring him that the emperor's letters "were not meant to convey anything unfavourable or unpleasant to the Embassy or myself, but he wished to remind me that the laws and usages of China were invariable, and that the Emperor was so strictly observant of them that no consideration could ever induce him to infringe them. That he was therefore upon his guard against the slightest appearance of innovation, and had declined any immediate compliance with the particular requests we had made; but that we were not to infer from thence a disinclination in him towards us or our concerns, for that notwithstanding any surmises of others, he entertained very kind intentions with regard to us, and that the English at Canton would soon find the good effects of them."[5]

The Chinese system of government, Songyun explained, left "a great deal to the discretion and recommendation the Viceroys, whose conduct might possibly be sometimes not unexceptionable." Now, however, "as a particular mark of attention to us," Changlin had been named viceroy of Guangdong. The British would marvel at his "justice and integrity" and his "remarkable benignity to strangers." It was his task to "make the most minute inquiries at Canton into such vexation and grievances as may exist there, and, . . . to rectify everything amiss by the most effectual exertion of his authority."[6]

Macartney took that ball and ran with it. Would it not be possible to put these good words in writing? A "third letter from the Emperor, confirming the flattering hopes now given me, would be very desirable." Songyun replied that this raised a problem of protocol. Since the embassy had now left the capital, no further correspondence could be exchanged between the court and the envoy.

In his effort to soothe the visitor whom he was now ushering out of the country, Songyun insisted that many favorable remarks about the embassy had been made in the letters he had been receiving from the court. In fact Songyun had in his possession stern directives designed to inspire "terror" among the barbarians if need be, but he had also been supplied with affable written remarks which he was authorized to reveal to the barbarians in order to elicit "their boundless gratitude." He therefore emphasized the "kindness" of the emperor, who had allowed the British to remain in Zhoushan to care for their sick seamen and to make various transactions in Ningbo on financially favorable terms.

Macartney was navigating through hostile territory, but his guides had been told to assure him that the hand of the Son of Heaven lay upon him "like a caress," *usque ad blanditias*, in the words of the priest-translators.[7]

So much for Macartney's account of this discussion. We also have Songyun's version. The same facts, a different point of view. The facts: two men talked over tea. The viewpoint: two different worlds, poles apart. Macartney reports to himself, analyzing, posing questions, contemplating. Songyun reports to his sovereign, adding a few more couplets to the unending epic of the immobile order.

> Your prostrated slave reports as follows for Your information.
>
> The tributary envoy, his deputy, and his interpreter came aboard my junk and told me: "We have benefitted from the kindness of the Great Emperor; we were wholly ignorant of the institutions of the Celestial Court, and we formulated improper requests. We now fear that our king may hold this against us."
>
> In conformity with Your instructions, Your slave replied: "The Emperor has flatly rejected those requests which are not in accordance with our customs. Go in peace."
>
> They replied: "The requests we submitted were in accordance with our king's will." I understood that I had not placated them; I therefore added: "Our Emperor will not hold it against your king

that he expressed these wishes, for in His immense benevolence, the Great Emperor intends to save face for your king. But if he were to present another request contrary to the practices of the Empire, he would inevitably suffer a rebuff."

They bowed their heads and spoke again: "One point remains unclear to us, that in which the edict refuses the practice of religion. We requested nothing of the kind." I explained to them: "From ancient times the Holy Emperors have left teachings that rigorously distinguish Chinese from Barbarians. The population respects this law and would not agree to allow a heterodox discourse to be spread in the country."

The envoy was pleased, and was effusive in his thanks: "All the measures taken by the Great Emperor are based on wisdom; we now understand this; we are sincerely convinced. He agrees to protect our trade in Macao. We shall advise our king immediately upon our return, and our king will be happy."[8]

SO BE IT. But the penultimate paragraph is significant in three respects. First, Songyun recognizes that Macartney made no request to proselytize for Anglicanism. In other words, this was a Chinese initiative meant to preempt any possible future request along these lines. Second, the wording tends to support the suspicions of those historians who believe that the Portuguese priests surreptitiously intervened on this issue.[9] Finally, it clearly heralds restrictions on—and even the persecution of—the freedom to preach. Such restrictions, indeed, would not be long in coming.

ON OCTOBER 22 the embassy continued its river journey through fields of cotton. The river was so sinuous that in the space of a few hours the travelers found the sun on their left, on their right, behind them, and in front of them. Enormous crowds of curious onlookers poured out of the great walled city of Liuqingzhou. The riverbank was lined with poplars and aspens much larger and taller than those of Europe.

Toward evening the flotilla left the river and sailed into a narrow canal, through a "kind of lock or gateway which I did not notice," says Thomas.[10] This was the beginning of an artificial waterway that the embassy would follow for more than a thousand miles. "This great work," Macartney wrote, "was executed for the purpose of laying open to each other the northern and southern provinces of the empire. It is more properly an improved river than an entirely artificial canal, . . . for it has a descent in almost every part, and generally runs with considerable velocity." In swampy areas the canal is "cut very deep below the surface of the ground" and is enclosed "between two high banks raised above the inundated country with incredible labour and expense." When proceeding "through a rising country," the canal is "often thirty and forty feet below the surface of the ground."[11] The embassy, Thomas notes on October 23, was "going on very well."[12]

Sir George could not contain his lyricism: "This enterprise, the greatest and most ancient of its kind, . . . [extends] about five hundred miles, not only through heights and over valleys, but across rivers and lakes. . . . This great work differs much from the canals of Europe, which are generally protracted in straight lines within narrow bounds, and without a current."[13] He especially admired the locks, which Hüttner counted: there were seventy-two in all.[14] "One man stands on the prow of the boat, steering it with a kind of oar, while others, having climbed upon the edge of the channel, where they stand holding cushions stuffed with hair, prepare to drop these into the gap to lessen the shock. At night the passages are illuminated by powerful lanterns."[15]

The boatmen paid a small toll when they crossed the gates of the locks, which opened at set times. "When the nature of the country has not answered the wishes for," Winder says, "the vessels are drawn up a glacis from one canal to the other, by means of a windlass, which is fixed on the bank. It is manned with sixteen people; it is drawn up and launched in three or four minutes."[16] Dinwiddie, ever the exacting man of science even when struck with admiration, timed the operation: it took between two and a half and three minutes for a junk to clear a lock.

Staunton, though clearly dazzled by this gigantic project, which antedated the canals of Europe by twelve centuries, nevertheless believed that Chinese technique could be improved upon if some Western ideas were borrowed. He tried to point out several respects in which European canals were superior. No luck. Discouraged, he concluded that the Chinese believed that everything in their country was excellent and that any attempted improvement would be at best superfluous and at worst culpable.

Half a century later, Father Huc wrote: "Any man of genius is instantly paralyzed by the thought that his efforts will be met with punishment instead of recompense."[17] Macartney, too, ascribed this technical immobility to the Chinese mentality.[18] Ritual was the enemy of improvement.

STAUNTON DESCRIBES the immemorial process of rice cultivation.

> After the mud [left by the flooding of the river] has lain some days upon the plains . . . preparations are made for planting them with

rice. For this purpose, a small spot of ground is inclosed by a bank of clay; the earth is ploughed up; and an upright harrow with a row of wooden pins in the lower end, is drawn lightly over it by a buffalo. The grain which had previously been steeped in dung diluted with animal water, is then sown very thickly on it. A thin sheet of water is immediately brought over it . . . by channels. . . . In a few days the shoots appear above the water. . . . As soon as the shoots have attained the height of six or seven inches, they are plucked up by the roots, the tops of the blades cut off, and each root is planted separately. . . . Water is brought over them a second time. . . . As the rice approaches to maturity, the water by evaporation and absorption, disappears entirely; and the crop, when ripe, covers dry ground. The first crop or harvest . . . happens towards the end of May or beginning of June. The instrument for reaping, is a small sickle, dentated like a saw, and crooked. Neither carts nor cattle are used to carry the sheaves off from the spot where they were reaped; but they are placed regularly in frames, two of which, suspended at the extremities of a bamboo pole, are carried across the shoulders of a man to the place intended for disengaging the grain from the stems which had supported it. This operation is performed not only by a flail, . . . or by cattle treading . . . but some-times also by striking it against a plank set upon its edge. . . . After being winnowed it is carried to the granary.[19]

Fresh plantings are prepared immediately after the first harvest, and the second crop is gathered in October or November. These same lands "are found equally suitable for raising an excellent crop of sugar canes. . . . Satisfied with two crops of rice or one of sugar cane in the year, the Chinese husbandman generally suffers the land to remain at rest till the following spring, when the same process is repeated."[20] Actually there was also a harvest of vegetables between the rice harvests. The land never lay fallow.

But rice is a vulnerable grain. "A frost in its early stages withers it on the ground; and an inundation, when nearly ripe, is equally destructive. The birds and the locusts, more numerous in this country than an European can well conceive, infest it more than any other kind of grain."[21]

During droughts the emperor fasted, thus attempting to intercede with Heaven. In 1689 the emperor Kangxi issued an edict in reply to the pleas of various high mandarins who anxiously urged the sovereign to take better care of himself. "It is only right," he wrote, "that we should be the first to sorrow and the last to rejoice. On account of the persistent drought that has lasted for such a long period we have been filled with anxiety, and so have grown thin and lost our strength. . . . Through the mercy of Heaven, rain has now fallen. When enough rain has fallen we may allow ourselves some relief from care."[22]

It seems unlikely that present-day Chinese leaders fast during droughts. The birds have been driven away, and insecticides have put the locusts to flight. But three centuries after Kangxi and two after Qianlong, little else has changed in the manner of cultivation of the queen of cereals.

55

An Unrivaled Postal System

(October 20–24, 1793)

THE BRITISH NOTED the steady flow of imperial correspondence, and they marveled at the diligence of the postal system, calculating times and distances and comparing Chinese to British performance in this domain. Good sports that they were, they hailed the Chinese accomplishments. "The Chinese couriers are so expeditious that, I am told, it is no uncommon thing to convey a letter fifteen hundred miles in ten or twelve days."[1]

Official letters were carried by couriers using horses bred on special military stud farms. Relay stations, run by "transmission officers," formed a kind of web centered on Peking. As the embassy got farther from the capital, the reports were dispatched more rapidly. Whereas letters to Tientsin traveled at the rate of 400 *li* (about 130 miles) per day, those going to the far south were carried at 600 *li* per day, the top speed.[2]

Judging from the dates of the correspondence between the court and the embassy, it took about five days for a letter to get from the capital to Hangzhou and ten to get to Canton, a distance our travelers would cover in eighty days. In other words, commentaries on the embassy traveled about eight times faster than the embassy itself.

British admiration was fully justified, since the most brilliant performance claimed by the English postal system at the time was far inferior to the Chinese.

On the other hand, only official letters traveled in this way. As we have seen, it was exceptional for the imperial post to carry private mail, and in all such cases (without exception) censorship was the price of passage. The letters of the missionaries generally took about three months to cover the distance between Peking and Canton.[3] Sometimes the priests might manage to slip a letter into the official post with the cooperation of a mandarin accomplice,[4] but such letters were invariably read before they reached their destinations.

In England, as in the rest of Europe, the postal system was a public service. It permitted countless forms of social communication without seeking to control them. In China the state alone communicated, and only with itself. When private individuals were granted the favor of having a letter carried, they effectively became hostages to the bureaucracy.

The Chinese mail outdid itself in guaranteeing the emperor's satisfaction, and so it had been since the Tang dynasty. Ten centuries after the establishment of the Chinese postal system, the Marquise de Sévigné marveled that thanks to the recent improvements in the Royal Post in France, it took only eight or nine days for a letter from her daughter in Grignan to arrive in Vitré.[5] That works out to about ninety miles a day, roughly one-third the Chinese rate.

Marco Polo described couriers on foot and on horseback who wore little bells to alert the relay stations to their approach, and the Manchu emperors had pedestrian couriers too. They formed relays, trotting at an average speed of about four and a half miles an hour. Some of them were drafted for set terms, while others held the position on a hereditary basis, despite low wages and harsh working conditions: delays or damaged envelopes were punishable by "bambooing," and the couriers had to venture out regardless of the weather.[6]

At the end of the seventeenth century the average distance between relay stations was seventy to a hundred *li*, and horses were often taxed to exhaustion. Many new stations were established during Qianlong's reign, primarily to assist military campaigns. The imperial administration bought thousands of horses, and a major relay station might have as many as a hundred of them on hand. Only a very few officials—such as specialists in explosives during provincial revolts—had the right to use them.[7]

There were even popular legends about the imperial relay stations. The beautiful Yang Guifei, a favorite of the emperor Xuan Zong in the beginning of the eighth century, was especially fond of lichis, which were grown only in Guangdong, three thousand *li* from Xi'an, then the capital. The Son of Heaven ordered his couriers to satisfy her craving, and since lichis spoil in three days, the couriers had to cover a thousand *li* a day, more than three hundred miles.

Our travelers noticed these mounted couriers on several occasions. Anderson, for instance: "We saw this day the Chinese post pass along the road, on the side of the canal, with great expedition." Strapped to his back the courier carried a large bamboo basket containing letters and packages. The key to this letter box "is given to the custody of one of the attendant soldiers, whose office it is to deliver it to the post-master; the box . . . is decorated at the bottom with a number of small bells, which being shaken by the motion of the horse, make a loud jingling noise, that announces the approach of the post. The post-man is escorted by five light-horsemen to guard him from robbery or interruption."[8] Roads were not safe in China—nor in England: the Portsmouth mail coach, for example, had been hijacked in 1757.[9]

Our travelers honestly acknowledged the inferiority of the British mail, to which many witnesses testified: "The post is the slowest means of communication commanded by the United Kingdom, and the least secure: to avoid losses resulting from thefts, it is customary to tear bank notes or stock certificates in half and to send the two pieces in different posts."[10] Paul Valéry noted: "Napoleon moves as slowly as Caesar did."

Europe never did catch up to China in horseback mail, but the postal performances of the two cultures were nevertheless reversed. The Middle Empire not only failed to progress, but actually regressed, while Europe leaped ahead through innovation. Chappe's optical telegraph became operational in 1796. The steamboat arrived a decade later, and two decades after that the railroad. China, which had once led the way, was left behind.

But British admiration might well have paled had they been able to read the letters these couriers were carrying. Songyun, for example, sent this one to the emperor: "On October 17 I received Your Majesty's edict on the terms of sale for the British and on the freedom of movement that they should be granted. In accordance with Your directives, Changlin, Jiqing, and I will assign officials to see that the Barbarians are accompanied by reliable courtiers. . . . The tributary envoy is docile in his obedience and seems sincerely grateful for Your benevolence. He is also impressed by our laws, by the Empire's military power, and by the prosperity of its inhabitants."[11]

And here is the letter court officials reverentially placed in the courier's basket on October 21:

> To Songyun, Changlin, and Jiqing,
> We were fully reassured by Songyun's report. He has perfectly understood the instructions which we communicated to him orally in Jehol and which were repeated at the time of his departure from Peking. He must see to it that the tributary envoy remains calm. To this end, he will apply the inviolable regulations. Barbarian trickery is well known. We note that Jiqing has assumed his post in Zhejiang. We expect that Changlin, in turn, will arrive there toward mid-November. As soon as he has made his purchases, the tributary envoy must embark. It would be appropriate to explain this to him clearly and to prevent him, by any means necessary, from procrastinating.
> Let these orders be obeyed![12]

"A Couple of English Frigates Could Reduce Their Coasts to Famine"

(October 24–28, 1793)

The Chinese, it is true, are a singular people, but they are men formed of the same materials and governed by the same passions as ourselves. They are jealous of foreigners, but are they jealous of us without reason?

MACARTNEY, January 1794[1]

THE CANAL CLIMBED higher from lock to lock, leaving the flat, silted land-scape behind. "Lord Macartney went again this morning to converse with Songyun," writes Thomas on October 25. "The banks of the canal being generally higher often prevents our seeing the face of the country from our windows."[2] His father explains: "On the twenty-fifth of October the yachts arrived at the highest port of the canal. . . . Here the river Luen, the largest by which the canal is fed, falls into it with a rapid stream in a line which is perpendicular to the course of the canal. A strong bulwark of stone supports the opposite western bank; and the waters of the Luen striking with force against it, part of them follow the northern and part the southern course of the canal: a circumstance which . . . gave the appearance . . . that if a bundle of sticks be thrown into that part of the river, they would soon separate and take opposite directions."[3] From here the convoy would now descend to the Yellow River.

Lines of cleavage also appeared in human behavior. After a banal conversation with the ever amiable Songyun, Macartney drifted into musings full of menace for China.

Songyun had informed the ambassador of the emperor's satisfaction that the journey was going so well. This imperial approval was accompanied by a gift of cheese and sweets. Macartney does not describe with what ceremony he received them, but Songyun does:

> Since the envoy was suffering from a headache, it was the vice-envoy who came aboard Your slave's vessel and declared: "Our joy was immense in learning that His Imperial Majesty has been so charitable as to grace us with provisions. But the tributary envoy has unfortunately been taken ill and is bedridden." Although Your slave knew that the envoy was ill, he could not allow the Barbarians to act as they wished. The following morning the said tributary envoy ordered his vessel to halt and, striving to overcome his indisposition, came to Your slave's vessel. The tributary envoy and the others removed their hats and bent their knee. Joy could be read on their faces. They declared: "We have received numerous favors from His Imperial Majesty. Today He has again given us cheese. We are touched to the bottom of our hearts. To benefit, during such a long journey, from the precious foodstuffs His Charity has bestowed upon us is, for us, like acquiring a treasure." Clearly, their intentions were perfectly sincere.[4]

They chatted briefly, Songyun tirelessly repeating that this new gesture was fresh proof of his sovereign's benevolence. And all because of a bit of cheese! It was more than the ambassador could take, and he vented his spleen in his journal: "If the Court of Peking is not really sincere can they possibly expect to feed us long with promises? Can they be ignorant that a couple of English frigates would be an overmatch for the whole naval force of their empire, that in half a summer they could totally destroy all the navigation of their coasts and reduce the inhabitants of the maritime provinces, who subsist chiefly on fish, to absolute famine?"[5]

Had this possibility occurred to Qianlong? If he had not discouraged Changlin from training his Dan fishermen, it was exactly because he was aware of the risk. At that very moment divers may well have been practicing drilling holes in the hulls of old junks. The emperor took various precautions that testified to his anxiety. But while his correspondence implicitly recognized the sea power of the British, it emphasized their weakness on land.

England, however, was making great technical strides in land weaponry as well, and the day would come when London would have the resources to alter the course of Chinese history. Why hadn't Qianlong taken the trouble to test the rapid-fire cannon Macartney had given him and proposed to export to China? *Après moi, le déluge* is a highly implausible attitude for the sovereign of a state that had endured for millennia. Qianlong surely expected his descendants to reign for centuries over an immortal empire. Why, then, had he refused to supply his entire army with firearms? Perhaps he feared that such weapons would make future revolts more dangerous. Historically, after all, palace coups were the greatest peril faced by dynasties. But the more likely explanation is that he was instinctively repelled by novelty of any kind.

ONCE THEY PASSED the highlands of Shandong, the ambassador and his retinue discovered new and exciting vistas. "Continued our course on the canal," Macartney wrote on October 26, "which is now supplied from a very extensive lake on our left hand. . . . The prospect of it at sunrise was most delightful, the borders fringed with wood, houses, and pagodas on the sloping grounds behind, and the lake itself covered with numberless vessels crossing it in different directions, according to all the various modes of navigation that poles, paddles, oars and sails can supply. On our right are many villages on the bank, which is here and there pierced with sluices. . . . The weather has been uncommonly fine, neither too cold nor too warm, much like our mild October in England."[6]

The child was enchanted: "Today we found the canal to go through several pretty large but not deep lakes with several little islands, great numbers of fishing boats and an abundance of a beautiful flower (which we saw before near Peking) called the nenuphar [water lily]."[7] The weather, he writes, was "warmer than before."[8]

On October 26 Macartney noted: "The idea of the great canal of Russia which at certain distances runs about parallel to the shores of the Ladoga and is filled from it seems to have been borrowed from hence."[9] The next day the canal crossed a great marsh, "above which it is raised and embanked by immense mounds of earth very high and very thick. It is a most stupendous work. . . ."[10]

Thomas was having fun: "I forgot to observe that we go day and night, which is easily accomplished by a continual and regular change of the trackers, who notwithstanding particular attention often run away and consequently delay the boats while they are getting others. This, however, only happened to some of the Mandarine and carriage boats."[11] The evacuation of the barbarians would suffer no delays. They were always the first to be assigned haulers.

Dinwiddie set his telescope into its tripod so that he could view more distant curiosities, but several times this instrument drove away crowds of Chinese who, convinced that the British were the world's fiercest people, took it for a cannon.[12] The mandarins persuaded the British to dismantle the instrument. The Chinese do not appreciate too sharp a gaze when the gaze is barbarian.

ON OCTOBER 28 young Staunton reports: "This morning we entered the province of Jiangsu. In some places the land was higher than usual, so they were obliged to cut several feet lower in the ground to be able to continue the canal. . . . It was very warm and comfortable today."[13] The embassy was introduced to bird fishing: the Chinese fished both with and for birds.

A variety of cormorant, a kind of white-throated brown pelican with a yellow beak and blue eyes, had been trained to fish. The lake was crowded with thousands of small boats or simple rafts, each one bearing a man and up to a dozen fishing birds. "On a signal from their master, they dive and shortly emerge from the water with enormous fishes in their beaks." Ropes were tied around the birds' necks to prevent them from swallowing, until eventually they were trained not to devour any prey without permission. If a fish was too heavy for a single bird, a second would help out. The fishermen had no equipment except their boats, which were light enough to be carried on their shoulders. This technique of fishing was so effective that "possession of a cormorant was subject to exorbitant taxes payable to the Emperor."[14]

While the cormorants hunted for fish, the fishermen hunted cormorants. Both Stauntons found this amusing. The fishermen floated large gourds on the water, until the birds got used to them. Then they waded into the water with gourds on their heads and snuck up on the cormorants. They would grab one and pull it silently into the water, being careful not to alarm the others. The captured cormorants were stuffed into satchels, and the fishermen continued their hunt until the satchels were full.[15] This strange style of fishing is still practiced in many parts of China today. I have seen it myself in such scattered places as Ningbo, Zhejiang, Guilin, and Guangxi.

The British also saw another original technique, plank fishing: "To one side of a boat a flat board, painted white, is fixed, at an angle of about forty-five degrees, the edge inclining towards the water. On moonlight nights, the boat is so placed that the painted board is turned to the moon, from whence the rays of light striking on the whitened surface, give to it the appearance of moving water, on which the fish being tempted to leap as on their element, the boatman raising with a string the board, turns the fish into the boat."[16]

If the Chinese were ingenious in devising techniques for catching fish, it was out of necessity.[17] The British, famous even then for their roast beef, were struck by the scarcity of meat. China raised very little livestock. "The beasts find asylum only in the mountainous districts, where the labor of farming would be exhausting and futile. No good land is devoted to pasturage."[18] Barrow affirms that the Chinese made no effort whatever to improve the breeds of their livestock. "They have no knowledge of the modes of improvement practised in the various breeds of cattle."[19]

The "common people have little opportunity of ever tasting [the meat of farm animals], unless of such as die by accident or disease. In such cases, the appetite of a Chinese surmounts all scruple."[20]

Even today, the Chinese have a horror of rare steaks, preferring their meat well done, though they are none too exigent about exactly what is cooked. "Quadrupeds that can find some resources for subsistence about dwelling-houses, such as hogs and dogs, are the most common animal food, and are sold at the public markets. Persons not so opulent as to be delicate, are sometimes found to ransack every department of nature to satisfy their appetites. And even the vermin that prey upon uncleanly persons, have been known to serve as a prey in their turn to them."[21] Barrow confirms: "The highest officers of state make no hesitation of calling their attendants in public to seek in their necks for those troublesome animals, which, when caught, they very composedly put between their teeth."[22] Still true. Ah Q, a character in a story by Lu Xun, complained that fate had unjustly visited fewer fleas upon him than upon his neighbors, thus giving him less to eat.[23]

The members of the embassy noted that Chinese vegetable production was quite well organized, while meat production lagged. The Chinese, Staunton comments, "have no conception of any thing beyond a moderate subsistence. The spirit of gain by working on an extensive plan, and by new methods, for supplying multitudes with a particular article, is not prevalent among the Chinese, unless in large and maritime towns. Some there are, however, in almost every village, who seek to accumulate wealth by taking advantage of the wants of the people round them. Shops for lending money upon pledges, are common everywhere. Very high interest upon loans is allowed by law."[24]

The exploitation of poverty by usurers was all China knew of capitalism. Even this, however, was not really capitalism, but its opposite: money was made not to be invested but to be spent.

If a merchant amassed a fortune, his immediate descendants would use it to acquire rank, spending fabulous sums in an endless quest for social prestige. This particular feature of Chinese life, inimical to capitalism, was compounded by two additional obstacles to development, one psychological, the other social: the traditional preference for investment in land and the surfeit of manual labor. In the West the development of machinery outstripped population growth, thus permitting savings of both time and labor. But since China's demographic growth occurred well before the introduction of machinery, the availability of cheap, superabundant labor tended to curb the search for labor-saving techniques.[25] The perspicacious Barrow noted: "The great advantages attainable from the use of mechanical powers are either not understood or, purposely, not employed. In a country of such vast population, machinery may perhaps be considered as detrimental."[26]

Except during famines, the Chinese did manage to survive. But their system did not lend itself to development. It was an economy that would never really get off the ground, but no one took that amiss. Confucius, after all, spoke "rarely" of "profit," while celebrating "culture" and the centrality of "the rites."[27] And as the British observed, these were not exactly the engines of progress.

57

Qianlong's Wrath

(October 28–November 1, 1793)

ON OCTOBER 28 Songyun received a short, placid message from the emperor. The eviction of the embassy was proceeding smoothly. They would embark in Zhoushan and sail on to Canton, where, under unobtrusive surveillance, they would rejoin their compatriots. But Qianlong was still haunted by one obsession: "Changlin, who will by then have arrived in Guangdong at a forced march, must apply himself to neutralizing any possible collusion between the British and the other Western Barbarians."[1]

The viceroy of Zhejiang reassured the court: "I have instructed my officers to inspect the military posts situated along the delegation's route of march and to see to it that those which are in poor condition are immediately repaired."[2]

But bad news arrived on October 29. An imperial instruction, dated October 26 and dispatched to the convoy at top speed, informed Songyun that the commander of the Dinghai garrison had just reported that four of the British ships had raised anchor. The British officers had told him that they were leaving because of their serious concern for their sick sailors. Only the *Hindostan*, with its crew of 120 men, had stayed behind. Governor Jiqing, who sent this news to the court on October 18, claimed that the "great ship" had remained in Zhoushan as a personal concession to him from Gower. The emperor lost his temper:

> First the English asked to remain in Zhoushan to care for their sick, and now they claim to be leaving because of these same sick men! More abrupt reversals so typical of Barbarians! Let Songyun inform the envoy that a ship is still waiting for him in Zhoushan! The governor of Zhejiang has visited the site in person and confirms that the remaining ship is large enough to accommodate the entire delegation. If the envoy claims that the ship is too small and uses this as a pretext for delay, Songyun shall dissuade him most energetically.

The English Barbarians have not obtained satisfaction; they are crafty and sly, and they may attempt to take revenge for their failure. We must guard against that possibility. Their country is very far away, separated from the Empire by great oceans. If they seek to cause incidents, it will take them two or three years to do so. The envoy has seen our strength and determination. For the moment, it is sufficient to guarantee the defense of our coasts and ports. Unless you are otherwise instructed, there is no reason to enroll the Dan divers in military units. They know nothing of the craft of weaponry and are at present usefully practicing their trade at home.[3]

The insistence with which the emperor keeps coming back to his fear of reprisals demonstrates that he was well aware of British naval and military superiority, even if he would not acknowledge it openly. Anxious to get rid of these barbarians as quickly as possible, he seized upon Jiqing's suggestion that the *Hindostan* alone could carry the entire embassy to Canton.

Songyun duly informed the envoy of the situation. Macartney was indignant: it was out of the question to sail on the *Hindostan*. "Thus," he wrote, "from the suspicious character of the Court which is so disposed to imagine some deep design in almost every proceeding of an European, we are now very seriously disappointed. Sir Erasmus Gower, hearing nothing from me, and knowing nothing of the state of things in Europe, is gone to the eastward and will not return before May."[4]

Gone to the eastward. In other words, to Japan. Macartney assumed that Sir Erasmus was carrying out the instruction he himself had been given, which he had formally delegated to Gower should appropriate circumstances arise. Gower, in turn, must have assumed that the ambassador would be spending the winter and spring in Peking. If he returned from Japan only in May, the missed connection in Zhoushan could be catastrophic for the return trip: "Our valuable China ships must therefore sail home without a convoy which, should we have a French war, would be attended with very great danger."[5]

Macartney was making a number of gloomy assumptions, among them that the Chinese, with their usual suspicion, had held up his second letter to Gower just as they had the first, and that it had therefore arrived too late. We now have evidence that he was right about this.

Macartney's letter, which left Peking on October 4, should have reached the new viceroy of Zhejiang on October 8 or 9. Only a deliberate delay can account for its failure to arrive in Dinghai before the sixteenth. Now that they had sailed, no imperial messenger could possibly catch up to the *Lion* and the three brigs.

It is not impossible that the viceroy of Zhejiang deliberately let the *Lion* leave, knowing that the *Hindostan* would not cast off without its captain. He may also have believed, in good faith, that the entire embassy could fit aboard the remaining ship. That would be killing two birds with one stone. He would get rid of the *Lion*, an impressive and dangerous warship, and would soon be rid of the rest of the embassy as well, gaining both time and money. This honorable mandarin was so unschooled in naval affairs that he was not even able to identify the *Hindostan* correctly: "It is the ship on which the envoy and his second arrived," Jiqing wrote on October 28. "This vessel is as vast as can be."[6]

Qianlong was too angry even to consider his next moves. He could not understand how these ships could have cast off on their own initiative: "What kind of institutions do these Englishmen have?"

This was the major diplomatic incident of Macartney's return trip, and it was caused primarily by the zigzags and prevarication of mandarins terrified at the prospect of an imperial rebuke. The memoranda, imperial rescripts, and instructions constantly contradicted themselves. The court began by putting pressure on the ships to leave, but then decided that if they stayed a little longer, the envoy could quit the empire sooner.

Macartney's refusal to embark on the *Hindostan* infuriated the emperor, who never imagined that he would be defied so openly. Having assumed that the embassy was as good as gone, he had treated the British to one final token of his benevolence: "The envoy should be at sea on [the lunar] New Year's Day [February 1, 1794]. We are therefore sending him a Fu [happiness] character for his king, written in our own hand, and another for himself and his officers, since they will be spending the year at sea."[7] But now British obstinacy had upset these calculations. The ambassador's journey would last twice as long as expected and would cost twice as much.

For his part, Songyun did his very best to convince Macartney, "summoning the tributary envoy to my junk" and telling him of the departure of his ships and of the emperor's wish that he embark on the remaining vessel. The barbarian objected that "he and his retinue had arrived on five ships and that it was impossible for them to leave on a single vessel, despite their great desire to return home."[8]

The Grand Councillor pointed out that "Governor Jiqing had personally confirmed that the ship was large enough." The envoy replied "that he was aware of his ships' capacity" and that the embarcation of too many men "would lead to a recrudescence of illness; all the members of the embassy would perish." And: "He added, his voice choked by sobs: 'We entreat the Emperor to allow us to travel to Canton over land; such exceptional grace would spare our lives. Let us abandon the heavy baggage in Zhoushan, with part of our retinue. We would never forget this favor, as high as Heaven and as deep as the Earth.' His tears were sincere: this was not a pretext for procrastination. I await Your orders with deference."[9]

Was Songyun trying to mollify his master by claiming that a tearful Macartney had begged to be allowed to proceed to Canton over land? The alleged scene does sound more Chinese than British. But there must have been two delicate conversations one right after the other, because Thomas writes, on the same day: "Today the great mandarine Songyun went aboard Lord Macartney's junk and had a pretty long conversation with him."[10]

What accounts for Macartney's rapid change of heart? At first he had been anxious to embark in Zhoushan, but now he "begged" to be allowed to continue to Canton on the riverine route. Once again the silver-tongued Thomas reveals his lordship's true feelings: "Today we were very sorry to hear that the *Lion* and brigs had left Zhoushan."[11] The "very sorry" would tend to confirm that the British were sincere: they really had hoped to cast off from Zhoushan.

But now Macartney was just as determined as he had been about the kowtow: he would go on to Canton by the river route. Why was he so insistent on flouting imperial injunctions? Surely not, as he claimed, simply to avoid the discomfort of cramming the embassy's personnel onto a ship designed to carry goods and not passengers. The spacious *Hindostan*, pride of the company fleet, was outfitted with comfortable cabins. If it was really too small to accommodate the entire embassy, Macartney and the other gentlemen could have gone aboard while sending the soldiers, musicians, servants, and other supernumeraries to Canton by the canals.

But that idea never even occurred to him. Only one explanation seems plausible: Macartney did not want to miss the chance of spending another forty days in the company of one of the leading figures of the state. He wanted to prolong the contacts he had managed to establish during this lengthy journey with Songyun, especially since it was now proposed that Prince Changlin, the new viceroy of Guangdong and therefore the chief interlocutor for the company and the British merchants in the years to come, should accompany him.

Though the ritual embassy had failed, the real embassy could continue. Macartney was seeking close and amiable contact with court personalities who might be persuaded to look more favorably on British requests—just the sort of diplomatic activity an ambassador would normally conduct among a sovereign's entourage in Europe. Had he been seeking rest and personal comfort, he would have completed the brief journey to the *Hin-*

dostan and sailed for Canton. But concern for his mission impelled him to take the fullest possible advantage of the unexpected opportunity now open to him.

Meanwhile, the smooth Songyun sought to placate both Qianlong and Macartney, inventing British tears for the former and imperial smiles for the latter. Macartney fell for it. On October 31 he wrote that Songyun "made me a visit" to report that the emperor had explained "in his last dispatch" that "the more he reflected on the circumstances of the Embassy, the better he was pleased with it, being now convinced that it had not been sent from any improper views or mischievous curiosity, but solely to do him honour and solicit commercial privileges and protection."

Macartney took advantage of these fine words to reiterate his request for a third letter. Songyun replied that he had written to the court about this matter but that he did not expect that the emperor would act "contrary to usage." Moreover, it was Qianlong's "style to give general assurances, not specific promises."[12]

Songyun's report of this interview was rather less mellow. He surmised that increasingly strict orders would come down from Peking, and indeed, on November 1 the emperor instructed him to tell the envoy: "There is no question of granting you in Huangpu* the favor the Empire earlier bestowed upon the Portuguese in Macao. The English may not build houses there, nor forts armed with cannon. Ships may gather there in autumn. That is the custom; to ask more would run counter to the Empire's institutions." This firm response, Qianlong noted, "will dissuade the envoy from renewing his troublesome requests."[13]

"I went aboard the envoy's junk several times out of concern for his illness," Songyun wrote to Qianlong.[14] Macartney makes no mention of any illness. Was the Grand Councillor inventing an excuse to prevent the emperor from chiding him for having lost face by visiting the envoy's junk? "I emphasized that his requests contravened the Empire's institutions and that he therefore need not fear that his king might blame him for having failed. But, I added: the Barbarians of your nation will always be treated equitably in Macao."

According to Songyun, Macartney replied: "Our king, motivated by sincere admiration, will not fail to rejoice at the protection the Great Emperor has been kind enough to bestow upon our trade in Macao. We are reassured about this. Changlin will not fail to foster our trade in Macao. But we also know that if any incidents occur, he will act harshly." Next

---

* An island in the Pearl River about ten miles downstream from Canton. It served as a moorage for foreign ships.

"the envoy confessed his past errors, promising that the Barbarian merchants of his nation would no longer dare to provoke incidents."[15]

Songyun then said to the envoy: "How can you so readily demand a new imperial edict?" At this rhetorical question Macartney "bowed," acknowledging that in light of Songyun's explanations, he "would soon be completely cured of his malady. When he mentioned Your Imperial Majesty, his face assumed a joyful expression. The recognition and reverence expressed by the Barbarians seemed to me even more sincere than before. When I present them with the Fu character drawn in Your own hand and the ceremonial robe for their king, they will immediately redouble their expressions of gratitude, so great is Your Majesty's bounty."[16]

Qianlong's only marginal note to this report, which he received the following week, is illegible. But that matters little. What could he have possibly said in reply to the echo of his own voice?

58

A Rooster Sacrificed

(November 2–6, 1793)

ON NOVEMBER 2 the flotilla sailed into the Yellow River. "The canal . . . now . . . brought us to a very large city, where we came to an anchor at six o'clock in the morning, having passed a fort at the entrance, by which the fleet had been saluted." An "inconceivable number of junks . . . were moored at its quays and wharfs."[1]

What city was it? Anderson could find no one to tell him, but Thomas's journal gives us the answer: Qingjiang.[2]

The fleet "entered the bay, with an alarming rapidity, through a large lock."[3] The flotilla now had to cross the Yellow River and then follow its turbulent current downstream to a new section of the Grand Canal farther south. It was a perilous maneuver, and the sailors wanted to appease the river god before attempting it.

"For this purpose, the master, surrounded by the crew of the yacht, assembled upon the forecastle and holding, as a victim, in his hand a cock, wrung off his head, which committing to the stream, he consecrated the vessel with the blood spouting from the body, by sprinkling it upon the deck, the masts, the anchor, and the doors of the apartments."[4] Why a rooster? Perhaps because the Chinese word *ji* means both "rooster" and "favorable." If so, the fortuitous pun cost the poor bird its life.

Next "large bowls filled with meat" were set on the deck, "before which had been placed a cup filled with oil, another of tea, a third of brandy, and a fourth of salt." The pilot kowtowed, holding his hands aloft and murmuring prayers.

During this ceremony a gong was rung and sticks of incense and sheets of silverfoil and tinfoil were burned; fireworks were also set off. The pilot then poured the oil, tea, brandy, and salt into the river. "All the ceremonies being over, and the bowls of meat removed, the people feasted on it; and launched afterwards, with confidence, the yacht into the current. As soon as she had reached the opposite shore, the captain returned thanks to heaven, with three inclinations of the body."[5]

But God helps those who help themselves, so in addition to performing this ritual, the Chinese also made every effort to counter the violence of the current. "Some [junks] stemmed the stream without losing much ground; while others were hurried by it with rapidity to a considerable distance below the opposite point, and were obliged to be tracked back with no little human labour."[6]

On that day, as the flotilla was crossing the river, the emperor was informed that the envoy had refused to embark on the one ship remaining in Zhoushan. After a brief and final burst of rage, Qianlong resigned himself to the change in plans: "Let Songyun tell the envoy that, as a token of my distinguished kindness, I grant him permission to bring his baggage and a part of his retinue aboard in Dinghai, while he himself may continue to Canton over land, escorted by Changlin."

Although he was once more giving ground, the emperor could not resist treating the British to a short lecture: "Let Songyun say to the envoy: 'Never does one of our ships cast off or drop anchor without having been ordered to do so. Were such a thing to occur, those responsible would be severely punished. What laws have you and what is your system of government that you are unable to make your sailors obey you?' Finally, let Songyun also say to the envoy: 'Inform your king of this insubordination, and may the guilty ones be punished.' "[7]

The British must not escape Chinese justice, neither in China (their impertinent request notwithstanding) nor after returning home. The barbarian would have his way again, but let him at least be advised that he was still no more than a barbarian.

ON NOVEMBER 3 they passed through Qingjiang, "an immense town; from its extent on both sides of the water and the prodigious number of vessels and people, I should suppose it to be nearly equal to Tientsin."[8] South of the Yellow River the junks were carried along by a swift current.

The land became so marshy that agriculture would have been impossible without Chinese ingenuity. "They forms rafts or hurdles of bamboo, which they float upon the water, or rest upon morasses: on these rafts they spread a layer of soil, from whence they raise various kinds of vegetables, in like manner as successful attempts are made, in miniature, to produce small vegetables on ship-board by laying seeds on moistened soil, or even on pieces of flannel, placed in frames, and wetted."[9]

They left the province of Shandong and entered Jiangsu. To this point the haulers, like all the peasants, had been dressed in the universal ragged blue cotton. But when the British crossed the provincial border, fresh haulers arrived wearing conical caps and brand new clothes with red trim. Was the viceroy of this province, who had been instructed not to greet the envoy,[10] doing honor to the embassy or to the imperial banner flying from the masts of the junks?

The ambiguous homage was accompanied by noisy music.[11] Thomas noticed tea growing on the hillsides, and he reports that he was given ewe's milk, "which we found like cream."[12]

These regions were the empire's richest, and the barbarians were able to take some measure of their prosperity, albeit only from their boats. When a few of the embassy personnel tried to slip ashore, they were seized *manu militari* and escorted back to their junks. The Grand Councillor assured Staunton that these "strict rules were motivated purely by concern for our safety."

On the evening of November 4 they arrived in Yangzhou, which young Staunton had been told was "very famous in China for its size and the beauty of its buildings." Unfortunately, he could see nothing but the walls bordering the canal. "We were saluted with near 250 soldiers, some with bows and arrows, others with matchlocks."[13] But the boy was not unduly impressed by this display of the Celestial armed forces.

At dawn on November 6 the flotilla reached the Yangtze, or Blue River, which was even mightier than the Yellow but equivalent in color despite its name. "In order to gain the canal on the other side of the Yangtze, the yachts sailed a little way along the northern shore of that great river. ... The waves rolled like those at sea, and porpoises are said to be sometimes seen leaping amongst them."[14]

Just outside the city of Zhenjiang, Macartney was struck by a landscape that seemed to have come straight out of a Chinese painting. In the middle of the river stood an enormous "conical rock"; "from the water's edge to the top" it was covered with "temples, turrets and belvederes on regular terraces or stories one above the other, intermixed with evergreen trees of various volumes and shades of verdure."* It looked like "a fairy edifice suddenly raised upon the river by the magic of an enchanter." Macartney sketched it in his notebook and added that the people called it "the Golden Mountain." He announced that he was "now inclined to think" that "the extravagant paintings of China fans and screens" had "been done from real views and not from the fancy of the artist."[15]

On that same day the emperor issued another instruction for Songyun,

---

* Tourists today can climb this Jinshan, or Golden Mountain, and visit the pagoda at its peak.

Changlin, and Jiqing: "The envoy, claiming fear of illness, has begged to be given permission to continue to Canton by the river route. If he respectfully insists on this, it is difficult to refuse the request. This will entail some additional expense, but no more. The Barbarians will recognize this as yet another token of Our benevolence."[16]

Money isn't everything. The court had spent five weeks deciding on the itinerary by which the barbarians would leave the empire, but in the end Qianlong yielded to Macartney's persistence.

THE CELESTIAL INTELLIGENCE system functioned as smoothly as the automatons the emperor so admired. "On November 5 the delegation sailed into the Blue River. The Barbarians did not go ashore in any place where they might have encountered the population. Viewing the multiplicity of fields and the luxuriance of the people and things, they contemplated with admiration this tableau of Great Peace."[17]

In Zhenjiang they were treated to a vast military display. But Macartney noted that the city walls were "much out of repair and going fast to decay," which tended to undermine the impressive deployment of some two thousand soldiers on parade, with banners and music. Their weaponry consisted of bows and arrows, halberds, lances, swords, and a few matchlocks. From a distance, their helmets gleamed like metal, but Macartney suspected that they were "only of burnished leather or glittering pasteboard." Their uniforms were "very showy," but the troops had a "slovenly, unmilitary air," and their "quilted boots and petticoats" made them "look heavy, inactive and effeminate."[18]

Wang explained that these ceremonial uniforms were used only "on great holidays and occasions like this." The helmets, he said, were "merely for show and . . . too heavy to be used on active service." Macartney asked to see one close up, but permission was denied. Defense secrets.

The Celestial officers, however, were in deadly earnest about this demonstration. Not a hair was out of place. General Wang Bing, commander of the brigade, wrote to the court: "All the military units behaved with discipline and seriousness. The tributary envoy and his retinue were quite impressed."[19] Mission accomplished.

Far from feeling intimidated, the British took this display as evidence that a landing would easily succeed. In fact, they were so sure of this that half a century later they were surprised when they encountered valiant resistance in some places. In the middle of the Blue River is an island called Jiaoshan. Visitors today can still admire its fortifications, from which the British were repelled during the Opium War in a military exploit now commemorated by a quotation from Friedrich Engels, another invader who conquered China with more subtle weapons.

Why was it that the Chinese preferred their crude muskets to the more advanced rifles in use throughout Europe? When Barrow asked Wang this question, the military mandarin replied that in Tibet these rifles had proved less effective than the muskets. The "superior steadiness of the fire from the matchlocks," Barrow retorted, "might possibly be owing to their being fixed, by an iron fork, into the ground." But he had no illusions. "It is difficult to combat prejudices."[20] In this case the British had little interest in doing so.

Wang and Qiao explained that the omnipresent army, immersed among the Chinese people, included a million infantrymen and 800,000 cavalry. Barrow was skeptical, but both mandarins, speaking separately, gave identical figures. They estimated the population at 330 million and the annual state revenue at the equivalent of 50 million or 60 million pounds sterling, of which 10 million went into the emperor's coffers, while 8 million was earmarked for military spending, a sum that would be adequate to maintain the level of forces cited by the mandarins.[21]

The precision of their statistics is somewhat surprising, but all signs are that they were accurate. If the imperial bureaucracy was aware of the doubling of the population under Qianlong, why did it fail to perceive the dangers of impoverishment and explosion? The government had exact figures, yet it remained immobile.

After calculating that China was "about eight times as big as France, infinitely more populous in comparison to its extent, far better cultivated and receiving annually for ages a great commercial balance in its favour," Macartney decided that the mandarins "may not be guilty of so much exaggeration" after all.[22]

But war seemed the furthest thing from the daily concerns of this army. Apart from the Tartar cavalry, which was deployed along the northern borders and in the conquered provinces, the Celestial troops functioned mainly as a police force. Some soldiers acted as jailers, others as lock keepers on the canal. Yet others collected taxes or guarded the public granaries, highways, rivers, and canals. ("These posts . . . are placed at the distance of three or four miles asunder. At one of these posts there are never fewer than six men.")[23] In other words, for the most part they were adjuncts of the civil administration.

When all was said and done, these recruits—unlike the Manchu "banners"—were not really soldiers, but militiamen. The emperor gave them plots of land, and they married where they were stationed. And: "After the salutes were over, the gaudy dresses or uniforms of the soldiers, . . . together with their arms, were said to be deposited in the storehouse . . . until they should again be wanted. . . . They certainly thus become more useful in time of peace; but must have less of the spirit and discipline which fit for scenes of war."[24]

Apart from being responsible for their own uniforms and horses, these soldiers also had to provide for their families' subsistence, which military pay was inadequate to secure.[25] They were less warriors than peasants. Barrow remarked that some of them saluted Macartney with their fans instead of their muskets. They remained seated or crouched until their officers ordered them to stand. "Whenever we happened to take them by surprise, there was the greatest scramble to get their holiday dresses out of the guard-house, which, when put on, had more the appearance of being intended for the stage than the field of battle."[26]

There is a very old Chinese proverb that says a lot about the role of this rabble soldiery and the low esteem in which it was held: "There is no point in using fine iron to make nails."

For actual combat the emperor relied not on these mediocre "nails," but on his Manchu "banners," a war machine about which Macartney gathered as much information as he could. These military companies had been organized at the beginning of the seventeenth century by Nurhaci, the founder of the dynasty. They were called banners because each detachment was known by the color of its standard: yellow, white, blue, or red. Posted at strategic locations in the country, they were the backbone of the Chinese armed forces. The hereditary members of these banners, like the nobles of feudal Europe, were exempt from all labor and duties —except for the shedding of blood.[27]

If the banners were the regime's elite corps, they were also a nation in arms—a very small nation whose 300,000 members had subjugated 300 million Chinese. Neither Alexander, nor Rome, nor Spain had done as much. In fact, Britain in India provided the only comparable numerical disparity between a conquered nation and its conquerors: a thousand to one. Each banner was commanded by a Tartar-Manchu general, and nearly every Manchu male was a soldier. In fact, they were rarely permitted to practice another profession. There were no Manchu craftsmen or peasants, and certainly no Manchu merchants. The only other position a Manchu could hold was that of mandarin. Another form of service to the same supreme power.

59

China's Paradise: Suzhou

(November 7, 1793)

"IT HAD BEEN a very foggy night," Anderson writes, "and the weather continued to be hazy till ten o'clock, when the fog cleared away, and a fine day succeeded, which unfolded to the view a charming and fertile country, bounded by hills, whose summits were crowned with pagodas."[1] Macartney mentions "a very noble bridge of three arches, the centre one so high that my yacht had no occasion to lower her masts in going under it." This was not always the case. Winder explained that the junks often had two masts, and that in places where there were many bridges, the boatmen would dismantle the main mast and raise the second, which was mounted on hinges so that it could be lowered and raised instantaneously.[2]

The population, however, "looked dispirited."[3] The people of this province had never recovered from the transfer of the capital from Nanking to Peking three centuries earlier. The entire Jiangnan region had suffered from the move, and Macartney noted that only the most compelling political considerations could have induced the emperor to move the capital north, nearer the Tartar lands, since Jiangnan was one of the most beautiful of the empire's provinces, having a most pleasant climate and very fertile soil.

That evening the flotilla reached the city of Suzhou. Young Staunton describes the mutual curiosity of the travelers and the native onlookers: "The houses are built to the edge and sometimes even some way into the water upon stakes or piles. Immense crowds of people, both men and women, were collected at the doors and windows of the houses and even in the boats and junks to see us."[4]

The amazed page notes that "this evening we saw a very long bridge . . . of above 90 small arches."[5] "It happened to catch the attention of a Swiss servant," said Barrow, "who, as the yacht glided along, began to count the arches, . . . [until] he ran into the cabin, calling out with great eagerness, 'For God's sake, gentlemen, come upon the deck, for here is a bridge such as I never saw before; it has no end.'" The arches, running parallel to the Grand Canal, seemed to bound ahead into infinity, disappearing into the darkness of the night. Actually, this was not a bridge but a kind of causeway that enabled junks to enter a large contiguous lake by passing under the road bordering the canal. "I lament exceedingly," commented Barrow, "that we passed this extraordinary fabric in the night. . . . From the highest point, or what appeared to us to be the central arch, I counted forty-five to the end."[6]

This structure, known as the Bridge of the Precious Belt, is still intact. It was built under the Tangs, a thousand years before the British saw it.

HAVING LITTLE to do or even to see, our travelers put their imaginations to work. Suzhou was known as "China's Venice," not only because of its canals, bridges, and "gondolas," but also "because of the pleasures it offers," at least in those places "where the painted boats sail and the flutes and drums resound, where all the city's courtesans and singers gather."[7]

The austere Staunton found he liked the women here: "The gentlemen of the Embassy also thought the women of Suzhou handsomer, fairer, and dressed in better taste, than most of those they had seen to the northward. . . . The ladies . . . are sometimes distinguished by a small cap on the forehead brought down to a peak between the eye-brows. . . . They likewise wear ear pendants of chrystal or gold."[8] The seven traditional charms of Chinese women were listed for him: "The winning eye, the honey mouth, the supple waist, the nimble foot, the modest profile, the graceful neck, the tapered nails."[9]

Their mandarin guides taught the British a proverb that can still be heard today: "Marry in Suzhou, eat in Canton, die in Lanzhou." In another forty days a series of banquets would let them test the truth of the second stage of this ideal itinerary. Lanzhou, they were told, produced a high-quality wood that made the best coffins, though this did not tempt them to test the third stage. As for Suzhou, they soon realized that marriageable women were by no means the sole attraction of this town.

On the outskirts of the city lay the "beautiful lake of Taihu, surrounded by a chain of picturesque hills." The inhabitants of Suzhou fished in the lake, but most of all it was a "place of public resort and recreation. Many of the pleasure boats were rowed each by a single female. Every boat had a neat and covered cabin; and the rowers were supposed to follow more than one profession."[10]

These "painted boats," floating facilities for sexual encounters, are widely celebrated in Chinese popular literature. The British, now in the middle of a two-year journey without women, must have done considerable daydreaming as their junks glided past these gondolas. But their virtue was not to be tested, for they were not given time to stop.

Hüttner, the pedagogue, questioned his Chinese guides about accounts given by the missionaries, and he learned that Suzhou was "the stopping place of the richest merchants and the training ground of the greatest artists and most skillful actors. It determines the patterns of Chinese taste and boasts of the most beautiful women, the smallest female feet, and the latest fashions. It is the site of the most voluptuous licentiousness and serves as a rendezvous for all the libertines of China. The Chinese have a saying: 'Above us stands paradise; here below lies Suzhou.' "[11]

The houses of the merchants were more beautiful here than elsewhere. But some of them were "abandoned," their inhabitants "spending all their time" on the varnished gondolas that plied the lake day and night, carrying flower-girls whose bloom revealed their station. The rich dissipated fortunes in these girls' arms. Indeed, not a few wealthy merchants, having come to Suzhou to peddle their wares, were soon "reduced to beggary, so lavishly did they indulge in the pleasures here offered."[12]

Dinwiddie put his telescope to work, focusing on the oarswomen perched on the prows and poops. "Here girls in neat attire and the handsomest I yet saw," Winder writes, "steered and sculled the pleasure boats."[13] Hüttner's view was sharper: "A glass-enclosed room in the center of a gondola occasionally offered a glimpse, through gauze, of young people playing music while reclining on sofas strewn with cushions, in the company of scantily clad females far too gay to be accounted decent, pupils of the academy for which this city has long been famous, for in this land, as in all of Asia, the pleasures of the flesh are an object of study and, moreover, a branch of trade."[14]

Oarswomen row similar black-lacquered, flower-painted boats in Suzhou and Hangzhou today. They are still pleasing to the eye, skilled in their sculling, and cheerful in their commentary, but there is never the slightest doubt of their morality. Until 1949 they practiced quite different skills and offered a wide variety of types, from proud waterborne courtesans to poverty-stricken girls making three-sapek propositions while pulling at the oars.

It is true that the art of love has long been cultivated throughout the Far East, partly as a counterweight to the constraints of arranged marriages.[15] "Behind the gauze curtains and brocades of these meeting houses, the pleasures of love are harvested in profusion, for how can one know its sweetness without having great personal experience of it? And quite wrong it would be to believe that the ignorant rustic disbursing gold as though it were sand necessarily wins the lady whose eyes are most enchanting and whose spirit is superior." Unlike common prostitutes ("damaged goods coated with make-up and daubed with powder"),[16] these courtesans had to be *courted*, in accordance with strict rites, before they would yield.[17]

After many long months of abstinence and careful self-control, our travelers suddenly felt titillated. Recreation. A breath of spring.

60

Brides for Sale

(November 8, 1793)

"Is there no way at all to help your daughter?"
"She is their daughter-in-law; they are free to beat her and to
reprimand her as they wish. There is nothing I can say."

YE SHENGTAO, 1919[1]

HAVING BROACHED this intriguing subject, the British now widened their
inquiries, and they soon discovered that prostitutes were not the only
women in China who had a market price. "The instant a comely girl
appears under any household's roof," one Chinese storyteller wrote, "the
competition of engagement gifts begins. Her parents will give her to him
who pays the highest price."[2] The young girl had no choice: she was simply
awarded to the highest bidder. All Chinese women, regardless of their
social status, were sold, whether by the hour or for life.

Barrow noted that "the man, . . . in this respect, has no great advantage
on his side, as he is not allowed to see his intended wife until she arrives
in formal procession at his gate. If, however, on opening the door of the
chair, in which the lady is shut up, and of which the key has been sent
before, he should dislike his bargain, he can return her to her parents; in
which case the articles are forfeited that constituted her price; and a sum
of money, in addition to them, may be demanded, not exceeding, however,
the value of these articles."[3]

Barrow found it hard to understand these marital arrangements, in
which sentiment played no part. Marriages of convenience were still the
rule in most of Europe at the time, but in Britain they were declining in
favor of marriages of choice. "No previous conversation is allowed to take
place, no exchange of opinions or comparison of sentiments with regard
to inclinations or dislikes; all the little silent acts of attention and kindness,
which so eloquently speak to the heart, and demonstrate the sincerity of
the attachment, are utterly unfelt. . . . The man takes a wife because the
laws of the country direct him to do so, and custom has made it indis-

pensable."[4] Anyone still a bachelor beyond the age of twenty was scorned as a male old maid.[5]

Confucian society denied women nearly all rights save one: to be married and thereby to be granted the chance of giving birth to boys, the sole path to power for a woman.

In her husband's home, Barrow writes, the newly married young woman becomes first of all "the same piece of inanimate furniture she was in her father's house."[6] A disdainful Father Huc later wrote: "To beat one's wife is considered such good form that any husband would be wary of failing to do so, lest he compromise his dignity and appear foolish."[7]

But revenge, too, was a Chinese dish, and our travelers might have had a less one-sided view of the battle of the sexes had they been able to read Chinese tales about the misadventures of husbands beaten by their wives.[8] The most agreeable form of revenge, however, was infidelity, and Chinese literature abounds in satires that sound as if they came out of *Così fan tutte* or *Rigoletto*:

> Woman is as fluid as water,
> Ever ready to deceive her husband.[9]

That particular theme is common to all cultures, but there was a more original factor that eluded the British: every young wife is a servant to her mother-in-law. When a young woman enters a new family in China, she is more daughter-in-law than wife. The Chinese do not say *take a wife*, but *take a daughter-in-law*.[10]

The young husband's subordination to his parents prevents him from taking his wife's side against his mother, and the wife has more obligations to her in-laws than to her husband. Only time inverts this situation: the daughter-in-law herself becomes a mother-in-law. These are the three stages in a Chinese woman's life—child, daughter-in-law, and mother-in-law. Finally, as a grandmother, she becomes the household's most respected personage.[11]

The British did, however, notice polygamy, which was seen as part of the order of things. When a husband brings "a second, or a third woman" into the house, Barrow explains, the first feels no "jealousy or disturbance (at least it is prudent not to shew it)."[12] A judicious qualification, since silence does not efface bad feeling: "It is difficult for several spoons not to collide in the same cup of tea," comments one character in "Flower in a Flask of Gold."[13]

The idea of concubinage outraged Barrow, who had a cynical explanation for it: "Nor is any disgrace attached to the condition of a concubine, where every marriage is a legal prostitution."[14]

But polygamy, he observed, "is an evil that, in great degree, corrects itself. Nine-tenths of the community find it difficult to rear the offspring of one woman by the labour of their hands; such, therefore, are neither in circumstances, nor probably feel much inclination, to purchase a second. The general practice would, besides, be morally impossible. In a country where so many female infants are exposed, and where the laws or custom oblige every man to marry, any person taking to himself two wives must leave some other without one. . . . It is indeed among the upper ranks only and a few wealthy merchants (whom the sumptuary laws, prohibiting fine houses, gardens, carriages, and every kind of external shew and grandeur, have encouraged secretly to indulge and pamper their appetite in every species of luxury and voluptuousness) where a plurality of wives are to be found."[15] Father de Grammont plaintively attributed the low number of conversions to the fact that the Chinese were "mired in the morass of the pleasures of the flesh."[16]

"Every great officer of state," Barrow says, "has his haram consisting of six, eight, or ten women, according to his circumstances and his inclination for the sex. Every merchant also of Canton has his seraglio."[17] We now know that the sex lives of wealthy Chinese consisted of a great variety of diversions, mostly conducted in "remote apartments."[18] There were also countless "bedroom manuals": "Closely aligned one against the other, they detailed the twenty-four tableaus of the frieze, the various manners of springtime love being depicted with polished artistry. After filling their hearts with joy, they would abandon the armchair for the bed, there to test the excellence of these lessons on their own persons."[19]

Our travelers, poised midway between Merry England and Victorian Britain, were not quite sure whether to be outraged or jealous. But when they were told of the emperor's harem, with its hundreds of lovely women, they were most of all intrigued. How had he managed it, even at a much younger age?

They were unaware of Taoist physiological theories and their consequent sexual practices. According to this doctrine, the male principle, or *yang*, affords man an inexhaustible energy, but only under certain conditions. He must be in frequent contact with the feminine principle, the *yin*; he must absorb all the energy of the *yin* by bringing the woman to her own flowering; and he must conduct himself with the greatest concentration, never unleashing his own force. He thereby increases his longevity and reinforces his vigor.

By having frequent relations with many concubines without allowing himself to climax, the Chinese man can satisfy a large harem; in fact, he will be especially pleasing to his women, since their satisfaction is required for the reinforcement of his *yang*. When he decides to procreate, he will engender vigorous male heirs who will assure the continuity of familial worship.[20]

But the feminine *yin* has its own interest, contradictory to that of the masculine *yang*. It gains greater strength the more often the *yang* climaxes. Certain expert women are able to parry male maneuvers and bring their partners to abandon, thereby winning victory in this particular battle of the sexes: the energy of their *yin* is enriched by that of the *yang*.[21] Taoist tradition ascribes endurable magic to these women who are able to "harvest the fruits of the battle."[22]

SUZHOU WAS the capital not only of women but also of their most precious of wrappings: silk. The Grand Canal ran through many mulberry plantations, and one of the embassy's objectives was to gather information about silk production—cultivation of the mulberry tree, the raising of the moth, the unraveling of the cocoon—with a view to introducing it in India. But the Chinese were on the alert. Silk had been a state secret in the empire since ancient times, the property of the entire nation. Its revelation was punishable by death.

The countryside on either side of the canal was dotted with houses surrounded by vast fields of mulberry bushes. But most were stripped of their leaves. "The owners of the mulberries do not tend to the raising of the silkworms," Hüttner explains. "Instead they sell the leaves, by weight, to the inhabitants of the cities, and it is they who raise the worms."[23] The British were given no opportunity to take samples of the plants or the worms.[24] Silk would remain a mystery.

ON NOVEMBER 8 Songyun sent the emperor a report that was not at all to his liking.

> Your slave had strictly forbidden the envoy to continue to Canton on the river route. But the Barbarians were so distressed by this that I transmitted their entreaty to Your Majesty. The envoy has now humbly confessed his contrition for the deplorable disorders caused by the indiscipline of his sailors. When I was able to confirm the grace Your Holy Majesty has bestowed upon him, the envoy's face was illuminated with joy. He doffed his hat, bent his knee, and brimming with gratitude, declared: "The mercy the Emperor has shown us has saved our lives."

Nevertheless, while still on his knees, he added this indecent request: "We have little money with us. The ship still moored in Zhoushan is freighted with Western products. Might we exchange them for the promised tea and silk?"

Your slave immediately reiterated that there was no merchant guild in Ningbo, that nothing could be bought without money, and that it was necessary for them to repair to Macao or Huangpu, where His Majesty, in his infinite grace, would exceptionally permit duty-free trade on this one occasion.

In the margin of this report the emperor wrote in his vermilion brush: BARBARIANS ARE NEVER SATISFIED.[25]

61

Glimmers in the Gloom

(November 8–11, 1793)

AFTER 475 MILES on the Grand Canal, the convoy approached Hangzhou, where Songyun was to be replaced by Changlin. Since the *Lion*'s unexpected departure and Macartney's refusal to embark on the *Hindostan* had upset the previous plans, it was now decided that the new viceroy of Canton, en route to take up his post, would accompany the embassy the rest of the way.

But first Songyun performed his final task: to predispose Macartney in Changlin's favor, by telling the ambassador that the emperor's designation of a man of Changlin's quality to the Canton post was a measure of his determination to establish better relations with the British merchants. Would this nomination be the sole concrete result of the embassy? In any event, Songyun's psychological ploy proved effective. It put some polish on Qianlong's image in Macartney's eyes, and the envoy began to harbor fresh hope, as is shown by the documents he now drafted for Captain Mackintosh to take back to London aboard the *Hindostan*.

Changlin, indeed, seemed to be the perfect man of the moment. The new viceroy of Guangdong was a Manchu and a relative of Qianlong's.[1] He had a reputation for righteousness, having recovered from the disgrace of his earlier efforts (in 1792) to absolve several people falsely accused of conspiracy by Heshen.*

The first contact between Macartney and Changlin was crucial, each seeking to take the other's measure. Imperial correspondence does not reveal what Changlin thought of Macartney (the Chinese tended not to set great store in psychological analysis, being far more inclined to moral

---

* Changlin remained in Canton for only fifteen months, and his career seems to have "received a setback at this time, possibly because of his brush with Heshen or because of his friendliness towards Macartney. However, after the death of Heshen he filled other great offices. He died in 1811."[2]

judgments), but Macartney, a good Westerner, carefully recorded his impressions and related their conversation in detail.

On the morning of November 9 the flotilla stopped near Hangzhou, and the viceroy's junk pulled alongside the ambassador's. After conferring with Songyun, Macartney says, Changlin came "to welcome us on our arrival here."*

The Briton was quite favorably impressed. Apart from his perfect manners, Changlin exuded frankness and distinction. A real gentleman. But what he had to say matched Songyun's comments word for word. Changlin reiterated that the emperor had instructed him "to pay the greatest regard to the English at Canton." He said that "on every occasion" they would have "free access to him in person or by letter."

It is hard to see how the Chinese managed not to laugh out loud at these Westerners, who seemed to combine the most sordid acquisitiveness with the most inane gullibility. The perfect gentleman now brimming with friendship for the British envoy was the same man who had recommended to Qianlong that Dan fishermen be taught to sabotage the barbarian ships.

Changlin ran through the customary banalities, noting that "it was very flattering to the Emperor to have an embassy sent to him from so great a distance" and that "the Emperor had charged him to repeat his satisfaction from it." He then gave Macartney a few more imperial gifts for his king: "some pieces of gold silk,† some purses taken from his own person and—what was of very high value—the 'paper of happiness' inscribed by the Emperor's own hand, which is known to be the strongest mark a Sovereign of China can give to another prince of his friendship and affection."[4] Here Macartney was almost certainly writing with his future British readers in mind. The "paper of happiness" was in fact just another Fu character drawn by the Celestial hand, a gesture none too costly to the emperor and a slender enough success for such a colossal enterprise as this embassy.

Moreover, it will be recalled that in Qianlong's mind this character, representing "good luck," was tantamount to a goodbye gift to the embassy,‡ which he had expected would embark from Zhoushan. The change in its itinerary lent the Fu character a somewhat comical aspect that eluded

---

* Young Staunton reveals that in fact it was Macartney who visited the viceroy.[3] No surprise there.

† According to the Imperial Archives, this was actually a ceremonial robe. Macartney either did not understand or could not bring himself to picture King George in Chinese dress.

‡ Scholars in Peking still give their diplomat friends handwritten copies of this character as goodbye gifts. On New Year's Day it is hung upside down on doors, to show that luck descends from Heaven.

Macartney. Nor did he realize that these gifts were supposed to have been given to him by Songyun, who, good comrade that he was, devolved the task to Changlin, thus enabling him to begin his new mission auspiciously.

One year later a Dutch ambassador, terribly mistreated and systematically humiliated, was also given a Fu character drawn in the emperor's own hand. It was meant as a gift for the king of Holland—though no such person existed.[5]

The convoy spent several days in Hangzhou, where the men and baggage were divided into two groups, one that would go on to Zhoushan with Captain Mackintosh and embark on the *Hindostan*, another that would accompany Macartney and Changlin to Canton.[6]

The *Hindostan* was waiting not only to take its captain on board, but also for authorization to barter for some local goods. The British assumed that since the ship was moored in a Chinese port, they might as well fill its holds. Who knows, it might even set a precedent. For their part, the Chinese realized that what was at stake here was not a few tons of tea, but a principle. Changlin therefore treated Macartney and Mackintosh to a glittering display of the art of evasion.

The merchants of Zhoushan, he explained, "were not accustomed, like those of Canton, to trade with Europeans and to purchase English goods; ... they were probably not at present provided with such articles as Captain Mackintosh might want, and . . . whatever they sold to him they would expect to be paid for in ready money"[7] (of which Changlin knew that the British had none). Macartney, probably at Mackintosh's urging, had proposed a swap. He did not make clear exactly what he wanted to trade for what, but the Grand Council archives ring with imperial indignation.

Qianlong took a personal interest in this affair, and he was most displeased by the excuse for the British offered up by Songyun:

"We had already authorized the Barbarians to purchase tea and silk in Ningbo. That is why, lacking cash, they now wish to exchange their goods for these products."

"This is truly contemptible," wrote Qianlong in the margin. "Let us tell them, yet again, that trade has always been conducted in Macao and Huangpu."[8]

But the wily emperor did authorize Heshen to suggest a compromise: "Let us relax the order and exceptionally allow the envoy to barter *a little* of his merchandise against the foodstuffs we have shipped to Ningbo. If, on the other hand, he seeks large quantities of them, then let us tell him that this is impossible, for it would contravene usage. Then have all the shipments of tea and silk earmarked for this transaction transferred to Macao."

Qianlong added: "If we were to heed them, they would make demands without limit."[9]

Changlin ran through the litany of objections that Macartney had already heard a hundred times from Songyun, and the ambassador finally let the matter drop. The administrative obstacles were insurmountable, and private individuals were powerless to act, since the "felonious merchants" had apparently been put out of commission. In any case, there was little point in trying to conclude private deals that the Celestial hierarchy would do its utmost to obstruct. Macartney therefore clung to the meager compensation that was offered him, the viceroy declaring that, as a very special favor, the *Hindostan* "would be exempt from the payment of measurage and duties at Canton."[10] Macartney was weary of the endlessly repeated ritual phrases and the ever-present meaningless smiles. Yet he told himself that these imperial favors, deviations (however slight) from the immemorial rules, did suggest that his embassy had not been wholly in vain and that it might be possible to introduce new practices little by little.

Thomas, who sensed how the ambassador and his own father felt, insisted: Changlin "was very civil and obliging."[11]

Macartney was certainly under the man's spell. He felt better and better about having insisted on traveling to Canton over land, sending only a part of the expedition home on the *Hindostan*. The prospect of several weeks in the company of the man on whom the fate of the Europeans in Canton and Macao would depend looked more and more like a serendipitous extension of his mission. One last chance to salvage his embassy.

THE NEXT DAY, November 10, the viceroy visited the ambassador again and picked up his usual refrain, repeating "in still stronger terms than yesterday the assurances and declarations of the Emperor's favour and of his own particular good wishes and disposition towards us." Macartney, ever the diplomat, sought to get something concrete out of these good dispositions. He now attacked on another front, expressing curiosity about the secrets of silk production. He had already asked "the people of my yacht what kind of mulberries chiefly grow here" and had been "informed by some that it was the red and by others the white." Which was it? The viceroy claimed complete ignorance of the subject. In his journal Macartney commented that the "shyness and jealousy of the Chinese in all matters where they observe us to be curious and inquisitive are inconceivably great."[12] They were constantly on their guard against espionage.

But Staunton apparently managed to ferret out some industrial secrets nevertheless. "The insects are nurtured in small houses erected for that purpose . . . in order to be retired from all noise, for the Chinese have an idea that even the barking of a dog will do some injury to the worms."[13] And further: "The insects are always suffocated before the silk is reeled off; for this purpose the cocoons or silk balls are placed in a basket, or in vessels pierced with holes, and exposed to the steam of boiling water. . . . After the silk is wound off, the aurelias furnish an article for the table."[14] If vermin were pleasing to Chinese palates, they could hardly be expected to resist the allure of the silk caterpillar.

Chinese suspicion of Western curiosity extended beyond silk production to include the city itself. In accordance with Qianlong's reiterated instructions—"No contact with the population; the Barbarians must never leave their junks"—the British spent the few days of their stay in Hangzhou confined to their boats. Truly these barbarians had no idea how much vermilion ink had flowed on their account.

Thomas's journal confirms the quarantine. "We did not come near the walls of the city but slept in the middle of the suburbs," he wrote on November 10.[15]

Sir George relates a significant incident. Some of the baggage meant for Canton was mistakenly loaded onto the junks headed for Zhoushan. Three Britons were sent to sort out the error, since they alone could identify the misplaced baggage. Accompanied by a mandarin and his servant, they set out on horseback, skirting the city to the east. A breath of freedom! When they reached the riverbank, they transferred to wagons, each drawn by three yoked buffalo led along by ropes piercing their nostrils. The teams of buffalo went as far into the river as they could, and the British then climbed out of the wagons and into a boat. On the other side of the river, palanquins were waiting to carry them to the Zhoushan canal.

On the return trip, the British mounted their horses and headed for Hangzhou at a full gallop. When they came within sight of the city walls, the mandarin following along behind them called out to the guards to close the gates. The British were then told that they could not be reopened, since only the governor had the keys. They therefore had to skirt the town again. But the order to close the gates had set off an alert, and Wang "laughed heartily at the idea of three Englishmen creating an alarm in one of the largest and strongest cities of the Chinese empire."[16]

The day after their arrival, however, Wang had taken Barrow and Mr. Plumb to have a look at the sites of embarkation south of Hangzhou, and they had crossed the city to get there. "They returned," writes Staunton junior, "with a very splendid account of the town and shops."[17] Their companions, who had had to stay aboard their junks, grew increasingly impatient at their seclusion.

HANGZHOU, the great hinge between north and south, lay between the Qiantang River and the Grand Canal and served as the point of passage for merchandise moving from the one to the other in either direction, "a circumstance which renders . . . [it] the general emporium for all articles that pass between the northern and southern provinces. Its population is indeed immense: and is supposed to be not very much inferior to that of Peking. It has . . . shops and warehouses; many not inferior to the most splendid of the kind in London. A brisk and extensive trade seems to be carried on in silks, and not a little in furs and English broad cloths."[18]

Countless inhabitants thronged the narrow streets, which were paved with broad, flat stones; the mere sight of the barbarians was enough to obstruct passage. The women were attractively but uniformly made up, the only variety being in the colors of their hats and of the flowers in their hair. They wore silk jerseys instead of shirts, fur-lined jackets, and baggy trousers, the entire outfit being covered by a long satin robe belted at the waist.

Chinese women "reckon corpulence a beauty in a man," but "they consider it as a palpable blemish in their own sex, and aim at preserving a thinness and delicacy of shape. They suffer their nails to grow, but reduce their eyebrows to an arched line."[19]

Alexander, the painter, described them this way: "The generality of females we had hitherto seen, certainly had no pretentions to beauty. The lower class are seen in crowds stumping along on their little feet, while those of the middle and superior orders are seldom seen except through the gauze blind of their windows, or when they sometimes venture to peep through them when nearly closed. Some of this description were seen at a distant habitation by means of a telescope; these appeared handsome, but possibly they owed much to the assistance of paint, which they use liberally, white and red."[20]

THEN AS NOW, tourism in China was never left to chance. Wang was kind enough to invite Mr. Barrow and several others for a ride on the Lake of the West in a "splendid yacht." Barrow notes: "Vast numbers of barges were sailing to and fro, all gaily decorated with paint and gilding and streaming colours; the parties within them apparently all in pursuit of pleasure. The margins of the lake were studded with light aereal buildings, among which one of more solidity and greater extent than the rest was said to belong to the Emperor."[21] Nothing has changed in this tableau, of which the *Chronique indiscrète des mandarins* affirmed, without much exaggeration: "The Lake of the West is the most beautiful landscape of mountains and waters under heaven."[22]

In the middle of the woods "several thousand tombs, generally built in the form of small houses, about six or eight feet high, painted mostly blue, and fronted with white pillars," formed little streets. "In this public burying place, a night seldom passes without a visit by persons accompanied by torches, to pay their respects to their deceased relations. . . ."[23]

Several pagodas stood at the crest of a mountain. One of them, built on the edge of a promontory, is known as the Pagoda of Thundering Winds. Its "top," Staunton reports, "was in ruins, . . . grass, shrubs, and mosses growing" upon it. "It is confidently asserted to have been erected in the time of Confucius."[24] This famous pagoda is the setting for the classical opera *The White Serpent.*

62

"Mollifying Them While Conceding Them Nothing"

(November 11–13, 1793)

IN HANGZHOU Macartney was given a letter from Erasmus Gower, the squadron commander. It had been written nearly a month earlier and explained the reasons for the *Lion*'s sudden departure from Zhoushan: the crew was "very sickly, . . . the surgeon and his first mate not being likely to recover." Moreover, "the ship was in such want of medicines, particularly of bark [quinine] and opium, that it became necessary to have a speedy supply of both." Gower had therefore decided to sail for Canton. He added that he would then return north "without delay."

This letter had obviously traveled at the same speed as the one informing Peking of the *Lion*'s departure, and Songyun had told Macartney about that two weeks ago. The ambassador attributed the delay in the delivery of Gower's letter to "the singular jealousy and suspicion of the Chinese Government."[1]

The British were not the only ones to suffer from the slowness of the normally efficient Chinese postal system. For the past two months Father Raux had been trying to establish contact with Fathers Hanna and Lamiot, who were still aboard the *Hindostan*. In the end he decided to write to them in Macao, inevitably their ultimate destination. "In August," he complained, "when you were so very near to us, I moved heaven and earth to obtain imperial authorization for your disembarcation. It was, however, suspected that you might be English, and I was therefore summoned to the Palace, where innumerable questions in your regard were put to me. . . . It was impossible for me to write to you aboard your vessel or to communicate with you through the returning embassy. . . . Father Amiot was taken from us suddenly during the night of the eighth and ninth of this month of October; pray for him in your masses. I trust that you are well; be gay, patient, and courageous."[2]

Poor Father Raux had spent many long years exhorting his colleagues to patience. On June 25, 1789, he had written, "I beseech you not to lose heart at the prospect of all the delays of the Chinese. These are indeed mortifying, yet ineluctable."[3]

But Gower's letter, tardy as it was, did bring some welcome news. Macartney was relieved to learn that the *Lion* had not sailed for Japan after all, and he immediately drafted a letter to a company representative in Canton asking that Gower be instructed "to remain off Macao till he either saw me or heard from me again." The viceroy promised to send that letter "this night by a special messenger."[4]

That was a promise kept, since Macartney's desire to hold the *Lion* in Canton tallied with the determination of the Chinese to be rid of the British as soon as possible. The authorities in Canton had already expressed concern that if the *Lion* left for Japan and "this delegation of a hundred men is unable to embark on the merchant ships now moored in Huangpu, they might seek to remain indefinitely." They had therefore taken the precaution of "dispatching a naval detachment to await the arrival of the English ships and to convey them to the moorage."* "Correct," Qianlong wrote in the margin when he received this message.[5] Everything was finally in place to get these barbarians out of China.

THOSE MEMBERS of the embassy who were to join the *Hindostan* in Zhoushan left Hangzhou on November 13, escorted by Songyun and Jiqing, the viceroy of Zhejiang, who were to supervise the embarcation.

Songyun paid "a farewell visit" to Macartney, and "seemed to be quite melted at parting from us. Among other things, he said to me in a strain of liberality scarcely to be expected in a Tartar or a Chinese, that as all distant countries must necessarily have different laws and customs, we should not be surprised that theirs varied from ours, that we owed each other mutual indulgences, and he therefore hoped I should not carry with me to Europe any impressions to the disadvantage or disparagement of China."[6]

Seeking to convince himself that these fine words represented more than Songyun's personal sentiments, Macartney noted that they must also be "agreeable to his Court, as no part of [what he said] can be concealed

---

* The same memorandum also states that Guo Shixun was making inquiries in Macao about *A-na* and *Lama-ete*, Fathers Hanna and Lamiot.

or misrepresented; for notwithstanding his high rank and situation, such is the caution and circumspection of this Government, that two considerable Mandarins . . . were always present at our conferences."[7] He concluded that Songyun's pleasantries boded well. Actually, they were merely part of his assignment, as is shown by the Imperial Archives: "We must send the English away as quickly as possible, mollifying them while conceding them nothing."

Songyun was marvelously suited to the task. While declining the presents Macartney offered him, he "excused himself" in such a "becoming and unaffected manner" that the ambassador never dreamed of taking offense. Yet in refusing these gifts, Songyun was acting on the very same instruction that had led Heshen to reject the famous carriage.

If the Grand Councillor was truly enamored of the ambassador, he certainly concealed the sentiment from the emperor. His final report, dated November 13, concludes: "On the twelfth the envoy came aboard my junk to present me with thanks to Your Sacred Majesty. Once again he cited the immense beneficence and favors the Great Emperor had bestowed upon him, a Barbarian ignorant of our institutions and our rites. These words were spoken with insistence and with evident sincerity."[8]

On the same day young Staunton wrote, "Today Songyun came aboard my papa's junk. . . . I wrote a letter to my mama to go by Captain Mackintosh."[9] Macartney also reports visits from Songyun on the twelfth and thirteenth. The Grand Councillor, however, told the court that it was the envoy who came aboard his vessel, and not the other way around. The hierarchical principle is as inhibiting in authoritarian societies as the egalitarian principle is in democratic ones.[10] It is the tributary envoy who owes the Grand Councillor respect.

ALL THE BRITISH were now on their way to Canton, some by sea, others by land. None of them suspected that as they traveled, the emperor in Peking and his representatives in the south were conducting an ongoing dialogue through the imperial post.

On October 21 Qianlong had sent an edict to the military governor of Canton and to all the governors of the coastal provinces, informing them of the "unseemly requests" of these barbarians, who were demanding "a small island where they could reside permanently," either in Zhoushan or near Canton.[11]

Guo Shixun replied just twelve days later, on November 1. Eleven days after that, on November 12, Qianlong annotated the response. Here is the text of their dialogue, which sealed Macartney's defeat:

GUO SHIXUN: When they arrive in Macao, the English will have to rent their lodgings from the Portuguese, whose guests they will thus become. That is why the envoy has requested that they be accorded a place in which they can store their merchandise. Such a site would be for them what Macao is for the Portuguese.

QIANLONG: This is absolutely impossible.

GUO SHIXUN: This gives us the full measure of the covetousness and guile of the English.

QIANLONG: Exactly!

GUO SHIXUN: The Portuguese settlement dates back to the Mings, more than two hundred years ago. These Barbarians have grown to love this land, wherein they bask in the Emperor's benevolent influence. They are no different from the rest of the Empire. It is especially impossible to allow the English Barbarians to settle on this coast, since it is so near to Canton.

QIANLONG: Exactly.

GUO SHIXUN: The envoy will not easily abandon his ill-considered request. In accordance with your sacred instructions, the coast must be rigorously defended. Along with Changlin, I will ensure that all the military posts are prepared for any eventuality: the English Barbarians will not be able to settle on even the smallest parcel of the Empire's territory.

QIANLONG: Execute this immediately.

GUO SHIXUN: Should the Barbarians who arrive in Guangdong seek to take up residence in the region, they will attempt to avail themselves of the services of internal felons capable of providing them with information.

QIANLONG: We must be especially alert to prevent this.

GUO SHIXUN: I have issued secret orders to the local authorities to keep a close watch on everything. If any guild interpreters or ordinary subjects make contact with the Barbarians to aid them in settling in the region, they must be arrested, tried, and sentenced so as to quash any such attempt.

QIANLONG: Absolutely.[12]

The clear skies Macartney had deduced from Songyun's affability were actually darkened with storm clouds.

IN HANGZHOU Macartney put the final touches on a twenty-eight-page report to King George, formally addressed to Henry Dundas and entrusted to Mackintosh. This was the ambassador's first opportunity to send some news of his mission back to Europe, and the tone of the document (which has never been published) is in sharp contrast not only to the pitiless imperial correspondence, but also to the impressions the ambassador and his companions record in their journals. Though suffused with a melancholy recognition of failure, it nevertheless glimpses a flickering glimmer of hope: "I had the satisfaction of finding that the report of an intended communication between the Courts of London and Peking had already begun to produce some effect on the minds of the Chinese in favour of the English merchants."[13]

But Macartney first describes a number of formidable obstacles, beginning with "the intrigues and misrepresentations of other European Factories. . . . We had every sort of opposition to expect from the Portuguese, whose ambition was to maintain an influence at Peking exclusive of other European Nations. They were likewise apprehensive of our desiring, if successful, a settlement independent of Macao which, in such case, must inevitably fall in ruine, as it subsists in great measure by the residence of the English there during the season when they are no longer allowed to continue at Canton."[14]

Then there was the suspicion of imperial officials: "Notwithstanding the hospitality with which we were treated, there was, too, perceptible on the part of every Tartar Chief a mistrust of our designs, as if we came to pry into the situation of the country."[15]

Swamped in the obligations of protocol, the embassy had been unable to negotiate anything of substance: ". . . the principal business for which I came was scarcely yet begun in the short space of time I had been here, most of which was necessarily employed in the previous ceremonies. There appeared no chance of obtaining any material object of my mission, without persevering a little longer in the hope of rendering the sentiments of this government more propitious towards us."[16]

Fortunately, the return journey on the Grand Canal had finally permitted the establishment of cordial relations with a Grand Councillor: "Songyun quoted out of the Emperor's letters received almost daily by him. I was privately informed. From the most carefull observations he was convinced we had really no other views than that of procuring advantages for our trade . . . however trifling in the eye of a Chinese statesman and unworthy of the trouble of such an expedition for the purpose of promoting it."[17]

Macartney then dealt with the disappointing content of the two edicts the emperor had addressed to King George: "I made a few remarks to Songyun on the Emperor's two letters to His Majesty the King—and observed of the first that except the subject of a minister to reside in Peking, which is denied, not the least notice was taken of any other, His Imperial Majesty thinking it sufficient generally to promise that he would treat our merchants kindly. That of the second letter, besides a refusal of the requests that are justly stated, none of which are supposed by him to be authorized by His Imperial Majesty, others, particularly those relating to Canton, are in some degree disfigured, as if to enable him [the emperor] to reject them with the greater ease; that these last, however, were of such moment that without speedy and equitable consideration of them, I was apprehensive the hardships suffered by our people at the port would become intolerable and force us to abandon this commerce altogether.[18] . . . I had the consolation of hearing that the Emperor entertained himself the best regard for us and our nation, and that he was determined to protect our trade; that he had indeed refused particular requests, not so much perhaps that they really were in themselves improper, as that they were introductive of something new, which at the advanced period of his life he did not think prudent to adopt, at least upon the sudden."[19]

Perhaps a younger successor to this senile sovereign would take a more flexible attitude. An Englishman never admits defeat, and the feeble flame of hope had to be kept burning.

V

NEW DEVELOPMENTS, FRESH HOPES

(November 1793–September 1794)

If a man is able to govern a state by observing the rites and showing deference, what difficulties will he have in public life? If he is unable to govern a state by observing the rites and showing deference, what good are the rites to him?

CONFUCIUS[1]

The Chinese say to their emperor: you are our father and our mother; it is through you that we live, and through you that we are what we are; deign to cast a glance of compassion upon us once more; learn of our misfortune, deign to see for yourself that which we dare not tell you, and rescue us.

FATHER J.-M. AMIOT, S.J., 1774[2]

Man is a sentient, reflective, thinking being who walks freely upon the face of the earth.

DIDEROT, 1751[3]

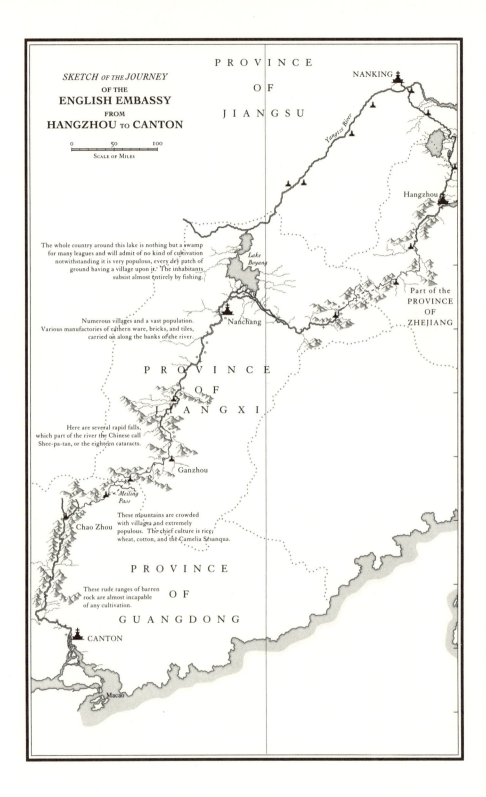

SKETCH *of the JOURNEY*
OF THE
ENGLISH EMBASSY
FROM
HANGZHOU TO **CANTON**

0   50   100
SCALE OF MILES

P R O V I N C E

O F

J I A N G S U

NANKING

Yangtze River

Hangzhou

Part of the
PROVINCE
OF
ZHEJIANG

Lake Boyang

The whole country around this lake is nothing but a swamp
for many leagues and will admit of no kind of cultivation
notwithstanding it is very populous, every dry patch of
ground having a village upon it. The inhabitants
subsist almost entirely by fishing.

Numerous villages and a vast population.
Various manufactories of eathern ware, bricks, and tiles,
carried on along the banks of the river.

Nanchang

P R O V I N C E

O F

J I A N G X I

Here are several rapid falls,
which part of the river the Chinese call
Shee-pa-tan, or the eighteen cataracts.

Ganzhou

Meiling Pass

These mountains are crowded
with villages and extremely
populous. The chief culture is rice;
wheat, cotton, and the Camelia Sesanqua.

Chao Zhou

P R O V I N C E

O F

These rude ranges of barren
rock are almost incapable
of any cultivation.

G U A N G D O N G

CANTON

Macao

63

The Patriarch's Testament

(November 9–10, 1793)

AS HE WORKED on his report to Dundas, Macartney carefully reread the letter he had received from Father Amiot on October 3, the very day the first imperial edict was delivered.[1] At the time, the ambassador had paid little attention to this message from the priest's deathbed, taking it as mere charitable consolation for his disappointment at the edict. But upon reflection he sensed its true depth and incisiveness. Had he known that Father Amiot had died on October 9, just six days after writing this letter, he might well have considered it the patriarch's testament.

Amiot explained to Macartney that since the Chinese regarded an embassy as no more than a formal exchange of presents, it could last no longer than the gift-giving ceremonies required: none of the embassies sent from Europe had been "of any considerable duration, and the last from Portugal, though very well received, [lasted] . . . less than six weeks." The Chinese, Amiot added, "had little notion of entering into treaties with foreign countries; . . . much might be obtained from them by time and management, but nothing suddenly."[2]

Foreign trade in Canton was "the victim of subordinate officials," and because of their pressure, there was but one alternative: either "renounce trade altogether" or make "severe remonstrances" to the central government through an embassy. But many years would inevitably elapse between the decision to organize such an embassy and the achievement of any results.

Macartney "would have met with fewer difficulties" if his embassy "had arrived before the Government had been alarmed by the news of great troubles in Europe." The internal upheavals in France had so "frightened" the Chinese authorities that they were now even more than usually "hostile to the most innocent innovation."

Here the Jesuit may well have been ascribing his own fears to the

Chinese, but Staunton, too, believed that the French Revolution had aroused Chinese suspicions: "It is said that in the French zeal for propagating principles of democracy, their Declaration of the Rights of Man had been translated into one of the languages of India, and distributed there. It is not, indeed, likely to cause any fermentation in the tranquil, submissive, and resigned minds, with the weak and delicate constitutions, of the Hindoos; but it might be otherwise among the Chinese people, who are more susceptible of such impressions, their disposition being more consonant to enterprize."[3] Staunton, however, may have been somewhat overzealous in seeking extenuating circumstances that might account for the embassy's failure. Charpentier-Cossigny, a French observer in Canton, commented: "I doubt very much that the government of China would be alarmed by the French Revolution, whose principles it could scarcely even comprehend. The Chinese government has no greater idea of democracy than does the king of Siam, who merely laughed when he was told that the Dutch had no king."[4]

But Father Amiot assured Macartney that his embassy had "made such an impression in the country, as must in the end be productive of very happy consequences, notwithstanding any different appearance at present." Once the uncertainties aroused by the mission had receded and the Chinese authorities became accustomed to the novelties that had initially shocked them, the ambassador's proposals might well be reconsidered.

Father Amiot advised Macartney to consolidate the bonds that had been woven, to follow up with "an intercourse of letters between" the British king and the Chinese emperor, "which annual ships might convey." In addition, "a person resident at Canton, with the king's commission," could be assured "access to the Viceroy" and would be able "to appear at Court, and negotiate with authority, in case he should be invited to attend there on occasion of the accession of a new Emperor, or any other solemnity." Such a permanent chargé d'affaires could keep the lines of communication open. In other words, those who had "planned the Embassy and had undertaken it might well forgo the satisfaction of momentary promises in favour of the more solid and permanent advantages which must gradually follow from it."[5]

Was it possible that Father Amiot wrote this letter at the behest of the Chinese? The missionaries, after all, were in China only by the emperor's sufferance, renewed from day to day. They were so completely dependent on the mandarin hierarchy that it was difficult for them to avoid acting as accomplices to the imperial will, whether consciously or otherwise. Yet they had no interest in a hostile expulsion of the British. On the contrary, they had reason to hope that an expansion of trade might improve their own living conditions and offer fresh opportunities for their apostolate. Father Amiot knew, Macartney wrote, "that without a better intercourse between Europe and China, or a miraculous interposition from above, the Gospel is likely to make but slow progress in this part of the world; and he knows that if the trade of China were once properly opened to us, it would wonderfully facilitate the business of conversion, and those of his own faith would still have the vineyard to themselves, for he has no jealousy of the English interfering with them in the proselyte branch."[6]

Staunton concluded from Amiot's letter that there was no reason to be disheartened by the court's rejection of Macartney's requests, for "such was the nature and practice of the Chinese government, that however adverse in the beginning to any new propositions, . . . the same matters might be brought again, when the offensive novelty of the idea was over, into a more serious and dispassionate consideration."[7]

In short, in this letter the aged missionary repeated what he had already written in 1789, though Macartney had not believed it: "Embassies are received in China only inasmuch as they can be regarded as tokens of submission."[8] Events had proved him right. Was he also right to amend this observation by holding out the prospect of change? The ambassador certainly hoped so, and he and his Chinese interlocutors soon sought to implement the old Jesuit's suggestion that the embassy be followed up with exchanges of letters and gifts through Canton.*

Hence Macartney's optimism in his report to the company directors, written the day after his letter to Dundas. Macartney told them that he was firmly convinced that British trade would benefit from the embassy. Much information had been gathered about the needs and morals of the inhabitants of northern China, and this should enable the company to increase its exports through Canton, until a more direct route of penetration was eventually found.[9]

On December 23 he wrote to Dundas again: "I acknowledged to the viceroy that the first perusal of the answers from the Court of Peking, made an impression on my mind which would naturally have led me to represent the China government as indifferent or inimical to that of Great Britain; but that the explanations which the Emperor's minister who accompanied me to Hangzhou, as well as he, the viceroy, gave me of His

---

* George III wrote to Qianlong in 1795; he also sent a message and a number of gifts to Jiaqing upon the new emperor's accession to the throne in 1796. The Chinese, of course, took these as marks of homage.

Imperial Majesty's real sentiments, had fully reconciled my mind." Songyun's words still echoed in his ears: "You will be even more at ease once you have met Viceroy Changlin."[10]

Give it time. That was Father Amiot's most pressing advice: The Chinese "might be rendered sensible of them ["treaties with distant powers"] if applied to and solicited without precipitation, and managed with caution and adroitness."[11]

64

On to the Deep South

(November 14–17, 1793)

THE BULK OF the embassy headed south on November 14, having been granted imperial dispensation to travel through Hangzhou.[1]

Young Staunton gives a vivid description of the departure: "Early this morning we set off in a procession with the soldiers through the city of Hangzhou to get to the River Jiang, where there were junks waiting for us. There were umbrellas of ceremony carried before, an honor done to us for the first time. Hangzhou is a very large and handsome city. We passed under several triumphal arches, all of which were of stone and curiously carved."[2]

The delighted page—and probably his compatriots as well—imagined that these arches had been erected in the embassy's honor, but clearly they were pai-lou of the sort the British had seen in Peking. Generally they were made of wood, but sometimes, as here, of stone.

Thomas also admired the "very good and large" shops, outside of which "valuable furs" were hanging.[3]

Upon leaving the city, the cortege was saluted by "guns, music, and several hundred of soldiers."[4] Anderson saw ten times as many as Thomas did: "a very large body of troops . . . were drawn up in regular order; the whole consisting . . . of several thousand men."[5]

"The river being very shallow towards the shore, the junks lay at the distance of fifty yards from it, and were ranged in a line close to each other. A platform was erected from the triumphal arch to the junk appointed to receive the Ambassador, which consisted of a great number of carts fastened together, with split bamboo laid across them." An immense crowd gathered to view the spectacle, onlookers perched on wagons drawn by buffalo or on the backs of these docile animals, who seemed not even to notice. "The buffalo," Anderson writes, "is very much used in this country in every kind of draught labour, and particularly in the occupation of husbandry."[6] The observation applies only to the south, where the British had now indeed arrived.

They were so struck by the military parade that most of them mention it in their journals. The "grandeur of the whole apparatus was enlivened by a great number of gaudy standards and ensigns. The artillery troops were dressed in blue, and had figures of the ordnance embroidered on their cloaths, by way of distinction. They consisted of several companies, and were stationed in the center, and on the flanks of the lines. Their cannon were by much the largest we had seen in China; and as the British cavalcade passed through the two very elegant triumphal arches, it was saluted by a discharge of artillery."[7] Macartney, however, found these cannon "very heavy and very clumsy, the thickness of the metal at the mouth being equal to the bore of the gun."[8]

As the British marched past, the Chinese soldiers saluted them "by falling down on their knees."* As many as a thousand Chinese soldiers were "drawn up to receive us at the waterside, dressed and armed in their best manner." Macartney thought the Chinese showed a "marked admiration" for the British guards, and he in turn felt that these imperial troops "looked more like soldiers than any I had seen in China before."

The two sides sized each other up. Macartney the diplomat, realizing that he had lost a battle, now assessed, with a soldier's eye, his chances of winning a war. But nearly half a century would pass before that war broke out.

By about five o'clock the British had boarded their canvas-sailed junks,[10] and the flotilla cast off. The vessels drew "very little water, not more than ten inches even when laden with two tons and a half weight."[11]

Once they passed Zhenjiang, where the Yangtze meets the Grand Canal, the travelers were truly in the south of China. This was another country, quite different from the north, a wealthy land of rice and tea, of rivers teeming with fish, and of people living lives of relative plenty.

"Friday the 15th," writes Thomas Staunton. "On our waking this morning we found ourselves encompassed by the most beautiful country I ever remember to have seen."[12] Macartney, too, found the landscape "beautiful and romantic."[13] "On one side," writes Thomas, "was an extended plain planted with eatables, . . . but on the other side the mountains rose immediately out of the water in the forms of rock or steep precipices. . . . Tho this river is so fine, yet it seldom exceeds 4 feet in depth. The

---

* Father Lamiot disputes that this genuflection was meant to honor the embassy, claiming that it was actually for Changlin, whose banners fluttered from the junks.[9] He is most likely right about this.

bottom is a bed of round stones which are covered with a greenish matter. Our junks . . . often rubbed . . . against them."[14]

Hüttner wondered about the risks of navigating such shallow waters. The oars struck rocks constantly, and the jolts made him fear "shipwreck." Each junk was drawn by about twenty men, whose shouts, joined to those of the sailors, "would be intolerable were it not for the distraction of the landscape's charm."[15]

Actually, the British were no longer traveling on the great north-south waterway. A direct route from Peking to Canton would not have taken them through Hangzhou. They would have sailed more than 150 miles up the Yangtze instead of merely crossing it to enter the final section of the Grand Canal. But they had taken an eastward detour to bring them closer to the Zhoushan Islands. The court had decreed this itinerary under the assumption that all the British would embark on the *Lion*, and it was maintained under the subsequent assumption that Macartney would agree to leave on the *Hindostan*. But now the flotilla had to double back, and Macartney proudly noted that no European had ever ventured so deep into China—not even Marco Polo, who went only as far as Fuzhou, and certainly not the various missionaries and foreign ambassadors, all of whom had been restricted to the imperial canal. This journey, like his stay in Jehol, was a first.

They reached the latitude of Cairo, and the land now had a heady scent of exoticism. "There are fields of rice, plantations of sugar cane, groves of orange, grapefruit, and pomegranate trees, chestnut trees, vegetables, tea, camphor, and bamboo."[16]

Young Staunton was fascinated by the "red and green" tallow trees, which he found "very handsome." He seemed surprised to find that "candles are made" from this tree.[17] The white fruit, ringed by red leaves, contains pits filled with a soapy, flourlike substance that burns remarkably evenly. Chinese candles were shorter and thicker than European ones, and their wicks were of wood.[18] Where the boy marveled, the father explained: "The flat and fleshy substance is separated from the kernels by crushing and boiling them in water. The candles made of this fat are firmer than those of tallow, as well as free from all offensive odour."[19] The manufacturing process was much cheaper too. Yet another Chinese technological achievement that would soon be eclipsed—by gas and electric lights.

ON NOVEMBER 16 the ambassador had a visit from the viceroy. He was accompanied by Wang and Qiao, who had originally been scheduled to leave the embassy in Hangzhou. Macartney was delighted that these two mandarins were still with him, and he attributed their continued presence to Changlin: "As they were well-known to the Viceroy, and as he observed that they were agreeable and accustomed to us, he desired them to come on and accompany the Embassy to Canton."[20] But this, like much else, was pure fantasy. The Imperial Archives tell us that the court had decided as early as October 15 that these two functionaries should accompany their charges through the mission's embarcation.

"In China, too, there are orange trees!" exclaimed Thomas, in much the same tone as the astonished director of a cooperative vineyard in the Crimea once said to me, "You mean you make champagne in France too?" Herr Hüttner, however, knew that the German name for this fruit, *Apfelsine*, meant "Chinese apple" and that "the Portuguese imported it to Europe. The first European orange tree is in Lisbon."[21]

Hüttner went on to explain that the Chinese had three categories of orange. The best was the "mandarin orange": its reddish skin was easily peeled, its flesh juicy. Next came the "captain's orange," yellowish in color and less tasty. Finally there was the "coolie orange," the one that had been imported to Europe.

ON NOVEMBER 17, the third day of the journey, Macartney and Changlin had a serious conversation. Once again his lordship began to hope that he might finally be able to accomplish something.

The new viceroy of Canton came aboard Macartney's junk and "began of his own accord to talk to me of the trade carried on between Great Britain and China of which he owned he was but imperfectly informed. He therefore desired me to explain to him the principal points in which I wished his assistance when we came to Canton. When I had done this he requested me to give it to him in writing, which I told him should be done as soon as possible. He said his reason for asking it was that he might read it at his leisure, in order to be master of the subject, for he was determined to be equitable and proper, to grant what was reasonable and to deny what was not." He acknowledged that "some change of conduct towards us would be right, both for the sake of justice and the reputation of his country."[22]

Changlin explained that "his affinity to the Emperor and his rank in the state" would give him some freedom of action, but he also noted that there would be opposition "at Canton from those who may perhaps be interested in the continuance of those very grievances we suffered." Moreover, "some of the great people at Court" were hostile to Great Britain, "particularly Fukang'an, his predecessor, who would not be much pleased to see him adopt a new system the reverse of his own." The viceroy "candidly" mentioned that he was aware of Macartney's "disappointment" at Heshen's rejection of the embassy's requests, and he urged the ambassador not to act "in such manner as to defeat any indulgences" that he, Changlin, meant to grant the British. This might "render him culpable for any representations he might make in our favour."[23]

Macartney replied to Changlin as he had to Songyun, "with the utmost frankness." He explained that "from the reception my requests had met with, I naturally concluded the Court of Peking to be indifferent, if not unfriendly to Great Britain." But because of the "pains" Songyun had taken "to impress me, as he declared he had the highest authority to do, with the Emperor's favourable sentiments towards us and our concerns," and because Changlin himself had "confirmed them at the first conference I had with him in the presence of Songyun," Macartney had sent no negative reports to London. He hoped that "notwithstanding what had passed at Peking, . . . I could not doubt of a very serious attention being paid to my representations." Macartney had so informed the Court of St. James, and "thus the matter now stood." He added that "it rested with him [Changlin] to determine whether I had deceived my own Court or not. It was from what he would do, not what I should write, that they would form a judgment."[24]

The ambassador felt that he was finally getting somewhere. Such conversations were well worth the detour of this trip. "Soon after the Viceroy left me he sent presents of tea, fans, and perfumes to me, and to all the gentlemen of the Embassy."[25] Thomas adds that there were also "presents of silk."[26]

PLEADING INEXPERIENCE, Changlin had urged Macartney to start the ball rolling. But he also stated the limits of his goodwill, acknowledging that he could well understand that the English might react vindictively to the court's apparent lack of cooperation but warning that any such conduct would block positive changes. Macartney had no way of knowing that the new viceroy, like Songyun before him, had been explicitly ordered to guard against any possible British violence, if necessary through a show of force. Changlin had been adroit enough to share this imperial apprehension with Macartney, while balancing it against the commercial advantages that might be forthcoming in its absence, thus skillfully turning the potential threat against the British themselves.

Macartney responded in kind. While making no promises about British behavior, he tried to box the Chinese in, telling Changlin that it was now up to him to confirm, through his actions, the favorable report that Macartney had made to His Britannic Majesty.

The ambassador no longer bothered to demand a written document (although he himself had been asked to supply one this time), Songyun having apparently convinced him that none would be forthcoming in any case and that he would do better to rely on tangible acts rather than words, whether spoken or written.

The most tangible factor of all seemed to be Changlin himself, the man who now held the fate of European trade in his hands. In any event, he was Macartney's only hope.

65

Keeping Hope Alive

(November 18–20, 1793)

ALL THIS DIPLOMACY did not prevent the British from pursuing another aspect of their mission—industrial espionage—and for once their tenacity made some headway against Chinese suspicion. As we have seen, Lord Cornwallis, the governor-general of India, wanted to initiate silk and tea production in Bengal, and Macartney had been instructed to pursue this objective, which was shared by the company.[1] In fact, this may well have been a secondary reason for his "entreating" Songyun to let him travel to Canton over land.

Nanking silk, perfectly white when manufactured locally, yellowed when prepared elsewhere, and the British wanted to know why. To find out they had to study the mulberry trees, the insects themselves, the nature of the terrain, and the composition of the water used in unraveling the cocoons. Macartney did not realize how much effort this would entail, and while he did not achieve everything he had hoped for,[2] he did at least manage to come away with some silkworm eggs.

Silk had been an exclusively Chinese product for twenty centuries. It was forbidden to export either the cocoons or the secret of the manufacturing process. Various thieves, however, had brought this secret out of China. In 555 two Nestorian monks hid some eggs in a reed cane and smuggled them back to Byzantium. In the seventh century Princess Wencheng introduced silk to Tibet, hiding some cocoons in the buns of her hair. Nine centuries later, Olivier de Serres used his wife's ample bosom as the hiding place for cocoons brought back to Vivarais from Italy. Macartney, too, sent silkworms to India, along with some information about the manufacturing process. But despite all this, the British made little progress.

They had better luck with tea, a plant that fascinated the English, who were as devoted to the beverage as the Chinese were. Today it is hard to imagine either nationality without thinking of tea, but in fact tea drinking became widespread in China only toward the middle of the first millennium after Christ, a thousand years after Confucius. As for England, it was only in 1660 that Samuel Pepys savored his first cup of tea in a London cafe.[3] By the eighteenth century, however, love of tea was one of the few things the British and the Chinese had in common, though the identity of taste may well have masked a distinct difference in culture.

Our travelers thirsted insatiably for information about tea. "Tea was their constant drink from morning till night," Dr. Gillan wrote of the Chinese.[4] "Such immense quantities of tea are consumed in China, that a sudden failure of a demand from Europe, would not be likely to occasion any material diminution of its prices at the Chinese markets," wrote Staunton, denying the law of supply and demand.[5] He considered tea drinking a major virtue: "One of the best qualities, perhaps, of it is, that the taste for it, and the habit of drinking it, at all times lessens the relish for fermenting and inebriating liquors."[6] A pungent remark, coming from a man whose compatriots were as fond of gin and beer as they were of tea. Staunton also noted that harvested tea was pressed into chests "by the naked feet of Chinese labourers, as grapes are pressed by the wooden shoes of European peasants. . . . Notwithstanding this uncleanly operation of Chinese packers, the upper ranks in China are as fond of tea as the people are, and particularly solicitous in their choice of it."[7]

Did the English realize that the Chinese drank their tea "while holding a morsel of candied sugar in their mouths"?[8] Or that certain beautiful women served their lovers a frothy mixture of tea, hazelnuts, and salted bamboo shoots, supposedly an aphrodisiac?[9]

Enamored of the beverage, they were ever on the lookout for the plant, and they noticed it growing in these southern fields.[10] Staunton admired the rows of plants terraced into the hills—marshy land was reserved for rice. The tea's "perpendicular growth is impeded, for the convenience of collecting its leaves."[11] Anderson thought they looked like currant bushes. He recorded his first encounter with tea plants on October 18, but his date is almost certainly off by at least two weeks: in mid-October the British were too far north for tea; judging by the season and the latitude, it seems more likely that Anderson was actually looking at cotton plants. But he was quite right to point out that "imperial tea" was made from the first blossoms of the season, while "gunpowder tea" was made from successive blossoms.*[12]

---

* Gunpowder tea owes its name to the crackling sound made by its furled leaves when hot water is added to them. The Chinese call it *zhucha*, or "pearl tea." It is exported to the Middle East, where it is commonly drunk with mint.

Macartney himself later wrote to Cornwallis (on February 28, 1794): "I was supposed, if possible, to procure some shoots of the best tea plants. Thanks to the benevolence of the new viceroy of Canton, with whom I travelled the best tea-growing regions of the country, I was able to observe and take samples of subjects of the highest quality. I have entrusted these to Dr. Dinwiddie, who will bring them to Calcutta, where he will arrive aboard the *Jackall*."*[13] As the group traveled through the "charming fruitful country," Macartney's Chinese escorts allowed him to gather samples of tea, "varnish trees,"† and tallow trees.[15] In the course of the next century, the profits made from the introduction of these plants in India would repay the costs of this entire journey more than a hundredfold.

Macartney's samples were carefully transported to Bengal, along with their soil. Colonel Kyd, a British officer who had founded the Calcutta Botanic Gardens and convinced the company to invest in tea plantations in India, where the plant had been unknown, was to take charge of the new species. The unfortunate colonel died just before Dinwiddie arrived with his precious cargo, but the plantations (as well as groves of tallow and varnish trees) were developed just as he had urged. The Calcutta Botanic Gardens nurtured the plants and sent shoots to all the nurseries of India. In 1823 a species of wild tea was discovered in Assam and crossbred with the Chinese strain, but it is very likely that a good part of today's "Indian" tea is in fact descended from the samples taken from China by Macartney.[16]

The *Bounty*, whose story would later be recounted by Barrow, had earlier been dispatched to Tahiti in search of breadfruit, which the British cabinet wanted to introduce in the West Indies. The Enlightenment had a passion for botany, and the London government felt that scientific, maritime, colonial, commercial, and industrial progress were wholly intertwined: only the simultaneous pursuit of them all could guarantee world supremacy.

AT NIGHTFALL the flotilla stopped within sight of a mountain range. Wang and Qiao came aboard Macartney's junk to introduce him to two envoys of the king of the Liu-Kiu Islands—colleagues, in a sense. Every other

---

* The *Jackall* left the rest of the Europe-bound squadron in mid-April 1794 and sailed for Bengal.[14]

† The varnish tree, which grows in a few regions of China and Cambodia, produces a latex that the Chinese learned to harvest as early as the days of Confucius.

year the prince of these islands sent tribute to Xiamen, in Fujian province, the only Chinese port in which his ships were authorized to moor.

Macartney describes the envoys as "tolerably fair complexioned." Thomas, on the other hand, says that they were "almost black."[17] But the ambassador and the page were both favorably impressed. Macartney found the envoys "well-bred, conversable, and communicative," while Thomas thought them "well-looking." They were dressed in "a very fine sort of shawl made in their own country, dyed of a beautiful brown colour and lined with a squirrel skin." They also wore turbans, one yellow, one purple.[18]

Macartney was still looking for some way of penetrating China, and these islands seemed to offer promising prospects. They were close to the continent, vassals of the empire but foreign to it, and apparently well-disposed to foreigners. Perhaps the French plan for Cochin China could be applied to the Liu-Kiu Islands: they might serve as a trading post just off the empire's coast, fueled by Chinese trade while lying beyond the reach of Chinese officialdom.[19]

The envoys seemed willing to talk, and Macartney gathered what information he could. They reported that their country had never been visited by European ships, but expressed a willingness to receive them. The archipelago boasted a large, deep-water port, near the capital.

Macartney's information was eventually followed up. In 1816, during the second British mission to China, Lord Amherst's ship paid a brief visit to the Liu-Kiu Islands after dropping the ambassador off in Tientsin. In the end, however, it was Japan that took possession of this strategically located archipelago, which became famous during the Second World War. Its main island is Okinawa.[20]

ON NOVEMBER 19 Qianlong issued a frantic instruction. He had just learned that two British brigs, soon to be joined by the *Lion*, had sailed into the Tiger's Mouth, the section of the Pearl River that flows through Canton.

Once they are resupplied, they must not be permitted to depart! Keep them there! The English Barbarians must be denied any form of settlement in Huangpu! Let no felonious merchant assist them in any way! Let Changlin escort the rest of them to Canton as quickly as possible, that they may embark on their vessels! Should these ships leave without waiting for the others, the envoy will use this as an excuse to remain indefinitely. This must be prevented at all costs. The Barbarians procrastinated long enough in Zhejiang; it would be intolerable to allow them to begin this contemptible game again in Guangdong. There must be no further incidents and no futile complications!

In the event that, despite all your vigilance, the Barbarian ships leave Canton before the envoy's arrival, then you must see to it, discreetly but without fail, that the Barbarians have no contact with Chinese merchants: we must make absolutely sure that they foment no conspiracy with anyone.

Let the embassy be properly resupplied, with neither too much nor too little. But no more banquets or receptions! They must proceed to Canton at a forced march.

The tax relief that has been granted applies only to the ships forming part of the envoy's squadron. Where will it lead if we bestow ill-considered favors upon one nation? All countries must be treated on an equal basis.[21]

WHILE THE EMPEROR fulminated, the viceroy held out the possibility of a second embassy. The English, after all, had themselves requested more frequent relations: "This evening [November 20] . . . the Viceroy visited me and . . . seemed still somewhat apprehensive . . . that I must feel much dissatisfaction at bottom, as I certainly do, . . . and that consequently my representations home might be the occasion of future trouble or mischief."[22]

Macartney repeated his earlier assurances, but Changlin seemed "still doubtful of my sincerity." The viceroy "was desirous of putting it to a test, by his asking me whether I would authorize him to tell the Emperor that the King my master would always continue in friendship with him, and in testimony of it would write to him, and send an ambassador again if the Emperor were willing to receive him."[23]

A clever proposal. If England accepted such periodic visits, perhaps it might become a regular tributary, much like the Liu-Kiu Islands, for example. Macartney parried: "I said that though what I solicited was refused, yet in every other respect I had no reason to complain, as the Embassy had been very honourably received and entertained. . . . As to matters of business, they stood on a different ground. That the King's original idea was to have an ambassador usually resident in China, . . . but that frequent or temporary embassies from so great a distance were attended with much trouble and expense to both Courts. Nevertheless, I thought that possibly another Minister might be sent to China if there was good ground to expect that such a measure would be requited by adequate advantages."[24]

Adequate advantages? Changlin had no wish to follow up that line of discussion. Instead he asked how quickly a second embassy could be arranged. Macartney replied that it was beyond his power to answer such a question, but assured the viceroy that he had "received the greatest satisfaction" from the various conversations they had had. Changlin replied that he would immediately write to the emperor, who would be "highly pleased in every respect with his accounts" of the embassy.

Indeed. Here is the statement that Changlin attributed to *Ma-ga-er-ni* in his memorandum to Qianlong:

> It is with the greatest humility that our King sent us to bring his tribute to the Great Emperor. Even before our departure, he spoke of a second expedition. He has observed, however, that it could take place only several years after the first. The distances make it impossible to set an exact date, but we will subsequently propose one. We will not fail to send a list of the presents to the viceroy of Canton, who alone is suited to transmit it to the Court. We will consider it an immense favor to be granted the right to present our tribute to His Imperial Majesty.[25]

It seems a flagrantly false report, but Changlin surely would not have considered himself a liar. He was simply interpreting Macartney's vague formulations in the light of the logic of the Celestial Order. Reality was less important than respect for principles. Changlin attributed to Macartney the only initiative permitted by the court, including a preliminary presentation of the list of gifts in Canton, a formality Macartney had failed to observe on this mission, thus outraging Peking even before his arrival.

Yet Changlin's punctilious account of Macartney's alleged declaration nevertheless bears out Father Amiot's observation: "It is in the nature and practice of the Chinese . . ." to be "adverse in the beginning to any new propositions. . . ."[26] The court wanted the Englishman to agree to pay homage a second time, while the Englishman wanted to make sure that no bridges were burned.

In the meantime, the ambassador was quite content with the viceroy: "Every time we see this gentleman he gains upon our good opinion, and I do not despair of the company's receiving many advantages by his means. It is true that he has art and address, and an air of candour to disguise them with, but he has prudence, sagacity, and a sense of character."[27] Macartney was still chasing the chimera of personal relations, which he hoped might enable him to circumvent the rigidity of the immutable system.

In response to Changlin's request, Macartney drafted a new memorandum on Anglo-Chinese trade.[28] This document, containing fifteen points, reiterates the earlier requests—ranging from the issue of transit duties between Macao and Canton to the right of the British to practice "equitation" and other "favoured sports"—and adds others: "That the English be allowed to trade with any merchants, and not be confined with the merchants of the guild. That Chinese be allowed to instruct the English in the language of their country. That in criminal cases persons of the same nation not guilty of the offense should not be held responsible."

One final point had to do with the new United States: "That the English not be identified with those people who speak a similar language, but are a different nation and live in another part of the world, named America."

The Americans, in fact, had sent their first ships to Canton in 1784, less than a decade after declaring their independence. In 1790 they posted a consul to the city. They were wasting no time, and they, too, were eager not to be confused with their former masters.[29]

66

A Passage over Land

(November 21, 1793)

THE EXPEDITION now had to take a land route across the high ground separating the basins of the Tong and Xiu rivers. The passage was completed in a single day, November 21.

Thomas Staunton was enthusiastic about this mountainous, terrestrial interlude: "This morning we left our boats and set off in sedan chairs* thro the country for 22 miles to another river where there were other boats to take us on towards Canton. We had an excellent road all the way, not very wide but made like the gravel walks in a garden, and when we went thro the wet rice grounds it was made so high as not to be at all damp. We saw no marks of wheels upon the road. Several young fir trees were planted on the otherwise barren mountains, at the roots of which we saw several tombs, which have the appearance of small stone houses, with little grated windows. The valleys are planted with rice and vegetables."[2]

Once again Macartney was amazed at the intensive agriculture: "I did not see a spot in the whole way that was not cultivated with infinite industry and compelled to produce every grain and vegetable of which it was capable. . . . Wherever the sides of the hills admit of it they are wrought into terraces, graduated with different crops and watered by the chain pump. . . . There are never less than two crops in the year and often there are three."[3]

"This," says young Staunton, "is the division between the two provinces Zhejiang and Jiangxi. Every mile or two we went thro a village. . . . We saw several people using what looked like our chain pumps† to raise the

---

* Anderson notes: "The mandarin Wang always consulted the suite as to the mode of travelling which they preferred, and never failed in accommodating them to their respective inclinations."[1]
† In regard to the chain pumps, Hüttner notes that "the English themselves assert that they borrowed this idea from the Chinese,"[4] and it is true that these pumps date back to the first century after Christ in China, whereas Europe began using them only in the fifteenth century.[5]

water, which is conducted through the rice grounds and other plantations.
. . . We came through some very extensive suburbs to a walled town of
the third order called Sue-Shan-Shien. We soon got thro' the town . . .
[and] at last turned down a long flight of steps down to the side of a river,
where we found boats ready for us, but something smaller than those we
had before."[6]

Macartney was struck by the zeal of the farmers in collecting human
excrement: "The care with which everything convertible into manure is
preserved would appear ridiculous elsewhere, but is here fully justified by
the effect."[7] During this brief passage over land the British had a chance
to observe this long-standing Chinese practice at their leisure.* "The
Chinese prefer human manure to any other," Thomas noted, "and on that
account have people and places for the collecting of it."[8] This strange
custom was by no means peculiar to this part of China or to the epoch.

Hüttner treated the delicate subject most gingerly, giving the roadside
latrines a mythological name: "These temples of Cloacine have been constructed not for the convenience of the public, but for the profit of those
who collect their offerings."[9]

The "temples of Cloacine" were in fact large, half-buried earthenware
jars "used by passersby and later emptied so as to put their contents to
use." Staunton reports that the "collection of manure is an object of so
much attention with the Chinese, that a prodigious number of old men
and women, as well as children, . . . are constantly employed about the
streets, public roads, banks of canals and rivers, with baskets tied before
them, and holding in their hands small wooden rakes to pick up the dung
of animals and offals of any kind that may answer the purpose of manure."[10]
Barrow had earlier noted that this basic fertilizer was enriched with additional refuse: "And as hair is considered an excellent manure, every
barber carries with him a small bag to collect the spoils of his razor."[11]
But most of all, "every family has its large vase, which, when full, is readily
exchanged for vegetables and fruits."[12] From jar to manure to vegetables,
the cycle was complete.

When blended with soil, the human manure was molded into "cakes
which are dried in the sun. In this manner a feeble old man may yet be
of some use to the family that feeds him."[13]

The British observed this same technique in Canton: "Half of the
buildings consisted, however, of places of convenience, to which passengers

---

* It will be recalled that Sir George expressed astonishment at it when he first disembarked
in the Zhoushan Islands. Possibly out of modesty, most of our witnesses made no mention of
it at that time, but none of them neglects it now.

might retire to obey the calls of nature; and the doors, or rather openings into such erections, were always invitingly fronting the street. To each single dwelling . . . was annexed a fabric of this description. Each was constructed upon a large terrace cistern, lined with such materials that no absorption could take place; and straw and other dry rubbish are thrown in by the owners, from time to time, to prevent evaporation. In one of the streets of Canton is a row of buildings of this kind, which, in so warm a climate is a dreadful nuisance, but the consideration of preserving that kind of manure, which by the Chinese is considered as superior for forcing vegetation to all others, has got the better of both decency and prudence."[14]

Had Barrow, Hüttner, and Staunton read Freud, they might have wondered about the effects of this practice on Chinese behavior patterns. Psychoanalysis has shown that training in cleanliness plays a pivotal role in personality formation, fostering a sense of order, neatness, self-discipline, and financial parsimony.[15] Erich Fromm has even interpreted the spirit of enterprise as a sublimation born of the desire to leave a trace of civilization to compensate for this abject trace. In his view, it is in Protestant education that disgust for filth is most pronounced, and the need for self-affirmation most exalted.

Is there a link between certain collective traits often described by the Chinese themselves—puerility, confusion, gregariousness, indiscipline, waste, dirtiness—and an anal stage experienced without the requisite rigor? Is it possible that, generation after generation, a society suffers upheavals acquired and transmitted by a culture that retards and even paralyzes its own development? Has the virtually religious use of excrement, gathered as precious instead of rejected as shameful, century after century, damaged the psyche of the Chinese to the point of perpetuating inhibiting neuroses? More than one psychoanalyst might be tempted to respond affirmatively, but let us merely pose the question.[16]

THERE WAS no hostelry "thought fit for the reception of the Embassy" that night. The British were therefore lodged in the "public building in which the young men of the district were examined for their degrees. . . ."[17]

This was the mission's first direct contact with one of the mirages of the Chinese system much admired by Enlightenment Europe and especially by the Jesuit propagators of this admiration, who transplanted the practice to their own colleges in France during the eighteenth century, organizing a hierarchy of examinations and competitions culminating in the prestigious Concours Général. These examinations, Staunton writes of the Chinese model, "are said to be always public. The body of auditors who attend, as well as the presence of the governor and chief magistrates of the district, who preside, must awe any disposition to partiality in the judges. Some oral questions are put, and some are given in writing, to the candidates, as in English colleges. The rewards of those who succeed, are not confined to the honour of the university, for these become the ascending steps which lead to all the offices and dignities of the state."

These careers are "open to all classes of men" and the "general persuasion . . . that authority has been acquired through merit, must contribute to insure respect and obedience to it."[18] Staunton warmly approved: "Such a system of government promises indeed great benefit to society."[19]

It is not clear whether the British actually saw candidates flocking to an examination, or whether they were merely told of such sessions by their escorts. It is also possible that they were simply repeating, with touching naiveté, legends already widespread in their century.

But there is always another side to the coin. What becomes of officials recruited in this way? Staunton sensed the answer: they form a redoubtable bureaucracy that exploits or rejects those who lack wealth or knowledge. "The poor and private individuals of China, who have no means of communicating their complaints, or declaring their sentiments on the conduct of their particular rulers, are left in great measure at their mercy; and foreigners, when, in the same predicament, are equally liable to suffer."[20] Here he hit upon the chief defect of the system, criticized for twenty-five centuries by the Chinese themselves, beginning with Confucius, by whom the system claimed to have been inspired but who, five centuries before Christ, denounced the tendency of government officials "to be miserly in the actual giving" even when "something has to be given to others anyway."[21] Less than a hundred years ago, a Chinese wrote, "When a citizen is mistreated by a mandarin, he has no choice but to resign himself."[22]

While denouncing the dismal dictatorship of these minor local chieftains, the British were dazzled by the revelation that a social system could actually be organized otherwise than by hereditary power. They criticized that system not in the name of the aristocracy that still held sway in their own society, but in the name of the democracy toward which Britain was now moving. Public administration in the service of the people and under their control was the uncontested ideal.

Yet the members of the embassy, like the Jesuits and the *philosophes*, still admired the China of competitive examinations, much as Western enthusiasts took revolutionary China as a model in the 1960s and 1970s. The British aristocrats were just as fascinated as the European Maoists of 1968.

Implicitly, Macartney's companions compared the Chinese method of recruiting state functionaries with the patronage system under which all British officials, from customs inspectors to ministry secretaries, were selected at the time. This patronage was a decisive element in what was commonly called "the old corruption" typical of the monarchies of the Ancien Régime. The seeds of the bureaucratic chimera of the Jacobins or of Napoleon can be glimpsed in the enthusiasm of the British visitors.

In China itself, however, there had long been rumblings that talent was neither a necessary nor a sufficient prerequisite for getting ahead under this system. In the *Chronique indiscrète des mandarins* a butcher says to his son-in-law: "To become a gentleman you have to be a star. Look at the Chang family in the city: a great fortune, rosy faces. What chance do you think you have, with your pointy chin and monkey snout? Forget it!"[23]

"In our village those who are straight are quite different," said Confucius. "Fathers cover up for their sons, and sons cover up for their fathers. Straightness is to be found in such behaviour."[24] How, then, could families be blamed for striving to perpetuate their positions just as jealously as they preserved their patrimony? There were more scions than scholarships in the Celestial examination system.

The method of teaching was based on the repetition of texts by rote until they were learned by heart. Composition was subject to strict rules that prevented inspiration. The system's goal was to teach recitation, not creation, and still less to foster judgment or criticism. The ideal was conformity to preestablished models.[25] "I drink always from the well of the classics," one schoolmaster declared. "Never could I manage anything of my own devising."[26] As a Confucian principle put it: "I was not born with knowledge but, being fond of antiquity, I am quick to seek it."[27]

While the British trumpeted their admiration for this system, Qianlong himself condemned its ineffectiveness, though without challenging its foundation. "Whatever their rank," he wrote, "the agents of the State rarely act with level-headedness. When they do not commit excesses, it is merely because they are timorous."[28]

In many respects, the British were beginning to penetrate the smokescreen in which the Enlightenment had enveloped the Middle Empire. But they had not shed all their illusions. They believed that power was held by an aristocracy of knowledge. For every Songyun with his traveling library, however, there were countless pedantic brutes. The members of the embassy were probably unaware of the true story of Heshen's path to power, nor did they know of the throngs of people he bought and sold or whose careers he made and ruined.

The Chinese system has often been likened to the civil service in republican France. But would French officials be sanctioned as Chinese were? A swarm of locusts descends on a rural district, and the governor is beaten and deposed. Another is docked a year's pay for exhibiting excessive good humor in public, thereby undermining the dignity of his office. Any advice that proves inadequate is punished.[29]

Confucius was asked, "What are the four wicked practices" of government? He named "cruelty, tyranny, causing injury, and officiousness."[30] Could he have guessed that all four would coexist in an immutable society in which an essential role was played by houses of examination established to perpetuate his own doctrine?

The Chinese system, a mirage for Europeans, was a dream for the Chinese—but one that was occasionally realized. Countless fathers have told their sons, "My ancestors were common people. If only you succeed in your examinations, I could die in peace!"[31] Even today, nothing so warms the heart of a Chinese peasant as having a son who graduates and lives in a house "steeped in the scent of books."[32]

No system is perfect. Every society has always favored the heirs of the privileged. Let us therefore acknowledge the positive aspect of the Chinese competitive examinations: despite their enormous defects (strenuously denounced by the Chinese themselves), they did introduce a measure of social mobility in this immobile empire.

The formalistic, literary organization of society persisted until the end of the empire. The revolution then sought to sweep aside both the advantages and the flaws of this two-thousand-year-old meritocracy. In this it did not entirely succeed.

67

"A Stroke of Luck for Our Country"

(November 15–22, 1793)

AS MACARTNEY headed south, the other branch of the expedition made its way to Zhoushan, traveling through the province of Zhejiang. This smaller contingent included Lieutenant Colonel Benson, Dr. Dinwiddie, the painter Alexander, Captain Mackintosh, some of the soldiers of the guard (including Holmes), and a number of mechanics to look after the equipment.[1]

They passed through the town of Ningbo, the prefecture of Zhejiang, where the British had once had a trading post and factory from which they were ousted because of their "bad behavior," recovering it by armed force only in 1859. A port on the southern rim of the Gulf of Hangzhou, Ningbo was then the commercial center of the region, a role later assumed by a larger metropolis on the northern rim: Shanghai.

In Ningbo the thorny question of Mackintosh's trading plans arose again, though Macartney was never informed of this development.

Qianlong, it will be recalled, was determined to prevent the British from trading in the city. All "felonious merchants" had been expelled, along with descendants of the compradors who had traded with the British earlier in the century. Captain Mackintosh had already been warned not to engage in any transactions, and the emperor now reiterated, "Trade is conducted in Macao and Canton."

According to Holmes, however, not everyone shared the emperor's view of Ningbo as a commercial desert. In fact, the city seemed more like a beehive of activity. ". . . on the 15th [of November we] came in sight of the famous city of Ningbo, situated on the side of a rugged mountain, as barren and uncouth as the hills of Derbyshire." The inhabitants treated the barbarian delegation with "unusual respect," and the "principal men" appeared to be the most attentive of all. The British found them "more communicative than their countrymen had hitherto been. . . . They carry on a great trade from this city to Batavia, the Philippine Islands, and other settlements in the Chinese seas, in their own vessels; and they supply the European ships, by way of Canton."[2]

The leading mandarins gave the British presents of silk, tea, nankins (printed cotton cloth), tobacco, and other trinkets, and generally tried to make their stay as pleasant as possible. But bad weather held the expedition up for about a week. "Being eager to get on board the *Hindostan*, which lay at no greater distance than ten leagues, made us very fractious and impatient, which the mandarins took notice of, but did not appear displeased."[3] "The rain has been unceasing, falling constantly on the roofs of the junks," Alexander noted on November 22. "From rain and wind, which found their way into our berth, we have passed a sleepless night."[4]

Suddenly bundles of tea and silk appeared. The governor of Zhejiang had specially ordered the silk, since none was produced locally. It was an elegant gesture, with nothing demanded in return. In other words, though the British were forbidden to trade in the city, the empire demonstrated a generosity that Qianlong hoped would elicit undying gratitude from the barbarians.

Songyun supplied the emperor with reports of the progress of this branch of the expedition:

> On November 18 we arrived in Ningbo. The Barbarian officers openly expressed their admiration for Hangzhou silk, though without daring to suggest that they purchase any. The best way of avoiding any idle discussion of this possibility was therefore to present them with a bit of tea and silk as gifts, in Your name. We told them that Ningbo was not disposed to engage in trade with foreigners, but that they could conduct such trade in Canton. In the meantime, each of the Barbarian officers received four pieces of Hangzhou cloth, fifty pounds of tea, and six pounds of raw silk, while each soldier of the contingent will also receive some tea and cloth. The Barbarian officers cast themselves to their knees and touched their foreheads to the ground to thank Your Imperial Majesty.
>
> The military governor, Wang Hui, and his men will hold themselves in readiness to intervene when Prefect Keshina escorts the English to their ship.[5]

This latter bit of information was undoubtedly accurate, while the former was not. But in both cases Songyun was simply reporting what the emperor wanted to hear.

Its holds loaded with silk, tea, and the English cloth that had been vainly brought from home, its decks crowded with the extra personnel of the embassy, the *Hindostan* finally set sail, leaving a long trail of yellow mud in its wake.[6]

MEANWHILE, the ambassador's progress toward Canton was also halted by rainstorms, accompanied by the squalls common in these southern latitudes. "The waters of the river roared like a tiger, breaking against the mountains, devouring columns of rain in its swirling eddies, pounding, roiling, tumbling, surging."[7] "We have been detained all day at this place (Yushanxian)," Macartney wrote on November 22, "by the violent rain which has now fallen for four and twenty hours without intermission."[8]

The next day the ambassador took advantage of the delay to draft the "note of compliment" that Changlin had suggested he send to the emperor. "Observing the character of the writing to be remarkably neat, he [Changlin] inquired who had transcribed it, and when I informed him that it was little Thomas Staunton, he would scarcely believe that a boy of twelve years old could have already made such progress. Nor was he perfectly satisfied till he had actually seen him add, at the bottom of the paper in Chinese characters, that it had been written by him."[9]

Though a copy of this extraordinary "note of compliment," written in English by Macartney and transcribed into Chinese by the page, was sent to Henry Dundas, I found no trace of it in the British archives. It was, however, carefully preserved in the Imperial Archives, which on the other hand contain no copies of any of Macartney's notes outlining King George's requests. Communications dealing with wretched commerce apparently had no business being filed among His Sacred Majesty's correspondence. The compliment copied out by the Sinified child, however, was an inestimable tribute well worth preserving.

Ritual required that the scribe begin a new line every time the word *Emperor* appeared (in this case, seven times). Young Thomas, more flexible than his master where ceremony was concerned, observed this rite:

The ambassador of England, Ma-ga-er-ni, thanks
the Great Emperor for his favors. Our sovereign sincerely desires that
the Great Emperor enjoy great happiness and longevity. Now that we
    have been received by
the Great Emperor, our sovereign authorizes us to express
    once again to
the Great Emperor the desire that he live ten thousand times ten
    thousand years, and that our sovereign hear his moral teachings

ten thousand times ten thousand years. In truth, the manifestation of the favors of

the Great Emperor is a stroke of luck for our country.

The Great Emperor has not only held nothing against us, but has given most freely of His time. For this we are grateful, and more than words can express do we appreciate His attitude in our regard. Our sovereign, in turn, will be unfailingly grateful. We entreat the Great Personage* to thank, on our behalf,

the Great Emperor for His favors.

This text has been written by the hand of Duo-ma Si-dang-dong [Thomas Staunton].[10]

Undoubtedly a pastiche, but it made the essential point: a stroke of luck for our country. While conforming to the requisite rites, it yet maintained some dignity. Probably too much, in the view of Bernardo d'Almeida, the Portuguese Jesuit who had been assigned to translate a similar letter sent to Qianlong several days earlier by Macartney to thank him for the Fu character. D'Almeida must have considered this insufficiently obsequious thank-you note deficient in enumerating the many favors the emperor had granted. The missionary therefore confected a pastiche of a pastiche, also conserved in the archives of the Grand Council. It begins this way:

Ma-ga-er-ni, the ambassador of the country of the men of red hair, prostrates himself to the earth before

the Great Emperor.

He has benefited, throughout his journey, from the favors of

the Great Emperor.

The Great Emperor has bestowed food and presents upon him. In Zhejiang the envoy once again received the favors of

the Great Emperor, who offered his king a satin purse and a calligraphy of the character Fu.

The Great Emperor has granted the envoy of the men of red hair permission to travel to Guangdong, by way of Jiangxi, from Hangzhou.[11]

And so on.

The lower, the better.

---

* The letter was meant to be read to the emperor by one of the embassy's escorts, probably Changlin himself, upon his return to the court.

68

Corporal Punishment

(November 23–27, 1793)

The chief ends proposed by the institution of punishments in the empire, have been to guard against violence and injury, to repress inordinate desires, and to secure the peace and tranquillity of an honest and unoffending community.

KANGXI, 1662–1722[1]

DESPITE A THICK FOG, the mission set out again on November 23, moving through a ghostly landscape. "The mist grew every moment darker and heavier," Macartney wrote, "and so magnified the objects around us that no wonder our senses and imaginations were equally deceived and disturbed, and that the temples, turrets, and pagodas appeared to us through the fog, as we sailed along, like so many phantoms of giants and monsters flitting away from us, and vanishing in the gloom."[2] Young Staunton was especially impressed by the mountains, which rose steeply from the riverside and were topped with pines. That night, when the fog lifted, the British saw their first sugarcane plantations. Thomas noted the "small mills for sugar. Some of these mills were built in the middle of the river, which being very shallow was easily close. The waterwheel is turned by the current."[3] The British were surprised that these were the first mills they had seen, for there was no lack of wind or water.

The next day the river wound through enormous rocks. "In some parts I observed people cutting the stone into the shape of bricks, and in others, there were large heaps of them, which were of a deep red. Several of these huge stones had been excavated with great labour, and formed a sort of dwelling, many of whose inhabitants came forth to see our fleet pass along before them. Some of the intervals between these stones were of sufficient extent to admit of gardens with their buildings and pagodas, which produced very picturesque, romantic, and delightful pictures. . . . This very singular and stupendous scenery continued, for a length of several miles."[4]

Only in China could visitors see roads hewn from the flanks of cliffs and human habitations hanging over the abyss.

They came out of the mountains on November 26, and the river suddenly widened, entering the famous Lake Boyang.[5] But we learn from Thomas that they never really saw it: "Last night I am told that we passed thro' a part of the great Lake Boyang."[6]

The boy's father, apparently unaware that he would be betrayed by his big-mouth son, could not resist describing what he had not seen: "The travellers . . . entered soon into that great extent of flat and swampy land, in the midst of which is the Boyang lake,* being the largest collection of water within the Chinese dominions." The lake fed various canals, which were protected by strong dikes to hold back "the billows of the lake," which, according to "Chinese mariners," rise "sometimes to such a height, as to render it . . . as dangerous as the sea."† Huts had been built on the banks; the residents, generally poor, lived from fishing. "Each inhabitant seemed to have his own fishing grounds. Their ponds were divided into small portions, in which their fish were bred and fattened. Some of them were a small species like sprats, which dried and salted, become an object of commerce throughout the empire."[8]

It was at this crossroads lake that the convoy reentered the normal Peking-to-Canton route.

Thomas noticed that the Chinese had arranged for the flotilla to pass through cities only at night. Life on the junks was unvaried: military posts greeted the visitors with petards, the soldiers supposedly showing the tiger's teeth; haulers were recruited and driven with whips; the populace was carefully isolated from any contact with the barbarians.

The monotony was broken on November 25. "Today two of our gentlemen who were walking on shore were violently attacked by two soldiers in the presence of a Blue Buttoned mandarine," writes Thomas.[9] Staunton senior reports that the embassy's escorts ordered the soldiers whipped immediately, but appealed to the viceroy to punish the mandarin.[10] "The viceroy," Thomas explains, "deprived the mandarine of his button and then flogged him. The soldiers were put in the cangue [yoke] and would have had their back bambooed if Lord Macartney had not begged off that part of the punishment."[11]

---

* They crossed the lake in order to get from the mouth of the Xinjiang, down which they had sailed, to that of the Gan, up which they now turned.[7]
† This lake was known as a sort of Chinese Bermuda Triangle. Even today ships sometimes sink in its turbulent waters.

The incident offered our travelers an opportunity to discourse on Chinese justice, a delicate subject on which Voltaire had written: "The constitution of their empire is the finest in the world, it alone being founded entirely on patriarchal power—which, however, does not prevent the mandarins from treating their children to powerful blows of the stick."[12] Spare the rod and spoil the child.

"The obvious object of the government," Staunton explains, "in seeking to maintain the general tranquillity and welfare, seems to have overlooked all precautions for the personal security of individuals."[13] A death sentence is "seldom . . . inflicted without the confirmation of the Emperor; but it takes place sometimes by order of the Viceroy of the province in cases of emergency, such as rebellion or sedition." Normally, "criminals for execution are all transferred to Peking, where a revision of the sentence is had before the great tribunal allotted for that purpose." Executions take place once a year, in autumn, heads falling along with the leaves. The number of capital sentences is "seldom above two hundred . . . very small for so vast and populous an empire." Fines, imprisonment, flagellation, and exile were the more usual punishments, "except in crimes against the state or Emperor, or in cases of blood, which admit of no pardon or commutation; nor is there any distinction between murder and manslaughter. Theft is never punished with death; nor is robbery, unless the act be accompanied with personal injury and cruelty."*[15]

Staunton felt that the "moderation of those punishments seems to imply the infrequency of the offence."[16] As an example of this "moderation," he cited the use of the cangue, or yoke, admittedly more lenient than the rope with which English thieves were hanged at the time. "It consists of an enormous tablet of wood with a hole in the middle to receive the neck, and two smaller ones for the hands of the offender. It is a kind of permanent and ambulatory pillory, which the culprit is sentenced sometimes to wear for weeks or months together. He is suffered, provided his strength will enable him, to walk about; but is generally glad, for the support of his awkward and degrading burden, to lean against a wall or tree. If a servant or runner of the civil magistrate takes it into his head that the culprit has

---

* The figure of two hundred executions a year sounds quite low, if it is meant to include all murderers. As late as 1830 hundreds of death sentences were pronounced each year in France, which had perhaps a twelfth of China's population. Other witnesses make different estimates. "Those criminals who are condemned to die in the autumn," Father Lamiot writes, "are executed in all the capitals of the provinces, unless the Emperor grants them clemency. There are provinces in which several hundred people are executed annually."[14] This figure does not include those who died during beatings with bamboo.

rested too long, he beats him with a whip, made of leather thongs, till he rises."[17]

Staunton questioned the mandarins of the escort, one of whose tasks was to satisfy their guests' curiosity. He was told that "confinement for debt is only temporary. . . . [But] in China the interests of the Emperor are always made the first object. No property can be secure against his claims." The Chinese were little inclined to litigation: "Property beside, whether real or personal, is held by tenures too simple to occasion much difference of opinion as to the right to it." Within families, "union" tends to hold sway.[18]

Staunton's comments are just about as "edifying" as those of the Jesuits. Our travelers apparently knew nothing of the boots and thumbscrews that crushed fingers and feet, or the bamboo beatings conducted even in court, supposedly in an effort to elicit the truth. Not a word about the corruption that was (and remains) the scourge of prison life. Nor about prisoners who died of hunger when their families were unable or unwilling to send them food. Nor about the secrecy surrounding the political prisons. One wonders whether the British were simply using the Chinese example to excoriate the West, China serving as a kind of fun-house mirror in which creative Western masochism sought the reflection of its own cruel truths.

69

Pleasures and Frustrations of Tourism

(November 27–December 4, 1793)

JINGDEZHEN, "the town of Great Virtue," was and remains the capital of China's porcelain industry, a huge imperial hearth that dwarfed Sèvres. At the time its production was reserved for the emperor, and we know from the loquacious Staunton junior that the British actually skirted the city, being unable even to enter it, let alone visit any factories or observe the processes of porcelain manufacture.

Staunton senior notes matter-of-factly: "A village or unwalled town called Kin-te-Chin, was not very far distant from this part of the traveller's route, in which three thousand furnaces for baking porcelain, were said to be lighted at a time, and gave to the place, at night, the appearance of a town on fire."[1] Staunton never saw the town, but he had apparently read the Jesuits: "In Kin-te-Chin there are some three thousand furnaces for porcelain. At nightfall it is as if an entire great city were in flames."[2] Both texts also speak of "the genius of fire." A curious coincidence.

Here Staunton is caught red-handed. Father Huc later repeated the same passage virtually word for word,[3] adding (he was, after all, a Gascon) that the city had more than a million inhabitants. All these "travelers" brazenly copied from one another, but the child revealed the truth.

The British entered the province of Jiangxi during the season when wheat began to grow and sugarcane was ready for harvesting. Staunton reports that the female peasants of the province were not subjected to the cruel practice of foot binding and were "so remarkably robust and laborious, that peasants have been known to come to purchase what they call, a working wife, in Jiangxi."[4] He adds that the "wives were distinguished from the maidens, by the latter allowing the hair near the forehead to hang down towards the eyebrows, while the former had all theirs bound together upon the crown of the head."[5] This is still the case in Jiangxi today, where married and unmarried women may be recognized by their concealed or exposed foreheads. Even fashion tends not to vary much in China.

Women were harnessed to the plow like beasts of burden. "A farmer in that province has been seen to drive, with one hand, a plough, to which his wife was yoked, while he sowed the seed with the other hand in drills."[6] A sight that may still be seen today, though more rarely. The Chinese, in fact, have often satirized themselves for such practices. One seventeenth-century tale tells us that "the men, arms hanging slack, feet extended under the table, think only of lounging about, while their wives and daughters toil in the fields, under the leaden sun, mean scarves knotted over their heads, even wading in the mud and hoeing the weeds."[7]

Mutilated feet were therefore a mark of social elevation for women, announcing their emancipation from work in the fields. A woman with unbound feet was a woman condemned to labor, while she whose feet were bound was exempt from toil. This may be part of the reason why women became accomplices in their own mutilation.

MACARTNEY AND STAUNTON, their curiosity piqued by the questionnaire Arthur Young had drawn up for them, inquired into the structure of rural property ownership. In Jiangxi province land was leased for terms of three, five, or seven years in a kind of sharecropping system. The landlord and farmer shared the harvest equally, while the former paid the taxes, theoretically 5 percent of the harvest's value but in practice often "a tenth of the whole."[8]

Staunton does not mention the fact that poorly paid local mandarins supplemented their incomes by taking a cut of the tax receipts, which explains the difference between the theoretical 5 percent and the actual 10 percent: the overage went into the mandarins' pockets. Careful moderation in theory, extensive corruption in practice.

The British tourists, like many of their successors in our own time, failed to perceive the gap between theory and reality. "It is, certainly, a wise policy in the government of China to receive the greater part of the taxes in the produce of that country; and is a considerable spur to improvement and industry in every class of the people, who are to get their bread by the exertions of genius, or the sweat of their brow."[9] Barrow was equally impressed: "The taxes raised for the support of government are far from being exorbitant or burthensome to the subject. They consist in the tenth of the produce of the land usually in kind, in a duty on salt, on foreign imports, and a few smaller taxes, that do not materially affect the bulk of the people."[10]

Barrow makes no mention of forced labor, but Winder does: "A kind of feudal tenure" is imposed on the farmers, who are "obliged, under the penalty of personal service," to supply haulers for passing boats.[11]

Chinese vox populi described the situation in adages rather more realistic than the reports of our dazzled travelers. Like: "The mandarins suck the people's marrow." Or: "Fire goes to the roast like money to the mandarin."[12] In the British mind, however, the China of the *philosophes* had not entirely yielded to the cold light of reality.

THE FLOTILLA SAILED up the Gan, and on December 1 they reached the mountains in which this river has its source. Thomas described the rituals practiced by the boatmen to mollify the river: "Each boat has its Fo [Buddha] or god to whom they make large sacrifices on their departure from any place, of silvered paper, paper boats, meat, salt, etc. which they throw into the water."[13]

Some of the mountaintops were crowned with buildings, "which have the appearance of watchtowers, somewhat resembling those I have seen on the coast of Spain between Carthagena and Malaga."* Macartney also noticed "some very pretty white pagodas of nine stories high, newly built on lesser eminences near the banks."[14]

That night, at Jianfu,† the British were treated to an unusually warm welcome: "From the crowd of people, the bustle made by the attendants of the mandarin, with the discharge of artillery, and the firing of rockets, such a scene of noise and confusion took place, as would have alarmed the whole British embassy on its first arrival in this country."[15]

Hadn't the local mandarins been told not to organize any welcoming ceremonies for the men of red hair? "Several temporary buildings were erected on purpose, as it appeared, to display a complimentary illumination of great magnificence, which was formed by a profusion of lamps, candles, and flambeaux."[16]

Temporary buildings? Once again the British seem to have mistaken pai-lou for temporary constructions. Or perhaps Anderson (or his imaginative editor) was merely hallucinating. "We saw little of the town," says

---

* These Spanish *atalayas* were of Arab origin, and it is possible that the Arabs, who traveled the Silk Road, may have copied Chinese models.
† Macartney calls the city Ki-gan-fu, while Staunton junior writes "Singafou" and Anderson "Chinga-foo."

Thomas, "as it was dark."[17] The child's report is probably the more reliable.

The next day the river was suddenly crowded. The flotilla passed "a great many" boats and balsa-wood rafts, "some of several hundred feet long." These were "navigated with a mast and sail and have houses raised upon them for the habitation of the skippers and their families. Such numbers of children as poured out from them to see us can only be compared to bees rushing from their hives at the time of swarming."[18]

The flotilla sailed deeper into Jiangxi, in our own day a rather poor province with a great revolutionary tradition.

ON DECEMBER 4 Thomas noted that the river was strewn with reefs. Winder recognized this stretch of water as the "eighteen cataracts" described by terrified Jesuits, and though he saw "many wrecks," he seemed unimpressed.[19] Barrow ascribed the locale's dangerous reputation to Chinese incompetence: "The Chinese have no great dexterity in the management of their vessels. They are so easily alarmed, that they frequently miscarry through timidity, when a little recollection and resolution would have secured them success."[20] Once again it is the boy who strikes the right note: the rapids "are dangerous to pass only at night."[21] They are less perilous for those traveling upstream, as this flotilla was, but it took two days to clear the obstacles.

At the fifteenth rapid, several of the boats capsized on the rocks, frightening the boatmen, who, Barrow writes (with the mocking phlegmaticism already typical of the Western visitor to exotic lands), "began to implore the assistance of the river god by sounding the gong, in order to rouse his attention and, by regaling his olfactory nerves with the smoke of burning sticks of sandalwood matches."[22]

On that same day, in Peking, an innocent man who had suffered much grief on account of this embassy was finally released from his ordeal: Guo Jieguan, the man suspected of unauthorized linguistic expertise, who had been prudently removed from Ningbo to Peking by order of the emperor, was cleared of all charges. As it turned out, he had never had the slightest contact either with the English or with their language, of which he knew not a word. His father had indeed traded with the barbarians, but that was forty years ago. He therefore represented no danger.[23] But his involuntary trip to Peking had not been for nothing: at least it set the emperor's mind at rest and inspired the Celestial bureaucracy to greater vigilance.

Also on December 4, Anderson noticed a beautiful building. Was it a temple or the harem of a high-ranking mandarin? The former, he was told, but he much preferred to believe the latter. He admired Chinese artistry in integrating buildings into the natural beauties of their settings.[24]

What Anderson did not know was that geomancy and hierarchy both played major roles in architecture. The location of entrances and the place-ment of buildings were determined so as to avoid evil spirits and attract the good graces of the divinity. The heights of buildings were proportional to their owners' ranks in the social pyramid. The beauty of the results owed more to taste than to geomancy, but it may be that the Chinese mind was so imbued with the powerful order of mountains, rivers, and landscapes that taste and geomancy had become one.

70

The Match of Progress

(December 4–6, 1793)

The imitative slave is born and vanishes, while only to the inventive is life promised.

ANDRÉ CHÉNIER[1]

THE VICEROY, accompanied by Wang and Qiao, came to visit Macartney at eight in the evening on December 4, spending four hours with him. Changlin was even more courteous than usual, speaking freely "on a great variety of things." He asked about "the value and amount" of British trade in Canton and also inquired about "that of other nations." He admitted that he suspected the Canton mandarins of embezzling money from the empire, but Macartney replied with "proper reserve saying that, as I had never been at Canton, I could not speak with precision, but that when I arrived there I would endeavour to procure for him any information in my power that he wished to have."[2]

At one point in the conversation Changlin took out his pipe. The viceroy's servant was absent, so Macartney reached into his pocket for "a small phosphoric bottle, and instantly kindled a match at it." Changlin was stunned that a man could carry "fire in his pocket" without being burned, and Macartney "explained to him the phenomenon and made him a present" of the rudimentary lighter.[3]

It seems remarkable that Changlin had never seen such a device, since the invention of matches in the sixth century is mentioned in Chinese texts of the tenth. At that time matches were known as "light-bearing slaves."[4] But even at the peak of the dynasty's power, China under the Qings had apparently forgotten them. In the nineteenth century the Chinese began calling matches *yanghuo*, or "foreign fire." (The term *yang* generally applies to anything imported from overseas, especially the West.) This is one of the many instances in which China, having been centuries (sometimes even a millennium or two) ahead of the West, had subsequently fallen behind, losing track of manufacturing processes that China itself had invented.

This "little incident led to a conversation upon other curious subjects, from which it appeared to us how far the Chinese (though they excel in some branches of mechanics) are yet behind other nations in medical or surgical skill and philosophical knowledge. Having often observed numbers of blind persons, but never having met a wooden leg or a deformed limb here, I concluded that good ocultists were very rare and that death was the usual consequence of a fracture."[5]

The viceroy confirmed that Macartney's supposition was accurate. "But when I told him of many things in England, and which I had brought people to instruct the Chinese in, if it had been allowed, such as the reanimating of drowned persons by a mechanical operation, restoring sight to the blind by extraction or depression of the glaucoma, and repairing or amputating limbs by manual dexterity, both he and his companions seemed as if awakened out of a dream, and could not conceal their regret for the Court's coldness and indifference to our discoveries."[6]

This conversation alone justified Macartney's decision to travel to Canton with Changlin instead of embarking on the *Hindostan* in Zhoushan. The viceroy had given the ambassador an opportunity to expound on some of the realities of which the Celestial hierarchy was (or pretended to be) unaware.

As late as the sixteenth century, China was still far ahead of the West. Its technical expertise was unparalleled (though its science was less elaborate, most Chinese inventions owing more to ingenuity than to theoretical speculation).

The Chinese used the decimal system five centuries before Europe. A thousand years before Macartney's visit they had an arithmetical notation that included zero and negative numbers. They invented the chest-and-collar harness a thousand years before its use became generalized in the Europe of Philippe Auguste and Frederick Barbarossa. Fifteen centuries before the Europeans, the Chinese detected sunspots, manufactured porcelain, invented magic lanterns, and used calliper rulers. They sowed their fields in rows, weeded vegetable gardens, and employed metal plows more than two thousand years before the rest of the world. The rotary threshing machine, which the West discovered in the eighteenth century, and the seeder, whose ingenuity Macartney's companions so openly admired, had been known in China for more than twenty centuries. The same might be said of the piston bellows, the smelting of steel, the technique of drilling for natural gas, and the construction of suspension bridges.

The enumeration of Chinese inventions takes up fifteen volumes of Joseph Needham's monumental work on China's science and civilization. This British scholar showed that many of the innovations that shook the West during the Renaissance originated in China and were brought to

Europe much later, either during the Crusades (through contact with Islam) or as a result of the great maritime explorations.

Granted, Needham sometimes displays the systematic relentlessness of a researcher who has decided in advance what his research must reveal, and the speculation of William Golding (who claims in his *Envoy Extraordinary* that a Greek traveler of Marcus Aurelius's time was actually responsible for many of the discoveries later attributed to the Chinese) cannot be entirely ruled out.[7] But there is little doubt that some of the major achievements of European civilization were based on discoveries that came originally from China, in particular some of the weapons with which the West later conquered the world. Long before the Europeans, the Chinese invented the compass and the rear rudder,* which made sea voyages possible; paper and printing, which permitted the explosion of reading and culture; paper money, which fostered the expansion of trade and the banking system; gunpowder and firearms, which changed the face of military combat. But none of these inventions had such sweeping effects in China itself, and with time several of them were actually lost.

At the beginning of the fifteenth century the eunuch admiral Zheng He, commanding four hundred junks outfitted for war, explored the shores of the Pacific and the Indian Ocean, from Timor to the Red Sea, possibly going as far as the Cape of Good Hope. Yet by the end of that century, when Vasco da Gama sailed into the Indian Ocean from the opposite direction, the Middle Empire had definitively abandoned maritime exploration. It was as if the country's mental energy, like that of the autistic child described by Bettelheim, was "made to serve only one goal: to protect sheer life by doing nothing about outside reality."[9]

The Ming emperors called upon their subjects to return to the strict observance of Confucian precepts, to imitate the ancients in all respects, and to reject pernicious foreign influences. They decreed immobility at the very moment that Europe, having recovered from the horrors of the Black Death, was grasping the means to speed the slow advance that had led them from the darkness of the tenth century to the outer boundaries of the known world. As the human adventure swept across the planet, the Chinese turned in on themselves, secure in their sense of their own superiority. But the country could not remain closed forever, and traders and missionaries soon began arriving on their shores.

---

* Needham argues that the Chinese also invented the sextant, but theirs was a primitive version of the instrument. It was later perfected by Westerners, while it fell out of use in China— another example of Chinese backsliding. Dinwiddie affirms that the Chinese had no apparatus for measuring a star's elevation above the horizon, adding that their only navigational instrument was a fairly crude compass.[8]

Now Europe was knocking at the gates in earnest, bringing news of the extraordinary further development of inventions that even the Chinese themselves no longer realized had originated in their country. The West had nurtured seedlings that China had allowed to wither, and it was China, more than Europe, that now stood to gain from trade and interpenetration. China was still mired in superstition, while the West was tearing itself away from it. The Chinese always paint a pair of eyes on the prows of their ships, a sarcastic Dinwiddie commented. If you ask them why, they reply, "How else could they see where they are going?"[10]

Now, near the end of his mission, Macartney had finally made contact with interlocutors capable of understanding the gap that had arisen between these two civilizations, and they were riveted by his account of Western progress: "From the manner of these gentlemen's inquiries, the remarks which they made, and the impressions which they seemed to feel, I have conceived a much higher opinion of their liberality and understanding."[11]

On February 1, 1793, while on his way to China, Macartney had written in his unpublished journal, "The art of flying in a balloon is now become almost as easy as that of driving in a Whisky. Dr. Hawes and the Human Society raise the dead without difficulty by a mechanical operation."[12] Here the ambassador's imagination had run ahead of the reality of scientific progress, but it is true that William Hawes had demonstrated the possibility of artificial respiration in 1773, and soon afterward John Hunter invented a mechanical device for the purpose. Eye surgery had taken a leap forward with Jacques Daviel's operation to cure cataracts and George Joseph Beer's for the treatment of glaucoma. As for the balloon fad, it began in Paris in 1783 and spread to Edinburgh in 1784; in 1785 a Frenchman and an American became the first to cross the English Channel in a hot-air balloon similar to the one Macartney had brought along to show the Chinese.

The ambassador did his best to communicate his enthusiasm for the progress of science and technology, and he was pleased with the responses of Changlin, Wang, and Qiao. He wondered whether Heshen was "really inferior to them, or whether he acts upon a certain public system, which often supersedes private conviction."[13]

Macartney had been shocked at Heshen's lack of interest in scientific and technological exchange: "In a conversation with him in Jehol, when I mentioned to him some recent inventions of European ingenuity, particularly that of the air balloon, and that I had taken care to provide one at Peking with a person to go up in it, he not only discouraged that experiment, but most of the others, which from a perusal of all the printed accounts of this country we had calculated and prepared for the meridian of China."

Macartney regretted that "whatever taste the Emperor Kangxi might have shown for the sciences, as related by the Jesuits in his day, his successors have not inherited it with his other great qualities and possessions. For it would now seem that the policy and vanity of the Court equally concurred in endeavouring to keep out of sight whatever can manifest our pre-eminence, which they undoubtedly feel, but have not yet learned to make the proper use of."[14] Had a hot-air balloon risen over Peking, all China would have known of Western superiority. An unthinkable outrage. Father Amiot commented in 1789, "Of all the new inventions of which I have had the opportunity to speak [in Peking], aerial navigation is the one that has aroused the least excitement. Aerostatic balloons are seen as mere objects of curiosity."[15] And even that curiosity soon faded. At the end of the nineteenth century, Yenfu wrote: "The virtuous descendants of Kangxi had to confront rapid changes occurring in the world. Instead of taking inspiration from the living spirit of their ancestor, they remained faithful to the dead institutions he had left behind."[16] The observation perfectly suits Qianlong and Heshen as well. Theirs was an ostrich policy.

Macartney and Changlin both sensed that while Chinese inventions were the product of mere tinkering, Western ones were increasingly the fruit of science. "All their technological processes," wrote one of our French observers in Canton, "are due only to experience and observation."[17]

Apparently Macartney had not read the Jesuits carefully enough, for Father Parennin had remarked upon Chinese scientific backwardness as early as 1740: "They are devoid of that uneasiness whose name is curiosity and which drives science forward with such great strides."[18] If necessity is the mother of invention, it is hard to see what might have goaded Qianlong to innovation, since he was fully convinced that his empire needed nothing.

Macartney concluded his account of this important meeting with a profession of faith quite typical of its time: "It is . . . in vain to attempt resisting the progress of human knowledge. The human mind is of a soaring nature and having once gained the lower steps of the ascent, struggles incessantly against every difficulty to reach the highest." Macartney's friend Samuel Johnson observed that "the desires of man increase with his acquisitions; every step which he advances brings something within his view, which he did not see before, and which . . . he begins to want."[19] But the Celestial system seemed to reject both this eternal curiosity and these insatiable desires.

For how long would the Chinese tolerate this system? Dinwiddie took heart (recovering from the depression born of the stubborn obstinacy of his interlocutors in Peking) when, in Canton, he succeeded in interesting some Chinese in his scientific demonstrations.[20] As for Macartney, he felt that the "Tartar government" would not long be able to "stifle the energies of their Chinese subjects." The frequency of revolt, he wrote, was "a strong symptom of the fever within."

Macartney returned to this theme of popular agitation several times: "There are certain mysterious societies in every province who are known to be disaffected, and although narrowly watched by the government, they find means to elude its vigilance and often to hold secret assemblies, where they revive the memory of ancient glory and independence, brood over recent injuries, and meditate revenge."[21]

Had Macartney found out about these societies from the mandarins escorting the embassy? The missionaries seem a more likely source of such information, but one way or the other, the ambassador's conclusions were confirmed over the next century. The secret societies, thriving on popular discontent, kindled anti-Manchu nationalism when their members were Han Chinese and anti-Han nationalism when they were composed of non-Chinese minorities. This was the only form of organization that eluded government control, and the only one that seemed to its members capable of promoting progress. The secret societies, as Hegel might have put it,[22] were alone in escaping the terrifying and venerable father figure who embodied not only the ancestors of the entire population, but also the empire's successive dynasties and the collective Chinese soul, reigning over what Western individualists would have called the inviolable domain of individual conscience. By gathering together in secret, the members of the underground societies overcame their own isolation and impotence, forming, as Durkheim showed,[23] a psychic entity far more dynamic than the sum of their individual components.

We now know that Qianlong's reign was marked by numerous revolts, and news of some of them reached the missionaries and the Europeans in Macao. The British knew of several that had occurred in the years before the embassy's arrival, and later there were others.* In 1800 our good friend

---

* The Jinchuan, a mountain people in western Sichuan, rebelled on various occasions between 1771 and 1776. The Muslims of Gansu revolted in 1784. In 1787 there was an uprising of Chinese settlers in Taiwan who hoped to reestablish the Mings. In 1791–92 the Gurkhas rebelled in Tibet. These upheavals were followed, in 1795, by a revolt of the Miao tribes in the border regions between Sichuan and Hunan, crushed by our old friend General Fukang'an, a renowned specialist in repression. The rebellions led by the White Lotus (Bai Lian Jiao) sect were more explicitly political and anti-Manchu in content. This group had its base among the populations of Hubei, who suffered oppression by local officials. The rebellion began in 1795 and ended only in 1804.

Wang was killed during the repression of one of them, the White Lotus revolt in Shanxi province.[24]

Father de Grammont's papers include his translation of a report from the viceroy of Shanxi published in an unidentified newspaper in Peking:

> I had been advised that an evil sect was holding meetings and reciting prayers. The local mandarin had dispatched bowmen to halt this disorder, and his people had been manhandled. I myself went to *Ho-tchéou*. These rebels numbered more than two thousand and were well armed. They formed up in battle lines. Their chief had at his side two women, their hair disheveled, holding unsheathed swords in one hand and banners in the other. They hurled a thousand curses. The rebels fought fiercely, and the battle lasted five hours.
>
> Upon visiting the battlefield, I found their chief stretched out on the ground, the two women beside him. I had the heads of these offenders cut off and displayed to the public in cages. The people are joyful.[25]

Father de Grammont complained that on Christmas Eve the year before, the Catholic community of this same province of Shanxi had been branded a "secret society" and denounced as a "foreign association." Qianlong made little distinction between rebels and Christians.

Behind the façade of the immutable apparatus, there was turmoil in the corridors of the empire, and the Manchu regime was uneasy. The threats it faced undoubtedly account for its fiercely defensive reaction to any potential challenge to its power. The British visitors were troublemakers in an already troubled order.

CHANGLIN DULY reported his conversations with Macartney to Peking. The ambassador's memorandum on trade, delivered to the viceroy on November 20, was likewise forwarded to the emperor. On December 1 the Grand Council issued an edict signed by Qianlong that, while failing to respond to any of Macartney's fifteen points, not only registered the possibility of a new embassy, but also treated the possibility as a promise.

At nine o'clock in the evening on December 9, just after the embassy's arrival in Nan'anfu, the viceroy showed Macartney this imperial letter, a copy of which would be delivered to him later. It said, in substance:

> Having been unaware of the usages of the Empire, you presented indecent requests. You now express your intention to return again bearing tribute. Observing your respectful reverence, We condescend

to grant you this favor. The date may be set at your convenience. You shall inform your sovereign that the Great Emperor agrees not to hold him responsible for the errors he has committed with regard to Celestial institutions, of which he was ignorant.[26]

Though a copy of this haughty letter remained among his papers, Macartney refrained from recording its content in his journal, even in a bowdlerized form. Instead he summarized Changlin's amiable presentation of it, adding that "it seems conceived in very friendly terms, saying that if the King should send a Minister again to China he would be well received." But the ambassador realized that his putative successor would have to conform strictly to the rites required of tributary envoys, in particular by arriving first in Canton. This was an implicit "disapprobation of our having come up the Gulf of Beizhili" to Tientsin. "Nevertheless," Macartney added, he had no regrets about having come by that route, "as by these means we are now masters of the geography of the north-east coasts of China, and have acquired a knowledge of the Yellow Sea, which was never before navigated by European ships."[27] Another tacit admission that military reconnaissance was one of the tasks of this mission. And Macartney's information was later put to use: in 1816 Lord Amherst's embassy also bypassed the imperial requirement and arrived by way of the Yellow Sea.

Changlin had accompanied Macartney's memorandum to Peking with protestations of the profound respect now allegedly manifested by the finally repentant barbarians. But the emperor rejected the British requests as sharply as ever, treating the embassy to a stinging, if paternal, lecture. The viceroy passed on the imperial reprimands in the gentlest possible tone, and Mr. Plumb softened them even further in his translation. Macartney presents a rose-colored summary, while Staunton does not even mention the document.

Misunderstanding continued to deepen with each successive exchange, the emperor pretending that he had heard Macartney say what he had not said, Macartney pretending that he had not heard the emperor say what he had. Changlin saved face for Qianlong, Macartney for George III, and both thereby maintained the serenity of their joint journey. The spirit of the late Father Amiot, who had spent more than forty years in the Chinese court, seems present at these conversations of December 1793. Conform to custom and be patient, the priest had advised. But in his journal Macartney makes no secret of his satisfaction at having prepared the way for more forceful action.

71

Descent Toward Canton

(December 6–14, 1793)

THE FLOTILLA CONTINUED its journey up the Gan River, which now flowed through high hills terraced with sugarcane plantations. On the evening of December 5 they arrived in Ganzhoufu, a "large walled city of the first order," where they were treated to a "profusion of military honours," including banners, music, and a three-gun salute.[1]

On December 7 the river became so shallow that the British had to disembark to lighten the boats, even though the Chinese dug a channel "by removing the stones and gravel with iron rakes."[2] On December 9, after two more days of slow sailing, they reached Nan'an, where the river was no longer navigable at all. For the second time they had to cross high ground over land, traveling through the Meiling pass, famous not for its altitude (barely 350 yards above the plain), but because it was the sole terrestrial interruption in the normal 1,500-mile riverine route between Peking and Canton. (The earlier land passage had been required only because of the convoy's detour through the province of Zhejiang.)

"*Tuesday, December 10,*" writes Macartney. "This morning we set out by land . . . [traveling] in the same manner as in our former expedition, some in palanquins and some on horseback, according to the conveyance they liked best." Actually, except for Staunton, his companions were offered only their choice of horses. The British rode fifteen miles "through a romantic Alpine country and over a mountain that divides the provinces of Jiangxi and Guangdong."[3] This winding road enabled them to avoid what would have been a long detour. They then descended into a land of rice paddies, moving from river to river, covering about thirty miles in nine hours. In 1710 the Jesuit Father Ripa reported that this route was so crowded with travelers that it resembled a pathway in a fairgrounds. There seems to have been less traffic in 1793.

Macartney admired the agile gait of the four bearers of his palanquin. Most people would expect this vehicle, a means of transport favored by illustrious personalities, to travel at a processional pace, but in fact the bearers "ran at full speed, more swiftly than the birds."[4] Official palanquin carriers were supposed to cover a hundred *li* a day, or about thirty miles. It was scarcely an enviable job, described this way in a ballad written during Qianlong's reign:

> The unhappy man, accompanying dignitaries,
> Bears the palanquin and runs without respite,
> While his shoulders, bruised by the friction,
> Soon are covered with open sores. . . .[5]

For the British, such practices were evidence of the "industry of the Chinese." Macartney seemed amazed: "In our navigation from Hangzhou the boatmen were usually wet up to their knees twenty times in a day, and sometimes almost the whole day, dragging our yachts along and often actually lifting them by mere bodily force over the shallows that occurred so often. . . . I have seen two Chinese raise nearly a ton weight between them, and pass it from one vessel to another. I doubt whether the labour of a negro in our West Indies be near so constant, harassing, toilsome, or consuming as that of the Chinese boatmen. They seem to work night and day with very little intermission and every exertion they make is accompanied by such vocal efforts, such a screaming symphony as would alone exhaust an European more than any manual employment."[6]

The ambassador concluded that rice must be a "very strong and wholesome food. The common people who live chiefly upon it and who have but a spare allowance are extremely vigorous, hardy and cheerful, four of them carrying my palanquin without effort and stepping under it with agility."[7]

The other members of the embassy were led to a circular corral and offered their choice among some three hundred horses. On disembarking from the junks, each man was given a cardboard receipt to be exchanged for a horse and saddle. Anderson was unhappy with his mount, but "had delivered my ticket, and was obliged to abide by my choice, such as it was." The "diplomatic cavalry" then set off, closely supervised by a strong detachment of Chinese soldiers.

Horseback riding was part of every gentleman's education, but not all the members of the embassy were of the upper classes: "Such a troop of equestrians are not often seen in China, or any other part of the world. . . . The mechanics, soldiers, and servants, were all on horseback; many of whom were indifferent riders, and some of them now found themselves obliged to ride for the first time."[8]

At the mountain pass the trail was so narrow that they had to dismount.

At Lee-con-au they paused for lunch. The Chinese provided an honor guard of soldiers, but Anderson preferred to look at the women, who seemed to be "allowed a greater share of liberty, than in the country through which we had lately passed."[9]

After completing the perilous ascent and negotiating the pass, the reluctant horsemen descended the gentler grades of the southern slopes, "transported with joy." By nightfall they reached Nanxiong, on the plain below, where every shop and home seemed to be illuminated with lanterns. Soldiers helped the procession clear a path through the crowd to a "prefect's palace." A meal was served in the brilliantly lit courtyard. "Illumination is a very principal feature of Chinese magnificence,"[10] Anderson commented.

Most of the gentlemen of the embassy spent the night in this building, but since Macartney's junk was "ready prepared," he preferred "settling" himself "in it at once." Both Macartney and Thomas Staunton inform us that the rest of the embassy slept not in a "governor's palace" but in a "public edifice . . . where the provincial candidates for literary degrees . . . are examined and received."[11] Every piece of baggage transferred to the junks bore a ticket indicating which boat it belonged in.[12] More Chinese efficiency.

Changlin had now entered "his" province, and the new viceroy left the contingent to go on to Canton alone. At first Macartney assumed that Changlin wanted to "get there a little before us to prepare for our reception," but he later realized that it would have been inappropriate for an imperial official to take up his post in the company of barbarians. Changlin left early not to prepare to receive the embassy, but to take some distance from it.

Before leaving he had another amiable conversation with Macartney: "He told us that he had written to the Emperor in such terms upon our subject that he was persuaded we should leave China, not only without dissatisfaction but with essential proofs of the Emperor's favour." The ambassador replied that Qianlong's "indulgence to the King my master's subjects at Canton would be the most essential and acceptable favour he could possibly confer upon me." In his journal Macartney seems confident in Changlin's goodwill and in the sincerity with which Wang and Qiao "have endeavoured to promote our interests."[13]

Thomas comments that the river "is so shallow our boats, tho drawing so little water, often got aground and are obliged to be pushed off with the force of men."[14] In other words, the British hobbled along, while Changlin galloped ahead. The viceroy's rapid departure set Hüttner yearning: "We were now but a few leagues distant from the place at which we were so eager to arrive, having had no news of Europe for fifteen months, and that during a time of disruption."[15]

As the British moved south, the eye of the dragon was ever upon them. On December 12, as they left the jurisdiction of Chen Huai, viceroy of Jiangxi, he reported to the emperor as follows:

> On November 21 the delegation, led by Viceroy Changlin and including seventy-seven Barbarians and one hundred ninety-seven pieces of baggage, entered Jiangxi, where General Wang-li awaited them. On November 22 the baggage was loaded; on the twenty-third the signal for departure was given. On the twenty-ninth the Barbarians reached Nanchang, where, discreetly, I was able to meet with Changlin, who informed me that all was well. On December 9 the palanquins and horses were waiting for the delegation. The next day the Barbarians crossed the mountain and entered Guangdong. A letter from Changlin informed me of his satisfaction: the discipline of the troops of the province had made a strong impression on the Barbarians.[16]

Couriers set out at top speed to deliver this message to Peking. The evacuation of the barbarians was proceeding apace, and the dragon would soon be able to fall into slumber again.

THE FINAL LEG of the journey to Canton was a 260-mile passage along the Bei River through Guangdong province, one of China's richest. Its northern reaches, however, were relatively undeveloped. Young Staunton notes that larches had been planted on the high ground, and that small houses could occasionally be seen in some of the fields. Stone dikes controlled the flow of the river, whose waters rushed quickly through the open locks.[17]

At the confluence of this river and another coming from the northwest lay the city of Shaozhou, whose environs Barrow describes as "beautiful." The "country was now in a high state of tillage; the chief products were rice, sugarcanes, and tobacco."[18] The mountains, Thomas writes, are "very rocky and . . . rising bluff from the water with little or no verdure upon them. . . . The small boats that we saw were often sculled by women."[19] Anderson adds: "It is not, indeed, by any means, uncommon to see a woman, with a child tied by a linen bandage to her back, and another suckling at her breast, while the mother herself is employed in handling the oar, or guiding the helm."[20] But more often they saw young women dressed in white skirts, jackets, and straw hats.

Barrow moralized: "To the occupation of ferrying passengers over the river, it seemed they added another, not quite so honourable, for which, however, they had not only the consent and approbation of their parents, but also the sanction of the government, or perhaps, to speak more correctly, of the governing magistrates, given in consideration of their receiving a portion of the wages of prostitution."[21]

Staunton, too, suspected that the state took its cut of the income generated by the activities of these ladies, but Father Lamiot protested that any husband who acted as his wife's pimp would be "bambooed and exiled."[22] The criminal code, after all, condemned extramarital relations of any kind, whether the woman in question was married or not. The prescribed penalty was seventy strokes of bamboo if the woman was unmarried and eighty if she was married.[23] According to the Lazarist, the moral order held sway in Canton just as it did in Peking. One may believe whom one wills.

72

Where the Barbarian Devils Were Hated

(December 15–18, 1793)

Among the primitive, "foreigner" is synonymous with "enemy" and "evil." Everything our nation does is good; everything other nations do is bad.

CARL GUSTAV JUNG, 1931[1]

UNTIL NOW the British had had the unpleasant suspicion that they were a source of amusement to the Chinese, but on their arrival in the province of Guangdong they were stunned to find that here they were actually hated.

This seemed particularly surprising, since this was the part of China where people were most familiar with them. But instead of showing respectful curiosity, the peasants who came out of their houses to watch the foreigners pass by shouted, *Guizhe fangui!*—"Barbarian devils." A sarcastic Barrow reports that such "epithets . . . are bestowed by the enlightened Chinese on all foreigners."[2]

The closer the members of the embassy came to Canton, the more insolence they encountered. A timely rebuke, however, given to the governor of Nan-cheun-fou by Wang, for applying the above-mentioned opprobrious epithets to the British embassy, had a good effect on the Canton officers.[3] In Guangdong the British discovered the explosive mixture of pride and servility typical of colonial relations. The Chinese were willing to perform the most menial tasks for British merchants, but in return they treated them with contempt, acting as though they considered "them as placed, in the scale of human beings, many degrees below them."[4]

The British were not the only targets of this hostility. Our French observer in Canton notes: "Along with several Frenchmen, I took a turn in a palanquin through the outskirts of the city; when we passed through a village, the children threw stones at us, as well as showering us with insults to which we were urged to pay no heed."[5]

One day Barrow noticed a servant drying the leaves of the tea he had just been served at lunch. When questioned, the servant explained that he intended to mix these dried leaves with fresh tea and sell it. Barrow chided him for cheating his compatriots, but the servant protested, "My own countrymen are too wise to be so easily cheated, but yours are stupid enough to let us serve you such like tricks." And he added: "Any thing you get from us is quite good enough for you." When Barrow got angry, the servant claimed that his real targets were only "second chop Englishmen"—in other words, Americans.[6]

In all likelihood this encounter was actually an instance of second-chop insolence, since in fact the Chinese prefer leaves the second time around, sometimes even throwing away tea from the first infusion.

A "LONG GORGE between steep mountains" had been turned into a coal mine, and the British examined this ore that they knew so well. The tunnels are "worked horizontally," along the hillsides, the page observes.[7] The coal was loaded directly into boats and transported to the porcelain factories. The Chinese also used coal dust, pressed into briquettes, for cooking rice.[8]

Thomas was astonished to find that the coal was extracted "by the labour of men," without "any kind of machine." The British were proud of their windlasses, rails, and iron coal-carriers, and the child, imbued with the spirit of the industrial revolution already shaking his country, was surprised by the Celestial Empire's backwardness.[9] But the use of machinery would have aggravated unemployment among an already superabundant work force.

There is something very strange about the Chinese disdain for coal, which they had discovered centuries ago. (It was one of the wonders that astonished Marco Polo.)[10] Woodlands had been stripped bare in the quest for firewood, and deforestation had already had tragic effects. In fact, wood had become as precious as the rice and noodles on which the Chinese diet was based, and for a hundred generations masses of Chinese had complained that the bulk of their money went straight into the coffers of the rice and wood merchants.[11] Why didn't they burn coal instead? A mystery of nondevelopment.

THE RIVER WENDED its way through the coal-streaked hills, and on the evening of December 14 the flotilla entered the gorges of the Huashin

Mountains.[12] In the background, looming over the river, was a mountain of "such stupendous magnitude, as the description which I am about to give, will not be able to convey."[13] A famous Buddhist temple had been cut into these cliffs.

At dawn on December 15 Macartney and a few favored companions were taken on one of the rare excursions of this long journey. A launch carried them upstream to a creek, where they disembarked on a narrow ledge between the cliff and the water. Entering the mouth of a cave, they found themselves at the foot of a "staircase hewn in the rock, long, narrow, steep, and rugged."

They mounted the steps, using the glimmer of a "feeble taper" up above as their "pole star." When they reached the top, they were met by "an ancient, bald-headed bonze" who guided them through a "subterraneous labyrinth." He began by taking them to a large room that seemed to be the "grand hall or refectory" of the temple, an "excavation forming nearly a cube of twenty-five feet, through one face of which is a considerable opening that looks over the water and is barricaded with a rail." There were highly varnished tables and chairs, as well as gauze and paper lanterns of various colors, "in the middle of which was suspended a glass lantern of prodigious size made in London, the offering of an opulent Chinese bigot [devotee] at Canton."

Next they mounted "many difficult steps to the temple itself," where "the god Pusa* is displayed in all his glory—a gigantic image with a Saracen face, grinning horribly from a double row of gilded fangs, a crown upon his head, a naked scimitar in one hand and a firebrand in the other." Macartney reports that he was able to "learn very few particulars of this colossal divinity. Even the bonzes who live by his worship scarcely knew anything of his history."[15]

Macartney supposed that he was "some great Tartar prince or commander of antiquity." The "magnificent altar . . . dressed out at his feet" had "lamps, lanterns, candles and candlesticks, censers and perfumes, strongly resembling the decorations of a Romish [Catholic] chapel." The walls were covered with "numerous tablets inscribed in large characters with moral sentences and exhortations to pious alms and religion." Opposite the statue was "a wide breach in the wall, down from which the perpendicular view requires the finest nerves and the steadiest head to resist its

---

* A *pusa* (or *poussah*) is the Chinese equivalent of a bodhisattva in India or Tibet: an enlightened being who has earned the right to become a buddha and thus to attain Nirvana, but who, like the Buddha, agrees out of compassion to continue to be reincarnated. Lamaist Buddhists believe that the bodhisattva Cherenzi, an avatar of Avalokitesvara, has been reincarnated for centuries in the person of the Dalai Lama.[14]

impression. The convoluted rocks above shooting their tottering shadows into the distant light, the slumbering abyss below, the superstitious gloom brooding upon the whole, all conspired to strike the mind with accumulated horror and the most terrifying images."[16]

Their guide led the visitors through long narrow galleries to the other rooms: kitchens, cells, cellars, and other recesses in the rock. The bonzes lit torches, and Macartney was able to see "the interior of the *souterrain*, and to examine into the nature of its inhabitants and their manner of living in it. Here we beheld a number of our fellow-creatures, endowed with faculties like our own . . . buried under a mountain and chained to a rock, to be incessantly gnawed by the vultures of superstition and fanaticism." Macartney, who had an obvious obsessional phobia about monasticism, was appalled: "Their condition appeared to us to be the last stage of monastic misery, the lowest degradation of humanity. The aspiring thoughts and elegant desires, the Promethean heat, the nobler energies of the soul, the native dignity of man, all sunk, rotting or extinguished in a hopeless dungeon of religious insanity. From such scenes the offended eye turns away with pity and disdain, and looks with impatience for a ray of relief from the light of reason and philosophy."[17]

Upon leaving "this wretched community" Macartney left "a small donation, which was, however, so far above their expectations that I think it not unlikely they will insert a new clause in their litany, and heartily pray that the Chinese Government may adopt a more liberal policy, and open the country to the free inspection and curiosity of English travellers."[18]

At this point in his journal Macartney inserts a footnote explaining that he had lately read his impressions of the temple to several members of the embassy who had visited it along with him. Though they "perfectly agree in their recollection of the principal features of the place," they found the ambassador's description "rather heightened and surcharged." Macartney notes that he wrote this account "immediately on my returning to my yacht," but acknowledges that "scarcely any two travellers . . . see the same objects in the same light, or remember them with the same accuracy. . . . I have therefore often thought what amusement and instruction might be derived from a perusal of the journals kept (if such have been kept) by the different persons belonging to my Embassy. Even the memorandums of a *valet de chambre* might be of some value."[19]

The valet in question is Anderson, who presents a somewhat more clement view of this same scene, with clear differences in culture and class. Unlike his master, Anderson was not steeped in gothic novels, and for him the cavern was an object of curiosity rather than horror. The steep staircase had a railing. The refectory had a pretty painted door. The statue of the god was lighted by a window, and what Macartney called a "wide breach in the wall" was, for Anderson, a "balcony . . . from whence there is a delightful prospect of the river."[20]

The visit to the temple led Winder to relate a story told to him by one of the mandarins. It seems that a *pusa* inhabited the body of a young girl. She was bathing in a limpid wave, when there suddenly appeared to her a wonderful water lily. She found it so beautiful that she devoured it. She was soon discovered to be with child and gave birth to a boy, whose education she entrusted to a humble fisherman. The boy grew up, learned to read, became erudite, then wise, and finally, after his death, in turn a god. His mother was thereafter venerated as a Holy Virgin.[21]

These Westerners lost no opportunity to seek evidence in the East that would bolster their own convictions, in this case at the expense of the Catholic cult of the Virgin. But Holmes admits that he was unable to draw the Chinese out about their religion: The mandarins of Ningbo were "more communicative than their countrymen had hitherto been, excepting some particulars which respected their religion; this seemed a mystery which they could not explain, nor could we form a judgment what they are, or in what belief. Their idols are numerous; every petty village, and almost every house of note, has its particular god for public or private worship."[22]

For Thomas Staunton, a temple cut from a cavern and inhabited by bonzes was no big deal. The cavern, he wrote, was "open to the day in three places one above another. The first is close to the water side, the next is about 50 feet above the water and the uppermost 90 or 100. In each of these apertures fronting the light is an altar, idol, and everything belonging to their devotions. The rock is of marble."[23] Each observer saw the temple in his own way. The matter-of-fact Thomas paid most attention to the inscriptions, which he was now able to decipher, having made sufficient progress in Chinese. Macartney, on the other hand, detected no human or peaceful touch in this temple.

That night Thomas saw "immense and singular rocks jutting upright from the side of the river . . . in every singular form and attitude that can be imagined, and again in the interstices between these, growing out, plants and shrubs as singular as the rocks that bore them."[24] This child was more disturbed by nature's works than by humankind's.

The river flowed through verdant but fallow hills. Wang and Qiao explained that uncultivated land was the property of the emperor. All that was needed to become a landowner was to inform the nearest magistrate of your intention to bring fresh land under cultivation, but little such land was left. In China, Macartney noted, "there is no such thing . . . as a waste or common depending upon a manor or lordship for the purpose of feeding the game or the vanity of an idle paramount."[25] Another swipe at Europe, using China as a foil.

THE LONG RIVER journey finally ended. In ten weeks our travelers had crossed most of China from north to south, and they now reached the suburbs of Canton. Just before noon on December 18 they arrived at a summer pavilion belonging to the merchant guild, and here they had the first, emotional reunion with several of their compatriots: Messrs. Brown, Irwin, and Jackson, commissioners of the East India Company, and Mr. Hall, the secretary. These gentlemen "brought with them our letters and packets from Europe, which after a fifteen months' absence were singularly acceptable."

The letters brought Macartney the not unexpected news that war had broken out between Britain and France. The execution of Louis XVI, on the other hand, was a surprise. Alexander writes in his journal: "Captain Montgomery, of the *Bombay Castle*, who left England in January last [1793], communicated to us the execution of the King of France, [and] that the trial of Thomas Paine, etc. . . . had excited some fermentation in London."*[26]

The next day the embassy entered Canton—or rather, passed through it. The *Lion* was moored downriver in the port.†

All these British movements were closely followed by Chinese troops. Macartney had frequently been treated to military honors during his stay in China, but never so often as here in the environs of Canton. Changlin had done his work well, and the ambassador understood that the Chinese meant "to impress us with an idea of the vigilance and alertness of the troops, and to show that they were not unprepared against an enemy."

But in mobilizing so openly, the Chinese also demonstrated their weakness: "As they are . . . armed only with matchlocks, bows and arrows, and heavy swords, awkward in the management of them, of an unwarlike

---

* Thomas Paine had been granted French citizenship on the strength of his republican convictions. Though elected to the Convention in 1792, he never took the floor in the chamber, since he did not know French. Consistent with his opposition to capital punishment, he, like Condorcet, refused to vote for the execution of Louis XVI. His incarceration was a consequence of Robespierre's extreme suspicion of foreigners resident in France, whether as refugees or otherwise. Paine was released after the ninth of Thermidor.

† The *Lion* had arrived in Macao two months earlier. After the crew had recovered its health, Sir Erasmus Gower, believing that Macartney would winter in Peking, made several attempts to sail for Japan, but bad weather prevented his departure,[27] until finally he received Macartney's order to wait in Canton.

character and disposition, I imagine they would make but a feeble resistance to a well-conducted attack. The circumstance of greatest embarrassment to an invader would be their immense numbers, not on account of the mischief they could do to him, but that he would find no end of doing mischief to them. The slaughter of millions would scarcely be perceived, and unless the people themselves soon voluntarily submitted, the victor might indeed reap the vanity of destruction, but not the glory or use of dominion."[28]

This prediction is very nearly stunning in its accuracy. Macartney considered the Chinese masters of evasion, but he knew that they had other strengths as well: their cultural specificity, which screened them against foreign influence; the country's great geographical size, which would allow the empire to fragment into local centers of rearguard resistance; its huge population, which would permit the formation of large "reserve armies," however ill armed. It would therefore be next to impossible to vanquish China completely. Teilhard de Chardin made a similar point in 1937, during the Japanese invasion: "When attacked, China defends itself by crumbling to dust—dust which invaders would never succeed in re-cementing."[29]

73

Canton

(December 19–23, 1793)

ON THE MORNING of December 19 the embassy set out for Canton on imperial barges, which carried them down the Pearl River. Two and a half hours later, they disembarked on the small island of Honam, where they had been assigned a palace. Viceroy Changlin, the military governor Guo Shixun, the superintendent of customs (hoppo) Suleng'e, and the principal mandarins of the region, all in ceremonial dress, waited for them on a rug-covered platform. The entire party, Macartney writes, then retired to "a very large apartment, with double semi-circular rows of arm-chairs on each side."[1] This sumptuous reception sounds very similar to the lavish welcomes enjoyed by "distinguished visitors" to the People's Republic nearly two centuries later.

But wait a minute! His lordship neglects to mention a preliminary ceremony described in young Thomas's journal: "We went through the tent and entered a handsome furnished room with a throne at the end. There we met the Suntoo* with the other great Mandarines who were preparing to make nine bows and three genuflections to the throne at the end of the room, as thanking the Emperor for our safe and pleasant arrival here. We followed their example."[2]

Doubt rears its head again, especially since one of the witnesses, the hoppo Suleng'e, affirmed in 1816 that he had seen Macartney kowtow to the throne in Canton. Thomas does not explain exactly how the British "followed their example." Did they finally bow to Celestial custom, or did they merely perform the British version of the kowtow, bringing one knee to the ground a single time? Young Staunton's laconism is troubling.

It seems inconceivable that Macartney, having created such a stir by

---

* Thomas Staunton's journal is strewn with phonetically transcribed Chinese words. *Suntoo* is clearly a version, based on Manchu pronunciation, of *zong du*, which means "viceroy" of a province.

refusing to kowtow to the emperor himself, would agree to prostrate himself before an empty throne. Yet the British were caught in another awkward situation: a collective ceremony. The most likely possibility is that they followed the crowd's lead, just as they had at the emperor's first appearance in Jehol, going down on one knee three times and bowing their heads nine times, thus conforming to the Celestial rhythm in a compromise that neither Macartney nor Qianlong wished to acknowledge.

"This ceremony being ended, we retired with the Mandarines to a large and handsome hall."[3] This was the room to which Macartney takes us directly, concealing the distressing detour.

The mandarins took their seats opposite the British, and an hour-long conversation followed, mostly about various incidents of the journey from Peking and the arrival of the *Lion*, which had been given permission by the viceroy to moor at the island of Huangpu along with the foreign merchant vessels, a signal privilege for a warship.

The party "then adjourned to the theatre, on which a company of comedians (who are reckoned capital performers, and had been ordered down from Nanking on purpose)* were prepared to entertain us. And here we found a most magnificent Chinese dinner spread out upon the tables, and a display of the presents upon this occasion. The Viceroy conducted the whole ceremony with the greatest dignity and propriety, distinguishing us by the most pointed marks of respect and regard (things quite new and astonishing to the Chinese here, who are totally unused to see foreigners treated with any attention), and evincing in every instance the high consideration which the Embassy was held in by the Government."[4] Or so Macartney wanted to believe. But that night young Staunton wrote in his terrible little notebook: "We all sat down according to our ranks. He [the viceroy] then offered us tea and milk. The Suntoo, after he had said several polite things, got up and, attended by other great Mandarines, conducted us to the house (or rather palace) that he had prepared for us. After having stayed here for a few minutes, they all returned."[5]

Tea and milk. A few pleasantries. A few minutes. Thanks to Thomas, we know that it was in their new residence—away from the viceroy and his assessors—that the banquet was served: the viceroy "sent a very grand dinner in their way." Next came the show: "The Suntoo ordered to be

---

* Nanking was the birthplace of *kunqu*, the refined style favored by the court, later to be replaced by that of the Peking Opera. It must have taken the troupe at least a month to get to Canton.

built a stage in one of the courts of our habitation, where he entertained us the whole day with the acting of Chinese plays."[6]

The ambassador's residence, on an island in the river, was a palace in the Chinese style: a collection of large pavilions. Some were furnished like European houses, with glass windows and fireplaces whose comforts Macartney appreciated in this month of December, even on the edge of the tropics. A large garden was adorned with ponds and flower beds, trees and shrubs.

On the opposite bank of the river was the English factory, which probably would have afforded more comfortable quarters than any Chinese residence, but "it was so repugnant to the principles of the government for an Embassador to take up his abode in the same dwelling with merchants, that it was thought expedient to indulge their notions in this respect."[7]

That evening, the page notes with relief, "we dined in the English fashion (everything that we wanted being supplied by the Factory)."[8]

Early the next morning, when Macartney opened his windows, he found that the stage had been moved to face his room and that the show had already begun. The actors had been ordered to perform in relays for the entire length of the ambassador's stay, but an exasperated Macartney managed to have the troupe dismissed. To their "no small astonishment," Barrow writes, "our Chinese conductors . . . concluded . . . that the English had very little taste for elegant amusements."[9]

Macartney wondered how a Chinese ambassador would have reacted had the Lord Chamberlain Salisbury commissioned the stars of the Covent Garden Theatre to perform outside his window for days on end.

Staunton junior explains that this second performance, unlike the first, was an offering from the hoppo and not the viceroy. But the boy was unimpressed: The hoppo "has been here only two months. He has the character of being still more avaricious and avid than his predecessor, and he has already forced out by unjust means from some Chinese merchants here two hundred thousand dollars, and has even tried to extort duties on our ships notwithstanding the Emperor's order to the contrary."[10] Macartney and his deputy were apparently so bitter that they had spoken openly of their disappointment in the presence of the perceptive Thomas, whose disparaging remark about the hoppo heralds the collapse of the mission's very last hopes.

Barrow is even more explicit: "In consideration of the *Hindostan* having carried presents for the Emperor, an order was issued from Court that she should be exempt from duties at any of the ports where she might take in cargo. It happened that the guild merchants had already paid the *Hindostan*'s duties with those of the other ships, of which her particular share was 30,000 ounces of silver. The Hoppo or collector was therefore requested to return this sum agreeably to the order from Court, but he refunded only into Mr. Browne's hands 14,000 dollars, which can be reckoned as little more than 11,000 ounces, observing, that so much was the exact amount of the Emperor's duties. As in this instance of a public nature the collector could not be supposed to act without circumspection, we may conclude how very small a proportion of the duties extorted from foreigners trading to Canton, finds its way into the Imperial treasury."[11] The incident speaks for itself: of thirty thousand ounces paid, nineteen thousand were embezzled by local officials, the Treasury collecting less than 40 percent of the total.

The company commissioners, obstinately sticking to the facts, had already begun to undermine Macartney's hopes. After describing the "extortions" in which the Chinese mandarins indulged, Barrow reports this "common answer": "Why do you come here? We take in exchange your articles of produce and manufacture, which we really have no occasion for, and give you in return our precious tea, which nature has denied your country, and yet you are not satisfied. Why do you so often visit a country whose customs you dislike? We do not invite you to come among us, but when you do come, and behave well, we treat you accordingly. Respect, then, our hospitality, but don't pretend to regulate or reform it."[12]

The voice of China, singing the refrain typical of any nation that feels its identity threatened.

On December 21 Thomas notes: "This morning the Dutch and Spanish commissioners came to salute Lord Macartney. This evening Qiao sent for some Nankinese jugglers for our diversion, who performed several curious things."[13] Spinning plates, whirling jars, and flying knives—the boy had not tired of the sort of performance he had earlier seen in Jehol.

IN EUROPE, Canton was known as the gateway to China, but the British now found that there was more than one gate. Canton is in fact no closer to the sea than Paris is to the mouth of the Seine, and to arrive at the "gateway" travelers coming by ship had to negotiate various obstacles.

The first of these was Macao, a dangerous, reef-strewn detour where pilots and transit visas were expensive. Next there was the Tiger's Mouth, a strait defended by two forts. Then three perilous sandbars rising out of the shallows. To cross them ships had to wait for three successive high tides. Finally, all European ships were halted at the island of Huangpu.

But as one of our French witnesses reports, this was not because of Chinese harassment: "Large Chinese junks can sail upriver to Canton, but European vessels draw far too much water."[14] There were three toll stations between Huangpu and Canton, and every launch was meticulously inspected at each one before being allowed through to the factories.

On the northern bank of the river were the British, French, Dutch, Spanish, and Swedish factories, identified by national flags flying from their masts. The British factory was ringed by covered galleries called *veranden*, from the Hindi word *varandā*, from which *veranda* is derived. The factories were one-story buildings, spacious and "tastefully furnished."[15]

An enormous Chinese bazaar of shops and workshops had grown up around them. Europeans were authorized to reside in these factories only during autumn and the beginning of winter. For the rest of the year they were relegated to Macao. Though Canton lies at the same latitude as the West Indies, winter can be harsh enough to require furs, and Anderson noticed well-made coats of leopard, fox, bear, and sheepskin, worn with the fur on the inside.[16] Furs and fireplaces—a strange kind of tropical winter.

Suspicious Chinese authorities were everywhere, and life was difficult for Europeans: "Since we are unable to make any purchases by ourselves without being subject to great vexation, our expenses are half again as high as those of our agents in Bengal."[17]

In his journal Macartney admits that he was virtually confined to his residence. "The Viceroy of Canton paid the British Ambassador only one visit during his stay here," Anderson reports.[18] Changlin was no longer the escort of a barbarian ambassador but a viceroy, and his character changed with his function. He was now as haughty as he had earlier been attentive. His lordship, Dinwiddie writes, was always "narrowly watched" and rarely left his residence.[19]

Life became so routine that Macartney ceased making routine entries in his journal. One social function shaded into the next, and conversations spun in circles. Macartney gives general accounts of them, as though they were numerous: "These three days [December 21–23] have been chiefly taken up in receiving visits from the Viceroy, the Fuyen or Governor, the Hoppo or Treasurer, . . . and several other great mandarins," some of whom, the ambassador notes with a touch of self-flattery, "are come from a considerable distance to see us." He makes it sound as though the whole three days were spent negotiating, but we know from the page and the valet that in fact Macartney had just one meeting with the viceroy and the superintendent (on December 22), and this meeting was notable primarily for the hostility of the hoppo, who "was averse to any alterations and wished everything to remain as he found it." Macartney hoped that help might be forthcoming from the viceroy, who "thought every reasonable alteration should be made" and who "debated [with the hoppo] with great earnestness for a considerable time."[20]

Unable to reconcile himself to having accomplished so little, Macartney gave free rein to his imagination. On December 23 he wrote a message to Dundas suggesting two possible courses of action. Either the *Lion* could escort a convoy of company ships home, protecting them from the French revolutionaries ("Nothing but the motive of guarding so valuable a fleet could warrant me in indulging the idea of returning home this season, without having made all the exertions in my power for attaining the objects of my mission out of China").[21] That would effectively put the blame for the embassy's premature departure on the French Revolution. Or the merchant convoy could leave Canton without the *Lion*'s protection, in which case Macartney would use the warship to attempt a mission to Japan: "When I called at Cochinchina, I received abundant encouragements to return there; but I have since found that the Court of Peking considers that kingdom as tributary, and might therefore perhaps take offence at any separate transaction with its supposed vassal. But no such objection applies against endeavouring to try Japan."[22]

Macartney hoped that if he undertook such a mission, he could return to Macao and Canton in October 1794, by which time he would be able to verify the positive effects of the new viceroy's actions:

> Changlin, whom I took every opportunity of cultivating his society, considered, as he said, that not only justice to us, but the honour of his own country required a change in its conduct towards the English; that he would be happy to be the instrument of effecting such a change. . . . At any rate, it was some indication that from a sense of our land forces in India and our strength everywhere by sea, the British nation was felt to be too powerful not to require some management. . . .
>
> I ventured to say that His Majesty the King had from the beginning intended to have, if not constantly, at least occasionally, a minister resident in China. . . . An answer came from the Emperor—it was considered as particularly gracious on the part of His Imperial Majesty,* and his desire to have an English minister in China, after the argument in his former letters against such a measure, shows a favourable change in his sentiments towards the British nation. . . .

---

* The reference is to the edict summarized in chapter 70, yet another letter from a sovereign to his vassal.

It might be one object of the minister at Peking fully to undeceive the government there in relation to our supposed assistance to the enemies of the Chinese in Thibet. . . . Next minister may from thence lay the foundation of an alliance, of which very advantageous conditions in our favour, or cession of territory for the convenience of our trade may be gained by promise of support on the side of India.[23]

Macartney had fallen into outright oneiric delirium. It was as if he had forgotten all the rebuffs he had suffered and had learned nothing from his daily contact with Chinese officials over five months. But there may have been a dash of subtle hypocrisy in his letter to Dundas: if he was unable to bring these wonderful projects to fruition, it would be because of the war, which, by forcing him to return home prematurely, would turn a great diplomat into a modest maritime escort.

74

Encounters

(December 22, 1793–January 1, 1794)

WHILE MACARTNEY remained effectively confined to his residence, the members of his retinue had more freedom, and their accounts of their activities afford us precious images of Sino-European Canton. As usual, the most vivid of these come from young Staunton.

> Sunday the 22d. Today I went over the river, which is here a good deal wider than the Thames, to the English Factory, which is indeed very elegantly built. However, we did not stay there long, but went to look at the principal shops in the neighbourhood. I was very much surprised to see upon the doors of each of the shops the names of the shopkeeper and often even what was to be sold within in Roman characters and still more so in finding that most of the shopkeepers spoke very intelligible English. Most of the streets are very narrow and crowded. We saw a very large China warehouse as full and well stocked as any of our English ones. In all the streets where we were there appears to be only shops and no private houses, and indeed altogether the streets much resemble those in the Merceria at Venice.[1]

Canton is quite unlike the rest of China. Even today there are many signs in Roman characters, and English is widely spoken.

"Tuesday the 24th. Today I again went across the water. Among other shops we went in that of a painter and into that of a modeller. In the first we saw several small but handsome paintings in oil colours in the Chinese and English fashion, also some very pretty paintings on glass. In the second we saw great numbers of dressed figures in painted clay, in the manner of large dolls, and we were told that the body was as perfectly done under the clothes as the face and hands that were uncovered." Chinese modesty, however, prevented the boy from being allowed to verify that claim. There were also porcelain figures "with nodding heads, such as I have often seen . . . in England."[2]

Thomas wandered the Canton bazaar with his tutor, Hüttner, who also recorded his impressions. "Everything that is made in Europe has been perfectly imitated here: furniture, tools and utensils of all varieties, silverwork, trunks. It is all as well fabricated as in England, and quite considerably cheaper."[3] Europe manufactured fake Chinese antiquities, while Canton made fake Western novelties.

As it turned out, this knockoff industry had a great future, and its establishments can still be seen in Canton today, especially in the free market not far from the Confucian temple. "Chinese tailors," Hüttner wrote, "could rival those of London, but their prices are lower by half." Locally produced silk and cotton were also high in quality and low in price: "Nowhere can one dress less dearly than in Canton."[4] Still true as far as price is concerned, but for clothes of British cut and cloth, visitors do better to press on to Hong Kong.

"The whitening performed by the laundries is quite superior in execution and far cheaper than in any European capital."[5] Chinese laundries had already established the reputation they would later carry to America. "Very good bargains are available, provided one is careful not to be cheated," since in Chinese eyes, "dishonesty, when aimed at foreigners, is regarded merely as ingenuity." These Chinese devils had made fraud a high art: "Rare is the European who has not discovered this talent to his own cost."[6] One gets the feeling that Hüttner was not among the happy few.

An intriguing bit of linguistic information: Anglo-Portuguese pidgin had already developed, one impertinent but canny Chinese informing the German Hüttner, "You no savey English talkey."[7]

The tutor escorted his charge to a "clock-work factory," where they saw "a little automaton who drew perfectly well, . . . another little automaton that danced and made divers odd attitudes upon the tight rope, . . . and dancing dogs and bears. . . . All these machines accompanied their motion with very pretty music of bells."[8] The Chinese were especially enamored of these machines and copied them assiduously. Which may be why Dinwiddie's apparatuses had had a less than stunning effect on the blasé Peking court.

Thomas, however, far from being bored, was ever ready for more. "We . . . went to see how the Chinese cut glass, which they do with a steel instrument instead of a diamond. . . . We then went to see the making of small looking glasses, having some leaf tin of the proper size upon which they spread some quicksilver, and then lay it on the glass, which finishes the operation. We then went to see the burning and painting of the china ware. The first was done by heating the ware in fires of different degrees till it should be able to bear the heat of the furnace, where it remains till it is red hot. . . . The gold paint is used hot."[9]

THE RANK-AND-FILE members of the embassy celebrated Christmas with His Majesty's seamen on board the *Lion*, while the dignitaries spent the day at the English factory. "Today we all went over the water to dine at the Factory," Thomas reports, ". . . in a very large and handsome room adorned with several large and beautiful paintings."[10] According to Dinwiddie, the holiday meal was shared by no fewer than sixty "gentlemen."[11]

The astronomer, who had arrived by sea with his scientific instruments, gave a series of lectures on physics, to which various of the "English and European" residents seemed "well disposed." Several English-speaking Chinese seem to have had somewhat more difficulty: One of the "natives," who had "a merchant's soul" and therefore assumed that Dinwiddie must have had something to sell if he had taken the trouble to speak so wisely, asked him what percentage return he expected on his products. Dinwiddie reports the remark, but no longer seems particularly exercised about Chinese attitudes: "The ideas of a Chinese contrast strangely with those of an European." One of the merchants of the guild asked him whether he could, without rising from his seat, "conjure away a picture hanging on the wall."[12]

At three in the afternoon on New Year's Eve the gentlemen held another banquet in the English factory. Young Thomas attended, but was taken back to the residence at nightfall, while the "other gentlemen stayed to supper."[13] The twelve-year-old, who alone among the seven hundred Britons was able to get along in Chinese, was still just a boy, and now was treated as such.

But the life of the British among their own was not always so affable. Thomas tells us that during the *Lion*'s stay in the Zhoushan Islands three duels were fought, involving six British officers.[14] There is no mention of this particular barbarian custom in the correspondence of the Chinese. They may well have been unaware of it, but they would surely have taken it as confirmation of English "ferocity." The Chinese were just as attentive to questions of honor as the British, but they did not believe in saving face by skewering the stomach.

In Europe the French supporters of the Convention found little cause for complaint in their first de-Christianized Christmas, for victory was their companion. On December 23 the Vendeans were crushed at Savenay. "La Vendée has ceased to exist," General Westermann wrote proudly to the Convention that very night. "I have just now buried it, crushing the children under horses' hooves and massacring the women. Not a single prisoner weighs against me. I have extermined everything."[15]

BARROW HAD the rare privilege of being invited to a Chinese party by Wang and Qiao, who had become his fast friends. The gravity of their mission had compelled the members of the embassy to a puritanical ascesticism, but Barrow now discovered that the mandarins did not always behave as strict Confucians: "Where any degree of confidence prevails among these people, they sometimes enjoy their moments of conviviality."

Wang and Qiao had run into an old mandarin friend, who "gave them an evening entertainment on the river, in a splendid yacht to which I was privately invited." Barrow found that the three mandarins had arranged for female companionship: each of them was accompanied by "a young girl . . . very richly dressed, the cheeks, lips, and chin highly rouged, the rest of the face and neck whitened with a preparation of ceruse. I was welcomed by a cup of hot wine from each of the ladies, who first sipped by way of pledging me."

A supper was served whose quantity and quality exceeded anything Barrow had yet seen in China. During the meal the young women played flutes and sang. Their musical skills were not commensurate with their looks, but Barrow didn't seem to mind: "We passed a most convivial evening free from any reserve or restraint." Just before leaving, Barrow was advised by his hosts not to mention the party, lest "their brother officers might condemn their want of prudence in admitting a barbarian to witness this occasional relaxation from good morals." Especially since Barrow understood that the ladies, having been "hired for the occasion," would remain after his departure.[16] Would Barrow have admitted it if Wang and Qiao had invited him to stay?

75

Extern Brothers
and Felonious Merchants

(January 1–8, 1794)

> Beneath the charming exterior of Pan-ke-qua, the chief of
> the guild in Canton, lurks the wickedest soul that ever has
> inhabited a human body. Yet in their incredible blindness,
> the witnesses to and victims of his constant perfidy continue
> to accord him the fullest confidence, even believing that they
> enjoy his as well. He calls himself the "father of Europeans,"
> and they reward him by clasping his hands with the ut-
> most joy.
>
> CHARLES DE CONSTANT[1]

AS BARROW PARTIED and Staunton junior visited the workshops of the bazaar,
his father and Macartney tried to get better acquainted with the merchants
of the guild.

These men were the eighteenth-century counterparts of today's "communist capitalists" of Hong Kong, the businessmen who control the channels of trade between the formally British "colony" and the supposedly
red empire. The Middle Empire supported a similar system in 1793: a
handful of men, closely supervised by the Celestial bureaucracy, were responsible for all trade relations with barbarians. Even a convent needs
some contact between the cloister and the outside world, and the members
of the Canton merchant guild were the extern brothers who provided the
link.

In the nineteenth century these intermediaries of foreign trade came
to be called *compradors*, from the Portuguese word for "buyers." In the
twentieth they formed a caste that played a central role in Guomindang
(Nationalist) China. The Soong family, for instance, to which Jiang Jieshi's
(Chiang Kai-shek's) wife belonged, made its fortune through its dealings
with international capitalism. That was why the Communists considered

this class their most formidable domestic enemy. It remains to be seen whether Deng Xiaoping's policies of "opening" and "modernization" herald their return.

Macartney met their forerunners. "Pan-ke-qua,"* he wrote, "is one of the principal [merchants], a shrewd, sensible, sly fellow. Chi-chin-qua is the next in point of consequence, but not inferior in point of opulence. The latter is the younger man and of a franker character." Or so Macartney decided, when he "declared without reserve his willingness to try experiments in trade with any new articles our Factory desired him."[3] His lordship seems to have exhibited just the sort of naiveté complained of by our Swiss witness, Charles de Constant.

The British were astonished to find that these men, though members of the despised class of merchants, wore mandarins' insignia. Strangely, Pan-ke-qua, the highest in rank, "wears a white opaque button on his cap, and Chi-chin-qua wears a crystal one, which is a degree superior to Pan-ke-qua's, but I soon learned the reason. Pan-ke-qua is more prudent and less ostentatious. Chi-chin-qua owned to me that he had also a blue button [higher in rank than the crystal], but that, although he wears it at home in his own family, he never appears with it abroad, lest the Mandarins in office should visit him on that account and make use of it as a pretence to squeeze presents from him, naturally supposing that a man could well afford them who had given ten thousand taels . . . for such a distinction."[4]

The mandarin buttons, Macartney explains, "are sold here to the wealthy merchants, but confer no official authority." Actually, they were not exactly sold, at least not officially, "but the suitor certainly buys them by the large presents which he makes to the great men at this extremity of the Empire who have interest enough at Court to procure them."[5]

According to our French and Swiss witnesses and the private papers of the missionaries, if anything Macartney's information understates the reality. At a time when Voltaire was singing the praises of the mandarin examination system, a mafialike structure linked high-ranking officials and rich merchants.[6] The most lucrative fields of commerce—the salt business and foreign trade—were often leased through a kind of kickback system by the salt inspectors and the maritime customs officials. Most of the mandarins in territorial government posts were Han Chinese, but the guild was too strategically important to be entrusted to Chinese, and its

---

* Pan Youdu, known to foreigners in Canton as Pan-ke-qua—which was actually the name of his father (1714–80), from whom he inherited his fortune—served as chief of the Canton guild from 1793 to 1808.[2] He died in 1821.

leaders were generally Manchus, Mongols, or "Chinese of the Banners" (Chinese assimilated by the Manchus). Some were even princes of the imperial clan.

These privileged officials were expected to shower government ministers with gifts in exchange for promotions, or simply in exchange for having their terms renewed; at the same time, they were playthings of the merchants, who filled their coffers with taels.[7] The consequent generalized venality, the buying and selling of decorations and tokens of prestige, the constant prevarication, and the various other features of the precapitalist economy all reflect what Max Weber called "patrimonialism," a system that makes no distinction between the public and the private. It is the ethic of "that which belongs to everyone is mine," an ideology that continues to prevail in much of the Third World today.

As he talked to these merchants, Macartney realized how right the company had been to try to open new markets in central and northern China. The guild members "seemed to know as little of Peking as of Westminster; not one of those whom I conversed with had ever been in the capital. They scarcely ever stir from the place of their nativity, unless compelled by authority or incited by the strongest motives of interest, but grovel on at Canton from generation to generation very unlike the Chinese whom I have had occasion to see in other places."

The guild's activities, Macartney wrote, did not extend beyond Nanking, where they shipped much of the merchandise they bought from Europeans and from which they received most of the goods they exported to Europe. Nanking, in fact, "is the great commercial metropolis," and "the Nanking merchants are in fact the real masters of the Chinese market; a circumstance which renders our admission to trade directly to Zhoushan and Ningbo doubly desirable."[8] Macartney now realized why it had been impossible to gain authorization to trade in either place: such permission, apart from contravening custom, would have threatened the merchants and mandarins of Canton, who at this point were the only Chinese who had a personal interest in Western trade. They had limited access to outlets in the south, but were completely isolated from the north, and they behaved much like the palace eunuch who endeavors to prevent others from engaging in activities of which he himself is incapable.

Far from seeking to develop trade, the Canton guild therefore curbed it. In addition, the guild was completely dependent on a multitude of mandarins and was unable to take any initiative without the hierarchy's approval. It bore no greater resemblance to the free merchant guilds of the West than the Canton city government did to a free European municipality. China was tightly enveloped by the Celestial bureaucracy, and quite innocent of the local and corporative exemptions from central control that had been won in medieval Europe.

Only during periods of fragmentation of the empire had Chinese commerce enjoyed sufficient freedom of development to generate a proto-capitalist economy. Whenever the country was united under the triumphant bureaucracy, the economy languished. Investment plummeted, and the profits of trade served mainly to widen official corruption and to purchase promotions for merchants within the social hierarchy.[9] Administrative and economic power in the Manchu dynasty was a single brick embedded in the imperial structure.

Macartney speculated that the difficulties in Chinese-British relations would have been infinitely lessened had a class of politically powerful and economically influential merchants existed in China.[10] The government's constant fear that "felonious merchants" might spontaneously establish contact with the barbarians constitutes striking *a contrario* evidence that he was right.

AS A KIND OF European New Year's gift, Qianlong sent Macartney a copy of the December 1 edict, which the emperor apparently thought would help the ambassador justify himself before his king. Thomas, laconic as usual, reports the incident: "Wednesday the 1st of January. This morning we heard that the Emperor's edict was come. We then went into a hall before our house, where the Suntoo [viceroy] was, where we all sat down."

The edict lay on a palanquin covered in yellow silk. The palanquin was then carried across the room, accompanied by musicians, soldiers, and parasol bearers, just as if the emperor had been present. The Chinese kowtowed. "We kneeled and bowed to it as it passed. . . . The Suntoo then presented the edict to Lord Macartney, who received it with all due ceremony."[11] All due ceremony? We will never know how deeply Macartney bowed, for the boy speaks of this ceremony as coyly as his elders do of human fertilizer.

The ambassador's description of this encounter is rather more flattering to his potential British readers. As he tells it, the viceroy came to his residence, "in great ceremony," to report that "he had received a letter from the Emperor, the contents of which he was ordered to communicate to me." There were no surprises: "It contained, as usual, a repetition of the Emperor's satisfaction from the Embassy, his good disposition towards the English, and promises to them of his future favour and protection."

It also mentioned the prospect of a second embassy and justified the rejection of British requests as being "incompatible with Chinese usage; it
was therefore not in his power to satisfy them."[12]

The message exonerated the ambassador of any blame his government
might ascribe to him. It explained everything: why the expedition had
failed, and why the empire was immobile.

The viceroy was "particularly courteous and caressing." He "told us
he had already issued two proclamations, denouncing the severest punishments against any persons who should attempt to injure Europeans, or
practise extortion in dealing with them." Macartney wrote that he hoped
that these would "have a good effect."[13]

If the Chinese were tireless in repeating themselves, the Briton, who
now submitted yet another memorandum, was equally obstinate. His stay
in Canton had given him a much better sense of the local situation. Until
now, most of his information had been based on the directives he had been
given sixteen months earlier, in the company headquarters in London, and
those directives in turn were based on messages that had taken eight months
to reach London from Canton. Effectively, the information was two years
old. Now that he had assessed the situation in Canton personally, Macartney
regretted having allowed the viceroy to talk him into submitting his November 20 memorandum, to which the Chinese had quickly replied with
vague assurances, before Macartney had had the time to prepare a complete
and updated dossier.

His new note therefore summarized the factory's latest demands: that
taxes no longer be levied on every vessel coming from Macao, that company
ships be allowed to bypass Macao and sail directly to Huangpu, that weights
be standardized so as to avoid disputes; that the British be permitted to
buy some land or to enlarge their factory, that they be allowed to hire
dockers and seamen without having to ask for special authorization, that
they be granted personal access to the viceroy whenever they had grievances
to present.[14]

It took no less than half a century—and one war—for the Chinese to
respond to the items on that wish list.

76

Rearguard Actions

(December 29, 1793–January 13, 1794)

ON THE NIGHT of December 29 the embassy was informed of the arrival in Macao of the *Walsingham*, a company ship that had left England last June 7. It brought dramatic news: three other company ships had been left in the Strait of Malacca, and the *Princess Royal*, another Indiaman, had been captured by three French warships, one of sixty-six guns, another of fifty, and a large frigate.*[1]

The next day the letters and packets sent from England on the *Walsingham* were delivered. Though seven months old, they contained the latest available information about friends, family, and the war.

The three delayed ships arrived on January 2, joining the annual gathering of the company fleet in Canton. On December 19, when the embassy arrived, five British ships had been moored at the dock; now there were eighteen. Some had come from Manila, others from the Coromandel coast. They were to take on cargo in Canton before heading back to Europe.

This was the maritime rhythm of the steady growth of British wealth and power: it took from six to nine months for a ship to arrive from England, a month or two to unload and reload in China, six or seven months to sail back to London, and another month or two to unload and reload.

The news of the war brought Macartney down to earth, and he realized that the time had come to resign himself to bringing this mission to a close. In his journal he struck a solemn yet touching tone of restrained melancholy:

---

* In addition to the *Princess Royal*, taken in September 1793, a second British ship, the *Polly*, was captured in October by a French privateer.[2] On May 26, 1793, the Convention, angered by Barère's report on the "crimes of England against the French people," voted to take no British prisoners in the future.

After maturely considering all the circumstances before me, re-flecting upon the state of the ships now ready to sail and upon the value of the cargoes provided for loading the ships lately arrived and those still expected this season (which cargoes, when sold, I can scarcely estimate at less than three millions sterling), ascertained of the capture of the *Princess Royal* in the Straits of Sunda and of a French force there; carefully perusing the letters lately received from Batavia, having no notice or intelligence of any convoy intended to be sent from home, aware of the present situation in Cochin China. . . . I have now, however painful to me, been obliged to dismiss from my mind many of the flattering ideas which I had entertained at the commencement of my Embassy, of distinguishing it by some happy discovery, some signal and brilliant success, in the prosecution of our political and commercial interests in these distant parts of the world.[3]

There was no longer any time to try to compensate for failure in China with an approach to Japan, "which . . . had been always with me a favourable adventure as the possible opening of a new mine for the exercise of our industry and the purchase of our manufactures."[4]

There was certainly no point in waiting fifteen months for a response to any request for instructions that he might send to London now. Ma-cartney had to make the decision himself.

For the moment, however, there was no particular hurry. The merchant fleet would need two months to take on all its cargo and prepare for departure. In the meantime, Macartney and his men could simply rest, and the Chinese left them in peace.

THE DECREES PROMISED by Changlin were promulgated on January 2 and 5. Until then the British had received only verbal assurances, delivered privately. Now they finally had written texts that could be held up to third parties and to the local authorities themselves, to whom they were ad-dressed. At bottom, however, they offered only "hollow verbiage."[5] The first stipulated penalties "for anyone who molested, plundered or defrauded the English. But it was aimed chiefly against the small fry who sold strong drink to the sailors." The second "was aimed at magistrates, military officers and others who might use their position to extort money from Europeans. But here again it was aimed only at the lesser officials."[6] It soon transpired that these decrees would change little in the current system. And there was no response to Macartney's memorandums.

The embassy continued to be closely watched. Dinwiddie, walking along the riverbank, noticed a variety of indigo unknown to him. When he stooped to pick a sample, a Chinese soldier materialized out of nowhere and menacingly stopped him. Similar incidents occurred several times.[7]

Macartney noted that the gentlemen of the company, restricted to their factory beyond the city walls, were not allowed to enter Canton. He was therefore more than a little proud to be given permission to visit this metropolis, a household name in Europe even though few Europeans had ever laid eyes on it. "I had a strong curiosity to see it," Macartney wrote. "I entered it at the great water-gate and traversed it from one end to the other. It covers a great extent of ground and is said to contain a million of inhabitants. This account may possibly exaggerate, but the population everywhere in China is so vastly disproportionate to what we have been accustomed to observe in Europe that it is difficult for us to determine upon any rule or standard of our own to go by.[8]

"All the people seemed very busily employed, chiefly in making either silk boots or straw bonnets, in the working of metals, and the labours of the forge, and most of them wore spectacles on their noses." The streets "are narrow and flat paved. . . . No wheel carriages are admitted, nor did I see any horses in the town except those which my servants rode upon. It is full of shops and trade, and has in general a gloomy appearance, except in two or three large open squares, where the Viceroy and other great men reside." The usual military intelligence: "The walls are kept in good repair, but no guns are mounted on them."[9]

We know from young Staunton that curiosity was not the sole motive for this visit: "Tuesday the 7th. This morning we went in a boat toward the city walls. On landing we entered sedan chairs in which we were carried through the city to the Suntoo's palace, where being arrived we met one of the attendants, who begged us not to trouble ourselves in walking in. Upon which we immediately returned, in that consisting the Chinese ceremony."[10]

In other words, Macartney left without saying a word to Changlin, too vexed even to mention this singular sample of Chinese courtesy in his journal.

MACARTNEY FOUND the relations between the British and the Chinese in Canton exceedingly strange, and he was not sure what to expect from Changlin's decrees. Some foreigners had already been victimized by minor instances of extortion since their promulgation. True, the malefactors had been punished, but Macartney did not see this as a solution: "There are many other things that depend a good deal on ourselves which, I believe, would be more likely to secure us than proclamations and punishments."[11]

To begin with, he felt that the Europeans, instead of flaunting their rivalries, ought to unite in resolute opposition to the exactions of venal and dishonest mandarins. Charles de Constant, our Swiss observer, had written just a few months before the arrival of the British embassy: "All those who know the Chinese agree that this quite pusillanimous people has always yielded to firmness and perseverance. The merchants are quite certain that if the Europeans residing in Canton were to gather together and issue demands unanimously, that would suffice to rid them of the vexations to which they are ceaselessly subjected."[12]

Most of all, however, it was up to the Europeans to make an effort to improve their relations with the population. "We keep aloof from them as much as possible," Macartney wrote. "We wear a dress as different from theirs as can be fashioned. We are quite ignorant of their language (which, I suppose, cannot be a very difficult one, for little George Staunton has long since learned to speak it and write it with great readiness, and from that circumstance has been of infinite use to us on many occasions)."[13]

The result: "We therefore almost entirely depend on the good faith and good-nature of the few Chinese whom we employ, and by whom we can be but imperfectly understood in the broken gibberish we talk to them. I fancy that Pan-ke-qua or Mahomet Soulem would attempt doing business on the Royal Exchange to very little purpose if they appeared there in long petticoat clothes, with bonnets and turbans, and could speak nothing but Chinese or Arabic."[14]

Macartney felt that "by a proper management," the British might "gradually and in some years be able to mould the China trade (as we seem to have done the trade everywhere else) to the shape that will best suit us. But it would certainly require in us great skill, caution, temper and perseverance, much greater perhaps than it is reasonable to expect."[15] The most important point of all, he reiterated, was to learn the language.[16]

Here the fault was not solely with the Europeans, however. The Chinese government forbade its subjects to teach their language to foreigners. The British therefore had to communicate through interpreters who, though they had learned English and were employed by the company, remained under the control of the imperial authorities. All efforts to get around this ruling had so far failed, and a request to lift the prohibition had been included in Macartney's November 20 memorandum. Naturally, there was no response.

Little has changed in this respect. Today it is impossible for a Chinese to become the interpreter, servant, or aide of a foreign resident without having first been selected by the authorities of the People's Republic, to whom he or she continues to report, albeit without payment for the service.

MACARTNEY STILL HOPED that he might have a chance to establish some further contact with the Chinese during his remaining two months in Canton. But there had been no serious conversations since December 22, and even the issuing of Changlin's decrees had not occasioned any meeting. In this it was reminiscent of the dismal ceremony in Peking heralding Macartney's dismissal. The decrees seemed largely irrelevant, and the attempt to visit the viceroy's home had resulted in a snub.

Macartney therefore decided to withdraw to Macao before being expelled. But he was now astute enough to cast the announcement of his departure in gallant terms: "Unwilling to trespass further on the hospitality of the Court of China, . . . I told the Viceroy of my intention of going to Macao, and of waiting there till our ships should be ready to sail for England under the *Lion*'s convoy. And to prevent his taking umbrage, or imagining I was not perfectly pleased with my reception and residence here at Canton . . . I put my removal chiefly upon the ground of my state of health, which has been much impaired, and which it is thought the sea air would be favourable to."

Changlin was only too pleased, and Macartney "fixed with him the time of my departure for to-morrow": January 8, 1794. But before raising anchor, Macartney tried one last initiative: "As I proposed to embark from the wharf of the Factory, I invited him to breakfast with me there, in order that I might have the opportunity (which he had before promised me) of introducing and recommending the Company's Commissioners to him, to the Fuyen [military governor], and the Hoppo in the most public and distinguished manner." The viceroy accepted the invitation, but was somewhat perplexed as to "these gentlemen's office and rank." Macartney "endeavoured to explain the matter to him as well as I could, but there is no making the Chinese understand the wide difference there is between an English merchant and a merchant of any other nation."[17]

They could not understand this difference, Hüttner explained, primarily because "the lowliest mandarin believes himself superior to the richest merchant."[18] Especially barbarian merchants—insulted, battered, and beaten down until they huddled helplessly in their factories.*

But there was another reason why it was especially difficult for Ma-

---

* Hüttner notes that the mandarin who was demoted and whipped for attacking the British was from Canton, where he had undoubtedly picked up these bad habits.[19]

cartney to convince the Chinese of the superiority of English merchants, and that was that they had a detestable reputation in Canton. Hüttner, who was neither English nor Chinese, noted both poles of the contradiction: "Merchants are scorned in China, while their status is respected in all the civilized countries of Europe. . . . The English traders suffer doubly," because they are "especially revered in their own country" but regarded in China as "the most ferocious of all Barbarians."[20]

Hüttner exaggerated the respect in which merchants were held in Europe. The fact is that hostile prejudices against trade, not very different from those prevailing in China, were still widespread in France and Italy, Spain and Portugal, and even a good part of Germany.* But he was right that the Chinese considered the English the worst of all barbarians. The French observer d'Entrecasteaux wrote that "the Chinese have perceived that this enterprising nation aspires to exclusive trade in Asia" and "is increasing the number of ships it dispatches to China, most of which could easily be transformed into warships at any moment."[21]

The Chinese did not understand that the British saw merchants as the very expression of the nation's genius and as the vanguard of civilization. But Macartney shared the Chinese contempt for merchants of other nationalities.

ON JANUARY 8 the viceroy, the governor, and the superintendent of customs duly arrived for breakfast at the factory, where they were introduced to the company commissioners. The mandarins promised to accord the commissioners all the attention they deserved, and seemed highly satisfied with the meal prepared in their honor. They especially appreciated the sweet wine and cherry brandy.

At one in the afternoon Macartney, Staunton, Sir Erasmus Gower, and Lieutenant Colonel Benson embarked on the *Lion*'s barge. The other gentlemen of the embassy, along with Wang and Qiao, boarded launches provided by company ships, and the flotilla sailed down the Pearl River.

The emperor's eye was still upon the British as they prepared to raise anchor. General Tuo'erhuan, commander of the Huzhou brigade, reported to Peking on January 9: "Viceroy Changlin assigned me to oversee the embarcation of the envoy's retinue. On January 8 the wind was calm; the Barbarians paid final homage to Your Imperial Majesty and then set sail."[22]

The trip downriver, writes Thomas, "took about an hour and a quarter.

---

* This reprobation had not changed since Voltaire devoted one of his most penetrating *Lettres philosophiques* to it.

We first passed before all the Indiamen, who . . . hailed us as we passed. There were a few American, Spanish, Dutch, and Genoese [ships].* Most . . . have struck the masts [for fear of typhoons], except the *Lion* and *Hindostan*. We at last got aboard the *Lion*, who indeed looks very handsome. She fired us a salute of 19 guns. Qiao, Wang, and his brother Mandarine dined with us and ate very heartily. The former two were very much affected on leaving us after being so long continually with us."[24]

Wang and Qiao, Macartney writes, "shed tears at parting, and showed such marks of sensibility and concern as could proceed from none but sincere and uncorrupted hearts. If I ever could forget the friendship and attachment of these two worthy men, or the services they rendered us, I should be guilty of the deepest ingratitude."[25]

The next day Wang and Qiao sent "a most liberal present of fruit and vegetables of all kinds in twenty large baskets, . . . as a farewell token of their remembrance. Their respective duties and employments now call them away to very distant provinces, and they are not likely to see any of us again. Of this little attention I therefore confess myself the more sensible."

His emotion at being separated from these men, whom he considered his "private friends," led Macartney to jump to conclusions about what the future held for them. An incorrigible Westerner, he believed that personal friendship could annul the effects of a system that denied individuality and stifled personal relations. Countless Western diplomats in China today harbor similar illusions about their close "personal contact" with second-ranking Chinese officials. The fact was—and remains—that only the highest leaders could overcome the system's inertia.

Qiao, Macartney wrote, "is a man of letters and capacity" who "stands high in the opinion of the Viceroy" and whose "universal reputation, joined to his connexion to the Imperial family, will probably elevate him one day to the first situation at Court. I have more than once talked with Qiao on the subject of office and preferment, and from his prospects of advantage being enlarged by what he has seen here, his pretensions heightened by his connexion with us, and his ambition dilated by the patronage of the Viceroy, I think it not at all improbable that he may soon be sent here in a high employment." Macartney dreamed that Qiao might someday be named hoppo in Canton, and "if he ever obtains the appointment we shall receive the most essential advantages by it."[26]

Anyone who knows anything about China, then or now, could not

---

* But no French vessels. One of our French witnesses would write in 1801 that no French ship had docked in the harbor "in ten years."[23]

help smiling at Macartney's assumption that Wang and Qiao's assignment to the British embassy would assure their promotion and that British interests would someday be served by having two reliable personalities at the summit of state power. In fact, Wang died just six years later during military operations against an obscure peasant revolt, and Qiao retired from government service in the ninth year of Jiaqing's reign (1804–05), having served as chief justice in three different provinces over a period of five years.[27]

IT TOOK THREE DAYS for the embassy to get from its Huangpu moorage to the mouth of the Pearl River, since they had to wait for the evening high tide to cross each of the sandbars.[28]

On January 13 the *Lion* passed the two forts that guarded the Tiger's Mouth. Macartney found both "very despicable . . . when viewed in the light of defence. There are a great many embrasures, but several are unfurnished with guns and of the few guns which they have the largest does not exceed a six pounder. The passage between the two forts is less than a mile across and any ship might go through it almost harmless with the wind and tide in her favour."[29]

The last Chinese "military parade," with "standards, colours, streamers, music and other appurtenances of war," was held as the embassy sailed by. Macartney was unimpressed. There were several "armed junks . . . crowded with soldiers who took great pains to show themselves on deck," but they did not salute the embassy as the soldiers of the forts had, and for good reason: they had "nothing but swivels mounted on their quarters, though they had several sham ports below."[30] His lordship may well have wondered whether these ships were not the very image of China itself.

77

Tomorrow, China

(January 13–15, 1794)

> We, believers in the future, who put our faith in hope and
> look toward dawn.
>
> JULES MICHELET[1]

AS HE PREPARED to leave China, Macartney, who had erred so often in his efforts to decode the behavior of his interlocutors, wrote some speculations whose incisive penetration remains gripping even today.[2]

His experiences had opened his eyes, and he recorded his thoughts at a time when many members of the embassy, speaking privately in the comfort of the drawing rooms of their ships, were also lamenting their lost illusions, most of them arguing that with the failure of this mission, "more direct methods" would be required to open China to British trade. Macartney did not agree with this inflammatory view, but he was quite explicit in assessing the damage China and Britain might inflict on each other in the event of an armed conflict.

China, he felt, would suffer most. "If, indeed, the Chinese were provoked to interdict us their commerce, or do us any material injury, we certainly have the means easy enough of revenging ourselves, for a few frigates could in a few weeks destroy all their coast navigation and intercourse from the island of Hainan to the Gulf of Beizhili." Moreover: "The Koreans, if they once saw ships in the Yellow Sea acting as enemies to China might be induced to attempt the recovery of their independence. The thread of connexion between this Empire and Formosa is so slender that it must soon break of itself, but a breath of foreign interference would instantly snap it asunder."[3] It would also be quite easy to use Bengal as a base from which to foment trouble in Tibet, which had little need of encouragement in any event.

"The Portuguese . . . as a nation, have been long really exanimated and dead in this part of the world, although their ghost still appears at Macao," which is "now chiefly supported by the English. . . . If the

Portuguese made a difficulty of parting with it to us on fair terms, it might easily be taken from them by a small force from Madras,* and the compensation and irregularity be settled afterwards. Or with as little trouble and with more advantage we might make a settlement in Lantao or Cowhee, and then Macao would of itself crumble to nothing in a short time."

This was only 1794, and Macartney very nearly foretells the course of nineteenth-century history in this part of the world. His expedition had sketched the future, and subsequent events would fill in the outlines much as he predicted.

In January and February Lieutenant Parish, aboard the *Jackall*, surveyed the islands between Macao and Hong Kong. His report indicated that Lantao, a "large island near Hongkong" whose "western extremity points towards Macao," would be ideal for an English settlement. As it happened, the British decided on Hong Kong instead (in 1842), but Macartney was right about the consequences: its colonization brought a rapid decline of Macao. Another of his predictions came true as well: the two forts at the mouth of the Pearl River were easily captured in February 1841, during the Opium War.

Macartney expected that the demolition of the forts would give the British control of the Pearl River, in which case "the whole trade of Canton and its correspondencies" could be "annihilated in a season. The millions of people who subsist by it would be almost instantly reduced to hunger and insurrection. They must overrun the country as beggars or as robbers, and wherever they went would carry with them misery and rebellion." In that event, Macartney speculated, Russia would not be likely to "neglect the opportunity of recovering Albazin and re-establishing her power upon the Amur. . . . Would the ambition of the great Catherine, that has stretched beyond Onalaska to the eastward, overlook the provinces and partitions within grasp at her door?"[4] Because of his experience in the Russian court and his conversations with Songyun, Macartney was well acquainted with the dispute between China and Russia over the Amur River and the Albazin fort on that river, which had been twice conquered by Cossacks and twice retaken by Chinese troops.

But war would bring a halt to trade, and this would seriously damage the United Kingdom as well. "Our settlements in India would suffer most severely by any interruption of their China traffic which is infinitely valuable to them, whether considered singly as a market for cotton and opium

---

* Such a force did seize Macao in 1808, following Macartney's plans to the letter, on the pretext of the French occupation of Portugal. The operation ultimately failed because of the immediate and decisive Chinese reaction. (See chapter 84.)

[finally the word is spoken aloud!], or as connected with their adventures to the Philippines and Malaya." To "Great Britain the blow would be immediate and heavy. Our great woolen manufacture, the ancient staple of England, would feel such a sudden convulsion as scarcely any vigilance or vigour in Government could for a long time remedy or alleviate." The Canton trade in wool was already valued at more than half a million pounds sterling annually and was expected to double within several years. Britain would also "lose the other growing branches of export to China of tin, lead, copper, hardware, and of clocks and watches, and similar articles of ingenious mechanism. We should lose the import from China not only of its raw silk, an indispensable ingredient in our silk fabrics, but of another indispensable luxury, or rather an absolute necessary of life: tea. We should also in some measure lose an excellent school of nautical knowledge, a strong limb of marine power, and a prolific source of public revenue."[5]

Macartney felt that in the end none of this damage would prove irreparable. Other markets might be found, and lost ones recovered. He was convinced that the rising British economy would ultimately triumph.

Moreover, many of the negative consequences of war might well come to pass even "without any quarrel or interference on our part. . . . The Empire of China is an old, crazy, First rate man-of-war, which a fortunate succession of able and vigilant officers has contrived to keep afloat for these one hundred and fifty years past, and to overawe their neighbours merely by her bulk and appearance, but whenever an insufficient man happens to have the command upon deck, adieu to the discipline and safety of the ship. She may perhaps not sink outright; she may drift some time as a wreck, and will then be dashed to pieces on the shore; but she can never be rebuilt on the old bottom."[6]

Macartney predicted that the "breaking-up of the power of China . . . would occasion a complete subversion of the commerce, not only of Asia, but a very sensible change in the other quarters of the world. The industry and ingenuity of the Chinese would be checked and enfeebled, but they would not be annihilated. Her ports could no longer be barricaded; they would be attempted by all the adventures of all trading nations, who would search every channel, creek, and cranny of China for a market, and for some time be the cause of much rivalry and disorder. Nevertheless as Great Britain, from the weight of her riches and the genius and spirit of her people, is become the first political, marine, and commercial power on the globe, it is reasonable to think that she would prove the greatest gainer by such a revolution as I have alluded to, and rise superior over every competitor."[7]

On the other hand, "our present interests, our reason, and our humanity equally forbid the thoughts of any offensive measures with regard to the Chinese, whilst a ray of hope remains for succeeding by gentle ones." Macartney regarded the "project of a territory on the continent of China," which he had "heard imputed to the late Lord Clive," as "too wild to be seriously mentioned." He hoped that now that his embassy had given the Chinese "an opportunity of knowing us," they would be led "to a proper way of thinking and of acting towards us in the future."[8]

To pursue this prospect required that "a King's Minister, or a Company's Minister with a King's commission," be "always resident at Canton, totally unconcerned with trade of any kind and clearly known to be so."[9] That suggestion had earlier been made by Father Amiot and endorsed by Charpentier-Cossigny: "This agent, who would have no direct interest in mercantile activities, would represent his nation and would have a more impressive character in the eyes of the Chinese government than a trading company."[10]

"The first object" of this representative of the Crown, Macartney wrote, would be "to preserve the ground we have lately gained." It had been "no small advantage arising from the Embassy that so many Englishmen have been seen at Peking," and that "a most favourable idea has been formed of the country which sent them." The "principal persons of rank" in China, having had "opportunities of observing our manners, tempers and disciplines," had now "dismissed the prejudices they had conceived against us, and by a generous transition grew to admire and respect us as a nation and to love us as individuals." Although the Chinese were "in public ceremonious, in private they were frank and familiar. Tired of official formalities they seemed often to fly to our society as a relief, and to leave it with regret." An "able Minister" would be able to "improve" such "dispositions" through his dealings with the viceroy, the governor, and the hoppo.

Macartney seemed convinced that the emperor's rejection of permanent diplomatic relations, as expressed in the letter he was carrying for George III, had been superseded by the last imperial edict. In this he was mistaken, having failed to realize that if the Chinese seemed accommodating, it was only in order to remove any possible motive for British reprisals. Macartney was wrong to think that most Chinese officials regarded him with the affectionate attitude of Wang and Qiao.

But his deep-seated humanism enabled him to perceive similarities between the Chinese and the British, despite the vast difference in mores. True, the Chinese were "a singular people." But they were "men formed of the same materials and governed by the same passions as ourselves.

They are jealous of foreigners; but are they jealous of us without reason? Is there any country on the globe that Englishmen visit where they do not display that pride of themselves and that contempt of others which conscious superiority is apt to inspire? Can the Chinese, one of the vainest nations in the world, and not the least acute, have been blind and insensible to this foible of ours? And is it not natural for them to be discomposed and disgusted by it?"[11]

A humanist and an optimist, Macartney, like Montesquieu, believed that the source of prejudice was ignorance of oneself and of others. He would have agreed with Goethe, who after reading the Chinese novel *Two Sisters*, noted that commonality of human feelings outweighed exoticism.[12]

Would the presence of a British minister in Canton have been sufficient to advance the cause of friendship between the two peoples?[13] How much freedom of action would the Chinese have granted such an envoy? Those questions never arose: Macartney's proposal was buried by company inertia.

The Frenchman J.-B. Piron,* who observed Macartney's embarcation, wrote that the "embassy was far from achieving the success that had been expected of it."[15] Ten years later, he analyzed Macartney's failure in these terms: "We saw him return to Canton, with all his retinue and a part of his presents, without having been able to obtain the least advantage from the Chinese government. Why had they come? Surely not simply in order to increase their trade, which is already brilliant. 'What do they want here?' the Chinese asked themselves, and they concluded, 'They must be trying to interfere in our affairs, as in India.' "[16]

ON JANUARY 8 Robespierre denounced his rivals on the "left" and the "right," the *Enragés* and the *Indulgents*. On January 13 Fabre d'Eglantine, one of the latter, was arrested on charges of corrupt practices in the liquidation of the French East India Company.

In the bay of Canton the *Lion* unfurled its sails and headed south, toward the islands of Hong Kong and Lantao. There lay the future. Macartney had already charted its course.

---

* This agent of the French East India Company had been sent to China in 1791 to inventory and liquidate the company's holdings; he had remained in the city ever since, without orders.[14]

More Prosperous Chinese

(January 13–February 1, 1794)

Begone, and leave us to our most ancient customs.

SAINT-JOHN PERSE[1]

ON JANUARY 13 the *Lion* dropped anchor some six miles from Macao. A strong wind forced the ship to spend the next day at its moorage, and on January 15 it finally docked in Macao, where the British would stay for two months, in the conditions described by a mandarin in a previously quoted report to Qianlong: "When they arrive in Macao, the English will have to rent their lodgings from the Portuguese, whose guests they will thus become."[2] Relations between Portugal and China were more or less analogous: in Macao the Chinese were landlords, the Portuguese tenants, and the British subletters.

Macartney and his retinue were received by Dom Manuel Pinto, the governor of Macao, and Dom Lazaro da Silva Ferreira, the *desembargador*, or chief justice.[3] A company of soldiers, "mostly negroes and mulattoes, but commanded by European officers, were drawn up in military order on the quay, and endeavoured to make as good an appearance as they could. Their undersize, motley complexion, and shabby regimentals impressed us, however, with no very high ideas in their favour."[4] The governor and his wife were warm hosts. After the hostility of the Portuguese missionaries in Peking, the British were astonished by the welcome they received here. "Such a cordial reception in a Catholic country was no little surprising to us," wrote Holmes. "The clergymen even seemed concerned to outdo the civilian and military officials in kindness."[5] The *desembargador*, Macartney wrote, was a man of "observation and address" who spoke "very good French." (Even today the priests and officials of Macao prefer French to English, despite—or perhaps because of—Hong Kong's proximity.)

Most of the embassy was lodged at the British factory, but Macartney stayed in a house "in the upper part of the town" loaned to him by a company official. "It is most delightfully situated, and has a very pleasant romantic garden adjoining to it of considerable extent. The tradition of Macao says it was formerly the habitation of the celebrated Camoens [Camões], and that here he composed his *Lusiad*."*⁶

The Portuguese national poet's name is still as magical in Macao as it is in Coimbra. Driven from the Court of Lisbon for having written passionate poems to the wrong lady, he was subsequently exiled (in 1553) after killing a military officer in a brawl. Eventually he made his way to Macao, where he was appointed trustee for the dead and absent, a post that left him plenty of free time to compose his epic celebrating the voyages of the intrepid Vasco da Gama and the other great Portuguese explorers of the time. On his way back to Lisbon in 1572, Camões was almost killed when his ship foundered in a storm. But he managed to swim to safety, supposedly while holding his precious manuscript above the water.

ANDERSON DESCRIBES the setting: "Macao is generally supposed to be situated on an island; but the fact is otherwise; nor is there any natural barrier which separates it from the Chinese territory. The whole extent of the Portuguese possessions does not exceed four miles in length and one and a half mile in breadth: the limits of which are accurately determined, and cannot be passed without danger."⁷ Still true.†

Built on rock, the city featured European-style houses lining narrow, winding streets. There were also churches, convents, the council palace (known as the senate), the governor's house, and the British factory. The population at the time included some ten thousand Chinese, who were "under the government of a mandarin stationed here by the Emperor," and about a thousand Portuguese, plus other Europeans resident in the factories and "a great number of Negro and Asiatic slaves."⁸ The harbor, though well sheltered, could not accommodate large ships at its docks. The city was dominated by a fortress equipped with many artillery pieces capable of being turned to defend against an attack from any direction. "The Chinese have a fort that looks toward the Portuguese territory, and it is the principal duty of the garrison to prevent strangers from passing the limits of it."⁹

How was it that the proud empire tolerated this irritating eyesore?

---

* This house, adjacent to a public garden and not far from a grotto (both named for Camões), has since been turned into a museum. In 1986–88 it held a fine exhibit honoring both Camões and four centuries of the Portuguese colony. There was no mention that Macartney had briefly lived in the house.

† Except that a second *sas*, or Special Economic Zone, in Zhulai now abuts Macao, as the Shenzhen zone abuts Hong Kong.

The fact is that Portuguese sovereignty was by no means as absolute as the West imagined. This colony, much like Macartney's genuflection in Jehol, was viewed quite differently by the two sides, Peking considering Macao just as Chinese as Lisbon considered it Portuguese. Hüttner explained the secret of this strange cohabitation: "The Emperor of China receives from the Portuguese an enormous tribute of five hundred thousand ducats. Moreover, the Portuguese governor inevitably refrains from any action that might vex the Chinese mandarins."[10] "The place is divided in its jurisdiction between the Portuguese and Chinese over their respective peoples," Anderson writes. "The latter, however, exact very heavy duties on all goods landed, or shipped, on account of the European factories."[11] In the event of armed conflict, the Portuguese fortifications would be quite ineffective.[12]

"We . . . went into the Senate House," Thomas writes on January 30, "in which we saw several charters which were granted to the Town of Macao engraved in Chinese characters upon stone."[13] These "charters" actually amounted to Macao's subjugation, and the Chinese characters underscored the colony's strict subordination to the Celestial Order. Father Lamiot confirms Thomas's assessment: "In this Senate there are two or three stones on which the mandarins have inscribed restrictive decrees that are in such complete opposition to the notion of the cession of territory that the Portuguese do not enjoy exhibiting them."[14]

Staunton senior commented: "In the senate house, which is built of granite, and two stories high, are several columns of the same material, with Chinese characters cut into them, signifying a solemn cession of the place from the Emperor of China."[15] Once again the minister plenipotentiary was more credulous than his astute son. As a Portuguese boasted to the father about Peking's imaginary concessions to Portugal, the son simply read the characters that revealed the truth.

Although the Chinese never went so far as to starve the Portuguese out, they did hector them in more subtle ways. The Portuguese, for instance, once sent deputies to Peking "to protest against a tax that they considered unjust." The Chinese of Macao decided to "avenge" this violation of Order (which, incidentally, had been in vain): "For three days they paraded through the streets with their idols, well aware that the Portuguese, terrified by these artifacts as they were, would refuse to venture from their homes." The bishop had to "offer the Chinese a considerable sum to call a halt to these processions."[16] Such parades are still held in both Macao and Hong Kong during the great holidays of the lunar calendar, and those Chinese who seem most Westernized are especially devoted to them: it is their way of remaining faithful to their identity.

Unpublished correspondence preserved in the archives of the Grand Council indicates that the Portuguese had reached an intelligent modus vivendi with the Middle Empire. They made no claim of sovereignty before the Chinese, but reserved their rodomontades strictly for European visitors. They submitted without protest to the kowtow, sent two or three embassies every century, paid heavy tribute, and did signal service for the emperor: "The Portuguese settlement dates back to the Mings. These Barbarians have grown to love this land, wherein they bask in the Emperor's benevolent influence. . . . The profound kindness of our Emperor has touched them deeply."[17]

These were barbarians who had allowed themselves to be baked in the slow fires of Civilization's hearth.

The British, in contrast, remained obstinately raw. Hence the Celestial emperor's violent reaction when they attempted to oust the Portuguese from Macao.

The British were intensely jealous of this enclave. They saw no reason why the Portuguese, who were incapable of exploiting their position, should enjoy such favor, and they were well on their way to supplanting their rivals. The Dutch, Swedish, French, and Spanish factories were nothing compared to theirs. "Far more numerous and much richer," writes Hüttner, "the British occupy large houses built and furnished in the English style, which they rent from the Portuguese."[18] The latter are "so lazy" and "so little concerned with seeking new resources that all of them live in the most dire poverty." Among themselves, the English whispered that the Portuguese even sank so low as to prostitute their women. "This poverty has made them jealous, especially of the English, who are detested by the bishop and the clergy as the most execrable of heretics."[19]

The Portuguese, a brilliant and conquering people in the fifteenth and sixteenth centuries, had now been colonized in their own colonies and even in their metropolitan territory. And the British were not alone in viewing Macao as a wasted opportunity. "If it belonged to an active and industrious nation," one of our French observers wrote, "Macao would soon attain a high degree of prosperity. Its location would attract enormous trade."[20] Which is exactly what later happened to Hong Kong.

Ultimately, however, it was the Chinese who prospered most from Macao. The huge sums spent by foreign (especially British) traders went straight into the pockets of the Chinese, who, once they acquired the requisite individual autonomy, proved industrious, efficient, and skilled at imitation and adaptation. They manufactured a wide variety of products, which they sold to the Europeans. The British had earlier been impressed with the economic gains of the Chinese in Java, where they had overwhelmed the Dutch. "They build all the houses; no labor seems too arduous or base to them, provided they are paid for it. They are the sole servants of foreigners, while the Portuguese have only Negro slaves."[21]

A striking portrait of this cosmopolitan enclave: the Portuguese were shunted to the sidelines by their poverty, the British were isolated by their wealth, the other Europeans lived in ghettos, the Chinese made money from them all. They felt quite at home in this Portuguese colony, where they were able to escape the Celestial bureaucracy's straitjacket and thereby to enrich themselves.

For that very reason, however, the bureaucracy was as uncomfortable with the Chinese of Macao as Qianlong had been with his compatriots in Batavia. Chinese living by trade and polluting themselves through contact with barbarians! "The Chinese nation is represented in Macao only by that which is most base about it," wrote Father Amiot. "These are men whom China barely numbers among its own."[22]

In addition to serving as a trading post, Macao was the base of the missionaries. The Office of Propagation of the Faith was headed by a resident official, an Italian, "who disbursed to the missionaries in the provinces of China the money which he received from Chinese seminary students in Italy and assigned freshly arrived missionaries to their dioceses."[23] But that was sometimes easier said than done, as we have seen in the case of Fathers Lamiot and Hanna.

Thomas paid a visit to the convent of Saint Joseph,* where his friend Mr. Plumb had spent the year 1773, just before setting out for the "Chinese college" of Naples.[24] The British now offered Mr. Plumb a job in England. What greater recompense could they bestow upon a Chinese than the chance to live among them? But "though he appeared to part from his European friends with a sensible regret, he very naturally preferred to return to the bosom of family and friends, from whom he had been so long separated."[25]

Father Li remained in China to pursue his evangelical calling. In 1801 and 1802 he wrote letters to Macartney from the province of Shanxi, telling his former employer in one of them that "the way here from Macao is almost blocked because of the fury of the rebellion which is daily growing in the provinces of Huguang,† Shanxi and Sichuan."[26] It is possible that

---

* The same convent where I met the astonishing Father Teixeira.

† By Huguang he means Hubei and Hunan, to which might be added Henan. In other words, five of the eighteen provinces involved in the White Lotus rebellion, which raged from 1795 to 1804.

Mr. Plumb, like so many other missionaries, may have lost his life in one of these rebellions. In any event, we have no further news of him.

AS IN MADEIRA and Rio, the British Protestants (and the German Hüttner) saw a link between the evident decadence of the Portuguese and the spectacular domination of Catholicism.[27] The astronomer noted that there were priests and monks everywhere, and crosses were ubiquitous, even among the banners of the fortress, as though they formed part of the arsenal of defense.[28] Staunton junior noted on January 19 that the church bells had been "ringing all day."[29] He counted thirteen churches and visited several of them, describing them as "very handsome, painted and adorned in the Roman Catholic style."[30]

On Ash Wednesday[31] the British observed a religious procession in the city: Death, carrying his scythe, led the march; behind him walked a person dressed in black and bearing a blood-stained cross; then there were statues of the Virgin, Jesus, and numerous saints, each placed on a bier covered with black cloth. Other marchers carried banners, crosses, and bells.[32]

A few hours later there was a Chinese counterdemonstration. Fishermen, carrying lanterns and large fish made of paper or silk, paraded to the sound of gongs. Some of these brightly painted paper fish had "moving jaws and fins." In general, the good humor of the Chinese was in sharp contrast to the lugubrious solemnity of the Portuguese.

According to a Chinese quoted by Dinwiddie, however, the British were far from expert in matters of religion. When the astronomer visited a Chinese temple in Macao, he found two sailors placing offerings on the altars. One of them informed Dinwiddie that he was not welcome in this holy place. "English," he said, "no savey much about religion."[33]

Indeed, their Protestantism was so discreet that the British were taken for "unbelievers" throughout the Far East. In Macao they had even been denied the right to a graveyard of their own. Anderson reports that the tombs of his compatriots lay in a cemetery "exclusively occupied by Chinese" and by non-Catholic Europeans, "as the papists have particular places of interment for those who depart this life in the faith of their church."*[34] The valet almost sounds like a Chinese lamenting the solitude of his dead countrymen, condemned to eternal rest so far from their ancestors.

---

* The Portuguese later granted the company permission to establish a cemetery of its own adjacent to the Camões house where Macartney had stayed.

A Surprising Request for
a Military Alliance

(February 1–March 17, 1794)

THE EMBASSY WAS now truly at its end: in late January, Changlin refused to accept a letter sent by Macartney from Macao, on the grounds that Peking had already been advised of the ambassador's departure.[1] Barred from any further dealings with the Chinese government, Macartney continued to meet with other foreigners, including Russians and Swedes. During one visit to a Russian gentleman, the captain of the *Lion* encountered the commander of a French ship "which Sir Erasmus chased into" the environs of Macao.[2] Now that the chase was done, the former adversaries shared their table amicably.

The British also met other Britons. The page wrote of going "to see the gentlemen play at kriket."[3] The English could feel at home anywhere, provided they were able to practice their national sports (which, in fact, had been among Macartney's urgent requests to the emperor).

The Chinese New Year broke the monotony. "There was a great show of gift ornaments and artificial flowers," says Thomas. And fireworks: "They began to fire crackers many days before" the New Year.[4] The houses had a festive air. "All the Chinese adorn . . . the fronts of their houses with gilt and painted paper." And everyone wore new clothes: "If ever so poor [they] yet make it a rule to put on a new suit of clothes on this day, which lasts the poorer sort throughout the year."[5]

Macartney brought his journal to a close upon leaving Canton; young Thomas, tired of recording tedious courtesy visits, made no entries in his after February 1.

AS MACARTNEY PREPARED to leave China, he was unaware of two edicts issued by Qianlong on January 25, before the Chinese New Year.

The first, though completely ignored by history, is surely of interest, for it reports that Macartney had proposed an Anglo-Chinese military alliance against France.

The emperor's edict, carefully drafted so as to be understood by all barbarians, reproduces word for word a report from Changlin informing the emperor of the British initiative. The three principal European missionaries in Peking, Fathers d'Almeida, Raux, and Poirot, were solemnly summoned to the court to listen to a reading of this edict: "England desires military aid from the Celestial Court, probably because of the reverses it is now suffering against the French. It is completely unaware that the Great Emperor, in exercising his authority over foreigners, has never showed the slightest partiality in favor of one or another. China has never been concerned with which country dominates the other in wars fought by Barbarians among themselves. The Great Emperor has never had the slightest disposition toward one Barbarian country over another."

The priests reportedly replied: "We are ignorant of the reasons for the war between England and France, two countries which the Great Emperor regards with equal benevolence. We know that he has never exhibited any preference among small states."[6]

It seems doubtful that this alleged proposal for a military alliance was merely a figment of Changlin's imagination. Although Chinese courtiers had a mania for telling the emperor what he wanted to hear, they never concocted news their master did not expect. Neither Macartney, nor Staunton, nor any documentation I was able to uncover in the archives of the Foreign Office or the India Office makes any mention of such a request. Yet it is not completely implausible. Dundas had urged Macartney to portray the French as predators eager to get their hooks into India as a base for exporting their revolution to China, and the idea of a British-Chinese military alliance had been raised by the company well before Macartney's mission: in 1783 George Smith proposed an offensive and defensive treaty of alliance against France.[7]

It is therefore possible that Macartney, having received the latest news of the conflict between the Jacobin Republic and the rest of Europe and convinced that Changlin was a receptive interlocutor, may have decided to play this card. If so, he was careful to put nothing in writing, whereas he drafted note after note on such issues as his efforts to obtain a trading post and even the right of the British to practice their favorite sports. It is therefore likely that Changlin interpreted a brief exploratory conversation as a formal proposal.

Macartney was an imaginative man, equally adept at pondering ways of sinking the debilitated Chinese ship of state or of bringing "the most powerful nation of the West" and "the greatest empire of the East" together against a common enemy. The backing of Chinese ports, and even of Chinese troops, would be precious if France ever revived Louis XVI's old ambitions in Indochina or regained the dominant position in the Indian Ocean it had briefly enjoyed under Suffren. The French might even occupy Portugal and lay claim to Macao. On the other hand, the Chinese might well have found it useful to have the British police their eastern waters.

But Qianlong rejected the extravagant proposal. The Celestial Order was quite unconcerned with quarrels among barbarians, so long as they did not impinge on China. But one of the questions he had put most insistently to the British had been, Are you at peace with your neighbors? The British had been equally insistent in replying that they were. Yet now, as their embassy departed, they suddenly proposed to draw China into *their* war.

THE SECOND EDICT involved a point of pride for the emperor. Formally, it was addressed to the dynasty and its allies: the Manchu and Mongol princes and the Grand Council. But the real target was the entire Chinese people, "now and in times to come." The edict was therefore widely published and distributed.

> The English envoy has now set sail. The Barbarians have been notified of a benevolent edict authorizing them to bring tribute once more. The joy they felt upon hearing this news could be read on their faces, and they redoubled their expressions of respect and reverence. Among all the countries beyond the seas, there is none that has not submitted and come to offer its treasures. As the English embassy returns to its country, it is already preparing to return again with tribute. An act of allegiance from so distant a land is without precedent in history.[8]

The prickly cactus of Jehol had lost his thorns. The farther from China the embassy got, the more rosy the official memory of it became.

This song of triumph had a no less obliging accompaniment on the other side of the world. In 1803 Barrow persisted in claiming that "the late embassy, by shewing the character and dignity of the British nation in a new and splendid light, to a court and people in a great measure ignorant of them before, however misrepresented by the jealousy of rivals, or impeded by the counteraction of enemies, has laid an excellent foundation for great future advantages, and done honour to the wisdom and foresight of the statesman who planned the measure, and directed its execution."[9]

During the next few weeks the company ships were loaded, the convoy was assembled, and Lieutenant Parish continued his exploration of the islands near Hong Kong.[10] When the time came for the embassy to cast off, Anderson reports, "The troops were all drawn out on the beach on the occasion, with six brass field-pieces, from which they fired a salute of nineteen guns, which was answered by several forts."[11]

The British raised anchor in a martial atmosphere, diplomacy falling silent at the crackle of gunfire, "the last word of kings," as the Latin slogan engraved on Louix XIV's artillery pieces put it.

For the moment they were firing blanks, but that would change soon enough. Macartney's departure was like a farewell to peace.

80

Oceans at War

(March 17–September 6, 1794)

EIGHTEEN MONTHS EARLIER, when the embassy set out, England had been at peace. Macartney traveled in a warship purely out of regard for the dignity of his mission. But the return convoy, although composed mainly of merchant ships, was outfitted for war. Recent successes scored by French troops had "caused some uneasiness."[1]

On March 17 the *Lion* was joined by a group of company vessels that had taken on cargo in Canton. A Spanish and a Portuguese ship, both of them armed as well,* also signed on for British protection. "Sir Erasmus Gower assigned its station, in case of action, to each of the English ships, over which he was authorized to assume command."[2]

The return voyage was to take only five and a half months, with stopovers for reprovisioning in Java and Saint Helena. The convoy would spend a little over a month in the China Sea, two months in the Indian Ocean, and another two in the Atlantic. When they set sail, Robespierre was scoring triumphs against the Hébertistes and was about to prevail against Danton; by the time they docked in Portsmouth, he had fallen to the guillotine.

The voyage back to England offers little information about China, but it affords us some insight into the world the expedition inhabited.†

A French squadron was known to be cruising the Strait of Sunda, and the British expected that their paths might cross at any moment. On March 29 a sail was sighted at the latitude of Singapore, and the *Lion* gave chase. Holmes was disappointed when it turned out to be only a small

---

* All merchant ships sailing to the Far East were heavily armed to defend themselves against pirates.
† Macartney closed his journal when the diplomatic part of his mission ended. During the return trip he spent many days editing the longhand notes he had taken day by day, polishing his account of the mission.[3] Of all our witnesses, only Staunton senior, Holmes, and Dinwiddie discuss any incidents of the voyage back to England.

fishing boat: "All hands were in high spirits, and anxious to have a brush with their old and natural enemy."[4]

On April 2 the squadron crossed the equator. On the fourth it entered the Strait of Banka, where a ship at anchor was spotted: "at 9 she fired two guns, and hoisted the Hon. East India Company's colours." The ship, out of Bombay, had been pursued in the Strait of Sunda by "four French privateers; and it was the general opinion that they were lurking about to pick up some of our homeward bound Indiamen; and we were in hopes of catching some of them."[5] No such luck. Frustrated at the missed naval skirmish, Staunton consoled himself with the thought that the French were afraid: "On hearing of the China ships having the convoy of a ship of war; and fearing the union of superior force against them, [they] had quitted the station, where they had expected to encounter only unprotected merchantmen."[6]

The China Sea was home to more Chinese and Malay pirates than French cruisers.[7] On April 7, near the Sunda Islands, the squadron sighted a dozen Malay ships flanking a Dutch-built eighteen-gun brig that "probably had been captured by the Malays."[8] The British, having "too important a charge, to be diverted from it by any occasional occurrence," decided not interfere with the pirates,[9] but on their arrival in Java they repented of their clemency: "The crew . . . consisting of about thirty Dutchmen, were all inhumanly murdered. . . . All hands were vexed that these savages . . . should not meet with the punishment they so justly merited."[10]

On April 11 there was a new alert. Two ships flying the Union Jack were spotted, but a ruse was suspected, and the *Lion* gave chase, "not doubting but they were some of the French cruizers. I never saw such alacrity, such spirit, and such anxiety as appeared throughout the *Lion* during the chase. The moment the drums beat to quarters every one obeyed the summons as cheerfully as though they had been ordered to splice the main brace." But the lead ship ran up the British flag again, "lowered her top-gallant sails, and saluted with fifteen guns."[11]

The *Lion*'s quarry proved to be a British ship sent from Bengal "to clear these seas of the French privateers."[12] Another disappointment. "Their being friends and countrymen did not give us half the satisfaction we should have received, to have found them our old and natural enemies, whom we wished to have a brush with. Each seaman and soldier left his quarters in sullen disappointment. The can of grog, which soon followed, revived their spirits, and many a hearty loyal toast rung throughout the ship."[13]

The British sailors were delighted to have recovered their freedom of action after so many long months of restraint, and they were jubilant in their conviction that they were as superior to the French as they were to any other nation. Perhaps the Chinese were not so far wrong in considering the English "the fiercest of the Western Ocean Barbarians."

THE FRENCH HAD captured the *Princess Royal* and turned it into a Republican vessel. Since 1792, however, the expression "the French" had been ambiguous, for the kingdom was deeply split. The captain of the Bengal fleet came aboard the *Lion* and told Macartney of a little-known incident of the Franco-French war: "Captain Mitchell also informed us, that two frigates, one under royal, the other under national colours, came into port near Batavia. East of Java they fought an obstinate battle; but the democrats were beat, and the prisoners sent ashore amongst the Malays, who in all probability did not treat them much better than their countrymen, and the royalists returned after the action to Old France."*[14]

The Count of Villèle, then cruising in the Indian Ocean, confirms: "Crews greeted one another with shouts of *Long live the king!* or *Long live the nation!* before exchanging cannon fire."[15] (Similarly, in 1864, during the American Civil War, a Union and a Confederate ship fought a battle in the English Channel during which the *Alabama*, an armored frigate, was sunk.)

Trickery also played its part in the war at sea. Two British ships captured two "American" vessels, which, after being sent on to Batavia, turned out to be French, flying the American flag but carrying cargo belonging to France.[16]

On April 14 the fleet reached Anguera, a supply station on the coast of Java. "Before we quitted . . . we had several proofs of the thievish disposition of the Malays; there was scarcely a boat went ashore from our ship, or the Indiamen, but they made some attempt upon. . . . We had large parties washing on shore, near the watering place, and they were artful enough to convey several shirts and other articles away unperceived."[17] The British took revenge against these Malays for the unpunished crimes committed by their countrymen: "Several of them were desperately wounded with the axes of the wooding parties, who spared none that appeared suspicious, but drove them back into the woods to their lurking places, bruised and wounded in a shocking manner: but nothing could prevent these savages from attacking our people whenever they appeared to have an advantage."[18]

---

* My research in the French national naval archives turned up no mention of this episode. It may have involved privateers.

On April 16 the *Jackall*, with Dinwiddie on board, left the squadron and headed for Calcutta with Macartney's precious plants.

On that same day, in France, the Terror was centralized. The decree of the twenty-seventh of Germinal, Year II, ordered that "conspirators" from "all points of the Republic be brought to the Revolutionary Tribunal in Paris."

In the Indian Ocean, however, the British convoy sailed on without incident, subject only to a restriction typical of such convoys: "Some of the Indiamen were intolerable dull, heavy sailors; the Portuguese in particular detained the whole fleet; five or six knots an hour were the most we could get out of her, in a breeze that would have carried us nine or ten."[19]

Aboard the *Lion*, the only amusement of the return voyage was offered by a Papuan who had been found aboard the French brigantine *L'Amélie*, captured off Macao by Sir Erasmus. This Papuan was a most diverting savage: He "plunged frequently from the gunwale of the vessel into the sea, to catch dollars thrown into it for that purpose. He caught them before they reached the bottom. . . . He would also bring up two dollars at once, one thrown towards the head and another towards the stern of the ship. . . . He would suffer two Europeans to throw spears at him at the same time, both of which he would divert with, or take in, his hands as they approached him."[20]

China had been an impenetrable world in which civilization had taken a different path and attained different heights from those of Europe. But at least they were heights. The Papuan also hailed from an impenetrable world, but one whose origin was common to all. The British saw him as a specimen of man in his natural state, neither Western nor Chinese. A gifted animal. It must have been difficult for Macartney to resist the notion that the Chinese somehow stood midway between Papuans and Englishmen.

At the latitude of Madagascar the squadron entered a zone of autumn storms, and the British were able to test the reliability of their mercury barometers: "The fluid suddenly descended by more than a quarter of an inch." Precautions were taken against the weather: "Scarcely was all, in technical language, made snug, when the tempest burst by one of the most tremendous crashes of thunder ever heard, together with several successive flashes of the most vivid lightning. The air was likewise so dense that one end of the ship was not visible from the other."[21]

On May 7 Robespierre inaugurated the cult of the Supreme Being.

THE SQUADRON ENTERED the latitudes known as the Roaring Forties, and on May 23 the *Hindostan* sprung its foremast.[22] They rounded the cape on

June 2 and headed for Saint Helena, a haven in a hostile sea. This fortified island belonged to the company and provided the only moorage beyond the cape where its ships returning from India or Canton could dock. But it was so small that the squadron commanders were afraid they might miss it,[23] a prospect that made them especially anxious since illness was ravaging the crews: about a hundred men were "on the surgeon's list" aboard the *Lion* alone.

"At sunrise on the 18th [of June] the *Exeter* and *Abergavenny* being ahead, made a signal for seeing land, and several strange sails."[24] Once again the squadron drew up into battle formation, and once again it was a false alarm. The other ships were part of a second flotilla that had been sent from England to meet the company convoy, the admiralty being unaware that the ships were sailing under the *Lion*'s protection.

The first view of the island was discouraging: its "lofty sides . . . bear so terrific and inhospitable an appearance, that . . . this apparent heap of rocks" might well have been called "inaccessible." But the ships anchored near "a road opposite to a valley, of which the pleasing scenes are justly said, by an ingenious traveller, 'to be laid in the lap of horror.' "[25] The crewmen and passengers who stopped here sometimes outnumbered the inhabitants. There was no inn, but "every house is open for the reception of strangers, who are considered, for the time, as a part of the family."[26] The family being the company.

When a squadron docked, the island sprang to life, and when it departed, the little colony sank back into immobility and "intestine divisions sometimes revive; it is, however, an object of government to divert their minds from private feuds, by engaging them in . . . dramatic entertainments."[27] One wonders whether Napoleon read this passage in 1805, as he skimmed the French translation of Staunton's book while en route to Austerlitz. If so, he surely could not have imagined that the British government would one day offer its far-off subjects the "dramatic entertainment" of the imprisoned Ogre.

THE CONVOY BURIED its dead, reprovisioned its holds, and gave its sick seamen time to recover. On July 1, 1794, the ships set sail again. Macartney's vessels were now joined by the second squadron, as well as five more company ships from Bengal and Bombay and a whaler returning from the far South Atlantic, near Antarctica.

Sir Erasmus set the course, and "the *Lion* kept just ahead of the Indiamen, so as to direct the movements of the whole."[28] Trade winds carried the convoy quickly across the equator, but near the Cape Verde islands the wind died, and the squadron was becalmed for ten days.

The ships were barely under way again when, on July 21, the lookouts sighted another squadron of eleven vessels to the northeast. The alarm was sounded yet again. Flags and signals were invisible in the fog. "The *Lion* was cleared for action. Several cumbersome articles were thrown overboard. Nothing remained upon the decks, except powder and ball, and cannon."[29] The Stauntons had an argument: "The passengers were to act as volunteers; except a boy, whom his father, who was present, thought much too young for such a situation, and proposed to send with the surgeons to the cockpit. The youth, however, though not affecting to be insensible of the danger, revolted from the idea of screening himself from it, while his parent was exposed, and earnestly solicited to remain with him upon deck. This contest of sentiment and affection was, indeed, soon decided, by the disappearance of the fog, which discovered the opposite ships close to each other, but all of them English."[30] It was learned that the "British fleet, under Lord Howe, had gained a complete victory over the French."*[31]

Meanwhile, in Paris, Robespierre had been ousted by the Convention. Wounded and dying, he was executed—along with five hundred supporters, among them Saint-Just. It was the ninth of Thermidor.

The squadron passed well to the east of the Azores and headed for Ireland. "On September 2 the flotilla came within sight of the southern extremity of Ireland." It encountered a Danish vessel that, on August 29, had been visited by seven French warships. It "appeared, upon computation, that Sir Erasmus Gower's much weaker ships must have passed a very few days before,"[32] barely eluding the French vessels.

The alarm had also been sounded among the French, who had just learned of the arrival of Macartney's convoy: "20th of Fructidor, Year II, Brest, from the Commissioner of the Navy to Admiral Villaret-Joyeuse: prepare a strong contingent of vessels of the highest speed to seek out the convoy coming from India."[33] But it was too late. The order reached the admiral on September 6, the day the British squadron entered Portsmouth harbor, "after an absence of near two years."[34]

For many, the absence was eternal. Dysentery had ravaged the crews

---

* This is the British version of the May 28–June 1, 1794, naval battle between Howe and Villaret-Joyeuse, whose fourteen vessels were escorting a convoy carrying grain, sugar, and flour from the West Indies and the United States. Six French ships were captured in the engagement, but despite Howe's numerical superiority, Villaret-Joyeuse managed to lead the rest of the merchant convoy back to Brest safe and sound. The French version of the battle features the legend of the republican *Vengeur*.

during the return voyage. Aboard the *Lion* alone, "near ninety seamen, and seven officers" out of a crew of four hundred had died since leaving Batavia in March. Five of Macartney's guards had also perished.[35] Such was the human cost of long-distance ocean travel in that era. But the dead were soon forgotten in the joy of the living at their safe return.

Macartney proudly informed the gentlemen of the company that the prey had eluded the French hunter:

> It is my pleasure to inform you that not only the thirteen ships which set out with us from China have arrived safely to port, but five others as well, coming from Bengal and Bombay, which joined us at Saint Helena, carrying Company products with a value of several millions of sterling.
>
> I defer, until we meet in London, a full account of the advances which will permit your agents in China to live and work on a footing completely different from that which they have known until now. I have, however, urged the youngest of your agents there to learn the Chinese language, failing which they will remain at the mercy of men disposed to abuse them.
>
> The exterior marks of respect shown the Embassy by order of the Emperor have had a salutary effect upon the mentality of the Chinese: the English are no longer subjected to their scorn and insults. The dispositions of the Chinese are henceforth more favourable in our regard. It is up to the Company to see to it that this state of affairs is reinforced.[36]

Illusion upon illusion.

For the members of the embassy, this was the happy end of a perilous adventure, and most of them felt that life would bring no greater thrills than those they had experienced in these two years. "We said to each other," wrote Holmes, that "we should think but trifling of the hardships of soldiering hereafter, having so severely felt that of sailoring."[37] For Staunton, "The scenes and objects which the rest [of the embassy, apart from the ambassador] had an opportunity of observing, left a gratifying and durable impression upon the minds of them, beyond all the events of the former period of their lives."[38] With these sober and modest words the plenipotentiary brings his account of the expedition to a close.

The mission was over. But despite what Macartney said, it had not been accomplished.

VI

AFTER MACARTNEY OR A SPIRAL OF MISFORTUNE

Events are greater than men know, and even those which appear to be the work of accident, individuals, special interests, or external circumstance have far deeper sources and quite an unsuspected scope.

FRANÇOIS GUIZOT, 1823[1]

Competition has neither heart nor pity. Woe to the vanquished! In this struggle, many crimes must inevitably be committed; this fratricidal struggle is moreover a continuous crime against human solidarity, which is the only basis of all morality.

MIKHAIL BAKUNIN, 1870[2]

The conquest of the earth, which mostly means the taking it away from those who have a different complexion or slightly flatter nose than ourselves, is not a pretty thing when you look into it too much.

JOSEPH CONRAD, 1902[3]

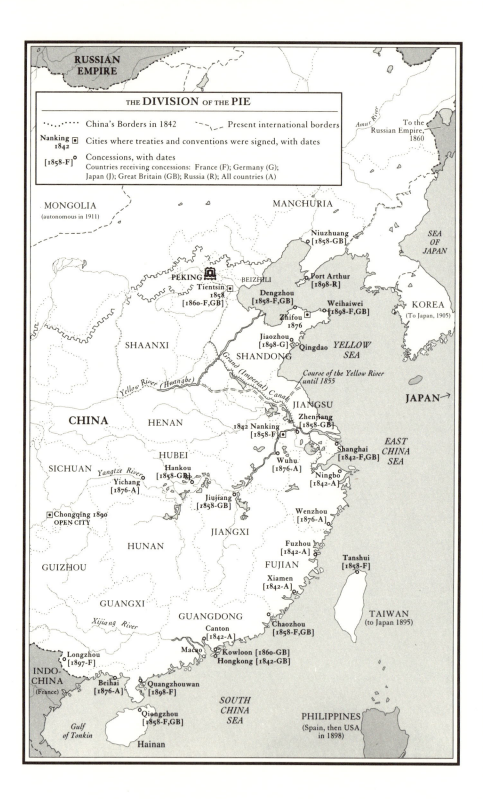

THE **DIVISION** OF THE **PIE**

.... China's Borders in 1842   — — — Present international borders

Nanking ▣ Cities where treaties and conventions were signed, with dates
1842

[1858-F]° Concessions, with dates
Countries receiving concessions: France (F); Germany (G);
Japan (J); Great Britain (GB); Russia (R); All countries (A)

RUSSIAN
EMPIRE

Amur River
To the
Russian Empire,
1860

MONGOLIA
(autonomous in 1911)

MANCHURIA

SEA
OF
JAPAN

Niuzhuang
[1858-GB]

Port Arthur
[1898-R]

KOREA
(To Japan, 1905)

PEKING   BEIZHILI
Tientsin
1858
[1860-F,GB]

Dengzhou
[1858-F,GB]

Weihaiwei
[1898-F,GB]

SHAANXI

Zhifou
1876

Jiaozhou
[1898-G]   Qingdao

YELLOW
SEA

SHANDONG

Yellow River (Huanghe)

Grand (Imperial) Canal

*Course of the Yellow River
until 1855*

JAPAN →

CHINA   HENAN

JIANGSU

Zhenjiang
[1858-GB]

EAST
CHINA
SEA

1842 Nanking
[1858-F]

HUBEI

Shanghai
[1842-F,GB]

SICHUAN   *Yangtze River*   Hankou
[1858-GB]

Wuhu
[1876-A]

Ningbo
[1842-A]

Yichang
[1876-A]

Jiujiang
[1858-GB]

▣Chongqing 1890
OPEN CITY

JIANGXI

Wenzhou
[1876-A]

HUNAN

GUIZHOU

FUJIAN

Fuzhou
[1842-A]

Tanshui
[1858-F]

Xiamen
[1842-A]

TAIWAN
(to Japan 1895)

GUANGXI

Xijiang River

GUANGDONG

Canton
[1842-A]

Chaozhou
[1858-F,GB]

Longzhou
[1897-F]

Macao   Kowloon [1860-GB]
Hongkong [1842-GB]

INDO-
CHINA
(France)

Beihai
[1876-A]

Quangzhouwan
[1898-F]

SOUTH
CHINA
SEA

PHILIPPINES
(Spain, then USA
in 1898)

*Gulf
of Tonkin*

Qiongzhou
[1858-F,GB]

Hainan

The End of Europe's China Fad

(1794–1816)

This Great Empire, too well assured of the competency of
its own natural and artificial resources, . . .

THOMAS STAUNTON, 1810[1]

MACARTNEY HAD ELUDED the French cannon, but now, safely back in England, he had to face an even more formidable challenge to his proud ego: severe criticism. The country had followed this unprecedented adventure so passionately that secrecy had been impossible, and rumors of failure had arrived in advance of the ambassador.

Up to June 1794, the London press published highly favorable reports, albeit nine or ten months after the fact. *Gentleman's Magazine* offered its readers flattering descriptions of the pomp and warmth with which the mission had been greeted. But Macartney's dispatches from Hangzhou, with which Mackintosh set out for England in November 1793, arrived in July 1794. Merchant ships had also brought news from European residents in Canton. England was an open society with freedom of the press, and the public was soon privy to a good deal of information about the embassy, either from official leaks or from the uncontrollable operation of private channels of communication. The newspapers had printed reports about the friction caused by the kowtow controversy, the interdiction on meetings with the missionaries, the embassy's precipitate departure from Peking, and the rejection of all the ambassador's requests. Headlines in *Gentleman's Magazine* underscored the scope of the disaster.[2]

The public reacted immediately. One reader wrote to the magazine: "Of the propositions tendered by Lord Macartney to this sulky court and which were all rejected, did ever a one stipulate for the residence of British women in the Factory . . . or were the settlers to profess celebacy? The use of chintzes, China and tea should be discontinued by the females of all ranks in every part of Europe, till the monarch of Tartar race shall have taken off the embargo on them."[3] The ladies' honor was at stake. A boycott for a boycott.

One sample quotation gives a sense of the acerbic tone with which Macartney would be greeted on his return: "Great expenses were incurred, and many exertions made to render this embassy worthy of the country from which it was sent; but, perhaps, after all that was done, we shall not err in saying, it was better calculated to succeed with a nation of Indians, or with a petty African prince, than with the government of China." The author of this phrase was most probably still convinced of "Chinese superiority": "If the court of Peking was to be swayed by splendour, much more ought to have been done to have accomplished it than was done."[4] Most often, however, even when the government and the ambassador were chided, China was not excused. Patriotic sensibilities had been bruised, and the public reaction was ambivalent: there was resentment at the cabinet for having subjected the nation to unacceptable humiliation.

The subsequent publication of the various accounts of the mission, combined with gossip circulating in the salons of London, decisively altered Europe's image of China. The philosophical smokescreen, already thinning out over the preceding two decades, was now dissipated completely. Macartney's expedition was supposed to have demonstrated, by peaceful means, that Great Britain was the world's leading power. Its failure accelerated the demystification of China that prepared the way for the armed confrontations of the next century.

BURGEONING RUMORS created a ticklish situation for government officials. It was impossible to hide everything, but neither could all be revealed. Macartney's journal was often quite frank, but he refrained from publishing it. Nor did he release his "Observations on China," probably the most lucid reflections on that country anyone had ever written. He now knew that the colossus had feet of clay, and that even the slightest blow might bring it crashing down.

With the agreement of the Court of St. James, he assigned Staunton to write an account of the mission that, while retaining credibility, would be careful to preserve British honor. Staunton's semiofficial narrative duly appeared in 1797. It made no attempt to conceal the mission's failure, but it did seek to remove any suspicion that the diplomats may have made mistakes that could justify the Chinese position. Staunton also tried to counter the impression that Britain had suffered humiliation without reacting. He embellished the truth in an effort to make it more palatable, lying only by omission. He also left bits and pieces of China's legendary image intact.

But there was another reason for this cautious approach: the British did not want the Chinese to find out that they had ceased to view China as the Chinese wanted the empire to be viewed. Here the motivation was the same as the Jesuits'. If the ambassador were to reveal everything, all the efforts of the eighteenth century, culminating in this expedition, might be compromised. Diplomatic exigencies therefore led Macartney to urge his deputy to present a portrait of the Chinese Empire that departed only partially from the myth. But it departed enough to contribute to dissipating it. The view of the empire projected by the embassy was therefore a prelude to Western dealings with China in the nineteenth century. Macartney's expedition was a kind of hinge in the history of relations between the West and the Far East, simultaneously a point of culmination and of departure. It brought a century of diplomatic and commercial initiatives to a close and stimulated a refashioning of China's image in the West.

Admittedly, the revelations of this mission were not exactly a thunderbolt in a clear blue sky. As we have seen, Montesquieu, for one, had already rejected the picture painted by Leibniz, Voltaire, and the Jesuits: that China was a land of milk and honey.[5] Le Gentil, whose *Voyage autour du monde* began appearing in 1731, had been especially hard on the Chinese: "The permanence of their institutions is no evidence of their superiority, for it prevents all progress."[6] And in his memoirs, published in 1741, Admiral Anson had been the first to preach gunboat diplomacy, almost exactly a century before the Opium War.

But there were so many Western hostages in China, both missionaries and merchants, and such extensive financial and commercial interests were at stake, that political leaders were cautious—at least in public. And while private correspondence from company agents in Canton kept London informed of all the humiliations suffered or feared in that city, the company was still anxious not to do anything that might damage its ability to trade, fearing that any confrontation would entail the loss of the advantages that had been won.

A French agent, who had less to lose, expressed his impatience more freely. "It is time," Louis-Chrétien de Guignes wrote from Canton, where he had been living for four years, "that China began to view Europe in a light different from that which has prevailed till now."[7] That did not happen. But after the Macartney mission, England (and later the West as a whole) did begin to look at China very differently.

The country's image quickly paled, and the writings of Hegel may be taken as testimony to the degradation. We know that he had read the

Lettres édifiantes et curieuses of the missionaries as well as Staunton's book. But it was from the latter that he acknowledged having drawn the elements of his very succinct view of China: "The Chinese . . . empire is the realm of theocratic despotism. . . . The individual has no moral selfhood. . . . History is still predominantly unhistorical, for it is merely the repetition of the same majestic process of decline. . . . No progress results from all this restless change."[8]

Goethe, who had read neither Staunton nor Hegel, continued to advocate the older view. His knowledge of China came mainly from a Chinese novel that he found reminiscent of his own *Hermann und Dorothea*: "It is about a young man so pure and honest that he was granted the honor of speaking to the Emperor, and about a couple so chaste that, when obliged to spend the night together in the same room, they do not touch each other. . . . Morals and propriety. It is thanks to this strict moderation that the Chinese Empire has lasted for thousands of years and will long continue to endure."[9] But Goethe was already behind the times.

IN A FREE COUNTRY, the official story does not always prevail, for editors and publishers may give the floor to other witnesses. The books written by nonranking members of the embassy further dimmed the Chinese star in the utopian heaven.

Anderson's ghostwriter, Coombes, gave a systematically pro-Chinese cast to his client's work, hoping to ensure the book's success by pandering to the presumed convictions of its potential readers. Anderson's account is therefore riddled with satirical jabs at British society, but the bias is occasionally fissured by telling anti-Chinese thrusts. The legend of the empire's prosperity is undermined by the mention of Chinese who recover and avidly devour rotten meat cast into the sea.[10] As an Englishman proud of his country's navy, Anderson condemns Chinese "prejudice in favour of long-established habits" and ignorance of "mechanics," which explains why "they have not made any advancement in the science of naval architecture."[11] He was shocked by the eunuchs[12] and by the sight of soldiers using whips to drive crowds back.[13] He found Chinese food filthy[14] and was irritated by the hilarity aroused by the British.[15] The Chinese generally come across as a "childish" people who will have to be "educated" in the years to come.

Hüttner notes condescendingly that the Chinese are wholly ignorant of the art of preparing leather;[16] ocean navigation is unknown to them;[17] their pleasure junks are devoid of "conveniences";[18] their architecture, apparently brilliant when viewed from a distance, reveals its crude workmanship and inferior gilding when seen close up.[19] Finally, the world's greatest potentate, "the old man who now reigns, is deceived by his courtiers much like any other sovereign."[20]

Holmes, the plain-speaking soldier, was quite horrified by China. The Chinese had supposedly invented gunpowder, but they were terrified by the mere sight of a cannon shooting blanks.[21] They treat you politely, but are so incredibly suspicious that they will not let you to take a single unescorted step in any city.[22] And they are ignorant beyond belief: "They have scarcely an idea of there being any other country than their own."[23]

The information offered by Anderson, Hüttner, and Holmes, who held no official posts and therefore felt no compulsion to espouse any particular line, was itself sufficient to erode the edifice erected by the Jesuits and the *philosophes*. Their accounts painted a picture of a backward, degenerate country unworthy of its reputation for high civilization.

By the time Barrow's ambitious book appeared, ten years after the embassy's return, Britain's view of China had changed dramatically. The ties to Peking maintained so laboriously during Qianlong's time began to unravel under Jiaqing, whose reign was racked by increasingly violent convulsions. Barrow therefore had less reason for caution, and the war against Napoleonic France also encouraged a more open flaunting of British superiority. Barrow's readers were most impressed by the critical passages of his book.

The prestigious *Edinburgh Review*[24] applauded the "demolition" of a "semi-barbarian race. . . . What else do we know with certainty of the Chinese, but their abject submission to a despotism upheld by the sordid terror of the lash—but the emprisonment and mutilation of their women—but their infanticide and unnatural vices—but their utter and unconquerable ignorance of all the exacter sciences, and all the branches of natural philosophy—but the stupid formalities which incomber their social intercourses—but their cowardice, uncleanliness, and inhumanity?"[25] Moreover, in "their penury of all rational entertainments, the Chinese, like other half-civilized nations, are addicted to games of chance."[26] As for their language: "The fact appears to be quite undeniable, that they have gone for many thousands of years pittering to each other in a jargon which resembles the chuckling of poultry more than the language of men."[27] And: "The great merit of Mr. Barrow's book is the sound good sense and candour which distinguish most of his observations."[28]

But this searing revision of the British view of China culminated with the work of Macartney's page, whose merciless judgment was based on his unparalleled knowledge of the Chinese.

When the mission ended, Thomas Staunton continued to concern himself with China, spending much time in Canton between 1798 and 1816, as an employee, commissioner, and finally senior executive of the company. In 1800, at the age of nineteen, he obtained a copy of the text of the Ta T'sing Leu Lee (Da Qing Lüli), the Chinese criminal code. Westerners had long complained of the arbitrary fiats of the mandarins, and Thomas felt that the publication of this code, hitherto concealed from them, would be enormously useful. He therefore undertook to translate it, publishing the results in 1810. The *Quarterly Review* hailed Staunton's achievement as historic: "The very first work ever rendered out of that language [Chinese] directly into our own."[29]

Thomas Staunton had become a leading expert on the Chinese view of the world. The Lazarist Father Richenet wrote to him in 1810: "With so much experience, after so many struggles, you are surely fully acquainted with all the ruses of the mandarins and have become a formidable adversary to them."[30] The priest was quite right to describe Thomas's relation to China in confrontational terms, for a kind of cultural war had been declared.

In the preface to his translation, Thomas went straight to the heart of this conflict: "The short residence in China of Lord Macartney's embassy . . . was amply sufficient to discover that the superiority over other nations, in point of knowledge and virtue, which the Chinese have long been accustomed to assume to themselves and which some of their European historians have too readily granted them, was in great measure fallacious."[31]

Staunton's readers got the point, and serious journals helped to spread awareness of his conclusions. "The laws of a people," wrote the *Edinburgh Review*,[32] ". . . are actual specimens of their intellect and character. . . . In an introduction of considerable length . . . he confesses that the romantic ideas which had been diffused by the writings of some of the missionaries, were far indeed from being realized by an actual inspection of the Chinese. 'Their knowledge,' he observes, 'was perceived to be defective in those points in which we have, in Europe, recently made the greatest progress.' "[33]

There was now a widening gap not only between the utopian China and the real one, but also between the real China and Europe. The feeling grew that, as the *Edinburgh Review* put it, a "nation that does not advance must retrograde, and finally fall back to barbarism and misery." Those were in fact Macartney's words.[34] Though the ambassador had never published his assessment, fifteen years after his return from China it had become the conventional wisdom.

The reviewer for the famous Scottish journal suggested that "the intellectual condition of the Chinese must be a subject of more curious investigation, than the best of our accounts would lead us to believe."[35]

Not long ago the Chinese had been widely regarded as humanity's incomparable elite; now they were reduced to the status of mere objects of anthropological curiosity. "Now this extraordinary minuteness and oppressive interference with the freedom of private conduct is not to be considered merely as arising from that passion for governing too much, which is apt to infest all persons in possession of absolute power; but appears to us to indicate a certain stage in the progress of society, and to belong to a period of civilization, beyond which the Chinese have not yet been permitted to advance." In China "no sense of individual honor exists." This absence is "the gravest reproach that can be incurred by this remarkable people." And: "a nation is strong and happy strictly in proportion to the sense of honor that prevails within each of its members."[36]

What had earlier been admired about China—its venerable antiquity, for example—was now turned against it. "What places the Chinese above all the earth's peoples," Voltaire had seriously asserted, "is that in four thousand years neither their laws, nor their morals, nor the language spoken by their men of letters has changed."[37] The pragmatic British now considered that assertion nonsense.

Anderson's trenchant phrase—"We entered Peking like paupers; we remained in it like prisoners; and we quitted it like vagrants"—did the greatest damage. "It must not be difficult to impress the Chinese," Macartney had written before setting out on his voyage.[38] In this he had been proved wrong, and it was now thought that other methods would be required.

The average Englishman was deeply patriotic. He cared little that the Chinese were not what the philosophers of the Continent had imagined, and he paid scant attention to the flourishes of French or German rhetoric. But he was offended to learn that this far-off people had treated his envoys as barbarian vassals. For this they deserved to be put in their place, just like the bourgeois of Calais.

The British were determined to make China pay for its impudence, and they had sufficient collective tenacity to pursue long-range plans to that effect. It was as though they had taken to heart a Confucian precept that the Chinese themselves had long ago forgotten: "He who gives no thought to difficulties in the future is sure to be beset by worries much closer at hand."[39] Relations with China became increasingly strained, with flare-ups in 1808 and 1816. But nearly half a century passed before London finally took decisive action.

82

A Dutch Embassy Humiliated

(1794–95)

THOUGH MACARTNEY's embassy was the most ambitious endeavor of its kind, it was followed by three others that more clearly highlight the causes of his failure.

Macartney had barely arrived in Portsmouth when another European embassy asked to be received in Peking. This one came from the Netherlands, a country that had long had interests in the Far East. The ambassador, Isaak Titsing, was accompanied by a modest retinue, and he was more than willing to kowtow as often as necessary. Yet his mission failed no less completely than Macartney's, and in retrospect seems to justify Macartney's intransigence.

Ten years later a Russian embassy of two hundred people set out across the steppes of central Asia, but it got no farther than Urga (Ulan Bator), the capital of the tributary state of Mongolia.

Finally, just after Waterloo London made another attempt to penetrate China's isolation. The British economy's need for a world market was greater than ever, and the government was emboldened by the glory that had just been won in the war against Napoleon. But the ambassador, Lord Amherst, never even got to see the emperor. His deputy, Thomas Staunton, dissuaded him from performing the kowtow, and the embassy was sent back to Canton in pitiable conditions.

On his way back to England, Amherst stopped at Saint Helena, where the loser of the Battle of Waterloo lectured the victors on their inability to speak effectively to the Orient.

Europe had heard the call of the four points of the compass, but those whose compass had five points were silent.

ANDRÉ-EVERARD VAN BRAAM, chief executive of the Dutch East India Company in Canton, had long dreamed of gaining representation at the Court of Peking. The common view in Canton was that the British had failed because they had taken the wrong approach. Van Braam believed that he could show the world how to make a good impression on the Chinese. He yearned to teach haughty England a lesson in diplomatic savoir faire, and the ceremonies marking the start of the sixtieth year of Qianlong's reign seemed to offer a perfect opportunity to do so. He urged his Western colleagues in Canton to join him in paying homage to the Son of Heaven, and when they declined, he did not lose heart, for he had allies: the mandarins of Canton were eager to wipe out the memory of the snub the Peking court had suffered from Macartney.

Batavia and The Hague finally agreed to dispatch a Dutch embassy to congratulate Qianlong. Unfortunately for Van Braam, he would be only the deputy to Titsing, the former chief of the Dutch East India Company in Japan and Bengal.

The Titsing embassy was a nightmarish, caricatural reenactment of the Macartney mission, offering us a graphic depiction of what the Chinese truly considered an embassy to be. By contrast, it highlights what Macartney managed to make of his own.

The Canton mandarins did not want the Dutch envoy to present any requests to the court, and Changlin and Suleng'e extracted a promise from Titsing that he would simply greet the emperor.[1] In that sense, the embassy was a failure even before it set out. The viceroy summoned Titsing in mid-October 1794 to inform him that the emperor would receive him before the Chinese New Year, which fell on January 21, 1795.

The Dutch mission left Canton on November 22, 1794. Apart from Titsing and Van Braam, it included seven other people, among them Louis-Chrétien de Guignes, who had lived in Canton for ten years and knew the Chinese well.* Guignes served as Titsing's interpreter, and the corrosive verve of his account of the adventure provides a welcome counterpoint to Van Braam's rose-colored memoir.

They had to move fast, for they were given only fifty days to get to Peking over land, crossing most of China from south to north. Along the way they were treated to uncomfortable lodgings, inconsiderate local officials, and putrid food. The oil-paper coverings of their palanquins were shredded by curious passersby, and there were disputes over the baggage, the Chinese urging the Dutch to go on ahead, the Dutch refusing to be separated from their gifts, lest they arrive at the court without them.[3]

It was a bitterly cold winter, and the travelers faced impassable roads

---

* Forgotten by the king, the Convention, and the Directoire, he returned to France only in 1801.[2]

and unheated lodgings. Rain poured into the palanquins. Beyond the Yangtze there was snow, which the Canton Chinese had never seen.[4] One incident after another marred the journey. They had to cross a river on rafts crowded pell-mell with men, baggage, and horses: "Our effects arrived partly damaged and decidedly wet."[5] The baggage bearers left the travelers in the middle of the road and went off to have lunch. Van Braam's palanquin broke under his weight, and he finished the trip in a wheelbarrow.[6] "We arrived in Peking exhausted and nearly starving, after traveling some six hundred leagues in forty-nine days."[7] Quite a contrast with the reception Macartney's five ships had enjoyed. If Van Braam's aim was to demonstrate the superior effectiveness of the humble approach, the enterprise had begun badly.

On January 11, the day after the ambassador's arrival in Peking, a mandarin delivered a gift from the emperor: "a sturgeon weighing three hundred pounds." Titsing and his deputy "prostrated themselves, as they were invited to do,"[8] before this imperial offering. Guignes is more precise: "They touched their foreheads nine times to the floor."[9] Citing the flattering remarks made by his Chinese escorts, Van Braam writes: "In the esteem of the sovereign and the prime minister, we stand well above the English."[10]

They were told that the audience would be held the next day. "We raised countless objections, but in vain. In the end the Ambassador agreed. Our mandarins were unstinting in their caressing praise. The Ambassador was shown how he must greet the Emperor, and he imitated the procedure: several reverences upon the ground."[11]

The Dutch were awakened at three in the morning. Told to leave their swords behind, they were escorted to the palace, where they mingled with the Mongol and Korean envoys, settling in for the long wait in the icy night. "The mandarins wielded their whips this way and that, the Koreans receiving a goodly share of the blows."[12]

When the palace doors opened, the Chinese had the personnel of all the embassies kneel. Qianlong was carried in on his palanquin. He glanced at the Koreans and ordered his bearers to halt before Titsing. "His second minister, Fuchang'an, who was walking on the left of the palanquin, took the gilded box from His Excellency's hands and carried it to His Majesty. We then all performed the greeting of honor, lowering our heads three times to the floor, three different times."[13] The emperor asked Titsing whether his sovereign was in good health, then went on his way.

Guignes sums up the encounter this way: "The Emperor received the Ambassador in a courtyard outside the palace; with the exception of the two or three words he spoke and the trifles he sent for lunch, he paid no further attention to the Ambassador, even though he was but two paces distant and within clear sight."[14]

That same night, the Chinese came to collect the watches the Dutch had brought along for the emperor. It was so cold that Van Braam asked for some coal and a few furnishings. They promised him everything he asked for but delivered nothing.[15] The following day the Dutch were escorted to the palace a second time and shown into a chilly room filled with tobacco smoke. Van Braam consoled himself for his Spartan quarters by noting that the ministers were in the same boat. And to think that "these apartments were part of the imperial palace!"[16] He complained of the peddlers of illusions: "This tableau ill-accorded with the brilliant reports sent to Europe by the missionaries on the subject of this capital and the Emperor's palace, but I must describe what I saw, though it scarcely matches what I expected to find."[17]

Fuchang'an asked the Dutch whether they were bothered by the cold and immediately left them.[18] There was no political discussion, but the Dutch had given their word on that in any event. On January 15 the emperor sent them some raisins, which Van Braam accepted with a kow-tow. The promised coal was finally delivered,[19] but though the Dutch were held "in higher esteem" than the English, it was impossible for them to meet with the missionaries. Eighteen months earlier, the priests had been forbidden to see Macartney only after it had been decided to dismiss his embassy. "A letter from my friend de Grammont was brought to me secretly," writes Van Braam on January 18. "He states his intense desire to communicate some important matters to me. I have given my reply to the bearer, and there is still hope that we may correspond."[20]

That hope proved as futile as the embassy itself, especially in view of the fact that on the same day, thousands of leagues from Peking, the *Stathouder* of Holland fled to England before the advancing armies of the Convention. The Dutch ambassador to China was about to become the envoy of a state that no longer existed—but it would be eighteen months before he found that out.

Guignes had written a note to Father Raux that Van Braam promised to deliver to the first missionary he encountered. On January 18 the French interpreter was summoned by Heshen and interrogated by a group of mandarins about the reasons for his presence in Peking and the content of the note. Guignes excused himself by appealing to his friendship for Father Raux, in whose company he had traveled from Europe to China.[21] This scene, like many others, might well have taken place at a far more recent date.

THE DUTCH REMAINED in the capital for a little over a month, somewhat longer than Macartney. But in all that time they accomplished nothing— apart from attending a few festivals and waiting long hours to watch the emperor pass by, honoring him by "touching their foreheads." They were proud to be told that "no European had ever been allowed so far into the palace," but on the Chinese New Year they were awakened at two in the morning to attend the emperor's passage, only to be told at three o'clock that he would not be coming after all.[22]

In this entire trip, they had just one brief moment of satisfaction: when they noticed the carriage Macartney had given Qianlong standing forlornly in one corner of a room. The scant attention paid to it went some way toward soothing the raw wounds inflicted on their own self-esteem.

The final audience was held on February 10 in a vast courtyard, before an immense crowd, and the humiliating ceremony was now compounded by a public tongue lashing: "The mandarins took great care to ensure that the ambassador and Mr. Van Braam prostrated themselves the requisite number of times. The latter having risen too soon, they obliged him to recommence." Under the threat of the whip.[23]

Van Braam finally met Father Raux, but "the mandarins watched us closely to see that no piece of paper was handed to him."[24] The priest explained that if the embassy had come directly from Europe instead of from Canton, its members would have been able to communicate with the missionaries more freely. "The Chinese fear those who know a little something of China."[25] Still true in the twentieth century.

On February 15 the embassy left Peking, carrying with them the imperial edict they had worked so hard to obtain. "In the sixty years since we received this Empire from Heaven," Qianlong had written, "we have governed it so well, with munificence and terror alike, that peace and happiness reign everywhere. O Prince, preserve an eternal memory of Our kindness and, touched by what we have done for you, apply yourself to governing your own people with care and justice. Thus do we enjoin you."[26]

This message never got to its addressee, for the "prince" in question had in the meantime given way to the Batavian republic.

BOTH EMBASSIES, the British and the Dutch, ended in failure, the former with dignity, the latter in humiliation. Van Braam's experience made him a sadder but wiser man. "This people," he wrote, "is so secluded that it can forgo all those artificial needs from whose lack we would suffer were they to go unsatisfied. The sight of the masterworks of European technique, though delivered annually to the Chinese, will not open their eyes, for they regard these marvels as mere superfluities."[27]

Guignes considered both embassies equally damaging: "In refusing to bow his head, Macartney did great harm to his own interests and offended the pride of a people that regards itself as standing above all others." On the other hand, "the agreement of the Dutch to perform the prescribed duties" was viewed by the Chinese as "mere recompense for the insult delivered by the English." The reception of the two embassies, then, "was not what might have been expected." It was therefore "a mistake to send an embassy to the Chinese until they learn, from experience, that they owe the preservation of their political existence only to their remote geographical position and that the high opinion in which they hold themselves is chimerical. The day will come when the Chinese, who now scorn foreigners as mere merchants, will recognize how formidable are the peoples whom they treat so outrageously. It will not be long before these peoples, once becoming aware of the Chinese nation, come to understand that this country, situated at the world's extremity, is likewise the last among nations in strength."[28]

Golovkin:
An Embassy Aborted

(Autumn 1805)

RUSSIA, NOT HOLLAND, was Britain's only real rival in Peking. Catherine II had pursued the Volga Tartars in their flight toward China. Her army guarded the Chinese border, and she had welcomed Jesuit refugees expelled from Catholic countries, an act of kindness not without afterthoughts of Asia.[1]

While Macartney was en route to China, a Russian mission, led by Lieutenant Laxman, had disembarked in Hokkaido in an unsuccessful approach to Japan. London had followed the preparation of this modest undertaking almost as closely as St. Petersburg had followed the Macartney mission,[2] and it will be recalled that Songyun, the Grand Councillor who escorted Macartney as far as Hangzhou, had recently returned from successful negotiations with the Russians in Mongolia.

Catherine II died in 1796, but her successors followed her example. Alexander I decided to try to establish relations with the Chinese not along the border, but in Peking itself. The prime mover in this enterprise was the Polish prince Czartoryski,* the tsar's minister of foreign affairs and an eager reader of the various accounts of the Macartney mission. The Russian empire, China's neighbor, had no intention of being outdone by far-off England.

The Russian mission set out in the autumn of 1805, as most of Europe, including Russia, was coalescing in the third coalition against France. The designated ambassador, Count Golovkin, organized a large contingent, consisting of sixty soldiers and a host of cavalry. Count Jan Potocki, a great Polish nobleman and cousin and friend of Czartoryski, offered to accom-

---

* The man whose *ex libris* adorns the translations of the works of Staunton, Barrow, and Hüttner that inspired the present book.

pany Golovkin in his capacity as a "scholar of the galvanic sciences"—in other words, electricity. Potocki, an intelligent and cultured man, believed (as Macartney had) that he would succeed in convincing the Chinese that they had every interest in dealing with Russia, more advanced in science and technology than the Middle Empire. But he considered himself primarily a political adviser to Golovkin, who, however, had no intention of listening to anyone.[3] When Potocki suggested that the ambassador might benefit from a reading of Staunton, Barrow, and the missionaries, the French-educated Golovkin replied that "nothing under the sun is worth so much as a good cook and fine wines." He fully expected that the splendor of his retinue, the tsar's prestige, and his own talent would be more than enough to make a stirring impression on the emperor Jiaqing, Qianlong's son and successor.

Potocki, however, later wrote that "it was because he had not read the reports of the Macartney embassy that we became mired in the great misunderstanding that caused the failure of our embassy. . . . The words 'God is good, go forward' were inscribed on Golovkin's vehicles, and he set out at the head of a light and brilliant troupe."[4]

The embassy passed through Irkutsk and had not yet reached Kazan when a letter arrived from the wang* of Urga (Ulan Bator) suggesting that the bulk of the escort remain at the border and informing the ambassador that the authorities eagerly awaited a list of the presents the embassy was carrying. Golovkin replied that an envoy of his importance required a retinue of at least 250 people.[5]

The embassy received a second letter in Selenginsk. The wang now reiterated: "Reduce the escort and supply the list of presents." Impressed by this tenacity, Golovkin agreed to cut ninety people out of his company. The wang's third letter reached Golovkin in Troitsk, the last Russian stopover before the border. "Ambassador," the wang wrote, "if you wish to behold the august face of the Emperor of China, you will enter with no more than seventy."[6]

Potocki noted in a letter to his brother: "Everything I have observed about them convinces me that in the long run the inertia of their system will overwhelm any effort that might be undertaken against them."[7]

In the end the Chinese agreed to accept a delegation of 124 people, provided that the ambassador would formally commit himself to perform the kowtow. Golovkin was only too happy to agree. What he did not know was that the wang had been ordered to bring the embassy to Peking for the Chinese New Year, submerging it in the broader influx of tributaries.

---

* A Mongol prince governing in the emperor's name.

The mission entered China on December 18, 1805, to the clatter of Russian salvos and Chinese fireworks.

It was so cold that ice crystals formed on the surface of hot tea the moment it was poured.[8] In Urga the wang, flanked by his Manchu *amban*,* assured Golovkin that he was eagerly expected in Peking. They invited him to an imperial banquet two days later.[9]

Golovkin was escorted to the banquet by a splendid cavalcade of Russians and Mongols.[10] The wang led him to the "table of perfumes" and said: "In offering you a banquet in Urga, the Emperor of China grants you an exceptional honor. For this you must thank him. You shall now join me in the ceremony I shall perform before these burning scented candles."[11] The ambassador merely removed his hat. Chided by the wang, the Russian replied that no one could possibly convince him that these burning candles were the emperor. The argument grew bitter, and the wang lost his temper. Eventually he calmed down, but the atmosphere was chilly as the two men parted.

Negotiations began again two days later, but Golovkin was stonewalled. "The Tribunal of Rites must be satisfied," he was told. "Its prescriptions are imperative." The wang also resorted to an argument that had earlier surprised the British: "These reverences, after all, are not such a weighty matter."[12] Perhaps not, but refusal to perform them would entail the failure of an embassy. The wang then announced that he had reported back to Peking and that there could be no further discussions until he received the court's reply. That would take about twenty days. In the meantime, it was unbearably cold in the yurts.

When the answer came in from Peking, the wang invited the emissaries to a new conference. "I have been authorized to send you away," the wang said. "How will you account for your behavior before your emperor?" The envoy replied that his emperor would reward him amply. Send us away if you will, he challenged the wang, who replied that he could not for the life of him understand Golovkin's attitude: "You have been sent to Peking, yet you are doing your best not to arrive there."[13]

He proposed that the ambassador ask the emperor's forgiveness for failing to kowtow in Urga and commit himself in writing to kowtowing as often as necessary in Peking. This letter, he explained, should state that commitment three times, in accordance with the Chinese rhetorical formula of repetition. Golovkin agreed to write a letter, but said he would state his willingness to kowtow only once and declined to ask forgiveness for

---

* A high-ranking official sent from Peking to oversee the indigenous princes of vassal regions (such as Tibet or Mongolia). It was the *amban* who held real power.

his infraction in Urga. He then withdrew to compose the letter, but Mongol horsemen soon arrived at his camp to return presents that the wang and his officers had initially accepted. They also delivered another letter: "You are a daft race. Begone!"[14] Golovkin ordered his frozen retinue to break camp and head back to Russia.

THE BRITISH HAD tried and failed to widen China's narrow southern gate. The Russians aspired to open the northern gate but never even got close enough to try. Like the British, they had assumed that a demonstration of strength would do the trick, but they seemed even more arrogant than the Far Westerners. The emperor therefore decided that there was no point in allowing them into Peking only to throw them out.

This new failure had no immediate effect on Europe's destiny. But in the long run China's closure, now confirmed north and south alike, would change the fate of the world.

84

Amherst's Embassy Rejected

(1816–17)

IN AN UNPUBLISHED letter dated December 1794 Macartney offered an optimistic assessment of his embassy, which had freed the English traders "from the tyranny of an inimical and rapacious viceroy, and placed them under the protection of an upright and friendly one. . . . Above all, it has laid a foundation of amity, good offices, and immediate intercourses with the Imperial Court."[1]

He believed that these direct relations were the best way of opening the eyes of the Chinese. In February 1795, as the angry Dutch left Peking, Macartney urged the British government to send George Staunton to Canton as a resident minister.[2] Unfortunately, Sir George suffered a stroke, and Macartney's project was buried with its putative envoy. Years later Thomas picked up where his father left off, though his attitude was quite different.

In the meantime, London followed Father Amiot's advice, seeking other ways to maintain contact with the Celestial Court.

IN LATE DECEMBER 1795 the *Cirencester* dropped anchor at Canton. It carried an array of gifts and letters: from the king to the emperor, from Macartney to the viceroy, from the company to the hoppo. But British luck was running bad. Changlin was no longer viceroy, and his successor refused to accept letters and presents meant for his predecessor. The hoppo stated that he was not authorized to deal with foreigners. All the personalities in place in the autumn of 1793 had left Canton—in the time it took for a single postal exchange.[3]

The letter from the king to the emperor, however, eventually made its way to Peking, and Qianlong replied to it at the beginning of February 1796:

Our Celestial dynasty, which sways the wide world, attaches no value to the costly presents which are offered at Our Court: what We appreciate is the humble spirit of the offerers. We have commanded our Viceroy [in Canton] to accept your tribute in order that your reverence may be duly recognized.[4]

Qianlong then raised the issue of Tibetan affairs again, acknowledging that the English had not opposed Chinese interests, but emphasizing that their position had had no influence on the war's outcome. China, he insisted, had no need of outside help:

Our commander in chief duly informed Us of your having dispatched a mission into Tibet, with a petition to Our resident, stating that you had advised the Nepalese to surrender. But at the time of your petition Our troops had already gained a complete victory and the desired end had been attained. We were not obliged to trouble your troops to render assistance. You . . . are doubtless ignorant of the precise course of events in Nepal, as your tribute mission was on its way to Peking at the time of these occurrences. Nevertheless, O King, you entertained a clear perception of your duty towards Us, and your reverent acknowledgment of Our dynasty's supremacy is highly praiseworthy.[5]

This edict was the very last to be signed by the aging emperor, who abdicated the next day, relinquishing power as he had promised he would in a solemn edict issued in the autumn of 1794:

Next year will witness the sixtieth anniversary of my succession to this goodly heritage of the Throne: few, indeed, of my predecessors in this and other dynasties, have completed a sixty-year cycle. . . . Today I am eighty-four, and my natural strength is not abated. I rejoice in the possession of perfect health, and my descendants to the fourth generation surround me. Immeasurably thankful as I am to the Almighty for His protection, I feel encouraged to yet further endeavour. On New Year's Day of my sixtieth year an eclipse of the sun is due, and on the Festival of Lanterns there will be a lunar eclipse. Heaven sends these portents as warnings. . . . During the course of next year, I shall prepare for my impending abdication, and the New Emperor will mount the Throne on New Year's Day of the year following. In recognition of the warning conveyed by these eclipses, I propose to hold no New Year's Court next year, and the customary banquet to the Princes will be omitted.[6]

Official superstition. The cast was changing, but the new actors would perform in the same play. And there was only one assigned role for barbarians: to kowtow.

Jiaqing, Qianlong's fifth son, had charmed his father with his beauty and obedience, but when Qianlong finally abdicated in his favor, the new emperor enjoyed little more than the appearance and trappings of power. Only on the death of the patriarch in 1799 did he come into his own, and it may have been during this transitional period that Jiaqing acquired his morbid devotion to etiquette, perhaps as compensation for his lack of real authority. In any event, the life of the court was soon marked by a maniacal delirium.[7]

The empire was racked by convulsions. Pirates ravaged the coasts. The White Lotus peasant rebellions were followed by those of the Celestial Order, and the various revolts had accomplices even in the court itself, where in 1813 there was an unprecedented attack on the emperor's life.

Several years earlier there had been an even more shocking event: the violation of Chinese soil by English barbarians. The French had just invaded Portugal, and in September 1808, on the pretext of preventing them from laying claim to Macao, the commander of the British fleet in Bengal, Admiral Drury, occupied the city of Macao, to the jeers of the Chinese and Portuguese inhabitants. Peking reacted vigorously, organizing a blockade and issuing an ultimatum. Macao was cut off, and the British evacuated the city.[8] The operation had been for nothing. Or rather, worse than nothing: not only had the English lost face, they had also frightened the Chinese. And for that they would pay dearly.[9]

Trade in Canton stagnated, disrupted by conflicts great and small, and China retreated ever more resolutely into its own proud seclusion, in action and spirit alike.

But the British, having vanquished Napoleon, now had the means—and the need—to try one last diplomatic approach. Perhaps twenty-three years of war had convinced the Chinese of what Macartney had sought to demonstrate: that Britain was the West's most powerful nation. The cabinet duly informed Peking of the collapse of the French empire—and received a reply of sovereign indifference: "Your Majesty's kingdom is at a remote distance beyond the seas, but is observant of its duties and obedient to our law, beholding from afar the glory of our Empire and respectfully admiring the perfection of our Government."[10]

The serene isolationism that had led to the rejection of Macartney's overtures seemed unbreakable, but London now decided to send a new embassy, headed by Lord William Pitt Amherst, nephew and heir of the victor of Montreal. Though less experienced than Macartney, he was accompanied by Europe's leading China expert, Thomas Staunton, who had penetrated the empire's language, history, and mystery and was now the president of the Canton Select Committee, the company's executive organ. Though he knew the Celestial Empire intimately, Staunton had never fallen under its spell, and he would now do all he could to avenge the failure of the enterprise that had so deeply marked his childhood.

The Chinese feared Staunton. When the news that he would serve as Amherst's deputy reached Peking, he was strongly advised not to make the trip. He replied that he would go wherever his king commanded. The Chinese yielded, but they remained on their guard.

Actually, Staunton shared the cautious attitude of the company, which was no more enthusiastic about this new venture than it had been about Macartney's. The directors explained their position in a detailed report from Canton that arrived in London at the beginning of the year: "Not to dwell on the fact that the disturbed and unsettled state of the Government ever since the attempt to assassinate the Emperor in 1813, must render the Government less disposed to receive complimentary communications than in times of greater tranquillity," there was ample reason to believe that the "violent injustice and despotism" suffered by foreign traders in Canton had the support of "the Sovereign himself. Under these circumstances we cannot doubt that any measures on our part which should disclose or seem to imply the probability of a remonstrance being intended to be addressed to the latter against the former, would be almost equally unwelcome to both."[11] In a note to the cabinet Thomas Staunton explained that two major issues—regular communication between Canton and Peking and access to another port farther north—had already been rejected during the earlier embassy, and "must be brought forward and treated with great delicacy."[12]

Lord Amherst embarked in the warship *Alceste* on February 8, 1816, and reached the China Sea in half the time it had taken Macartney, arriving at the end of June. There he was joined by Thomas Staunton and the rest of the embassy's "Cantonese" component. "Several days later" the mission received authorization—"expressed in the usual strain of arrogance and affected superiority"[13]—to enter the Gulf of Beizhili.

The *Alceste* sailed into the gulf on July 28, and the question of the kowtow came up almost immediately. Lord Amherst had no hard and fast position on the matter, and his advisers were divided. Henry Ellis, the third-ranking member of the embassy, argued that the kowtow was a meaningless formality. Staunton opposed that view,[14] vigorously stating his objections in a note presented to Lord Amherst on the eve of their arrival in Tientsin: "The compliance [of the kowtow] will be unadvisable, even

although the refusal should be attended with the hazard of the total rejection of the Embassy. . . . Such compliance, judging from the result of
the Dutch embassy of 1795, would not be likely to promote the attainment
of any one of the objects we have in view."[15]

The British cabinet had taken a pragmatic stance: the purpose of the
mission was to get results, and the kowtow should be evaluated in that light.
But the company directors urged consideration of the effects a kowtow
would have in Canton: if the objective was to win greater respect for British
honor, such a goal would be ill served by the abasement of a kowtow.[16]

If Amherst ultimately decided to refuse to kowtow, it was because he
soon realized that this mission was in fact a test of strength. The mandarins
who came aboard the *Alceste* on August 4 were stone-faced. One of them
was Suleng'e, who had been hoppo of Canton in 1793. The British raised
various issues, but obtained no satisfaction whatever, nor even any response.
The letter from the prince regent* to the emperor was returned with
horror to the ambassador. It began, "Sir, my Brother. . . ."[17]

Amherst invoked the Macartney precedent, but the mandarins swore
that Macartney had kowtowed: they had seen it with their own eyes. Jiaqing
issued an edict affirming: "At that time your Ambassador performed the
ceremony required of him with the greatest respect and committed no
breach of decorum or etiquette."[18]

In Tientsin the British were brought before a table, covered in yellow
silk, on which scented candles burned. As the Chinese kowtowed, Amherst
remained erect, removing his hat and bowing slightly. At the subsequent
dinner, the British had to sit cross-legged on the floor. The mandarins
made no secret of their disdain for the behavior of these barbarians: there
could be no question of allowing them anywhere near the emperor so long
as they exhibited such uncivilized manners. Amherst promised to kneel,
along with his retinue. The mandarins requested an immediate demonstration. When he refused, Thomas Staunton, who no doubt remembered
how useful children could be, suggested that the gesture be performed by
Lord Amherst's son Jeff, who was serving as page.

After Tientsin, pressure was brought to bear on another front. The
Chinese now complained that the ambassador's retinue was too numerous,
even though it had only seventy-five members, as opposed to the ninety-
five of the Macartney mission.[19] The order to reduce it, however, had come
from Jiaqing himself. Thomas reports that the text of the edict was annotated in the emperor's vermilion ink.[20] The mandarins suggested that

---

* King George III had gone insane, and his eldest son assumed the regency in 1811, holding
it until his father's death in 1820 and ruling thereafter as George IV.

the musicians be sent away. They were told that this was impossible, since the ships had already sailed. Keenly irritated, they responded by raising the issue of the kowtow again, insisting that the emperor would tolerate no infringement of the rites. Amherst proposed the compromise that Macartney had originally suggested: a mandarin whose rank was equivalent to his own would kowtow to a portrait of the prince regent while Amherst kowtowed to Jiaqing; alternatively, Chinese ambassadors to Britain would state their willingness to kowtow to His Gracious Majesty. The Chinese fumed with indignation. Finally the envoy announced that he would kneel three times, bowing his head three times with each genuflection[21]—exactly the ceremony Thomas Staunton had seen his master perform in 1793. That was as far as Amherst would go.

The Chinese harassed the embassy as it made its way to Peking. Despite a driving rain, the travelers were denied the use of palanquins, which in the immediate proximity of the capital would offend imperial dignity.[22] Three Russian missionaries requested permission to meet the embassy, but were rebuffed.[23] The two company commissioners, Staunton and Ellis, were denounced as "merchants" unworthy of an audience with the emperor.[24] Finally, there was a rumor[25] that an edict was being prepared to explain the reasons for the embassy's impending expulsion.[26] One of the mandarins produced a copy of an imperial document affirming that Lord Macartney had kowtowed to Qianlong.[27]

In an instruction dated August 25, however, Jiaqing suddenly called for a "degree of moderation in the protocol demands made to Barbarians who have come from so great a distance." He told his mandarins to simply "do your best."[28] But his subjects did better than their best. The zealous Celestial bureaucracy had escaped its master's control.

Finally the emperor sent his own brother-in-law, Heshitai, to see Amherst. This Tartar nobleman treated the Briton coolly, not inviting him to sit down and explaining that the ceremony Macartney had performed before Qianlong would no longer be acceptable under Jiaqing. Either Amherst would kowtow or the embassy would be dismissed. "As there is only one sun, there is only one Jiaqing Emperor; he is the universal sovereign, and all must pay him homage."[29]

The procession arrived in Peking—dirty, frustrated, and exhausted—on the night of August 28.[30]

They were taken directly to the Forbidden City. It was nearly midnight, and the ambassador asked to be shown to his quarters, but the Chinese told him that he would have to wait: Heshitai was on his way. The scene seemed carefully choreographed: despite the late hour, high-ranking mandarins and princes of the blood were present, in ceremonial dress. All at once the British were told that the audience with the emperor had been moved up and would take place immediately. Only the ambassador, the two company commissioners, and the interpreter, Morrison, would be admitted. Heshitai arrived and urged Amherst to agree to kowtow.[31]

An extraordinary row then broke out, as a horde of mandarins seized the British and tried to drag them bodily to the throne room, pushing, shoving, and screaming at Amherst and his companions. The ambassador resisted, citing his exhaustion, the state of his dress, and the unseemly hour. He protested the violence, reaffirmed his refusal to kowtow, and asked to withdraw.[32] His resistance was reported to the emperor, and a furious Jiaqing demanded the embassy's immediate departure. The mission was ordered out of Peking that very night.

Since it was impossible to admit openly that a barbarian envoy had refused to kowtow, the officially stated reason for the expulsion was different. But the edict establishing this version of events was written purely for the record, and for the edification of future generations:

> On the morning of the 7th I partook of breakfast, and at 6:30 a.m. issued a decree saying I was about to proceed to the Throne Hall, where I would receive the Mission in audience. To this Heshitai . . . replied . . . "The Chief Ambassador has had a severe gastric attack; it will be necessary to postpone the audience, giving him time to recover." . . . I directed that the Ambassador be taken back to his lodging, and supplied at once with medical aid, after which I desired the immediate attendance of the Deputy Ambassador. To this Heshitai replied that the Deputy Ambassador had also been attacked by sickness, and that both would attend together on the Chief Ambassador's recovery.
>
> China is lord and sovereign of the world; was it possible for Us to submit calmly to such a wanton display of irreverent arrogance? Therefore I issued a decree, commanding the expulsion of the Mission from China. Nevertheless, I inflicted no punishment upon the Ambassadors.[33]

Probably out of fear of British reprisals. Heshitai, on the other hand, was reprimanded (for having exposed his sovereign to an affront), and the escort mandarins were demoted.[34] Bad advice was a punishable offense, and the emperor's servants had overstepped their master's will. The sanction against them was an a posteriori sop to the British.

THE MISSION'S JOURNEY to Peking had been arduous enough, but the return trip was outright torture. The roads were in disrepair, the Chinese intrusive, the escort openly hostile. Beggars were encouraged to throng the route of march. Ellis speaks of "the stench of putrefying garlic on a much used blanket."[35]

The Amherst embassy followed more or less the same itinerary as Macartney's, but they, even more than the visitors of 1793, were treated to constant displays of Chinese pride and denied any possibility of manifesting their own country's greatness. Peking's policy of amiability had given way to invective. The "retreat from China" took four months and eight days.

The emperor's letter to the prince regent, delivered in Canton with the usual solemnity,[36] offered little hope for the future:

> If you but show the sincerity of your heart and study good will, one could then say, without the necessity of sending annual representatives to our Court, that you make progress towards civilized transformation. It is to the end that you continue your obedience that I send you this Imperial command.[37]

Just as in 1794, however, the Chinese were concerned about possible consequences, and a number of local decrees favorable to European trade were issued. In Huangpu, Ellis notes, "The crew gave three cheers, which the Englishmen found it impossible to hear without strong emotion. There was an awful manliness in the sound so opposite to the discordant salutations and ridiculous ceremonies of the nation we were quitting."[38]

In Macao there was a surprise: the viceroy of Canton ordered his troops to cross the fortifications isolating the peninsula, and Chinese soldiers held a military parade to salute the ambassador's departure, on January 28, 1817.[39]

Another gesture of consolation came from the Select Committee, exponent of dignity that it was: "Greatly as we must feel the treatment Your Excellency met at the Yuanming Yuan and the insolent manner in which the negotiation was broken off by the Court of Peking, we cannot but congratulate Your Lordship on the subsequent edicts issued by the Emperor of China evincing a degree of repentance and a wish to remove the merited censure from himself that could not have been expected from this arbitrary monarch." The message concluded with a profession of faith: "Submission . . . only leads to degradation and disgrace, whereas a firm and decided tone will generally carry a point in China provided the grounds are just and reasonable, however it may be urged that the point is contrary to established rules and customs."[40]

Thomas Staunton spoke in similar terms twenty-three years later, on the eve of the Opium War.

85

Amherst at Saint Helena

(June–August 1817)

ON THE RETURN voyage to England, Amherst, like Macartney, stopped at Saint Helena. Between these two visits, the island had acquired a most distinguished involuntary resident.

Napoleon Bonaparte was informed of the embassy's approach in March 1817, and the news rekindled his old oriental yearnings, in which China had held a prominent place. Eight and a half years earlier, in 1808, he had ordered the preparation of a Chinese-French-Latin dictionary,[1] compiled by none other than our Canton observer Louis-Chrétien de Guignes, whose *Voyage à Pékin* had just appeared.[2]

Nor had he forgotten the memorandum that had been submitted to him in 1811 by Renouard de Sainte-Croix, who had recently returned from a four-year journey that had taken him to Canton, where he met Thomas Staunton. Sainte-Croix suggested that an embassy be sent to Peking to "recover the prestige France enjoyed before the Revolution." The mission, he wrote, would "inform them of Your Majesty's great feats and request the exclusion of the English from the China trade. It would be especially well received were it to be composed of military officers and scholars, for the Chinese government has the greatest of contempt for peoples engaged in commerce." Sainte-Croix argued that the Russian embassy had failed primarily because of its unseemly ceremonial pretensions. He recommended that the French embassy travel to Peking through Siberia; the tsar, he wrote, would not be able to deny it passage in the name of the Continental blockade. (As it happened, it was the Grand Army, and not an embassy, that entered Russia the following summer.)[3]

Napoleon had no doubt that Amherst would want to meet the captive

Eagle, and he had three months to prepare for the visit. He therefore read—or reread—the various accounts of the Macartney embassy.*

"I WAS DESIROUS of paying my respects at Longwood, Bonaparte's residence," Amherst wrote, adhering to the English custom of referring to the prisoner as "Bonaparte." He used the word *Emperor* only when quoting Napoleon's companions, and even then he underlined the term to emphasize its incongruity.[4]

Napoleon had definite ideas about China, and since he had acquired a typical prisoner's penchant for monologues, he treated his companions in exile to frequent and lengthy expositions of them. The deposed emperor dreamed that the Celestial Empire might someday avenge him by battering British pride.

As early as March 1817 Napoleon chided the British cabinet for not having ordered Amherst to conform to the customs of the country to which he had been sent—"otherwise they ought not to have sent him at all."[5] "It is my opinion that whatever is the custom of a nation, and is practised by the first characters of that nation towards their chief cannot degrade strangers who perform the same. Different nations have different customs. . . . In Italy you kiss the pope's toe, yet it is not considered a degradation. A man who goes into a country, must comply with the ceremonies in use there, and it would have been no degradation whatever for Lord Amherst to have submitted to such ceremonies before the emperor of China, as are performed by the first mandarins of that empire." He complained to O'Meara: "You say that he was willing to render such respect as was paid to his own king. You have no right to send a man to China to tell him they must perform certain ceremonies, because such are practised in England."

Napoleon did not mince words in making his point: if the English custom had been to kiss the king's ass instead of his hand, would you have asked the emperor of China to "let down his breeches . . . because it was the practice in England?"[6] He acted out the gesture as he spoke, and both he and O'Meara had a good laugh.[7]

A moment later he continued, "If I had sent an ambassador to China, I would have ordered him to ask the mandarins to instruct him in the ceremonies practised before the Emperor and to conform to them if that

---

* Napoleon's Irish physician, Barry O'Meara, wrote a volume of memoirs; O'Meara's account is complemented by Amherst's unpublished journal, several extracts from which Mr. Michael Galvin of Santa Barbara, California, has kindly granted me permission to reproduce.

was what was requested of him. You [the British] now risk losing China's friendship, not to mention great commercial advantages, as a result of this stupidity." Such was Napoleon's thinking on the matter three months before his meeting with Amherst.

"Napoleon," Chateaubriand reports, "agreed to meet Lord Amherst upon the return of his embassy from China . . . No trace of color remained in Bonaparte's face, his head now resembling a marble bust slightly yellowed with age. His apparent calm suggested that the flame of his genius was extinguished. He spoke slowly. Now and again his gaze was dazzling, but the brilliance quickly faded."[8]

But we have too many eyewitnesses to be satisfied with an imaginary account, no matter how illustrious its author. The *Mémoires d'outre-tombe*, for example, make no mention of a fact reported by the English travelers: the deposed emperor of the French was just as concerned with protocol as the ruling emperor of the Chinese. Lord Amherst may well have thought that it was as difficult to get an audience with Napoleon as with Jiaqing.

The most immediate problem was Hudson Lowe, the governor of Saint Helena, who insisted on accompanying Amherst. Napoleon, however, refused to receive Amherst in the governor's presence.[9] As eagerly as the ex-emperor had looked forward to this meeting, he preferred to forgo it rather than to admit the hated jailer to his residence. Lowe wanted Amherst to cancel the meeting in deference to him, but in this he was disappointed.

The encounter was meticulously prepared. "On Sunday, the 29th [of June]," Amherst writes, "I received a visit from Count Bertrand at Plantation House. He said the *Emperor* was still suffering from pain in his face, but that he was desirous to see me, and would do so if possible before I left the Island, and that if I would send to Longwood the following morning I should receive a positive answer."[10] The answer arrived on Monday: Count Bertrand invited "me, & the gentlemen of my suite, to an interview with the *Emperor* the following afternoon, between 3 and 4 o'clock."[11]

As these negotiations went on, Amherst examined the terms of Napoleon's imprisonment, and he was surprised at the space the deposed emperor had been granted. He was able to ride "about 12 miles" without the supervision of any British officer. Bonaparte's complaints that he had been deprived of exercise were "groundless."[12] Indeed, the British merchants in Canton would have been overjoyed to enjoy such liberty.

Clarke Abel, the expedition's physician, reports: "We were majestically received. A valet dressed in the livery of Napoleon at the height of his glory stood at the door, the ghost of vanished splendour. Led by Bertrand, we were greeted by Montholon, Lord Amherst being immediately introduced to Bonaparte. An hour later, Mr. Ellis was in turn shown in, followed, half an hour later, by His Excellency's retinue.

"A circle being formed about Napoleon, he walked round, addressing successively each person on some subject connected with his particular pursuit or situation in the Embassy, and gave a neat and complimentary turn to all his remarks. His object was evidently to please as much as possible, and he certainly succeeded. But had we left the island without knowing that he had obtained a list of the persons of the Embassy, and of their particular situations in it, previously to our introduction to him, we should have gone away with a much higher opinion of his address in conforming the subject of his conversation to individual characters."[13]

Lord Amherst held a private audience with Napoleon, to which he is our only witness:

> Bonaparte was standing up towards a window on the right hand as you enter the room. He was draped in a plain green coat with covered buttons, the rest of his dress was white; he wore silk stockings & shoes & buckles; a plain cocked hat under his arm; on his breast, the star of the Legion of Honor. The drawings I had lately seen of him represented him as bloated. This was by no means the case. He is rather corpulent & his neck short; but his limbs are well formed, and I should judge that he was perfectly capable of even violent exercise. His face is sallow, broad in the upper part, but of an oval form. Its expression is stern and intelligent, & becomes animated in speaking. . . . His conversation might fairly divide itself into four parts, my own history, China, his treatment on the Island, and European politics.

In the part of the discussion dealing with China, Amherst reports, Napoleon was good enough not to criticize his lordship's conduct: He "then passed to my late residence in China, enquired about the Tartar Ceremony, but made no observation (as I expected him to have done) on the propriety of my withholding or performing it. . . . [he] asked me several questions about the details of my voyage in that country." But what Napoleon "most dwelt upon" was "the circumstances of his present situation." He "complained bitterly" and "insinuated that but for the fear of committing or embarrassing me he might perhaps have made me the bearer of his complaints in writing; but as I had already to render to my government a report of an Embassy which had not been successful, it would perhaps be inconsiderate to commission me with any other business." Napoleon then had Mr. Ellis come in, followed soon after by the "rest of the gentlemen." Upon being introduced to Amherst's son Jeff, Napoleon "exclaimed *jolie figure*" and asked him "what curiosities he had brought back with him from China."[14]

Amherst, it appears, expected to be lectured for having refused to kowtow, which suggests that his British informants, primarily O'Meara and Hudson Lowe, had alerted him to Bonaparte's views, with which they were undoubtedly familiar. Why was it that Napoleon spared Amherst the tirades his own companions had so often heard? Perhaps he was concerned not to compound the humiliation the ambassador had already suffered. Napoleon must have known that Amherst had been informed of his views, and he thus treated the Briton to a lesson in international savoir faire and delicacy.

But Napoleon attached such great importance to this subject that he raised it again with O'Meara several weeks after Amherst's departure: "Your ministers, . . . who did foresee difficulty in etiquette, had, in sending out Lord Amherst, authorized him to comply with it; and it appears, that his private opinion was, that he ought to perform it [the kowtow], and that in refusing to do so, he suffered himself to be guided by bad advisers."[15]

It is hard to see how Napoleon could have known of these details unless he heard them from Amherst himself, who may thus have broken ranks with Thomas Staunton after the fact. On the other hand, Napoleon may simply have heard what he wanted to hear. Five years later Amherst wrote to Staunton: "I have never for a moment regretted that I suffered myself to be guided by your opinion. It is impossible that even *you* should feel more gratified than I do at the complete fulfilment of all your predictions."[16]

Napoleon raised his criticism to the level of doctrine: "It is an error, but one which is very generally believed, that an ambassador represents the sovereign. An ambassador, however, does not represent his sovereign, as in fact none of the stipulations of affairs which he signs are valid until after a ratification; and as to his rank in etiquette, there never has been an example of sovereigns having treated them as equals."[17] And: "A man charged with a diplomatic mission ought to have performed the kowtow; and could not refuse it without being wanting in respect to the emperor. . . . Lord Macartney, and it appears Lord Amherst, . . . proposed . . . that by a public declaration the Chinese monarch should promise that if he sent an ambassador to England, he should perform the kowtow. The Chinese rejected these proposals, and with good reason. If a Chinese ambassador were received in London, . . . he ought to follow the same etiquette in the presence of the king of England as that observed by the princes, ministers of state, and the knights of the garter. . . . These proposals [of Macartney and Amherst] were therefore unreasonable."[18]

He concluded on a peremptory note, saying that the ambassador to the Porte "is not admitted to the feet of the sublime sultan, unless he is clothed in a caftan, and is obliged to perform such ceremonies as the civilization of the Porte . . . have prescribed. . . . Every sensible man in your country therefore can consider the refusal to perform the kowtow no otherwise than as unjustifiable and unfortunate in its consequences."[19]

Here Napoleon sounds much like an edict from the Son of Heaven himself. He had read the reports of the Macartney mission carefully and had listened attentively to Amherst. But he seems not to have grasped that the kowtow represented far more than a mere act of courteous reverence: it signified that there was but one emperor and that all other sovereigns were his vassals; to these vassals the ranking dignitaries of the Middle Empire owed no kowtow. Admittedly, there were constant kowtows in traditional China: soldiers kowtowed to officers, merchants to subprefects, sons to their fathers, entire families to a dying member. These, however, were mere signs of veneration. Even today, despite "liberalization," "de-Confucianization," and other cultural revolutions, children kowtow to their grandparents on the day of the Spring Festival, and the student demonstrators during the "Peking Spring" of 1989 kowtowed to the first of their dead. But the kowtow was an exclusive feature of the Chinese Order, reserved above all for the man who interceded before Heaven on behalf of that order. It was not an anecdotal gesture of homage, but the acknowledgment of the subordination of a lower to a higher power. Like it or not, to perform it was to be incorporated into the Celestial hierarchy.

HAVING DELIVERED his lesson on the past, Napoleon turned to the future: "You say that you might awe them by means of a maritime argument, and thus force the mandarins to submit to the European etiquette. This idea is madness. You would be very badly advised indeed, if you were to call to arms a nation of two hundred millions of inhabitants."*[20]

The pragmatic Napoleon noted that England, a "nation of shopkeepers," would be well advised to follow another road: "If a million francs had been given to the first mandarin, everything would have been settled, and it would not have been a reproach to the nation; as that embassy was not one which regarded the honour of the country. It was, and ought to

---

* Napoleon seriously underestimates the population of China, which, according to the 1812 census, had risen to 361 million (from 330 million in 1792).

be considered more as an affair of merchandise than as one immediately affecting the nation."[21]

Affairs of "merchandise" are not of direct interest to the nation. Only affairs of honor count, and the exchange of commodities does not engage a nation's honor. Spoken like a true Frenchman. A few decades later Napoleon III, Bonaparte's nephew, acting with the full support of the legislature, declared war on Prussia in response to a dispatch cleverly formulated by Bismarck to elicit exactly that response. Meanwhile, international trade developed beyond the borders of France.

Napoleon firmly opposed the idea (already widespread in London) of opening China to British trade by force. "It would be the worst thing you have done for a number of years, to go to war with an immense empire like China, and possessing so many resources. You would doubtless, at first, succeed, take what vessels they have, and destroy their trade; but you would teach them their own strength. They would be compelled to adopt measures to defend themselves against you; they would consider and say, 'We must try to make ourselves equal to his nation. . . . We must build ships, we must put guns into them, we must render ourselves equal to them.' They would get artificers, and ship builders, from France, and America, and even from London; they would build a fleet, and in the course of time, defeat you."[22]

As it turned out, it was not the Chinese but the Japanese who followed that path. Why was it that the Chinese disappointed Napoleon's hopes? Why is it that to this day they have failed to justify his famous prediction: "When China awakens, the world will tremble"?

NAPOLEON—a man who knew as well as anyone how intoxicating the clatter of arms could be—now spoke as an apostle of peace. More than twenty years earlier Macartney had written, not without nobility: "Our present interests, our reason, and our humanity equally forbid the thoughts of any offensive measures with regard to the Chinese, whilst a ray of hope remains for succeeding by gentle ones."[23]

Gentle measures had now failed for the second time, yet Napoleon the Impatient preached patience, Napoleon the Proud humility. Considering its source, it is hardly surprising that the lesson fell on deaf ears. The diplomats would not absorb a third defeat. It would soon be time for soldiers to take over.

86

In Exchange for Tea: Opium

(1817–40)

BETWEEN THE PATHETIC departure of the diplomats and the triumphal march of the soldiers came the sly penetration of the opium traders. Where the diplomats had tried unsuccessfully to open China's gates, the smugglers slipped in through the back door. Once inside, they chased down every possible outlet.

The original aim of the opium trade had been more modest: to balance the West's trade deficit. Huge quantities of tea were being exported from China, while almost nothing was imported, Qianlong having insisted that there was no demand for any European product in his empire. British smugglers therefore set about creating that demand—for a product equally as inessential as tea but somewhat less inoffensive. Clandestine imports of opium compensated for official exports of tea.

Opium devastated China. Individuals were destroyed by its ravages, the system by its clandestineness. But it also undermined the company's monopoly.

Chinese exports of tea doubled between 1813 and 1833, while imports of opium quadrupled.[1] Money flowed out of China to pay for the poison that gnawed at the country. Two parallel, watertight channels of currency circulation arose: the emperor accumulated money from the tea trade, while Chinese subjects paid for their drug in cash. The empire was tottering, and opium was one of the reasons why. Moreover, the authorities knew it.

In 1820 the viceroy of Canton finally launched an attack on the traffic. (It is likely that this action had been long delayed by the percentage of the take he had been receiving, whether in cash or in kind.) He began by arresting Chinese dealers, but business continued to flourish on the nearby island of Lintin, where ships were freely unloaded out of the sight of Chinese officials. The cargoes, however, still had to pass through Canton, and for that the mandarins had to be paid off.[2]

Just as the viceroy began to move against the traffic, the market exploded. Competition between British and Portuguese suppliers and among individual dealers drove prices down, and that helped to widen demand. "Opium," one agent said, "is like gold. I can sell it anytime."[3]

In 1832 the most prosperous of the "private" British traders, Jardine —the founder of one of the largest international trading firms, later based in Hong Kong and with headquarters in Bermuda and Singapore today —decided to try his luck farther north. Speedy, well-armed coastal launches began selling the drug directly in small, isolated creeks and inlets along the coasts of Fujian and Zhejiang. New customers emerged, and sales climbed.

In 1833, forty years after the Macartney mission, the viceroy of Canton (still the only Chinese official authorized to deal with foreigners) appealed to the king of Great Britain and Ireland in the name of . . . the rights of man. Opium, he complained, was forbidden in Britain itself. Why, then, did the king allow sinister, greedy merchants to "poison" the Chinese people?[4] This state official and man of letters was actually asking that the British and Chinese peoples be treated equally. Macartney and Amherst never would have believed it.

Shortly afterwards a petition sent to the emperor Daoguang by the censor Yuan Yulin indicated just how anxious some officials had become. The empire, Yuan wrote, had never faced such a danger in its entire history. The poison was debilitating the people, drying up their bones, eating at their hearts. Whole families were being ruined.[5] "I have many friends who smoke," wrote Lieou Ngo. "None believes that he is addicted, but all, having begun smoking opium as a pastime, have finished by spending all their time at it."[6]

The smugglers succeeded where Macartney and Amherst had failed. But these were smugglers only in appearance, for they were backed by British power. To its honor, a part of British public opinion objected to their government's role in creating "languid, shattered individuals with idiotic smiles on their faces."[7] But the dissenters were told that opium was essential to British trade, and trade was an expression of the highest values: personal endeavor and freedom of enterprise.

The normally cautious Canton Select Committee went so far as to write in a petition to the Commons that the failures of the Macartney and Amherst embassies "will forcibly suggest to your Honourable House how little is to be gained in China by any refinements of diplomacy." And war, of course, is the continuation of diplomacy by other means. The committee declared that the Chinese people were hostile to Britain only because of the "jealousy of the government." The agents of the company "fully believed that the common Chinese, oppressed by magistrates and taxed by Hoppos, could not help but approve what internal Chinese merchants had been unable to carry out for centuries: the destruction of bureaucratic restraints on commerce, even if it meant force of arms."[8] War would be waged against China in the interests of the Chinese.

Confident of their power and exasperated by the pretensions of the Chinese dragon, now clearly in its death agony yet still demanding homage from the entire planet, the British identified opium with trade itself, claiming that the fight for freedom and national honor required that a powerful war machine be hurled against the last remaining forces of the Manchu empire.

Opium was already undermining Chinese civilization. The war that would now be waged in its support would do little to convince the Chinese that Westerners were not barbarians. Opium had anesthetized the Chinese. Would the war waged in its name in turn awaken them?

IN 1832 Captain Hugh Lindsay was secretly assigned to verify the military observations of the Chinese coast made by the Macartney mission in 1793 and 1794.[9] At one point his frigate, the *Amherst*, was suddenly ringed by a fleet of war junks, but managed to drive them off, leading the captain to conclude that "thousands of Chinese war junks could not stand up to a single British frigate." Lindsay also noted that "the best ports—such as Xiamen or Ningbo—are still protected only by derisory batteries incapable of interdicting access."[10] Chinese military organization had not changed, for the very idea of a seaborne landing seemed inconceivable. The emperor still commanded an army of a hundred thousand Manchus, but these troops were trained primarily to put down domestic rebellions. The coasts were defended only by local militias and a few small forts barely capable of repelling incursions by pirates.

In 1833 London abolished the company's monopoly, and a "superintendent" of British trade was appointed in Canton. It was also decided to accredit a consular representative authorized to deal directly with the viceroy—in effect implementing Macartney's old proposal.[11]

William John Napier, the consul-designate, arrived in Canton in July 1834, but his letter of accreditation was rejected, and he was ordered to withdraw to Macao. When he refused, the viceroy ordered trade halted and blockaded the British factory. Napier sent two warships up the Pearl River and called for reinforcements from India, but eventually he was forced to take refuge in Macao, where he died of malaria in October.[12]

The Chinese were now convinced that Westerners in Canton would never be anything more than hostages and "paper tigers." For their part, the British were beginning to understand that Macartney had been right to point out that if peaceful, patient methods failed, a serious war effort would be required to turn the situation around. Nevertheless, the suggestion of a third embassy to Peking was raised, to be headed by Sir Thomas Staunton. He, however, opposed the idea, fearing that Britain would be negotiating from a position of weakness.

In the meantime, trade continued, though the Canton guild was disconcerted by the elimination of the company's monopoly. Guild officials wondered how business could be controlled if the barbarians were allowed to trade individually.[13] Western-style personal responsibility—freedom with a thousand faces—was unfathomable to the Chinese, and the guild found it impossible to deal with fifty-five independent firms and two thousand seasonal British traders. Eventually the monolithic structure was forced to give way to compradors, intermediaries who escaped official control and amassed colossal fortunes. The expansion of British capitalism thereby fostered the rise of Chinese capitalists.[14] The "felonious merchants" feared by Qianlong proliferated, gradually acquiring pride of place.

By refusing to establish natural ties of trade with the West, the emperor probably made inevitable an aggressive confrontation that would leave the empire broken and dismembered.[15] His obsessional attachment to the Rites may have made him the person ultimately most responsible for the fall of his dynasty and the decay of his country. Macartney had accurately predicted this facet of nineteenth-century history: "The Chinese are now . . . awaking from the political stupor they had been thrown into by the Tartar impression, and begin to feel their native energies revive. A slight collision might elicit fire from the flint, and spread flames of revolt from one extremity of China to the other."[16]

As British impatience mounted, the Middle Empire clung immutably to pride in a long-vanished supremacy. The obstinate dynamism of the British and the unmitigated intransigence of the Chinese were mutually exasperating. Wars are always justified by arousing passion for some "good cause" raised to metaphysical status. For the Chinese the cause was definitive perfection, for the British perfectible progress. These two countries lived in different mental universes, and the more contact there was between them, the less inclined either was to accept the other's point of view.

IN 1836 the Chinese Empire ran a trade deficit for the first time. Opium accounted for three-quarters of the total value of Chinese imports.[17] In 1837 the scholars of the Hanlin Academy denounced the "ten million taels" spent each year to stupefy a growing number of Chinese. The viceroy of Hubei warned the emperor Daoguang that if His Majesty allowed things to continue in this way, China would soon have no soldiers to defend it nor any money to pay them with.[18]

Not only the state, but society itself was threatened, and the anguish of social decomposition was aggravated by the Confucian obsession with order. If the people continue to abandon themselves to this drug, the censor Yuan Yulin declared, "fathers would no longer be able to admonish their wives; masters would no longer be able to restrain their servants; and teachers would no longer be able to train their pupils. . . . It would mean the end of the life of the people and the destruction of the soul of the nation."[19] The evil was now ubiquitous. Even the commander of the imperial fleet, Admiral Han, transported opium in exchange for a cut of the cargo. The great mercantile houses of Canton, which initially tried to steer clear of the illegal traffic, eventually became immersed in it.

"Moralists" denounced opium as a "heretical religion" that was dissolving social relationships and erasing the distinction between Chinese and barbarians.[20] But others answered these warnings with a "political" argument: prohibition was utopian; the real problem was the massive outflow of money, and the logical solution was to legalize the traffic and either levy taxes on the imported opium or cultivate the poppy locally.[21] The debate in China was as bitter as the one now raging in the United States about the uncontrollable drug invasion. Except that today's smugglers do not claim to be acting in the name of great principles.

After deliberating on the matter in May 1836, the troubled emperor finally came down on the side of the moralists. In 1837 two thousand dealers were arrested, and a judge closed the opium dens of Canton.[22] Lin Zexu, a leading man of letters and exponent of the moralists' school, went so far as to advocate the death penalty, admittedly a brutal punishment, for opium smokers. The drug, he argued, was a mortal danger to society, and the drug smoker was morally ill. It would not be just to execute morally ill individuals for breaking the law, but it was nonetheless just and necessary to terrorize drug addicts by threatening them with death unless they abandoned their addiction: "To get rid of the habit of smoking is not a difficult task; what is difficult is to reform the mind. If we want to reform that mind which constantly tends to neglect the law, how can we refrain from promulgating laws that will threaten the mind?" Lin called for state sanatoriums to be opened to help addicts quit, and argued that the year between the promulgation of the death sentence and its execution should be divided into four phases with increasingly harsher penalties.[23]

In December 1838 the emperor named Lin Zexu imperial commissioner in Canton, with full powers. His instructions to his subordinates were clear: terrify users and dealers alike. But no one thought this would lead to war with the barbarians. Since the outside world was inconsequential, the Peking court never considered the foreign consequences of its policy.[24]

Lin set to work in March 1839, immediately upon his arrival in Canton. He asked the Westerners to take inventory of their stocks of the drug, which would then be destroyed. Six weeks later, 20,619 crates of opium —a total of about 2,000 tons—were publicly emptied into vats of quicklime on the Humen beach opposite Canton.[25] These measures hit the foreigners like a thunderbolt, and Charles Elliot, the new British superintendent, began organizing a resistance, dealing piecemeal with the various isolated incidents and playing for time until reinforcements could be sent from Europe and India.[26]

Lin addressed Queen Victoria on the essence of the problem. Opium, he pointed out, was strictly forbidden in her own kingdom. It was regarded as damaging to Britain, yet the British were content to damage other countries. Why? China, he went on, has countless products needed by other countries, while the products imported by China were trifles it could easily do without. Opium was a product of Britain's Indian possessions, and he called upon the queen to destroy the poppy plantations in favor of food production.[27]

But London did not view the issue in the same terms as the Chinese. For Lin, the heart of the matter was the fight against drugs; for London, it was the sacrosanct right of trade and free enterprise.

IN 1836 Thomas Staunton had written a polemical article that helped to forestall an armed conflict. By 1839, however, his attitude had changed. He now believed that "the unprovoked outrages of the Chinese had placed right on *our* side." On various occasions, both in Parliament and in private, he told Lord Palmerston, the head of the Foreign Office, that the time for half-measures was past. He characterized Lin's behavior as "violent" and "treacherous."[28] In his memoirs he proudly notes his role in the decision that led to war.

In January 1840, after several exchanges of cannon fire, Lin closed the port of Canton to British vessels and banned the British from all trade.[29]

The China lobby, headed by Jardine, mobilized in London. Demands for resolute action poured in from all the industrial cities of the kingdom. When Lin organized a second public destruction of opium, Palmerston protested: "Let us give China a good thrashing and explain ourselves afterwards."[30]

On April 7, 1840, Sir Thomas Staunton addressed the House of Commons again. The contemporary parliamentary record summarizes his speech this way: "With regard to the immediate cause of the rupture, that was entirely attributable to the conduct of Imperial Commissioner Lin. The only answer he would give would be to state what he actually had done under circumstances somewhat similar. When he accompanied Lord Amherst to Peking, similar threats had been held out to him; he was told that his life would be forfeited if he did not advise the ambassador to perform the ceremony of the kowtow; he did not tremble at the order; he did not advise the ambassador to perform the ceremony. The ceremony was not performed, and the embassy was dismissed in safety, and on its returning from Peking, received even greater honours than had been accorded to the preceding embassy of Lord Macartney. . . . He believed he had been actuated by a sincere desire to benefit his country, and that he had exhibited a total disregard to his personal safety in the execution of his duty."[31]

On that same day the historian Macaulay exhorted the British to recall the example of Rome, noting that Britain "had not degenerated since her great Protector vowed he would make the name of Englishman as respected as ever had been the name of Roman citizen."[32]

Gladstone condemned the argument of the government and its majority: "I am not competent to judge how long this war may last, or how protracted may be its operations, but this I can say, that a war more unjust in its origins, a war more calculated in its progress to cover this country with permanent disgrace, I do not know, and I have not read of. . . . [The British] flag is hoisted to protect an infamous contraband traffic."[33]

The war resolution passed by a mere five-vote margin.

Debate continued to rage in Britain: about the horrors of opium and about the rights of the Chinese, the British, and trade itself. This was, after all, a parliamentary system, with a government and an opposition. But Thomas Staunton observed: "I took an active, and, I have reason to believe, effectual part in vindicating the Government policy, which appeared to me to have been opposed solely on party grounds. It was afterwards carried out with vigour, and to the fullest extent, by its most strenuous opponents, the moment they came into power."[34] It took time, but eventually all of Britain went to war against China.

87

Military Action

(1840–60)

Our present relations with China present a vast field for
British enterprise. . . . Our missionaries, merchants, and men
of science, have already visited many places in the interior of
China previously untrodden by British footsteps.

THOMAS STAUNTON, 1846[1]

IN JUNE 1840 a British fleet of forty ships and four thousand soldiers arrived
near Canton from Bengal. There was no time to waste. Admiral Elliot,
like Macartney and Amherst, wanted to negotiate in Peking, not Canton.
On August 11, forty-seven years after Macartney, Elliot docked in Dagu,
the port attached to Tientsin, and transmitted London's demands to the
Peking government: financial compensation for the opium Lin had ordered
destroyed in Canton, the opening of new ports, the signing of a customs
agreement, the concession of a trading post. The emperor pretended to
yield, disavowing Lin and appointing Qishan, an advocate of the legali-
zation of opium, as plenipotentiary. He promised that if the British would
only withdraw to Canton, their grievances would be dealt with.[2]

But the arrangement concluded by Elliot and Qishan, a master of
compromise, was soon disavowed by both sides.

The emperor considered these enemies paper tigers. He had been told,
after all, that if the barbarians were "deprived of China's tea and rhubarb
for a few days, they would suffer constipation and a loss of vision that
would endanger their lives."[3]

For its part, London wanted more. Elliot was replaced by Sir Henry
Pottinger, and the squadron headed north. The emperor was shaken out
of his torpor in October 1841, when three cities, among them Ningbo,[4]
were taken by the British fleet. One of his nephews was put in charge of
stopping the barbarian advance. After a dream in which he was promised
victory, the nephew armed his soldiers with swords and ordered an assault.

The British met the attack with murderous firepower, and three successive clashes resulted in disaster for the Chinese, who could not understand how four thousand "Barbarian devils" racked by illness and fighting so far from their homes had been able to rout twenty thousand of the empire's elite soldiers.[5]

Well aware that the prime concern of the Chinese was to defend the sanctuary of Peking, the British established a base in the Zhoushan Islands. In the spring of 1842 they sailed up the Yangtze toward Nanking, the crossroads of all the great trade routes and the Grand Canal, and thus the linchpin for the provisioning of the capital. They were now resolved to strike at China's heart.[6]

The Chinese armed forces were gripped by a stupefying paralysis.[7] Pottinger treated the Chinese generals to a demonstration of his artillery, with which they were almost as impressed as Admiral Tojo was with the bombing of Hiroshima a century later. On August 29, 1842, the Treaty of Nanking was signed aboard the admiral's flagship, the *Cornwallis*.[8] Cannon fire obtained what traders and diplomats had coveted for so many long years: the opening of the ports of Canton, Xiamen, Fuzhou, Ningbo, and Shanghai; consular representation; unvarying tax rates; abolition of the guild; equal treatment of Western and Celestial officials; the cession of Hong Kong to Britain.

As for opium, the Chinese were compelled to pay an indemnity of fifteen million taels for the drugs destroyed in 1839, and it was now understood that opium would be treated like any other commodity. Thomas Staunton wrote: "In April 1843 I spoke at considerable length in the House in support of Lord Ashley's Motion against the Opium Trade, and I afterwards published my speech. I did not take up the question (as Lord Ashley did) exclusively on the *moral* ground, but argued it more especially on the ground that any sanction or countenance of such contraband trade with China, was wholly inconsistent with our treaty of peace and amity with that Empire, and, therefore, likely in a short period to occasion another rupture. The Chinese government having, however, since practically (although without any specific enactment) legalised this traffic, the international argument against it, of course, falls to the ground."[9] Thus was the British conscience eased.

Would war now succeed in imposing what peaceful cooperation might otherwise have brought about through a gradual evolution of ideas and technology? The gate had been violently forced open, just as Macartney had feared. But for a very long time the Chinese would have no greater wish than to slam it shut on their aggressors' fingers.

"IN VIEW OF China's great resources in land and population," Father Huc wrote in the 1840s, echoing the views of both Macartney and Napoleon, "one wonders what this people lacks to shake the world. Should a far-sighted Emperor come forward, determined to break boldly with the old traditions and to initiate his people into the progress of the West, the course of regeneration would be rapid."[10]

But no such emperor appeared. Faced with foreign demands, the Manchu dynasty retreated to its defensive bunker and encouraged bursts of xenophobia. The task of "regeneration" fell to the people themselves; but while nationalism did finally succeed in rousing China from its slumber, the awakening required successive revolutions. From this point on there were three major players on the scene: the entrenched power of the Manchu dynasty and the closely associated Celestial bureaucracy; popular nationalism; and the West. China was paralyzed by this infernal trio. None of the three protagonists was able to establish sufficient control over the country to reshape it, and their conflicts mired it in underdevelopment. The interweaving of conflicting forces in a country so vast as to constitute a world unto itself produced earthquakes whose aftershocks are with us still.

Faced with relentless Western demands for greater privileges, the mandarin regime increasingly resorted to a new tactic: passive resistance. The people came to know the foreigners, learning both to serve them and to scorn them. Daoguang's successor, the emperor Xianfeng, dismissed the mandarins who had negotiated the Treaty of Nanking and deliberately fostered paralysis within the bureaucratic apparatus. The Europeans, however, were unconcerned: such measures simply offered fresh opportunities for armed action.

Antiforeign rioting in 1857 provided the pretext. In the spring of 1858 an Anglo-French fleet sailed into the waters of Tientsin, and the court immediately agreed to sign a second "unequal treaty": eleven additional ports were opened, and a Westerner was put in charge of customs. The "seventh request"—the one never made by Macartney but rejected by Qianlong—was finally granted: Catholic and Protestant missionaries were authorized to settle in the interior of the country and to preach freely. They were to be protected by law and, if necessary, by soldiers. But they would never shake the accusation that they had been carried into China on military wagons, just like the crates of opium. The religious hierarchy was later assimilated to the Chinese dignitaries, the bishops to viceroys.[11]

The humble patience recommended by Fathers Amiot and Raux had vanished.

A few months later, Peking violated the Treaty of Tientsin. English and French negotiators were tortured and murdered. The West then struck at China's nerve center with military force. British, French, and American troops entered Peking on October 13, 1860, ignoring the sacred banners and emblems displayed from the ramparts by soldiers and civilians alike. It was another clash of two cultures: paper dragons against Lord Elgin's and Cousin-Montauban's well-equipped troops; magic formulas against mortars.

Five days later, the invading troops were turned loose against the Summer Palace. An Anglo-French army sacked and burned the Yuanming Yuan, destroying, in particular, the replica of Versailles designed by the French Jesuits, the building in which Macartney, Dinwiddie, and Barrow had tried unsuccessfully to demonstrate England's scientific superiority. Stunned by the riches they were plundering, the soldiers found most of the presents Macartney had left there intact, including the planetarium and the artillery pieces. The West was destroying the West as well as the East. But most of all it was destroying any chance for the kind of peaceful exchanges that might have permitted cultural cross-fertilization.

As Europe rejoiced in its victory, at least one Western writer, himself an exile fleeing another empire, understood that this armed victory was in fact the terrible symbol of an offense against civilization itself:

> Once, in a distant corner of the world, there was a great wonder, a wonder known as the Summer Palace. Everything born of the imagination of an almost superhuman people was there. . . . Build a dream of marble, of jade and bronze and porcelain; cover it with precious stones; drape it in silk; make of it a sanctuary, a harem, a citadel; fill it with gods and monsters; varnish it, enamel it, gild it, adorn it; let poet-architects build the thousand and one dreams of the thousand and one nights; add gardens and ponds, fountains of water and foam, swans, ibises, and peacocks, a dazzling cavern of the human imagination. . . .
>
> It had taken the patient work of generations to create it, and people spoke of the Parthenon of Greece, the Pyramids of Egypt, the Coliseum of Rome, the Summer Palace of the Orient. . . .
>
> This wonder is no more.
>
> There came a day when two bandits entered that Palace. One plundered it, the other put it to the torch. Involved in this we find

the name of Elgin,* which fatally reminds us of the Parthenon. What one Elgin began at the Parthenon has now been repeated at the Summer Palace, but more completely, such that nothing at all remains. All the treasures of all our cathedrals taken together would not have equaled this formidable and splendid museum of the Orient. A great exploit, a true godsend! One of the conquerors filled his pockets, the other his coffers, and the two returned to Europe arm in arm, in laughter.

We Europeans are civilized, and to us the Chinese are barbarians. Here is what civilization has done to barbarism!

History shall call one of these bandits France, the other England. But I protest!

The French Empire has pocketed half the spoils of this victory, and today, with a proprietor's naiveté, it displays the splendid bric-a-brac of the Summer Palace. But I hope the day will come when France, cleansed and delivered, will return its booty to despoiled China.

Until then, what we have is theft, and two thieves.

I take note.

Such, Sir, is the degree of approbation I bestow upon the China expedition.

This little-known letter bears the signature of Victor Hugo.[12]

ADMITTEDLY, Hugo exaggerates the splendor of the Summer Palace. He repents of the misdeeds of Napoleon le Petit, and loudly trumpets the "white man's lament." The sack of Rome by the most Catholic Charles V, the plunder of the Palatinate by Louis XIV, and countless other exactions in countless other wars show that China's fate was by no means unique. But Hugo was quite right about the gravity of the trauma for the collective consciousness of the Chinese.

This fresh "victory" was followed by the signing, in Peking, of a third "unequal treaty." The peninsula of Kowloon was attached to Hong Kong; the foreign concessions became completely autonomous; Western warships were authorized to sail six hundred miles up the Yangtze. Finally—and this was not the least painful of its clauses—permanent representatives were exchanged. No more kowtows. Standard international practices were finally accepted, sixty-seven years after Macartney. The Westerners were

---

* The Lord Elgin who sacked the Yuanming Yuan was none other than the son of the former British ambassador to Turkey, the man who plundered the treasures of the Acropolis, bringing the Parthenon friezes to London.

no longer tributary barbarians; instead their accredited diplomatic missions would deal with a Chinese Ministry of Foreign Affairs expressly created for the purpose.

The inequality between China and the outside world that had prevailed since the beginning of time was thereby abolished. The Chinese call these treaties, imposed by force, "unequal." But what treaty isn't? In the view of the West, the treaties replaced the inequality of force with the lasting rule of law, halting the destructive logic of unequal combat in favor of the peaceful logic of relations between equals. In Chinese eyes, however, order and justice required that China and its tributaries be unequal. The new inequality they so deeply resented was the imposition of equality. The rightful vassal was elevated to the same status as the legitimate sovereign. An outrage.

This innovation was so damaging to the mentality of the Chinese that many years passed before it was assimilated. It overturned their entire view of life, imposing rationality upon them and wrenching them away from magical thought. But it also wounded them in the depths of their soul, somewhat like an autistic child struck in the face by a companion trying to teach him that he is not alone in the world. Uprisings, xenophobia, and civil war would be required to heal the wound.

88

Implosion

(1850–1911)

AS THE CELESTIAL ORDER was being shaken by the blows of barbarians, it was also imploding under the internal pressure of nationalist popular reactions that the Manchu rulers were no longer able to control.

The humiliation of the ruling dynasty by barbarians was taken as a sign that the Mandate of Heaven had been withdrawn. Secret societies had been a feature of Chinese life even in Macartney's day, but by the 1850s they were extraordinarily widespread, eventually culminating in the Taiping Rebellion. Though motivated primarily by Chinese nationalism, this revolt was also a sign of the times, for nationalism was now beginning to appropriate Western weapons, the better to combat the West. The leader of the Taipings, Hong Xiuquan, was a young peasant of Guangdong province who had had contact with Europeans in Canton. He had learned two things from them: the superiority of their technology and the rudiments of the Protestant religion. In his own crude and utopian way, he was the first to combine Western ideas with Chinese nationalism.

Hong called himself the "younger brother of Jesus Christ." His followers, known as Worshipers of God, prayed twice a day, observed the Ten Commandments, and banned alcohol, tobacco, and gambling. They also preached the equality of the sexes and demanded that land be shared, recurrent themes that were precursors of Mao. They were roused to action by the aggravation of peasant poverty during the nineteenth century, a consequence of the combination of population growth and social immobility.

In 1851 Hong proclaimed himself emperor and "King of Heaven." Millions of Chinese hostile to the Manchu dynasty followed him. In 1853 he took control of Nanking, and the self-proclaimed emperor was soon in command of eleven of China's eighteen provinces. But cracks began to appear in his power base, and eventually he went too far, organizing an attack on Shanghai. It was the West that ultimately rescued the Manchu dynasty from the Taiping Rebellion, supplying the government forces with weapons, ammunition, advisers, and mercenaries, beginning in 1861. The popular spirit, already fractured by dissension, was crushed by the military machine, and the King of Heaven poisoned himself. His body was cut into ten thousand pieces. One more death among the twenty million caused by the rebellion.[1]

The year 1861 also saw the death of the emperor Xianfeng, who was formally succeeded by his four-year-old son, Tongzhi. But it was Tongzhi's mother, the imperial concubine Cixi (Tseu-hi), who wielded real power, and she held it for half a century. Intelligent and unscrupulous, she was a devotee of the inexhaustible validity of Confucian thought, and she was as convinced as Qianlong and Jiaqing had been of Manchu superiority over the Chinese and Chinese superiority over Westerners.

But nothing could ever be quite the same as before. Cixi tried to reorganize the army, construct arsenals and steam-powered ships, combat corruption, adopt manuals of Western technology, and encourage the teaching of foreign languages. But she never attacked the system itself. Her half-measures were not sufficient to restore Confucian authority or to turn China into a modern state. "A piece of rotten wood cannot be carved," Confucius himself might have said.[2]

The Celestial bureaucracy proved powerful enough to defeat both the Taiping Rebellion and the attempt at reform from above. Although the peasant revolt did not destroy the empire, it did seriously threaten the ruling caste of officials-literati-landowners. This caste was unable to accept reform, for to do so would have been to give way to new elites whose power was already growing: the compradors and the army officers shaped by the military reforms of 1895–1900, the future cadets of Huangpu who would later be led by a Jiang Jieshi (Chiang Kai-shek), trained in Japan and Moscow, or a Zhou Enlai upon his return from France. The mandarin ruling class, while obstinately continuing to live in its own dream, now had to contend simultaneously with these new forces and the constant threat of insurrectional turmoil.

Meanwhile, the barbarians continued to gnaw at the empire. In 1885 France sliced off Annam, and in 1886 Britain swallowed Burma. Ten years later, the Sino-Japanese War compounded China's shame, as a people who had been contemptuously referred to as "the Dwarfs"* vanquished the

---

* Japan, which had a celestial emperor of its own (the *tennō*), had actually ceased to be a vassal of China in the sixth century. Sino-Japanese relations were based on a compromise: it was not the emperor of Japan, but his "first minister," the *shōgun*, who sent messengers to the Chinese court to deliver tribute and perform the kowtow.

country from which they had drawn the essence of their civilization. Korea was the apple of discord between China, its theoretical suzerain, and rapidly modernizing Japan, which aspired to become Korea's ruler in practice. On September 17, 1894, at the mouth of the Yalu River, the Japanese routed the Chinese fleet and invaded Manchuria, cradle of the dynasty. Less than a year later, China was forced to sue for peace. The "division of the pie" continued.*

On the eve of the battle, a British launch brought a message from the Japanese admiral Ito to his former comrade and friend but current adversary, the Chinese admiral Ting. This letter from one soldier to another epitomizes the contrast between Japanese and Chinese reactions to "the rapidity of changes in the world."[3] Here is the gist of the text:

> The present situation of your country . . . results from a system under which you designate a man to fulfill a function solely on the basis of his literary knowledge. It is a millennial custom. This system was probably a good one so long as your nation remained isolated, but it has now become outdated. In the present state of the world, it is no longer possible to live in isolation.
>
> You know what an arduous situation Japan faced thirty years ago, and how we applied ourselves to escaping the difficulties, rejecting the old system and adopting a new one. Your homeland, too, must adopt this new manner of living. If it does so, all will be well. If it does not, it will inevitably perish.
>
> He who loyally serves his country must not accept being carried along by the great tide that threatens it, but would do better to reform the world's oldest empire, which possesses a glorious history and an immense territory, striving to make it forever unshakable.
>
> Come to my country, there to await the moment when your homeland requests your participation in an enterprise of reform.[4]

After the battle Admiral Ting respectfully turned to face Peking and committed suicide.

SOME OF THE LITERATI did demand that China change. Under their influence, the emperor Guangxu, who succeeded Tongzhi in 1875 at the age of twenty-four, attempted to throw off the yoke of Cixi, his aunt and adoptive

---

* Korea became independent; Taiwan and the Pescadores went to Japan; Russia acquired Port Arthur and a sphere of influence in Manchuria; the British won the right to trade on the Yangtze, the French the right to intervene in the provinces bordering Tonkin; Germany was granted a concession in Shandong.

mother. In effect, Guangxu told his people that the empire was now encircled by the Western nations, and that if China refused to adopt their methods, its ruin was ineluctable.

This was the dynasty's last chance, and for a hundred days, from June 11 to September 20, 1898, the young emperor tried to grasp that chance, enacting many innovative measures of the sort inspired by Peter the Great and the Meijis. Young people were sent abroad to study; a national budget was published; literary competitions were abolished; a university was founded in Peking; ministries of Agriculture, Technology, Trade, and Railroads were created; laws were passed dealing with inventions and economic initiative; the courts were overhauled; uncultivated military lands were distributed to the peasants; political journalism was encouraged; subjects of the empire were authorized to submit petitions to the emperor.

The retinue of the dowager empress was outraged by this wave of diabolical moves. "You poor fool!" Cixi thundered, declaring Guangxu feebleminded and ordering him confined to a pavilion on an island in the middle of a lake in what was then the Summer Palace. The room in which the emperor was held was called the "Empty Chamber."[5] She then ordered the reformers arrested and executed.

IN HER EFFORTS to save the dynasty, Cixi exploited xenophobia. Playing a double game, she encouraged the creation of village militias, with an eye toward a general insurrection against the "Barbarian devils" to whom she was apparently so accommodating. Within these militias a secret society called the Fist of Justice arose; its adherents were known as Boxers. The most untutored elements of the population were now urged to revolt by the most conservative cliques of the literary oligarchy, the very people who had made China, in Lu Xun's words, "a windowless house whose many people, slumbering inside, will die asphyxiated."[6]

In June 1900 Cixi declared war on the barbarians and appealed to the populace "to eat their flesh and sleep in their skins."[7] The mass rising of popular anger claimed its first victims among the missionaries and their flocks and among foreign diplomats, but it was unable to prevail against the Western and Japanese forces that hastily disembarked in Tientsin. The court fled, and negotiations were eventually held, but not before Peking was abandoned to pillage.

Once again the West rescued the regime it had undermined, thereby contributing to China's paralysis and helping to ripen it for future revolutions. But Europe, carried away by its own dynamism, also marveled at the prospect of what might someday be produced by this immense reservoir of labor and talent. But how? "To bring out these resources, the administration would have to be entrusted to European hands, as in Egypt, Tunisia, or Turkey,"[8] commented the president of the administrative council of the French concession in Shanghai. What China needed, he felt, was greater tutelage. An outrageous notion? Perhaps. But during the same period, Yenfu wondered whether "before undertaking anything at all," China ought not to "take the road of India or Poland."[9] Perhaps servitude was the tribute his country would have to pay the laws of Darwin.

THICK AS THEY may be at any given moment, thieves inevitably fall out. The Russo-Japanese War of 1904–05 was triggered by a quarrel over control of Manchuria, and the astonished world discovered that an Asian nation was now capable of crushing Europe's largest state. Westerners were not invincible after all! In China the war convinced both traditionalists and progressives, each in their own way, that their country, too, had finally to undertake the sort of structural reforms that had led the Empire of the Rising Sun to its new power. The army, for example, was reorganized: there were to be no more demonstrations in which "horsemen shot arrows over their shoulders, never missing an oak leaf at a distance of a hundred paces."[10]

Revolution from above and revolution from below were now in open competition. Rebellions broke out in 1906, 1907, and 1908. In that year, when Cixi died, the Mandate of Heaven passed to a three-year-old boy named Puyi. His uncle, acting as regent, yielded to the insurrection, convoking provincial assemblies in 1909 and a consultative assembly in 1910. He may well have been trying to move to a constitutional monarchy, but the Manchu dynasty itself was now increasingly under attack. On October 10, 1911, almost by accident, an uprising broke out in the Russian concession in Hankou. The garrison rallied to the insurgents, and revolution suddenly spread like wildfire. In a gesture symbolic of their liberation, Chinese men began cutting off the pigtails the Manchus had imposed since 1644.

A republic was proclaimed in Nanking, and the new state was officially inaugurated on January 1, 1912. The Gregorian calendar replaced the Chinese astrological calendar, and Sun Yatsen assumed the presidency. But on February 14 he ceded power to a dictator, General Yuan Shikai. There had been just forty-five days of democracy, the only ones China has ever known in its four-thousand-year history.

The grand machinery of Heaven had finally revolved, and a new era began. Macartney's gloomy prophecy had come to pass, largely because the hand he had extended 120 years earlier had not been grasped.

Conclusion

The Planetarium and
the Cloisonné

Liberty is a principle profoundly mistrusted by the saints and
sages of China ever since ancient times.

YEN FU, 1895[1]

Things had gone so far in China that the only possibility left
was extremism.

CHARLES DE GAULLE, 1964[2]

THE MOST SPLENDID of Macartney's gifts to Qianlong, intended to demonstrate Britain's modernity, was the planetarium, a working model of the
solar system. In return Qianlong gave the ambassador various objects of
traditional arts and crafts: jade sculptures, silk purses, and cloisonnés,
decorated enameled vases whose partitions, set off by fine brass wires,
created compartmentalized scenes.

These gifts could hardly have been more symbolic of the cultures the
two men represented. For Great Britain, exchange was the source of scientific and technological progress and of the wealth and power of nations.
Though its population still numbered fewer than ten million, the country
was already imbued with a winner's pride. Having chosen to explode across
the globe, it commanded the world's largest merchant marine and its most
powerful fleet of warships. Its explorers and privateers enjoyed full government support, as did its chartered companies, which were the world's
most active. Canada and India had been seized from France, and when
London was forced to recognize the independence of the United States
(which nevertheless remained a British customer), it resolved to compensate
for the loss by expanding in Southeast Asia and the Pacific. The British
were convinced that universal domination would fall to the society that

was most open and mobile and that commanded the most far-flung presence in an interrelated world all of whose regions had now been charted.

Qianlong's China, in the meantime, had conquered the greatest empire humanity had ever known. Its own territories were ringed by vassal states that paid tribute and acted as buffers. Pax Sinica held sway from the Caspian Sea to the Ryukyu Islands, from Lake Baikal to the gulfs of Bengal and Siam.

This immense domain was protected by a belt of arid deserts, impassable mountains, and seas infested with pirates and ripped by furious storms. But there were other protective structures as well: the Great Wall, a spiritual wall of deeply rooted prejudices, and the unshakable conviction that the Middle Empire was home to "the only Civilization under Heaven." The peoples beyond its sphere of influence were crude barbarians. Anything they produced was intrinsically deleterious and worthy of rejection, and any of their nationals who entered China were inevitably ill intentioned and therefore had to be regarded with constant suspicion. Conversely, any Chinese who left the empire otherwise than on a mission for the emperor was a civic deserter, dead in Chinese eyes.

Internally, China was divided into groupings that resembled castes more than classes, and the partitions between them were nearly as inviolable as those separating Chinese from barbarians. They could be crossed only through the study of Confucian culture, verified in the competitive examinations. Chinese sociologists often point to the social mobility permitted by this system, in which heredity played a minor role. But the requisite course of study inculcated the rules of social partitioning, of which all mandarins, however humble their origins, became the guarantors, acting as delegates of the emperor, who in turn answered for these rules before Heaven, from which he had received the mandate to preserve them. It was an order that no one could escape.

Together with its vassals, from Korea to Burma, and its traditional clients, such as India, the Philippines, and Java, China constituted a gigantic yet autarkic bloc, active and bustling, yet set in its ways, rejecting exchange with the outside world,[3] yet practicing it widely within its own borders, forming what Braudel called an economic universe. But this world, unlike the British economy, was unable to reach beyond its own borders, for it lacked a "sufficiently strong periphery to stimulate the heartland."[4] In the absence of any real competitor, China's economic power was inevitably subjugated by the ideological order. As Balazs has shown, germs of genuinely competitive capitalist development took root in China only during periods when the political order was deeply shaken.[5]

In ethnic and political terms, however, it would be wrong to call China a monolith. During the reign of Qianlong, for example, Han Chinese, Manchus, Tibetans, and others coexisted, as is shown by the many stelae from that era bearing inscriptions in these four languages, one on each side, often including calligraphic engravings of Qianlong's name.

But China was nevertheless an internally compartmentalized society sealed at its perimeter. The Macartney mission brought it into contact with a society of global free circulation, leading to a confrontation between two empires, one open, the other closed.

Each side boasted of its own superiority. China regarded its civilization as superior by nature, and expected that it would expand at the expense of inferior, baked barbarians. Britain considered its civilization superior because it was modern: founded on science, the free circulation of ideas, and the mastery of commercial exchange. Mutual misunderstanding and contempt made genuine communication impossible.

In the introduction to this book I raised the question of why China so quickly lost its centuries-long lead over other civilizations. The Macartney mission suggests at least two explanations: first, at a time when Western nations were expanding across the world, China turned in on itself; second, China obstinately curbed innovations, while Europe nurtured them.

CHILDREN SOMETIMES like to play a game walking up a down escalator. If they stop, they descend. If they take normal steps, they stay in one place. To ascend they have to scurry on all fours. Nations find themselves in much the same situation in the long convoy of humanity: those that do not move up decline; those that advance slowly mark time. Only those that rush ahead progress.

Relative movement and immobility of this kind are detectable only over long periods. Eighteenth-century China was rich in incident, and Sinologists who devote their lives to studying this period might well balk at calling this empire immobile. On the other hand, an Anglicist might fail to notice the soaring rise of British power during that same century. After all, there were poverty and shortage, turmoil and revolt; peasants were driven from their land by the draconian enclosure laws; the insolent oligarchy suffered defeats at the hands of France and the American insurgents; the annual growth rate was modest, never exceeding 2 percent.

But comparative analysis reveals that British agriculture modernized rapidly at a time when most French peasants were still living in medieval conditions, and that the synergism of its banking system, large-scale industry, and expanding trade gave Britain a lead not only over other continents, but also over the other countries of Europe.

When two straight lines diverge, an initially barely perceptible gap between them eventually becomes enormous. The Macartney expedition affords us a critical moment for measuring the growing distance between a nation on the rise in the West and an Eastern empire which, though smug in the certainty of its own global supremacy, had already fallen into lethargy.

The mission and its failure represent a microcosm of the confrontations that marked the two centuries to come: the cultural collision of the West and the Far East; the clash of the industrialized countries and the Third World.

Yet the encounter between the Lion and the Dragon brooks no oversimplified comparisons. In remaining closed to the outside world, China was obeying its own logic. Britain's attempt to force an opening, on the other hand, entailed a measure of inconsistency. Confronted with the originality of Chinese civilization, Macartney and his companions were no more open-minded than China was in assessing the West. Though well aware that they were dealing with a refined culture, they approached the empire no differently than second-rate captains and merchants approached minor peoples of Africa. They were men of their time, Enlightenment adventurers of technology and the market, and they viewed the noble savage and the refined exotic in the same way: as a potential exchange partner, an object of commerce, someone who had never read Adam Smith and never would. They made little distinction between the four Chinese who sailed with them and the Papuan they brought back.

The British were more than happy to spend many a guinea in their effort to charm the grown child with their mechanical instruments, just as they charmed Africans with glass beads. This was a more costly seduction, but the procedure was essentially the same. Except that it didn't work. "The Chinese are timid and superstitious and naturally disinclined to innovation," said a company report given to Macartney before his departure.[6] This assessment was largely confirmed by events, and the Chinese rejection of novelty was itself taken as evidence of backwardness. The British refused to recognize the right of civilizations to be different.

They felt that it was their right, perhaps even their duty, to open China to international trade, in accordance with rules established by the West. If China refused to bend to the practices of European traders, then it was simply in the wrong.[7] Macartney acted as a merchant of exoticism, offering the British not only tea, silk, lacquer, and porcelain, but also the pleasure of satisfying dreams of far-off adventure. He meant to appropriate the originality of this civilization, which had aroused the covetousness of consumers all over Europe, for the benefit of the United Kingdom. He lamented only that he was unable to inspire any reciprocal desire. "It has been difficult, nay almost impossible, to persuade them of the advantage which would result to themselves from extending the import of foreign articles in China."[8] These poor people rejected the benefits of commerce and civilization, of which Britain was the heart.

Macartney's conduct effectively denied the validity of Chinese civilization. His rejection of the kowtow, his disgust at sitting cross-legged, and his haughty amusement at scenes of everyday life show that his view was as one-sided as that of the Chinese: there was only one civilization toward which all humanity must strive, and England was its flower and its driving force. This unique and universal cultural model was the WASP civilization in which the Bible was crossbred with rationalism, and predestination was supplanted by the duty of enterprise. Macartney's task was to extend this culture to China, and his experiences convinced him that the effort required would be superhuman and that violence would someday be necessary.

The history of the nineteenth and twentieth centuries evolved on the basis of these prejudices, leading to Europe's colonization of peoples of color and their subsequent revolt. The conflicts emerged with the very first instances of contact, which could instead have abolished them.

But at least their haughty examination of the Chinese taught the British something about themselves. Societies, like individuals, acquire self-knowledge through knowledge of the other. Every discovery of a difference raises two questions: Why are they like that? and Why aren't I?

In the course of their journey, the attitude of the British shifted from enthusiasm to scorn. But on the return trip, Macartney, aided by Sir George, had plenty of time to ponder his "Observations" at his leisure. Excerpts of them were published for the first time only in 1908, a more complete version appearing in 1962. They are in fact more than mere observations. Rising to the level of ethnology and philosophy of history, they establish Macartney as a penetrating and farsighted thinker, a fact that modern Chinese historians are now beginning to acknowledge.[9]

Like Tocqueville in America and Custine in Russia, Macartney was an honest observer: "If I venture to say anything upon the manners and character of the Chinese, I must begin by confessing that I am very far from being a competent judge of them. . . . I am sensible that it was impossible to avoid falling into mistakes. . . . I may have formed wrong judgments and have deceived myself; but as I do not mean that others should be deceived, I fairly own my disadvantages and give previous notice of the nature of the information that may be expected from me. It will be chiefly the result of what I saw and heard on the spot, however imperfectly, not of what I had read in books or been told in Europe."[10] Difference makes visible what one fails at first to notice. To understand oneself, one must first view the other. Macartney and his companions had spent years preparing their Chinese mirror. Now that they dipped the glass into the irreplaceable magic liquid of reality, the layer of tin had formed, and the mirror reflected the image of their own society. China taught them to perceive the West, and as they pondered the characteristics of their own world, they were astonished at the opposite characteristics of Celestial society.

Having noted Chinese immobility, they gained a clearer sense of their own motion. Their appreciation of individual initiative was enhanced as they noted that individuals in China could undertake only what society expected of them. They grasped more sharply the strength of the human personality in the West by observing that the only recognized human entity in China was the collective. They took the measure of the role of competition in their own country when they saw that no one in China could escape his assigned place, for to do so would offend against the established hierarchy. They saw more clearly how important merchants were in Britain by observing how deeply they were scorned in China. They became aware of their own devotion to the new by discovering the cult of the immutable. In short, they gained a clearer insight into the fact that individualism, competition, and innovation were the wellsprings of their own wealth and power.

GREAT EMPIRES are founded by great centralizers capable of molding unformed clay in their iron hands: Nebuchadnezzar, Xerxes, Alexander, Caesar, Charlemagne, Peter the Great, Napoleon, Stalin, Mao. These giants mastered rebellious elements and imposed hierarchical organizations that long survived them, great pyramids able to withstand assaults. None was more solidly constructed than the Chinese Empire, whose architects were Confucius and Qin Shihuangdi. Everything was ordered so as to ensure the durability and grandeur of the state; the individual was annihilated and humanity exalted only in its collective dimension. Every subject of the empire was incorporated into some hierarchy, and individual consciousness was filed down and polished by common values universally imposed.

All intermediary groups—corporations, orders, estates, castes—were instruments in the consolidation of the overall architecture, forming an assemblage of juxtaposed miniature societies each closed into itself, nested one within another. The social pyramid, with its smooth and impenetrable outer surface, was united against the outside world. But it was honeycombed within. The division of labor reinforced both the separation of groups and their interdependence, and the society built on this blueprint reproduced itself indefinitely. The whole commanded the parts.

At the peak of the monument stood the Son of Heaven, the earthly incarnation of the deity. Immediately below him, cementing the pyramid's summit and its edges, stood the Grand Council, the viceroys, the governors, and the entire hierarchy of literati–cum–state functionaries. As the only ones capable of reading and writing the language of the elite, they were charged with transmitting the emperor's will and the empire's values to the masses. Next came the peasants, the great mass necessary to the subsistence of the whole. They were the real producers, the other classes serving solely to allow them to produce. Below the peasants stood the artisans, of whom it was asked only that they provide the tools the peasants needed to cultivate the land. Below the artisans stood the merchants, who were not producers but mere parasites. Living only from exchange, they created nothing* but simply harvested money at others' expense. The mere fact that they grew rich accorded them no dignity.

Such was the shape of Chinese society from the third century before Christ to the beginning of the twentieth. It was a construction as solid as granite, defying time. Little freedom was left to individuals, who were regarded as incapable of discerning what was good for them. In this it was the converse of a free society, in which each person, taken singly, is considered the embodiment of all humanity, and individuals are assumed to know better than the collective what is best for them.

The consciousness of the Chinese Macartney encountered had been shaped by this extraordinarily long-lived system and the principles that lay beneath it. They knew that the empire's longevity depended on constant defense of the established rules, which had to be eternally respected. They had every reason in the world—in *their* world—to reject the advances of this "long nose" who came to speak to them of adventure. Qianlong and his mandarins were proud of their system, and for good reason. They were devoted to the centralizing bureaucracy, a masterwork that through the centuries had dominated a diversity of historical situations and endured despite profound transformations.

Contrary to the claims of wooden Marxist jargon, the system abolished by the revolution of 1949 was not "feudalism," which may be defined as a system in which personal status is *received* at birth and not *acquired*, and in which relations of personal dependence on a hereditary nobility prevail.

---

* Not until 1986 did China include the tertiary sector (services and trade) in the calculation of the gross national product.

Hereditary nobility had been abolished in China in the third century before Christ.*

A fully centralized state arose at that time, impersonally administered (in accordance with universally imposed rules) by interchangeable, salaried officials liable to revocation by a stroke of the imperial pen. Beginning with the Tang dynasty (in the seventh century), these officials were recruited through anonymous competitions. The empire's administrative districts, all subordinate to a single ruler, were quite unlike feudal fiefs, whose extents varied according to their suzerain's expertise with the sword. All public officials were appointed by the emperor, who, doling out rewards and punishments, maintained strict control of the bureaucratic network in which the country was bound. All power was concentrated in his hands.

The goal of the system was power and effectiveness. Most of all it had to win wars and sustain agricultural production. The dynasty was responsible for order and subsistence. If it failed in this double task, the Mandate of Heaven was withdrawn from it. The dynasty was simply the first servant of the empire, which antedated it and would endure after it.

This system worked so well in China that it spread to other countries, such as Korea and Vietnam. In some respects it even served as a model in the West, helping to inaugurate examinations and competitions in France under Louis XV, for instance. Its advantages are obvious. It provided a stable structure for a territory larger than Europe from the Atlantic to the Urals, with lines of defense, roads, a postal system—an entire web of command. The state controlled the market through its massive grain purchases, its taxes, and the inventories it stockpiled in public warehouses. Only at a far more recent date did the countries of Europe attain the centralized state established by the Chinese model.

Laws had been uniform ever since the age of Qin Shihuangdi, and so were currency, taxes, weights and measures, and even the permissible wheelbase of handcarts. A uniform writing system was imposed, and later exported to the peripheral monarchies of Korea, Japan, and Vietnam. For more than twenty centuries Chinese civilization spread with incomparable power and continuity; the duration of its brilliance is unparalleled in human history.

BUT THIS CONSTRUCTION had its Achilles' heel, and its weakness was exposed when the germs of power sown by individualism began to flower in West-

---

* Only rarely did elements of feudalism persist under the centralized state. The Manchu nobility under the Qings and the recognized descendants of Confucius are two examples.

ern societies, first of all in England. The slow process of germination took many centuries, but the harvest was sudden. The model of centralized order, regarded as perfect at its conception and virtually unchanged for two millennia, was suddenly confronted with the nascent, turbulent, incomplete yet already strangely effective model of social freedom.

The gap between the "developed" and "developing" countries arose in a very brief period relative to the duration of human existence. When Western explorers first encountered them, even the most primitive tribes of South America or equatorial Africa had reached technological levels attained by the populations of Europe two thousand years before Christ. The Chinese had attained a level comparable to that of France under Louis XIV. This unevenness is easily accounted for by the geographical and historical circumstances that drove some societies forward and held others back, causing the intermixing of the former and the isolation of the latter. A development gap of thirty-five centuries represents about a thousandth of the total span of human existence, which is roughly three and a half million years. There is no possible justification for any notion of racial superiority of white people over people of color.

Macartney's retinue approached China in the certainty that they were superior to all other Europeans. They returned with a new certainty: that they were also far superior to the Chinese. They found that the empire whose wonders had been hailed since Marco Polo's day was actually quite backward. And why? Because it scorned progress, science, and the spirit of enterprise.

Macartney and his companions made a notable contribution to the exaltation of Anglo-Saxon superiority that spread through the world during the next two hundred years. The repercussions of their accounts bolstered the dogma of European superiority, which in turn served to legitimate the annexation of countless territories of Asia, Africa, and the Pacific. Jules Ferry and the Third Republic spoke an identical language, claiming to be bringing "civilization" to "savages."

The West's virtually messianic faith in itself created a terrible contradiction, for it was incompatible with the universalist principles crystallized in the French Revolution and ultimately shared by all of Europe: the populations subjected to European domination were denied liberty, equality, and fraternity. This contradiction ran so deep that in the end the West came to hate itself for having built colonial empires, and the era of decolonization, which should have brought it back into harmony with its own genius, instead brought a mood of self-flagellation.

For their part, the dominated countries were inevitably outraged by the brutality with which the West ravaged their traditions. They had pride, and rightly so, for a people without pride loses its taste for life, especially if, like India or China, their home is the hearth of an ancient, refined civilization. The revolt of the peoples of the Third World against the West was a healthy rejection of foreign domination that had denied their identity. For any people with the resources to form a nation, no price is too high to pay for independence. But the thirst for independence is rooted in depths of passion, and decolonization also brought a flowering of misguided ideas.

Marxists and pro-Marxists managed to convince not only the socialist countries and the Third World, which were only too happy to believe it, but also the intelligentsia of the West that the development of the colonizing countries and the underdevelopment of the colonies were consequences of the plunder of the latter by the former. This allegation ignored the fact that the Third World's poverty predated colonization and likewise survived it (or, more often, was reborn after it). Underdevelopment, which really ought to have been called *nondevelopment*, is a permanent, universal phenomenon. Ignorance, disease, multiple forms of subjugation (slavery, the oppression of women, dependence of one group on another), malnutrition, and fear of illness, famine, and war have been the common lot of the species since humanity's appearance on earth. Underdevelopment is not an anomaly; development is a miracle, and a recent one at that.

It is true, of course, that the irruption of advanced civilization destabilized and eventually destroyed the traditional societies from within. But that is no reason to idealize them retrospectively. In China, as in the primitive societies of Africa, Asia, the Americas, and the Pacific, terrible scourges existed long before the West's arrival: drought, leprosy, malaria, infant mortality, mutilation of women, not to mention cannibalism. These occurred not consequent to but prior to colonization, which in most cases actually alleviated them.

What the colonizers brought to the colonized was not poverty but subjugation, which in the long run was intolerable and debilitating. And that is where the contradiction lies: this subjugation was by no means the best method of exporting the reflexes that had been responsible for launching the West on its path to development. Western civilization could not be transmitted by colonization, but only by freedom and exchange, the factors that lay at its roots.

In point of fact, colonization was of little profit to the West, even in economic terms. Spain and Portugal, the most dynamic countries of the fifteenth and sixteenth centuries, were undermined by their colonies in subsequent centuries. Britain prospered before its imperial conquests, and it is now estimated that at its apogee the empire was responsible for only a small portion of its wealth. The countries that have undergone the most astonishing economic miracles since 1945—Germany, Japan, and Italy—had been divested of their colonies. Those that lost empires with which they had lived symbiotically—the Netherlands, France, Belgium—experienced rapid economic growth precisely from the moment that they were relieved of their colonies. The richest countries of Europe—Switzerland and Sweden—never even had any. The reason for this is that while trade brings profits, colonization eventually becomes costly. Even in the 1780s, when Macartney was governor of Madras, he realized that India was costing Britain more than it was returning. Only a triangular trade with China would permit the deficit to be made up.

Colonization was so foreign to the Western spirit that it was most often an unexpected result of unforeseen difficulties. Except in the case of virtually unpopulated territories, the colonizers generally began by proposing not to annex countries but merely to trade with them, which would have been to their mutual advantage. Expanding Europe needed new markets, and the traditional societies would have been able to modernize had they accepted trade. This was especially true of China. The objective of all the missions sent to Peking from the end of the sixteenth to the beginning of the nineteenth century was to propose economic exchange. The resort to force, the cession of territories, and the move to impose direct administration were only consequences of the Manchu dynasty's rejection of these overtures—or, later on, of its inability to honor commitments made grudgingly. The British had earlier been obliged to take over direct management of India in order to deal with anarchy. The West's preference would have been for trading posts scattered along the edges of these vast empires, but their collapse compelled the assumption of direct responsibilities it would happily have done without.

Yes, colonization entailed unacceptable effects of domination. But who shall cast the first stone? Why should the West stand alone in the dock? The Arabs colonized a large part of Africa and introduced slavery long before the Europeans picked up that baton. Islam converted more than half of Asia by the scimitar. China, after being conquered by the Mongols and the Manchus, in turn occupied Mongolia and Manchuria and annexed Tibet and Turkestan. India, Burma, and Indochina were colonized by the Mongols and the Chinese before being taken over by the British and French. Korea was ruled by China, then by Japan, before being split in two, half falling under Soviet, half under American control. And Russia was the last great colonial power.

The colonizers always proclaimed their civilizing mission, a pretext never more justified than in the case of the West, which introduced medicine and hygiene, reduced famine and mortality, and rationalized production, bringing traditional societies hitherto immobilized by under-development into the mobile era of development. Is the West any more guilty than any of the great nations that have sought to make their mark on the outside world?

No more guilty than the floods or tidal waves that inundate countries. The only reasonable candidate for prosecution in such cases would be the omnipotent leader of the victimized country if he refused to recognize such natural phenomena even after witnessing a succession of them. And that is more or less what Qianlong did by scornfully rejecting the resources of progress offered him by the British, in the name of the inviolable order of which he was the guarantor. His fierce hatred of "felonious merchants" was reprised by the Chinese Communist party after 1949.

THE MIDDLE EMPIRE rejected commercial accords that could have brought it into the network of international production. But it lacked the means with which to shield its subjects from consumerist temptations. China was abruptly incorporated into the world market not as a commercial and industrial power but as a consumer of drugs.

By rejecting a process of opening in 1793, it was condemned to suffer future aggression, whereas had it acted otherwise, it could have drawn its own regeneration from British competition. Determinists, of course, would argue that this was impossible. But what happened in Russia during the century before Macartney and in Japan during the century after him makes it tempting to believe that it was in fact quite possible. A perceptive people acting with farsightedness can cast off decadence and take its place in the convoy of progress.

In 1695 Peter the Great, halted at the walls of Azov and unable to defeat the Turks, realized how backward his country was. He decided to go west—to France, Holland, and England—in search of the innovations and technical assistance he needed. During this journey, in 1697 and 1698, this most imperious of despots became a humble borrower of ideas. On his return to Russia, he placed the nobility and the clergy in check, cut off the beards and shortened the dress of the ruling class, sent it to the Western school, reformed the army and the tax system, created ministries and a senate, developed education, adopted a mercantile policy that fostered exports, and brought forth a flowering of factories.

He died a detested man in 1725, but he had launched Russia's modernization.

THE SUDDEN EMERGENCE of Japan in the last third of the nineteenth century is further evidence that a nation can absorb the lessons of a cultural collision and make centuries of progress in a single generation.

Japan had always "received China's wisdom." In the middle of the seventeenth century the country was closed to all foreign influence, the sole contact with the outside world being a Dutch ship that docked in Nagasaki once a year.

In 1853, sixty years after the Macartney expedition, the American commodore Matthew Perry forcibly entered the port of Shimoda, in Tokyo Bay, and delivered a note to the Japanese government. Six months later he returned for the response, and in March 1854 Japan signed the Treaty of Kaganawa, which opened two of its ports to Western ships year round. Forty-one years later, in 1895, the Japanese fleet and army crushed China. In 1904–05 they annihilated the Russian forces in the Far East, on land and sea alike. In just four decades Meiji Japan emerged from its isolation with its head high, entering the concert of powers.

The Japanese dealt with the West in order to imitate it and catch up to it. If they pretended humility, it was in order to achieve domination later on. They were awakened by the cultural collision of 1853. After some years of hesitation, they sent missions to the most advanced countries of the West, and they borrowed forms of political, economic, and social organization from the Westerners: an English-style parliament; French civil and penal codes; a French police force; a Prussian army. And most of all, after a long period of state control of the economy, Anglo-Saxon-style companies, free trade, ports, and banks.

No doubt it was easier for Japan than for China to enroll in the Western school. The Chinese were convinced of their own perfection, while the Japanese had had centuries of practice at remaining true to themselves while borrowing from others. In shifting their compass from China to the West, they were merely changing models. They realized that they had to imitate or perish.

The Celestial Empire, on the contrary, was unprepared for any such leap into the unknown. In the last years of the nineteenth century the Yang Wa—or Movement for Western Affairs—took inspiration from the same principles as the Meijis. But it faced far too much resistance all along the social pyramid, from base to summit.

"The Japanese deeply detest the Westerners," a Chinese man of letters observed just after the Sino-Japanese War.[11] "Yet they devote themselves to Western studies, with a heavy heart, but also with courage and perseverance. They know that without these studies they would be incapable of preserving their country." The author of these lines, Yenfu, deplored the fact that "the mentality and mores of China do not recognize the course of history."

The world turned without China, trying with increasing urgency to draw the Middle Empire into its orbit. But China did not respond to the pull. To do so would have required a mental metamorphosis that no single cultural revolution would have sufficed to bring about.

TO ENTER another's school, the Chinese would have had to jettison a millennial pride. It took two centuries of tragedy for them to begin to get used to this idea, and it is far from certain that they have fully grasped it even now.

Between 1793 and 1978 China remained devoted to its own model. Despite several attempts (each swiftly renounced), it refused to humble itself at any foreign school. There was no civilization save China's. Anything evil inevitably came from abroad. Anything good came from within.

Not until the ouster of the Gang of Four and the reexamination of Mao's legacy did a revision of this interpretation of China's past begin. But official historiography has been slow to reassess the past two hundred years in the light of the courageous choices of 1978.* Even after the third plenum of the Eleventh Congress of the Chinese Communist party, it continued to quote Mao, for whom foreign capitalism played a predominant role in the decomposition of the Chinese economy.[13] Freedom of trade was stigmatized as a euphemism for the "machinery of the world capitalist market"[14]—in other words, of the open world. Qianlong's and Cixi's rejection of planetary realities was still endorsed, albeit in Marxist phraseology.

Has anything really changed, or is history simply repeating itself in Peking? Marxism is as foreign to the Chinese as the Manchu dynasty was, yet like the dynasty, it has reinforced China's isolation. It is important not to forget the circumstantial element in the attitude of Qianlong and his successors. It so happened that when the West came knocking at the gate, the guardian of that gate was a Manchu emperor. But the Qings had become zealous devotees of the Chinese cult of self-worship. By pandering to the most extreme Sinicity, they strove to ensure their domination of the Chinese people, and the reflex of closure was encouraged by the fragility

---

* In a 1988 thesis the young historian Zhu Yong broke with the view upheld in the bulk of all previous works and severely criticized the closure policy of the Manchu dynasty.[12]

of this dynasty of foreign origin. The survival of an invariant system had to be guaranteed by shutting out the outside world. This may have flattered Chinese pride, but it was good for Manchu power as well.

Manchus and Marxists, foreigners and internationalists—both were more Chinese than the Chinese themselves. The unshakable conviction that China was sufficient unto itself was the ideological premise underlying any number of claims and policies: Qianlong's reply to King George, announcing that China had no need of his country's products; the persecution of foreign religions, especially the Christian communities, to make them cease their efforts to alter Chinese mores; Cixi's protestation after China's crushing military defeat by Japan that no one could have anticipated an attack by the Dwarfs; Mao's expulsion of Russian experts, his proclamation that China must rely on its own strength, and his scorning of America as a paper tiger.

How many Chinese intellectuals today continue to uphold China's fidelity to its own self-sufficient uniqueness! How many would endorse this statement of that fascinating thinker Yenfu, an Anglophile earlier in his career, made during the revolution of 1912: "In three centuries of progress, the peoples of the West have elaborated three principles: egotism, murder, and dishonesty. How different are the principles of Confucius and Meng-tzu, vast and deep as Heaven and Earth"![15]

Such narcissism inevitably results in an immense failure of self-understanding. How was it that a handful of Western soldiers some twelve thousand miles from their bases were able to cut the Chinese army to pieces on its own soil? What accounts for the heavy burden of underdevelopment today? So many masterworks, so much invention, so much intelligence, so much ardor and toil, so much collective genius! Forty centuries of brilliant civilization, forty years of revolutionary regeneration! And for what? To attain a standard of living comparable to that of some tropical republic whose ancestors were still mired in the Stone Age during the nineteenth century?

ALL PEOPLE ARE born equal in rights and dignity. But not all people, let alone all societies, have an equal aptitude for technological, market, and industrial civilization. Some spurt wealth as a geyser spurts water, while others cannot, do not want to, or do not know how. What was lacking among the Chinese was not individual aptitude but a cultural environment.

In Batavia, even before their arrival in China, Macartney's companions noted that the Chinese, drawn by "the desire of accumulating wealth in a foreign land, . . . apply to every industrious occupation, and obtain whatever either care or labour can accomplish. . . . They do, at length, acquire fortunes, which they value by the time and labour required to earn them."[16] They observed a similar situation in Macao. In Hong Kong, Taiwan, and Singapore, overseas Chinese have attained such great levels of productivity that their standard of living over the past forty years has risen ten or twenty times as high as that of their brothers, sisters, and cousins in the People's Republic, whose starting point was equivalent. Today, as in the past, some of the world's most daring entrepreneurs, skillful financiers, and talented merchants are Chinese. So long as they do not remain in China.

Nor can there be any doubt about the effectiveness of the Chinese state when it acts in its natural domain. Brilliant successes have been achieved in the launching of missiles and satellites. China moved from atomic fission to thermonuclear fusion in half the time it took France. But when the same people achieve a growth rate unequaled in the world during forty years of a market economy, while stagnating under a bureaucratic system of state planning, certain obvious conclusions must be drawn.

The Communist regime has perpetuated the Celestial bureaucracy of the Qianlong era. It is hostile to profit, to merchants, to foreign trade, to the very presence of foreigners, and to any initiative that does not come from itself. The small states of Southeast Asia peopled by Chinese released from this tutelage have taken to production and commerce with ease. In their daily contacts with other nationalities, both Japanese and Western, they have shed the millennial conviction that China's is the only civilization and that all other peoples are mere barbarians.

EVERY COUNTRY has a tendency to consider itself the center of the world. Every people is ethnocentric. The Gê Indians of central Brazil wept when the ethnologist Kurt Unkel left their lands, because they did not believe that he could survive if separated from the only people who led lives worth living: themselves.[17] But rarely has any nation carried this defect as far as China has. Its present inferiority flows largely from its sense of superiority.

Underdevelopment is a combination of isolation and immobility, linked by demography. Development is the marriage of openness and the reciprocal exchange of innovation. Qianlong and Macartney were each convinced that they represented the world's most powerful nation. However embryonic Britain's power may have been at the time, the history of the subsequent century proved Macartney right.

Had the ambassador presented his offer differently, had the emperor received it differently, China would likely have "awakened" without the world having to "tremble." Its creativity might have diversified; its capacity for progress might have soared. Instead the confrontation between arrogance and self-sufficiency robbed humanity of incalculable riches.

But the lessons of this abortive rendezvous remain. Qianlong and Macartney are not dead but live among us still, reincarnated in this century. Perhaps they are immortal.

Biographical Notes on
Major Personalities

EUROPEANS

ABEL, CLARKE (b. 1780), physician in Amherst's retinue and author of an account of the Amherst mission.

ADEODATO, FATHER PIERO (c. 1755–1822), Italian Augustine missionary. Arrived in China 1784. Clockmaker and mechanic, assigned to assist the personnel of the Macartney mission in setting up the exhibit of scientific presents in the Yuanming Yuan. Driven out of Peking in 1811 by persecution of missionaries.

ALEXANDER, WILLIAM (1767–1816), leading painter of the Macartney expedition, later a conservator at the British Museum. Produced a collection of watercolor prints and an unpublished journal.

ALMEIDA, FATHER JOSÉ BERNARDO D' (1728–1805), Portuguese Jesuit missionary. Arrived in Peking 1759. Astronomer, physician, and pharmacist, named president of the Tribunal of Mathematics 1783. Openly hostile to the British. Macartney rejected his services as interpreter.

AMHERST, WILLIAM PITT (1773–1857), nephew of Baron Jeffrey Amherst (commander of victorious British forces in Canada during the Seven Years' War), named after William Pitt the elder, his uncle's patron. Led the embassy sent by George III to the emperor Jiaqing in 1816; met Napoleon in Saint Helena in July 1817. Governor-general of India 1826. Author of an unpublished journal of his China mission.

AMIOT, FATHER JOSEPH-MARIE (1718–93), French Jesuit missionary. Arrived in China 1750. Mathematician, physicist. Correspondent of the Académie des Sciences and the Royal Society. Qianlong's official interpreter for Western languages, spiritual leader of the missionaries in Peking. Illness prevented him from meeting Macartney; died two days after the ambassador's departure from Peking. Author of a vast and largely unexplored corpus of correspondence.

ANDERSON, AENEAS, Macartney's valet. Gave his notes and memoirs to a publicist, Coombes, who edited and published them in 1795.

BARROW, JOHN (1764–1848), comptroller on the Macartney mission and mathematics tutor to young Thomas Staunton. George Staunton's librarian 1794, secretary to Macartney 1800. Author of many travel books, including two (1804 and 1806) on the Macartney expedition. A founder of the Royal Society of Geography and the author of *The Mutiny and the Piratical Seizure of H.M.S. Bounty* (1831).

BENSON, LT. COL. GEORGE (born c. 1755), commander of Macartney's guard (twenty artillerymen, twenty infantrymen, ten light dragoons) during the China mission, former collaborator of Macartney (with rank of captain) in India. Promoted to lieutenant colonel to enhance prestige of embassy.

BERTRAND, HENRI (1773–1844), accompanied Napoleon to Saint Helena after loyally serving him during Egyptian campaign. Author of *Cahiers de Sainte-Hélène*.

CHARPENTIER-COSSIGNY, J. F. (1730–1809), civil engineer in Mauritius, traveled to Batavia and Canton for several months. Author of *Observations*, on Staunton's account of the Macartney mission.

CONSTANT, CHARLES DE (1762–1833), cousin of Benjamin Constant. Lived in Canton September 1789–January 1793 during third trip to China. Encountered Macartney's squadron in Strait of Sunda; predicted failure of the mission.

COUSIN-MONTAUBAN, GEN. CHARLES-GUILLAUME (1796–1878), commander of French troops in Tientsin in 1860, victor in the Battle of Palikao. Participated in the taking of Peking, October 1860, and allowed soldiers to plunder the Yuanming Yuan.

CZARTORYSKI, ADAM JERZY (1770–1861), Polish prince held hostage in St. Petersburg after partition of Poland. Became friends with Grand Duke Alexander, who, upon accession to throne, 1802, named him foreign minister. Organizer of the Golovkin mission to China and the man to whom Potocki addressed his reports.

DINWIDDIE, JAMES (1746–1815), mathematician and expert in scientific experimentation. Met Macartney in Dublin after several speaking tours of Britain. Custodian of the planetarium and hence designated the mission's astronomer. Continued his scientific work in India until 1805; returned to Britain rich. Author of journal of the Macartney mission published 1868 by his grandson, W. Proudfoot-Jardine.

DUNDAS, HENRY (FIRST VISCOUNT MELVILLE; 1742–1811), leading British politician and merchant. Member of Parliament 1774, close friend of William Pitt the younger, member of Board of Control of East India Company 1784, president of board 1793. Minister of the Interior 1791. Played decisive role in organizing Macartney mission. Minister of War 1794, First Lord of the Admiralty 1804.

EADES, HENRY (c. 1750–93), mechanic, first member of Macartney mission to die in China; buried with great ceremony August 20, 1793.

ELGIN, JAMES LORD (1811–63), son of British ambassador to Ottoman Turkey, commander of British troops in Tientsin and Peking 1860. Allowed his troops to plunder Yuanming Yuan October 1860. First viceroy of India 1862.

ELLIOT, CHARLES (1801–75), superintendent of British trade in Far East during tenure of Commissioner Lin in Canton (1839). Advised Westerners to resign themselves to loss of the opium burned by Lin on Humen beach in July. His attitude, meant to avert confrontation, caused sharp reaction in London.

ELLIOT, GEORGE (1784–1863), British admiral, commander of fleet that attacked China 1840–41. Relieved by Pottinger 1841.

ELLIS, HENRY (1777–1855), naval officer employed by East India Company. Secretary to Lord Amherst and third-ranking member of 1816 mission to China, after Thomas Staunton. Author of a journal of the mission.

ENTRECASTEAUX, JEAN-ANTOINE D' (1739–93), French admiral, commander of Indian Ocean fleet 1785, charged with intelligence mission to investigate British forces east of Cape of Good Hope. In Canton February 1787, tried to alert Chinese authorities to British expansionism. Died at sea in search of La Pérouse.

GEORGE III (1738–1820), king of Great Britain and Ireland 1760–1811. Policies helped trigger American War of Independence. Ardently supported Macartney expedition to China. After crises of madness 1765, 1788, and 1803–04, sank definitively into insanity 1810. His son, future George IV, became regent 1811.

GILLAN, HUGH (c. 1745–98), physician of Macartney mission, chosen to gather information on Chinese medicine, pharmacology, and chemistry. Author of extensive notes on these themes.

GOLOVKIN, YURI ALEXANDROVICH, ambassador of Tsar Alexander I to emperor of China 1805. Got as far as Urga (Ulan-Bator), Mongolia, whereupon he was sent back to Russia.

GOVEA, ALEXANDRO (1751–1808), Portuguese missionary, arrived in China 1784. Bishop of Peking and member of Tribunal of Mathematics, despite ignorance of subject.

GOWER, SIR ERASMUS (1742–1814), captain of the *Lion* and of naval squadron during Macartney expedition, knighted August 1792 to enhance prestige of embassy. Rear admiral 1799, vice admiral 1804, admiral 1809. Author of memoirs that include an account of the mission to China.

GRAMMONT, FATHER JEAN-JOSEPH DE (1736–1812), mathematician and musician, Jesuit missionary, younger brother of Marquis de Grammont. Arrived in Peking 1770. Authorized to return to Canton 1785 for reasons of health. Made contact with Europeans of all nationalities. Returned to Peking, offered services to Macartney 1793 and to Dutch ambassador Isaak Titsing 1795. Author of many illuminating unpublished letters on life of missionaries in China.

GUIGNES, LOUIS-CHRÉTIEN DE (1759–1845), official "French resident in China" 1784–1800, trustee of property of the Lazarists in Macao and Canton, close observer of Macartney embassy. Interpreter for Dutch ambassador Titsing 1794–95. Author of account of his stay in China, particularly of Dutch embassy.

HANNA, FATHER ROBERT (1762–97), French Lazarist missionary of Irish origin. Arrived Macao November 1788. Mathematician. Tried to move to Peking, traveling aboard the *Lion*, June 1793; barred in Tientsin, sent back to Canton aboard the *Hindostan*. Finally arrived Peking June 1794, became member of Tribunal of Mathematics.

HICKEY, THOMAS (1741–1824), painter with Macartney expedition.

HOLMES, SAMUEL, soldier of Macartney's guard; author of account of the mission published 1798; named sergeant major 1804.

HÜTTNER, HANS CHRISTIAN (1765–1847), Leipzig-born tutor of Thomas Staunton 1791–97. Author of account of Macartney mission.

KOSIELSKI, FATHER ROMUALD, Polish astronomer and only missionary allowed to meet with Macartney during mission's last days in Peking.

LAMIOT, FATHER LOUIS-FRANÇOIS-MARIE (1767–1831), French Lazarist missionary, arrived in Macao October 1791, tried to move to Peking June 1793, traveling aboard the *Lion* with Father Hanna. Both sent back to Canton aboard the *Hindostan*. Arrived Peking June 1794, served as court interpreter and superior of French mission 1812. Forced by persecution to withdraw to Macao 1819; refused permission to reenter France 1825. Author of abundant correspondence and copious observations on Macartney mission.

LINDSAY, HUGH HAMILTON, commissioner of East India Company, unofficially assigned

1832 to reconnoiter coasts of central China aboard the *Amherst*. March–September entered ports of Xiamen, Fuzhou, Ningbo, and Shanghai (all officially closed to foreign ships).

LOWE, SIR HUDSON (1769–1844), governor of Saint Helena and Napoleon's jailer. Author of memoirs.

MACARTNEY, GEORGE LORD (1737–1806), created Baron of Lisanoure, later Viscount of Dervock in Irish peerage, Knight of the Order of Bath, ambassador extraordinary to emperor of China. Previously ambassador to Russian court, secretary for Ireland, governor-general of British West Indies, governor of Madras. Made an earl upon return from China, later Baron of Parkhurst in English peerage and envoy to Count of Provence (future King Louis XVIII), Verona. Ended career as governor of the Cape. Died without issue. Author of journal of his embassy to China and of "Observations" on China, as well as voluminous correspondence and notes covering entire career—mostly unpublished, at his own request.

MACKINTOSH, WILLIAM, agent of East India Company and commander of the *Hindostan*. Had extensive personal interest in ships he commanded and enjoyed broad support from British cabinet.

MAXWELL, ACHESON (born c. 1750), private secretary to Macartney in Madras and secretary of China embassy. Named commissioner at the Exchequer upon return from China.

MONTHOLON, CHARLES (1783–1853), general, chamberlain of the French Empire. Followed Napoleon to Saint Helena; confidant and executor of Bonaparte, author of *Mémoires* and *Récits de la captivité de Napoléon*.

MORRISON, ROBERT (1782–1834), first Protestant missionary to China, arrived 1807; interpreter for Amherst mission 1816. Published Chinese translation of the Bible and *Sage Advice*, proselytizing pamphlet that had great influence on Hong Xiuquan, future leader of Taiping Rebellion. Died of cholera in Canton.

NAPIER, WILLIAM JOHN (1786–1834), first superintendent of British trade in Far East, appointed 1833 after abrogation of East India Company's monopoly. Arrived in Canton July 1834 and tried to meet viceroy while circumventing Chinese merchant guild. Two months later forced to withdraw to Macao, where he died in October.

NAPOLEON I (1769–1821), emperor of the French, prisoner at Saint Helena from October 1815; met Lord Amherst and his entourage July 1817, during their return from China.

O'MEARA, BARRY EDWARD (1786–1836), Irish doctor, Napoleon's physician at Saint Helena, author of memoirs.

PANZI, FATHER GIUSEPPE (1733–1812), Italian Jesuit missionary attached to French mission. Painter.

PARIS, BROTHER CHARLES (known as BROTHER JOSEPH; 1738–1804), French Lazarist, self-educated and multitalented, clockmaker at imperial palace, Peking.

PARISH, LT. HENRY WILLIAM (?–1798), artillery officer and geometer of Macartney expedition, commander of artillery demonstrations. Produced maps and charts of Bay of Tourane (Da Nang), Zhoushan Islands, the Great Wall, and Bay of Hong Kong. Later named aide-de-camp to Marquess Richard Wellesley, governor-general of India. Died at sea.

PIRON, JEAN-BAPTISTE (C. 1735–C. 1805), employee of French East India Company, sent to Canton 1791 to liquidate company holdings in China. Observer of Macartney mission. Agent of Ministry of Foreign Relations under the Directoire, the Consulat, and the empire. Author of notes now archived in Quai d'Orsay.

PITT, WILLIAM II (1759–1806), younger son of William Pitt, Member of Parliament 1781, Chancellor of the Exchequer, Prime Minister 1783. Governed until 1801 and again 1804–06. Stabilized British rule in India, reorganized government general, undermined smuggling by lowering taxes on tea. Pressured East India Company to support Macartney mission. Initially friendly to French Revolution, became ardent opponent when troops of the French Republic crossed Belgian border. Resolute enemy of Napoleon.

POIROT, FATHER LOUIS DE (1735–1814), French Jesuit missionary to China, painter and interpreter, summoned to Jehol August 1793. Translated second imperial edict delivered to Macartney October 7, 1793.

POTOCKI, COUNT JAN (1760–1815), Polish diplomat assigned by his cousin, Prince Adam Jerzy Czartoryski, to accompany Golovkin to Peking as "scientific" (actually political) adviser. Author of memoirs and correspondence on China expedition, written in French.

POTTINGER, SIR HENRY (1789–1856), British admiral, commander of second phase of Opium War, 1841 to August 1842. Captured Zhoushan Islands, sailed up Yangtze and seized Nanking, where he imposed first of the "unequal treaties," August 29, 1842.

PROCTOR (CAPTAIN), agent of the East India Company, commander of the *Endeavour*, sent June 1793 to meet Macartney squadron in Yellow Sea.

RAUX, FATHER NICOLAS-JOSEPH (1754–1801), French Lazarist, superior of French mission in China. Arrived in Peking 1785 as mathematician. Visited Macartney frequently before embassy's departure for Jehol. Translator, along with Poirot, of second imperial edict, October 1793. Author of rich, unpublished correspondence.

RODRIGUES, FATHER ANDRÉ (1729–96), Portuguese Jesuit missionary, arrived in Peking 1759, mathematician and astronomer. President and vice president of Tribunal of Mathematics.

SCOTT, WILLIAM, naval physician and surgeon attached to Macartney mission.

STAUNTON, SIR GEORGE LEONARD (1737–1801), doctor of medicine, University of Montpellier, doctor of laws, Oxford, met Macartney in Grenada and accompanied him to India, rendering services that earned him knighthood. Macartney's deputy and minister plenipotentiary during embassy to China. His account of the mission, published 1797, was translated into several languages and was a success throughout Europe.

STAUNTON, SIR GEORGE THOMAS (1781–1859), first British Sinologist, son of Sir George Leonard, Macartney's page during China expedition. Later commissioner and then director of East India Company in Canton. Deputy to Amherst during 1816 embassy to China. Member of Parliament 1823, advocate of war against China 1840. Author of journal of Macartney mission, journal of Amherst mission (both unpublished), and memoirs. Produced (1810) abridged translation of Manchu penal code (Ta T'sing Leu Lee), along with substantive introduction.

TITSING, ISAAK (1745–1811), former surgeon, agent of Dutch East India Company 1768; delegated to Japan to 1785, then to Bengal to 1792. Ambassador of Dutch Stathouder to Peking 1795. Author of unpublished account of his embassy.

VAN BRAAM, ANDRÉ-EVERARD (1739–1801), naval officer, agent of Dutch East India Company 1758. Long stays in Macao and Canton until 1775. Agronomist in Holland, and later in United States. Returned to Canton 1790, organized Dutch embassy, in which he served as deputy. His account of it (in French) published in Philadelphia, 1797.

WINDER, EDWARD (born c. 1760), relative of Macartney (whose mother's maiden name was Winder) and private secretary to him during China mission. Author of unpublished journal.

CHINESE AND MANCHUS

AGUI (1717–97), Manchu, dean of Grand Councillors, empire's "most competent and most popular servant" (Father Amiot). During Macartney mission participated in government only as elder statesman. Court letters often bear his signature, along with Heshen's.

AN (NGAN), FATHER, Chinese Catholic priest educated at Collegium Sinicum, Naples, granted free passage from Portsmouth to Macao by George Staunton. Helped Thomas Staunton in first Chinese lessons.

CHANGLIN (c. 1745–1811), Manchu prince, relative of emperor, governor of Zhejiang province early 1793, named viceroy of "the two Guangs" in Canton. Met Macartney in Hangzhou November 1793 and accompanied him to Canton. Author of many reports to the emperor during the embassy. Organized reception of Dutch embassy 1794. Career temporarily set back by clashes with Heshen.

CIXI (TSEU-HI; 1835–1908), concubine of emperor Xianfeng and mother of his son, future emperor Tongzhi (b. 1856). Became regent in Tongzhi's name 1862; initiated timid reforms. On death of Tongzhi had her four-year-old nephew Guangxu proclaimed emperor and continued to wield real power. Reign marked by successive disasters (Franco-Chinese War of 1885, Sino-Japanese War of 1894–95). When Guangxu tried to assert power in 1898 (leading to a hundred days of reform), had him declared simpleminded and reigned alone, supporting Chinese nationalism while also collaborating with West to preserve Manchu dynasty.

DAOGUANG (1782–1851), emperor of China 1820–51, son and successor of Jiaqing. Sent Lin Zexu to Canton 1838 with orders to end opium trade. Accepted Treaty of Nanking at end of Opium War (1842). Aware that he had allowed empire to be diminished, ordered that no posthumous stela be erected for him.

FUCHANG'AN (c. 1760–1817), Manchu leader, younger brother of Fukang'an. General 1779, Grand Councillor 1789. A creature of Heshen, to whom he was very close. Sometimes called "second minister" or "vice prime minister"; was sentenced to death at same time as Heshen, but was pardoned.

FUKANG'AN (c. 1750–96), Manchu general, elder brother of Fuchang'an. Adjunct to Agui in general staff 1773, military governor of many provinces beginning 1780, specialist in repression of revolts (Taiwan, Fujian, Tibet). Viceroy of Canton when

British opened negotiations about Macartney mission. Led campaign against Gurkhas in Tibet, 1791–92. Viceroy of Sichuan 1793. Openly hostile to British.

GUANGXU (1871–1908), emperor of China 1876–1908, cousin and successor of Tongzhi, placed on throne by Cixi, from whom he distanced himself in 1898, opening a hundred-day period of reforms aimed at modernization. Ousted and confined as feebleminded by Cixi.

GUO SHIXUN, military governor of Guangdong province, governor-general in viceroy's absence. Author of many reports to emperor September 1792–November 1793.

HESHEN (1745–99), soldier of imperial guard and later favorite of Emperor Qianlong, who considered him reincarnation of a lost love of his youth. Rapidly promoted to viceroy, then to all-powerful chief minister during 1770s. British called him "Prime Minister" or "Grand Colao." Held tight, corrupt grip on empire and rejected negotiations with Macartney. Gained greater power after Qianlong's abdication, but outlived his master by only ten days. Condemned to commit suicide by Emperor Jiaqing.

HESHITAI (born c. 1775), Manchu dignitary, brother-in-law of Emperor Jiaqing. Assigned to accompany Amherst mission August 20–28, 1816. Tried to drag ambassador before the court, triggering the rupture. Relieved of his prerogatives by Jiaqing.

HONG XIUQUAN (c. 1814–64), peasant of Guangdong province, unsuccessful candidate in mandarin examinations. After reading Morrison's Chinese pamphlet on the Bible, decided that he was younger brother of Jesus Christ. Preached an ascetic, communalist morality and roused peasants to revolt. Proclaimed himself King of Heaven 1851 and announced era of Great Peace, or Taiping. Eleven of China's eighteen provinces fell under his sway. Attack on Shanghai 1862 caused West to come to aid of Manchu dynasty. Committed suicide.

JIAQING (1760–1820), fifth son and successor of Qianlong as emperor of China. Proclaimed emperor after his father's abdication 1796, but began to rule in earnest only after Qianlong's death in 1799. Forced suicide of Heshen and eliminated his coterie of supporters. His reign was shaken by revolts. Survived an attempted assassination in 1812. Initiated violent persecution of Christians 1805, 1811, and 1818. Died when struck by lightning in Jehol.

JIN JIAN (c. 1720–95), imperial dignitary of Korean origin. Minister of the Imperial House 1772. Took part in restoration of Ming Tombs 1785. Oversaw organization of exhibition of Macartney's gifts to Qianlong. Author of various reports on Macartney embassy, often co-signed with Zhengrui.

JIQING, viceroy of Shandong province. Author of various reports on Macartney mission.

LI (FATHER JACOBUS LI; born c. 1750), Catholic priest trained in Naples and recruited by Sir George Staunton to act as interpreter for Macartney. Nicknamed "Mr. Plumb" (*li* meaning "plum tree" in Chinese) by Thomas Staunton and often referred to as such by other members of the mission. Remained in China after the embassy and wrote letters to his British friends as late as 1802.

LIANG KENTANG (1715–1802), high-ranking Chinese official who served in various posts in the hierarchy, from district magistrate to viceroy of Beizhili province, the position he held during Macartney embassy. Received British in Dagu and Tientsin. Author of various memoranda December 1792 and summer 1793.

LIN ZEXU (1785–1850), eminent man of letters and high-ranking official. Partisan of prohibition in the opium controversy, sent to Canton 1838 to eradicate the drug. His efficacy convinced Elliot, superintendent of British trade, to advise Westerners to hand over their stocks, which were destroyed July 1839. This action led to Opium War (1840–42) and Treaty of Nanking (1842). Removed from office by emperor, Lin returned to favor in 1845. In 1850 was put in charge of suppressing first Taiping insurrections in Guangxi, but died before taking any action.

PUYI (1906–67), the "last emperor," 1908–11. Chosen by Cixi to succeed his uncle Guangxu, he abdicated in 1912 but remained a "distinguished guest" in the Forbidden City until 1924.

QIANLONG (1711–99), fourth Qing (Manchu) emperor, fourth son of Emperor Yong-zheng, his predecessor. Reigned from 1736 to his abdication in 1796.

QIAO RENJIE (c. 1745–1804), Chinese civilian mandarin and one of two main escorts of Macartney's expedition July 1793–January 1794. Ended career as "supreme judge" in Beizhili province.

SONGYUN (1752–1836), Mongol prince and Grand Councillor. Imperial agent in border regions 1786–92, when he signed an accord with Russia. Grand Councillor 1793. Accompanied Macartney from Peking to Hangzhou. Later governed several provinces, among them Guangdong, where in 1810 he again encountered Thomas Staunton, then a commissioner of East India Company.

SULENG'E (c. 1745–1828), Manchu superintendent of customs (hoppo) in Canton from summer 1793. Received Macartney along with Changlin and organized reception of Titsing embassy. During Amherst embassy of 1816, which he accompanied in his capacity as minister of public works, affirmed that he had seen Macartney kowtow to Qianlong.

TONGZHI (1856–75), son and successor of Xianfeng as emperor, 1861–75.

WANG, FATHER, Chinese priest trained in Naples along with Father An.

WANG WENXIONG (c. 1740–1800), Chinese mandarin, colonel, and escort of Macartney mission July 1793–January 1794, along with Qiao. Authored no reports, since his rank did not entitle him to write to emperor. Died during a military campaign to suppress a rebellion.

XIANFENG (1831–61), son and successor of Daoguang as emperor, 1851–61. Reign was marked by xenophobic reaction leading to first Treaty of Tientsin (1858), second Western military intervention (1859–60), and second Treaty of Tientsin, after seizure of Peking (1860). Taiping Rebellion broke out during his reign. His concubine, Cixi, was mother of his son Tongzhi (born 1856), a future emperor.

YILING'A, vice minister of public works and adjunct to Jin Jian. Co-signed some of the memoranda of August 1793.

ZHENGRUI (c. 1733–1815), Manchu salt-tax commissioner and imperial legate assigned to accompany Macartney to Jehol. Qianlong was unhappy with his performance of this task. Authored many memoranda between May and October 1793. After the embassy, career experienced various ups and downs, until he finally attained post of vice minister of works.

ZHOU (FATHER PAULUS; born c. 1750), Chinese Catholic priest educated at Collegium Sinica in Naples and recruited by George Staunton to serve as interpreter. Broke his contract and disembarked in Macao for fear of government reprisals.

Money and Currency

The Chinese unit of currency during the reign of Qianlong was the tael, also called the *liang*. A tael was considered equal in value to one ounce of silver, and sums drawn in taels were payable in carefully weighed ingots or shavings of silver. The tael was subdivided into ten *ma*, one hundred *condorin*, and one thousand sapeks. The sapek (or *sien*) was a copper coin pierced by a square hole. A thousand sapeks strung on a cord were known as a ligature, worth one tael.

Along the Chinese coast a unit of currency of Spanish American origin was in common use. The British called it the Spanish dollar, the French the piastre, and the Chinese the *fan ping yuan* (foreign disk), or *yuan* for short. This dollar had no connection with the U.S. currency adopted in 1793, but was in fact the *peso gordo* of the Spanish Empire, which spread into the Pacific basin, primarily from Mexico, toward the end of the sixteenth century.

The *yuan* was worth .72 tael, or .25 pound sterling. The British pound was therefore worth about 3 taels, or 4 Spanish dollars.

Notes

Full bibliographical details of the sources that appear in the notes may be found in the Bibliography, divided into listings of primary and secondary sources. A list of abbreviations frequently used in the notes follows. Most of these refer to the locations of documents cited as primary sources. For fuller explanations, see Bibliography, Primary Sources.

AL	Archives of the Lazarists
AMAE	Archives of the (French) Ministry of Foreign Affairs
AN	Archives Nationales (of France)
ASJ	Archives of the Society of Jesus
BIF	Bibliothèque de l'Institut de France
BL	British Library, Manuscript Department
CUMC	Cornell University, Macartney's Correspondence
CUMP	Cornell University, Macartney's Papers
DU	Duke University, Durham, North Carolina
IOCA	India Office, China, Amherst
IOCC	India Office, China, Cathcart
IOCM	India Office, China, Macartney
NLD	National Library, Dublin
PR	Public Record Office, Kew
PRONI	Public Records Office of Northern Ireland
TB	Toyo Bunko (The Oriental Library), Tokyo
UAGC	Unpublished Archives of the Grand Council, Peking
WI	Wellcome Historical Medical Institute, London
ZGCB	*Zhongghu Congbian*, Peking

EPIGRAPHS

1. Cranmer-Byng, p. 219.
2. *Lectures on the Philosophy of World History. Introduction: Reason in History*, trans. H. B. Nisbet, Cambridge, 1975, pp. 199–200.
3. *La Bureaucratie céleste*, p. 34.

INTRODUCTION

1. *Règne de Charles XII*, 1751, preface.
2. "Chez la Veuve Lepetit, rue Pavée-Saint-André-des-Arts."
3. Including accounts of Cook's three circumnavigations of the world, in 1768, 1772, and 1776; Bougainville's in 1771; and La Pérouse's in 1785. *Voyage en Egypte et en Nubie*, by Norden, and *Voyage aux sources du Nil*, by Bruce, between 1768 and 1772; *Voyage à l'océan Pacifique du Nord, exécuté par ordre de Sa Ma-* jesté britannique entre 1790 et 1795 par le capitaine Vancouver; *Voyage dans l'Amérique septentrionale*; *Voyage dans l'intérieur de l'Afrique*, by Frédéric Horneman.

4. Including a two-volume atlas, with plates.

5. The most reliable population estimates for the years 1790–95 are as follows: China 330 million; England and Wales 8.5 million (1.5 million for Scotland and 5 million for Ireland); Europe 180 million (36 million for Russia, 28 million for France); Africa 100 million; America 24 million; India 180 million. The global figure was 950 million. These estimates are taken from Colin MacEverdy and Richard Jones, *Atlas of World Population History* (Harmondsworth, 1978), and the pathbreaking article by Dr. J. N. Biraben, "Essai sur l'évolution du nombre des hommes," in the journal *Population*, January–February 1979.

6. *Considérations sur les causes de la grandeur des Romains et de leur décadence*, Paris, 1987, p. 123.

7. A translation of Staunton's book, by J. Castéra, was published in Paris in 1798, and a second translation, by J. B. J. Breton, in Paris in 1804. A translation of Barrow's *Travels in China* by Castéra was published in 1805, and another, by Breton, in 1807, both in Paris.

8. Some of his sketches and drawings are now in a Tokyo institute, the Toyo Bunko, others in the India Office in London. A limited-edition album of about fifty of his watercolor engravings, financed by subscription, was published in 1805.

9. Young Thomas Staunton, the son of George Staunton, Macartney's deputy.

10. AL, notes of Father Lamiot on the English embassy, 1807.

11. Published by his grandson, W. Proudfoot-Jardine, in 1868.

12. A copy of which is in the Toyo Bunko in Tokyo. There is another copy in Nottingham, England.

13. The Cranmer-Byng edition is more complete than that of Helen Robbins, especially as regards the section entitled "Observations on China."

14. Of which Duke University in North Carolina possesses the precious manuscript.

15. Manuel Teixeira, *Annales de Macao*, 1979.

16. *Les Manifestes de Yen fou*, trans. F. Houang, Paris, 1977, p. 77.

17. See Will, *Bureaucratie et famine en Chine au XVIIIᵉ siècle*.

PROLOGUE

1. Quoted by Paul Hazard, *La Pensée européenne au XVIIIᵉ siècle*, vol. 1, p. 375.

2. Westerners generally use the word *yurt* to refer to the rigid, cylindrical tents of the Mongols and Turkomans in central Asia. Actually this usage is incorrect. In Mongolian, *yurt* means "pastureland," while the word for tent is *ger*.

3. *Hansard's Parliamentary Debates*, 1840, vol. 53, p. 739.

4. Ibid., p. 745.

PART ONE

EPIGRAPHS

1. *The Spirit of the Laws*, trans. Anne M. Cohen, Basia Carolyn Miller, and Harold Samuel Stone, Cambridge, 1989, 9, 27, p. 329.

2. AN, *Fonds Colonies* C 1/16, letter to the missionaries of Peking, February 1787.

3. *Reflections on the Revolution in France*, Penguin Classics, Harmondsworth, 1986, p. 149.

CHAPTER I

1. Staunton, vol. 1, p. 28.

2. Ibid., p. 26.

3. Mr. de Restif, a French naval agent, noted on September 21: "Lord Macartney is about to set out on his embassy to China, with the *Lion*, a vessel of the King, the *Hindostan*, a vessel of the Company, and a brig." His next dispatch reports their departure on September 22, four days before the date given by all other sources. But four days was not considered so important in a journey that would last eight months. Restif also described the *Lion* as having seventy-four guns, ten more than the other sources report. AMAE, *Correspondance politique Angleterre*, vol. 582, pp. 280–82.

4. Robbins, *Our First Ambassador to China*, p. 172.

5. In the House of Commons, May 1791.

6. IOCM, 93, 25.

7. Barrow, *A Voyage to Cochinchina*, pp. 1–2.

8. Holmes, p. 3.

9. Staunton, vol. 1, p. 30.

10. WI, Macartney, Memoranda from London to China, f° 13.

11. Earl H. Pritchard, *The Crucial Years of Anglo-Chinese Relations, 1750–1800*, p. 279.

12. Ibid.

13. *Parliamentary History*, 1782–83, XXIII, p. 646.

14. Pritchard, *The Crucial Years*, pp. 147–50.

15. CUMP, *Official MSS. of Macartney's Embassy*, vol. 1, October 25, 1791, "Questions Raised by the Directors."

16. IOCC, 90, Fitzburgh to Smith, August 29, 1787.

17. BL, MSS Add. 38310, *Hawkesbury's letters-book*, 1780–94, April 1791.

18. Pritchard, *The Crucial Years*, p. 272.

19. IOCM, G/12/91, Macartney to Dundas, January 4, 1792.

20. Ibid.

21. Pritchard, *The Crucial Years*, p. 269.

22. Ibid., pp. 278–81.

23. *Hansard's Parliamentary History*, March 30, 1790.

24. IOCM, 92, Macartney to Dundas, February 17, 1792.

25. Louis Dermigny, *La Chine et l'Occident: le commerce à Canton au XVIIIᵉ siècle, 1719–1833*, vol. 3, pp. 931ff.

26. H. B. Morse, *The Chronicles of the East India Company Trading to China*, vol. 2 (1635–1834), appendix G, p. 232.

27. Ibid., p. 235.

28. Ibid., p. 236.

29. IOCM, G/12/91, letter to Dundas, January, 4, 1792.

30. Morse, p. 240.

31. Louis XIV never sent an embassy, but in 1689 he did exchange (rather banal) letters with the emperor Kangxi. He also sent presents (astronomical instruments, now displayed in the Nanking Observatory) and donated money to establish a Peking branch of the Academy of Sciences (including a "school of languages"). The priests taught science, and their young pupils taught them Chinese language and literature. See D. Elisseeff, *Nicolas Fréret: réflexions d'un humaniste du XVIIIᵉ siècle sur la Chine*.

32. J. K. Fairbank and S. Y. Teng, "On the Ch'ing Tributary System," p. 188.

33. G. T. Staunton, *Ta T'sing Leu Lee*, p. iii.

34. See Mark Mankall, *Russia and China: Their Diplomatic Relations to 1728*.

CHAPTER 2

1. *The Idler*, September 8, 1759.

2. Holmes, p. 5.

3. Staunton, vol. 1, pp. 36–37.

4. Ibid., pp. 35–36.

5. Ibid., p. 37.

6. D. B. Quinn, *Raleigh and the British Empire*, London, 1947.

7. "The Traveller."

8. See Bosquet, *Adam Smith*, Dalloz, 1950.

9. John W. Derry, *William Pitt*, p. 46.

10. *The Adventurer*, June 26, 1753.

11. See Paul Mantoux, *La Révolution industrielle au XVIIIᵉ siècle*, p. 415, n. 2.

12. See Joël Mokyr, *Industrial Revolution and the New Economic History*, pp. 1–2.

13. Carrington, *History of England*, pp. 603–4.

14. Mokyr, p. 2.

15. See Fernand Braudel, *Civilisation matérielle, économie et capitalisme, XVᵉ–XVIIIᵉ siècle*, vol. 3, p. 483.

16. H. B. Morse, *The Chronicles of the East India Company Trading to China*, vol. 2 (1635–1834), appendix G.

17. Vincent T. Harlow, *The Founding of the Second British Empire, 1763–1793*, vol. 2, pp. 528–29.

18. L.-M. Langlès, "Observations sur les relations politiques et commerciales de l'Angleterre et de la France avec la Chine," preface to the French translation of Holmes, *Voyage en Chine et en Tartarie*, Paris, 1805, pp. xii ff.

19. Confucius, *The Analects (Lun yü)*, trans. D. C. Lau, Harmondsworth, 1979, 9: 1, p. 96.

20. Holmes, p. 6.

21. Staunton, vol. 1, p. 44.

22. Holmes, p. 10.

23. Staunton, vol. 1, p. 60.

24. Holmes, p. 10.

25. Ibid., pp. 8–9.

26. Barrow, *A Voyage to Cochinchina*, p. 28.

27. Peter Roebuck, *Macartney of Lisanoure, 1737–1806*, pp. 17–18.

28. Ibid., p. 22.

29. Ibid., p. 312.

30. Ibid., p. 7.

31. Robbins, *Our First Ambassador to China*, p. 8.

32. The average cost has been estimated at £1,000 to £3,000. See C. Hibbert, *The Grand Tour*, London, 1987, p. 20.

33. Robbins, p. 10.

34. Sir Gavin de Beer, ed., *Voltaire's British Visitors*, 1967.

35. Ibid.

36. Mantoux, p. 45, n. 2.

CHAPTER 3

1. Barrow, *A Voyage to Cochinchina*, p. 64.

2. *The Journal of Elizabeth Lady Holland*, ed. the Earl of Ilchester, London, 1908, vol. 1, p. 229.

3. Mr. de Bausset to the Duke of Choiseul, December 23, 1766, from St. Petersburg. AMAE, Paris, *Corresp. politique, Russie, 1766–1767*, vol. 8, p. 139.

4. Roebuck, p. 57.

5. Robbins, p. 162.

6. Roebuck, p. 85.

7. AN, *Fonds Marine* B4 163, Paris.

8. Macartney to Lord Germain, July 5, 1779. See also Roebuck, pp. 123–24.

9. AN, *Fonds Marine* B4 163, Paris.

10. Roebuck, p. 152.

11. G. T. Staunton, *Memoirs of the Chief Incidents of the Public Life of Sir G. T. Staunton,* p. 38.

12. N. Wraxall, *Historical Memoir of My Own Time*, London, 1904, p. 321.

13. He was paid £15,000 a year, plus travel expenses of £1,000.

14. Roebuck, chapter 5.

15. Ibid.

16. *Hansard's Parliamentary Debates*, 1806, vol. 6, p. 762.

17. BL, *MSS* 22461, Macartney to Mercer, May 28, 1785.

18. Private collection, quoted in Robbins, p. 163.

19. *Gentleman's Magazine*, June 1786.

20. Robbins, p. 159.

21. Macartney doc., CUMP.

22. By Cornelius de Pauw (Berlin: Decker, 1773), 2 vols.

23. Robbins, p. 193.

24. Barrow, *A Voyage to Cochinchina*, p. 95.

25. They are all included in the Macartney Archives at Cornell University.

26. *Weekly Review*, January 1708.

27. *L'An deux mille quatre cent quarante*, p. 368.

28. Huc, vol. 4, p. 203.

29. Danielle Elisseeff, *Moi, Arcade, interprète chinois du Roi-Soleil*, pp. 146–47.

30. Ibid., p. 93.

31. Paul Hazard, *La Crise de la conscience européenne 1680–1715*, p. 29.

32. Collins, *Lettre à Dodwell sur l'immortalité de l'âme* (French translation 1709), p. 289.

33. Quoted by Hazard.

34. Boulainvilliers, *La Vie de Mahomet*, 1730, p. 180.

35. Quoted by *Bulletin Ecole française d'Extrême-Orient*, p. 139.

36. Quoted in Appleton, *A Cycle of Cathay*, p. 58.

37. See Harder, Colloque sinologie, Chantilly, 1980, p. 83.

38. Phrase attributed to him by his friend Guasco, quoted in ibid., p. 86.

39. *The Spirit of the Laws*, 8, 21, pp. 127–28.

40. Ibid., 19, 20, p. 321.

41. Dedication to M. le duc de Richelieu for *L'Orphélin de Chine*, 1755.

42. The reference is to a poem about Mukden written by Qianlong: *Epître au roi de la Chine*, 1771.

43. Letter to d'Alembert, November 6, 1775.

44. Ange Goudar, author of many books on economics and politics, *L'Espion chinois ou l'Envoyé secret de la cour de Pékin pour examiner l'état présent de l'Europe*, 1774, vol. 2, p. 91.

CHAPTER 4

1. Barrow, *A Voyage to Cochinchina*, p. 74.

2. Staunton, vol. 1, p. 78.

3. Ibid., p. 79.

4. Holmes, pp. 16–17.

5. Ibid., p. 16.

6. WI, Macartney, Memoranda from London to China, f° 54.

7. Staunton, vol. 1, p. 86.

8. Ibid., p. 87. Of the 6 million Africans "sold" between 1701 and 1810, Brazil absorbed nearly a third (1,891,000), nine-tenths of whom were transported by Portuguese ships, but under the protection of the British navy.

9. Ibid.

10. Ibid.

11. P. V. Malouet, *Mémoires*, vol. 1, p. 10. Gold production in Brazil had fallen since 1760, but England was buying more and more cotton.

12. Pliny the Elder, *Natural History*, 6:54.

13. Seneca, *De beneficiis*, 7:9.

14. Paper was introduced in Italy only at the end of the thirteenth century, but had been used in China since the third. Xylography, which combined seals and engraving, was widespread in China from the eighth century and penetrated the West only six centuries later.

15. Staunton, vol. 1, p. 101.

16. Holmes, p. 20.

17. Roebuck, p. 62.

18. CUMC, letter of Father de Grammont

to Macartney, August 30, 1793, n. 214. See also Dermigny.

19. *Lettres édifiantes*, Paris, 1979, p. 92.

CHAPTER 5

1. Holmes, p. 27.
2. Ibid., p. 28.
3. Girault de Coursac, *Le Voyage de Louis XVI autour du monde*, Paris, 1985, p. 96.
4. Staunton, vol. 1, p. 104.
5. Ibid.
6. Ibid.
7. Braudel, vol. 1, p. 51.
8. Staunton, vol. 1, p. 113.
9. It is now known that lemons lose their effectiveness within a few days.
10. Robbins, p. 211.
11. Staunton, vol. 1, p. 118.
12. Holmes, pp. 42–43.
13. Staunton, vol. 1, p. 121.
14. Ibid., p. 126.
15. Ibid., p. 132.
16. Ibid., p. 121.
17. Ibid., p. 122.
18. Ibid., p. 129.
19. Ibid.
20. Barrow, *A Voyage to Cochinchina*, p. 169.
21. Staunton, vol. 1, p. 132.
22. WI, Macartney, Memoranda from London to China, f° 180, London.
23. Holmes, p. 63.
24. WI, Macartney, Memoranda, f° 181, unpublished, London.
25. Holmes, p. 62.
26. Staunton, vol. 1, p. 154.
27. Holmes, pp. 66–67.
28. Staunton, vol. 1, p. 159.
29. Ibid., p. 162.
30. Ibid., p. 172.
31. Ibid., p. 184.

PART TWO

EPIGRAPHS

1. Nicolas Trigault, *Histoire de l'expédition chrétienne au royaume de la Chine, 1582–1610*, Paris, 1617; reprint Paris, 1978, p. 123.
2. *Dictionnaire philosophique*, "Egalité."
3. Joseph-Marie Amiot, *Mémoires concernant*, Paris, 1789, vol. 14, p. 534.

CHAPTER 6

1. David Scott, like Captain Mackintosh, was both a "free trader" and an agent of the East India Company. This quotation was the conclusion of a memorandum he sent to the directors of the company on May 3, 1787. Cited in Harlow, *The Founding of the Second British Empire*, vol. 2, p. 535.
2. Staunton, vol. 1, p. 194.
3. IOCM, 93:43–49.
4. UAGC, October 22, 1792.
5. Ibid.
6. IOCM, 93:77–82.
7. UAGC, December 7, 1792.
8. Ibid., December 9, 1792.
9. Staunton, vol. 1, p. 196.
10. At the time the superintendent of customs in Canton, known as the hoppo, was Shengzhu, who was replaced the following September by Suleng'e. See Cranmer-Byng, p. 184.
11. Staunton, vol. 1, p. 193.
12. IOCM, 92, letter from Francis Baring to the viceroy of Canton, April 27, 1792.
13. Staunton, vol. 1, p. 195.
14. Nathaniel Peffer, *China, the Collapse of a Civilisation*, pp. 21–23.
15. Charpentier-Cossigny, p. 407.
16. Barrow, *Travels in China*, p. 611.
17. Pritchard, *The Crucial Years*, p. 305.
18. Hüttner, p. 220.
19. Staunton, vol. 1, p. 192.
20. Ibid.
21. Robbins, p. 245.

CHAPTER 7

1. Staunton, vol. 1, pp. 119–20.
2. William Hickey, *Memoirs of William Hickey 1749 to 1775*, London, 1913, pp. 202ff. Hickey's works figured prominently in Macartney's library (see catalogue at Cornell University).
3. J. B. Eames, *The English in China, 1600–1843*, pp. 75–76; Richard Walter, *Voyage Round the World in 1740–1744 with H.M.S. Centurion.*
4. Hickey, pp. 215–17.
5. Ibid., pp. 224–25.
6. Ibid., pp. 218–19. Captain William Elphinstone, younger son of Lord Elphinstone, made two trips to Canton aboard the *Triton* between 1766 and 1777. See also Dermigny, vol. 1, p. 228.
7. Eames, pp. 86ff.

8. Pritchard, *The Crucial Years*, pp. 133–34.

9. Ibid., p. 131.

10. Cranmer-Byng, p. 214.

11. Pritchard, *The Crucial Years*, pp. 133–34.

12. Louis-Mathieu Langlès, preface to the French translation of Holmes, pp. xiv and xvii.

13. Joseph-Marie Amiot, *Mémoires concernant*, Paris, 1789, vol. 14, p. 534.

CHAPTER 8

1. Hüttner, p. 4.

2. In 1811 the trip was still described as "very uncomfortable." See AL, letter of Father Richenet to Thomas Staunton, November 5, 1811.

3. UAGC, June 26, 1793, ref. 4 24 18.

4. Robbins, p. 245.

5. IOCM, 91: 155–63, letter to Dundas, February 17, 1792.

6. Staunton, vol. 1, p. 203.

7. Abbé Grosier, *Description générale de la Chine*, Paris, 1788.

8. Staunton, vol. 1, p. 203.

9. Ibid., pp. 203–4.

10. Ibid., p. 204.

11. Ibid., pp. 210–11.

12. Ibid., p. 207.

13. UAGC, July 9, 1793, ref. 4 24 21.

14. Staunton, vol. 1, p. 207.

15. Ibid., p. 208.

16. Ibid.

17. Charpentier-Cossigny, p. 270.

18. Staunton, vol. 1, p. 208.

19. Charpentier-Cossigny, p. 273.

20. AL, Father Lamiot's notes on the English embassy, 1807.

21. Hüttner, p. 30.

22. "Les Latrines de la fortune," trans. Lanselle, in *Le Cheval de jade*, p. 198.

23. Staunton, vol. 1, p. 208.

24. Ibid.

25. Ibid., pp. 208–9.

26. Ibid., p. 209.

27. Cranmer-Byng, p. 229.

28. Ibid.

29. R. Van Gulik, *Sexual Life in Ancient China*, p. 27.

30. *Jin Ping Mei*, trans. Lévy, vol. 1, pp. 71 and 88.

31. Etiemble, *L'Erotisme et l'amour*, p. 27.

32. Staunton, vol. 1, p. 211.

33. Ibid., p. 210.

34. Barrow, *Travels in China*, p. 74.

35. Staunton, vol. 1, p. 210.

CHAPTER 9

1. Staunton, vol. 1, p. 213.

2. Ibid.

3. Ibid., p. 214.

4. Barrow, *Travels in China*, p. 58.

5. Ibid., p. 59.

6. Ibid., pp. 59–60.

7. Ibid., pp. 36–37.

8. Anderson, p. 66.

9. Barrow, *Travels in China*, p. 38.

10. Ibid., p. 39.

11. Staunton, vol. 1, pp. 219–20.

12. Ibid., p. 219.

13. Barrow, *Travels in China*, p. 41.

14. Ibid.

15. Ibid.

16. Cranmer-Byng, p. 81.

17. Staunton, vol. 1, p. 215.

18. Ibid., p. 214.

19. Ibid., p. 215.

20. Ibid., p. 216.

21. Ibid.

22. UAGC, July 12, 1793, ref. 4 24 25.

23. Staunton, vol. 1, p. 217.

24. Holmes, p. 100.

25. Anderson, p. 57.

26. UAGC, July 18, 1793, ref. 2 24 29.

27. Ibid.

CHAPTER 10

1. Robbins, p. 248. See also Amiot, vol. 12, pp. 513–15.

2. IOCM, 92: 40–47.

3. Barrow, *Travels in China*, p. 603.

4. Staunton, vol. 2, p. 37.

5. IOCM, 92, secret committee, November 5, 1792.

6. UAGC, July 24, 1793, ref. 2 24 34.

7. Ibid., July 16, 1793, ref. 2 24 27.

8. Staunton, vol. 1, p. 222.

9. Holmes, pp. 100–101.

10. Robbins, p. 248.

11. Ibid., p. 249.

12. Ibid., p. 250.

CHAPTER 11

1. Staunton, vol. 1, p. 240.

2. UAGC, August 3, 1793, ref. 2 26 6.

3. Robbins, p. 251.

4. *Jing Ping Mei*, trans. Lévy, vol. 2, p. 854.

5. Their full names were Wang Wen-xiong, a colonel in command of the Tongzhou brigade, and Qiao Renjie, circuit supervisor in Tientsin. See UAGC, August 3, 1793, and July 16, 1793.

6. Robbins, pp. 251–52.

7. Staunton, vol. 1, p. 240.

8. Ibid., pp. 240–41.

9. Ibid., pp. 243–46, for following quotations.

10. UAGC, August 3, 1793, ref. 4 25 6.

11. Staunton, vol. 1, p. 246.

12. UAGC, August 10, 1793, ref. 4 25 21.

13. Staunton, vol. 1, pp. 241–42.

14. UAGC, August 3, 1793, ref. 4 25 6.

15. Robbins, p. 253.

16. Ibid.

17. NLD, Winder, MSS 8799.

18. Hüttner, p. 12.

19. Ibid.

20. Holmes, p. 121.

CHAPTER 12

1. Robbins, p. 255.

2. Staunton, vol. 1, p. 256.

3. Anderson, p. 35.

4. Robbins, p. 255.

5. Ibid.

6. Dinwiddie, p. 35

7. Adam Smith, *An Inquiry into the Nature and Causes of the Wealth of Nations*, Oxford, 1976, vol. 1, p. 224.

8. Mantoux, pp. 111–16.

9. Dinwiddie, p. 35.

10. The wood was from *qishu* (*Vornici-flua*), a shrub used to make lacquer. See Hütt-ner, pp. 14–16.

11. Hüttner, p. 16.

12. Robbins, p. 256.

13. Ibid. Mention is made of this "Temple of the Sea" in one of Zhengrui's earlier reports (UAGC, June 18, 1793, ref. 4 24 31). It had just been refurbished.

14. Robbins, p. 257.

15. Ibid.

16. Ibid., p. 258.

17. Barrow, *Travels in China*, p. 186.

18. Cranmer-Byng, note 4, p. 356.

19. Barrow, *Travels in China*, p. 186.

20. Macartney's journal does not even mention this. See Staunton, vol. 1, p. 238.

21. Robbins, p. 258.

22. Letter of Heshen to the legate Zhen-grui, dated August 6, 1793; because of the rapidity of the postal system, it arrived that same evening.

23. UAGC, August 7, 1793, ref. 4 25 12.

24. Robbins, p. 258.

25. Barrow, *Travels in China*, p. 190.

26. UAGC, August 6, 1793, microfilm 67.

27. Ibid., August 7, 1793, ref. 4 25 12.

28. Ibid., August 9, 1793, microfilm 25.

29. AL.

30. UAGC, August 7, 1793, microfilm 67.

CHAPTER 13

1. Robbins, p. 259.

2. Dinwiddie, p. 36.

3. NLD, Winder, journal, MSS 8799.

4. Robbins, p. 260.

5. Dinwiddie, p. 36.

6. Hüttner, pp. 23–24.

7. Cranmer-Byng, p. 81.

8. Anderson, p. 73.

9. Hüttner, p. 22.

10. Ibid., p. 93.

11. UAGC, August 6, 1793, microfilm 67.

12. Confucius, *The Analects*, 6:27, p. 85.

13. UAGC, August 6, 1793, microfilm 67.

14. *Qi Ju Zhu*, p. 4870, quoted by Zhu Yong, *Qingdai zongzufa yanjiu*.

15. IOCM, 92, letter to Dundas, November 9, 1793.

16. Dinwiddie, p. 36.

17. Staunton, vol. 1, p. 258.

18. Ibid., p. 259.

19. Anderson, p. 81.

20. Ibid.

21. Paul Claudel, Œuvre poétique, *Connaissance de l'Est*, p. 115.

22. Anderson, pp. 81–82.

23. Dinwiddie, p. 63.

24. Lin Yutang, pp. 317–18.

25. Dinwiddie, p. 39.

26. *The Spirit of the Laws*, 19, 20, p. 321.

27. Barrow, *Travels in China*, pp. 179–80.

28. Hüttner, p. 200.

29. Staunton, vol. 1, p. 266.

30. Anderson, p. 69.

31. Staunton, vol. 1, p. 267.

CHAPTER 14

1. Staunton, vol. 1, p. 268.

2. Barrow, *Travels in China*, p. 71.

3. Ibid., p. 79.

4. Ibid., pp. 79–80. Muhammed-bey al-

Alfi visited London in 1803 in an unsuccessful attempt to negotiate the return of the Mamlukes to power in Egypt.

5. Sigmund Freud, *Essai de psychanalyse*; PBP, p. 184.

6. Dinwiddie, p. 37.

7. Robbins, p. 261.

8. UAGC, August 6, 1793, microfilm 67.

9. Robbins, p. 262.

10. Staunton, vol. 1, pp. 273–74.

11. UAGC, August 9, 1793, microfilm 25.

12. Ibid. August 12, 1793, ref. 4 25 14.

13. Ibid., August 12, 1793, ref. 4 25 21.

14. Staunton, vol. 1, p. 274.

15. Ibid.

16. ASJ Chantilly, letters of J. de Grammont, 1767–88.

17. CUMC, no. 251.

18. The unpublished correspondence of the Lazarists (AL) shows that Father de Grammont did not have a great reputation. See, for instance, the letter of Father Raux to Father Aubin, June 25, 1789. See also the letter of Father de Poirot to Macartney, October 1794, CUMC, no. 308.

19. Robbins, p. 263.

20. Barrow, *Travels in China*, p. 188.

21. Cranmer-Byng, p. 223.

22. Anderson, p. 76.

23. Ibid., p. 77.

24. Dinwiddie, p. 37.

25. Ibid., p. 38.

26. Holmes, pp. 128–29.

27. Staunton, vol. 1, p. 294.

28. Holmes, p. 157.

29. Anderson, p. 77.

30. Ibid.

31. Lin Yutang, pp. 47 and 166.

32. Hüttner, p. 17.

33. Anderson, p. 80.

34. Ibid.

35. Ibid., p. 81.

36. Dinwiddie, p. 39.

37. Cranmer-Byng, p. 83.

38. Barrow, *Travels in China*, p. 84.

39. Ibid., pp. 84–85.

40. Anderson, p. 82.

41. Dinwiddie, p. 38.

42. Huc, vol. 3, p. 33.

43. Dinwiddie, p. 38.

44. Ibid., vol. 1, p. 295.

45. *Lettres de voyage, 1923–1939*, p. 101.

46. Confucius, *The Analects*, 7: 11, p. 87.

47. Robbins, p. 265.

CHAPTER 15

1. UAGC, August 14, 1793, ref. 4 25 16.

2. AL, Father Lamiot's notes on the English embassy, 1807.

3. Robbins, p. 265.

4. Ibid., p. 266.

5. Ibid.

6. Ibid.

7. UAGC, August 17, 1793, ref. 4 25 22.

8. Robbins, p. 268.

9. Ibid.

10. IOCM, 93: 264–325.

11. Robbins, p. 267.

12. Barrow, *Travels in China*, p. 22.

13. Robbins, p. 267.

14. Ibid., p. 268.

15. Barrow, *Travels in China*, p. 605. Macartney's embassy eventually cost the Peking government about £173,000, twice what it cost the company.

16. Robbins, p. 269.

17. Confucius, *The Analects*, 15: 40, p. 137.

CHAPTER 16

1. Anderson, p. 87.

2. Ibid., pp. 87–88.

3. Robbins, p. 270.

4. Anderson, pp. 87–88.

5. *Le Cheval de jade*, trans. Lanselle, p. 103.

6. Robbins, p. 257.

7. Anderson, p. 90.

8. Ibid.

9. Charles Commeaux, *La Vie quotidienne en Chine sous les Mandchous*, Paris, 1970, p. 197.

10. Huc, vol. 3, p. 242.

11. Ibid.

12. Teilhard de Chardin, p. 101.

13. Anderson, pp. 88–89.

14. Staunton, vol. 2, p. 5.

15. Ibid.

16. Dinwiddie, p. 42.

17. Staunton, vol. 2, p. 12.

18. Ibid.

19. Ibid.

20. Cranmer-Byng, p. 234.

21. Staunton, vol. 2, p. 13.

22. Ibid.

23. Ibid.

24. Commeaux, p. 262.

25. Staunton, vol. 2, p. 8.

26. Ibid.

27. *L'Ilusion comique*, vol. 1, p. 1.
28. Staunton, vol. 2, p. 9.
29. Hüttner, p. 46.
30. Lin Yutang, p. 301.
31. Barrow, *Travels in China*, p. 292.

CHAPTER 17

1. Anderson, p. 91.
2. Ibid., p. 92.
3. Ibid., p. 89.
4. Ibid., p. 94.
5. Staunton, vol. 2, p. 8. It is more likely that Staunton heard *fanqui*, which would mean "Barbarian devil of the South." "Black demon" would be *keigui*. In any event, Staunton was misinformed, since *Fan-quee* means "foreign devil," a term that encompasses both blacks and whites and has been endlessly applied to Europeans.
6. Barrow, *Travels in China*, p. 549.
7. Staunton, vol. 2, p. 206.
8. Anderson, p. 132.
9. Staunton, vol. 2, p. 6.
10. Ibid., p. 7. In the eighteenth century the imperial granaries did play an important role in preventing massive death by famine. Only after 1878 did China suffer famines that were fatal to millions. See Pierre-Etienne Will, *Bureaucratie et famine en Chine au XVIIIᵉ siècle*.
11. In the southern provinces, however, rich families did invest in social projects, particularly orphanages. See Angela Leung, *Etudes chinoises*, 1985.
12. Staunton, vol. 2, p. 11.
13. Ibid.
14. Ibid., p. 15, and J. Gernet, "Chine moderne, Chine traditionelle," in *Etudes chinoises*, 4 (spring 1985): 7–13.
15. Staunton, vol. 2, p. 15.
16. Mantoux, pp. 107–10.
17. Staunton, vol. 2, p. 16.
18. Lin Yutang, p. 131.
19. Staunton, vol. 2, p. 16.
20. Ibid.
21. *Mémoires concernant les Chinois*, vol. 12, p. 509.
22. Staunton, vol. 2, p. 17.

CHAPTER 18

1. CUMC, no. 217.
2. Robbins, p. 271.
3. UAGC, August 18, 1793, microfilm 25.
4. Confucius, *The Analects*, 20: 3, p. 160.

5. Robbins, p. 272.
6. Ibid.
7. Ibid.
8. Dinwiddie, p. 43. "From twenty to thirty," claims the ambassador (Robbins, p. 271), surely an exaggeration. "There were two different types," Holmes explains: mortars and howitzers.
9. Holmes, pp. 147–48.
10. Dinwiddie, p. 43.
11. Robbins, p. 273.
12. Anderson, p. 95.
13. Ibid., p. 96.
14. Ibid, pp. 96–97.
15. Confucius, *The Analects*, 20:1, p. 159.

CHAPTER 19

1. Dinwiddie, p. 42.
2. Ibid., p. 43.
3. Anderson, pp. 100–101.
4. Barrow, *Travels in China*, p. 88.
5. Ibid., p. 89.
6. Ibid., p. 90.
7. Cranmer-Byng, p. 92.
8. NLD, Winder, journal, MSS 8799.
9. Staunton, vol. 2, p. 19.
10. Ibid.
11. Ibid. This observation, confirmed by several other witnesses, suggests that Anderson had been fooled in Tongzhou, taking painted cannon for real artillery pieces.
12. Barrow, *Travels in China*, p. 96.
13. Ibid.
14. Ibid.
15. Ibid., pp. 89–90.
16. Anderson, pp. 101–2.
17. Ibid., p. 108.
18. Staunton, vol. 2, p. 23.
19. Anderson, p. 108.
20. Ibid., p. 109.
21. Staunton, vol. 2, p. 102.
22. Barrow, *Travels in China*, p. 95.
23. Ibid., p. 528.
24. Huc, vol. 4, p. 27.
25. NLD, Winder, journal, MSS 8799.
26. *Chronique indiscrète des mandarins*, Gallimard-UNESCO, vol. 2, p. 644.
27. Staunton, vol. 2, p. 19.
28. Ibid., p. 20.
29. Barrow, *Travels in China*, p. 93.
30. Teilhard de Chardin, p. 68.
31. Staunton, vol. 2, p. 20.
32. Dinwiddie, p. 44.

CHAPTER 20

1. Holmes, p. 134.
2. Dinwiddie, pp. 42–43.
3. Staunton, vol. 2, p. 24.
4. Quoted in I. and J.-L. Vissière, *La Mission française de Pékin*, colloquium in Chantilly, 1980.
5. BL, Alexander, journal, MSS Add. 35174.
6. Staunton, vol. 2, p. 24.
7. Anderson, p. 112.
8. Ibid.
9. Ibid.
10. Ibid., p. 113.
11. Winterbotham, p. 240.
12. Anderson, p. 114.
13. Holmes, p. 135.
14. Robbins, p. 274.
15. Ibid., p. 275.
16. ZGCB, 4, p. 38a.
17. Ibid. Lake Wanshou was an artificial lake. The dredged dirt was used to form a hill known as the Mount of Longevity.
18. ZGCB, 6, p. 336.

CHAPTER 21

1. Pfister says that Father d'Almeida was the last Portuguese to preside over the Tribunal of Mathematics. He also mentions that the Chinese confused the names Rodrigues and d'Almeida, which would explain why the court letter of August 19 refers to Rodrigues as the president of this tribunal.
2. Some of his paintings are exhibited in the Taipei museum.
3. The rivalries between the various Catholic religious communities are revealed by Barrow (*Travels in China*, pp. 445–48), who did not invent them out of hostility to the Roman church. The letters of Fathers Lamiot and Richenet (AL), in particular that of September 12, 1820, make these divisions painfully obvious.
4. UAGC, October 3, 1793, microfilm 26.
5. Robbins, p. 276.
6. Ibid., p. 277.
7. On several occasions Staunton mentions translations that had to go from English to Latin to Chinese. Hüttner was assigned to check the accuracy of the Latin. Anderson, the indiscreet footman, also mentions this technique.
8. Dinwiddie, p. 46.
9. Guignes, vol. 1, p. 255.

10. Dinwiddie, p. 45.
11. Ibid., p. 46.
12. Arthur W. Hummel, *Eminent Chinese of the Ch'ing Period*, pp. 59–160.
13. Court letter of August 16, 1793, quoted in UAGC, August 22, 1793, ref. 4 25 17.
14. UAGC, August 22, 1793, marginal note August 23, 1793, ref. 4 25 17.
15. Cranmer-Byng, p. 95.
16. Hüttner, pp. 42–43.
17. Staunton, vol. 2, p. 24.
18. Robbins, p. 279. Dinwiddie says that the throne was of Indian mahogany, a gift from the company.
19. Victor Segalen, *Stèle, Eloge et pouvoir de l'absence*.
20. UAGC, August 25, 1793, ref. 4 25 19.
21. Robbins, p. 279. *The Beggar's Opera* was first performed in London in 1728. Macartney noted the name and address of the clockmaker: George Clarke, Leadenhall Street. Clarke exercised his craft from 1725 to 1740. Macartney described the clock as being in "wretched old taste."

CHAPTER 22

1. Robbins, p. 280.
2. UAGC, July 16, 1793, and August 3, 1793, as well as October 15, 1793. He was administratively aware of their existence, but no more.
3. UAGC, August 6, 1793. The Chinese first faced this sort of European rhetoric in Baring's letter, which arrived in Canton in September 1792.
4. Confucius, *The Analects*, 13: 3, p. 118.
5. Victor Thibaut was a precision mechanic, a specialist in scientific instruments, Charles-Henri Petitpierre a Swiss clockmaker resident in London. After Macartney's mission he lived for a while in Canton, Manila, and Batavia, where he married a Javanese woman. He was murdered by Malay pirates. See Cranmer-Byng, p. 361, n. 13.
6. Robbins, pp. 280–81.
7. The ceremonial manual (*T'ai Tsing Toung-li*) was published in France by G. Pauthier as *Histoire des relations politiques de la Chine avec les puissances occidentales*, Paris, 1859. It distinguished tribute, objects offered *to* the emperor, from presents, objects offered *by* the emperor. See Pauthier, p. 184, n. 2. *Kungshi* (*gongsi*) were articles of the birthday tribute. It is therefore understandable that Ma-

cartney and Staunton would insist that the Chinese term designating the gifts they were carrying be *songli*.

8. Dinwiddie, p. 50.

9. The planetarium was the principal gift. It had been purchased by the East India Company from the Baron of Meylius for £600. It was then delivered to Vulliamy and Sons for repairs, modifications, and embellishments, which brought the price up to £656. According to Dinwiddie, it had been invented and manufactured by a German scholar, P. M. Hahn, and had taken thirty years to build. See UAGC, August 7, 1793, ref. 4 25 12; CUMC, no. 225; Dinwiddie, p. 26.

10. William Fraser of 3 New Bond Street, supplier to King George III, was a manufacturer of mathematical instruments. He formed his company in 1777 and ran it until 1812. Fraser furnished the East India Company with a superb astronomical machine for the sum of £105, along with a selection of "mathematical and philosophical" instruments. See CUMC, no. 225.

11. Robbins, p. 279.

12. The Vulliamys were a family of clockmakers of Swiss origin. The founder of the company, François-Justin, moved to England in 1730, and the reputation of Vulliamy clocks had risen steadily since then.

13. See N. Kendrick, "Josiah Wedgwood, an Eighteenth Century Entrepreneur," in *Economic History Review*, 2nd series, vol. 12, no. 3, 1960, pp. 426–28.

14. Barrow, *Travels in China*, p. 109.

15. Dinwiddie, p. 47.

16. Ibid.

17. UAGC, August 15, 1793, ref. 4 25 17.

18. Alfred Chapuis, *La Montre chinoise*, pp. 21–22.

19. Robbins, p. 279.

CHAPTER 23

1. Barrow, *Travels in China*, p. 110.

2. Henri Bernard-Maître, *L'Apport scientifique du P. Mathieu Ricci à la Chine*, Tientsin, 1935.

3. The trio astronomy-astrology-power played its part in Europe as well. In his *Le Désordre* (Paris, 1988) G. Ballandier discusses Dondi's *astrorium*, built in the fifteenth century for the podesta of Padua (pp. 47ff.).

4. Barrow, *Travels in China*, p. 285.

5. Huc, vol. 4, p. 40.

6. Barrow, *Travels in China*, p. 111.

7. Ibid., p. 190.

8. Ibid.

9. Ibid., p. 291.

10. Ibid.

11. Ibid., pp. 111–12.

12. Ibid., p. 112.

13. G. H. C. Wong, "China's Opposition to Western Science During the Late Ming and Early Ch'ing," *Isis*, 54 (1963): 37.

14. *Shuli ching-yun*, quoted by Wong, p. 39.

15. See Joseph Needham, *Science and Civilisation in China*, vol. 6.

16. Hsu Qangchi, quoted by Wong, pp. 42–43.

17. Wei Chun, quoted by Wong, p. 44.

18. Wong, p. 45.

19. Yang Kuangxian, quoted by Wong, p. 34.

20. Cranmer-Byng, p. x.

21. ZGCB, court letter, August 28, 1793, 7, p. 46.

CHAPTER 24

1. Barrow, *Travels in China*, p. 110.

2. Ibid.

3. Quoted in Simon Leys, *Ombres chinoises*.

4. *Lettres de voyage, 1923–1939*, p. 72.

5. Dinwiddie, p. 46.

6. Barrow, *Travels in China*, p. 115.

7. ZGCB, 7, pp. 29b and 40.

8. Barrow, *Travels in China*, p. 115.

9. Dinwiddie, p. 50.

CHAPTER 25

1. Robbins, p. 282.

2. Ibid.

3. *Jin Ping Mei*, vol. 2, p. 1001.

4. Anderson, p. 116.

5. ZGCB, p. 34a, August 16, 1793.

6. Anderson, p. 117.

7. Barrow, *Travels in China*, p. 195.

8. *Jin Ping Mei, passim*.

9. Barrow, *Travels in China*, p. 104.

10. Holmes, p. 135.

11. Ibid., p. 136.

12. Ibid., p. 137.

13. Hüttner, pp. 52–53.

14. Holmes, p. 138.

15. Ibid., p. 139.

16. Hüttner, p. 48.

17. "Le Châtiment du parasite," in *Le Cheval de jade*, trans. Lanselle, p. 91.

18. Staunton, vol. 2, p. 38.

19. Ibid.

20. Hüttner, p. 37.

21. Staunton, vol. 2, p. 39.

22. Ibid. This system was called *pao-chia*. See Ho Ping-ti, *Studies on the Population of China*, p. 36.

23. Staunton, vol. 2, p. 39.

24. AL, Father Lamiot's notes on the English embassy, 1807.

25. *Jin Ping Mei*, vol. 1, p. 255.

26. See Gillan, observations on Chinese medicine, in Cranmer-Byng, p. 287.

27. Braudel, vol. 1, pp. 62 and 68.

28. AN, J.-B. Piron letter to the Ministry of the Navy in Paris, March 4, 1804. *Fonds Colonies-missions d'Extrême-Orient* F5 A22.

29. Ibid.

30. Anderson, p. 255.

31. Dinwiddie, p. 50.

32. Huc, vol. 4, p. 162. Father Huc calls these bandits *kouan-kouen*, an idiosyncratic spelling of the pinyin *guangkun*, meaning "bare club."

CHAPTER 26

1. Cranmer-Byng, p. 232.

2. Robbins, p. 282.

3. AL, letter to his sister Anne-Marie, November 19, 1788.

4. J. J. L. Duyvendak, *The Last Dutch Embassy to the Chinese Court*, p. 84.

5. Robbins, p. 284.

6. AL, letter, June 25, 1789.

7. Robbins, p. 284.

8. Cranmer-Byng, p. 231.

9. ASJ, J. de Grammont, letter to his parents, November 12, 1770.

10. Robbins, p. 287.

11. Goubert and Denis, *1789, les Français ont la parole*, p. 19.

12. Barrow, *Travels in China*, p. 175.

13. Staunton, vol. 2, pp. 39–40.

14. Hüttner, p. 237.

15. Huc, vol. 4, p. 249.

16. Ho Ping-ti, *Studies on the Population of China*, pp. 36–46.

17. An article in the Hong Kong magazine *Jiushi Niandai* (September 1988) cites many cases and emphasizes the recent recrudescence of this scourge.

18. Robbins, p. 288.

19. AL, letter of August 9, 1793, Paris.

20. AMAE, *Fds Asie*, vol. 20, f° 235–38.

21. AL, letter to his sister Anne-Marie, October 17, 1789.

22. Staunton, vol. 2, p. 40.

23. Robbins, p. 289.

CHAPTER 27

1. According to Hummel, Qianlong had seventeen sons.

2. Robbins, p. 286.

3. See E. Backhouse and J. O. P. Bland, *Annals and Memoirs of the Court of Peking*, London, 1914, p. 315.

4. Ibid., p. 317.

5. Robbins, p. 286.

6. Ibid.

7. See Harold Kahn, *Monarchy in the Emperor's Eyes*, pp. 52–53.

8. CUMC, Father de Grammont, quoted in a letter of Father Hanna to George Staunton, March 1, 1794, no. 292.

9. Robbins, p. 286.

10. See Sven Hedin, *Jehol, City of Emperors*, p. 211.

11. Cranmer-Byng, n. 17. See also D. S. Nivison, "Hoshen and his Accusers," in *Confucianism in Action*, Stanford, 1959, p. 214.

12. The edict is translated in G. T. Staunton, *Ta T'sing Leu Lee*, pp. 498–502. See also Hummel, p. 288.

13. UAGC, September 10, 1793, microfilm 24.

14. Of the 145 Grand Councillors named between 1730 and 1911, 72 were Manchus, 67 Chinese, and 6 Mongols. Parity (one horse, one rabbit) was scrupulously respected. See Feuerwerker, *State and Society in Eighteenth Century China*, p. 47.

15. UAGC, August 9, 1793, microfilm 25.

16. Ibid., August 11, 1793, microfilm 25.

17. *Journal du Lion*, in the French translation of Anderson, vol. 2, pp. 180–86.

18. UAGC, August 27, 1793, microfilm 25.

CHAPTER 28

1. UAGC, August 28, 1793, microfilm 25.

2. Ibid., August 16, 1793, microfilm 25.

3. Ibid.

4. Ibid.

5. ZGCB, court letter, August 30, 1793, p. 47a.

6. Ibid., court letter, September 1, 1793, pp. 47b, 48a.

7. UAGC, September 1, 1793, ref. 4 25 20.

8. Robbins, p. 284.

9. Cranmer-Byng, p. 228.

10. Robbins, p. 284.

11. ZGCB, p. 50a.

12. Memorandum presented by the censor Wu Kotu, quoted in Charlotte Haldane, *The Last Great Empress of China*, p. 62.

CHAPTER 29

1. Louis Dermigny, *Les Mémoires de Charles de Constant sur le commerce à la Chine*, p. 428.

2. Robbins, p. 285.

3. See Fairbank and Teng, "On the Ch'ing Tributary System," p. 181, and Pauthier, *Histoire des relations politiques*, pp. 177–206.

4. Charpentier-Cossigny, p. 338.

5. Robbins, p. 285.

6. CUMC, 5, no. 214.

7. Ibid.

8. Robbins, p. 289.

9. CUMC, Letter from Father de Grammont, 5, no. 214.

10. Anderson, p. 122.

11. Ibid.

12. Ibid., pp. 122–23.

13. BL, Alexander, journal, MSS Add. 35175.

14. IOCM, G/12/91, letter of the directors to Henry Dundas, January 20, 1792.

15. Staunton, vol. 2, p. 33.

16. UAGC, September 1, 1793, ref. 4 25 16.

17. Robbins, p. 291.

PART THREE

EPIGRAPHS

1. *Lettres de voyages 1923–1939,* February 10, 1924, p. 72.

2. Morse, vol. 2, appendix I, p. 247.

3. Quoted in Nathan Wachtel, *La Vision des Vaincus*, Paris, 1971, p. 63.

CHAPTER 30

1. Anderson, p. 125.

2. Alexander, September 2, 1793.

3. Cranmer-Byng, p. 109.

4. Anderson, p. 125.

5. Ibid., p. 126.

6. UAGC, August 30, 1793, ref. 4 25 20.

7. ZGCB, August 17, 1793, p. 41b.

8. Anderson, p. 125.

9. Hüttner, p. 64.

10. Winder, f° 3.

11. Hüttner, p. 64.

12. Ibid., p. 67.

13. Cranmer-Byng, p. 108.

14. AL, letter to his sister Anne-Marie, September 9, 1788.

15. Anderson, p. 127.

16. Cranmer-Byng, p. 109.

17. Barrow, *Travels in China*, p. 299.

18. Li Liweng, quoted in Lin Yutang, p. 308.

19. Cranmer-Byng, p. 110.

20. Staunton, vol. 2, p. 48.

21. Barrow, *Travels in China*, p. 299.

22. Anderson, p. 188.

23. Staunton, vol. 2, p. 48.

24. Cranmer-Byng, p. 225.

25. Anderson, p. 188.

26. Huc, vol. 4, p. 180.

27. Staunton, vol. 2, p. 48.

28. See, for example, New China News Agency, quoted in *Financial Times*, August 10, 1987.

29. Staunton, vol. 2, p. 48.

30. Morse, vol. 2, appendix G, p. 239, Dundas to Macartney, September 9, 1792.

31. Van Braam, vol. 2, p. 299. A "crate" generally weighed about 132 pounds (60 kilos). The value of opium traded by Western merchants rose from £39,800 in 1773 to £355,000 in 1794. See Dermigny, vol. 3, p. 1261, n. 4.

32. Anderson, p. 127.

33. Huc, vol. 1, p. 200.

34. Anderson, p. 130.

35. Ibid.

36. Staunton, vol. 2, pp. 186–87.

37. UAGC, July 28, 1793, ref. 4 24 26; the July report goes for September and the following months as well.

38. Cranmer-Byng, p. 112.

39. See Sven Hedin, *Jehol, City of Emperors*, pp. 142–46.

40. Holmes, p. 141.

CHAPTER 31

1. Anderson, p. 133.

2. Cranmer-Byng, p. 114.

3. Ibid.

4. Hüttner, p. 61.

5. Ibid., p. 63.

6. Cranmer-Byng, p. 114.

7. Anderson, p. 135.

8. Ibid.

9. Confucius, *The Analects*, 20: 1, p. 159.

10. *Handbook of Jehol*, part 1, chapter 2, quoted in Hedin, p. 168.

11. Hüttner, pp. 60–61.

12. Cranmer-Byng, p. 114.

13. Ibid., p. 115.

14. Staunton, Jr., f° 103.

15. Cranmer-Byng, pp. 115–16; Anderson, p. 138.

16. Anderson, p. 138.

17. Ibid., pp. 138–39.

18. See Holmes, p. 143.

CHAPTER 32

1. *The Handbook of Jehol*, part 1, chapter 22, cited in Hedin, pp. 145–46.

2. Hüttner, pp. 70–71.

3. Anderson, p. 139.

4. Cranmer-Byng, p. 117.

5. Staunton, vol. 2, p. 64.

6. See Marcel Granet, *La Religion des Chinois*, p. 159.

7. "Do not let yourself be deceived by them, for they are evil nuns: how many reputations have they ruined!" writes André Lévy in his translation of *Jin Ping Mei*, vol. 2, p. 169.

8. See Anderson, p. 140.

9. Ibid., p. 139.

10. Ibid.

11. Ibid., p. 140.

12. IOCM, 92, 264–325.

13. Cranmer-Byng, pp. 117–18.

14. Staunton, vol. 2, p. 65.

15. Ibid., p. 66.

16. Staunton, Jr., f° 103.

17. Staunton, vol. 2, p. 67.

18. See A Kuo Liang-ho, "The Grand Council in the Ch'ing Dynasty," *Far Eastern Quarterly*, February 1952, pp. 167–69.

19. See the entire text in Morse, vol. 2, appendix I, pp. 244–47.

20. IOCM, 92, 68–71.

21. Staunton, vol. 2, p. 67.

22. Ibid.

23. ZGCB, p. 53.

24. UAGC, September 8, 1793, microfilm 26.

25. ZGCB, p. 54.

26. Ibid.

27. Cranmer-Byng, p. 119.

28. Staunton, vol. 2, p. 68.

29. Ibid.

30. Ibid.

31. ZGCB, p. 54.

CHAPTER 33

1. Staunton, Jr., f° 103. The legate's demotion is reported by Macartney in an entry dated September 8 (Cranmer-Byng, p. 118), but we know that the ambassador's journal was actually put together from scattered notes during the return trip. Young Staunton's diary seems more likely to be reliable on such a detail.

2. Cranmer-Byng, p. 118.

3. UAGC, August 3, 1793, and August 12, 1793, microfilm 25.

4. Ibid., August 12, 1793, and August 17, 1793, microfilm 25.

5. And not by two, as young Staunton says, and still less three, as Macartney claims (Cranmer-Byng, p. 118). Staunton (vol. 2, p. 87) specifies the color of the button both before (transparent blue) and after (opaque white). This shows that in fact Zhengrui was demoted from the fifth to the sixth class.

6. Barrow reports this detail (*Travels in China*, p. 116). In the course of his long career (he was active right up to his death, in his eighties), Zhengrui regained his peacock feather and lost it yet again. (See Cranmer-Byng, pp. 323–24.)

7. Cranmer-Byng, p. 252.

8. Barrow, *Travels in China*, p. 390.

9. Cranmer-Byng, p. 119.

10. Anderson, p. 141.

11. Ibid., pp. 142–43.

12. Ibid., p. 143.

13. Cranmer-Byng, p. 119.

14. Ibid., p. 122.

15. *Lettres de voyage, 1923–1939*, April 20, 1936, p. 201.

CHAPTER 34

1. *Qing shizao: Li Zhi*, chapter 10, p. 4a-b, quoted in Pritchard, *Le Kowtow et l'ambassade Macartney*, 1943, p. 190.

2. Backhouse and Bland, p. 321.

3. Ibid., pp. 382–83.

4. ZGCB, pp. 53–54, September 10, 1793.

5. Psalms 2.

6. *Li Ki*, vol. 101, p. 215; quoted in Marcel Granet, *La Civilisation chinoise*, p. 318.

CHAPTER 35

1. See Barrow, *Travels in China*, p. 117.
2. Ibid., pp. 117–18.
3. Cranmer-Byng, p. 120.
4. Morse, vol. 2, appendix G, letter from Dundas to Macartney, September 8, 1792.
5. Staunton, Jr., f° 103.
6. Cranmer-Byng, p. 121.
7. Ibid., p. 239.
8. ZGCB, p. 54a-b; *Ch'ing Shih-lu*, reign of Qianlong, chapter 1434, p. 11a-b.
9. Pritchard (*Kowtow*, p. 190, n. 87) reports that the Sinologist John Kullgen said that he was told by Dr. Yuan Tingli, a conservator at the National Library of Peking, that the report to the emperor presenting Macartney's case explained that the English genuflected on both knees only to God; that the most humble homage any mortal could render another was to go down on one knee; that the English did so before their king and were prepared to do so before the emperor. It was this reasoning that was judged sincere and acceptable. But I was unable to find any trace of this document, and the story may well have been handed down by word of mouth.
10. Backhouse and Bland, *Annals and Memoirs of the Court of Peking*, p. 384n.
11. Anderson, p. 144.
12. Amiot, quoted in Hedin, p. 155.
13. Cranmer-Byng, p. 122.
14. Anderson, p. 146.

CHAPTER 36

1. Anderson, p. 146.
2. Ibid., p. 238.
3. *Le Cheval de jade*, p. 110.
4. Anderson, p. 146.
5. See *Jin Ping Mei*, vol. 2, p. 1030.
6. Anderson, pp. 146–47.
7. Barrow, *Travels in China*, p. 420.
8. Cranmer-Byng, p. 122.
9. Anderson, p. 147.
10. Ibid.
11. Hüttner, p. 77.
12. Ibid., p. 78.
13. Ibid., pp. 78–80.
14. Ibid., p. 81.
15. Ibid., p. 82.
16. Ibid., p. 83.
17. Ibid., p. 85.
18. Staunton, vol. 2, p. 74.
19. Cranmer-Byng, p. 122.
20. Hüttner, p. 183.

21. Staunton, vol. 2, p. 76.
22. Van Gulik, p. 275.
23. UAGC, April 2, 1793, ref. 4 21 12.
24. IOCM, 93, 188–93.
25. Staunton, Jr., f° 104–5.
26. Staunton, vol. 2, p. 74.
27. AL, Father Lamiot's notes on the English embassy, 1807.
28. Staunton, vol. 2, p. 75.
29. Ibid.
30. Ibid.

CHAPTER 37

1. Staunton, vol. 2, p. 75.
2. BIF, letter to Mr. Bertin, MS 1517.
3. Van Braam, vol. 1, p. 180.
4. Hüttner, p. 84.
5. Winder, f° 6.
6. Cranmer-Byng, p. 123.
7. Staunton, Jr., f° 104.
8. Winder, f° 6. Emphasis added.
9. Ibid.
10. Staunton, Jr., f° 105.
11. Full text of the Chinese ceremonial, translated by Pauthier, 1859.
12. Cranmer-Byng, p. 122.
13. Ibid., pp. 122–23.
14. Ibid.
15. Staunton, vol. 2, p. 78.
16. Barrow, *Travels in China*, p. 150.
17. ZGCB, 7, p. 39.
18. Staunton, vol. 2, p. 78.
19. Ibid.
20. Cranmer-Byng, p. 124.
21. Ibid., p. 371, n. 44.
22. Ibid., p. 123.
23. *The Travels of Marco Polo*, trans. Waugh, p. 78.
24. Cranmer-Byng, p. 123.
25. Ibid.
26. Ibid.
27. Hüttner, p. 89.
28. Official Records, September 14, 1793, vol. 27, p. 172.

CHAPTER 38

1. Cranmer-Byng, p. 124.
2. Ibid.
3. Ibid., pp. 124–25.
4. See Hummel, p. 256. Shunzhi, Kangxi's father, had the Buddhist name Fulin.
5. Cranmer-Byng, p. 125.
6. See Staunton, Jr., f° 108.
7. Cited in Hedin, p. 158.

8. Ibid., p. 159.

9. Cranmer-Byng, p. 126.

10. Ibid., 125.

11. Ibid., p. 126.

12. AN, Paris, *Fonds Colonies-missions d' Extrême-Orient*, letter of Father Raux to Mr. de Castries, minister of the navy, October 14, 1788.

13. Cranmer-Byng, p. 271.

14. Ibid.

15. Ibid., p. 126. Barrow made much of these observations in *Travels in China*, pp. 126–37.

16. Cranmer-Byng, p. 127.

17. See Hummel, p. 691.

18. See Fairbank and Teng, pp. 193–94.

19. Cranmer-Byng, pp. 127–28.

20. Ibid., p. 128.

21. Ibid., p. 125.

22. Staunton, vol. 2, p. 84.

23. Ibid.

24. Cranmer-Byng, p. 129.

25. Staunton, vol. 2, p. 69.

26. Holmes, pp. 149–50.

27. See ZGCB, p. 65a.

28. Staunton, vol. 2, p. 70.

29. "Dr. Gillan's Observations on the State of Medicine, Surgery, and Chemistry in China," in Cranmer-Byng, pp. 280–82.

30. Cranmer-Byng, p. 129.

31. Staunton, vol. 2, p. 87.

32. Dr. Gillan, in Cranmer-Byng, p. 283.

CHAPTER 39

1. See Commeaux, p. 124. Each generation, however, could also win promotions of rank.

2. Cranmer-Byng, p. 130.

3. Ibid., p. 237.

4. Ibid.

5. Huc, vol. 4, p. 37.

6. Barrow, *Travels in China*, p. 412.

7. Ibid., pp. 412–13.

8. Ibid., p. 413.

9. See Commeaux, p. 126.

10. Barrow, *Travels in China*, p. 416.

11. See Lu Xun, *La Véridique Histoire d'Ah Q*, p. 61.

12. Barrow, *Travels in China*, p. 414.

13. Staunton, vol. 2, pp. 243–51.

14. G. W. F. Hegel, *The Philosophy of History*, trans. J. Sibree, New York, 1899, p. 134.

15. *Phenomenology of Spirit*, Gallimard, 1970, p. 410.

16. Barrow, *Travels in China*, p. 414.

17. Hüttner, p. 68.

18. Ibid., pp. 224–25.

19. See Marco Polo, p. 79.

20. Cranmer-Byng, p. 131.

21. Barrow, *Travels in China*, p. 315.

22. Cranmer-Byng, p. 131.

23. Ibid., p. 124.

24. Official Records, September 17, 1793, vol. 27, pp. 175–76.

25. Hüttner, pp. 99–100.

26. See Chavannes, *Ts'in Che-Houang*, p. 156, n. 1; Couvreur, *Dictionnaire chinois-français*, p. 755; Marcel Granet, *La Civilisation chinoise*, p. 49.

27. Cranmer-Byng, p. 131.

28. See Lu Xun, p. 65.

29. Winder, f° 5.

30. Cranmer-Byng, p. 131.

31. *The Handbook of Jehol*, part 1, chapter 2, quoted in Hedin, p. 185.

32. UAGC, September 22, 1793, microfilm 26.

33. *Journal du Lion*, in French translation of Anderson, vol. 2, pp. 191–92.

CHAPTER 40

1. Cranmer-Byng, p. 132.

2. Such as the Jesuit Father Attiret (another official painter) and Sir William Chambers.

3. Cranmer-Byng, p. 133.

4. Anderson, p. 153.

5. Cranmer-Byng, p. 134.

6. *The Handbook of Jehol*, quoted in Hedin, p. 15.

7. Cranmer-Byng, p. 135.

8. Ibid., p. 136.

9. Ibid.

10. Ibid.

11. Staunton, vol. 2, pp. 92–93.

12. Cranmer-Byng, p. 137.

13. See Hedin, pp. 176–77.

14. G. W. F. Hegel, *Reason in History*, p. 198.

15. Freud, *The Future of an Illusion*, Standard Edition of the Complete Psychological Works of Sigmund Freud, London, 1961, vol. 21, p. 49.

16. *Totem and Taboo*, trans. A. A. Brill, New York, 1946, p. 167.

17. Cranmer-Byng, p. 137.

18. Ibid.

19. Quoted in Hedin, p. 187.

20. Cranmer-Byng, pp. 137–38.
21. Ibid., p. 138.
22. Ibid.
23. Ibid., pp. 138–39.
24. Ibid., p. 139.
25. Ibid.
26. Ibid.
27. UAGC, June 19, 1793, and August 5, 1793, microfilm 67.
28. Cranmer-Byng, p. 140.
29. Ibid.

CHAPTER 41

1. See Commeaux, chapter 5.
2. Cranmer-Byng, p. 201.
3. See Hedin, p. 229.
4. H. Kahn, pp. 52–53.
5. Ibid., p. 55.
6. Hüttner, p. 231.
7. Staunton, vol. 2, p. 119.
8. Qianlong had two empress-consorts. The first died in 1738; the second, proclaimed empress in 1750, shaved her head and joined a convent in 1765, a decision the court ascribed to insanity. But not everyone was so indulgent about the sovereign's behavior. See Hummel, p. 372.
9. Though he was Qianlong's favorite grandson, Miencul never acceded to the throne; he died in 1822 or 1823, during the reign of his brother Daoguang. See Cranmer-Byng, p. 362, note 16.
10. Some of which were in Manchu. C. de Hartez argues that he created poetry in this language. See Eloge de Mukden, in rhymed distiches, which was translated into French by Father Amiot and criticized by Voltaire.
11. See Backhouse and Bland, pp. 334–35.
12. Cranmer-Byng, p. 202.
13. See Hedin, pp. 215ff. In the chapter on Xiangfei, Hedin refers to Qianlong's "all-powerful favourite" Heshen (p. 219). But this must be a mistake, since the episode occurred during the twenty-fourth year of Qianlong's reign (1759), and Heshen, born in 1745, would have been only fourteen years old at the time.
14. Backhouse and Bland, pp. 347–49.
15. Staunton, vol. 2, pp. 117–18.
16. Barrow, Travels in China, p. 230n. See also Gillan, in Cranmer-Byng, p. 284.

CHAPTER 42

1. Cranmer-Byng, pp 140–41.
2. Staunton, vol. 1, p. 290.

3. See AL, letter from Father Raux to de Guignes, August 9, 1793.
4. Cranmer-Byng, p. 141.
5. Staunton, Jr., f° 112.
6. Cranmer-Byng, p. 141.
7. See Pritchard, The Crucial Years, pp. 179–84.
8. Cranmer-Byng, p. 142.
9. Ibid.
10. Ibid.
11. Anderson, p. 146.
12. Barrow, Travels in China, p. 161.
13. Jin Ping Mei, vol. 2, p. 1245.
14. See Staunton, vol. 2, p. 204.
15. Anderson, p. 205.
16. Cranmer-Byng, p. 142.
17. Ibid., p. 143.
18. Hüttner, p. 121.
19. Ibid.
20. Under the French monarchy, the (eternal) "mystical body" of the king was considered quite distinct from his (mortal) physical body. Only the king and princes of the blood had the right to die in Versailles. Louis XV made an exception for Mme de Pompadour, but immediately after her death her body was carried on a stretcher to a bier in her hotel. See Ludovic Michel, Prestigieuse marquise de Pompadour, p. 356.
21. Staunton, Jr., f° 113.
22. Anderson, p. 168.
23. UAGC, September 21, 1793, microfilm 26.
24. Ibid.
25. ZGCB, 65a.
26. UAGC, September 22, 1793, microfilm 26.
27. See P. E. Will, Bureaucratie et famine en Chine au XVIII° siècle, pp. 79–81.
28. Cranmer-Byng, p. 143.
29. Staunton, Jr., f° 113–15.
30. Cranmer-Byng, p. 144.

CHAPTER 43

1. Staunton, Jr., f° 115.
2. CUMC, no. 259.
3. Staunton, vol. 1, pp. 128–29.
4. Cranmer-Byng, p. 144.
5. Anderson, p. 170.
6. Ibid., pp. 170–71.
7. ZGCB, 8, p. 63b.
8. Ibid.
9. Ibid., p. 64a.
10. Cranmer-Byng, p. 146.

11. Staunton, Jr., f° 115.

12. AN, letter from Father Raux to Mr. de Sartine, minister of the navy, November 16, 1788, *Fonds Colonies-missions d'Extrême-Orient*, F5 A22, Paris.

13. Dinwiddie, p. 51. See also Macartney, p. 146: "none of the missionaries . . . have been allowed to frequent us since we returned from Jehol."

14. See AL, letter from Father Raux to Fathers Hanna and Lamiot, October 28, 1793.

15. Cranmer-Byng, p. 144.

16. Anderson, p. 171.

17. Hüttner, p. 125.

18. Staunton, Jr., f° 116.

19. Van Braam, vol. 2, p. vi.

20. Staunton, Jr., f° 117.

21. Staunton, vol. 2, p. 121.

22. See Van Braam, I, 222.

23. Staunton, Jr., f° 117.

24. Cranmer-Byng, p. 145.

25. ZGCB, 8, pp. 68b–69a.

26. Barrow, *Travels in China*, p. 120.

CHAPTER 44

1. Staunton, Jr., f° 117.

2. It is Barrow who adds this detail, *Travels in China*, p. 121.

3. See Cranmer-Byng, p. 356, n. 3.

4. Cranmer-Byng, p. 146.

5. Dinwiddie, p. 52.

6. Ibid., p. 53.

7. Ibid.

8. Ibid.

9. Anderson, p. 171.

10. Holmes, p. 147.

11. See Cranmer-Byng, p. 367, n. 27. The carriages Macartney had given the emperor were also found unused.

12. Anderson, p. 180.

13. Staunton, vol. 2, p. 122.

14. Cranmer-Byng, p. 146. He also reports that the only missionary to continue to visit the British was a Pole named Father Kosielski. We have no further information about this priest, who may have been working for the tsar.

15. Dinwiddie, p. 51.

16. Ibid., p. 52.

17. Barrow, *Travels in China*, p. 121.

18. UAGC, June 19, 1793, microfilm 67.

19. Cranmer-Byng, p. 146.

20. Ibid.

21. Staunton, Jr., f° 118.

22. Dinwiddie, p. 53.

23. Cranmer-Byng, pp. 146–47.

24. Staunton, vol. 1, p. 274. See also AN, letter from Father Raux to the marquis de Castri, November 16, 1788, *Fonds Colonies-mission d'Extrême-Orient* F5 A22. See also Huc., vol. 4, p. 191.

25. Cranmer-Byng, p. 147.

26. Ibid.

27. Ibid.

28. Ibid.

29. Ibid.

30. Confucius, *The Analects*, 7: 11, p. 87.

31. ZGCB, 8, p. 68.

32. UAGC, September 22, 1793, microfilm 26.

33. Ibid., October 10, 1793, microfilm 68.

34. Ibid.

35. Ibid.

36. Ibid.

CHAPTER 45

1. Cranmer-Byng, p. 149.

2. Ibid.

3. Ibid.

4. Staunton, Jr., f° 118.

5. Cranmer-Byng, p. 150.

6. See above, chapter 34.

7. Anderson, p. 182.

8. Staunton, vol. 2, p. 127.

9. Cranmer-Byng, p. 150.

10. UAGC, October 3, 1793, microfilm 26.

11. Ibid.

12. *Histoire de l'expédition chrétienne au royaume de la Chine, 1582–1610*, Paris, 1978, p. 396.

13. Dinwiddie, p. 54.

14. Ibid., p. 50.

CHAPTER 46

1. See CUMC, Father Raux's letter to Macartney, September 29, 1794, no. 310.

2. UAGC, edict in reply to the king of England, n.d.; see also ZGCB, II, pp. 18a–19b. English translation in Cranmer-Byng, pp. 336–341.

3. See G. T. Staunton, *Miscellaneous Notices Relating to China*, pp. 78–86; *Lettres édifiantes et curieuses écrites des missions étrangères*, vols. 16–24; W. Devine, *The Four Churches of Peking*.

CHAPTER 47

1. Alexander.
2. IOCM, 92, pp. 259–61.
3. Macartney is alluding to the Russo-Chinese treaty of 1727, which authorized the Russians to open a trading post in Peking. Convoys accompanied by up to two hundred merchants were granted permission to come to the capital once every three years, but by the middle of the century this trade had stopped, and by the time of Macartney's embassy, the Russian colony in Peking had been reduced to just a few priests. (See CUMC, no 397. See also *Journal inédit des Jésuites de Saint-Pétersbourg*, ASJ.)
4. A thousand dollars in 1772; nine thousand in 1791.
5. Cranmer-Byng, p. 150.
6. Morse, vol. 2, appendix G, p. 239, letter from Dundas to Macartney, September 8, 1792.
7. Ibid., p. 240. and pp. 207–8.
8. Cranmer-Byng, p. 153.
9. Staunton, vol. 2, p. 128.
10. UAGC, October 4, 1793, microfilm 23.

CHAPTER 48

1. Staunton, Jr., f° 119.
2. Dinwiddie, p. 54.
3. Cranmer-Byng, p. 154.
4. Ibid., p. 155.
5. Ibid.
6. Anderson, p. 181.
7. See Cranmer-Byng, pp. 152 and 154.
8. Anderson, p. 182.
9. Dinwiddie, pp. 54–55.
10. Cranmer-Byng, p. 155.
11. See Pauthier, *Histoires des relations politiques de la Chine avec les puissance occidentales*, Rituel.
12. AMAE, letter of Father de Grammont to Van Braam, MD, *Asie 21*, f° 76–77, Paris.
13. Cranmer-Byng, p. 155.
14. Ibid., pp. 155–56.
15. AMAE, unpublished letter of Father de Grammont to Van Braam, MD, *Asie 21* f° 76–77, Paris.

PART FOUR

EPIGRAPHS

1. *The Analects*, 1: 9, p. 60.
2. *Democracy in America*, trans. Henry Reeve, New York, 1945, vol. 2, book 4, chapter 7, p. 239.

CHAPTER 49

1. *Souvenirs d'enfance et de jeunesse*, 1883, vol. 5, p. 2.
2. Cranmer-Byng, p. 156.
3. The Chinese text of this reply is to be found not in the ZGCB collection but in the *Ta Ch'ing Li-ch'ao Shih-lu*, vol. 1435, pp. 156–200.
4. *Ta Ch'ing Li-ch'ao Shih-lu*, vol. 1435, p. 156.
5. Ibid., p. 162.
6. Ibid., p. 174.
7. Ibid.
8. CUMC, no. 310.
9. Ibid.
10. Ibid.
11. P. Corradini ("Concerning the ban on preaching Christianity . . . ," *East & West*, 1968, pp. 89–91) raises the possibility.
12. BIF, letter of Father Amiot to Mr. Bertin, September 20, 1774, MS 1515, Paris.
13. CUMC, no. 444.
14. IOCM, 92, letter to Dundas, November 9, 1793.
15. Cranmer-Byng, p. 152.
16. Ibid., pp. 158–59.

CHAPTER 50

1. Cranmer-Byng, p. 159.
2. Anderson, p. 183.
3. Staunton, Jr., f° 120.
4. Dinwiddie, p. 55.
5. Anderson, p. 184.
6. Cranmer-Byng, p. 159.
7. Ibid.
8. UAGC, October 8, 1793, microfilm 26.
9. Cranmer-Byng, p. 159.
10. Staunton, vol. 2, p. 139.
11. From the Mongol blue banner (Hummel, p. 691).
12. Staunton, vol. 2, p. 139.
13. Cranmer-Byng, p. 160.
14. Ibid.
15. Ibid.

16. UAGC, October 11, 1793, microfilm 23.

17. Cranmer-Byng, p. 161.

18. Ibid.

19. See Staunton, Jr., f° 120–21.

20. Ibid., f° 121.

21. Staunton, vol. 2, p. 141.

22. Ibid., pp. 139–40.

23. Ibid., p. 140.

24. Staunton, Jr., f° 121–22.

25. Cranmer-Byng, p. 162.

26. UAGC, October 14, 1793, microfilm 26.

27. Staunton, Jr., f° 123.

28. UAGC, October 14, 1793, microfilm 26.

29. Cranmer-Byng, p. 162.

30. Ibid.

31. Ibid., pp. 162–63.

32. UAGC, October 14, 1793, microfilm 26.

CHAPTER 51

1. G. T. Staunton, *Ta Ts'ing Leu Lee*, p. 65.

2. Cranmer-Byng, p. 163.

3. AL, letters of Father Richenet to G. T. Staunton, 1811.

4. UAGC, October 5, 1793, microfilm 68.

5. Ibid., October 7, 1793, microfilm 26.

6. Ibid., October 11, 1793, microfilm 68.

7. Ibid., October 14, 1793, microfilm 26.

8. Ibid., October 17, 1793, microfilm 26.

9. Ibid., October 11, 1793, microfilm 26.

CHAPTER 52

1. Songshi, 179/3a-b, quoted in Balazs, *La Bureaucratie céleste*, p. 189.

2. Holmes, pp. 153–54.

3. Dinwiddie, p. 56.

4. Cranmer-Byng, p. 164.

5. Staunton, Jr., f° 124–25.

6. Dinwiddie, p. 57.

7. Cranmer-Byng, p. 164.

8. Staunton, vol. 2, p. 142.

9. AL, Father Lamiot's notes on the English embassy.

10. Barrow, *Travels in China*, p. 570.

11. See *Jin Ping Mei*, vol. 2, p. 1002.

12. UAGC, October 15, 1793, microfilm 26.

13. Ibid.

14. Ibid.

15. Bodleian Library, Oxford, MSS *English History*, C 1124.

16. Staunton, vol. 2, p. 148.

17. Ibid., pp. 143–44.

18. AL, Father Lamiot's notes on the English embassy.

19. See Labrousse, Romano, Dreyfus, *Les prix du froment en France au temps de la monnaie stable, 1726–1913*, EHESS, 1970, p. 246.

20. From the middle of the eighteenth century to the middle of the nineteenth, the population of China tripled, while the total area of land under cultivation barely doubled. See S. Naquin and E. Rawski, *Chinese Society in the Eighteenth Century*. Other estimates of population growth are somewhat more modest but still impressive.

21. AL, Father Lamiot's notes on the English embassy.

22. Zhu Yong, *Sino-English Relations Under Qianlong, 1736–1796*, introduction.

23. Staunton, vol. 2, p. 144.

24. Barrow, *Travels in China*, p. 559.

25. See Commeaux, p. 196.

26. Staunton, vol. 2, p. 143.

27. Van Gulik, chapter 8.

CHAPTER 53

1. Staunton, Jr., f° 125.

2. Cranmer-Byng, p. 165.

3. Dinwiddie, p. 57.

4. Staunton, Jr., f° 126.

5. Staunton, vol. 2, p. 149.

6. Staunton, Jr., f° 125.

7. Barrow, *Travels in China*, p. 501.

8. Ibid.

9. Hüttner, p. 237.

10. Staunton, Jr., f° 125.

11. Staunton, vol. 2, p. 14.

12. Ibid.

13. Ricci and Trigault, *Histoire de l'expédition chrétienne à la conquête du royaume de la Chine*, p. 49.

14. Cranmer-Byng, p. 165.

15. Staunton, vol. 2, p. 150.

16. Holmes, p. 174.

17. See AL, Father Lamiot's notes on the English embassy.

18. Cranmer-Byng, p. 233.

19. Barrow, *Travels in China*, p. 480.

20. See *Jin Ping Mei*, vol. 1, p. 1051.

21. See Commeaux, p. 191.

22. See *Jin Ping Mei*, vol. 2, p. 336.

23. Cranmer-Byng, p. 165.

24. Staunton, vol. 2, p. 146.

25. Quoted in Goubert and Denis, *1789, les Français ont la parole*, p. 193.

26. Barrow, *Travels in China*, p. 155.

27. *Jin Ping Mei*, vol. 1, p. 261, and vol. 2, p. 1078. See also Granet, pp. 13–14.

28. Staunton, vol. 2, pp. 146–47.

29. Charpentier-Cossigny, p. 400.

30. Barrow, *Travels in China*, p. 157.

31. Huc, vol. 4, p. 233.

32. "Les Latrines de la fortune," in *Le Cheval de jade*, p. 186.

33. UAGC, October 20, 1793, microfilm 26.

34. Ibid., October 15, 1793, microfilm 26.

CHAPTER 54

1. Staunton, Jr., f° 127.

2. Cranmer-Byng, p. 166.

3. Ibid.

4. Ibid., p. 167.

5. Ibid., p. 168.

6. Ibid.

7. Latin translation of the edict submitted October 3, 1793; IOCM, 92, letter from Macartney to Dundas, November 9, 1793, ann. no. 11.

8. UAGC, October 24, 1793, microfilm 26.

9. Especially P. Corradini. See n. 11 in chapter 49.

10. Staunton, Jr., f° 127.

11. Cranmer-Byng, pp. 268–69.

12. Staunton, Jr., f° 128.

13. Staunton, vol. 2, pp. 150–51.

14. Hüttner, p. 133.

15. Ibid., p. 134.

16. Winder, f° 7.

17. Huc, vol. 4, p. 81.

18. See Cranmer-Byng, p. 266.

19. Staunton, vol. 2, pp. 156–57.

20. Ibid., pp. 157–58.

21. Barrow, *Travels in China*, p. 586.

22. *Tung Hua Chen Lu*, cited in Hedin, p. 134.

CHAPTER 55

1. Cranmer-Byng, p. 159.

2. See J. K. Fairbank and S. Y. Teng, "On the Transmission of Ch'ing Documents," *Ch'ing Administration: Three Studies*, Cambridge, Mass., 1960, pp. 1–35.

3. A letter sent on February 13, 1789, for

example, arrived on May 24. See AL, correspondence of Father Raux.

4. Ibid.

5. See Madame de Sévigné, *Correspondance*, vol. 2, p. 136, October 20, 1675.

6. See Sylvie Pasquet, *L'Evolution du système postal sous les Qing*, pp. 46–49, 66–73.

7. Ibid., pp. 170–93.

8. Anderson, p. 189.

9. See Mantoux, p. 107.

10. See A. Anderson, *Chronological History of the Origin of Commerce*, p. 712, cited in Mantoux, p. 108, n. 5.

11. UAGC, October 21, 1793, microfilm 26.

12. Ibid., October 21, 1793, microfilm 68.

CHAPTER 56

1. Cranmer-Byng, p. 215.

2. Staunton, Jr., f° 129.

3. Staunton, vol. 2, p. 153.

4. UAGC, October 26, 1793, microfilm 26.

5. Cranmer-Byng, p. 170.

6. Ibid., pp. 170–71.

7. Staunton, Jr., f° 130.

8. Ibid., f° 131.

9. Cranmer-Byng, p. 170. China originated many inventions that the West adopted, most often without the Westerners' realizing it. I leave it to other researchers to verify Macartney's hypothesis.

10. Ibid., p. 171.

11. Staunton, Jr., f° 132–33.

12. Dinwiddie, p. 62.

13. Staunton, Jr., f° 133–34.

14. Hüttner, p. 142.

15. Staunton, vol. 2, p. 159.

16. Ibid., p. 158.

17. Ibid.

18. Old Nick, *La Chine ouverte*, p. 319.

19. Barrow, *Travels in China*, p. 567.

20. Staunton, vol. 2, pp. 158–59.

21. Ibid., p. 159.

22. Barrow, *Travels in China*, p. 77.

23. *La Véridique Histoire d'Ah Q*, pp. 43–44.

24. Staunton, vol. 2, p. 159. He estimated the interest rate at 30 percent a year (ibid.). Macartney confirms: "The legal interest of money is twelve per cent, but it is commonly extended to eighteen and sometimes even to thirty-six. Usury is punishable by the laws, but, as in most other countries, is rarely punished"

(Cranmer-Byng, p. 243). Two centuries earlier, *Jin Ping Mei* gave identical rates (vol. 1, p. 381). Balazs has established that they were the same even under the Tangs, between the seventh and ninth centuries (p. 300). The *Ta T'sing Leu Lee*, the legal code in force under Qianlong, also authorized a rate of 3 percent a month. The penalty for violation of the law was forty to one hundred strokes of bamboo, and in the case of a state official, exile up to a distance of three thousand *li* (see the translation by G. T. Staunton, p. 158).

25. See Balazs, pp. 310–11.
26. Barrow, *Travels in China*, p. 311.
27. Confucius, *The Analects*, 9: 1, p. 96, and 12: 15, p. 115.

CHAPTER 57

1. UAGC, October 24, 1793, microfilm 68.
2. Ibid., October 25, 1793, microfilm 26.
3. Ibid., October 26, 1793, microfilm 68.
4. Cranmer-Byng, p. 172.
5. Ibid.
6. UAGC, October 28, 1793, microfilm 26.
7. Ibid., October 27, 1793, microfilm 68.
8. Ibid., October 29, 1793, microfilm 27.
9. Ibid.
10. Staunton, Jr., f° 137.
11. Ibid., f° 135.
12. Cranmer-Byng, pp. 172–73.
13. UAGC, November 1, 1793, microfilm 68.
14. Ibid., November 1, 1793, microfilm 27.
15. Ibid.
16. Ibid.

CHAPTER 58

1. Anderson, p. 193.
2. Staunton, Jr., f° 139.
3. Anderson, p. 193.
4. Staunton, vol. 2, p. 161.
5. Ibid.
6. Ibid., p. 163.
7. Official Records, fifty-eighth year, Qianlong era, p. 214.
8. Cranmer-Byng, p. 173.
9. Staunton, vol. 2, p. 168.
10. See ZGCB, 8, pp. 68b–69a.
11. Staunton, vol. 2, p. 167.
12. Staunton, Jr., f° 141.
13. Ibid., f° 141–42
14. Staunton, vol. 2, p. 171.

15. Cranmer-Byng, p. 174.
16. UAGC, November 6, 1793, microfilm 68.
17. Ibid., November 7, 1793, microfilm 27.
18. Cranmer-Byng, p. 174. (In her edition, Robbins omits the adjective "effeminate.")
19. UAGC, November 8, 1793, microfilm 27.
20. Barrow, *Travels in China*, p. 411.
21. Ibid., p. 407.
22. Cranmer-Byng, p. 196. In his "Observations on China" the ambassador notes: "The revenues of this great empire are said to be a little less than 200 millions of taels (. . . but the Chinese, who have a fanciful predilection for odd numbers, call it 199,999,999), equal to £66,666,666 sterling, or about four times those of Great Britain, and three times those of France before the late subversion" (Cranmer-Byng, p. 247).
23. Barrow, *Travels in China*, p. 408.
24. Staunton, vol. 1, p. 294.
25. See Commeaux, pp. 100–101.
26. Barrow, *Travels in China*, p. 409.
27. See Hsie Pao Chao, *The Government of China, 1644–1911*, and the description of Nurhaci in Hummel, *Eminent Chinese*. The term *qi*, or "banner," is still used to designate administrative divisions in Inner Mongolia.

CHAPTER 59

1. Anderson, p. 205.
2. Winder, f° 9.
3. Cranmer-Byng, p. 175.
4. Staunton, Jr., f° 145.
5. Ibid., f° 146.
6. Barrow, *Travels in China*, pp. 520–21.
7. *Le Cheval de jade*, p. 37.
8. Staunton, vol. 2, pp. 173–74.
9. "Le Châtiment du parasite," in *Le Cheval de jade*, p. 83.
10. Staunton, vol. 2, p. 174.
11. Hüttner, p. 142.
12. Ibid., p. 143.
13. Winder, f° 9.
14. Hüttner, p. 146.
15. See Lin Yutang, p. 154.
16. "La Belle et le Lettré," in *Le Cheval de jade*, p. 25.
17. Lin Yutang, p. 155.

CHAPTER 60

1. *Treize récits chinois*, Paris, p. 82.
2. "La Belle et le Lettré," p. 25.

3. Barrow, *Travels in China*, pp. 145–46.
4. Ibid., p. 146.
5. "La Belle et le Lettré," p. 28.
6. Barrow, *Travels in China*, p. 146.
7. Huc, vol. 4, p. 146.
8. See P'ou Song-Ling, *Contes extraordi-naires du pavillon du loisir*, Gallimard/UNESCO, p. 170.
9. *Jin Ping Mei*, vol. 1, p. 82.
10. See Lin Yutang, p. 141.
11. See Marcel Granet, *La Civilisation chinoise*, p. 398. The character of great-grandmother Xia in *Le Rêve dans le pavillon rouge* represents the epitome of the role.
12. Barrow, *Travels in China*, p. 146.
13. *Jin Ping Mei*, vol. 2, p. 719.
14. Barrow, *Travels in China*, p. 235.
15. Ibid., pp. 147–48.
16. ASJ, letter of Father de Grammont to his family, November 15, 1770.
17. Barrow, *Travels in China*, p. 148.
18. *Jin Ping Mei, passim.*
19. Ibid., vol. 1, p. 268.
20. See Etiemble, *L'Erotisme et l'amour*, pp. 85–96.
21. *Zhulin Yeshi*, trans. Kontler, "Belle de Candeur," p. 25.
22. Ibid., pp. 25 and 134.
23. Hüttner, p. 152.
24. See Cranmer-Byng, p. 175.
25. UAGC, November 8, 1793, microfilm 27.

CHAPTER 61

1. Cranmer-Byng, p. 176.
2. See Cranmer-Byng, p. 373, note 51.
3. See Staunton, Jr., f° 148.
4. Cranmer-Byng, p. 176.
5. See Cranmer-Byng, p. 374, n. 54.
6. See Cranmer-Byng, p. 177.
7. Ibid.
8. UAGC, November 13, 1793, microfilm 27.
9. Ibid.
10. See Cranmer-Byng, p. 177.
11. Staunton, Jr., f° 148.
12. Cranmer-Byng, p. 177.
13. Staunton, vol. 2, p. 170.
14. Ibid.
15. Staunton, Jr., f° 148–49.
16. Staunton, vol. 2, pp. 183–84.
17. Staunton, Jr., f° 149.
18. Staunton, vol. 2, pp. 179–80.

19. Ibid., p. 180. See also C. Larre, *Les Chinois*, p. 318.
20. Alexander.
21. Barrow, *Travels in China*, p. 524.
22. *Chronique indiscrète des mandarins*, Gallimard/UNESCO, vol. 1, p. 215.
23. Staunton, vol. 2, pp. 182–83.
24. Ibid., p. 182.

CHAPTER 62

1. Cranmer-Byng, p. 177.
2. AL, letter from Father Raux to Fathers Hanna and Lamiot, October 28, 1793.
3. Ibid., Father Raux to Father Aubin, June 25, 1789.
4. Cranmer-Byng, p. 178.
5. See UAGC, November 4, 1793, microfilm 27.
6. Cranmer-Byng, p. 178.
7. Ibid.
8. UAGC, November 13, 1793, microfilm 27.
9. Staunton, Jr., f° 151.
10. See Louis Dumont, *Homo hierarchicus*, p. 15.
11. UAGC, October 21, 1793, microfilm 68.
12. Guo Shixun's report is dated November 1, 1793 (UAGC, microfilm 27). The marginal notes are from November 12, 1793.
13. IOCM, 92, November 9, 1793, letter to Dundas, first page.
14. Ibid., 2nd page.
15. Ibid., 10th page.
16. Ibid., 21st page.
17. Ibid., 24th page.
18. Ibid., 25th page.
19. Ibid., 26th page.

PART FIVE

EPIGRAPHS

1. Confucius, *The Analects*, 4, 13.
2. BIF, letter to Mr. Bertin, from Peking, September 20, 1774, MS 1515.
3. *Encyclopédie philosophique*, entry for "Man."

CHAPTER 63

1. Cranmer-Byng, p. 151.
2. Staunton, vol. 2, p. 127.
3. Ibid., p. 110.

4. Charpentier-Cossigny, p. 283.

5. Cranmer-Byng, p. 151.

6. Ibid., p. 153.

7. Staunton, vol. 2, p. 128. See also ASJ, unpublished journal of the Jesuits of St. Petersburg.

8. *Mémoires concernant les Chinois*, vol. 14, p. 534.

9. IOCM, 92, letter to the Board of Directors, November 10, 1793.

10. UAGC, November 1, 1793, microfilm 27.

11. See Cranmer-Byng, p. 151.

CHAPTER 64

1. Cranmer-Byng, p. 179.

2. Staunton, Jr., f° 151–52.

3. Ibid.

4. Ibid., f° 153–54.

5. Anderson, p. 210.

6. Ibid.

7. Ibid.

8. Cranmer-Byng, pp. 179–80.

9. See AL, Father Lamiot's notes on the English embassy.

10. Staunton, Jr., f° 154.

11. Cranmer-Byng, p. 179.

12. Staunton, Jr., f° 155.

13. Cranmer-Byng, p. 180.

14. Staunton, Jr., f° 155–57.

15. Hüttner, pp. 158–59.

16. Ibid., p. 160.

17. Staunton, Jr., f° 155.

18. Ibid., f° 156.

19. Staunton, vol. 2, p. 174.

20. Cranmer-Byng, p. 180.

21. Hüttner, p. 162.

22. Cranmer-Byng, pp. 180–81.

23. Ibid., p. 181.

24. Ibid., pp. 181–82.

25. Ibid., p. 182.

26. Staunton, Jr. f° 158.

CHAPTER 65

1. Letter from Macartney to Lord Cornwallis, from Batavia, March 6, 1793, in *Journal of the Bihar Research Society*, vol. 44, 1958, p. 86.

2. Ibid., p. 183.

3. See Braudel, vol. 1, pp. 214–15.

4. Cranmer-Byng, p. 286.

5. Staunton, vol. 2, p. 193.

6. Ibid.

7. Ibid., pp. 192–93.

8. Charpentier-Cossigny, p. 252.

9. See *Jin Ping Mei*, vol. 1, p. 779.

10. Staunton, Jr., f° 125 (October 17).

11. Staunton, vol. 2, p. 192.

12. Anderson, p. 186.

13. See *Journal of the Bihar Research Society*, p. 117.

14. See Dinwiddie, pp. 86ff.

15. Cranmer-Byng, p. 182.

16. Here I am merely summarizing the exhaustive explanations given by Cranmer-Byng, pp. 374–75, n. 57.

17. Staunton, Jr., f° 158.

18. Cranmer-Byng, pp. 182–83.

19. Ibid., p. 183.

20. See Cranmer-Byng, n. 58. The Liu-Kiu Islands (also known as Riou Kiou or Ryū Kyū) were also tributaries of the House of Satsuma, in Japan. In fact, Chinese suzerainty was purely nominal, even in Macartney's time.

21. UAGC, October 19, 1793, microfilm 68.

22. Cranmer-Byng, p. 184.

23. Ibid.

24. Ibid.

25. I was unable to find the original text of Changlin's memorandum, but a summary of it appears in an imperial edict dated December 1, 1793, microfilm 68.

26. Staunton, vol. 2, p. 128.

27. Cranmer-Byng, p. 185.

28. This memorandum, appended to Macartney's manuscript, is not included in the Cranmer-Byng edition. It is available in the company archives (IOCM, 92, pp. 411–14). An abridged version appears in Pritchard, *The Crucial Years*, p. 357.

29. See Cranmer-Byng, p. 389, n. 104.

CHAPTER 66

1. Anderson, p. 214.

2. Staunton, Jr., f° 161–62.

3. Cranmer-Byng, p. 186.

4. Hüttner, pp. 167–68.

5. See Temple, *Quand la Chine nous précédait*, p. 56.

6. Staunton, Jr., f° 162–63.

7. Cranmer-Byng, p. 186.

8. Staunton, Jr., f° 163. See also "Les Latrines de la fortune," p. 157 *et passim*.

9. Hüttner, pp. 171–72.

10. Staunton, vol. 2, p. 197.

11. Barrow, *Travels in China*, p. 564.

12. Ibid., p. 220.

13. Ibid., p. 558.

14. Ibid., p. 544.

15. See Freud, *Civilization and Its Discontents*, The Standard Edition of the Complete Psychological Works of Sigmund Freud, London, 1961, vol. 21, pp. 93–94 and 97.

16. See Erikson, *Identity: Youth and Crisis*, New York, 1968, pp. 107–14. It is true that the use of human fertilizer by no means implies pleasure in the handling of excrement or attachment of a sexual value to it. There is no mention of coprophagy or similar deviations in Chinese erotic literature. The Japanese also use human fertilizer, but they, unlike the Chinese, have an obsessional mania for cleanliness and bathing.

17. Staunton, vol. 2, p. 201.

18. Ibid.

19. Ibid.

20. Ibid., pp. 201–2.

21. Confucius, *The Analects*, 20: 2, p. 160.

22. Lieou Ngo, *Pérégrinations d'un clochard*, p. 93.

23. *Chronique indiscrète des Mandarins*, vol. 1, p. 40.

24. Confucius, *The Analects*, 12: 18, p. 121.

25. See Commeaux, chapter 3.

26. "Les Latrines de la fortune," p. 157.

27. Confucius, 7: 2, p. 88.

28. UAGC, October 15, 1793, microfilm 68.

29. See Commeaux, p. 89.

30. Confucius, 20: 2, p. 160.

31. "Les Latrines de la fortune," p. 186.

32. *Le Rêve dans le pavillon rouge*, vol. 1, p. 37.

CHAPTER 67

1. Anderson, p. 208.

2. Holmes, pp. 172–75.

3. Ibid., p. 176.

4. Alexander.

5. UAGC, November 21, 1793, microfilm 27.

6. Dinwiddie, p. 70.

7. Li Guantian, "Le Jugement des eaux," in *Treize récits chinois*, p. 221.

8. Cranmer-Byng, p. 187.

9. Ibid.

10. UAGC, November 21, 1793, microfilm 27.

11. UAGC, trans. of a note from Macartney (dated November 20, 1793), microfilm 27.

CHAPTER 68

1. Quoted in G. T. Staunton, *Ta T'sing Leu Lee*, p. lxvii.

2. Cranmer-Byng, p. 187.

3. Staunton, Jr., f° 165.

4. Anderson, pp. 216–17.

5. At the lakeside, Macartney inquired about a fish about which Thomas Pennant, a member of the Royal Society, had asked for information, but he was unable to find out anything (see Cranmer-Byng, p. 188 and n. 61). Cranmer-Byng could find nothing more about the incident, and neither could I.

6. Staunton, Jr., f° 167.

7. The map given by Cranmer-Byng (which makes the Yushan a tributary of the Gan, such that the British would have been able to sail up the Gan without going as far as the lake) is in contradiction with the account of young Staunton, f° 167. On the other hand, the map drawn at the time by Barrow's cartographer conforms to Thomas's account.

8. Staunton, vol. 2, pp. 208–9.

9. Staunton, Jr., f° 165.

10. Staunton, vol. 2, p. 204.

11. Staunton, Jr., f° 165–66.

12. *Dictionnaire philosophique*, p. 108.

13. Staunton, vol. 2, p. 204.

14. AL, Father Lamiot's notes on the English embassy.

15. Staunton, vol. 2, p. 205.

16. Ibid.

17. Ibid., pp. 205–6.

18. Ibid., pp. 206–7.

CHAPTER 69

1. Staunton, vol. 2, p. 194.

2. *Lettres édifiantes*, September 1, 1712, pp. 180–81.

3. Huc, vol. 4, pp. 280–81.

4. Staunton, vol. 2, p. 212.

5. Ibid.

6. Ibid.

7. "Les Latrines de la fortune," p. 175.

8. Staunton, vol. 2, p. 212.

9. Anderson, p. 135.

10. Barrow, *Travels in China*, p. 400.

11. Winder, f° 9.

12. *Le cheval de jade*, p. 145; see also *Jin Ping Mei*, vol. 1, p. 979.

13. Staunton Jr., f° 170–71.
14. Cranmer-Byng, p. 189.
15. Anderson, p. 223.
16. Ibid.
17. Staunton, Jr., f° 172.
18. Cranmer-Byng, p. 189.
19. Winder, f° 9.
20. Barrow, *Travels in China*, p. 536. Barrow gives the date as November 3, but this is obviously a mistake. December 4, the date given by Staunton junior (f° 173), is clearly the correct one.
21. Staunton, Jr., f° 175.
22. Barrow, *Travels in China*, p. 537.
23. See Official Records, vol. 27, p. 235.
24. Anderson, p. 226.

CHAPTER 70

1. *Poèmes*, "L'Invention," 1787.
2. Cranmer-Byng, p. 190.
3. Ibid.
4. Needham, *passim*; see also Temple, p. 99.
5. Cranmer-Byng, p. 190.
6. Ibid.
7. See William Golding, *The Scorpion God: Three Short Novels*, London, 1971.
8. Dinwiddie, p. 80.
9. See Bruno Bettelheim, *The Empty Fortress*, p. 73.
10. Dinwiddie, p. 83.
11. Cranmer-Byng, p. 191.
12. WI, Macartney, *Memoranda from London to China* (journal), f°s 129–30.
13. Cranmer-Byng, p. 191.
14. Ibid.
15. BIF, letter to Bertin, October 10, 1789, MS 1517.
16. *Les Manifestes de Yen fou*, trans. F. Houang, Paris, 1977, p. 135.
17. Charpentier-Cossigny, p. 358.
18. *Lettres édifiantes*, to Dorfous de Mairan, September 20, 1740, p. 363.
19. *The Idler*, November 11, 1758.
20. Dinwiddie, p. 83.
21. Cranmer-Byng, p. 239.
22. *Reason in History*, p. 200.
23. *Le Suicide*, 1897.
24. See Cranmer-Byng, pp. 325–26.
25. ASJ, letter from Father de Grammont, November 29, 1778.
26. UAGC, December 1, 1793, microfilm 68.
27. Cranmer-Byng, p. 193.

CHAPTER 71

1. Cranmer-Byng, p. 192.
2. Barrow, *Travels in China*, p. 542.
3. Cranmer-Byng, p. 193.
4. "La Belle et le lettré," in *Le Cheval de jade*, p. 52.
5. See Sylvie Pasquet, p. 124.
6. Cranmer-Byng, p. 193.
7. Ibid., p. 194.
8. Anderson, p. 236.
9. Ibid., p. 237.
10. Ibid., p. 238.
11. Cranmer-Byng, p. 194, and Staunton, Jr., f° 184–85.
12. Anderson, p. 239.
13. Cranmer-Byng, p. 194.
14. Staunton, Jr., f° 185.
15. Hüttner, p. 184.
16. UAGC, December 12, 1793, microfilm 27.
17. Staunton, Jr., f°s 186–99, *passim*.
18. Barrow, *Travels in China*, p. 600.
19. Staunton, Jr., f° 188–89.
20. Anderson, p. 255.
21. Barrow, *Travels in China*, p. 595.
22. See Staunton, vol. 2, p. 39, and AL, Father Lamiot's notes on the English embassy.
23. G. T. Staunton, *Ta T'sing Leu Lee*, p. 404.

CHAPTER 72

1. *L'Homme à la découverte de son âme*, p. 267.
2. Barrow, *Travels in China*, pp. 591–92.
3. Ibid., p. 592.
4. Ibid.
5. Charpentier-Cossigny, p. 270.
6. Barrow, *Travels in China*, pp. 592–93.
7. Staunton, Jr., f° 188.
8. Barrow, *Travels in China*, p. 595.
9. Staunton, Jr., f° 189.
10. *The Travels of Marco Polo*, p. 91.
11. *Chronique indiscrète des mandarins*, vol. 2, p. 461.
12. Anderson, p. 244. Mount Huashin (Xueshen) is 1,307 meters (4,288 feet) high.
13. Ibid.
14. See Cranmer-Byng, p. 378, note 68.
15. Cranmer-Byng, pp. 197–98.
16. Ibid., p. 198.
17. Ibid., pp. 198–99.
18. Ibid., p. 199.
19. Ibid.
20. Anderson, pp. 247–48.

21. Winder, f° 11.
22. Holmes, p. 173.
23. Staunton, Jr., f° 190.
24. Ibid., f° 195.
25. Cranmer-Byng, p. 200.
26. Alexander.
27. See Cranmer-Byng, pp. 380–81, n. 75.
28. Cranmer-Byng, p. 203.
29. *Lettres de voyage, 1923–1939*, p. 219.

CHAPTER 73

1. Cranmer-Byng, p. 203.
2. Staunton, Jr., f° 201–2.
3. Ibid., f° 202–3.
4. Cranmer-Byng, pp. 203–4.
5. Staunton, Jr., f° 203–4.
6. Ibid., f° 204.
7. Barrow, *Travels in China*, p. 609.
8. Staunton, Jr., f° 204.
9. Barrow, *Travels in China*, p. 609. See also Hüttner, p. 242.
10. Staunton, Jr., f° 206.
11. Barrow, *Travels in China*, p. 613.
12. Ibid., p. 610.
13. Staunton, Jr., f° 207–8.
14. Charpentier-Cossigny, p. 394.
15. Hüttner, pp. 195–96.
16. Anderson, p. 257.
17. AN, J.-B. Piron, letter to the French East India Company, November 25, 1792, *Fonds Colonies-missions d'Extrême-Orient* F5 A 22.
18. Anderson, p. 259.
19. Dinwiddie, p. 83.
20. Cranmer-Byng, p. 205.
21. IOCM, 92, 393–405.
22. Ibid., 406.
23. Ibid.

CHAPTER 74

1. Staunton, Jr., f° 209–11.
2. Ibid., f° 211–13.
3. Hüttner, p. 199.
4. Ibid., p. 200.
5. Ibid., p. 201.
6. Ibid.
7. Ibid., p. 216.
8. Staunton, Jr., f° 219–22.
9. Ibid., f° 227–30.
10. Ibid., f° 214.
11. Dinwiddie, p. 84.
12. Ibid., p. 77.
13. Staunton, Jr., f° 231.
14. Ibid., f° 234.

15. In Jean Tullard, *Les Révolutions*, Paris, 1985, p. 111.
16. Barrow, *Travels in China*, pp. 192–93.

CHAPTER 75

1. Louis Dermigny, *Les Mémoires de Charles de Constant*, p. 411.
2. See Cranmer-Byng, p. 381, n. 76.
3. Cranmer-Byng, p. 207.
4. Ibid.
5. Ibid. See also Morse, vol. 1, pp. 261–64.
6. See Ho Ping-ti, *The Ladder of Success in Imperial China*, pp. 26, 35, 45.
7. Ibid., p. 82.
8. Cranmer-Byng, pp. 207–8.
9. Balazs, pp. 300–301.
10. See Pritchard, *The Crucial Years*, p. 108.
11. Staunton, Jr., f° 226–27.
12. There is an English translation of the edict of December 1, 1793, in Robbins, pp. 380–81n, but it is abridged and bowdlerized.
13. Cranmer-Byng, p. 209.
14. See IOCM, 93, 253–63. The note addressed to the Chinese accompanies a dispatch to Dundas dated January 7, 1794 (IOCM, 92, 443–46). The latter is not included in the Cranmer-Byng edition.

CHAPTER 76

1. Staunton, Jr., f° 223–24.
2. Morse, vol. 2, p. 211.
3. Cranmer-Byng, pp. 205–6.
4. Ibid., p. 206. See also Morse, vol. 2, p. 241; G. A. Lensen, *The Russian Push toward Japan*, pp. 96–120; Cranmer-Byng, pp. 380–81, n. 75.
5. These two decrees were attached by Macartney to his dispatch of January 7, 1794. IOCM, 112, 475–78, 483–86, 513–14, 517–18.
6. Cranmer-Byng, introduction, p. 31.
7. Dinwiddie, p. 78.
8. Cranmer-Byng, p. 209.
9. Ibid., p. 210.
10. Staunton, Jr., f° 235–36.
11. Cranmer-Byng, p. 210.
12. Dermigny, p. 431.
13. Cranmer-Byng, p. 210.
14. Ibid.
15. Ibid.
16. Macartney's advice to his companions was of a piece with the times; three company employees in Macao were secretly learning

Chinese (see Susan Reed Stifler, "The Language Students of the Canton Factory," in *Journal of the North Asia Branch of the Asiatic Society* [69, 1938]: 46–82). During the nineteenth century, some Britons, French, and Americans were able to learn enough Chinese to do business in China. But there was also a local linguistic difficulty, mentioned by Guignes: "Mr. de Martigny, the French commissioner, speaks Chinese, but not Cantonese, and must follow his deputy, whose uncertainty is very great" (AN, letter, January 10, 1788, *Fonds Marine*, C7-135, Paris).

17. Cranmer-Byng, pp. 215–16.
18. Hüttner, p. 209.
19. Ibid., p. 210.
20. Ibid., p. 204.
21. AN, letter of d'Entrecasteaux to the missionaries of Peking, *Fonds Colonies* C1-6, Paris, February 1787.
22. UAGC, January 9, 1794, microfilm 27.
23. AMAE, Guignes, report dated 21 vendémiaire, Year X, Paris, vol. 7, 1793–1855.
24. Staunton, Jr., f° 239–41.
25. Cranmer-Byng, p. 216.
26. Ibid., pp. 216–17.
27. Ibid., pp. 328–31; assuming, of course, that the Chiao Jenchieh of his note and our Qiao Renjie are indeed the same person.
28. Staunton, Jr., f° 247–48.
29. Cranmer-Byng, p. 218.
30. Ibid.

CHAPTER 77

1. *Histoire de la Révolution française*, p. 412.
2. Passages of them, though not the full text, may be found in Cranmer-Byng, from which the following quotations have been taken.
3. Cranmer-Byng, p. 211.
4. Ibid.
5. Ibid., p. 212.
6. Ibid., pp. 212–13.
7. Ibid., p. 213.
8. Ibid.
9. Ibid., p. 214.
10. Charpentier-Cossigny, p. 406.
11. Cranmer-Byng, p. 215.
12. *Conversations de Goethe avec Eckermann*, January 31, 1827, Paris, 1949, p. 157.
13. Cranmer-Byng, p. 214.
14. See Dermigny, p. 12.
15. AN, letter to the minister of the navy

in Paris, January 17, 1794, *Fonds Colonies* 8 AQ 349.
16. AN, letter from J.-B. Piron to the minister of the navy, *Fonds Colonies-missions d'Extrême-Orient*, F5 A 22, March 4, 1804.

CHAPTER 78

1. *Anabasis*, 1924.
2. UAGC, November 1, 1793, microfilm 27.
3. Cranmer-Byng, p. 219.
4. Ibid.
5. Holmes, p. 196.
6. Cranmer-Byng, p. 219.
7. Anderson, p. 263.
8. Holmes, p. 194.
9. Anderson, pp. 262–63.
10. Hüttner, p. 248.
11. Anderson, p. 263.
12. Hüttner, p. 248.
13. Staunton, Jr., f° 268.
14. AL, Father Lamiot's notes on the English embassy.
15. Staunton, vol. 2, p. 255.
16. Hüttner, p. 250.
17. UAGC, November 1, 1793, microfilm 27.
18. Hüttner, p. 252.
19. Ibid., p. 253.
20. Charpentier-Cossigny, p. 408.
21. Hüttner, p. 254.
22. BIF, letter from Father Amiot to Bertin, from Peking, October 10, 1789, MS 1517.
23. Hüttner, p. 255.
24. Staunton, Jr., f° 258.
25. Anderson, p. 264.
26. Cranmer-Byng, p. 320.
27. Hüttner, p. 256.
28. Dinwiddie, p. 86.
29. Staunton, Jr., f° 259.
30. Ibid., f° 264.
31. February 13, 1794; that night, the fourteenth of the first lunar month, was also the Festival of Lanterns.
32. Dinwiddie, p. 86.
33. Ibid.
34. Anderson, p. 264.

CHAPTER 79

1. See Morse, vol. 2, p. 265.
2. Staunton, Jr., f° 264.
3. Ibid., f° 263.
4. Ibid., f° 265–66.

5. Ibid., f° 270.

6. UAGC, January 25, 1794, microfilm 68.

7. India Office, Home Miscellaneous, 434, f° 15.

8. UAGC, January 25, 1794, microfilm 68.

9. Barrow, *Travels in China*, pp. 621–22. The statesman in question was Henry Dundas, who had just gotten Barrow a job in the admiralty.

10. CUMC, no. 371.

11. Anderson, p. 264.

CHAPTER 80

1. Dinwiddie, p. 87.

2. Staunton, vol. 2, p. 258.

3. This probably accounts for the occasional chronological disagreement with the day-to-day notes made by his page.

4. Holmes, p. 199.

5. Ibid., pp. 201–2.

6. Staunton, vol. 2, p. 258.

7. Dinwiddie, p. 88.

8. Holmes, p. 203.

9. Staunton, vol. 2, p. 259.

10. Holmes, p. 210.

11. Ibid., pp. 204–5.

12. Ibid., pp. 205–6.

13. Ibid., p. 206.

14. Ibid., p. 208.

15. *Mémoires du comte de Villèle*, pp. 62–63.

16. Holmes, p. 209.

17. Ibid., pp. 212–13.

18. Ibid., p. 212.

19. Ibid., p. 216.

20. Staunton, vol. 2, p. 265.

21. Ibid., p. 260.

22. Holmes, p. 223.

23. Staunton, vol. 2, p. 260.

24. Holmes, p. 230.

25. Staunton, vol. 2, p. 261.

26. Ibid., p. 262.

27. Ibid., p. 264. See also Holmes, pp. 231–32.

28. Holmes, p. 243.

29. Staunton, vol. 2, p. 266.

30. Ibid., pp. 266–67.

31. Holmes, p. 247.

32. Staunton, vol. 2, p. 267, confirmed by BL, the log of the *Hindostan*, MSS add. 35174.

33. AN, *Fonds Marine*, BBA 37, f° 101.

34. Staunton, vol. 2, p. 267.

35. Holmes, p. 255.

36. IOCM, 92, 487–89.

37. Holmes, p. 256.

38. Staunton, vol. 2, p. 267.

PART SIX

EPIGRAPHS

1. *Essais*, 1823.

2. "Three Lectures to Swiss Members of the International," in *From out of the Dustbin, Bakunin's Basic Writings 1869–1871*, trans. and ed. Robert M. Cutler, Ann Arbor, Mich., 1985, p. 57.

3. *Heart of Darkness*, 1902, chapter 1.

CHAPTER 81

1. Preface to his translation of the *Ta T'sing Leu Lee*, p. iii.

2. *Gentleman's Magazine*, 1794, pp. 708–11.

3. Ibid., p. 815.

4. Winterbotham, *An Historical, Geographical and Philosophical View of the Chinese Empire*, 1795, appendix: "Narrative of the Embassy to China," p. 2.

5. *The Spirit of the Laws*, 8, 21, pp. 127–28. See also Masson, *Revue des deux mondes*, May 15, 1951, and Danielle Elisseeff, *Moi, Arcade*.

6. Le Gentil, *Voyage autour du monde*, September 1736, p. 129.

7. AN, *Fonds Marine*, C7-135, Paris.

8. *Reason in History*, pp. 199–200.

9. Goethe, pp. 156–57.

10. Anderson, p. 64.

11. Ibid., p. 66.

12. Ibid., p. 76.

13. Ibid., p. 77.

14. Ibid., p. 81.

15. Ibid., p. 100.

16. Hüttner, p. 9.

17. Ibid., p. 3.

18. Ibid., p. 16.

19. Ibid., pp. 42–43.

20. Ibid., p. 71.

21. Holmes, pp. 147–48.

22. Ibid., pp. 149–50.

23. Ibid., p. 158.

24. *Edinburgh Review*, January 1805, p. 259.

25. Ibid., p. 262.

26. Ibid., p. 265.

27. Ibid., p. 270.

28. Ibid., p. 280.

29. *Quarterly Review*, May 1810, p. 273.

30. AL, correspondence of Father Richenet to Thomas Staunton, December 8, 1810.

31. G. T. Staunton, *Ta T'sing Leu Lee*, preface, p. viii.

32. *Edinburgh Review*, August 1810, p. 476.

33. Ibid., p. 478.

34. Cranmer-Byng, p. 226.

35. *Edinburgh Review*, August 1810, p. 478.

36. Ibid., p. 498.

37. *Encyclopédie*, "History."

38. IOCM, G/12/91, letter from Macartney to Dundas, January 4, 1792.

39. Confucius, *The Analects*, 15: 12, p. 134.

CHAPTER 82

1. See Duyvendak, "The Last Dutch Embassy to the Chinese Court," in *T'oung Pao*, vol. 34, pp. 14–18.

2. See AMAE, *Fonds Marine, Extrême-Orient*, no. 1 691.

3. Guignes, vol. 1, pp. 318–19.

4. Ibid., p. 321.

5. Ibid., p. 310.

6. Ibid., p. 341.

7. Ibid., p. 358.

8. Van Braam, vol. 1, p. 153.

9. Guignes, vol. 1, p. 371.

10. Van Braam, vol. 1, p. 151.

11. BL, Titsing, *Journal d'un voyage à Pékin*, MSS add. 18102, f° 62.

12. Van Braam, vol. 1, p. 152.

13. Ibid., p. 145.

14. Guignes, vol. 1, p. 382.

15. Ibid., p. 384.

16. Van Braam, vol. 1, p. 162.

17. Ibid.

18. Guignes, vol. 1, pp. 385–86.

19. Ibid., p. 394.

20. Van Braam, vol. 1, p. 167.

21. Guignes, vol. 1, p. 430.

22. Ibid., p. 433.

23. Ibid.

24. Van Braam, vol. 1, p. 264.

25. Ibid.

26. Guignes, vol. 1, pp. 437–39.

27. Van Braam, vol. 1, pp. 181–82.

28. Guignes, vol. 3, pp. 165–66.

CHAPTER 83

1. See Cranmer-Byng, "Russian and British Interest in the Far East," *Canadian Slavonic Papers*, vol. 10, 1968, p. 363.

2. CUMC, nos. 17 and 119.

3. Potocki, *Voyages au Caucase et à la Chine*, p. 168.

4. Ibid., p. 169.

5. Ibid., p. 170.

6. Ibid., p. 171.

7. Potocki, letter to his brother Severin, from Kiakhta, November 20, 1805, ibid., p. 206.

8. Ibid., p. 172.

9. Ibid., p. 175.

10. Ibid., p. 177.

11. Ibid.

12. Ibid., p. 179.

13. Ibid., p. 185.

14. Ibid., p. 187.

CHAPTER 84

1. CUMC, no. 313.

2. IOCM, vol. 95, 217–19.

3. See Morse, vol. 2, pp. 273–75.

4. Backhouse and Bland, p. 332.

5. Ibid., pp. 332–33.

6. Ibid., pp. 318–19.

7. Morse, vol. 2, p. 336–38.

8. See Marques-Pereira, *Efemérides comemorativas da história de Macau*, 1868, p. 8. and *passim*.

9. See Morse, vol. 3, appendix T.

10. Soothill, *China and the West*, p. 97.

11. Morse, vol. 3, p. 257.

12. Thomas Staunton, unpublished journal of the Amherst embassy, p. 1.

13. Ibid., p. 10.

14. Ibid., p. 12.

15. Ibid., p. 13.

16. Morse, vol. 3, p. 264.

17. See Hibbert, *The Dragon Wakes*, p. 62.

18. Edict of Jiaqing, in Backhouse and Bland, p. 382.

19. Thomas Staunton, p. 20.

20. Ibid., p. 55.

21. Ibid., p. 67.

22. Ibid., p. 77.

23. Ibid., p. 83.

24. Ibid., pp. 85–86.

25. Ibid., p. 90.

26. Edict of Jiaqing, in Backhouse and Bland, p. 383.

27. Ellis, *Journal of the Proceedings of the*

Late Embassy to China, p. 154. See also Pritchard, "The Kowtow in the Macartney Embassy," p. 169.

28. *Wen-hoien Ts'ung-pien*, vol. 10, p. 30, in Pritchard, "The Kowtow," p. 173.

29. Hibbert, p. 64.

30. Ellis, p. 176.

31. Thomas Staunton, p. 94.

32. Ellis, pp. 180–81; Thomas Staunton, p. 11.

33. Edict of Jiaqing, in Backhouse and Bland, pp. 387–88; see also Morse, vol. 3, p. 264.

34. Thomas Staunton, p. 147.

35. Ellis, p. 382.

36. Morse, vol. 3, pp. 274–75.

37. Edict of Jiaqing, quoted in Hibbert, p. 68.

38. Ellis, p. 420.

39. AN, *Fonds Marine*, C 1-5, f° 92/93, Paris, letter of Mr. de Kergariou, from Macao, December 8, 1817.

40. Morse, vol. 3, pp. 276–77.

CHAPTER 85

1. By imperial decree, October 22, 1808.

2. See Louis-Chrétien de Guignes, *Dictionnaire chinois-français-latin*, 1813, introduction.

3. "Mémoire sur la Chine adressé à S. M. Napoléon Ier par M. Renouard de Sainte-Croix," quoted in H. Cordier, *Mélanges d'histoire et de géographie orientales*, Paris, 1914, vol. 1, pp. 193–200.

4. Amherst, "Embassy to China," unpublished manuscript, vol. 1, June 27, 1817, "Anchored at Saint Helena."

5. Barry O'Meara, *Napoleon in Exile*, vol. 1, p. 288.

6. Ibid., p. 289.

7. Ibid.

8. Chateaubriand, *Mémoires d'outre-tombe*, Garnier, vol. 4, pp. 80–81.

9. Memoirs of Hudson Lowe.

10. Amherst, vol. 1, June 29, 1817.

11. Ibid.

12. Ibid., June 30, 1817.

13. Clarke Abel, *Narrative of a Journey in the Interior of China*, London, 1818, pp. 315–16.

14. Amherst, vol. 1, July 1, 1817.

15. O'Meara, vol. 2, p. 98.

16. Thomas Staunton, *Memoirs of the Chief*

Incidents of the Public Life of Sir George Thomas Staunton, p. 68.

17. O'Meara, vol. 2, p. 98.

18. Ibid., p. 99.

19. Ibid., pp. 100–101.

20. Ibid., p. 100.

21. Ibid., p. 30.

22. Ibid., vol. 1, p. 290.

23. Cranmer-Byng, p. 213.

CHAPTER 86

1. Dermigny, *Le Commerce à Canton*, vol. 3, p. 1275.

2. Greenberg, *British Trade and the Opening of China*, p. 118.

3. Fairbank, *The Cambridge History of China*, vol. 10, p. 172.

4. A. Walley, *The Opium War Through Chinese Eyes*, p. 28.

5. Ibid.

6. Lieou Ngo, *Pérégrinations d'un clochard*, Paris, p. 219.

7. Lord Jocelyn, *Six Mois avec l'expédition de Chine*, 1842.

8. Fairbank, pp. 173–74.

9. Dermigny, vol. 3, pp. 1404–09.

10. Ibid., p. 1409.

11. Fairbank, p. 175.

12. Ibid.

13. Dermigny, vol. 3, p. 1395.

14. Ibid., p. 1441.

15. Ibid., pp. 1416–17.

16. Cranmer-Byng, p. 239.

17. See Greenberg, pp. 140–42.

18. Committee on the Modern History of China, *The Opium War*, Peking, 1979, p. 27.

19. Fairbank, p. 179.

20. Ibid.

21. Ibid., pp. 180–81.

22. Ibid., p. 181.

23. Lin Zexu, quoted in Fairbank, p. 184.

24. Fairbank, p. 187.

25. R. Grousset and G. Deniker, *La Face de l'Asie*, p. 305.

26. Committee on the Modern History of China, p. 30.

27. See Waley, pp. 28–31.

28. Thomas Staunton, *Memoirs*, pp. 84–86.

29. Committee on the Modern History of China, p. 40.

30. Ibid., p. 41.

31. See *Hansard's Parliamentary Debates*, April 7, 1840, vol. 2, pp. 744–45.

32. Ibid., p. 718.
33. Ibid., pp. 818–19.
34. Thomas Staunton, *Memoirs*, p. 87.

CHAPTER 87

1. Thomas Staunton, *Memoirs*, p. 207.
2. Committee on the Modern History of China, pp. 46–49; see also Grousset, pp. 305–6.
3. *Chinese Repository*, 1840, vol. 7, p. 311. See also Dermigny, p. 1403.
4. Committee on the Modern History of China, p. 76.
5. Ibid., p. 80.
6. Ibid., p. 83.
7. Ibid., p. 90.
8. Fairbank, p. 211.
9. Thomas Staunton, *Memoirs*, pp. 92–93.
10. Huc, vol. 4, p. 92.
11. E. Bard, *Les Chinois chez eux*, p. 353.
12. Letter to Captain Butler, Guernsey, November 25, 1861.

CHAPTER 88

1. The various uprisings of the second half of the nineteenth century caused an overall population decline of sixty-five million people and proportional losses in the area of land under cultivation. See Mi Rucheng, "Pertes humaines et économiques dues aux guerres contre-révolutionnaires," in *Zhongguo Sheshui Jingjishi Yanjiu*, 1986, no. 4, pp. 1–15.
2. Confucius, *The Analects*, 5: 10, p. 77.
3. Title of one of the manifestos of Yenfu, 1895. See *Les Manifestes de Yen Fou*, trans. F. Houang, Paris, 1977.
4. In Nagayo Agasarawa, *Life of the Admiral Togo*, pp. 135–38.
5. See Haldane, *Tsou-hsi*, pp. 126–29;

Brian Power, *La Vie de P'ouyi: le dernier empereur de Chine*, p. 33.
6. Lu Xun, preface to *Le Cri*, December 3, 1922, Peking: Foreign Languages Press, 1981, vol. 1, p. 30.
7. A traditional expression. See Old Nick, p. 374; Lu Xun, *Journal d'un fou*, Paris, p. 18.
8. Bard, p. 167.
9. Yenfu, p. 63.
10. Sheng Congwen, "Autres temps, autres mœurs," in *Treize récits chinois*, p. 95.

CONCLUSION

1. Yenfu, p. 39.
2. Press conference, January 31, 1964.
3. See Braudel, vol. 3, chapter 1.
4. Ibid., p. 223.
5. *La Bureaucratie céleste*, chapters 9–11.
6. *Second Report of the Secret Committee appointed to take consideration on the export trade from Great Britain to the East Indies*, London: East India House, December 29, 1791.
7. Ibid.
8. Ibid.
9. See Xiao Zhizhi and Yang Weidong, *Chronicle of Sino-Occidental Relations Before the Opium War, 1517–1840*, pp. 250–51.
10. Cranmer-Byng, p. 221.
11. Yenfu, pp. 136–37.
12. Zhu Yong, thesis, 1988.
13. Committee on the History of Modern China, p. 128.
14. Quoted in ibid., p. 129.
15. Yenfu, quoted in Etiemble, *Confucius* (Paris, Idées), p. 266.
16. Staunton, vol. 1, p. 128.
17. Claude Lévi-Strauss uses this example in a suggestive analysis of the relations between civilizations: *Race et histoire*, p. 54. See also *Tristes tropiques*, pp. 284 and 485.

Bibliography

PRIMARY SOURCES

UNPUBLISHED CHINESE ARCHIVES

UNPUBLISHED ARCHIVES OF THE GRAND COUNCIL (hereafter designated UAGC). The original documents, including Qianlong's handwritten rescripts, are preserved in the Imperial Archives in the Forbidden City in Peking. These documents include edicts signed by the emperor himself, court letters addressed to leading mandarins and signed by the Grand Council in the emperor's name, and memoranda sent to the emperor by these same mandarins. The sources on the Macartney embassy, written between October 20, 1792, and February 5, 1794, represent the equivalent of about 420 manuscript pages, microfilms of which were kindly supplied by the custodians of the Imperial Archives.

UNPUBLISHED ENGLISH ARCHIVES

INDIA OFFICE LIBRARY AND RECORDS, LONDON
Factory Records, G/12/90: Cathcart's Embassy to China. India Office, China, Cathcart (hereafter designated IOCC).
G/12/91–93: Macartney's Embassy to China. India Office, China, Macartney (hereafter designated IOCM).
G/12/196–98: Amherst's Embassy, India Office, China, Amherst (hereafter designated IOCA).

BRITISH LIBRARY, MANUSCRIPT DEPARTMENT (hereafter designated BL)
Alexander, W. A Journal of the Lord Macartney's Embassy to China, 1792–1794, Journey of a Voyage to Peking, the Metropolis of China, in the *Hindostan* Indiaman, accompanying Lord Macartney as Ambassador to the Emperor of China, Mss Add. 35174.
Gower, Sir E. A Journal of H.M.S. *Lion* beginning the 1st October 1792 and ending the 7th September 1794, MSS Add. 21106.

PUBLIC RECORD OFFICE, KEW (hereafter designated PR)
Colonial Office Papers 77/29, Correspondence of Lord Macartney with Henry Dundas and Sir Erasmus Gower.

WELLCOME HISTORICAL MEDICAL INSTITUTE, LONDON (hereafter designated WI)
Macartney (Lord). Memoranda from London to China (unpublished handwritten journal kept during the sea voyage, September 11, 1792, to June 15, 1793).

CORNELL UNIVERSITY, ITHACA, NEW YORK
Wason Collection on China and the Chinese, *Macartney's Papers* (21 vols.; hereafter designated CUMP) and *Macartney's Correspondence* (10 vols., hereafter designated CUMC).

TOYO BUNKO (THE ORIENTAL LIBRARY), TOKYO (hereafter designated TB)
Letters Book of Lord Macartney during his Embassy to China, 1792–94.
Lord Macartney. A Journal of the Embassy in 1792, 1793, 1794. 3 vols.

DUKE UNIVERSITY, DURHAM, NORTH CAROLINA (hereafter designated DU)
Staunton, Sir George Thomas. Diary (30th Aug. 1793–1st Feb. 1794) and Correspondence 1798–1818.

STAUNTON, SIR GEORGE THOMAS (texts printed in limited editions for private circulation)
Memoirs of the Chief Incidents of the Public Life of Sir G. T. Staunton, London, 1856.
Memoirs of the Life and Family of the Late Sir G. L. Staunton, collected by Sir G. T. Staunton, London, 1828.
Miscellaneous Notices Relating to China, London, 1823.
Notes of Proceedings and Occurrences during the British Embassy to Peking, 1816, London, 1824.

ROYAL GEOGRAPHICAL SOCIETY, LONDON
Else, Stephen. A Journal of a Voyage to the East Indies and an Historical Narrative of the Lord Macartney's Embassy to the Court of Peking, 1793.

PUBLIC RECORDS OFFICE OF NORTHERN IRELAND, BELFAST
Macartney's Papers (D 572, 6–19).

NATIONAL LIBRARY, DUBLIN (hereafter designated NLD)
Winder, E. Papers: Account of a Voyage to Brazil, Tristan da Cunha and the East Indies, 1793. MSS 8799.

UNIVERSITY OF WITWATERSRAND, JOHANNESBURG
The Earl Macartney Papers (catalogue compiled by Anna M. Cunningham). The 617 documents included in this file deal primarily with the period 1795–98. Two documents (nos. 15 and 16) deal with the embassy to China. Documents 22, 28, and 45 highlight the strategic position of the Cape for the East India Company.

PRIVATE COLLECTION
Amherst, Lord William Pitt. Embassy to China, handwritten journal, consulted and quoted by kind permission of its owner, Mr. Michael Galvin.

UNPUBLISHED FRENCH ARCHIVES

ARCHIVES NATIONALES (hereafter designated AN)
Correspondence of N. Raux, superior of the French mission in Peking, November 16, 1788.
Fonds Colonies-missions d'Extrême-Orient. Correspondence of J.-B. Piron, agent of the French East India Company, 1792–94, 1804.
Fonds de la correspondance de la Compagnie française des Indes orientales, 8 AQ 349. Letters of J.-B. Piron, 1794.

Fonds Marine B4 163. Documents and report of Macartney relating to the seizure of Grenada by Admiral Count d'Estaing.

Fonds Marine C-5. Letter from Commander de Kergariou to M. de Courson, commander of the *Cléopâtre*, Macao, December 8, 1817.

Letters from and about Macartney during his captivity in France, autumn 1779.

ARCHIVES OF THE MINISTRY OF FOREIGN AFFAIRS (hereafter designated AMAE)
Correspondance politique
>*Russie*, coded messages of the Marquis de Bausset to the Duke de Choiseul on the subject of Macartney, July 3, November 27, December 3 and 23, 1766.

>*Angleterre*, vol. 582, pp. 280–82, announcement of the departure of the Macartney embassy, September 1792.

Memoranda and Documents
>*Asie 17*: anonymous, July 20, 1801, from Peking to a correspondent in Canton on Sino-English relations after the Macartney embassy.

>*Asie 19*: unpublished correspondence of L.-C. de Guignes, 1787–91.

>*Asie 21*: letter from Father de Grammont to Van Braam, dated (erroneously) September 1793.

>Lamiot, L.-F.-M. Mémoire sur la Chine, Macao, n.d. (1821 or 1822).

>Richenet, J.-F. Note on the Lazarist mission in China, July 30, 1817.

>*Chine 17*: Father Joseph de Grammont, S. J., letter on the Dutch embassy of 1795, n.d.

BIBLIOTHÈQUE DE l'INSTITUT DE FRANCE (hereafter designated BIF)
Correspondence of M. Bertin, MSS 1515 and 1517: letters from Father Joseph-Marie Amiot, S.J., September 20 and October 1, 1774; October 10, 1789; August 20 and September 24, 1790.

ARCHIVES OF THE LAZARISTS, RUE DE SÈVRES, PARIS (hereafter designated AL)
Correspondence of the Lazarist missionaries residing in China from 1784 to 1801: letters of Fathers Ghislain (Jean-Joseph), Hanna (Robert), Lamiot (Louis-François-Marie), Richenet (Jean-François), and Raux (Nicolas-Joseph).

Correspondence of the missionaries of the Congregation of missions to Peking (1806–50; 3 bound registries).

Notes on the English embassy, anonymous (but most probably written by Father Lamiot in 1807), with commentary on the Castéra translation of Staunton's report on the Macartney embassy.

Letters from Chateaubriand (François-René) to Father Lamiot, from Paris, June 24, 1823.

Note from the captain of Bougainville's ship about Father Lamiot, Macao, January 1, 1825.

ARCHIVES OF THE SOCIETY OF JESUS, PROVINCE DE FRANCE, CHANTILLY (hereafter designated ASJ)
Letters of Father de Grammont to his family (1767–86).

Unpublished supplements to the *Lettres édifiantes* (1762–1808).

Unpublished journal of the Jesuits of St. Petersburg, 1805–07, Fds Brotier, vol. 134.

PERIODICALS
Le Mercure de France, September–October 1779.

OTHER UNPUBLISHED SOURCES

TITSING, ISAAK. *Journal d'un voyage à Pékin*, manuscript of French translation from the Dutch, British Library, MSS Add. 18102.

VAN BRAAM, ANDRÉ-EVERARD. *Le Voyage en Chine*. 4 vols. Archives Nationales, Paris, Colonies F3 108–111, Fonds Moreau de Saint-Méry, MSS in French.

PUBLISHED CHINESE SOURCES

The conservators of the Chinese Archives published some of the documents relating to the Macartney embassy in a bulletin entitled *Zhongghu Congbian* (Peking, 1928–29; hereafter designated ZGCB).

In addition, the history of the Qianlong era is very succinctly summarized in the Official Records.

Finally, English translations of a number of Chinese documents, some identical to those of the ZGCB, others different, were published in Backhouse and Bland's *Annals and Memoirs of the Court of Peking*. London: Heinemann, 1914.

PUBLISHED ENGLISH SOURCES

ABEL, CLARKE. *Narrative of a Journey in the Interior of China in the Years 1816–1817*. London: Longman and Hurst, 1818, 420 pp.

ANDERSON, AENEAS. *A Narrative of the British Embassy to China in the Years 1792, 1793 and 1794*. London: J. Debrett, 1795, 278 pp.

————. *Relation du voyage de lord Macartney à la Chine* (French translation of the above). Paris: Denné Le Jeune, 1797, with an appendix including the log of the *Lion*, August 5, 1793–October 28, 1793. (Reprint by G. Manceron, Aubier-Montaigne, 1978.)

BARROW, JOHN. *Travels in China*. London: Cadell and Davis, 1804, 632 pp.

————. *A Voyage to Cochinchina*. London: Cadell and Davis, 1806, 477 pp.

————. *Some Account of the Public Life and Selections from the Unpublished Writing of the Earl Macartney*. 2 vols. London: Cadell and Davis, 1807.

————. *An Autobiographical Memoir*. London: John Murray, 1847, 515 pp.

CRANMER-BYNG, J. L. *An Embassy to China. Being the journal kept by Lord Macartney during his embassy to the Emperor Ch'ien-lung 1793–1794*. London: Longman, 1962, 421 pp.

DINWIDDIE, JAMES (SEE PROUDFOOT-JARDINE)

ELLIS, HENRY. *Journal of the Proceedings of the Late Embassy to China*. London: John Murray, 1817, 528 pp.

GILLAN, HUGH. "Observations on the State of Medicine, Surgery and Chemistry in China," in CRANMER-BYNG.

HOLMES, SAMUEL. *The Journal of Mr. Samuel Holmes, Sergeant-Major of the XIth Light Dragoons, during his attendance as one of the guards on Lord Macartney's Embassy to China and Tartary*. London: W. Bulmer & Co., 1798, 256 pp.

MACARTNEY, LORD GEORGE (SEE CRANMER-BYNG, ROBBINS, and UNPUBLISHED SOURCES).

MORRISON, ROBERT. *A Memoir of the Principal Occurrences during an Embassy from the British Government to the Court of China in the Year 1816*. London: Hatchard & Son, 1820, 96 pp.

O'MEARA, BARRY. *Napoleon in Exile, or, A Voice from St. Helena*. 2 vols. New York: Redfield, 1853. (Original edition probably 1822.)

PROUDFOOT-JARDINE, W. *A Biographical Memoir of James Dinwiddie*. Liverpool: Howell, 1868, 138 pp.

ROBBINS, HELEN. *Our First Ambassador to China*. London: John Murray, 1908, 679 pp.

STAUNTON, SIR GEORGE LEONARD. *An Authentic Account of an Embassy from the King of Great Britain to the Emperor of China*. 2 vols. Philadelphia: 1799. (Original edition London: Stockdale, 1797.)

STAUNTON, SIR GEORGE THOMAS. *Ta T'sing Leu Lee* (The Penal Code of Qing China). Trans. from the Chinese language by G. T. Staunton. London, 1810, 581 pp. (Reprint Taipei: Ch'eng Wen Publishing Co., 1966.)

WINTERBOTHAM, W. *An Historical, Geographical and Philosophical View of the Chinese Empire, with an appendix: "Narrative of the Embassy to China."* London: Ridgeway and Buttom, 1795, 445 pp. + 114 pp.

PERIODICALS

Hansard's Parliamentary Debates, 1791–93, 1806, 1840.

Edinburgh Review, 1800–20.

Gentleman's Magazine, 1787, 1794.

Quarterly Review, 1810–20.

The Times of London, 1797–1818.

The Chinese Repository, 1832–41.

PUBLISHED FRENCH SOURCES

CHARPENTIER-COSSIGNY (or DE COSSIGNY, J.-F.). *Voyage à Canton, capitale de la province de ce nom. Observations sur le voyage à la Chine de lord Macartney et du citoyen Van Braam*. Paris: André, Year VII (1799), 607 pp.

GUIGNES, L.-C. DE. *Voyage à Pékin, Manille, et l'île de France*, 3 vols. Paris: Imprimerie Impériale, 1808.

HUC, FATHER EVARISTE. *Souvenirs d'un voyage dans la Tartarie, le Thibet et la Chine*. Paris, 1850. (Reprint Paris: Plon, 1925–28, 4 vols.)

LANGLÉS, L.-M. "Observations sur les relations politiques et commerciales de l'Angleterre et de la France avec la Chine." In Holmes, Samuel, *Voyage en Chine et en Tartarie* (French trans. of Holmes, above). Delance, 1805, pp. xii–xiv.

RENOUARD DE SAINTE-CROIX, FÉLIX. *Voyage commerciale et politique aux Indes orientales, aux Philippines, à la Chine, pendant les années 1803–1807*. Paris: Imprimerie Impériale, 1810.

VILLELE, J.-B., COUNT DE. *Mémoires et correspondance*, 5 vols. Paris: Perrin, 1888.

OTHER PUBLISHED SOURCES

HÜTTNER, HANS CHRISTIAN. *Nachricht von der Brittischen Gesandtschaftreise durch China*. Berlin: Vossicher Buchhandlung, 1797. French trans. by Winckler (Paris: Pillot, 1800).

———. *Voyage à la Chine*. In *Bibliothèque des voyages*. Paris: Vve Lepetit, 1804, 258 pp.

POTOCKI, JAN. "Account of the expedition to China 1805–1806." In W. Kotwicz, *Jan Hr. Potocki i jego prodroz do Chin*. Vilna, 1935.

———. French edition: *Voyages au Caucase et à la Chine, Mémoires et correspondance 1797–1798, 1805–1806*. Paris. Fayard, 1980, 251 pp.

VAN BRAAM, ANDRÉ-EVERARD. *Voyage de l'ambassade de la Compagnie des Indes orientales hollandaises vers l'empereur de Chine en 1794 et 1795.* Published in French, in collaboration with Moreau de Saint-Méry, Philadelphia, 1797.

SECONDARY SOURCES

ALLAN, C. W. *The Jesuits at the Court of Peking.* Shanghai: Kelly and Walsh, 1935.

AMIN, S., ET AL. *Le Tiers Monde et la gauche.* Paris, 1979.

AMIOT, JOSEPH-MARIE (see MÉMOIRES CONCERNANT . . .)

ARMOGATHE, JEAN-ROBERT. "Voltaire et la Chine: une mise au point," Actes du 1ᵉʳ colloque international de sinologie (Chantilly, 1974). Paris, 1976.

BAIROCH, PAUL. *Le Tiers Monde dans l'impasse.* Paris, 1971. (New edition, with postface, 1983.)

BALAZS, ÉTIENNE. *La Bureaucratie céleste.* Paris, 1968.

BALLANDIER, G., ET AL. "Sociologie des mutations," Actes du VIIᵉ colloque de l'Association des sociologues de langue française (Neuchâtel, October 1968). Paris, 1970.

BARD, E. *Les Chinois chez eux.* Paris, 1904.

BASTID, M., BIANCO, L., CADART, C., and VANDERMEERSCH, L. "Que savons-nous de la Chine?" *Esprit,* November 1972.

BERGER, K. H. "Henry Hayne Travelling through China with Lord Amherst." *Library Notes* (January 1982): no. 50, 13–21.

BERGÈRE, MARIE-CLAIRE. *L'Age d'or de la bourgeoisie chinoise.* Paris, 1986.

———. *La République populaire de Chine de 1949 à nos jours.* Paris, 1987.

BERNARD-MAÎTRE, HENRI. *Sagesse chinoise et philosophie chrétienne: essai sur leurs relations historiques.* Hautes Etudes, Tientsin, 1935.

BERVAL, RENÉ DE. *Présence du bouddhisme.* Paris, 1987.

BETTELHEIM, BRUNO. *The Empty Fortress.* Chicago, 1967.

BIANCO, LUCIEN. *Les Origines de la révolution chinoise.* Paris, 1969.

BOXER, C. R. "European Missionaries and Chinese Clergy, 1654–1810." In King, B., *The Age of Partnership: Europeans in Asia Before Dominions.* Honolulu, 1979.

BRAUDEL, FERNAND. *Civilisation matérielle, économie et capitalisme, XVᵉ–XVIIIᵉ siècle.* 3 vols. Paris, 1979.

BRIGGS, ASA. *The Age of Improvement 1783–1867.* London, 1959.

BRUCKNER, PASCAL. *Les Sanglots de l'homme blanc.* Paris, 1983.

CADART, C., and NAKAJIMA, M. *La Stratégie chinoise ou la Mue du dragon.* Paris, 1986.

CAMERON, N. "Kowtow: Imperial China and the West in Confrontation." *Orientations* (January 1971): 44–51.

CAMMAN, S. *Trade through the Himalayas. The Early British Attempts to Open Tibet.* Princeton, 1951.

CHANG HSIN PAO. *Commissioner Lin and the Opium War.* Cambridge, Mass., 1964.

CHARBONNIER, JEAN. *La Chine sans muraille.* Paris, 1988.

CHEONG, W. *Mandarins and Merchants: Jardine, Matheson & Co., a China Agency in the Early Nineteenth Century.* London, 1979.

CHESNAIS, JEAN-CLAUDE. *La Revanche du Tiers Monde.* Paris, 1987.

CHESNEAUX, J., and BASTID, M. *Histoire de la Chine,* 4 vols. Paris, 1969, 1977.

CHAUNU, PIERRE. *La Civilisation de l'Europe des Lumières.* Paris, 1971.

CHU CHENG. *Contributions des Jésuites à la Défense de la Chine des Ming face aux Mandchous* (thesis). University of Paris, 1970.

COEN, DEAN BUCHANAN. *The Encyclopedia and China* (thesis). Indiana University, 1962.

COHEN, PAUL A. *Reform in Nineteenth Century China.* East Asian Research Center, Harvard University, 1976.

COMMEAUX, CHARLES. *La Vie quotidienne en Chine sous les Mandchous*. Paris, 1970.

COMMITTEE ON THE MODERN HISTORY OF CHINA. *The Opium War*. Peking: Foreign Languages Press, 1979.

CONFUCIUS. *The Analects (Lun yü)*. Trans. by D. C. Lau. Harmondsworth, 1979.

CORDIER, HENRI. *Histoire générale de la Chine et de ses relations avec les pays étrangers depuis les temps les plus anciens jusqu'à la chute de la dynastie mandchoue*. Paris, 1920.

———. *Mélanges d'histoire et de géographie orientales*. Paris, 1914.

CORRADINI, P. "Concerning the ban on preaching Christianity contained in Ch'ien-lung's reply to the request advanced by Lord Macartney." *East and West* (1968): 89–91.

CRANMER-BYNG, J. L. "Lord Macartney's embassy to Peking in 1793 from official Chinese documents." *Journal of Oriental Studies* 4 (1957/1958): 117–87.

———. "The Chinese attitude towards external relations." *International Journal* no. 21 (1965/1966): 57–77.

CRANMER-BYNG, J. L., and LEVERE, H. "A case study in cultural collision: scientific apparatus in Macartney's embassy to China." *Annals of Science* no. 38 (1981): 503–25.

CROUZET, FRANÇOIS. *The First Industrialists*. Cambridge, 1985.

DANTON, B. H. *The Cultural Contact of the United States and China, the Earliest Sino-American Contact, 1784–1844*. New York, 1931.

DEDEYAN, CHARLES. *Le Retour de Salente, ou Voltaire en Angleterre*. Paris, 1988.

DEHERGNE, JOSEPH. *Répertoire des Jésuites de Chine de 1552 à 1800*. Paris, 1973.

———. "Voyageurs chinois venus à Paris au temps de la marine à voile, et l'influence de la Chine dans la littérature française du XVIIIᵉ siècle." *Monumenta Serica* no. 23 (1964): 372–97.

———. "Un problème ardu: le nom de Dieu en chinois." Actes du IIIᵉ colloque international de sinologie (Chantilly, 1980). Paris, 1983.

DEMIEVILLE, PAUL. "Premiers contacts philosophiques entre la Chine et l'Europe." *Diogène* 58 (1967): 81–110.

DERMIGNY, LOUIS. *La Chine et l'Occident: le commerce à Canton au XVIIIᵉ siècle, 1719–1833*. 3 vols. Paris, 1964.

———. *Les Mémoires de Charles de Constant sur le commerce à la Chine*. Paris, 1964.

DERRY, JOHN W. *Charles-James Fox*. London, 1972.

DEVÈZE, M. "L'Impact du monde chinois sur la France, l'Angleterre, la Russie au XVIIIᵉ siècle." Actes du Iᵉʳ colloque international de sinologie (Chantilly, 1974). Paris, 1976.

DUMONT, LOUIS. *Homo hierarchicus*. Paris, 1966.

DURAND, PIERRE-HENRI. *Lettrés et pouvoirs: un procès littéraire dans la Chine impériale, l'affaire du Nanshan Ji, 1711–1713*. Unpublished thesis. École des hautes études en sciences sociales, Paris, 1988.

DUVERGER, M., ET AL. *Le Concept d'empire*. Paris, 1980.

DUYVENDAK, J. L. L. "The Last Dutch Embassy to the Chinese Court" (supplementary document in *T'oung Pao*, vol. 34, bk. 4, pp. 1–137). Leiden, 1938.

EAMES, J. B. *The English in China, 1600–1843*. London, 1909. (Reprint London, 1974.)

ELISSEEFF, DANIELLE. *La Femme au temps des empereurs de Chine*. Paris, 1988.

———. *Moi, Arcade, interprète chinois du Roi-Soleil*. Paris, 1985.

———. "Imagerie populaire chinoise du Nouvel An." *Cahiers de l'Ecole française d'Extrême-Orient*, vol. 35. Paris, 1978.

———. *Nicolas Fréret: reflexions d'un humaniste du XVIIIᵉ siècle sur la Chine*.

ELISSEEFF, V. and D. *Civilisation de la Chine classique*. Paris, 1979.

ERIKSON, ERIK H. *Identity: Youth and Crisis*. New York, 1968.

ETIEMBLE. *L'Europe chinoise*. Vol. 1: *De l'Empire romain à Leibnitz*. Paris, 1988. Vol. 2: *De la sinophilie à la sinophobie*. Paris, 1989.

————. *Ouverture(s) sur un comparatisme planétaire.* Paris, 1988.

————. *Quarante ans de mon maoïsme.* Paris, 1976.

————. *Les Jésuites en Chine.* Paris, 1966.

————. *Connaissons-nous la Chine?* Paris, 1965.

————. *L'Orient philosophique au XVIIIᵉ siècle: missionnaires et philosophes.* 3 vols. Paris, 1959.

————. *Le Nouveau Singe pèlerin.* Paris, 1958.

————. *Confucius.* Paris, 1956.

EVANS, ERIC J. *The Forging of the Modern State: Early Industrial Britain 1783–1870.* London, 1983.

FAIRBANK, J. K. *The Great Chinese Revolution, 1800–1985.* London, 1987.

————. *The Cambridge History of China.* Vol. 10. Cambridge, 1978.

————. *Trade and Diplomacy on the China Coast: the Opening of the Treaty Ports (1842–1854).* Stanford, 1969.

————. *The Chinese World Order.* Cambridge, Mass., 1968.

————. *Ch'ing Documents, an introductory syllabus.* 2 vols. East Asian Research Center, Harvard University, 1965.

FAIRBANK, J. K., and REISCHAUER, E. D. *China, Tradition and Transformation.* Sydney, 1979.

————. *East Asia: The Modern Transformation.* Boston, 1965.

FAIRBANK, J. K., and TENG, S. Y. "On the Ch'ing Tributary System." *Harvard Journal of Asiatic Studies* (1941): 135–246.

————. "On the Transmission of Ch'ing Documents." In *Ch'ing Administration: Three Studies.* Cambridge, Mass., 1960.

FANON, FRANZ. *Les Damnés de la Terre.* Paris, 1961.

FAY, PETER WARD. *The Opium War, 1840–1842.* New York, 1976.

FEUERWERKER, ALBERT. *State and Society in Eighteenth Century China: the Ch'ing Empire in its Glory.* University of Michigan Center for Chinese Studies, 1976.

FRANÇOIS-XAVIER, SAINT. *Correspondance 1535–1552.* Paris, 1987.

FREUD, SIGMUND. *Civilization and Its Discontents.* Standard Edition of the Complete Psychological Works of Sigmund Freud, vol. 21. London, 1961.

————. *The Future of an Illusion.* Standard Edition of the Complete Psychological Works of Sigmund Freud, vol. 21. London, 1961.

————. *Totem and Taboo.* Trans. by A. A. Brill. New York, 1946.

FRODSHAN, J. D. *The First Chinese Embassy to the West: The Journal of Kuo Sung-tao, Liu Hsi-hung and Chang Te-yi.* Oxford, 1974.

FU LO-SHU. *A Documentary Chronicle of Sino-Western Relations, 1644–1820.* 2 vols. Tucson, 1966.

FURBER, HOLDEN. *Henry Dundas, First Viscount Melville, 1742–1811.* Oxford, 1931.

GAUBIL, FATHER ANTOINE. *Correspondance de Pékin, 1722–1729.* Geneva, 1970.

GEOFFROY-DECHAUNE, FRANÇOIS. *La Chine face au monde.* Private printing, Hong Kong, 1976; English edition, *China Looks at the World,* London, 1967.

GERNET, JACQUES. *Clubs, cénacles et sociétés dans la Chine des XVIᵉ et XVIIᵉ siècles.* Institut de France, Académie des Inscriptions et Belles Lettres. Paris, 1986.

————. "Chine moderne, Chine traditionnelle." *Etudes chinoises* 4 (1): 7–13.

————. *Chine et christianisme, action et réaction.* Paris, 1982.

————. *Le Monde chinois.* Paris, 1972 (second, expanded edition 1987).

GILDER, GEORGE. *Wealth and Poverty.* New York, 1981.

GOODRICH, L. C. *The Literary Inquisition of Qianlong.* New York, 1966 (reprint of 1935).

GOUBERT, P., and DENIS, M. *1789, les Français ont la parole.* Paris, 1964.

GRANET, MARCEL. *La Religion des Chinois.* Paris, 1951.

————. *La Pensée chinoise.* Paris, 1934.

————. *La Civilisation chinoise.* Paris, 1928.

GREENBERG, M. *British Trade and the Opening of China.* Cambridge, 1951.

GROSIER, ABBÉ. *Description générale de la Chine.* 5 vols. Paris: Montand, 1788.

————. *De la Chine, ou Description générale de cet empire d'après les mémoires de la mission de Pékin.* 7 vols. Paris: Piller, 1818.

GROUSSET, R., and DENIKER, G. *La Face de l'Asie.* Paris, 1955.

GUILAIN, ROBERT. *Orient-Extrême.* Paris, 1987.

GUILLEMIN, PHILIPPE. *Le Yuanming yuan, jeux d'eau et palais européens du XVIIIᵉ siècle à la Cour de Chine.* Paris, 1987.

GUILLERMAZ, JACQUES. *Une vie pour la Chine.* Paris, 1989.

GUILLOU, JEAN. "Les Jésuites en Chine aux XVIIᵉ et XVIIIᵉ siècles." *Académie du Var, bulletin* (1980): no. 148, 69–84.

GUO TINGJI. *Jianming Qingshi* (Short History of the Qings). Peking, 1980.

HALDANE, CHARLOTTE. *The Last Great Empress of China.* London, 1965.

HARDER, HERMANN. "La Question du gouvernement de la Chine au XVIIIᵉ siècle: Montesquieu et de Brosse chez Mgr Foucquet, à Rome." Actes du IIIᵉ colloque international de sinologie (Chantilly, 1980). Paris, 1983, pp. 79–92.

HARLOW, VINCENT T. *The Founding of the Second British Empire, 1763–1793.* London, 1964.

HAY, MALCOLM. *Failure in the Far East: Why and How the Breach Between the Western World and China First Began.* Wetteren: Scaldis Pub., 1956.

HAZARD, PAUL. *La Pensée européenne au XVIIIᵉ siècle.* 2 vols. Paris, 1946.

————. *La Crise de la conscience européene 1680–1715.* Paris, 1935.

HEDIN, SVEN. *Jehol, City of Emperors.* Trans. by G. Nash. London, 1932.

HIBBERT, CHRISTOPHER. *The Dragon Wakes.* London, 1978.

HOFSTEDE, GEERT. *Culture's Consequences: International Differences in Work Related Values.* London, 1980.

HOIZEY, DOMINIQUE. *Histoire de la médecine chinoise.* Paris, 1988.

HO PING-TI. *The Ladder of Success in Imperial China.* New York, 1980.

————. *Studies on the Population of China.* Cambridge, Mass., 1959.

HSIE PAO CHAO. *The Government of China, 1644–1911.* New York, 1966.

HUARD, PIERRE. "Le développement scientifique chinois au XIXᵉ siècle." *Cahiers d'histoire mondiale* 7 (1): 68–95.

HUDSON, G. F. *Europe and China, a survey of their relations, from the earliest time to 1800.* London, 1931.

HUEY, HERBERT. "A French Jesuit's Views on China." In *Papers on Far Eastern History,* no. 31, Canberra, 1985.

HUMMEL, ARTHUR W. *Eminent Chinese of the Ch'ing Period.* Original edition, Washington, Government Printing Office, 1943; reprint, Taipei, 1970.

HUXLEY, JULIAN, ET AL. *Le Comportement rituel chez l'homme et l'animal.* Paris, 1971.

JUNG, CARL-GUSTAV. *L'Homme à la découverte de son âme.* Trans. by Cahen-Sallabelle. Geneva, 1946.

KAHN, HAROLD. *Monarchy in the Emperor's Eyes.* Cambridge, Mass., 1971.

KOYRÉ, ALEXANDRE. *Etudes d'histoire de la pensée scientifique.* Paris, 1966.

LARRE, CLAUDE. *La Voie du Ciel, la médecine chinoise traditionnelle.* Paris, 1987.

————. *Les Chinois.* Paris, 1982.

LATOURETTE, KENNETH SCOTT. *A History of Christian Missions in China.* London: Society for Promoting Christian Knowledge, 1929.

LAURENT, ALAIN. *L'Individu et ses ennemis.* Paris, 1987.

LAURENTIN, RENÉ. *Chine et christianisme—après les occasions manquées.* Paris, 1977.

LECERF, Y., and PARKER, D. *Les Dictatures d'intelligentsia.* Paris, 1987.

LE COMTE, FATHER L. *Nouveaux Mémoires sur l'état présent de la Chine.* 3 vols. Paris, 1690–1700.

LEDUFF, R., and MAISSEU, A. *L'Antidéclin, ou les Mutations technologiques maîtrisées.* Paris, 1988.

LEGOUIX, SUSAN. *Image of China, William Alexander.* London, 1980.

LEITES, EDMUND. "La Chine et l'Europe des Lumières, recherches récentes faites aux U.S.A." Actes du IIe colloque international de sinologie (Chantilly, 1977). Paris, 1980.

———. "Le Confucianisme dans l'Angleterre du XVIIIe siècle: la morale naturelle et la réforme de la société." Actes du IIe colloque international de sinologie (Chantilly, 1977). Paris, 1980.

LENSEN, G. A. *The Russian Push toward Japan 1697–1875.* Princeton, 1959.

LEQUILLER, JEAN. *Nouveaux Mondes d'Asie: la Chine et le Japon du XVIe siècle à nos jours.* Paris, 1974.

LESSAY, JEAN. *Thomas Paine.* Paris, 1987.

Lettres édifiantes et curieuses écrites des missions étrangères par quelques missionnaires de la Compagnie de Jésus. Paris, 1702–76 (excerpts selected and presented by I. and J.-L. VISSIÈRE, Paris 1979).

LÉVY, ANDRÉ. *Nouvelles Lettres édifiantes et curieuses d'Extrême-Occident par des voyageurs lettrés chinois de la Belle Epoque.* Paris, 1986.

LEYS, SIMON. *Ombres chinoises.* Paris, 1978.

———. *La Forêt en feu.* Paris, 1976.

———. *Images brisés.* Paris, 1976.

LIANG QISHAO. *History of Chinese Science of the Past Three Hundred Years.* Shanghai: Minghi Shupi, 1929.

LIN YUTANG. *My Country and My People.* New York, 1938.

LI SHUCHANG. *Carnet de notes de l'Occident.* Trans. from the Chinese by Shi Kangqiang. Paris, 1988.

LOMBARD, D., and AUBIN J. *Marchands et hommes d'affaires asiatiques dans l'océan Indien et la mer de Chine, XIIIe–XXe siècle.* Paris, 1988.

MAILLA, FATHER J. DE. *Histoire générale de la Chine ou Annales de cet empire.* 13 vols. Paris, 1777–85.

MALINOVSKI, BRONISLAV. *Trois Essais sur la vie sociale des primitifs.* Paris, 1980.

MALTHUS, T. ROBERT. *An Essay on the Principle of Population.* London, 1798.

MANKALL, MARK. *Russia and China: Their Diplomatic Relations to 1728.* Cambridge, Mass., 1971.

MANN, SUZAN. *Local Merchants and the Chinese Bureaucracy, 1750–1950.* Stanford, 1987.

MANTOUX, PAUL. *La Révolution industrielle au XVIIIe siècle.* Paris, 1959.

MARIENSTRAS, ELISE. *Les Mythes fondateurs de la nation américaine.* Paris, 1976.

MARSEILLE, JACQUES. *Empire colonial et capitalisme français, histoire d'un divorce.* Paris, 1984.

MARTZLOFF, J. C. *Histoire des mathématiques chinoises.* Paris, 1988.

MARX, KARL. *Karl Marx on China 1853–1860* (articles in the *New York Daily Tribune*). Introduction and notes by Donna Torr. New York, 1975.

MARX, ROLAND. *La Révolution industrielle en Grande-Bretagne des origines à 1850.* Paris, 1970.

MA SHI. *Zhonghua diguo dui wai guanxi shi* (History of the Foreign Relations of the Chinese Empire). Peking, n.d.

MASPÉRO, HENRI. *Le Taoïsme et les religions chinoises.* Posthumous edition by M. Kaltenmark, Paris, 1971.

———. *Mélanges posthumes sur les religions et l'histoire de la Chine.* Paris, 1952.

Mémoires concernant l'histoire, les sciences, les arts, les moeurs, les usages des Chinois, by Father Amiot, et al. 15 vols. Paris, 1776–91.

MENG HUA. *Voltaire et la Chine.* Doctoral thesis. Sorbonne, Paris, 1988.

MEYER, CHARLES. *Histoire de la femme chinoise.* Paris, 1986.

MOKYR, JOËL. *The Economics of the Industrial Revolution.* Evanston, Ill., 1985.

MORSE, H. B. *The Chronicles of the East India Company Trading to China, 1600–1833.* 5 vols. London, 1927.

MOUSNIER, ROLAND. *Fureurs paysannes.* Paris, 1967.

MOUSNIER, R., and LABROUSSE, E. *Histoire générale des civilisations: le XVIIIe siècle.* Paris, 1963.

MÜHLMANN, WILHELM E. *Messianismes révolutionnaires du Tiers Monde.* Paris, 1968.

MYRDAL, GUNNAR. *Le Défi du monde pauvre.* Paris, 1971.

NAQUIN, S., and RAWSKI, E. *Chinese Society in the Eighteenth Century.* New Haven, 1987.

NAYAK, P. R., and KETTERINGHAM, J. M. *Douze Idées de génie auxquelles personne ne croyait.* Paris, 1987.

NEEDHAM, JOSEPH. *Science and Civilisation in China.* 16 vols. Cambridge, latest 1987.

———. *Clerks and Craftsmen.* Cambridge, 1970.

———. *Chinese Science and the West.* London, 1969.

NEVEU, B. "Nouvelle Archives mises à jour." Actes du Ier colloque international de sinologie (Chantilly, 1974). Paris, 1976.

NIZAN, PAUL. *Aden-Arabie.* Paris, 1931.

OLD NICK (E. DAURAN FORGUES). *La Chine ouverte.* Paris: Henri Fournier, 1845.

PALMER, R. R. *1789, les révolutions de la liberté et de l'égalité.* Paris, 1968.

PASQUET, SYLVIE. *L'Evolution du système postal: la province chinoise du Yunnan sous les Qing.* Paris, 1986.

PAUTHIER, G. *Histoire des relations politiques de la Chine avec les puissances occidentales.* Paris: Firmin Didot, 1859.

PEFFER, NATHANIEL. *China, the Collapse of a Civilisation.* London, 1931.

PELLIOT, PAUL. *L'Origine des relations de la France avec la Chine: le premier voyage de l'Amphitrite.* Paris, 1930.

PERKINS, D. H. "Government as an obstacle to industrialisation: the case of nineteenth century China." *Journal of Economic History* no. 27 (December 1967): 478–92.

PHILIPS, C. H. *The East India Company* (1784–1834). Manchester, 1940.

PINOT, VIRGILE. *La Chine et la formation de l'esprit philosophique en France, 1640–1740.* Paris, 1932.

POLIN, C., and ROUSSEAU, C. *Les Illusions de l'Occident.* Paris, 1981.

POLO, MARCO. *The Travels of Marco Polo.* Trans. by Teresa Waugh, from the Italian by Marie Bellonci. London, 1984.

PRITCHARD, EARL H. *The Crucial Years of Anglo-Chinese Relations, 1750–1800.* Research Studies of the State College of Washington, Pullman, Wash., 1936.

RANGEL, CARLOS. *Du bon sauvage au bon révolutionnaire.* Paris, 1976.

RAWSKI, EVELYN. *Education and Popular Literacy in Ch'ing China.* Ann Arbor, Mich., 1979.

REICHWEIN, A. *China and Europe.* London, 1925.

REILLY, ROBIN. *Pitt, the Younger.* London, 1978.

RICCI, FATHER MATTEO, and TRIGAULT, FATHER NICOLAS. *Histoire de l'expédition chrétienne à la conquête du royaume de la Chine.* Lille, 1617 (reprint Paris, 1978).

RIEMERSMA, J. C. *Religious Factors in Early Dutch Capitalism, 1550–1650.* The Hague–Paris, 1967.

RIOUX, JEAN-PIERRE. *La Révolution industrielle, 1780–1880.* Paris, 1971.

ROCHON, A. M. DE. *A Voyage to Madagascar and the East Indies.* Reprint of 1792, New York, 1971.

ROEBUCK, PETER. *Macartney of Lisanoure, 1737–1806.* Belfast, 1983.

ROWBOTHAM, ARNOLD. *Missionary and Mandarin, the Jesuits at the Court of China.* Berkeley, 1966.

SAUTTER, CHRISTIAN. *Les Dents du géant, le Japon à la conquête du monde.* Paris, 1987.

SCHNERB, ROBERT. *Histoire générale des civilisations: le XIXe siècle.* Paris, 1961.

SCHRAM, S. B. *Foundations and Limits of the State Power in China.* Hong Kong, 1987.

SHONFIELD, ANDREW. *Modern Capitalism.*

SMITH, ADAM. *An Inquiry into the Nature and Causes of the Wealth of Nations.* Oxford, 1976.

SONG PUZHANG. "Qingdai qianqi Zhong Ying haiyun maoyi yanjiu" (Research on the maritime trade between China and England at the beginning of the Qings). In *Haishi jiaotong yanjiu* (Research on Maritime Relations) no. 22 (1983).

SOOTHILL, J. *China and the West, a Sketch of Their Intercourse.* Oxford, 1925.

SORMAN, GUY. *La Nouvelle Richesse des nations.* Paris, 1987.

STEIN, ROLF. *Le Monde en petit: jardins en miniature et habitations dans la pensée religieuse en Extrême-Orient.* Paris, 1987.

SUN YATSEN. *Memoirs of a Chinese Revolutionary.* London, 1927.

TAINE, HIPPOLYTE. *Les Origines de la France contemporaine (1876–1894).* 2 vols. Paris, 1986.

TAMARIN, A., and GLUBOK, S. *Voyaging to Cathay.* New York, 1976.

TAN CHUNG. *China and the Brave New World: a Study of the Origins of the Opium War.* Durham, N.C., 1978.

TEILHARD DE CHARDIN, FATHER PIERRE. *Lettres de voyage et Nouvelles Lettres de voyages, 1923–1939/1939–1945.* 2 vols. Paris, 1956.

TEIXEIRA, MANUEL. *The Fourth Centenary of the Jesuits at Macao.* Macao: Salesian School, 1964.

———. "Relação dos missionarios da China." *Boletim eclesiástico* no. 68 (1970): 128–141.

TEMPLE, ROBERT. *Quand la Chine nous précédait.* Paris, 1986.

TENG SU-YÜ and FAIRBANK, JOHN K. *China's Response to the West: a Documentary Survey, 1839–1923.* New York, 1954; reedition Cambridge, Mass., 1979.

TREVOR-ROPER, H. R. *Religion, Reformation and Social Change.* London, 1956.

TRISTAN, FRÉDÉRIK. *Houng, les sociétés secrètes chinoises.* Paris, 1987.

URSEL, PIERRE D'. *La Chine de tous les jours.* Paris, 1985.

VAN DEN BRANDT, F. J. *Les Lazaristes en Chine, 1697–1935, dictionnaire biographique.* Peking: Press of the Lazarists, 1936.

VANDERMEERSCH, LÉON. *Le Nouveau Monde sinisé.* Paris, 1986.

VAN GULIK, R. *Sexual Life in Ancient China.* Leiden, 1961.

VAN KLEY, EDWIN. "Chinese History in Seventeenth Century European Reports." Actes du IIIe colloque international de sinologie (Chantilly, 1980). Paris, 1983.

VISSIÉRE, I., and J.-L. "Un Carrefour culturel: la mission française de Pékin au XVIIIe siècle." Actes du IIIe colloque international de sinologie (Chantilly, 1980). Paris, 1983.

WACHTEL, NATHAN. *La Vision des vaincus.* Paris, 1971.

WALEY, ARTHUR. *The Opium War Through Chinese Eyes.* London, 1958.

WATSON, W. "Interprétation de la Chine: Montesquieu et Voltaire." Actes du IIe colloque international de sinologie (Chantilly, 1977). Paris, 1980.

WEBER, MAX. *Gesammelte Aufsätze zur Religionssoziologie.* Tübingen, 1922.

WEI, LOUIS TSING-SING. *La Politique missionnaire de la France, 1842–1856.* Paris, 1960.

WERNER, EDWARD T. C. *Ancient Tales and Folklore of China.* London, 1922.

WILL, P.-E. *Bureaucratie et famine en Chine au XVIIIe siècle.* Paris, 1980.

WITEK, J. "Chinese Chronology: a Source of Sino-European Widening Horizons in the Eighteenth Century." Actes du IIIe colloque international de sinologie (Chantilly 1980). Paris, 1983.

———. "J. F. Foucquet, controversiste jésuite en Chine et en Europe." Actes du Ier colloque international de sinologie (Chantilly, 1974). Paris, 1976.

WU, SILAS. *Communication and Imperial Control in China: Evolution of the Palace Memorial System 1693–1735.* Cambridge, Mass., 1970.

XIAO YISHAN. *Qingdai tonshi* (General History of the Qings). Shanghai, 1928.

XIAO ZHIZHI and YANG WEIDONG. *Yapian zhanzheng qian Zhong Xi guanxi jishi 1517–1840* (Chronicle of Sino-Occidental Relations Before the Opium War, 1517–1840).

YENFU (YEN FOU). *Les Manifestes de Yen fou.* Trans. by F. Houang. Paris, 1977.

YOUNG, ARTHUR. *Voyages en France (1787, 1788, 1789).* 3 vols. Trans. by H. Sée. Paris, 1976.

ZHANG YIDONG. "Zhong Ying liangguo zui de jiechu" (On the First Contacts Between China and England). *Lishi Yanjiu* (Historical Research), 1955.

ZHU YONG. *Qingdai zongzufa yanjiu.* Changsha: Hunan jiayu Chubanshe, Boshi Iuncong, 1988.

———. *Sino-English Relations Under Qianlong, 1736–1796.* Institute for the Study of the History of the Qings, University of the Chinese People, Peking, 1988.

Index

A NOTE ABOUT THE AUTHOR

As writer, historical researcher and career diplomat, Alain Peyrefitte has had a long, distinguished and multifaceted career. For thirty-six years he served as the foreign envoy for Charles de Gaulle, and he has served in a similar capacity under the past three French presidents. In 1987 he was elected by a unanimous vote to the Academy of Moral and Political Science in Paris, where he now lives.

A NOTE ON THE TYPE

This book was set in a film version of Granjon, a type named
in compliment to Robert Granjon, but neither a copy of a
classic face nor an entirely original creation. George W. Jones
based his designs for this type on that used by Claude Garamond (1510–61) in his beautiful French books, and Granjon
more closely resembles Garamond's own type than does any
of the various modern types that bear his name.

Robert Granjon began his career as typecutter in 1523.
The boldest and most original designer of his time, he was
one of the first to practice the trade of typefounder apart from
that of printer. Between 1557 and 1562 Granjon printed about
twenty books in types designed by himself, following, after
the fashion, the cursive handwriting of the time. These types,
usually known as *caractères de civilité*, he himself called *lettres
françaises*, as especially appropriate to his own country.

Composed by PennSet, Inc.,
Bloomsburg, Pennsylvania

Printed and bound by The Haddon Craftsmen, Inc.
Scranton, Pennsylvania

Typography and binding design by
Dorothy Schmiderer Baker